Get the eBook FREE!

(PDF, ePub, Kindle, and liveBook all included)

We believe that once you buy a book from us, you should be able to read it in any format we have available. To get electronic versions of this book at no additional cost to you, purchase and then register this book at the Manning website.

Go to https://www.manning.com/freebook and follow the instructions to complete your pBook registration.

That's it!
Thanks from Manning!

Machine Learning with R, the tidyverse, and mlr

HEFIN I. RHYS

MANNING
SHELTER ISLAND

For online information and ordering of this and other Manning books, please visit www.manning.com. The publisher offers discounts on this book when ordered in quantity. For more information, please contact

Special Sales Department
Manning Publications Co.
20 Baldwin Road
PO Box 761
Shelter Island, NY 11964
Email: orders@manning.com

♾ Recognizing the importance of preserving what has been written, it is Manning's policy to have the books we publish printed on acid-free paper, and we exert our best efforts to that end. Recognizing also our responsibility to conserve the resources of our planet, Manning books are printed on paper that is at least 15 percent recycled and processed without the use of elemental chlorine.

Manning Publications Co.
20 Baldwin Road
PO Box 761
Shelter Island, NY 11964

Development editor: Marina Michaels
Technical development editor: Doug Warren
Review editor: Aleksandar Dragosavljević
Production editor: Lori Weidert
Copy editor: Tiffany Taylor
Proofreader: Katie Tennant
Technical proofreader: Kostas Passadis
Typesetter: Dennis Dalinnik
Cover designer: Marija Tudor

ISBN: 9781617296574
Printed in the United States of America

brief contents

contents

preface

While working on my PhD, I made heavy use of statistical modeling to better understand the processes I was studying. R was my language of choice, and that of my peers in life science academia. Given R's primary purpose as a language for statistical computing, it is unparalleled when it comes to building linear models.

As my project progressed, the types of data problems I was working on changed. The volume of data increased, and the goal of each experiment became more complex and varied. I was now working with many more variables, and problems such as how to visualize the patterns in data became more difficult. I found myself more frequently interested in making predictions on new data, rather than, or in addition to, just understanding the underlying biology itself. Sometimes, the complex relationships in the data were difficult to represent manually with traditional modeling methods. At other times, I simply wanted to know how many distinct groups existed in the data.

I found myself more and more turning to machine learning techniques to help me achieve my goals. For each new problem, I searched my existing mental toolbox of statistical and machine learning skills. If I came up short, I did some research: find out how others had solved similar problems, try different methods, and see which gave the best solution. Once my appetite was whetted for a new set of techniques, I read a textbook on the topic. I usually found myself frustrated that the books I was reading tended to be aimed towards people with degrees in statistics.

As I built my skills and knowledge slowly (and painfully), an additional source of frustration came from the way in which machine learning techniques in R are spread disparately between a plethora of different packages. These packages are written by different authors who all use different syntax and arguments. This meant an additional challenge when learning a new technique. At this point I became very jealous of the scikit-learn package from the Python language (which I had not learned), which provides a common interface for a large number of machine learning techniques.

But then I discovered R packages like caret and mlr, which suddenly made my learning experience much easier. Like scikit-learn, they provide a common interface for a large number of machine learning techniques. This took away the cognitive load of needing to learn the R functions for another package each time I wanted to try something new, and made my machine learning projects much simpler and faster. As a result of using (mostly) the mlr package, I found that the handling of data actually became the most time consuming and complicated part of my work. After doing some more research, I discovered the tidyverse set of packages in R, whose purpose is to make the handling, transformation, and visualization of data simple, streamlined, and reproducible. Since then, I've used tools from the tidyverse in all of my projects.

I wanted to write this book because machine learning knowledge is in high demand. There are lots of resources available to budding data scientists or anyone looking to train computers to solve problems. But I've struggled to find resources that simultaneously are approachable to newcomers, teach rigor and good practice, and use the mlr and tidyverse packages. My aim when writing this book has been to have as little code as possible do as much as possible. In this way, I hope to make your learning experience easier, and using the mlr and tidyverse packages has, I think, helped me do that.

acknowledgments

When starting out on this process, I was extremely naive as to how much work it would require. It took me longer to write than I thought, and would have taken an awful lot longer were it not for the support of several people. The quality of the content would also not be anywhere near as high without their help.

Firstly, and most importantly, I would like to thank you, my husband, Zand. From the outset of this project, you understood what this book meant to me and did everything you could to give me time and space to write it. For a whole year, you've put up with me working late into the night, given up weekends, and allowed me to shirk my domestic duties in favor of writing. I love you.

I thank you, Marina Michaels, my development editor at Manning—without you, this book would read more like the ramblings of an idiot than a coherent textbook. Early on in the writing process, you beat out my bad habits and made me a better writer and a better teacher. Thank you also for our long, late-night discussions about the difference between American cookies and British biscuits. Thank you, my technical development editor, Doug Warren—your insights as a prototype reader made the content much more approachable. Thank you, my technical proofreader, Kostas Passadis—you checked my code and theory, and told me when I was being stupid. I owe the technical accuracy of the book to you.

Thank you, Stephen Soenhlen, for giving me this amazing opportunity. Without you, I would never had the confidence to think I could write a book. Finally, a thank-you goes to all the other staff at Manning who worked on the production and promotion, and my reviewers who provided invaluable feedback: Aditya Kaushik, Andrew

Hamor, David Jacobs, Erik Sapper, Fernando Garcia, Izhar Haq, Jaromir D.B. Nemec, Juan Rufes, Kay Engelhardt, Lawrence L. Matias, Luis Moux-Dominguez, Mario Giesel, Miranda Whurr, Monika Jakubczak, Prabhuti Prakash, Robert Samohyl, Ron Lease, and Tony Holdroyd.

about this book

Who should read this book

I firmly believe that machine learning should not be the domain only of computer scientists and people with degrees in mathematics. *Machine learning with R, the tidyverse, and mlr* doesn't assume you come from either of these backgrounds. To get the most from the book, though, you should be reasonably familiar with the R language. It will help if you understand some basic statistical concepts, but all that you'll need is included as a statistics refresher in the appendix, so head there first to fill in any gaps in your knowledge. Anyone with a problem to solve, and data that contains the answer to that problem, can benefit from the topics taught in this book.

If you are a newcomer to R and want to learn or brush up on your basic R skills, I suggest you take a look at *R in Action*, by Robert I. Kabacoff (Manning, 2015).

How this book is organized: A roadmap

This book has 5 parts, covering 20 chapters. The first part of the book is designed to get you up and running with some of the broad machine learning and R skills you'll use throughout the rest of the book. The first chapter is designed to get your machine learning vocabulary up to speed. The second chapter will teach you a large number of tidyverse functions that will improve your general R data science skills.

The second part of the book will introduce you to a range of algorithms used for classification (predicting discrete categories). From this part of the book onward, each chapter will start by teaching how a particular algorithm works, followed by a worked example of that algorithm. These explanations are graphical, with mathematics provided optionally for those who are interested. Throughout the chapters, you will find exercises to help you develop your skills.

The third, fourth, and fifth parts of the book are dedicated to algorithms for regression (predicting continuous variables), dimension reduction (compressing information into fewer variables), and clustering (identifying groups within data), respectively. Finally, the last chapter of the book will recap the important, broad concepts we covered, and give you a roadmap of where you can go to further your learning.

In addition, there is an appendix containing a refresher on some basic statistical concepts we'll use throughout the book. I recommend you at least flick through the appendix to make sure you understand the material there, especially if you don't come from a statistical background.

About the code

As this book is written with the aim of getting you to code through the examples along with me, you'll find R code throughout most of the chapters. You'll find R code both in numbered listings and in line with normal text. In both cases, source code is formatted in a `fixed-width font like this` to separate it from ordinary text.

All of the source code is freely available at https://www.manning.com/books/machine-learning-with-r-the-tidyverse-and-mlr. The R code in this book was written with R 3.6.1, with mlr version 2.14.0, and tidyverse version 1.2.1.

liveBook discussion forum

Purchase of *Machine Learning with R, the tidyverse, and mlr* includes free access to a private web forum run by Manning Publications where you can make comments about the book, ask technical questions, and receive help from the author and from other users. To access the forum, go to https://livebook.manning.com/#!/book/machine-learning-with-r-the-tidyverse-and-mlr. You can also learn more about Manning's forums and the rules of conduct at https://livebook.manning.com/#!/discussion.

Manning's commitment to our readers is to provide a venue where a meaningful dialogue between individual readers and between readers and the author can take place. It is not a commitment to any specific amount of participation on the part of the author, whose contribution to the forum remains voluntary (and unpaid). We suggest you try asking some challenging questions lest their interest stray! The forum and the archives of previous discussions will be accessible from the publisher's website as long as the book is in print.

about the author

Hefin I. Rhys is a life scientist and cytometrist with eight years of experience teaching R, statistics, and machine learning. He has contributed his statistical/machine learning knowledge to multiple academic studies. He has a passion for teaching statistics, machine learning, and data visualization.

about the cover illustration

The figure on the cover of *Machine Learning with R, the tidyverse, and mlr* is captioned "Femme de Jerusalem," or "Woman of Jerusalem." The illustration is taken from a collection of dress costumes from various countries by Jacques Grasset de Saint-Sauveur (1757–1810), titled *Costumes Civils Actuels de Tous les Peuples Connus,* published in France in 1788. Each illustration is finely drawn and colored by hand. The rich variety of Grasset de Saint-Sauveur's collection reminds us vividly of how culturally apart the world's towns and regions were just 200 years ago. Isolated from each other, people spoke different dialects and languages. In the streets or in the countryside, it was easy to identify where they lived and what their trade or station in life was just by their dress.

The way we dress has changed since then, and the diversity by region, so rich at the time, has faded away. It is now hard to tell apart the inhabitants of different continents, let alone different towns, regions, or countries. Perhaps we have traded cultural diversity for a more varied personal life—certainly, for a more varied and fast-paced technological life.

At a time when it is hard to tell one computer book from another, Manning celebrates the inventiveness and initiative of the computer business with book covers based on the rich diversity of regional life of two centuries ago, brought back to life by Grasset de Saint-Sauveur's pictures.

Part 1

Introduction

While this first part of the book includes only two chapters, it is essential to provide you with the basic knowledge and skills you'll rely on throughout the book.

Chapter 1 introduces you to some basic machine learning terminology. Having a good vocabulary for the core concepts can help you see the big picture of machine learning and aid in your understanding of the more complex topics we'll explore later in the book. This chapter teaches you what machine learning is, how it can benefit (or harm) us, and how we can categorize different types of machine learning tasks. The chapter finishes by explaining why we're using R for machine learning, what datasets you'll be working with, and what you can expect to learn from the book.

In chapter 2, we take a brief detour away from machine learning and focus on developing your R skills by covering a collection of packages known as the *tidyverse*. The packages of the tidyverse provide us with the tools to store, manipulate, transform, and visualize our data using more human-readable, intuitive code. You don't need to use the tidyverse when working on machine learning projects, but doing so helps you simplify your data-wrangling processes. We'll use tidyverse tools in the projects throughout the book, so a solid grounding in them in chapter 2 can help you in the rest of the chapters. I'm sure you'll find that these skills improve your general R programming and data science skills.

Beginning with chapter 2, I encourage you to start coding along with me. To maximize your retention of knowledge, I strongly recommend that you run the code examples in your own R session and save your .R files so you can refer back to your code in the future. Make sure you understand how each line of code relates to its output.

1 Introduction to machine learning

This chapter covers

- What machine learning is
- Supervised vs. unsupervised machine learning
- Classification, regression, dimension reduction, and clustering
- Why we're using R
- Which datasets we will use

You interact with machine learning on a daily basis whether you recognize it or not. The advertisements you see online are of products you're more likely to buy based on the things you've previously bought or looked at. Faces in the photos you upload to social media platforms are automatically identified and tagged. Your car's GPS predicts which routes will be busiest at certain times of day and replots your route to minimize journey length. Your email client progressively learns which emails you want and which ones you consider spam, to make your inbox less cluttered; and your home personal assistant recognizes your voice and responds to your requests. From small improvements to our daily lives such as these, to big, society-changing ideas such as self-driving cars, robotic surgery, and automated scanning for other Earth-like planets, machine learning has become an increasingly important part of modern life.

But here's something I want you to understand right away: machine learning isn't solely the domain of large tech companies or computer scientists. *Anyone* with basic programming skills can implement machine learning in their work. If you're a scientist, machine learning can give you extraordinary insights into the phenomena you're studying. If you're a journalist, it can help you understand patterns in your data that can delineate your story. If you're a businessperson, machine learning can help you target the right customers and predict which products will sell the best. If you're someone with a question or problem, and you have sufficient data to answer it, machine learning can help you do just that. While you won't be building intelligent cars or talking robots after reading this book (like Google and Deep Mind), you will have gained the skills to make powerful predictions and identify informative patterns in your data.

I'm going to teach you the theory and practice of machine learning at a level that anyone with a basic knowledge of R can follow. Ever since high school, I've been terrible at mathematics, so I don't expect you to be great at it either. Although the techniques you're about to learn are based in math, I'm a firm believer that there are no hard concepts in machine learning. All of the processes we'll explore together will be explained graphically and intuitively. Not only does this mean you'll be able to apply and understand these processes, but you'll also learn all this without having to wade through mathematical notation. If, however, you are mathematically minded, you'll find equations presented through the book that are "nice to know," rather than "need to know."

In this chapter, we're going to define what I actually mean by *machine learning*. You'll learn the difference between an algorithm and a model, and discover that machine learning techniques can be partitioned into types that help guide us when choosing the best one for a given task.

1.1 What is machine learning?

Imagine you work as a researcher in a hospital. What if, when a new patient is checked in, you could calculate the risk of them dying? This would allow the clinicians to treat high-risk patients more aggressively and result in more lives being saved. But where would you start? What data would you use? How would you get this information from the data? The answer is to use machine learning.

Machine learning, sometimes referred to as *statistical learning*, is a subfield of artificial intelligence (AI) whereby *algorithms* "learn" patterns in data to perform specific tasks. Although algorithms may sound complicated, they aren't. In fact, the idea behind an algorithm is not complicated at all. An algorithm is simply a step-by-step process that we use to achieve something that has a beginning and an end. Chefs have a different word for algorithms—they call them "recipes." At each stage in a recipe, you perform some kind of process, like beating an egg, and then you follow the next instruction in the recipe, such as mixing the ingredients.

Have a look in figure 1.1 at an algorithm I made for making a cake. It starts at the top and progresses through the various operations needed to get the cake baked and

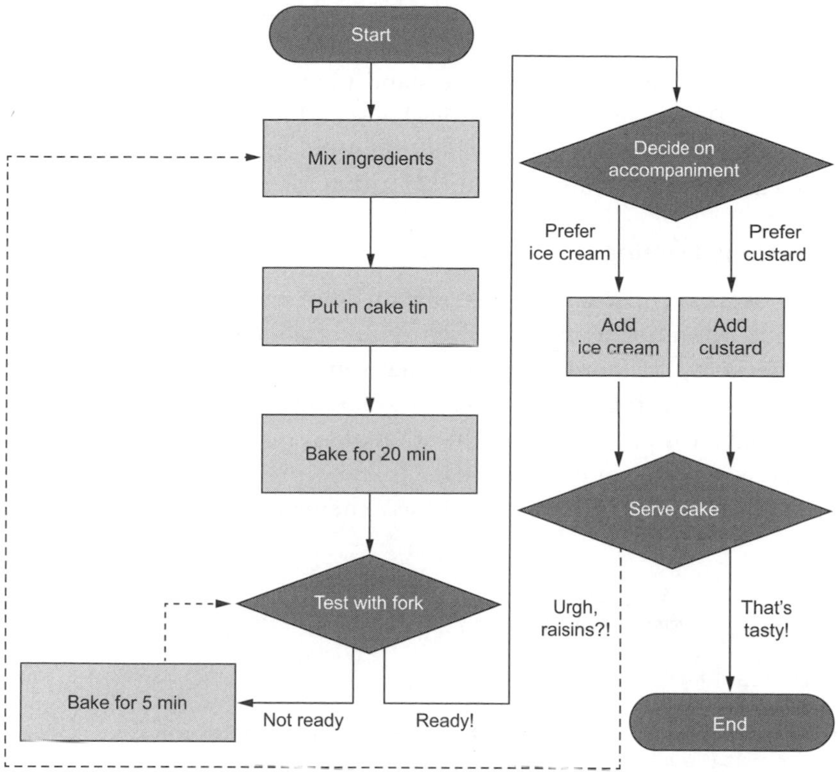

Figure 1.1 An algorithm for making and serving a cake. We start at the top and, after performing each operation, follow the next arrow. Diamonds are decision points, where the arrow we follow next depends on the state of our cake. Dotted arrows show routes that iterate back to previous operations. This algorithm takes ingredients as its input and outputs cake with either ice cream or custard!

served up. Sometimes there are decision points where the route we take depends on the current state of things, and sometimes we need to go back or *iterate* to a previous step of the algorithm. While it's true that extremely complicated things can be achieved with algorithms, I want you to understand that they are simply sequential chains of simple operations.

So, having gathered data on your patients, you train a machine learning algorithm to learn patterns in the data associated with the patients' survival. Now, when you gather data on a new patient, the algorithm can estimate the risk of that patient dying.

As another example, imagine you work for a power company, and it's your job to make sure customers' bills are estimated accurately. You train an algorithm to learn patterns of data associated with the electricity use of households. Now, when a new household joins the power company, you can estimate how much money you should bill them each month.

Finally, imagine you're a political scientist, and you're looking for types of voters that no one (including you) knows about. You train an algorithm to identify patterns of voters in survey data, to better understand what motivates voters for a particular political party. Do you see any similarities between these problems and the problems you would like to solve? Then—provided the solution is hidden somewhere in your data—you can train a machine learning algorithm to extract it for you.

1.1.1 AI and machine learning

Arthur Samuel, a scientist at IBM, first used the term *machine learning* in 1959. He used it to describe a form of AI that involved training an algorithm to learn to play the game of checkers. The word *learning* is what's important here, as this is what distinguishes machine learning approaches from traditional AI.

Traditional AI is programmatic. In other words, you give the computer a set of rules so that when it encounters new data, it knows precisely which output to give. An example of this would be using `if else` statements to classify animals as dogs, cats, or snakes:

```
numberOfLegs <- c(4, 4, 0)
climbsTrees <- c(TRUE, FALSE, TRUE)

for (i in 1:3) {
  if (numberOfLegs[i] == 4) {
    if (climbsTrees[i]) print("cat") else print("dog")
  } else print("snake")
}
```

In this R code, I've created three rules, mapping every possible input available to us to an output:

1. If the animal has four legs and climbs trees, it's a cat.
2. If the animal has four legs and does not climb trees, it's a dog.
3. Otherwise, the animal is a snake.

Now, if we apply these rules to the data, we get the expected answers:

```
[1] "cat"
[1] "dog"
[1] "snake"
```

The problem with this approach is that we need to know in advance all the possible outputs the computer should give, and the system will never give us an output that we haven't told it to give. Contrast this with the machine learning approach, where instead of telling the computer the rules, we give it the data and allow it to learn the rules for itself. The advantage of this approach is that the machine can "learn" patterns we didn't even know existed in the data—and the more data we provide, the better it gets at learning those patterns (figure 1.2).

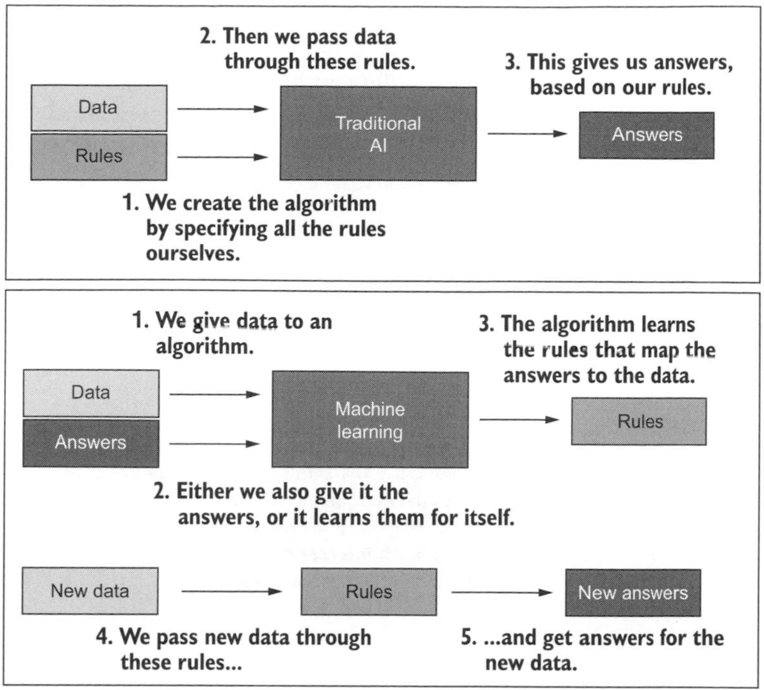

Figure 1.2 Traditional AI vs. machine learning AI. In traditional AI applications, we provide the computer with a complete set of rules. When it's given data, it outputs the relevant answers. In machine learning, we provide the computer with data and the answers, and it learns the rules for itself. When we pass new data through these rules, we get answers for this new data.

1.1.2 The difference between a model and an algorithm

In practice, we call a set of rules that a machine learning algorithm learns a *model*. Once the model has been learned, we can give it new observations, and it will output its predictions for the new data. We refer to these as models because they represent real-world phenomena in a simplistic enough way that we and the computer can interpret and understand it. Just as a model of the Eiffel Tower may be a good representation of the real thing but isn't exactly the same, so statistical models are attempted representations of real-world phenomena but won't match them perfectly.

> **NOTE** You may have heard the famous phrase coined by the statistician George Box that "All models are wrong, but some are useful"; this refers to the approximate nature of models.

The process by which the model is learned is referred to as the *algorithm*. As we discovered earlier, an algorithm is just a sequence of operations that work together to solve a problem. So how does this work in practice? Let's take a simple example. Say we have two continuous variables, and we would like to train an algorithm that can predict one (the *outcome* or *dependent* variable) given the other (the *predictor* or *independent* variable). The relationship between these variables can be described by a straight line that can be defined using only two parameters: its slope and where it crosses the y-axis (the y-intercept). This is shown in figure 1.3.

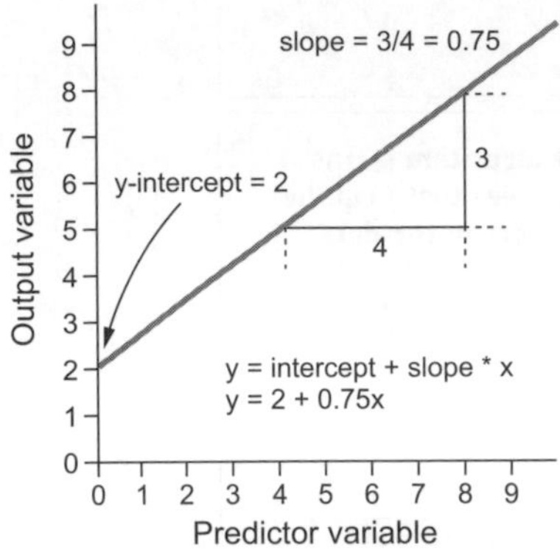

Figure 1.3 Any straight line can be described by its slope (the change in *y* divided by the change in *x*) and its intercept (where it crosses the y-axis when *x* = 0). The equation *y* = *intercept* + *slope* * *x* can be used to predict the value of *y* given a value of *x*.

An algorithm to learn this relationship could look something like the example in figure 1.4. We start by fitting a line with no slope through the mean of all the data. We calculate the distance each data point is from the line, square it, and sum these squared values. This *sum of squares* is a measure of how closely the line fits the data. Next, we rotate the line a little in a clockwise direction and measure the sum of squares for *this* line. If the sum of squares is bigger than it was before, we've made the fit worse, so we rotate the slope in the other direction and try again. If the sum of squares gets smaller, then we've made the fit better. We continue with this process, rotating the slope a little less each time we get closer, until the improvement on our previous iteration is smaller than some preset value we've chosen. The algorithm has iteratively learned the model (the slope and y-intercept) needed to predict future values of the output variable, given only the predictor variable. This example is slightly crude but hopefully illustrates how such an algorithm could work.

NOTE One of the initially confusing but eventually fun aspects of machine learning is that there is a plethora of algorithms to solve the same type of problem. The reason is that different people have come up with slightly different ways of solving the same problem, all trying to improve upon previous attempts. For a given task, it is our job as data scientists to choose which algorithm(s) will learn the best-performing model.

While certain algorithms tend to perform better than others with certain types of data, no single algorithm will always outperform all others on all problems. This concept is called the *no free lunch theorem*. In other words, you don't get something for

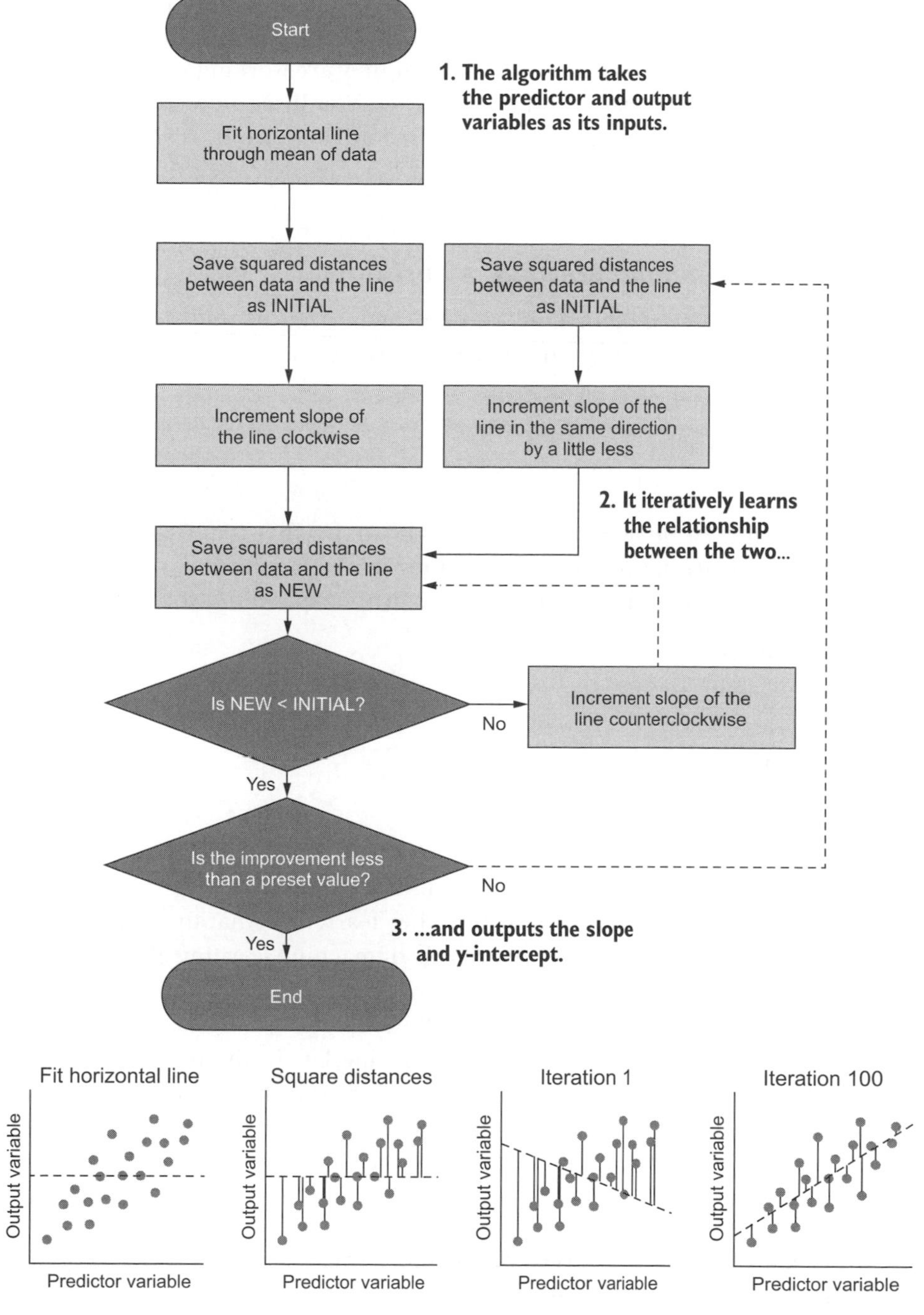

Figure 1.4 A hypothetical algorithm for learning the parameters of a straight line. This algorithm takes two continuous variables as inputs and fits a straight line through the mean. It iteratively rotates the line until it finds a solution that minimizes the sum of squares. The parameters of the line are output as the learned model.

nothing; you need to put some effort into working out the best algorithm for your particular problem. Data scientists typically choose a few algorithms they know tend to work well for the type of data and problem they are working on, and see which algorithm generates the best-performing model. You'll see how we do this later in the book. We can, however, narrow down our initial choice by dividing machine learning algorithms into categories, based on the function they perform and how they perform it.

1.2 Classes of machine learning algorithms

All machine learning algorithms can be categorized by their learning type and the task they perform. There are three learning types:

- Supervised
- Unsupervised
- Semi-supervised

The type depends on how the algorithms learn. Do they require us to hold their hand through the learning process? Or do they learn the answers for themselves? Supervised and unsupervised algorithms can be further split into two classes each:

- Supervised
  - Classification
  - Regression
- Unsupervised
  - Dimension reduction
  - Clustering

The class depends on what the algorithms learn to *do*.

So we categorize algorithms by how they learn and what they learn to do. But why do we care about this? Well, there are *a lot* of machine learning algorithms available to us. How do we know which one to pick? What kind of data do they require to function properly? Knowing which categories different algorithms belong to makes our job of selecting the most appropriate ones much simpler. In the next section, I cover how each of the classes is defined and why it's different from the others. By the end of this section, you'll have a clear understanding of why you would use algorithms from one class over another. By the end of the book, you'll have the skills to apply a number of algorithms from each class.

1.2.1 Differences between supervised, unsupervised, and semi-supervised learning

Imagine you are trying to get a toddler to learn about shapes by using blocks of wood. In front of them, they have a ball, a cube, and a star. You ask them to show you the cube, and if they point to the correct shape, you tell them they are correct; if they are incorrect, you also tell them. You repeat this procedure until the toddler can identify the correct shape almost all of the time. This is called *supervised learning*, because you, the person who already knows which shape is which, are supervising the learner by telling them the answers.

Now imagine a toddler is given multiple balls, cubes, and stars but this time is also given three bags. The toddler has to put all the balls in one bag, the cubes in another bag, and the stars in another, but you won't tell them if they're correct—they have to work it out for themselves from nothing but the information they have in front of them. This is called *unsupervised learning*, because the learner has to identify patterns themselves with no outside help.

A machine learning algorithm is said to be *supervised* if it uses a ground truth or, in other words, *labeled data*. For example, if we wanted to classify a patient biopsy as healthy or cancerous based on its gene expression, we would give an algorithm the gene expression data, labeled with whether that tissue was healthy or cancerous. The algorithm now knows which cases come from each of the two types, and it tries to learn patterns in the data that discriminate them.

Another example would be if we were trying to estimate a person's monthly credit card expenditure. We could give an algorithm information about other people, such as their income, family size, whether they own their home, and so on, including how much they typically spent on their credit card in a month. The algorithm looks for patterns in the data that can predict these values in a reproducible way. When we collect data from a new person, the algorithm can estimate how much they will spend, based on the patterns it learned.

A machine learning algorithm is said to be *unsupervised* if it does not use a ground truth and instead looks on its own for patterns in the data that hint at some underlying structure. For example, let's say we take the gene expression data from lots of cancerous biopsies and ask an algorithm to tell us if there are clusters of biopsies. A *cluster* is a group of data points that are similar to each other but different from data in other clusters. This type of analysis can tell us if we have subgroups of cancer types that we may need to treat differently.

Alternatively, we may have a dataset with a large number of variables—so many that it is difficult to interpret the data and look for relationships manually. We can ask an algorithm to look for a way of representing this high-dimensional dataset in a lower-dimensional one, while maintaining as much information from the original data as possible. Take a look at the summary in figure 1.5. If your algorithm uses labeled data (a ground truth), then it is supervised, and if it does not use labeled data, then it is unsupervised.

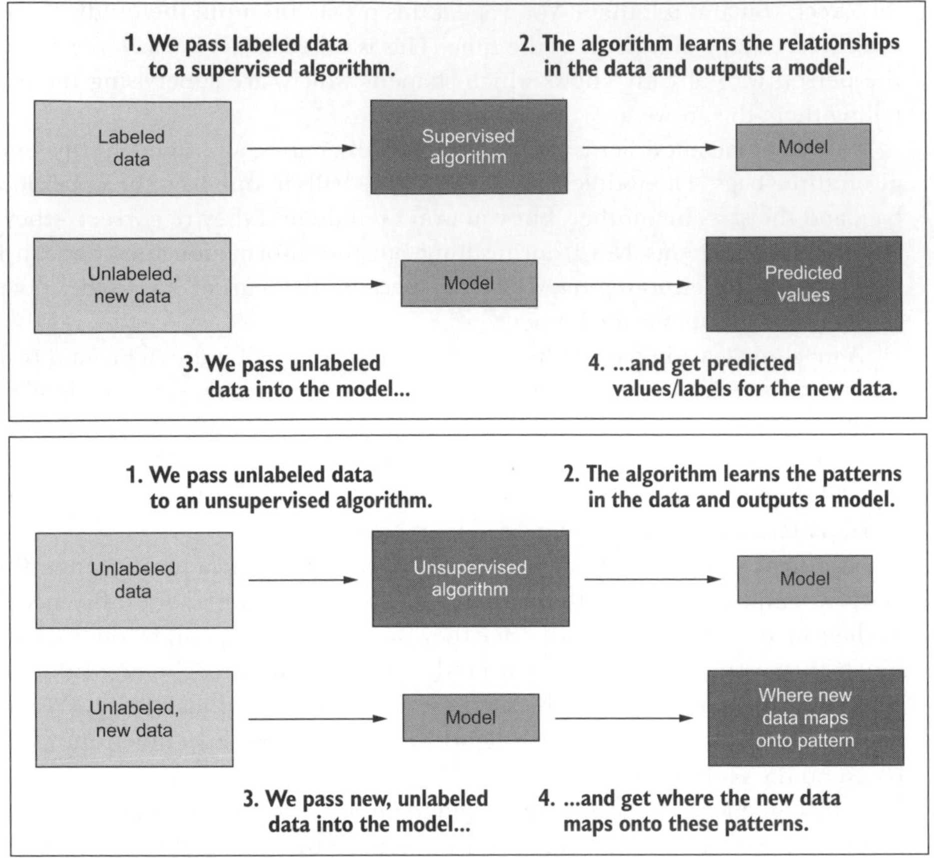

Figure 1.5 Supervised vs. unsupervised machine learning. Supervised algorithms take data that is already labeled with a ground truth and build a model that can predict the labels of unlabeled, new data. Unsupervised algorithms take unlabeled data and learn patterns within it, such that new data can be mapped onto these patterns.

Semi-supervised learning

Most machine learning algorithms will fall into one of these categories, but there is an additional approach called *semi-supervised* learning. As its name suggests, semi-supervised machine learning is not quite supervised and not quite unsupervised.

Semi-supervised learning often describes a machine learning approach that combines supervised and unsupervised algorithms together, rather than strictly defining a class of algorithms in and of itself. The premise of semi-supervised learning is that, often, labeling a dataset requires a large amount of manual work by an expert observer. This process may be very time consuming, expensive, and error prone, and may be impossible for an entire dataset. So instead, we expertly label as many of the cases as is feasibly possible, and then we build a supervised model using only the labeled data. We pass the rest of our data (the unlabeled cases) into the model to get their predicted labels, called *pseudo-labels* because we don't know if all of them are actually correct. Now we combine the data with the manual labels and pseudo-labels, and use the result to train a new model.

This approach allows us to train a model that learns from both labeled and unlabeled data, and it can improve overall predictive performance because we are able to use all of the data at our disposal. If you would like to learn more about semi-supervised learning after completing this book, see *Semi-Supervised Learning* by Olivier Chapelle, Bernhard Scholkopf, and Alexander Zien (MIT Press, 2006). This reference may seem quite old, but it is still very good.

Within the supervised and unsupervised categories, machine learning algorithms can be further categorized by the tasks they perform. Just as a mechanical engineer knows which tools to use for the task at hand, so the data scientist needs to know which algorithms they should use for their task. There are four main classes to choose from: classification, regression, dimension reduction, and clustering.

1.2.2 Classification, regression, dimension reduction, and clustering

Supervised machine learning algorithms can be split into two classes:

- *Classification algorithms* take labeled data (because they are supervised learning methods) and learn patterns in the data that can be used to predict a *categorical* output variable. This is most often a *grouping variable* (a variable specifying which group a particular case belongs to) and can be *binomial* (two groups) or *multinomial* (more than two groups). Classification problems are very common machine learning tasks. Which customers will default on their payments? Which patients will survive? Which objects in a telescope image are stars, planets, or galaxies? When faced with problems like these, you should use a classification algorithm.
- *Regression algorithms* take labeled data and learn patterns in the data that can be used to predict a *continuous* output variable. How much carbon dioxide does a household contribute to the atmosphere? What will the share price of a company be tomorrow? What is the concentration of insulin in a patient's blood? When faced with problems like these, you should use a regression algorithm.

Unsupervised machine learning algorithms can also be split into two classes:

- *Dimension-reduction algorithms* take unlabeled (because they are unsupervised learning methods) and high-dimensional data (data with many variables) and learn a way of representing it in a lower number of dimensions. Dimension-reduction algorithms may be used as an exploratory technique (because it's very difficult for humans to visually interpret data in more than two or three dimensions at once) or as a preprocessing step in the machine learning pipeline (it can help mitigate problems such as *collinearity* and the *curse of dimensionality*, terms I'll define in later chapters). Dimension-reduction algorithms can also be used to help us visually confirm the performance of classification and clustering algorithms (by allowing us to plot the data in two or three dimensions).

- *Clustering algorithms* take unlabeled data and learn patterns of clustering in the data. A *cluster* is a collection of observations that are more similar to each other than to data points in other clusters. We assume that observations in the same cluster share some unifying features that make them identifiably different from other clusters. Clustering algorithms may be used as an exploratory technique to understand the structure of our data and may indicate a grouping structure that can be fed into classification algorithms. Are there subtypes of patient responders in a clinical trial? How many classes of respondents were there in the survey? Do different types of customers use our company? When faced with problems like these, you should use a clustering algorithm.

See figure 1.6 for a summary of the different types of algorithms by type and function.

By separating machine learning algorithms into these four classes, you will find it easier to select appropriate ones for the tasks at hand. This is why the book is structured the way it is: we first tackle classification, then regression, then dimension reduction, and then clustering, so you can build a clear mental picture of your toolbox of available algorithms for a particular application. Deciding which class of algorithm to choose from is usually straightforward:

- If you need to predict a categorical variable, use a classification algorithm.
- If you need to predict a continuous variable, use a regression algorithm.
- If you need to represent the information of many variables with fewer variables, use dimension reduction.
- If you need to identify clusters of cases, use a clustering algorithm.

1.2.3 A brief word on deep learning

If you've done more than a little reading about machine learning, you have probably come across the term *deep learning*, and you may have even heard the term in the media. Deep learning is a subfield of machine learning (all deep learning is machine learning, but not all machine learning is deep learning) that has become extremely popular in the last 5 to 10 years for two main reasons:

- It can produce models with outstanding performance.
- We now have the computational power to apply it more broadly.

Deep learning uses *neural networks* to learn patterns in data, a term referring to the way in which the structure of these models superficially resembles neurons in the brain, with

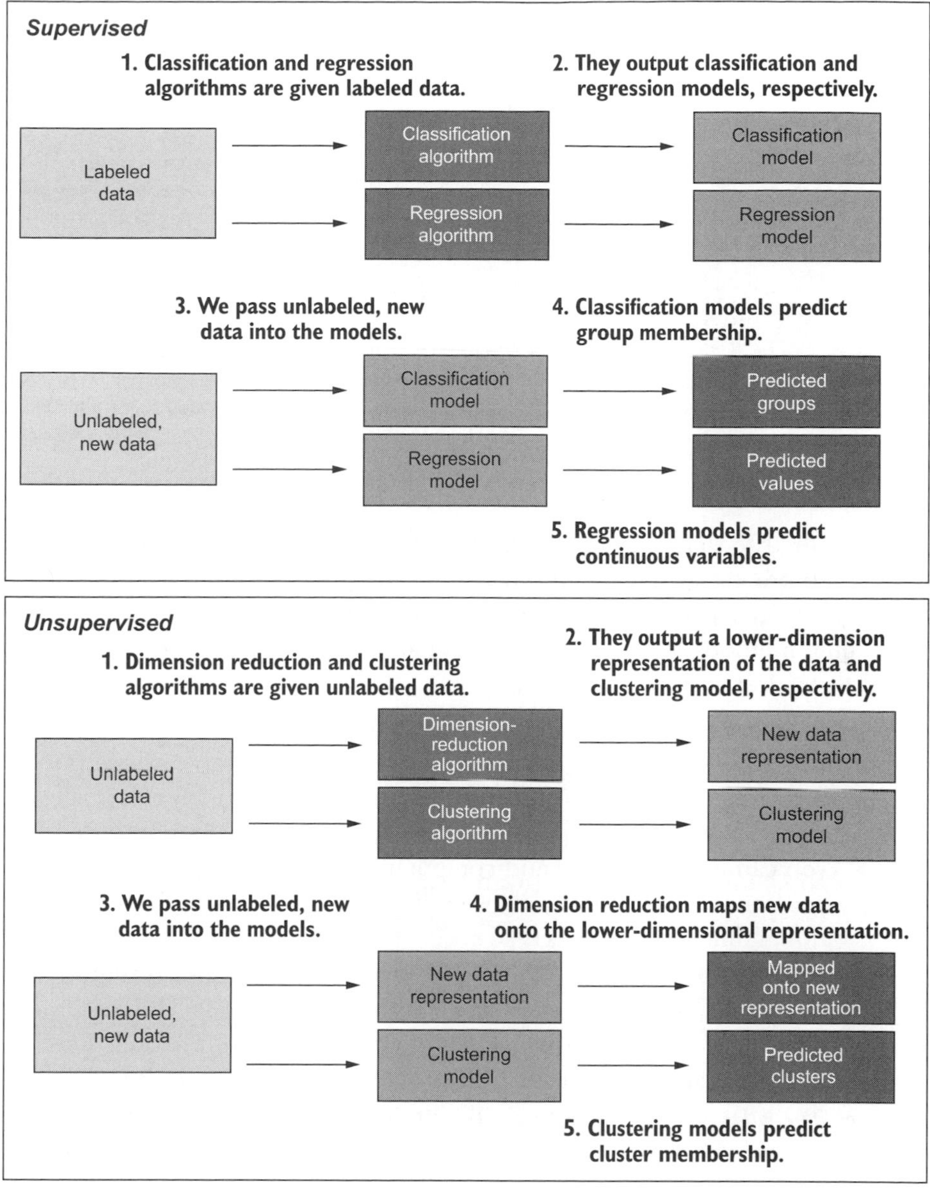

Figure 1.6 Classification, regression, dimension reduction, and clustering. Classification and regression algorithms build models that predict categorical and continuous variables of unlabeled, new data, respectively. Dimension-reduction algorithms create a new representation of the original data in fewer dimensions and map new data onto this representation. Clustering algorithms identify clusters within the data and map new data onto these clusters.

connections to pass information between them. The relationship between AI, machine learning, and deep learning is summarized in figure 1.7.

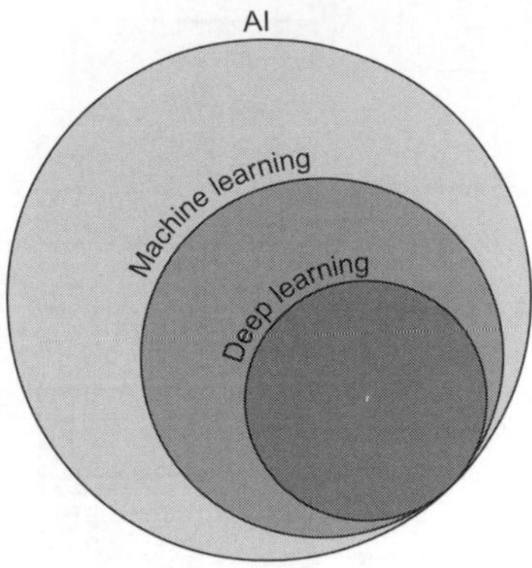

Figure 1.7 The relationship between artificial intelligence (AI), machine learning, and deep learning. Deep learning comprises a collection of techniques that form a subset of machine learning techniques, which themselves are a subfield of AI.

While it's true that deep learning methods will typically outperform "shallow" learning methods (a term sometimes used to distinguish machine learning methods that are not deep learning) for the same dataset, they are not always the best choice. Deep learning methods often are not the most appropriate method for a given problem for three reasons:

- *They are computationally expensive.* By expensive, we don't mean monetary cost, of course: we mean they require a lot of computing power, which means they can take a long time (hours or even days!) to train. Arguably this is a less important reason not to use deep learning, because if a task is important enough to you, you can invest the time and computational resources required to solve it. But if you can train a model in a few minutes that performs well, then why waste additional time and resources?
- *They tend to require more data.* Deep learning models typically require hundreds to thousands of cases in order to perform extremely well. This largely depends on the complexity of the problem at hand, but shallow methods tend to perform better on small datasets than their deep learning counterparts.
- *The rules are less interpretable.* By their nature, deep learning models favor performance over model interpretability. Arguably, our focus should be on performance; but often we're not only interested in getting the right output, we're also interested in the rules the algorithm learned because these help us to interpret things about the real world and may help us further our research. The rules learned by a neural network are not easy to interpret.

So while deep learning methods can be extraordinarily powerful, shallow learning techniques are still invaluable tools in the arsenal of data scientists.

NOTE Deep learning algorithms are particularly good at tasks involving complex data, such as image classification and audio transcription.

Because deep learning techniques require a lot of additional theory, I believe they require their own book, and so we will not discuss them here. If you would like to learn how to apply deep learning methods (and, after completing this book, I suggest you do), I strongly recommend *Deep Learning with R* by Francois Chollet and Joseph J. Allaire (Manning, 2018).

1.3 Thinking about the ethical impact of machine learning

Machine learning can be a force for good, whether that's helping people understand nature or assisting organizations to better manage their resources. But machine learning also has the potential to do great harm. For example, in 2017, a study was published showing that a machine learning model could predict—with startling accuracy—a person's sexual orientation from nothing but an image of their face.[1] While the authors had no sinister intentions, the study raised concerns about the potential misuse of machine learning. Imagine if a country in which it is still illegal to be gay (happily, Botswana legalized homosexuality in 2019, so this number should now be 71) used a model like this to persecute or even execute people?

Here's another example: in 2015, it was discovered that Google's algorithm for image recognition would classify images of people of color as images of gorillas.[2] The ethical consideration here is that the data the algorithm was trained on was biased toward images of white people and did a poor job of making accurate (and non-racist) predictions on images of non-white people. To avoid this kind of bias, it is imperative that our datasets are adequately representative of the population our model will be let loose on. Whether this is done using sensible sampling strategies or by testing for and correcting biases after training, it is our responsibility to ensure that our models aren't biased against particular groups of subjects.

An additional ethical concern with regard to machine learning research is one of security and credibility. While it may seem like something taken directly from a science fiction film, machine learning research has now reached a point where models can create videos of a person speaking, from just an image of their face. Researchers have used this so-called *deep fake* technology to produce videos of Barack Obama speaking whatever audio they provide.[3] Imagine misusing this technology to fabricate evidence of a defendant in a criminal trial making a statement they never made. Similar technology has also been used to replace one person's face in a video with another person's face. Sadly and notoriously, this has been misused to swap celebrities' faces into pornographic videos. Imagine the potential of this for ruining a person's career and dignity.

---

[1] Yilun Wang and Michal Kosinski, "Deep Neural Networks Are More Accurate than Humans at Detecting Sexual Orientation from Facial Images," 2017, https://osf.io/zn79k.

[2] Jessica Guynn, "Google Photos Labeled Black People 'Gorillas,'" *USA Today*, 2015, http://mng.bz/j5Na.

[3] Supasorn Suwajanakorn, Steven M. Seitz, and Ira Kemelmacher-Shlizerman, "Synthesizing Obama: Learning Lip Sync from Audio," *ACM Transactions on Graphics* 36 (4), article 95, 2017, http://mng.bz/WOQg.

The previous point brings me to the issue of data protection and consent. In order to train useful machine learning models that perform well, we need data. But it's important to consider whether the data you are using was collected ethically. Does it contain personal, sensitive, or financial information? Does the data belong to anyone? If so, have they given informed consent as to how it will be used? A spotlight was shined on these issues in 2018 when the consultancy firm Cambridge Analytica mined the social media data of millions of people without their consent. The subsequent media outcry and liquidation of Cambridge Analytica should serve as a stark reminder as to the importance of ethical data-collection procedures.

Two more ethical considerations are these:

- When a model suggests a particular course of action, should we follow its prediction blindly, or take it under advisement?
- Who is culpable when something goes wrong?

Imagine that we have a machine learning model that tells us whether to operate on a patient based on their diagnostic data. Would you be happy to follow the advice of the model if it had been shown to be correct in all previous cases? What about a model that predicts whether a defendant is guilty or innocent? You could argue that this second example is ridiculous, but it highlights my point: should humans be involved in the decision-making processes informed by machine learning? If so, *how* should humans be involved in these processes? The answers to these questions depend on the decision being made, how it affects the people involved, and whether human emotions should be considered in the decision-making process.

The issue of culpability poses this question: when a decision made by a machine learning algorithm leads to harm, who is responsible? We live in societies in which people are held accountable for their actions. When something bad happens, rightly or wrongly, we expect that someone will be found culpable. In 2018, a car with self-driving capability collided with and killed a pedestrian.[4] Who was culpable? The manufacturer? The person in the car? The pedestrian? Does it matter if the pedestrian was jaywalking? Ethical quandaries like these need to be considered and carefully worked out before such machine learning technologies are released into the world.

When you train a machine learning model, I request that you ask yourself these five questions:

- Are my intentions ethical?
- Even if my intentions are ethical, could someone else do harm with my model?
- Is my model biased in a way that can cause harm or discriminate?
- Has the data been collected ethically?
- Once deployed, how will humans fit into the decisions made by the model?

[4] "Death of Elaine Herzberg," Wikipedia, http://mng.bz/8zqK.

If the answer to any of them makes you feel uneasy, please carefully consider if what you're doing is ethical. Just because we *can* do something, doesn't mean we *should.* If you would like to explore a deeper discussion of how to perform ethical machine learning, I suggest *Towards a Code of Ethics for Artificial Intelligence* by Paula Boddington (Springer, 2017).

1.4 Why use R for machine learning?

There is something of a rivalry between the two most commonly used data science languages: R and Python. Anyone who is new to machine learning will choose one or the other to get started, and their decision will often be guided by the learning resources they have access to, which one is more commonly used in their field of work, and which one their colleagues use. There are no machine learning tasks that are only possible to apply in one language or the other, although some of the more cutting-edge deep learning approaches are easier to apply in Python (they tend to be written in Python first and implemented in R later). Python, while very good for data science, is a more general-purpose programming language, whereas R is geared specifically for mathematical and statistical applications. This means users of R can focus purely on data but may feel restricted if they ever need to build applications based on their models.

There really isn't an overall winner when pitching these two against each other for data science (although of course everyone has their favorite). So why have I chosen to write a book about machine learning in R? Because there are modern tools in R designed specifically to make data science tasks simple and human-readable, such as those from the *tidyverse* (we'll cover these tools in depth in chapter 2).

Traditionally, machine learning algorithms in R were scattered across multiple packages written by different authors. This meant you would need to learn to use new functions with different arguments and implementations each time you wanted to apply a new algorithm. Proponents of Python could use this as an example of why it was better suited for machine learning, because Python has the well-known scikit-learn package that has a plethora of built-in machine learning algorithms. But R has now followed suit, with the caret and mlr packages. While mlr is quite similar to caret in purpose and functionality, I believe mlr is more flexible and intuitive; so, we'll be using mlr in the book.

The mlr package (which stands for *machine learning in R*) provides an interface for a large number of machine learning algorithms and allows you to perform extremely complicated machine learning tasks with very little coding. Where possible, we will use the mlr package throughout this book so that when you're finished, you'll be proficient at using one of the most modern machine learning packages available.

1.5 Which datasets will we use?

To make your learning process as fun and interesting as possible, we will use real datasets in our machine learning pipelines. R comes with a considerable number of built-in datasets, which are supplemented by datasets that come with packages we'll be loading into our R sessions. I decided to use datasets that come with R or its packages, to make it easier for you to work through the book while offline. We'll use these datasets to help us build our machine learning models and compare how different models perform on different types of data.

> **TIP** With so many datasets to choose from, after completing each chapter, I suggest you apply what you've learned to a different dataset.

1.6 What will you learn in this book?

This book gives you a hands-on introduction to machine learning with R. To benefit from the book, you should be comfortable with basic R coding, such as loading packages and working with objects and data structures. You will learn the following:

- How to organize, tidy, and plot your data using the tidyverse
- Critical concepts such as overfitting, underfitting, and bias-variance trade-off
- How to apply several machine learning algorithms from each of the four classes (classification, regression, dimension reduction, and clustering)
- How to validate model performance and prevent overfitting
- How to compare multiple models to decide on the best one for your purpose

Throughout the book, we'll use interesting examples to learn concepts and apply our knowledge. When possible, we will also apply multiple algorithms to the same dataset so you get a feel for how different algorithms perform under certain situations.

Summary

- Artificial intelligence is the appearance of intelligent knowledge by a computer process.
- Machine learning is a subfield of artificial intelligence, where the computer learns relationships in data to make predictions about future, unseen data or to identify meaningful patterns that help us understand our data better.
- A machine learning algorithm is the process by which patterns and rules in the data are learned. A model is a collection of those patterns and rules that accepts new data, applies the rules to it, and outputs an answer.
- Deep learning is a subfield of machine learning, which is, itself, a subfield of AI.
- Machine learning algorithms are categorized/divided as supervised and unsupervised, depending on whether they learn from ground-truth-labeled data (supervised learning) or unlabeled data (unsupervised learning).

- Supervised learning algorithms are categorized/divided as classification (if they predict a categorical variable) or regression (if they predict a continuous variable).
- Unsupervised learning algorithms are categorized/divided as dimension reduction (if they find a lower-dimension representation of the data) or clustering (if they identify clusters of cases in the data).
- Along with Python, R is a popular data science language and contains many tools and built-in datasets that simplify the process of data science and machine learning.

2 Tidying, manipulating, and plotting data with the tidyverse

This chapter covers

- Understanding the tidyverse
- What is meant by *tidy* data
- Installing and loading the tidyverse
- Using the tibble, dplyr, ggplot2, tidyr, and purrr packages

I'm really excited to start teaching machine learning to you. But before we dive into that, I want to teach you some skills that are going to make your learning experience simpler and more effective. These skills will also improve your general data science and R programming skills.

Imagine that I asked you to build me a car (a typical request between friends). You could go old-fashioned: you could purchase the metal, glass, and other components; hand-cut all the pieces; hammer them into shape; and rivet them together. The car might look beautiful and work perfectly, but it would take a very long time to build, and it would be hard for you to remember exactly what you did if you had to make another one.

Instead, you could take a modern approach and use robotic arms in your factory. You could program them to cut and bend the pieces into predefined shapes and assemble the pieces for you. In this scenario, building a car would be much faster and simpler for you, and it would be easy for you to reproduce the same process in the future.

Now imagine that I make a more reasonable request and ask you to reorganize and plot a dataset, ready to be passed through a machine learning pipeline. You could use base R functions for this, and they would work fine. But the code would be long, it wouldn't be very human-readable (so in a month you'd struggle to remember what you did), and the plots would be cumbersome to produce.

Instead, you could take a more modern approach and use functions from the *tidyverse* family of packages. These functions help simplify the data-manipulation process, are very human-readable, and allow you to produce very attractive graphics with minimal typing.

2.1 What is the tidyverse, and what is tidy data?

The purpose of this book is to give you the skills to apply machine learning approaches to your data. While it isn't my intention to cover all other aspects of data science (nor could I, in a single book), I do want to introduce you to the tidyverse. Before you can input your data into a machine learning algorithm, it needs to be in a format that the algorithm is happy to work with.

The tidyverse is an "opinionated collection of R packages designed for data science," created for the purpose of making data science tasks in R simpler, more human-readable, and more reproducible. The packages are "opinionated" because they are designed to make tasks the package authors consider to be good practice, easy, and make tasks they consider to be bad practice, difficult. The name comes from the concept of *tidy data*, a data structure in which

- Each row represents a single observation.
- Each column represents a variable.

Take a look at the data in table 2.1. Imagine that we take four runners and put them on a new training regime. We want to know if the regime is improving their running times, so we record their best times just before the new training starts (month 0), and for three months thereafter.

Table 2.1 An example of untidy data. This table contains the running times for four runners, taken immediately before starting a new training regime and then for three months thereafter.

Athlete	Month 0	Month 1	Month 2	Month 3
Joana	12.50	12.1	11.98	11.99
Debi	14.86	14.9	14.70	14.30
Sukhveer	12.10	12.1	12.00	11.80
Kerol	19.60	19.7	19.30	19.00

This is an example of *untidy* data. Can you see why? Well, let's go back to our rules. Does each row represent a single observation? Nope. In fact, we have four observations per row (one for each month). Does each column represent a variable? Nope. There are only three variables in this data: the athlete, the month, and the best time, and yet we have five columns!

How would the same data look in tidy format? Table 2.2 shows you.

Table 2.2 This table contains the same data as table 2.1, but in tidy format.

Athlete	Month	Best
Joana	0	12.50
Debi	0	14.86
Sukhveer	0	12.10
Kerol	0	19.60
Joana	1	12.10
Debi	1	14.90
Sukhveer	1	12.10
Kerol	1	19.70
Joana	2	11.98
Debi	2	14.70
Sukhveer	2	12.00
Kerol	2	19.30
Joana	3	11.99
Debi	3	14.30
Sukhveer	3	11.80
Kerol	3	19.00

This time, we have the column Month that contains the month identifiers that were previously used as separate columns, and the Best column, which holds the best time for each athlete for each month. Does each row represent a single observation? Yes! Does each column represent a variable? Yes! So this data is in tidy format.

Ensuring that your data is in tidy format is an important early step in any machine learning pipeline, and so the tidyverse includes the package tidyr, which helps you achieve this. The other packages in the tidyverse work with tidyr and each other to help you do the following:

- Organize and display your data in a sensible way (tibble)
- Manipulate and subset your data (dplyr)

- Plot your data (ggplot2)
- Replace `for` loops with a functional programming approach (purrr)

All of the operations available to you in the tidyverse are achievable using base R code, but I strongly suggest that you incorporate the tidyverse in your work: it will help you keep your code simpler, more human-readable, and reproducible.

> **Core and optional packages of the tidyverse**
>
> I'm going to teach you to use the tibble, dplyr, ggplot2, tidyr, and purrr packages of the tidyverse. These are part of the "core" tidyverse packages, along with these:
>
> - readr, for reading data into R from external files
> - forcats, for working with factors
> - stringr, for working with strings
>
> In addition to these core packages that can be loaded together, the tidyverse includes a number of optional packages that need to be loaded individually.
>
> To learn more about the other tools of the tidyverse, see *R for Data Science* by Garrett Grolemund and Hadley Wickham (O'Reilly Media, 2016).

2.2 Loading the tidyverse

The packages of the tidyverse can all be installed and loaded together (recommended)

```
install.packages("tidyverse")
library(tidyverse)
```

or installed and loaded individually as needed:

```
install.packages(c("tibble", "dplyr", "ggplot2", "tidyr", "purrr"))
library(tibble)
library(dplyr)
library(ggplot2)
library(tidyr)
library(purrr)
```

2.3 What the tibble package is and what it does

If you have been doing any form of data science or analysis in R, you will surely have come across data frames as a structure for storing rectangular data. Data frames work fine and, for a long time, were the only way to store rectangular data with columns of different types (in contrast to matrices, which can only handle data of the same type), but very little has been done to improve the aspects of data frames that data scientists dislike.

> **NOTE** Data is *rectangular* if each row has a number of elements equal to the number of columns, and each column has a number of elements equal to the number of rows. Data isn't always of this kind!

The tibble package introduces a new data structure, the tibble, to "keep the features that have stood the test of time, and drop the features that used to be convenient but are now frustrating" (http://mng.bz/1wxj). Let's see what's meant by this.

2.3.1 Creating tibbles

Creating tibbles with the `tibble()` function works the same as creating data frames:

```
myTib <- tibble(x =  1:4,
                y = c("london", "beijing", "las vegas", "berlin"))

myTib

# A tibble: 4 x 2
      x y
  <int> <chr>
1     1 london
2     2 beijing
3     3 las vegas
4     4 berlin
```

Tells us it's a tibble with four rows and two columns (annotates `# A tibble: 4 x 2`)

Variable names (annotates `x y`)

Variable classes: <int> = integer, <chr> = character (annotates `<int> <chr>`)

If you're used to working with data frames, you will immediately notice two differences in how tibbles are printed:

- When you print a tibble, it tells you that it's a tibble and its dimensions.
- Tibbles tell you the type of each variable.

This second feature is particularly useful in avoiding errors due to incorrect variable types.

> **TIP** When printing a tibble, `<int>` denotes an integer variable, `<chr>` denotes a character variable, `<dbl>` denotes a floating-point number (decimal), and `<lgl>` denotes a logical variable.

2.3.2 Converting existing data frames into tibbles

Just as you can coerce objects into data frames using the `as.data.frame()` function, you can coerce objects into tibbles using the `as_tibble()` function:

```
myDf <- data.frame(x =  1:4,
                   y = c("london", "beijing", "las vegas", "berlin"))

dfToTib <- as_tibble(myDf)

dfToTib

# A tibble: 4 x 2
      x y
  <int> <fct>
1     1 london
2     2 beijing
3     3 las vegas
4     4 berlin
```

NOTE In this book, we'll be working with data already built into R. Often, we need to read data into our R session from a .csv file. To load the data as a tibble, you use the `read_csv()` function. `read_csv()` comes from the readr package, which is loaded when you call `library(tidyverse)`, and is the tidyverse version of `read.csv()`.

2.3.3 Differences between data frames and tibbles

If you're used to working with data frames, you'll notice a few differences with tibbles. I've summarized the most notable differences between data frames and tibbles in this section.

Tibbles don't convert your data types

A common frustration people have when creating data frames is that they convert string variables to factors by default. This can be annoying because it may not be the best way to handle the variables. To prevent this conversion, you must supply the `stringsAsFactors = FALSE` argument when creating a data frame.

In contrast, tibbles don't convert string variables to factors by default. This behavior is desirable because automatic conversion of data to certain types can be a frustrating source of bugs:

```
myDf <- data.frame(x =  1:4,
                   y = c("london", "beijing", "las vegas", "berlin"))

myDfNotFactor <- data.frame(x =  1:4,
                            y = c("london", "beijing", "las vegas", "berlin"),
                            stringsAsFactors = FALSE)

myTib <- tibble(x =  1:4,
                y = c("london", "beijing", "las vegas", "berlin"))

class(myDf$y)
[1] "factor"

class(myDfNotFactor$y)
[1] "character"

class(myTib$y)
[1] "character"
```

If you want a variable to be a factor in a tibble, you simply wrap the `c()` function inside `factor()`:

```
myTib <- tibble(x =  1:4,
                y = factor(c("london", "beijing", "las vegas", "berlin")))
myTib
```

Concise output, regardless of data size

When you print a data frame, all the columns are printed to the console (by default), making it difficult to view early variables and cases. When you print a tibble, it only prints the first 10 rows and the number of columns that fit on your screen (by default), making it easier to get a quick understanding of the data. Note that the names of variables that aren't printed are listed at the bottom of the output. Run the following code, and contrast the output of the `starwars` tibble (which is included with dplyr and available when you call `library(tidyverse)`) with how it looks when converted into a data frame.

Listing 2.1 The `starwars` data as a tibble and a data frame

```
data(starwars)

starwars

as.data.frame(starwars)
```

TIP The `data()` function loads into your global environment a dataset that is included with base R or an R package. Use `data()` with no arguments to list all the datasets available for your currently loaded packages.

SUBSETTING WITH [ALWAYS RETURNS ANOTHER TIBBLE

When subsetting a data frame, the `[` operator will return another data frame if you keep more than one column, or a vector if you keep only one. When subsetting a tibble, the `[` operator will *always* return another tibble. If you wish to explicitly return a tibble column as a vector, use either the `[[` or `$` operator instead. This behavior is desirable because we should be explicit in whether we want a vector or rectangular data structure, to avoid bugs:

```
myDf[, 1]

[1] 1 2 3 4

myTib[, 1]

# A tibble: 4 x 1
      x
  <int>
1     1
2     2
3     3
4     4

myTib[[1]]

[1] 1 2 3 4

myTib$x

[1] 1 2 3 4
```

NOTE An exception to this is if you subset a data frame using a single index with no comma (such as `myDf[1]`). In this case, the `[` operator *will* return a single-column data frame, but this method doesn't allow us to combine row and column subsetting.

VARIABLES ARE CREATED SEQUENTIALLY

When building a tibble, variables are created sequentially so that later variables can reference those defined earlier. This means we can create variables on the fly that refer to other variables in the same function call:

```
sequentialTib <- tibble(nItems = c(12, 45, 107),
                        cost = c(0.5, 1.2, 1.8),
                        totalWorth = nItems * cost)

sequentialTib

# A tibble: 3 x 3
  nItems  cost totalWorth
   <dbl> <dbl>      <dbl>
1     12   0.5          6
2     45   1.2         54
3    107   1.8        193
```

> **Exercise 1**
> Load the `mtcars` dataset using the `data()` function, convert it into a tibble, and explore it using the `summary()` function.

2.4 What the dplyr package is and what it does

When working with data, we often need to perform operations on it such as the following:

- Selecting only the rows and/or columns of interest
- Creating new variables
- Arranging the data in ascending or descending order of certain variables
- Getting summary statistics

There may also be a natural grouping structure in the data that we would like to maintain when performing these operations. The dplyr package allows us to perform these operations in a very intuitive way. Let's work through an example.

2.4.1 Manipulating the CO2 dataset with dplyr

Let's load the built-in CO2 dataset in R. We have a tibble with 84 cases and 5 variables, documenting the uptake of carbon dioxide by different plants under various conditions. I'm going to use this dataset to teach you some fundamental dplyr skills.

Listing 2.2 Exploring the CO2 dataset

```
library(tibble)

data(CO2)

CO2tib <- as_tibble(CO2)
```

```
CO2tib

# A tibble: 84 x 5
   Plant Type   Treatment   conc uptake
 * <ord> <fct>  <fct>      <dbl>  <dbl>
 1 Qn1   Quebec nonchilled    95   16
 2 Qn1   Quebec nonchilled   175   30.4
 3 Qn1   Quebec nonchilled   250   34.8
 4 Qn1   Quebec nonchilled   350   37.2
 5 Qn1   Quebec nonchilled   500   35.3
 6 Qn1   Quebec nonchilled   675   39.2
 7 Qn1   Quebec nonchilled  1000   39.7
 8 Qn2   Quebec nonchilled    95   13.6
 9 Qn2   Quebec nonchilled   175   27.3
10 Qn2   Quebec nonchilled   250   37.1
# ... with 74 more rows
```

Let's say we want to *select* only columns 1, 2, 3, and 5. We can do this using the `select()` function. In the `select()` function call in the following listing, the first argument is the data; then we supply either the numbers or names of the columns we wish to select, separated by commas.

Listing 2.3 Selecting columns using `select()`

```
library(dplyr)

selectedData <- select(CO2tib, 1, 2, 3, 5)

selectedData

# A tibble: 84 x 4
   Plant Type   Treatment  uptake
 * <ord> <fct>  <fct>       <dbl>
 1 Qn1   Quebec nonchilled   16
 2 Qn1   Quebec nonchilled   30.4
 3 Qn1   Quebec nonchilled   34.8
 4 Qn1   Quebec nonchilled   37.2
 5 Qn1   Quebec nonchilled   35.3
 6 Qn1   Quebec nonchilled   39.2
 7 Qn1   Quebec nonchilled   39.7
 8 Qn2   Quebec nonchilled   13.6
 9 Qn2   Quebec nonchilled   27.3
10 Qn2   Quebec nonchilled   37.1
# ... with 74 more rows
```

Exercise 2

Select all of the columns of your `mtcars` tibble except the `qsec` and `vs` variables.

Now let's suppose we wish to *filter* our data to include only cases whose uptake was greater than 16. We can do this using the `filter()` function. The first argument of `filter()` is, once again, the data, and the second argument is a logical expression that will be evaluated for each row. We can include multiple conditions here by separating them with commas.

Listing 2.4 Filtering rows using `filter()`

```
filteredData <- filter(selectedData, uptake > 16)

filteredData

# A tibble: 66 x 4
   Plant Type   Treatment  uptake
   <ord> <fct>  <fct>       <dbl>
 1 Qn1   Quebec nonchilled   30.4
 2 Qn1   Quebec nonchilled   34.8
 3 Qn1   Quebec nonchilled   37.2
 4 Qn1   Quebec nonchilled   35.3
 5 Qn1   Quebec nonchilled   39.2
 6 Qn1   Quebec nonchilled   39.7
 7 Qn2   Quebec nonchilled   27.3
 8 Qn2   Quebec nonchilled   37.1
 9 Qn2   Quebec nonchilled   41.8
10 Qn2   Quebec nonchilled   40.6
# ... with 56 more rows
```

Exercise 3

Filter your `mtcars` tibble to include only cases with a number of cylinders (`cyl`) *not* equal to 8.

Next, we would like to *group* by individual plants and *summarize* the data to get the mean and standard deviation of uptake within each group. We can achieve this using the `group_by()` and `summarize()` functions, respectively.

In the `group_by()` function, the first argument is—you guessed it—the data (see the pattern here?), followed by the grouping variable. We can group by more than one variable by separating them with commas. When we print `groupedData`, not much has changed except that we get an indication above the data saying that they are grouped, the variable by which they are grouped, and how many groups there are. This tells us that any further operations we apply will be performed on a group-by-group basis.

Listing 2.5 Grouping data with `group_by()`

```
groupedData <- group_by(filteredData, Plant)

groupedData

# A tibble: 66 x 4
# Groups:   Plant [11]
   Plant Type   Treatment  uptake
```

```
   <ord> <fct>  <fct>      <dbl>
 1 Qn1   Quebec nonchilled  30.4
 2 Qn1   Quebec nonchilled  34.8
 3 Qn1   Quebec nonchilled  37.2
 4 Qn1   Quebec nonchilled  35.3
 5 Qn1   Quebec nonchilled  39.2
 6 Qn1   Quebec nonchilled  39.7
 7 Qn2   Quebec nonchilled  27.3
 8 Qn2   Quebec nonchilled  37.1
 9 Qn2   Quebec nonchilled  41.8
10 Qn2   Quebec nonchilled  40.6
# ... with 56 more rows
```

TIP You can remove a grouping structure from a tibble by wrapping it in the `ungroup()` function.

In the `summarize()` function, the first argument is the data; in the second argument, we name the new variables we're creating, followed by an = sign, followed by a definition of that variable. We can create as many new variables as we like by separating them by commas. In listing 2.6, we create two summary variables: the mean of the uptake for each group (`meanUp`) and the standard deviation of the uptake for each group (`sdUp`). Now, when we print `summarizedData`, we can see that aside from our grouping variable, our original variables have been replaced with the summary variables we just created.

Listing 2.6 Creating summaries of variables using `summarize()`

```
summarizedData <- summarize(groupedData, meanUp = mean(uptake),
                            sdUp = sd(uptake))

summarizedData

# A tibble: 11 x 3
   Plant meanUp   sdUp
   <ord>  <dbl>  <dbl>
 1 Qn1     36.1  3.42
 2 Qn2     38.8  6.07
 3 Qn3     37.6 10.3
 4 Qc1     32.6  5.03
 5 Qc3     35.5  7.52
 6 Qc2     36.6  5.14
 7 Mn3     26.2  3.49
 8 Mn2     29.9  3.92
 9 Mn1     29.0  5.70
10 Mc3     18.4  0.826
11 Mc1     20.1  1.83
```

Finally, we will *mutate* a new variable from the existing ones to calculate the coefficient of variation for each group, and then we'll *arrange* the rows in the data so that the row with the smallest value of the new variable is at the top, and the row with the largest value is at the bottom. We can do this with the `mutate()` and `arrange()` functions.

For the `mutate()` function, the first argument is the data. The second argument is the name of the new variable to be created, followed by an = sign, followed by its definition. We can create as many new variables as we like by separating them with commas.

Listing 2.7 Creating new variables using `mutate()`

```
mutatedData <- mutate(summarizedData,  CV = (sdUp / meanUp) * 100)

mutatedData

# A tibble: 11 x 4
   Plant meanUp   sdUp    CV
   <ord>  <dbl>  <dbl> <dbl>
 1 Qn1     36.1  3.42   9.48
 2 Qn2     38.8  6.07  15.7
 3 Qn3     37.6 10.3   27.5
 4 Qc1     32.6  5.03  15.4
 5 Qc3     35.5  7.52  21.2
 6 Qc2     36.6  5.14  14.1
 7 Mn3     26.2  3.49  13.3
 8 Mn2     29.9  3.92  13.1
 9 Mn1     29.0  5.70  19.6
10 Mc3     18.4  0.826  4.48
11 Mc1     20.1  1.83   9.11
```

TIP Argument evaluation in dplyr functions is sequential, meaning we could have defined the `CV` variable in the `summarize()` function by referencing the `meanUp` and `sdUp` variables, even though they hadn't been created yet!

The `arrange()` function takes the data as the first argument, followed by the variable(s) we wish to arrange the cases by. We can arrange by multiple columns by separating them with commas: doing so will arrange the cases in the order of the first variable, and any ties will be ordered based on their value of the second variable, and so on with subsequent ties.

Listing 2.8 Arranging tibbles by variables using `arrange()`

```
arrangedData <- arrange(mutatedData, CV)

arrangedData

# A tibble: 11 x 4
   Plant meanUp   sdUp    CV
   <ord>  <dbl>  <dbl> <dbl>
 1 Mc3     18.4  0.826  4.48
 2 Mc1     20.1  1.83   9.11
 3 Qn1     36.1  3.42   9.48
 4 Mn2     29.9  3.92  13.1
 5 Mn3     26.2  3.49  13.3
 6 Qc2     36.6  5.14  14.1
 7 Qc1     32.6  5.03  15.4
 8 Qn2     38.8  6.07  15.7
 9 Mn1     29.0  5.70  19.6
```

```
10 Qc3       35.5  7.52  21.2
11 Qn3       37.6 10.3   27.5
```

TIP If you want to arrange a tibble in *descending* order of a variable's values, simply wrap the variable in `desc()`: `arrange(mutatedData, desc(CV))`.

2.4.2 Chaining dplyr functions together

Everything we did in section 2.4.1 could be achieved using base R, but I hope you can see that the dplyr functions—or *verbs*, as they're often called (because they are human-readable and clearly imply what they do)—help make the code simpler and more human-readable. But the power of dplyr really comes from the ability to chain these functions together into intuitive, sequential processes.

At each stage of our CO2 data manipulation, we saved the intermediate data and applied the next function to it. This is tedious, creates lots of unnecessary data objects in our R environment, and is not as human-readable. Instead, we can use the pipe operator, `%>%`, which becomes available when we load dplyr. The pipe passes the output of the function on its left as the first argument to the function on its right. Let's look at a basic example:

```
library(dplyr)

c(1, 4, 7, 3, 5) %>% mean()

[1] 4
```

The `%>%` operator takes the output of the `c()` function on the left (a vector of length 5), and "pipes" it into the first argument of the `mean()` function. We can use the `%>%` operator to chain multiple functions together to make the code more concise and human-readable.

Remember how I made a point of saying that the first argument of each dplyr function is the data? Well, the reason this is so important and useful is that it allows us to pipe the data from the previous operation into the next one. The entire process of data manipulation we went through in section 2.4.1 becomes the following listing.

Listing 2.9 Chaining dplyr operations together with `%>%`

```
arrangedData <- CO2tib %>%
  select(c(1:3, 5)) %>%
  filter(uptake > 16) %>%
  group_by(Plant) %>%
  summarize(meanUp = mean(uptake), sdUp = sd(uptake)) %>%
  mutate(CV = (sdUp / meanUp) * 100) %>%
  arrange(CV)

arrangedData

# A tibble: 11 x 4
   Plant meanUp   sdUp     CV
```

```
   <ord>  <dbl>  <dbl> <dbl>
 1 Mc3     18.4  0.826  4.48
 2 Mc1     20.1  1.83   9.11
 3 Qn1     36.1  3.42   9.48
 4 Mn2     29.9  3.92  13.1
 5 Mn3     26.2  3.49  13.3
 6 Qc2     36.6  5.14  14.1
 7 Qc1     32.6  5.03  15.4
 8 Qn2     38.8  6.07  15.7
 9 Mn1     29.0  5.70  19.6
10 Qc3     35.5  7.52  21.2
11 Qn3     37.6 10.3   27.5
```

Read the code from top to bottom, and every time you come to a `%>%` operator, say "and then." You would read it as "Take the CO2 data, *and then* select these columns, *and then* filter these rows, *and then* group by this variable, *and then* summarize with these variables, *and then* mutate this new variable, *and then* arrange in order of this variable and save the output as `arrangedData`. Can you see that this is how you might explain your data-manipulation process to a colleague in plain English? This is the power of dplyr: being able to perform complex data manipulations in a logical, human-readable way.

> **TIP** It is conventional to start a new line after a `%>%` operator to help make the code easier to read.

> **Exercise 4**
>
> Group the `mtcars` tibble by the `gear` variable, summarize the medians of the `mpg` and `disp` variables, and mutate a new variable that is the `mpg` median divided by the `disp` median, all chained together with the `%>%` operator.

2.5 What the ggplot2 package is and what it does

In R, there are three main plotting systems:

- Base graphics
- Lattice
- ggplot2

Arguably, ggplot2 is the most popular system among data scientists; and as it's part of the tidyverse, we will use this system to plot our data throughout this book. The "gg" in ggplot2 stands for *grammar of graphics*, a school of thought that says any data graphic can be created by combining data with layers of plot components such as axes, tick-marks, gridlines, dots, bars, and lines. By layering plot components like this, you can use ggplot2 to create communicative, attractive plots in a very intuitive way.

Let's load the iris dataset that comes with R and create a scatter plot of two of its variables. This data was collected and published by Edgar Anderson in 1935 and contains length and width measurements of the petals and sepals of three species of iris plant.

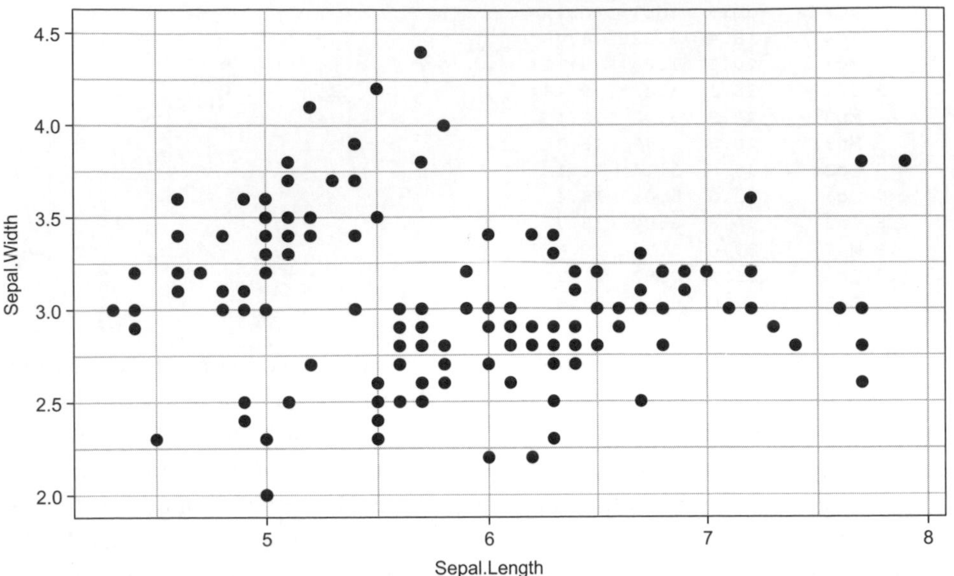

Figure 2.1 A scatter plot created with ggplot2. The `Sepal.Length` variable is mapped to the x aesthetic, and the `Sepal.Width` variable is mapped to the y aesthetic. A black-and-white theme was applied by adding the `theme_bw()` layer.

The code to create the plot in figure 2.1 is shown in listing 2.10. The function `ggplot()` takes the data you supply as the first argument and the function `aes()` as the second (more about this in a moment). This creates a plotting environment, axis, and axis labels based on the data.

The `aes()` function is short for *aesthetic mappings*, which, if you're used to base R plotting, may be new to you. An *aesthetic* is a feature of a plot that can be controlled by a variable in the data. Examples of aesthetics include the x-axis, y-axis, color, shape, size, and even transparency of the data points drawn on the plot. In the function call in listing 2.10, we have asked `ggplot()` to map the `Sepal.Length` and `Sepal.Width` variables to the x- and y-axes, respectively.

Listing 2.10 Plotting data with the `ggplot()` function

```
library(ggplot2)
data(iris)
myPlot <- ggplot(iris, aes(x = Sepal.Length, y = Sepal.Width)) +
  geom_point() +
  theme_bw()

myPlot
```

TIP Notice that we don't need to wrap the variable names in quotes; `ggplot()` is clever!

We finish the line with the + symbol, which we use to add additional layers to our plot (we can add as many layers as it takes to create our desired plot). Convention states that when we add additional layers to our plots, we finish the current layer with + and place the next layer on a new line. This helps maintain readability.

> **NOTE** When adding layers to the initial `ggplot()` function call, each line needs to finish with +; you cannot put the + on a new line.

The next layer is a function called `geom_point()`. *Geom* stands for *geometric object*, which is a graphical element used to represent data points, such as bars, lines, box and whiskers, and so on; the functions to produce these layers are all named `geom_[graphical element]`. For example, let's add two new layers to our plot: `geom_density_2d()`, which adds density contours; and `geom_smooth()`, which fits a smoothed line with confidence bands to the data (see figure 2.2).

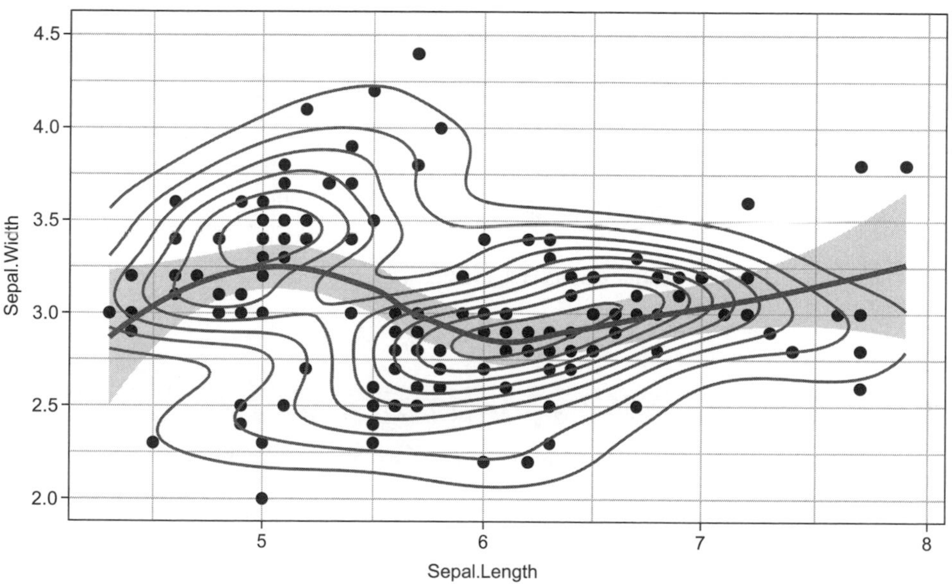

Figure 2.2 The same scatter plot as in figure 2.1, with 2D density contours and a smoothed line added as layers using the `geom_density_2d()` and `geom_smooth` functions, respectively.

The plot is reasonably complex, and to achieve the same in base R would take many lines of code. Here's how easy this is to achieve with ggplot2!

Listing 2.11 Adding geom layers to a `ggplot` object

```
myPlot +
  geom_density_2d() +
  geom_smooth()
```

NOTE You can save a ggplot as a named object and simply add new layers to that object, instead of creating the plot from scratch each time.

Finally, it's often important to highlight a grouping structure within the data, and we can do this by adding a color or shape aesthetic mapping, as shown in figure 2.3. The code to produce these plots is shown in listing 2.12. The only difference between them is that species is given as the argument to the shape or col (color) aesthetic.

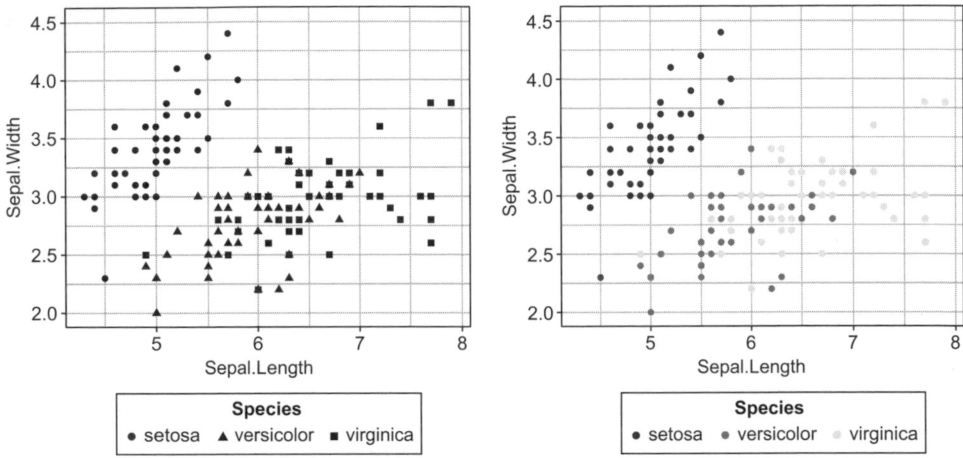

Figure 2.3 The same scatter plot as in figure 2.1, with the Species variable mapped to the shape and col aesthetics

Listing 2.12 Mapping species to the shape and color aesthetics

```
ggplot(iris, aes(x = Sepal.Length, y = Sepal.Width, shape = Species)) +
  geom_point()  +
  theme_bw()

ggplot(iris, aes(x = Sepal.Length, y = Sepal.Width, col = Species)) +
  geom_point()  +
  theme_bw()
```

NOTE Notice how ggplot() automatically produces a legend when you add aesthetic mappings other than x and y. With base graphics, you would have to produce these manually!

One final thing I want to teach you about ggplot() is its extremely powerful *faceting* functionality. Sometimes we may wish to create subplots of our data where each subplot, or *facet*, displays data belonging to some group present in the data.

For example, figure 2.4 shows the same iris data, but this time faceted by the Species variable. The code to create this plot is shown in listing 2.13: I've simply

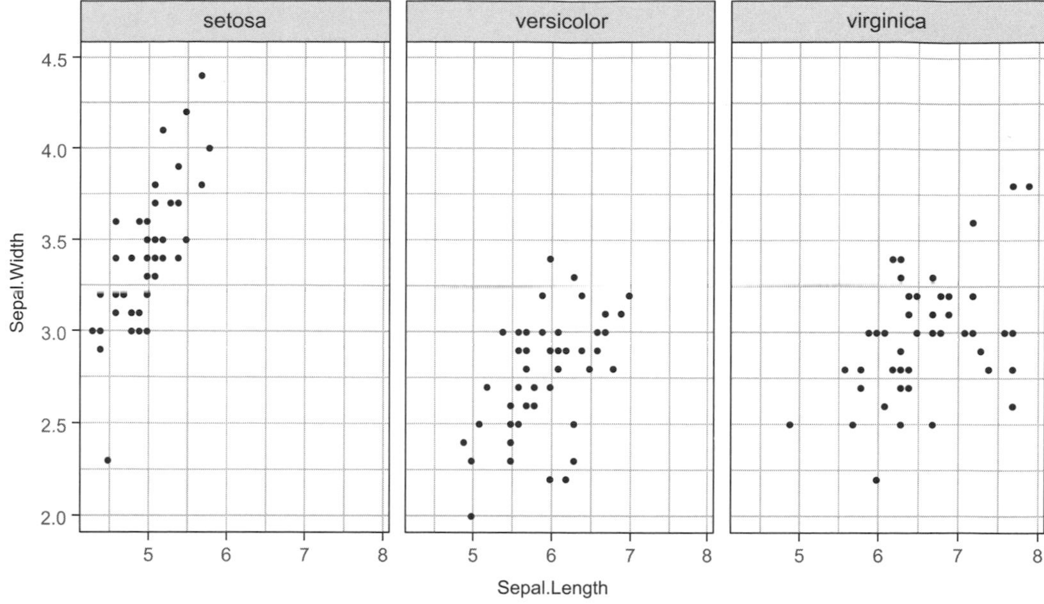

Figure 2.4 The same data is shown, but with different iris species plotted on separate subplots or facets.

added a `facet_wrap()` layer to the `ggplot` call, and specified I want it to facet by `(~ Species)`.

Listing 2.13 Grouping subplots with the `facet_wrap()` function

```
ggplot(iris, aes(x = Sepal.Length, y = Sepal.Width)) +
  facet_wrap(~ Species) +
  geom_point()  +
  theme_bw()
```

While there is much more you can do with ggplot2 than is presented here (including customizing the appearance of virtually everything), I just want to give you an understanding of how to create the basic plots needed to replicate those you'll find throughout the book. If you want to take your data-visualization skills to the next level, I strongly recommend *ggplot2: Elegant Graphics for Data Analysis* by Hadley Wickham (Springer International Publishing, 2016).

TIP The order of plot elements on a ggplot is important! Plot elements are layered on sequentially, so elements added later in a `ggplot()` call will be *on top* of all the others. Reorder the `geom_density_2d()` and `geom_point()` functions used to create figure 2.2, and look closely to see what happens (the plot might look the same, but it's not!).

Exercise 5

Create a scatter plot of the `drat` and `wt` variables from your `mtcars` tibble, and color the dots by the `carb` variable. See what happens when you wrap the `carb` aesthetic mapping in `as.factor()`.

2.6 What the tidyr package is and what it does

In section 2.1, we looked at an example of data that was not tidy and then at the same data after restructuring it in tidy format. Quite often, as data scientists, we don't have much control over the format data is in when it comes to us; we commonly have to restructure untidy data into a tidy format so that we can pass it into our machine learning pipelines. Let's make an untidy tibble and convert it into its tidy format.

Listing 2.14 shows a tibble of fictitious patient data, where patients' body mass index (BMI) was measured at month 0, month 3, and month 6 after the start of some imaginary intervention. Is this data tidy? Well, no. There are only three variables in the data:

- Patient ID
- The month the measurement was taken
- The BMI measurement

But we have four columns! Also, each row doesn't contain the data for a single observation: it contains all the observations made on that patient.

Listing 2.14 Untidy tibble

```
library(tibble)

library(tidyr)

patientData <- tibble(Patient = c("A", "B", "C"),
                      Month0 = c(21, 17, 29),
                      Month3 = c(20, 21, 27),
                      Month6 = c(21, 22, 23))

patientData

# A tibble: 3 x 4
  Patient Month0 Month3 Month6
  <chr>    <dbl>  <dbl>  <dbl>
1 A           21     20     21
2 B           17     21     22
3 C           29     27     23
```

To convert this untidy tibble into its tidy counterpart, we can use tidyr's `gather()` function. The `gather()` function takes the data as its first argument. The `key` argument defines the name of the new variable that will represent the columns we are "gathering." In this case, the columns we are gathering are named `Month0`, `Month3`, and Month6, so we call the new column that will hold these keys Month. The value argument defines the name of the new variable that will represent the data from the columns we are gathering. In this case, the values were BMI measurements, so we call the new column that will represent these values BMI. The final argument is a vector defining which variables to gather and convert into the key-value pairs. By using -Patient, we are telling gather() to use all the variables except the identifying variable, Patient.

Listing 2.15 Tidying data with the gather() function

```
tidyPatientData <- gather(patientData, key = Month,
                          value = BMI, -Patient)

tidyPatientData

# A tibble: 9 x 3
  Patient Month    BMI
  <chr>   <chr>  <dbl>
1 A       Month0    21
2 B       Month0    17
3 C       Month0    29
4 A       Month3    20
5 B       Month3    21
6 C       Month3    27
7 A       Month6    21
8 B       Month6    22
9 C       Month6    23
```

We could have achieved the same result by typing the following, instead (note that the tibbles returned by the two listings are identical).

Listing 2.16 Different ways to select columns for gathering

```
gather(patientData, key = Month, value = BMI, Month0:Month6)

# A tibble: 9 x 3
  Patient Month    BMI
  <chr>   <chr>  <dbl>
1 A       Month0    21
2 B       Month0    17
3 C       Month0    29
4 A       Month3    20
5 B       Month3    21
6 C       Month3    27
7 A       Month6    21
8 B       Month6    22
9 C       Month6    23

gather(patientData, key = Month, value = BMI, c(Month0, Month3, Month6))

# A tibble: 9 x 3
  Patient Month    BMI
```

```
  <chr>   <chr>  <dbl>
1 A       Month0    21
2 B       Month0    17
3 C       Month0    29
4 A       Month3    20
5 B       Month3    21
6 C       Month3    27
7 A       Month6    21
8 B       Month6    22
9 C       Month6    23
```

Converting data to wide format

The data structure in the `patientData` tibble is called *wide* format, where observations for a single case are placed in the same row, across multiple columns. Mostly we want to work with tidy data because it makes our lives simpler: we can see immediately which variables we have, grouping structures are made clear, and most functions are designed to work easily with tidy data. There are, however, some rare occasions where we need to convert our tidy data into wide format, perhaps because a function we need expects the data in this format. We can convert tidy data into its wide format using the `spread()` function:

```
spread(tidyPatientData, key = Month, value = BMI)

# A tibble: 3 x 4
  Patient Month0 Month3 Month6
  <chr>    <dbl>  <dbl>  <dbl>
1 A           21     20     21
2 B           17     21     22
3 C           29     27     23
```

Its use is the opposite of `gather()`: we supply the `key` and `value` arguments as the names of the key and value columns we created using the `gather()` function, and the function converts these into wide format for us.

Exercise 6

Gather the `vs`, `am`, `gear`, and `carb` variables from your `mtcars` tibble into a single key-value pair.

2.7 What the purrr package is and what it does

The last tidyverse package I'm going to show you is purrr (with three r's). R gives us the tools to use it as a functional programming language. This means it gives us the tools to treat all computations like mathematical functions that return their values, without altering anything in the workspace.

NOTE When a function does something other than return a value (such as draw a plot or alter an environment), it's called a *side effect* of the function. A function that does not produce any side effects is said to be a *pure* function.

A simple example of functions that do and do not produce side effects is shown in listing 2.17. The `pure()` function returns the value of `a + 1` but does not alter anything in the global environment. The `side_effects()` function uses the super-assignment operator `<<-` to reassign the object `a` in the global environment. Each time you run the `pure()` function, it gives the same output; but running the `side_effect()` function gives a new value each time (and will impact the output of subsequent `pure()` function calls as well).

Listing 2.17 Creating a list of numeric vectors

```
a <- 20

pure <- function() {
  a <- a + 1
  a
}

side_effect <- function() {
  a <<- a + 1
  a
}

c(pure(), pure())
[1] 21 21

c(side_effect(), side_effect())
[1] 21 22
```

Calling functions without side effects is usually desirable because it's easier to predict what the function will do. If a function has no side effects, it can be substituted with a different implementation without breaking anything in your code.

An important consequence is that `for` loops, which when used on their own can create unwanted side effects (such as modifying existing variables), can be wrapped inside other functions. Functions that wrap `for` loops inside them allow us to iterate over each element of a vector/list (including columns and rows of data frames or tibbles), apply a function to that element, and return the result of the whole iterative process.

> **NOTE** If you're familiar with the `apply()` family of base R functions, functions from the purrr package help us achieve the same thing, but using a consistent syntax and some convenient features.

2.7.1 Replacing for loops with map()

The purrr package provides a set of functions that allow us to apply a function to each element of a list. Which purrr function to use depends on the number of inputs and what we want our output to be; in this section, I'll demonstrate the importance of the most commonly used functions from this package.

Imagine that we have a list of three numeric vectors:

```
listOfNumerics <- list(a = rnorm(5),
                       b = rnorm(9),
                       c = rnorm(10))

listOfNumerics

$a
[1] -1.4617 -0.3948  2.1335 -0.2203  0.3429

$b
[1]  0.2438 -1.3541  0.6164 -0.5524  0.4519  0.3592 -1.3415 -1.7594  1.2160

$c
 [1] -1.1325  0.2792  0.5152 -1.1657 -0.7668  0.1778  1.4004  0.6492 -1.6320
[10] -1.0986
```

Now, let's say we want to apply a function to each of the three list elements separately, such as the `length()` function to return the length of each element. We could use a `for` loop to do this, iterating over each list element and saving the length as an element of a new list that we predefine to save time:

```
elementLengths <- vector("list", length = 3)

for(i in seq_along(listOfNumerics)) {
  elementLengths[[i]] <- length(listOfNumerics[[i]])
}

elementLengths

[[1]]
[1] 5

[[2]]
[1] 9

[[3]]
[1] 20
```

This code is difficult to read, requires us to predefine an empty vector to prevent the loop from being slow, and has a side effect: if we run the loop again, it will overwrite the `elementLengths` list.

Instead, we can replace the `for` loop with the `map()` function. The first argument of all the functions in the `map` family is the data we're iterating over. The second argument is the function we're applying to each list element. Take a look at figure 2.5, which illustrates how the `map()` function applies a function to every element of a list/vector and returns a list containing the outputs.

In this example, the `map()` function applies the `length()` function to each element of the `listOfNumerics` list and returns these values as a list. Notice that the `map()`

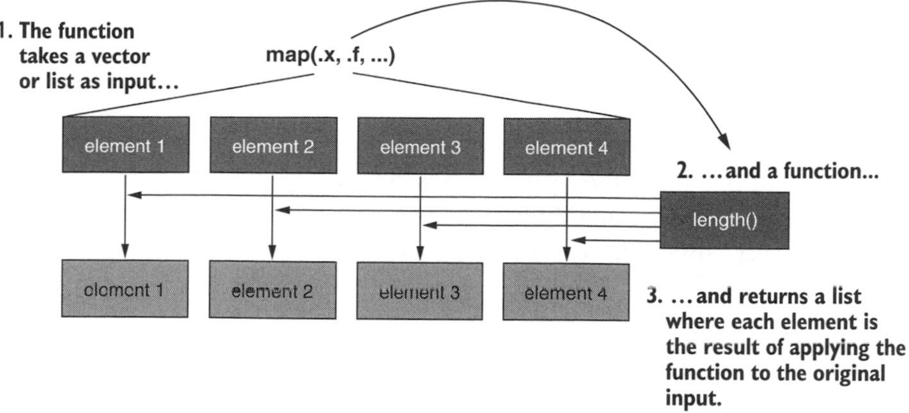

Figure 2.5 The `map()` function takes a vector or list as input, applies a function to each element individually, and returns a list of the returned values.

function also uses the names of the input elements as the names of the output elements (a, b, and c):

```
map(listOfNumerics, length)

$a
[1] 5

$b
[1] 9

$c
[1] 20
```

> **NOTE** If you're familiar with the apply family of functions, `map()` is the purrr equivalent of `lapply()`.

I hope you can immediately see how much simpler this is to code, and how much easier it is to read, than the `for` loop!

2.7.2 Returning an atomic vector instead of a list

So the `map()` function always returns a list. But what if, instead of returning a list, we wanted to return an atomic vector? The purrr package provides a number of functions to do just that:

- `map_dbl()` returns a vector of doubles (decimals).
- `map_chr()` returns a character vector.
- `map_int()` returns a vector of integers.
- `map_lgl()` returns a logical vector.

Each of these functions returns an atomic vector of the type specified by its suffix. In this way, we are forced to think about and predetermine what type of data our output should be. For example, as shown in listing 2.18, we can return the lengths of each of our `listOfNumerics` list elements just as before, using the `map_int()` function. Just like `map()`, the `map_int()` function applies the `length()` function to each element of our list, but it returns the output as a vector of integers. We can do the same thing using the `map_chr()` function, which coerces the output into a character vector, but the `map_lgl()` function throws an error because it can't coerce the output into a logical vector.

NOTE Forcing us to explicitly state the type of output we want to return prevents bugs from unexpected types of output.

Listing 2.18 Returning atomic vectors

```
map_int(listOfNumerics, length)

 a  b  c
 5  9 20

map_chr(listOfNumerics, length)

   a     b     c
 "5"   "9"  "20"

map_lgl(listOfNumerics, length)

Error: Can't coerce element 1 from a integer to a logical
```

Exercise 7

Use a function from the purrr package to return a logical vector indicating whether the sum of the values in each column of the `mtcars` dataset is greater than 1,000.

Finally, we can use the `map_df()` function to return a tibble instead of a list.

Listing 2.19 Returning a tibble with `map_df()`

```
map_df(listOfNumerics, length)

# A tibble: 1 x 3
      a     b     c
  <int> <int> <int>
1     5     9    10
```

2.7.3 Using anonymous functions inside the map() family

Sometimes we want to apply a function to each element of a list that we haven't defined yet. Functions that we define on the fly are called *anonymous functions* and can be useful when the function we're applying isn't going to be used often enough to warrant assigning it to an object. Using base R, we define an anonymous function by simply calling the `function()` function.

Listing 2.20 Defining an anonymous function with `function()`

```
map(listOfNumerics, function(.) . + 2)

$a
[1] 0.5383 1.6052 4.1335 1.7797 2.3429

$b
[1] 2.2438 0.6459 2.6164 1.4476 2.4519 2.3592 0.6585 0.2406 3.2160

$c
 [1] 0.8675 2.2792 2.5152 0.8343 1.2332 2.1778 3.4004 2.6492 0.3680 0.9014
```

NOTE Notice the `.` in the anonymous function. This represents the element that `map()` is currently iterating over.

The expression after `function(.)` is the body of the function. There is nothing wrong with this syntax—it works perfectly fine—but purrr provides a shorthand for `function(.)`: the `~` (tilde) symbol. Therefore, we could simplify the `map()` call to

```
map(listOfNumerics, ~. + 2)
```

by substituting `~` for `function(.)`.

2.7.4 Using walk() to produce a function's side effects

Sometimes we want to iterate over a function for its side effects. Probably the most common example is when we want to produce a series of plots. In this situation, we can use the `walk()` function to apply a function to each element of a list to produce the function's side effects. The `walk()` function also returns the original input data we pass it, so it's useful for plotting an intermediate step in a series of piped operations. Here's an example of `walk()` being used to create a separate histogram for each element of our list:

```
par(mfrow = c(1, 3))

walk(listOfNumerics, hist)
```

NOTE The `par(mfrow = c(1, 3))` function call simply splits the plotting device into two rows and four columns for base plots.

The resulting plot is shown in figure 2.6.

But what if we want to use the name of each list element as the title for its histogram? We can do this using the `iwalk()` function, which makes the name or index of

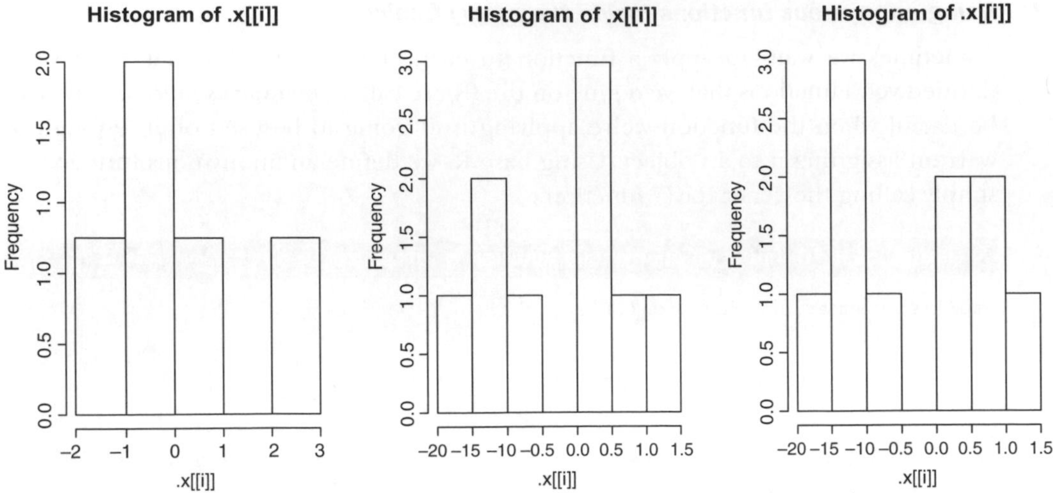

Figure 2.6 The result of "walking" the `hist()` function over each element of our list using `walk()`

each element available to us. In the function we supply to `iwalk()`, we can use `.x` to reference the list element we're iterating over and `.y` to reference its name/index:

```
iwalk(listOfNumerics, ~hist(.x, main = .y))
```

> **NOTE** Each of the `map()` functions has an `i` version that lets us reference each element's name/index.

The resulting plot is shown in figure 2.7. Notice that now each histogram's title shows the name of the list element it's plotting.

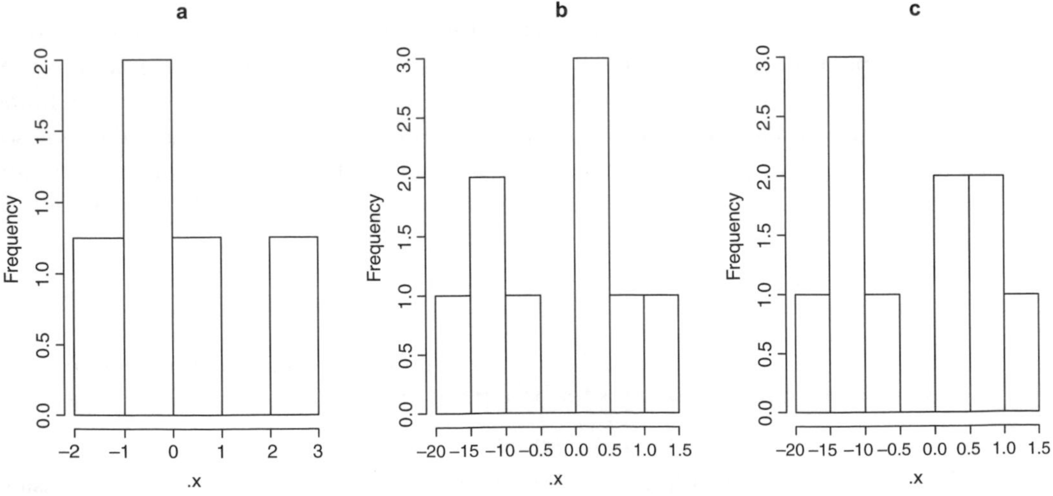

Figure 2.7 The result of "walking" the `hist()` function over each element of our list using `iwalk()`

2.7.5 Iterating over multiple lists simultaneously

Sometimes the data we wish to iterate over isn't contained in a single list. Imagine that we want to multiply each element in our list by a different value. We can store these values in a separate list and use the `map2()` function to iterate over both lists simultaneously, multiplying the element in the first list by the element in the second. This time, instead of referencing our data with `.`, we specifically reference the first and second lists using `.x` and `.y`, respectively:

```
multipliers <- list(0.5, 10, 3)

map2(.x = listOfNumerics, .y = multipliers, ~.x * .y)
```

Now, imagine that instead of iterating over just two lists, we want to iterate over three or more. The `pmap()` function allows us to iterate over multiple lists simultaneously. I use `pmap()` when I want to test multiple combinations of arguments for a function. The `rnorm()` function draws a random sample from the normal distribution and has three arguments: `n` (the number of samples), `mean` (the center of the distribution), and `sd` (the standard deviation). We can create a list of values for each and then use `pmap()` to iterate over each list to run the function on each combination.

We start by using the `expand.grid()` function to create a data frame containing every combination of the input vectors. Because data frames are really just lists of columns, supplying one to `pmap()` will iterate a function over each column in the data frame. Essentially, the function we ask `pmap()` to iterate over will be run using the arguments contained in each row of the data frame. Therefore, `pmap()` will return eight different random samples, one corresponding to each combination of arguments in the data frame.

Because the first argument of all `map` family functions is the data we wish to iterate over, we can chain them together using the `%>%` operator. The following code pipes the random samples returned by `pmap()` into the `iwalk()` function to draw a separate histogram for each sample, labeled with its index.

Listing 2.21 Using `pmap()` to iterate over multiple lists

```
arguments <- expand.grid(n = c(100, 200),
                         mean = c(1, 10),
                         sd = c(1, 10))

arguments

    n mean sd
1 100    1  1
2 200    1  1
3 100   10  1
4 200   10  1
5 100    1 10
6 200    1 10
7 100   10 10
8 200   10 10
```

```
par(mfrow = c(2, 4))

pmap(arguments, rnorm) %>%
  iwalk(~hist(.x, main = paste("Element", .y)))
```

The resulting plot is shown in figure 2.8.

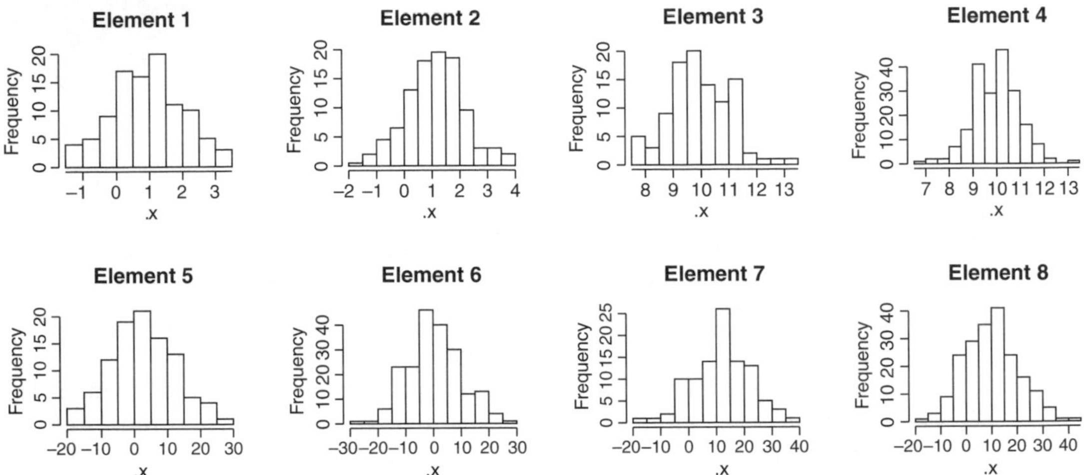

Figure 2.8 The `pmap()` function was used to iterate the `rnorm()` function over three vectors of arguments. The output from `pmap()` was piped into `iwalk()` to iterate the `hist()` function over each random sample.

Don't worry if you haven't memorized all of the tidyverse functions I just covered—we'll be using these tools throughout the book in our machine learning pipelines. There's also much more we can do with tidyverse tools than I've covered here, but this will certainly be enough for you to solve the most common data-manipulation problems you'll encounter. Now that you're armed with the knowledge of how to use this book, in the next chapter we'll dive into the theory of machine learning.

Summary

- The tidyverse is a collection of R packages that simplifies the organization, manipulation, and plotting of data.
- Tidy data is rectangular data where each row is a single observation and each column is a variable. It's often important to ensure that data is in tidy format before passing it into machine learning functions.
- Tibbles are a modern take on data frames that have better rules for printing rectangular data, never change variable types, and always return another tibble when subsetted using `[`.

- The dplyr package provides human-readable, verb-like functions for data-manipulation processes, the most important of which are `select()`, `filter()`, `group_by()`, `summarize()`, and `arrange()`.
- The most powerful aspect of dplyr is the ability to pipe functions together using the `%>%` operator, which passes the output of the function on its left as the first argument of the function on its right.
- The ggplot2 package is a modern and popular plotting system for R that lets you create effective plots in a simple, layered way.
- The tidyr package provides the important function `gather()`, which lets you easily convert untidy data into tidy format. The opposite of this function is `spread()`, which converts tidy data into wide format.
- The purrr package provides a simple, consistent way to iteratively apply functions over each element in a list.

Solutions to exercises

1. Load `mtcars`, convert it to a tibble, and explore it with `summary()`:

```
library(tidyverse)

data(mtcars)

mtcarsTib <- as_tibble(mtcars)

summary(mtcarsTib)
```

2. Select all columns except `qsec` and `vs`:

```
select(mtcarsTib, c(-qsec, -vs))
# or
select(mtcarsTib, c(-7, -8))
```

3. Filter for rows with cylinder numbers *not* equal to 8:

```
filter(mtcarsTib, cyl != 8)
```

4. Group by `gear`, summarize the medians of `mpg` and `disp`, and mutate a new variable that is the `mpg` median divided by the `disp` median:

```
mtcarsTib %>%
  group_by(gear) %>%
  summarize(mpgMed = median(mpg), dispMed = median(disp)) %>%
  mutate(mpgOverDisp = mpgMed / dispMed)
```

5. Create a scatter plot of the `drat` and `wt` variables, and color by `carb`:

```
ggplot(mtcarsTib, aes(drat, wt, col = carb)) +
  geom_point()

ggplot(mtcarsTib, aes(drat, wt, col = as.factor(carb))) +
  geom_point()
```

6 Gather `vs`, `am`, `gear`, and `carb` into a single key-value pair:

```
gather(mtcarsTib, key = "variable", value = "value", c(vs, am, gear, carb))
# or
gather(mtcarsTib, key = "variable", value = "value", c(8:11))
```

7 Iterate over each column of `mtcars`, returning a logical vector:

```
map_lgl(mtcars, ~sum(.) > 1000)
# or
map_lgl(mtcars, function(.) sum(.) > 1000)
```

Part 2

Classification

Now that we've covered some basic machine learning terminology, and your tidyverse skills are developing, let's finally start learning some practical machine learning skills. The rest of the book is split into four parts:

- Classification
- Regression
- Dimension reduction
- Clustering

Within each of these parts, each chapter will focus on a different algorithm (or algorithms). Each chapter will start by explaining the theory behind how the algorithm learns, in a graphical way, and the rest of the chapter turns our knowledge into skills by applying the algorithm to a real dataset.

Recall from chapter 1 that classification and regression are both supervised learning tasks. They're supervised because we have a ground truth we can use to train the models. We're going to begin by focusing on the prediction of categorical variables in chapters 3 through 8, so welcome to the classification part of the book. Alongside teaching you how the algorithms work and how to use them, I'll also be teaching you a range of other machine learning skills, such as how to evaluate the performance of your models and how to tune models to maximize their performance. By the time you've completed this part of the book, I hope you'll feel very confident using the mlr package in R for machine learning tasks. The mlr package creates a very simple, repetitive work flow for any machine learning task and will make your learning much simpler. Once we've completed the classification part of the book, we'll move on to predicting continuous variables in the regression part.

3 Classifying based on similarities with k-nearest neighbors

This chapter covers

- Understanding the bias-variance trade-off
- Underfitting vs. overfitting
- Using cross-validation to assess model performance
- Building a k-nearest neighbors classifier
- Tuning hyperparameters

This is probably the most important chapter of the entire book. In it, I'm going to show you how the k-nearest neighbors (kNN) algorithm works, and we're going to use it to classify potential diabetes patients. In addition, I'm going to use the kNN algorithm to teach you some essential concepts in machine learning that we will rely on for the rest of the book.

By the end of this chapter, not only will you understand and be able to use the kNN algorithm to make classification models, but you will be able to validate its performance and tune it to improve its performance as much as possible. Once the model is built, you'll learn how to pass new, unseen data into it and get the data's predicted classes (the value of the categorical or grouping variable we are trying to predict). I'll introduce you to the extremely powerful mlr package in R, which contains a mouth-watering number of machine learning algorithms and greatly simplifies all of our machine learning tasks.

3.1 What is the k-nearest neighbors algorithm?

I think the simple things in life are the best: playing Frisbee in the park, walking my dog, playing board games with my family, and using the kNN algorithm. Some machine learning practitioners look down on kNN a little because it's very simplistic. In fact, kNN is arguably *the* simplest machine learning algorithm, and this is one of the reasons I like it so much. In spite of its simplicity, kNN can provide surprisingly good classification performance, and its simplicity makes it easy to interpret.

NOTE Remember that, because kNN uses labeled data, it is a supervised learning algorithm.

3.1.1 How does the k-nearest neighbors algorithm learn?

So how does kNN learn? Well, I'm going to use snakes to help me explain. I'm from the UK, where—some people are surprised to learn—we have a few native species of snake. Two examples are the grass snake and the adder, which is the only venomous snake in the UK. But we also have a cute, limbless reptile called a slow worm, which is commonly mistaken for a snake.

Imagine that you work for a reptile conservation project aiming to count the numbers of grass snakes, adders, and slow worms in a woodland. Your job is to build a model that allows you to quickly classify reptiles you find into one of these three classes. When you find one of these animals, you only have enough time to rapidly estimate its length and some measure of how aggressive it is toward you, before it slithers away (funding is very scarce for your project). A reptile expert helps you manually classify the observations you've made so far, but you decide to build a kNN classifier to help you quickly classify future specimens you come across.

Look at the plot of data before classification in figure 3.1. Each of our cases is plotted against body length and aggression, and the species identified by your expert is indicated by the shape of the datum. You go into the woodland again and collect data from three new specimens, which are shown by the black crosses.

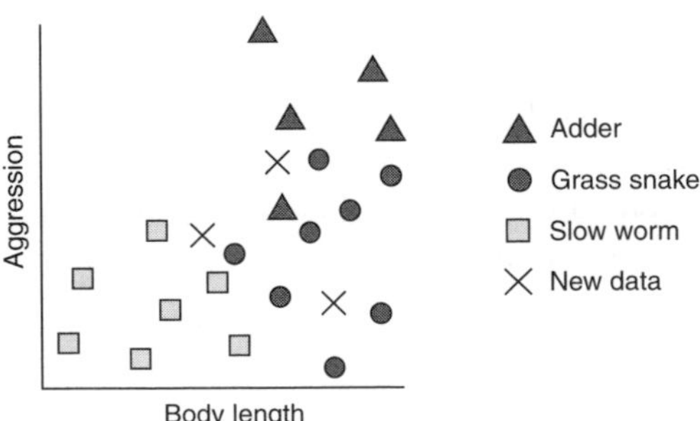

Figure 3.1 Body length and aggression of reptiles. Labeled cases for adders, grass snakes, and slow worms are indicated by their shape. New, unlabeled data are shown by black crosses.

We can describe the kNN algorithm (and other machine learning algorithms) in terms of two phases:

1. The training phase
2. The prediction phase

The training phase of the kNN algorithm consists only of storing the data. This is unusual among machine learning algorithms (as you'll learn in later chapters), and it means that most of the computation is done during the prediction phase.

During the prediction phase, the kNN algorithm calculates the *distance* between each new, unlabeled case and all the labeled cases. When I say "distance," I mean their nearness in terms of the aggression and body-length variables, not how far away in the woods you found them! This distance metric is often called *Euclidean distance*, which in two or even three dimensions is easy to visualize in your head as the straight-line distance between two points on a plot (this distance is shown in figure 3.2). This is calculated in as many dimensions as are present in the data.

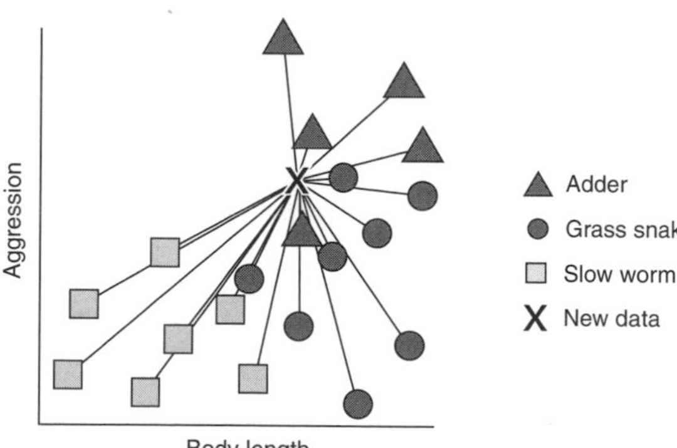

Figure 3.2 The first step of the kNN algorithm: calculating distance. The lines represent the distance between one of the unlabeled cases (the cross) and each of the labeled cases.

Next, for each unlabeled case, the algorithm ranks the neighbors from the nearest (most similar) to the furthest (the least similar). This is shown in figure 3.3.

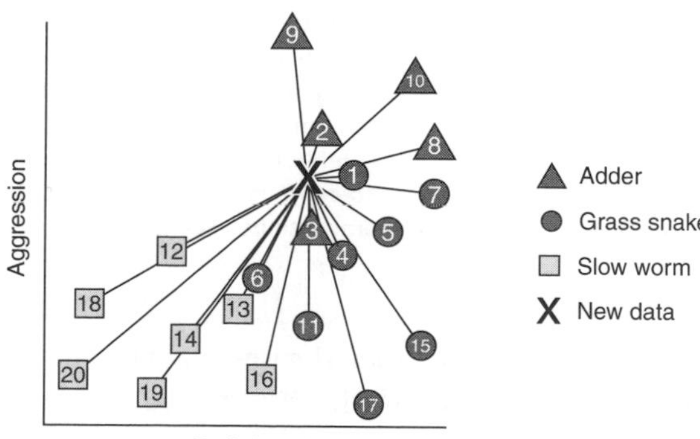

Figure 3.3 The second step of the kNN algorithm: ranking the neighbors. The lines represent the distance between one of the unlabeled cases (the cross) and each of the labeled cases. The numbers represent the ranked distance between the unlabeled case (the cross) and each labeled case (1 = closest).

The algorithm identifies the *k*-labeled cases (neighbors) nearest to each unlabeled case. *k* is an integer specified by us (I'll cover how we choose *k* in section 3.1). In other words, find the *k*-labeled cases that are most similar in terms of their variables to the unlabeled case. Finally, each of the k-nearest neighbor cases "votes" on which class the unlabeled data belongs in, based on the nearest neighbor's own class. In other words, whatever class most of the k-nearest neighbors belong to is what the unlabeled case is classified as.

> **NOTE** Because all of its computation is done during the prediction phase, kNN is said to be a *lazy learner*.

Let's work through figure 3.4 and see this in practice. When we set *k* to 1, the algorithm finds the single labeled case that is most similar to each of the unlabeled data items. Each of the unlabeled reptiles is closest to a member of the grass snake class, so they are all assigned to this class.

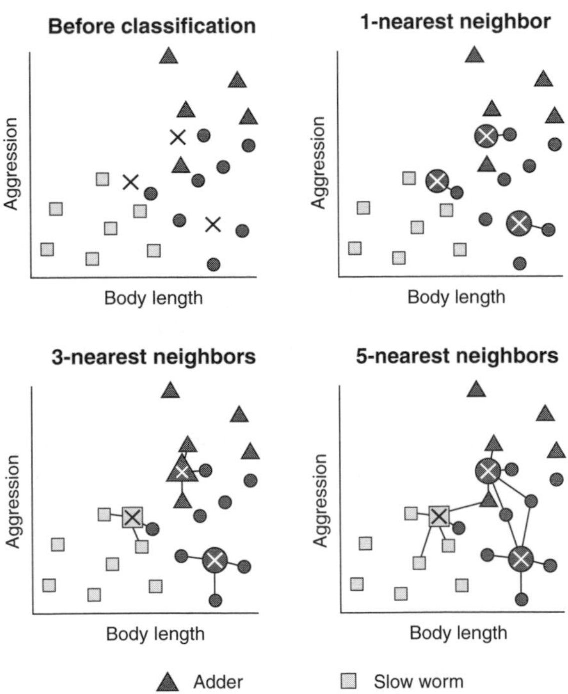

Figure 3.4 The final step of the kNN algorithm: identifying the k-nearest neighbors and taking the majority vote. Lines connect the unlabeled data with their one, three, and five nearest neighbors. The majority vote in each scenario is indicated by the shape drawn under each cross.

When we set *k* to 3, the algorithm finds the three labeled cases that are most similar to each of the unlabeled data items. As you can see in the figure, two of the unlabeled cases have nearest neighbors belonging to more than one class. In this situation, each nearest neighbor "votes" for its own class, and the majority vote wins. This is very intuitive because if a single unusually aggressive grass snake happens to be the nearest neighbor to an as-yet-unlabeled adder, it will be outvoted by the neighboring adders in the data.

Hopefully now you can see how this extends to other values of *k*. When we set *k* to 5, for example, the algorithm simply finds the five nearest cases to the unlabeled data and takes the majority vote as the class of the unlabeled case. Notice that in all three scenarios, the value of *k* directly impacts how each unlabeled case is classified.

> **TIP** The kNN algorithm can actually be used for both classification *and* regression problems! I'll show you how in chapter 12, but the only difference is that instead of taking the majority class vote, the algorithm finds the mean or median of the nearest neighbors' values.

3.1.2 What happens if the vote is tied?

It may happen that all of the k-nearest neighbors belong to different classes and that the vote results in a tie. What happens in this situation? Well, one way we can avoid this in a two-class classification problem (when the data can only belong to one of two, mutually exclusive groups) is to ensure that we pick odd numbers of *k*. This way, there will always be a deciding vote. But what about in situations like our reptile classification problem, where we have more than two groups?

One way of dealing with this situation is to decrease *k* until a majority vote can be won. But this doesn't help if an unlabeled case is equidistant between its two nearest neighbors.

Instead, a more common (and pragmatic) approach is to randomly assign cases with no majority vote to one of the classes. In practice, the proportion of cases that have ties among their nearest neighbors is very small, so this has a limited impact on the classification accuracy of the model. However, if you have many ties in your data, your options are as follows:

- Choose a different value of *k*.
- Add a small amount of noise to the data.
- Consider using a different algorithm! I'll show you how you can compare the performance of different algorithms on the same problem at the end of chapter 8.

3.2 Building your first kNN model

Imagine that you work in a hospital and are trying to improve the diagnosis of patients with diabetes. You collect diagnostic data over a few months from suspected diabetes patients and record whether they were diagnosed as healthy, chemically diabetic, or overtly diabetic. You would like to use the kNN algorithm to train a model that can predict which of these classes a new patient will belong to, so that diagnoses can be improved. This is a three-class classification problem.

We're going to start with a simple, naive way of building a kNN model and then gradually improve it throughout the rest of the chapter. First things first—let's install the mlr package and load it along with the tidyverse:

```
install.packages("mlr", dependencies = TRUE)

library(mlr)

library(tidyverse)
```

WARNING Installing the mlr package could take several minutes. You only need to do this once.

3.2.1 Loading and exploring the diabetes dataset

Now, let's load some data built into the mclust package, convert it into a tibble, and explore it a little (recall from chapter 2 that a tibble is the tidyverse way of storing rectangular data): see listing 3.1. We have a tibble with 145 cases and 4 variables. The `class` factor shows that 76 of the cases were non-diabetic (`Normal`), 36 were chemically diabetic (`Chemical`), and 33 were overtly diabetic (`Overt`). The other three variables are continuous measures of the level of blood glucose and insulin after a glucose tolerance test (`glucose` and `insulin`, respectively), and the steady-state level of blood glucose (`sspg`).

Listing 3.1 Loading the diabetes data

```
data(diabetes, package = "mclust")

diabetesTib <- as_tibble(diabetes)

summary(diabetesTib)

class          glucose          insulin               sspg
Chemical:36    Min.   : 70    Min.   :  45.0    Min.   : 10.0
Normal  :76    1st Qu.: 90    1st Qu.: 352.0    1st Qu.:118.0
Overt   :33    Median : 97    Median : 403.0    Median :156.0
               Mean   :122    Mean   : 540.8    Mean   :186.1
               3rd Qu.:112    3rd Qu.: 558.0    3rd Qu.:221.0
               Max.   :353    Max.   :1568.0    Max.   :748.0

diabetesTib

# A tibble: 145 x 4
   class  glucose insulin  sspg
 * <fct>    <dbl>   <dbl> <dbl>
 1 Normal      80     356   124
 2 Normal      97     289   117
 3 Normal     105     319   143
 4 Normal      90     356   199
 5 Normal      90     323   240
 6 Normal      86     381   157
 7 Normal     100     350   221
```

```
 8 Normal       85      301    186
 9 Normal       97      379    142
10 Normal       97      296    131
# ... with 135 more rows
```

To show how these variables are related, they are plotted against each other in figure 3.5. The code to generate these plots is in listing 3.2.

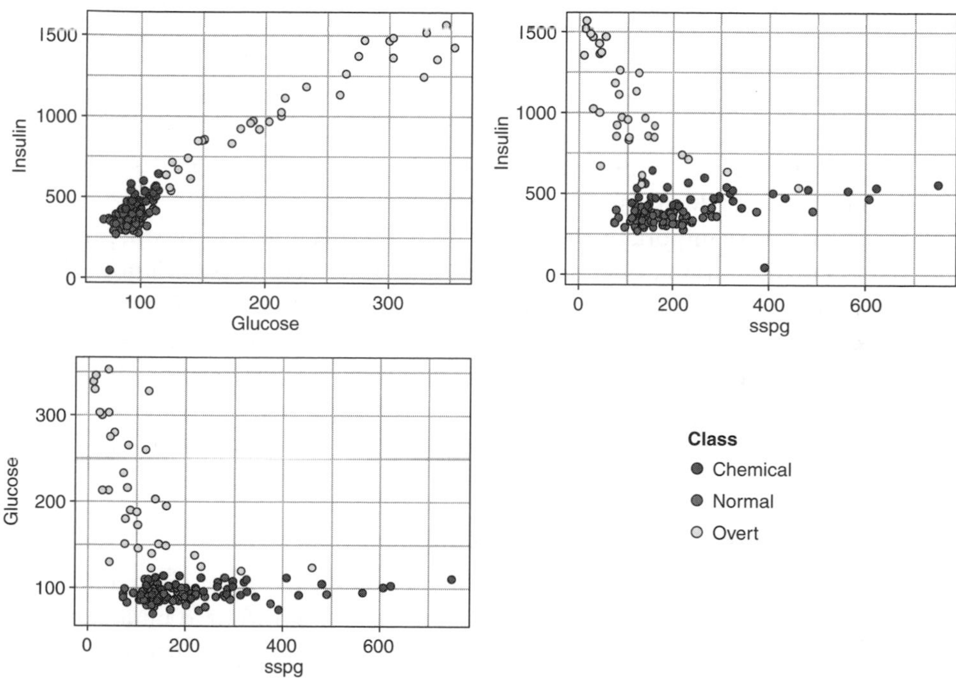

Figure 3.5 Plotting the relationships between variables in `diabetesTib`. All three combinations of the continuous variables are shown, shaded by class.

Listing 3.2 Plotting the diabetes data

```
ggplot(diabetesTib, aes(glucose, insulin, col = class)) +
  geom_point()  +
  theme_bw()

ggplot(diabetesTib, aes(sspg, insulin, col = class)) +
  geom_point() +
  theme_bw()

ggplot(diabetesTib, aes(sspg, glucose, col = class)) +
  geom_point() +
  theme_bw()
```

Looking at the data, we can see there are differences in the continuous variables among the three classes, so let's build a kNN classifier that we can use to predict diabetes status from measurements of future patients.

> **Exercise 1**
> Reproduce the plot of `glucose` versus `insulin` shown in figure 3.5, but use shapes rather than colors to indicate which class each case belongs to. Once you've done this, modify your code to represent the classes using shape *and* color.

Our dataset only consists of continuous predictor variables, but often we may be working with categorical predictor variables too. The kNN algorithm can't handle categorical variables natively; they need to first be encoded somehow, or distance metrics other than Euclidean distance must be used.

It's also very important for kNN (and many machine learning algorithms) to scale the predictor variables by dividing them by their standard deviation. This preserves the relationships between the variables, but ensures that variables measured on larger scales aren't given more importance by the algorithm. In the current example, if we divided the `glucose` and `insulin` variables by 1,000,000, then predictions would rely mostly on the value of the `sspg` variable. We don't need to scale the predictors ourselves because, by default, the kNN algorithm wrapped by the mlr package does this for us.

3.2.2 Using mlr to train your first kNN model

We understand the problem we're trying to solve (classifying new patients into one of three classes), and now we need to train the kNN algorithm to build a model that will solve that problem. Building a machine learning model with the mlr package has three main stages:

1. *Define the task.* The task consists of the data and what we want to do with it. In this case, the data is `diabetesTib`, and we want to classify the data with the `class` variable as the target variable.
2. *Define the learner.* The learner is simply the name of the algorithm we plan to use, along with any additional arguments the algorithm accepts.
3. *Train the model.* This stage is what it sounds like: you pass the task to the learner, and the learner generates a model that you can use to make future predictions.

TIP This may seem unnecessarily cumbersome, but splitting the task, learner, and model into different stages is very useful. It means we can define a single task and apply multiple learners to it, or define a single learner and test it with multiple different tasks.

3.2.3 Telling mlr what we're trying to achieve: Defining the task

Let's begin by defining our task. The components needed to define a task are

- The data containing the predictor variables (variables we hope contain the information needed to make predictions/solve our problem)
- The target variable we want to predict

For supervised learning, the target variable will be categorical if we have a classification problem, and continuous if we have a regression problem. For unsupervised learning, we omit the target variable from our task definition, as we don't have access to labeled data. The components of a task are shown in figure 3.6.

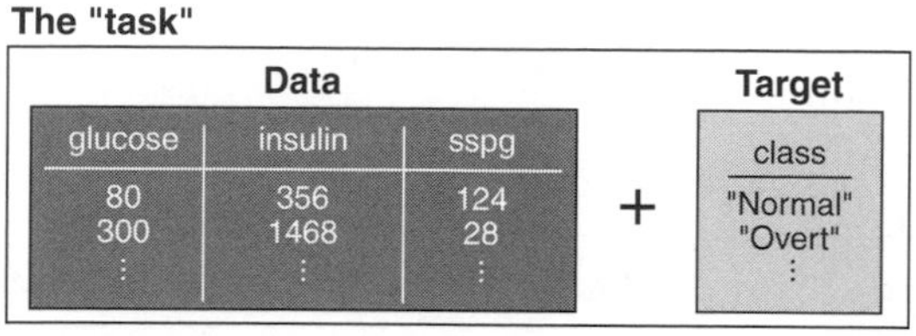

The "task"

Data				Target
glucose	insulin	sspg	+	class
80	356	124		"Normal"
300	1468	28		"Overt"
⋮	⋮	⋮		⋮

Figure 3.6 Defining a task in mlr. A task definition consists of the data containing the predictor variables and, for classification and regression problems, a target variable we want to predict. For unsupervised learning, the target is omitted.

We want to build a classification model, so we use the `makeClassifTask()` function to define a classification task. When we build regression and clustering models in parts 3 and 5 of the book, we'll use `makeRegrTask()` and `makeClusterTask()`, respectively. We supply the name of our tibble as the `data` argument and the name of the factor that contains the class labels as the `target` argument:

```
diabetesTask <- makeClassifTask(data = diabetesTib, target = "class")
```

> **NOTE** You may notice a warning message from mlr when you build the task, stating that your data is not a pure `data.frame` (it's a tibble). This isn't a problem, because the function will convert the tibble into a `data.frame` for you.

If we call the task, we can see it's a classification task on the `diabetesTib` tibble, whose target is the `class` variable. We also get some information about the number of observations and the number of different types of variables (often called *features* in machine learning lingo). Some additional information includes whether we have missing data, the number of observations in each class, and which class is considered to be the "positive" class (only relevant for two-class tasks):

```
diabetesTask

Supervised task: diabetesTib
Type: classif
Target: class
Observations: 145
Features:
```

```
   numerics      factors     ordered functionals
          3            0           0           0
Missings: FALSE
Has weights: FALSE
Has blocking: FALSE
Has coordinates: FALSE
Classes: 3
Chemical   Normal    Overt
      36       76       33
Positive class: NA
```

3.2.4 Telling mlr which algorithm to use: Defining the learner

Next, let's define our learner. The components needed to define a learner are as follows:

- The class of algorithm we are using:
  - `"classif."` for classification
  - `"regr."` for regression
  - `"cluster."` for clustering
  - `"surv."` and `"multilabel."` for predicting survival and multilabel classification, which I won't discuss
- The algorithm we are using
- Any additional options we may wish to use to control the algorithm

As you'll see, the first and second components are combined together in a single character argument to define which algorithm will be used (for example, `"classif.knn"`). The components of a learner are shown in figure 3.7.

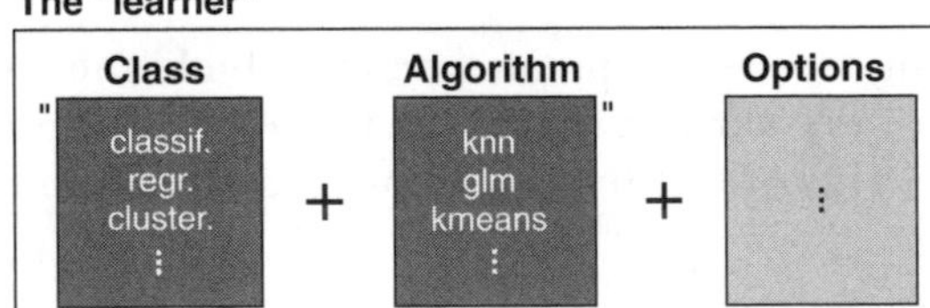

Figure 3.7 Defining a learner in mlr. A learner definition consists of the class of algorithm you want to use, the name of the individual algorithm, and, optionally, any additional arguments to control the algorithm's behavior.

We use the `makeLearner()` function to define a learner. The first argument to the `makeLearner()` function is the algorithm that we're going to use to train our model. In this case, we want to use the kNN algorithm, so we supply `"classif.knn"` as the argument. See how this is the class (`"classif.`) joined to the name (`knn"`) of the algorithm?

The argument `par.vals` stands for parameter values, which allows us to specify the number of k-nearest neighbors we want the algorithm to use. For now, we'll just set this to 2, but we'll discuss how to choose *k* soon:

```
knn <- makeLearner("classif.knn", par.vals = list("k" = 2))
```

> **How to list all of mlr's algorithms**
>
> The mlr package has a large number of machine learning algorithms that we can give to the `makeLearner()` function, more than I can remember without checking! To list all the available learners, simply use
>
> ```
> listLearners()$class
> ```
>
> Or list them by function:
>
> ```
> listLearners("classif")$class
> listLearners("regr")$class
> listLearners("cluster")$class
> ```
>
> If you're ever unsure which algorithms are available to you or which argument to pass to `makeLearner()` for a particular algorithm, use these functions to remind yourself.

3.2.5 Putting it all together: Training the model

Now that we've defined our task and our learner, we can now train our model. The components needed to train a model are the learner and task we defined earlier. The whole process of defining the task and learner and combining them to train the model is shown in figure 3.8.

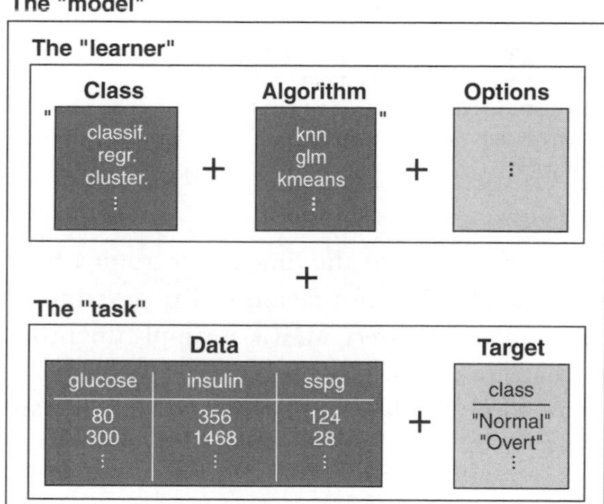

Figure 3.8 Training a model in mlr. Training a model simply consists of combining a learner with a task.

This is achieved with the `train()` function, which takes the learner as the first argument and the task as its second argument:

```
knnModel <- train(knn, diabetesTask)
```

We have our model, so let's pass the data through it to see how it performs. The `predict()` function takes unlabeled data and passes it through the model to get the predicted classes. The first argument is the model, and the data being passed to it is given as the `newdata` argument:

```
knnPred <- predict(knnModel, newdata = diabetesTib)
```

We can pass these predictions as the first argument of the `performance()` function. This function compares the classes predicted by the model to the true classes, and returns *performance metrics* of how well the predicted and true values match each other. Use of the `predict()` and `performance()` functions is illustrated in figure 3.9.

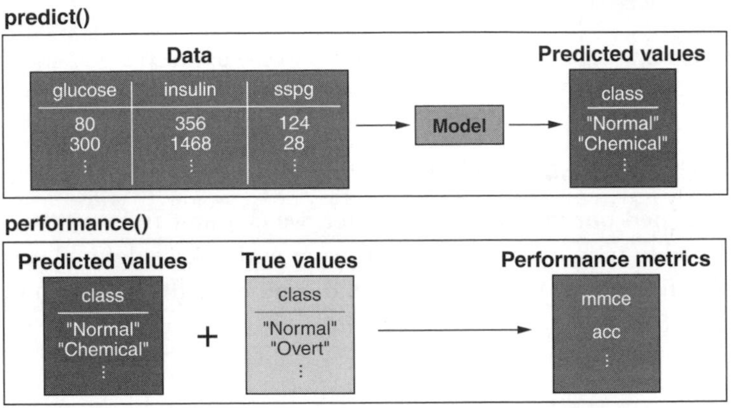

Figure 3.9 A summary of the `predict()` and `performance()` functions of mlr. `predict()` passes observations into a model and outputs the predicted values. `performance()` compares these predicted values to the cases' true values and outputs one or more performance metrics summarizing the similarity between the two.

We specify which performance metrics we want the function to return by supplying them as a list to the `measures` argument. The two measures I've asked for are `mmce`, the *mean misclassification error*; and `acc`, or *accuracy*. MMCE is simply the proportion of cases classified as a class other than their true class. Accuracy is the opposite of this: the proportion of cases that were correctly classified by the model. You can see that the two sum to 1.00:

```
performance(knnPred, measures = list(mmce, acc))

      mmce        acc
0.04827586 0.95172414
```

So our model is correctly classifying 95.2% of cases! Does this mean it will perform well on new, unseen patients? The truth is that *we don't know*. Evaluating model performance by asking it to make predictions on data you used to train it in the first place tells you very little about how the model will perform when making predictions on completely unseen data. Therefore, you should *never* evaluate model performance this way. Before we discuss why, I want to introduce an important concept called the bias-variance trade-off.

3.3 Balancing two sources of model error: The bias-variance trade-off

There is a concept in machine learning that is so important, and misunderstood by so many people, that I want to take the time to explain it well: the *bias-variance trade-off*. Let's start with an example. A colleague sends you data about emails your company has received and asks you to build a model to classify incoming emails as junk or not junk (this is, of course, a classification problem). The dataset has 30 variables consisting of observations like the number of characters in the email, the presence of URLs, and the number of email addresses it was sent to, in addition to whether the email was junk or not.

You lazily build a classification model using only four of the predictor variables (because it's nearly lunch and they're serving katsu curry today). You send the model to your colleague, who implements it as the company's junk filter.

A week later, your colleague comes back to you, complaining that the junk filter is performing badly and is consistently misclassifying certain types of emails. You pass the data you used to train the model back into the model, and find it correctly classifies only 60% of the emails. You decide that you may have *underfitted* the data: in other words, your model was too simple and was *biased* toward misclassifying certain types of emails.

You go back to the data, and this time you include all 30 variables as predictors in your model. You pass the data back through your model and find that it correctly classifies 98% of the emails: an improvement, surely! You send this second model to your colleague and tell them you are certain it's better. Another week goes by, and again, your colleague comes to you and complains that the model is performing badly: it's misclassifying many emails, and in a somewhat unpredictable manner. You decide that you have *overfitted* the data: in other words, your model was too complex and is modeling noise in the data that you used to train it. Now, when you give new datasets to the model, there is a lot of *variance* in the predictions it gives. A model that is overfitted will perform well on the data used to train it, but poorly on new data.

Underfitting and overfitting are two important sources of error in model building. In underfitting, we have included too few predictors or too simple a model to adequately describe the relationships/patterns in the data. The result is a model that is said to be *biased*: a model that performs poorly on both the data we use to train it and on new data.

> **NOTE** Because we typically like to explain away as much variation in our data as possible, and because we often have many more variables than are important for our problem, underfitting is less frequently a problem than overfitting.

Overfitting is the opposite of underfitting and describes the situation where we include too many predictors or too complex a model, such that we are modeling not only the relationships/patterns in our data, but also the *noise*. Noise in a dataset is variation that is not systematically related to variables we have measured, but rather is due to inherent variability and/or error in measurement of our variables. The pattern of noise is very specific to an individual dataset, so if we start to model the noise, our model may perform very well on the data we trained it on but give quite variable results for future datasets.

Underfitting and overfitting both introduce error and reduce the *generalizability* of the model: the ability of the model to generalize to future, unseen data. They are also opposed to each other: somewhere between a model that underfits and has bias, and a model that overfits and has variance, is an optimal model that balances the bias-variance trade-off; see figure 3.10.

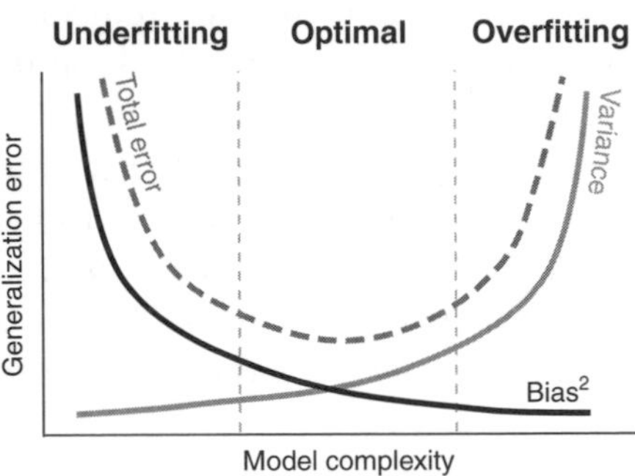

Figure 3.10 The bias-variance trade-off. Generalization error is the proportion of erroneous predictions a model makes and is a result of overfitting and underfitting. The error associated with overfitting (too complex a model) is variance. The error associated with underfitting (too simple a model) is bias. The error associated with overfitting (too complex a model) is variance. An optimal model balances this trade-off.

Now, look at figure 3.11. Can you see that the underfit model poorly represents the patterns in the data, and the overfit model is too granular and models noise in the data instead of the real patterns?

In the case of our kNN algorithm, selecting a small value of *k* (where only a small number of very similar cases are included in the vote) is more likely to model the

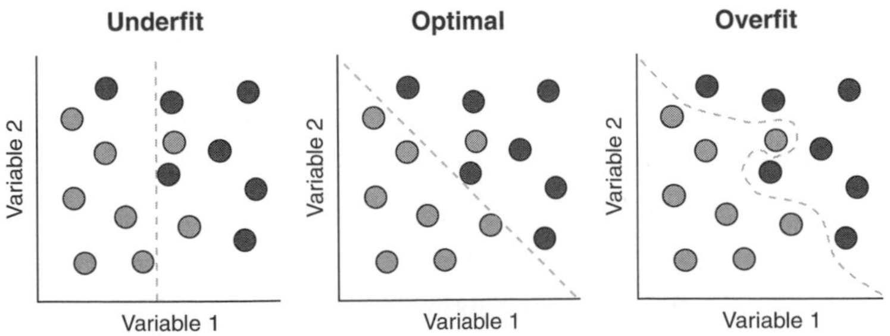

Figure 3.11 Examples of underfitting, optimal fitting, and overfitting for a two-class classification problem. The dotted line represents a decision boundary.

noise in our data, resulting in a more complex model that is overfit and will produce a lot of variance when we use it to classify future patients. In contrast, selecting a large value of *k* (where more neighbors are included in the vote) is more likely to miss local differences in our data, resulting in a less complex model that is underfit and is biased toward misclassifying certain types of patients. I promise you'll learn how to select *k* soon!

So the question you're probably asking now is, "How do I tell if I'm under- or overfitting?" The answer is a technique called *cross-validation*.

3.4 Using cross-validation to tell if we're overfitting or underfitting

In the email example, once you had trained the second, overfit model, you tried to evaluate its performance by seeing how well it classified data you had used to train it. I mentioned that this is an extremely bad idea, and here is why: a model will almost always perform better on the data you trained it with than on new, unseen data. You can build a model that is extremely overfit, modeling all of the noise in the dataset, and you would never know, because passing the data back through the model gives you good predictive accuracy.

The answer is to evaluate the performance of your model on data it hasn't seen yet. One way you could do this would be to train the model on all of the data available to you and then, over the next weeks and months, as you collect new data, pass it through your model and evaluate how the model performs. This approach is very slow and inefficient, and could make model building take years!

Instead, we typically split our data in two. We use one portion to train the model: this portion is called the *training set*. We use the remaining portion, which the algorithm never sees during training, to test the model: this portion is the *test set*. We then evaluate how close the model's predictions on the test set are to their true values. We summarize the closeness of these predictions with *performance metrics* that we'll explore in section 3.1. Measuring how well the trained model performs on the test set helps us determine whether our model will perform well on unseen data, or whether we need to improve it further.

This process is called *cross-validation* (CV), and it is an extremely important approach in any supervised machine learning pipeline. Once we have cross-validated our model and are happy with its performance, we then use all the data we have (including the data in the test set) to train the final model (because typically, the more data we train our model with, the less bias it will have).

There are three common cross-validation approaches:

- Holdout cross-validation
- K-fold cross-validation
- Leave-one-out cross-validation

3.5 Cross-validating our kNN model

Let's start by reminding ourselves of the task and learner we created earlier:

```
diabetesTask <- makeClassifTask(data = diabetesTib, target = "class")

knn <- makeLearner("classif.knn", par.vals = list("k" = 2))
```

Great! Before we train the final model on all the data, let's cross-validate the learner. Ordinarily, you would decide on a CV strategy most appropriate for your data; but for the purposes of demonstration, I'm going to show you holdout, k-fold, *and* leave-one-out CV.

3.5.1 Holdout cross-validation

Holdout CV is the simplest method to understand: you simply "hold out" a random proportion of your data as your test set, and train your model on the remaining data. You then pass the test set through the model and calculate its performance metrics (we'll talk about these soon). You can see a scheme of holdout CV in figure 3.12.

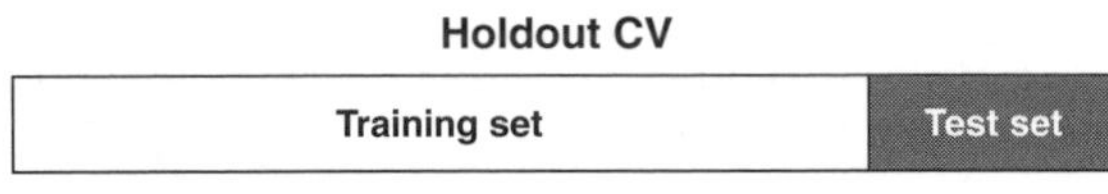

1. The data is randomly split into a training and test set.
2. A model is trained using only the training set.
3. Predictions are made on the test set.
4. The predictions are compared to the true values.

Figure 3.12 Holdout CV. The data is randomly split into a training set and test set. The training set is used to train the model, which is then used to make predictions on the test set. The similarity of the predictions to the true values of the test set is used to evaluate model performance.

When following this approach, you need to decide what proportion of the data to use as the test set. The larger the test set is, the smaller your training set will be. Here's the confusing part: performance estimation by CV is also subject to error and the bias-variance trade-off. If your test set is too small, then the estimate of performance is going to have high variance; but if the training set is too small, then the estimate of performance is going to have high bias. A commonly used split is to use two-thirds of the data for training and the remaining one-third as a test set, but this depends on the number of cases in the data, among other things.

MAKING A HOLDOUT RESAMPLING DESCRIPTION

The first step when employing any CV in mlr is to make a resampling description, which is simply a set of instructions for how the data will be split into test and training sets. The first argument to the `makeResampleDesc()` function is the CV method we're going to use: in this case, `"Holdout"`. For holdout CV, we need to tell the function what proportion of the data will be used as the training set, so we supply this to the split argument:

```
holdout <- makeResampleDesc(method = "Holdout", split = 2/3,
                            stratify = TRUE)
```

I've included an additional, optional argument, `stratify = TRUE`. It asks the function to ensure that when it splits the data into training and test sets, it tries to maintain the proportion of each class of patient in each set. This is important in classification problems like ours, where the groups are very unbalanced (we have more healthy patients than both other groups combined) because, otherwise, we could get a test set with very few of one of our smaller classes.

PERFORMING HOLDOUT CV

Now that we've defined how we're going to cross-validate our learner, we can run the CV using the `resample()` function. We supply the learner and task that we created, and the resampling method we defined a moment ago, to the `resample()` function. We also ask it to give us measures of MMCE and accuracy:

```
holdoutCV <- resample(learner = knn, task = diabetesTask,
                      resampling = holdout, measures = list(mmce, acc))
```

The `resample()` function prints the performance measures when you run it, but you can access them by extracting the `$aggr` component from the `resampling` object:

```
holdoutCV$aggr

mmce.test.mean  acc.test.mean
     0.1020408      0.8979592
```

You'll notice two things:

- The accuracy of the model as estimated by holdout cross-validation is less than when we evaluated its performance on the data we used to train the full model. This exemplifies my point earlier that models will perform better on the data that trained them than on unseen data.
- Your performance metrics will probably be different than mine. In fact, run the `resample()` function over and over again, and you'll get a very different result each time! The reason for this *variance* is that the data is randomly split into the test and training sets. Sometimes the split is such that the model performs well on the test set; sometimes the split is such that it performs poorly.

Exercise 2

Use the `makeResampleDesc()` function to create another holdout resampling description that uses 10% of the data as the test set and does *not* use stratified sampling (don't overwrite your existing resampling description).

CALCULATING A CONFUSION MATRIX

To get a better idea of which groups are being correctly classified and which are being misclassified, we can construct a confusion matrix. A *confusion matrix* is simply a tabular representation of the true and predicted class of each case in the test set.

With mlr, we can calculate the confusion matrix using the `calculateConfusionMatrix()` function. The first argument is the `$pred` component of our `holdoutCV` object, which contains the true and predicted classes of the test set. The optional argument `relative` asks the function to show the proportion of each class in the true and predicted class labels:

```
calculateConfusionMatrix(holdoutCV$pred, relative = TRUE)

Relative confusion matrix (normalized by row/column):
          predicted
true       Chemical  Normal    Overt     -err.-
  Chemical 0.92/0.73 0.08/0.04 0.00/0.00 0.08
  Normal   0.12/0.20 0.88/0.96 0.00/0.00 0.12
  Overt    0.09/0.07 0.00/0.00 0.91/1.00 0.09
  -err.-        0.27      0.04      0.00 0.10


Absolute confusion matrix:
          predicted
true       Chemical Normal Overt -err.-
  Chemical       11      1     0      1
  Normal          3     23     0      3
  Overt           1      0    10      1
  -err.-          4      1     0      5
```

The absolute confusion matrix is easier to interpret. The rows show the true class labels, and the columns show the predicted labels. The numbers represent the number of cases in every combination of true class and predicted class. For example, in this matrix, 11 patients were correctly classified as chemically diabetic, but one was erroneously classified as healthy. Correctly classified patients are found on the diagonal of the matrix (where true class == predicted class).

The relative confusion matrix looks a little more intimidating, but the principal is the same. This time, instead of the number of cases for each combination of true class and predicted class, we have the proportion. The number before the / is the proportion of the row in this column, and the number after the / is the proportion of the column in this row. For example, in this matrix, 92% of chemically diabetic patients were correctly classified, while 8% were misclassified as healthy. (Do you see that these are the proportions for the numbers I used for the absolute confusion matrix?)

Confusion matrices help us understand which classes our model classifies well and which ones it does worse at classifying. For example, based on this confusion matrix, it looks like our model struggles to distinguish healthy patients from chemically diabetic ones.

> **NOTE** Does your confusion matrix look different than mine? Of course it does! The confusion matrix is based on the prediction made on the test set;

and because the test set is selected at random in holdout CV, the confusion matrix will change every time you rerun CV.

As the performance metrics reported by holdout CV depend so heavily on how much of the data we use as the training and test sets, I try to avoid it unless my model is very expensive to train, so I generally prefer k-fold CV. The only real benefit of this method is that it is computationally less expensive than the other forms of CV. This can make it the only viable CV method for computationally expensive algorithms. But the purpose of CV is to get as accurate an estimation of model performance as possible, and holdout CV may give you very different results each time you apply it, because not all of the data is used in the training set and test set. This is where the other forms of CV come in.

3.5.2 K-fold cross-validation

In k-fold CV, we randomly split the data into approximately equal-sized chunks called *folds*. Then we reserve one of the folds as a test set and use the remaining data as the training set (just like in holdout). We pass the test set through the model and make a record of the relevant performance metrics. Now, we use a different fold of the data as our test set and do the same thing. We continue until all the folds have been used once as the test set. We then get an average of the performance metric as an estimate of model performance. You can see a scheme of k-fold CV in figure 3.13.

K-fold CV
Fold 1
Training set
Test set
Fold 2
Test set
Fold 3
Test set
Fold 4
Test set
Fold 5
Test set
1. The data is randomly split into *k* equal-sized folds.
2. Each fold is used as the test set once, where the rest of the data makes the training set.
3. For each fold, predictions are made on the test set.
4. The predictions are compared to the true values.

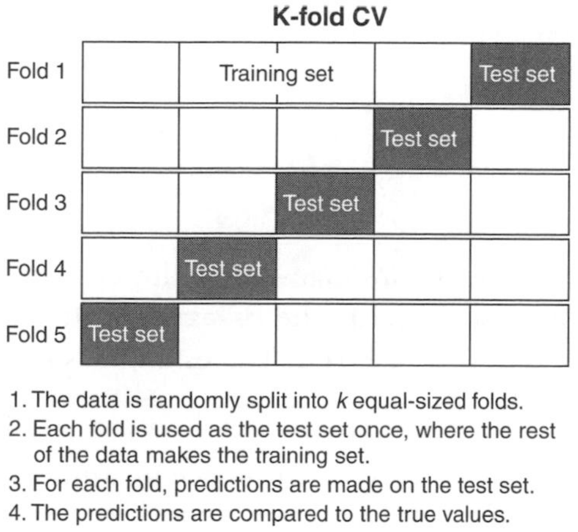

Figure 3.13 K-fold CV. The data is randomly split into near equally sized folds. Each fold is used as the test set once, with the rest of the data used as the training set. The similarity of the predictions to the true values of the test set is used to evaluate model performance.

NOTE It's important to note that each case in the data appears in the test set only once in this procedure.

This approach will typically give a more accurate estimate of model performance because every case appears in the test set once, and we are averaging the estimates over many runs. But we can improve this a little by using *repeated* k-fold CV, where, after the previous procedure, we shuffle the data around and perform it again.

For example, a commonly chosen value of *k* for k-fold is 10. Again, this depends on the size of the data, among other things, but it is a reasonable value for many datasets.

This means we split the data into 10 nearly equal-sized chunks and perform the CV. If we repeat this procedure 5 times, then we have 10-fold CV repeated 5 times (this is *not* the same as 50-fold CV), and the estimate of model performance will be the average of 50 different runs.

Therefore, if you have the computational power, it is usually preferred to use repeated k-fold CV instead of ordinary k-fold. This is what we'll be using in many examples in this book.

PERFORMING K-FOLD CV

We perform k-fold CV in the same way as holdout. This time, when we make our resampling description, we tell it we're going to use repeated k-fold cross-validation (`"RepCV"`), and we tell it how many folds we want to split the data into. The default number of folds is 10, which is often a good choice, but I want to show you how you can explicitly control the splits. Next, we tell the function that we want to repeat the 10-fold CV 50 times with the `reps` argument. This gives us 500 performance measures to average across! Again, we ask for the classes to be stratified among the folds:

```
kFold <- makeResampleDesc(method = "RepCV", folds = 10, reps = 50,
                          stratify = TRUE)

kFoldCV <- resample(learner = knn, task = diabetesTask,
                    resampling = kFold, measures = list(mmce, acc))
```

Now let's extract the average performance measures:

```
kFoldCV$aggr

mmce.test.mean  acc.test.mean
     0.1022788      0.8977212
```

The model correctly classified 89.8% of cases on average—much lower than when we predicted the data we used to train the model! Rerun the `resample()` function a few times, and compare the average accuracy after each run. The estimate is much more stable than when we repeated holdout CV.

> **TIP** We're usually only interested in the average performance measures, but you can access the performance measure from every iteration by running `kFoldCV$measures.test`.

CHOOSING THE NUMBER OF REPEATS

Your goal when cross-validating a model is to get as accurate and stable an estimate of model performance as possible. Broadly speaking, the more repeats you can do, the more accurate and stable these estimates will become. At some point, though, having more repeats won't improve the accuracy or stability of the performance estimate.

So how do you decide how many repeats to perform? A sound approach is to choose a number of repeats that is computationally reasonable, run the process a few times, and see if the average performance estimate varies a lot. If not, great. If it does vary a lot, you should increase the number of repeats.

> **Exercise 3**
> Define two new resampling descriptions: one that performs 3-fold CV repeated 5 times, and one that performs 3-fold CV repeated 500 times (don't overwrite your existing description). Use the `resample()` function to cross-validate the kNN algorithm using both of these resampling descriptions. Repeat the resampling five times for each method, and see which one gives more stable results.

CALCULATING A CONFUSION MATRIX

Now, let's build the confusion matrix based on the repeated k-fold CV:

```
calculateConfusionMatrix(kFoldCV$pred, relative = TRUE)

Relative confusion matrix (normalized by row/column):
          predicted
true       Chemical  Normal    Overt     -err.-
  Chemical 0.81/0.78 0.10/0.05 0.09/0.10 0.19
  Normal   0.04/0.07 0.96/0.95 0.00/0.00 0.04
  Overt    0.16/0.14 0.00/0.00 0.84/0.90 0.16
  -err.-        0.22      0.05      0.10 0.10


Absolute confusion matrix:
          predicted
true       Chemical Normal Overt -err.-
  Chemical     1463    179   158    337
  Normal        136   3664     0    136
  Overt         269      0  1381    269
  -err.-        405    179   158    742
```

NOTE Notice that the number of cases is much larger. This is because we repeated the procedure 50 times.

3.5.3 Leave-one-out cross-validation

Leave-one-out CV can be thought of as the extreme of k-fold CV: instead of breaking the data into folds, we reserve a single observation as a test case, train the model on the whole of the rest of the data, and then pass the test case through it and record the relevant performance metrics. Next, we do the same thing but select a different observation as the test case. We continue doing this until every observation has been used once as the test case, where we take the average of the performance metrics. You can see a scheme of leave-one-out CV in figure 3.14.

Because the test set is only a single observation, leave-one-out CV tends to give quite variable estimates of model performance (because the performance estimate of each iteration depends on correctly labeling that single test case). But it can give less-variable estimates of model performance than k-fold when your dataset is small. When

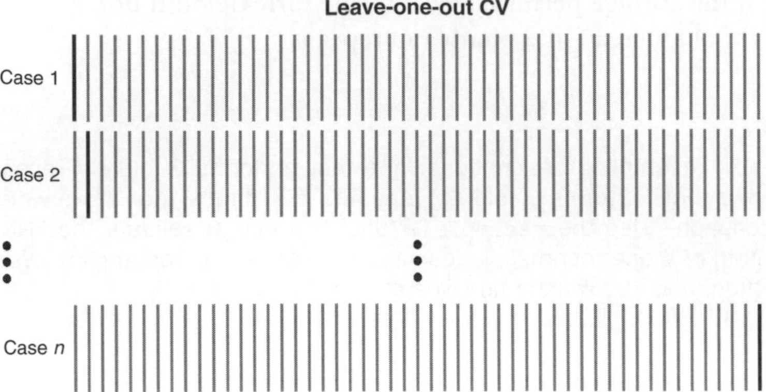
Leave-one-out CV
Case 1
Case 2
Case *n*
1. Use all of the data except a single case as the training set.
2. Predict the value of the single test case.
3. Repeat until every case has been the test case.
4. The predictions for each case are compared to the true values.

Figure 3.14 Leave-one-out CV is the extreme of k-fold, where we reserve a single case as the test set and train the model on the remaining data. The similarity of the predictions to the true values of the test set is used to evaluate model performance.

you have a small dataset, splitting it up into *k* folds will leave you with a very small training set. The variance of a model trained on a small dataset tends to be higher because it will be more influenced by sampling error/unusual cases. Therefore, leave-one-out CV is useful for small datasets where splitting it into *k* folds would give variable results. It is also computationally less expensive than repeated, k-fold CV.

> **NOTE** A supervised learning model that has not been cross-validated is virtually useless, because you have no idea whether the predictions it makes on new data will be accurate or not.

PERFORMING LEAVE-ONE-OUT CV

Creating a resampling description for leave-one-out is just as simple as for holdout and k-fold CV. We specify leave-one-out CV when making the resample description by supplying `LOO` as the argument to the method. Because the test set is only a single case, we obviously can't stratify with leave-one-out. Also, because each case is used once as the test set, with all the other data used as the training set, there's no need to repeat the procedure:

```
LOO <- makeResampleDesc(method = "LOO")
```

> **Exercise 4**
>
> Try to create two new leave-one-out resampling descriptions: one that uses stratified sampling, and one that repeats the procedure five times. What happens?

Now, let's run the CV and get the average performance measures:

```
LOOCV <- resample(learner = knn, task = diabetesTask, resampling = LOO,
                  measures = list(mmce, acc))

LOOCV$aggr

mmce.test.mean  acc.test.mean
     0.1172414      0.8827586
```

If you rerun the CV over and over again, you'll find that for this model and data, the performance estimate is more variable than for k-fold but less variable than for the holdout we ran earlier.

CALCULATING A CONFUSION MATRIX

Once again, let's look at the confusion matrix:

```
calculateConfusionMatrix(LOOCV$pred, relative = TRUE)

Relative confusion matrix (normalized by row/column):
          predicted
true       Chemical  Normal    Overt     -err.-
  Chemical 0.81/0.74 0.14/0.06 0.06/0.07 0.19
  Normal   0.05/0.10 0.95/0.94 0.00/0.00 0.05
  Overt    0.18/0.15 0.00/0.00 0.82/0.93 0.18
  -err.-        0.26      0.06      0.07 0.12


Absolute confusion matrix:
          predicted
true       Chemical Normal Overt -err.-
  Chemical       29      5     2      7
  Normal          4     72     0      4
  Overt           6      0    27      6
  -err.-         10      5     2     17
```

So you now know how to apply three commonly used types of cross-validation! If we've cross-validated our model and are happy that it will perform well enough on unseen data, then we would train the model on all of the data available to us, and use this to make future predictions.

But I think we can still improve our kNN model. Remember how earlier, we manually choose a value of 2 for *k*? Well, randomly picking a value of *k* isn't very clever, and there are much better ways we can find the optimal value.

3.6 What algorithms can learn, and what they must be told: Parameters and hyperparameters

Machine learning models often have *parameters* associated with them. A parameter is a variable or value that is estimated from the data and that is internal to the model and controls how it makes predictions on new data. An example of a model parameter is the slope of a regression line.

In the kNN algorithm, *k* is not a parameter, because the algorithm doesn't estimate it from the data (in fact, the kNN algorithm doesn't actually learn any parameters). Instead, *k* is what's known as a *hyperparameter*: a variable or option that controls how a model makes predictions but is *not* estimated from the data. As data scientists, we don't have to provide parameters to our models; we simply provide the data, and the algorithms learn the parameters for themselves. We do, however, need to provide whatever hyperparameters they require. You'll see throughout this book that different algorithms require and use different hyperparameters to control how they learn their models.

So because *k* is a hyperparameter of the kNN algorithm, it can't be estimated by the algorithm itself, and it's up to us to choose a value. How do we decide? Well, there are three ways you can choose *k* or, in fact, any hyperparameter:

- *Pick a "sensible" or default value that has worked on similar problems before.* This option is a bad idea. You have no way of knowing whether the value of *k* you've chosen is the best one. Just because a value worked on other datasets doesn't mean it will perform well on this dataset. This is the choice of the lazy data scientist who doesn't care much about getting the most from their data.
- *Manually try a few different values, and see which one gives you the best performance.* This option is a bit better. The idea here is that you pick a few sensible values of *k*, build a model with each of them, and see which model performs the best. This is better because you're more likely to find the best-performing value of *k*; but you're still not guaranteed to find it, and doing this manually could be tedious and slow. This is the choice of the data scientist who cares but doesn't really know what they're doing.
- *Use a procedure called hyperparameter tuning to automate the selection process.* This solution is the best. It maximizes the likelihood of you finding the best-performing value of *k* while also automating the process for you. This is the method we'll be using throughout the book.

NOTE While the third option is generally the best if possible, some algorithms are so computationally expensive that they prohibit extensive hyperparameter tuning, in which case you may have to settle for manually trying different values.

But how does changing the value of *k* impact model performance? Well, values of *k* that are too low may start to model noise in the data. For example, if we set $k = 1$, then a healthy patient could be misclassified as chemically diabetic just because a single chemically diabetic patient with an unusually low insulin level was their nearest neighbor. In this situation, instead of just modeling the systematic differences between the classes, we're also modeling the noise and unpredictable variability in the data.

On the other hand, if we set *k* too high, a large number of dissimilar patients will be included in the vote, and the model will be insensitive to local differences in the data. This is, of course, the bias-variance trade-off we talked about earlier.

3.7 Tuning k to improve the model

Let's apply hyperparameter tuning to optimize the value of *k* for our model. An approach we *could* follow would be to build models with different values of *k* using our full dataset, pass the data back through the model, and see which value of *k* gives us the best performance. This is bad practice, because there's a large chance we'll get a value of *k* that overfits the dataset we tuned it on. So once again, we rely on CV to help us guard against overfitting.

The first thing we need to do is define a range of values over which mlr will try, when tuning *k*:

```
knnParamSpace <- makeParamSet(makeDiscreteParam("k", values = 1:10))
```

The `makeDiscreteParam()` function inside the `makeParamSet()` function allows us to specify that the hyperparameter we're going to be tuning is *k*, and that we want to search the values between 1 and 10 for the best value of *k*. As its name suggests, `makeDiscreteParam()` is used to define discrete hyperparameter values, such as *k* in kNN, but there are also functions to define continuous and logical hyperparameters that we'll explore later in the book. The `makeParamSet()` function defines the hyperparameter space we defined as a parameter set, and if we wanted to tune more than one hyperparameter during tuning, we would simply separate them by commas inside this function.

Next, we define how we want mlr to search the parameter space. There are a few options for this, and in later chapters we'll explore others, but for now we're going to use the *grid search* method. This is probably the simplest method: it tries every single value in the parameter space when looking for the best-performing value. For tuning continuous hyperparameters, or when we are tuning several hyperparameters at once, grid search becomes prohibitively expensive, so other methods like *random search* are preferred:

```
gridSearch <- makeTuneControlGrid()
```

Next, we define how we're going to cross-validate the tuning procedure, and we're going to use my favorite: repeated k-fold CV. The principle here is that for every value in the parameter space (integers 1 to 10), we perform repeated k-fold CV. For each value of *k*, we take the average performance measure across all those iterations and compare it with the average performance measures for all the other values of *k* we tried. This will hopefully give us the value of *k* that performs best:

```
cvForTuning <- makeResampleDesc("RepCV", folds = 10, reps = 20)
```

Now, we call the `tuneParams()` function to perform the tuning:

```
tunedK <- tuneParams("classif.knn", task = diabetesTask,
                     resampling = cvForTuning,
                     par.set = knnParamSpace, control = gridSearch)
```

The first and second arguments are the names of the algorithm and task we're applying, respectively. We give our CV strategy as the `resampling` argument, the hyperparameter space we define as the `par.set` argument, and the search procedure to the `control` argument.

If we call our `tunedK` object, we get the best-performing value of *k*, 7, and the average MMCE value for that value. We can access the best-performing value of *k* directly by selecting the `$x` component:

```
tunedK

Tune result:
Op. pars: k=7
mmce.test.mean=0.0769524

tunedK$x
$k
[1] 7
```

We can also visualize the tuning process (the result of this code is shown in figure 3.15):

```
knnTuningData <- generateHyperParsEffectData(tunedK)

plotHyperParsEffect(knnTuningData, x = "k", y = "mmce.test.mean",
                    plot.type = "line") +
  theme_bw()
```

Now we can train our final model, using our tuned value of *k*:

```
tunedKnn <- setHyperPars(makeLearner("classif.knn"),
                         par.vals = tunedK$x)

tunedKnnModel <- train(tunedKnn, diabetesTask)
```

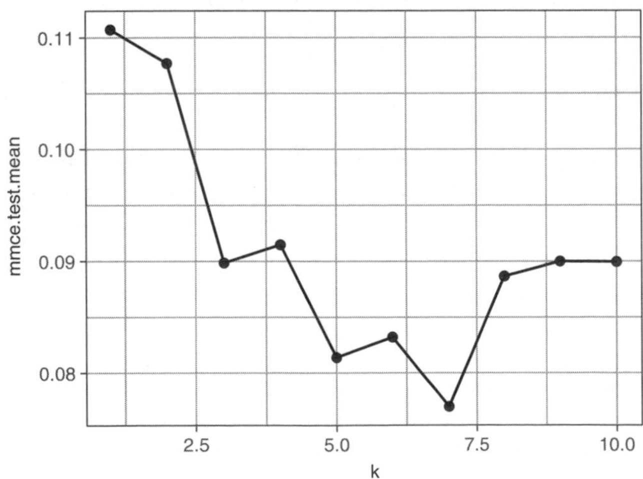

Figure 3.15 The MMCE values from fitting the kNN model with different values of *k* during a grid search

This is as simple as wrapping the `makeLearner()` function, where we make a new kNN learner, inside the `setHyperPars()` function, and providing the tuned value of *k* as the `par.vals` argument. We then train our final model as before, using the `train()` function.

3.7.1 Including hyperparameter tuning in cross-validation

Now, when we perform some kind of preprocessing on our data or model, such as tuning hyperparameters, it's important to include this preprocessing *inside* our CV, so that we cross-validate the whole model-training procedure. This takes the form of nested CV, where an inner loop cross-validates different values of our hyperparameter (just as we did earlier), and then the winning hyperparameter value gets passed to an outer CV loop. In the outer CV loop, the winning hyperparameters are used for each fold.

Nested CV proceeds like this:

1. Split the data into training and test sets (this can be done using the holdout, k-fold, or leave-one-out method). This division is called the *outer loop*.
2. The training set is used to cross-validate each value of our hyperparameter search space (using whatever method we decide). This is called the *inner loop*.
3. The hyperparameter that gives the best cross-validated performance from each inner loop is passed to the outer loop.
4. A model is trained on each training set of the outer loop, using the best hyperparameter from its inner loop. These models are used to make predictions on their test sets.
5. The average performance metrics of these models across the outer loop are then reported as an estimate of how the model will perform on unseen data.

If you prefer a graphical explanation, take a look at figure 3.16.

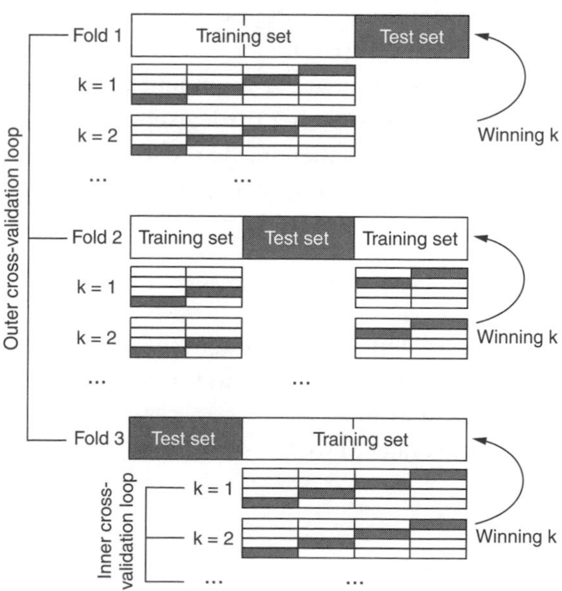

Figure 3.16 Nested CV. The dataset is split into folds. For each fold, the training set is used to create sets of inner k-fold CV. Each of these inner sets cross-validates a single hyperparameter value by splitting the data into training and test sets. For each fold in these inner sets, a model is trained using the training set and evaluated on the test set, using that set's hyperparameter value. The hyperparameter from each inner CV loop that gives the best-performing model is used to train the models on the outer loop.

In the example in figure 3.16, the outer loop is 3-fold CV. For each fold, inner sets of 4-fold CV are applied, only using the training set from the outer loop. This 4-fold cross-validation is used to evaluate the performance of each hyperparameter value we're searching over. The winning value of *k* (the one that gives the best performance) is then passed to the outer loop, which is then used to train the model, and its performance is evaluated on the test set. Can you see that we're cross-validating the whole model-building process, including hyperparameter tuning?

What's the purpose of this? It validates our entire model-building procedure, including the hyperparameter-tuning step. The cross-validated performance estimate we get from this procedure should be a good representation of how we expect our model to perform on completely new, unseen data.

The process looks pretty complicated, but it is extremely easy to perform with mlr. First, we define how we're going to perform the inner and outer CV:

```
inner <- makeResampleDesc("CV")

outer <- makeResampleDesc("RepCV", folds = 10, reps = 5)
```

I've chosen to perform ordinary k-fold cross-validation for the inner loop (10 is the default number of folds) and 10-fold CV, repeated 5 times, for the outer loop.

Next, we make what's called a *wrapper*, which is basically a learner tied to some preprocessing step. In our case, this is hyperparameter tuning, so we create a tuning wrapper with `makeTuneWrapper()`:

```
knnWrapper <- makeTuneWrapper("classif.knn", resampling = inner,
                              par.set = knnParamSpace,
                              control = gridSearch)
```

Here, we supply the algorithm as the first argument and pass our inner CV procedure as the `resampling` argument. We supply our hyperparameter search space as the `par.set` argument and our `gridSearch` method as the `control` argument (remember that we created these two objects earlier). This "wraps" together the learning algorithm with the hyperparameter tuning procedure that will be applied inside the inner CV loop.

Now that we've defined our inner and outer CV strategies and our tuning wrapper, we run the nested CV procedure:

```
cvWithTuning <- resample(knnWrapper, diabetesTask, resampling = outer)
```

The first argument is the wrapper we created a moment ago, the second argument is the name of the task, and we supply our outer CV strategy as the resampling argument. Now sit back and relax—this could take a while!

Once it finishes, you can print the average MMCE:

```
cvWithTuning

Resample Result
Task: diabetesTib
```

```
Learner: classif.knn.tuned
Aggr perf: mmce.test.mean=0.0856190
Runtime: 42.9978
```

Your MMCE value will probably be a little different than mine due to the random nature of the validation procedure, but the model is estimated to correctly classify 91.4% of cases on unseen data. That's not bad; and now that we've cross-validated our model properly, we can be confident we're not overfitting our data.

3.7.2 Using our model to make predictions

We have our model, and we're free to use it to classify new patients! Let's imagine that some new patients come to the clinic:

```
newDiabetesPatients <- tibble(glucose = c(82, 108, 300),
                              insulin = c(361, 288, 1052),
                              sspg = c(200, 186, 135))

newDiabetesPatients

# A tibble: 3 x 3
  glucose insulin  sspg
    <dbl>   <dbl> <dbl>
1      82     361   200
2     108     288   186
3     300    1052   135
```

We can pass these patients into our model and get their predicted diabetes status:

```
newPatientsPred <- predict(tunedKnnModel, newdata = newDiabetesPatients)

getPredictionResponse(newPatientsPred)

[1] Normal Normal Overt
Levels: Chemical Normal Overt
```

Congratulations! Not only have you built your first machine learning model, but we've covered some reasonably complex theory, too. In the next chapter, we're going to learn about logistic regression, but first I want to list the strengths and weaknesses of the k-nearest neighbor algorithm.

3.8 Strengths and weaknesses of kNN

While it often isn't easy to tell which algorithms will perform well for a given task, here are some strengths and weaknesses that will help you decide whether kNN will perform well for your task.

The strengths of the kNN algorithm are as follows:

- The algorithm is very simple to understand.
- There is no computational cost during the learning process; all the computation is done during prediction.
- It makes no assumptions about the data, such as how it's distributed.

The weaknesses of the kNN algorithm are these:

- It cannot natively handle categorical variables (they must be recoded first, or a different distance metric must be used).
- When the training set is large, it can be computationally expensive to compute the distance between new data and all the cases in the training set.
- The model can't be interpreted in terms of real-world relationships in the data.
- Prediction accuracy can be strongly impacted by noisy data and outliers.
- In high-dimensional datasets, kNN tends to perform poorly. This is due to a phenomenon you'll learn about in chapter 5, called the *curse of dimensionality*. In brief, in high dimensions the distances between the cases start to look the same, so finding the nearest neighbors becomes difficult.

Exercise 5

Load the iris dataset using the `data()` function, and build a kNN model to classify its three species of iris (including tuning the *k* hyperparameter).

Exercise 6

Cross-validate this iris kNN model using nested CV, where the outer CV is holdout with a two-thirds split.

Exercise 7

Repeat the nested CV as in the previous exercise, but using 5-fold, non-repeated CV as the outer loop. Which of these methods gives you a more stable MMCE estimate when you repeat them?

Summary

- kNN is a simple supervised learning algorithm that classifies new data based on the class membership of its nearest *k* cases in the training set.
- To create a machine learning model in mlr, we create a task and a learner, and then train the model using them.
- MMCE is the mean misclassification error, which is the proportion of misclassified cases in a classification problem. It is the opposite of accuracy.
- The bias-variance trade-off is the balance between two types of error in predictive accuracy. Models with high bias are underfit, and models with high variance are overfit.
- Model performance should never be evaluated on the data used to train it; cross-validation should be used, instead.

- Cross-validation is a set of techniques for evaluating model performance by splitting the data into training and test sets.
- Three common types of cross-validation are holdout, where a single split is used; k-fold, where the data is split into *k* chunks and the validation performed on each chunk; and leave-one-out, where the test set is a single case.
- Hyperparameters are options that control how machine learning algorithms learn, which cannot be learned by the algorithm itself. Hyperparameter tuning is the best way to find optimal hyperparameters.
- If we perform a data-dependent preprocessing step, such as hyperparameter tuning, it's important to incorporate this in our cross-validation strategy, using nested cross-validation.

Solutions to exercises

1 Plot the glucose and insulin variables against each other, representing the class variable using shape, and then using shape *and* color:

```
ggplot(diabetesTib, aes(glucose, insulin,
                        shape = class)) +
  geom_point()  +
  theme_bw()

ggplot(diabetesTib, aes(glucose, insulin,
                        shape = class, col = class)) +
  geom_point()  +
  theme_bw()
```

2 Create a holdout resampling description that uses 10% of the cases as the test set and does not use stratified sampling:

```
holdoutNoStrat <- makeResampleDesc(method = "Holdout", split = 0.9,
                                   stratify = FALSE)
```

3 Compare the stability of the performance estimates of 3-fold cross-validation repeated 5 times or 500 times:

```
kFold500 <- makeResampleDesc(method = "RepCV", folds = 3, reps = 500,
                             stratify = TRUE)

kFoldCV500 <- resample(learner = knn, task = diabetesTask,
                       resampling = kFold500, measures = list(mmce, acc))

kFold5 <- makeResampleDesc(method = "RepCV", folds = 3, reps = 5,
                           stratify = TRUE)

kFoldCV5 <- resample(learner = knn, task = diabetesTask,
                     resampling = kFold5, measures = list(mmce, acc))

kFoldCV500$aggr
kFoldCV5$aggr
```

4 Attempt to make leave-one-out resampling descriptions that use stratified sampling and repeated sampling:

```
makeResampleDesc(method = "LOO", stratify = TRUE)

makeResampleDesc(method = "LOO", reps = 5)

# Both will result in an error as LOO cross-validation cannot
# be stratified or repeated.
```

5 Load the iris dataset, and build a kNN model to classify its three species of iris (including tuning the *k* hyperparameter):

```
data(iris)

irisTask <- makeClassifTask(data = iris, target = "Species")

knnParamSpace <- makeParamSet(makeDiscreteParam("k", values = 1:25))

gridSearch <- makeTuneControlGrid()

cvForTuning <- makeResampleDesc("RepCV", folds = 10, reps = 20)

tunedK <- tuneParams("classif.knn", task = irisTask,
                     resampling = cvForTuning,
                     par.set = knnParamSpace,
                     control = gridSearch)

tunedK

tunedK$x

knnTuningData <- generateHyperParsEffectData(tunedK)

plotHyperParsEffect(knnTuningData, x = "k", y = "mmce.test.mean",
                    plot.type = "line") +
                    theme_bw()

tunedKnn <- setHyperPars(makeLearner("classif.knn"), par.vals = tunedK$x)

tunedKnnModel <- train(tunedKnn, irisTask)
```

6 Cross-validate this iris kNN model using nested cross-validation, where the outer cross-validation is holdout with a two-thirds split:

```
inner <- makeResampleDesc("CV")

outerHoldout <- makeResampleDesc("Holdout", split = 2/3, stratify = TRUE)

knnWrapper <- makeTuneWrapper("classif.knn", resampling = inner,
                              par.set = knnParamSpace,
                              control = gridSearch)
```

```
holdoutCVWithTuning <- resample(knnWrapper, irisTask,
                                resampling = outerHoldout)

holdoutCVWithTuning
```

7 Repeat the nested cross-validation using 5-fold, non-repeated cross-validation as the outer loop. Which of these methods gives you a more stable MMCE estimate when you repeat them?

```
outerKfold <- makeResampleDesc("CV", iters = 5, stratify = TRUE)

kFoldCVWithTuning <- resample(knnWrapper, irisTask,
                              resampling = outerKfold)

kFoldCVWithTuning

resample(knnWrapper, irisTask, resampling = outerKfold)

# Repeat each validation procedure 10 times and save the mmce value.
# WARNING: this may take a few minutes to complete.

kSamples <- map_dbl(1:10, ~resample(
  knnWrapper, irisTask, resampling = outerKfold)$aggr
  )

hSamples <- map_dbl(1:10, ~resample(
  knnWrapper, irisTask, resampling = outerHoldout)$aggr
  )

hist(kSamples, xlim = c(0, 0.11))
hist(hSamples, xlim = c(0, 0.11))

# Holdout CV gives more variable estimates of model performance.
```

4 Classifying based on odds with logistic regression

This chapter covers

- Working with the logistic regression algorithm
- Understanding feature engineering
- Understanding missing value imputation

In this chapter, I'm going to add a new classification algorithm to your toolbox: *logistic regression*. Just like the k-nearest neighbors algorithm you learned about in the previous chapter, logistic regression is a supervised learning method that predicts class membership. Logistic regression relies on the equation of a straight line and produces models that are very easy to interpret and communicate.

Logistic regression can handle continuous (without discrete categories) and categorical (with discrete categories) predictor variables. In its simplest form, logistic regression is used to predict a binary outcome (cases can belong to one of two classes), but variants of the algorithm can handle multiple classes as well. Its name comes from the algorithm's use of the *logistic function*, an equation that calculates the probability that a case belongs to one of the classes.

While logistic regression is most certainly a classification algorithm, it uses *linear regression* and the equation for a straight line to combine the information from multiple predictors. In this chapter, you'll learn how the logistic function works and how the equation for a straight line is used to build a model.

NOTE If you're already familiar with linear regression, a key distinction between linear and logistic regression is that the former learns the relationship between predictor variables and a *continuous* outcome variable, whereas the latter learns the relationship between predictor variables and a *categorical* outcome variable.

By the end of this chapter, you will have applied the skills you learned in chapters 2 and 3 to prepare your data and build, interpret, and evaluate the performance of a logistic regression model. You will also have learned what *missing value imputation* is, a method for filling in missing data with sensible values when working with algorithms that cannot handle missing values. You will apply a basic form of missing value imputation as a strategy to deal with missing data.

4.1 What is logistic regression?

Imagine that you're the curator of fifteenth-century art at a museum. When works of art, allegedly by famous painters, come to the museum, it's your job to determine whether they are genuine or fake (a two-class classification problem). You have access to the chemical analysis performed on each painting, and you are aware that many forgeries of this period used paints with lower copper content than the original paintings. You can use logistic regression to learn a model that tells you the probability of a painting being an original based on the copper content of its paint. The model will then assign this painting to the class with the highest probability (see figure 4.1).

NOTE The algorithm is commonly applied to two-class classification problems (this is referred to as *binomial* logistic regression), but a variant called *multinomial* logistic regression handles classification problems where you have three or more classes.

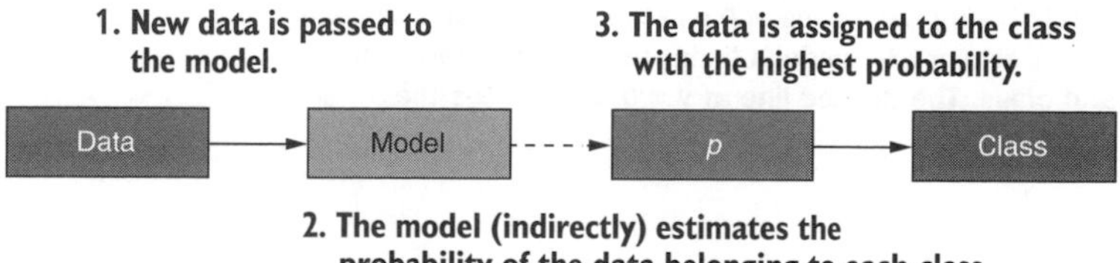

Figure 4.1 Logistic regression learns models that output the probability (*p*) of new data belonging to each of the classes. Typically, new data is assigned the class to which it has the highest probability of belonging. The dotted arrow indicates that there are additional steps in calculating the probabilities, which we'll discuss in section 4.1.1.

Logistic regression is a very popular classification algorithm, especially in the medical community, partly because of how interpretable the model is. For every predictor variable in our model, we get an estimate of just how the value of that variable impacts the probability that a case belongs to one class over another.

We know that logistic regression learns models that estimate the probability of new cases belonging to each class. Let's delve into how the algorithm learns the model.

4.1.1 How does logistic regression learn?

Take a look at the (imaginary) data in figure 4.2. I've plotted the copper content of a sample of paintings we know to be real or forgeries against their class as if it were a continuous variable between 0 and 1. We can see that, on average, the forgeries contain less copper in their paint than the originals. We *could* model this relationship with a straight line, as shown in the figure. This approach works well when your predictor variable has a linear relationship with a *continuous* variable that you want to predict (we'll cover this in chapter 9); but as you can see, it doesn't do a good job of modeling the relationship between a continuous variable and a *categorical* one.

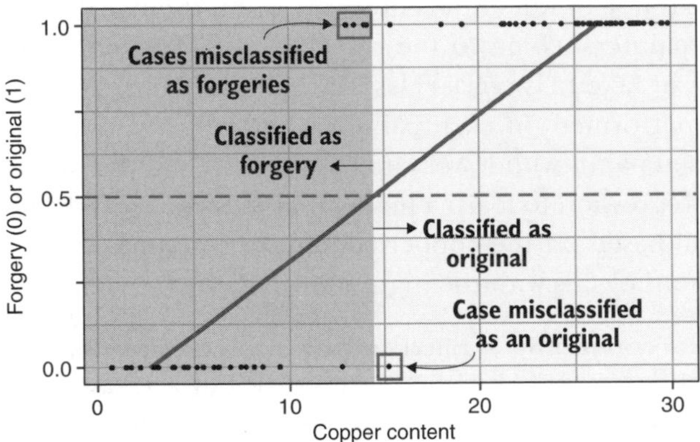

Figure 4.2 Plotting copper content against class. The y-axis displays the categorical class membership as if it were a continuous variable, with forgeries and originals taking the values of 0 and 1, respectively. The solid line represents a poor attempt to model a linear relationship between copper content and class. The dashed line at y = 0.5 indicates the threshold of classification.

As shown in the figure, we could find the copper content at which the straight line passes halfway between 0 and 1, and classify paintings with copper content below this value as forgeries and paintings above the value as originals. This might result in many misclassifications, so a better approach is needed.

We can better model the relationship between copper content and class membership using the *logistic* function, which is shown in figure 4.3. The logistic function is an S-shaped curve that maps a continuous variable (copper content, in our case) onto values between 0 and 1. This does a much better job of representing the relationship between copper content and whether a painting is an original or forgery. The figure shows a logistic function fit to the same data as in figure 4.2. We could find the copper

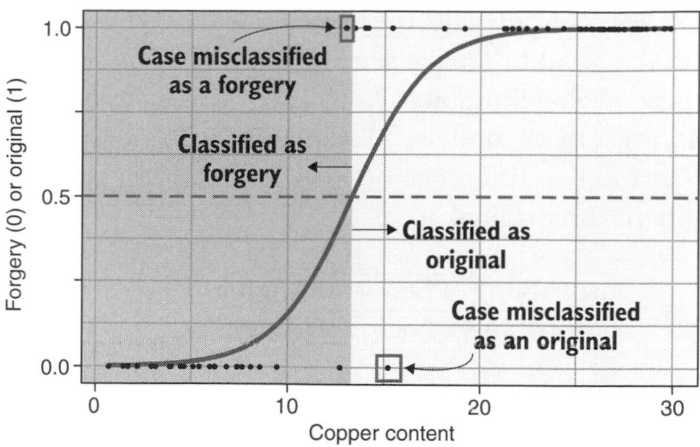

Figure 4.3 Modeling the data with the logistic function. The S-shaped curve represents the logistic function fitted to the data. The center of the curve passes through the mean of copper content and maps it between 0 and 1.

content at which the logistic function passes halfway between 0 and 1, and classify paintings with copper content below this value as forgeries and paintings above the value as originals. This typically results in fewer misclassifications than when we do this using a straight line.

Importantly, as the logistic function maps our *x* variable between the values of 0 and 1, we can interpret its output as the probability of a case with a particular copper content being an original painting. Take another look at figure 4.3. Can you see that as copper content increases, the logistic function approaches 1? This represents the fact that, on average, original paintings have a higher copper content, so if you pick a painting at random and find that it has a copper content of 20, it has a ~ 0.99 or 99% probability of being an original.

> **NOTE** If I had coded the grouping variable the other way around (with forgeries being 1 and originals being 0), then the logistic function would approach 1 for low values of copper and approach 0 for high values. We would simply interpret the output as the probability of being a forgery, instead.

The opposite is also true: as copper content decreases, the logistic function approaches 0. This represents the fact that, on average, forgeries have lower copper content, so if you pick a painting at random and find it has a copper content of 7, it has a ~ 0.99 or 99% probability of being a forgery.

Great! We can estimate the probability of a painting being an original by using the logistic function. But what if we have more than one predictor variable? Because probabilities are bounded between 0 and 1, it's difficult to combine the information from two predictors. For example, say the logistic function estimates that a painting has a 0.6 probability of being an original for one predictor variable, and a 0.7 probability for the other predictor. We can't simply add these estimates together, because they would be larger than 1, and this wouldn't make sense.

Instead, we can take these probabilities and convert them into their *log odds* (the "raw" output from logistic regression models). To introduce log odds, let me first explain what I mean by *odds*, and the difference between odds and probability.

The odds of a painting being an original are

$$\text{odds} = \frac{\text{probability of being an original}}{\text{probability of being a forgery}}$$ **Equation 4.1**

You may come across this written as

$$\text{odds} = \frac{p}{1-p}$$ **Equation 4.2**

Odds are a convenient way of representing the likelihood of something occurring. They tell us how much more likely an event is to occur, rather than how likely it is *not* to occur.

In *The Empire Strikes Back*, C3PO says that the odds of "successfully navigating an asteroid field are approximately 3,720 to 1!" What C3PO was trying to tell Han and Leia was that the probability of successfully navigating an asteroid field is approximately 3,720 times smaller than the probability of *unsuccessfully* navigating it. Simply stating the odds is often a more convenient way of representing likelihood because we know that, for every 1 asteroid field that was successfully navigated, 3,720 were not! Additionally, whereas probability is bounded between 0 and 1, odds can take any positive value.

NOTE Despite being a highly intelligent protocol droid, C3PO got his odds the wrong way around (as many people do). He *should* have said the odds of successfully navigating an asteroid field are approximately 1 to 3,720!

Figure 4.4 shows copper content plotted against the odds of a painting being an original. Notice that the odds are not bounded between 0 and 1, and that they take on positive values.

As we can see, though, the relationship between the copper content of the paint and the odds of a painting being an original is not linear. Instead, if we take the natural logarithm (log with a base of *e*, abbreviated as *ln*) of the odds, we get the *log odds*:

$$\text{log odds} = \ln\left(\frac{p}{1-p}\right)$$ **Equation 4.3**

TIP Equation 4.3, which converts probabilities into log odds, is also called the *logit* function. You will often see *logit regression* and *logistic regression* used interchangeably.

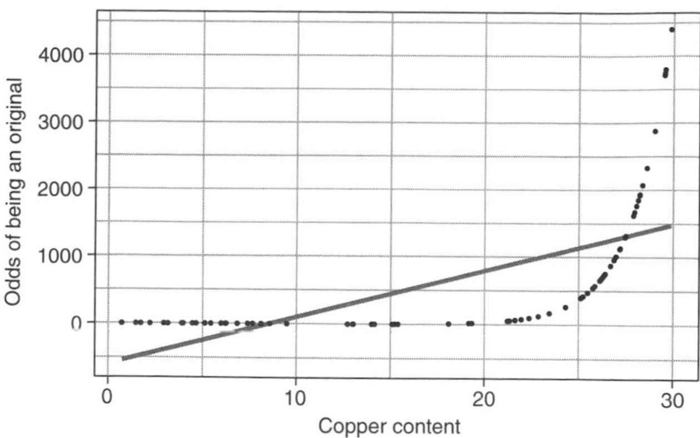

Figure 4.4 Plotting the odds of being an original against copper content. The probabilities derived from the logistic function were converted into odds and plotted against copper content. Odds can take any positive value. The straight line represents a poor attempt to model a linear relationship between copper content and odds.

I've taken the natural logarithm of the odds shown in figure 4.3 to generate their log odds, and plotted these log odds against copper content in figure 4.5. Hurray! We have a linear relationship between our predictor variable and the log odds of a painting being an original. Also notice that log odds are completely unbounded: they can extend to positive and negative infinity. When interpreting log odds

- A positive value means something is more likely to occur than to not occur.
- A negative value means something is less likely to occur than to occur.
- Log odds of 0 means something is as likely to occur as not to occur.

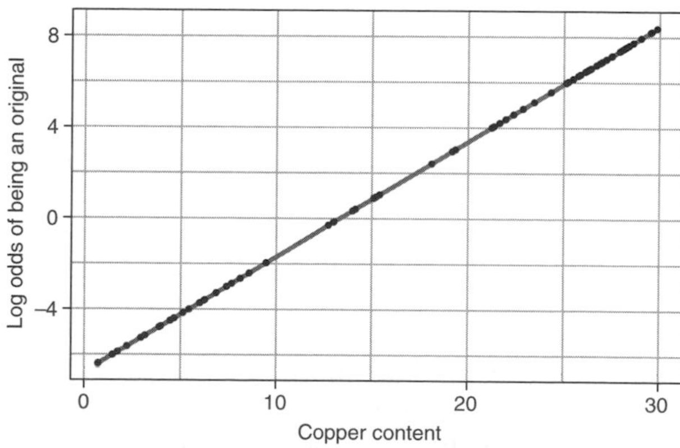

Figure 4.5 Plotting the log odds of being an original against copper content. The odds were converted into log odds using the logit function and plotted against copper content. Log odds are unbounded and can take any value. The straight line represents the linear relationship between copper content and log odds.

When discussing figure 4.4, I highlighted that the relationship between copper content and the odds of being an original painting was not linear. Next, I showed you in figure 4.5 that the relationship between copper content and log odds *was* linear. In fact, linearizing this relationship is why we take the natural logarithm of the odds. Why did I make such a big deal about there being a linear relationship between our predictor variable and its log odds? Well, modeling a straight line is easy. Recall from chapter 1 that all an algorithm needs to learn to model a straight-line relationship is the y-intercept and the slope of the line. So logistic regression learns the log odds of a painting being an original when copper content is 0 (the y-intercept), and how the log odds change with increasing copper content (the slope).

NOTE The more influence a predictor variable has on the log odds, the steeper the slope will be, while variables that have no predictive value will have a slope that is nearly horizontal.

Additionally, having a linear relationship means that when we have multiple predictor variables, we can add their contributions to the log odds together to get the overall log odds of a painting being an original, based on the information from all of its predictors.

Now, how do we get from the straight-line relationship between copper content and the log odds of being an original, to making predictions about new paintings? The model calculates the log odds of our new data being an original painting using

$$log\ odds = y\text{-}intercept + slope * copper$$

where we add the y-intercept and the product of the slope and the value of copper in our new painting. Once we've calculated the log odds of the new painting, we convert it into the probability of being an original using the logistic function:

$$p = \frac{1}{1 + e^{-z}} \qquad \text{Equation 4.4}$$

where p is the probability, e is Euler's number (a fixed constant ~ 2.718), and z is the log odds of a particular case.

Then, quite simply, if the probability of a painting being an original is > 0.5, it is classified as an original. If the probability is < 0.5, it is classified as a forgery. This conversion of log odds to odds to probabilities is illustrated in figure 4.6.

NOTE This threshold probability is 0.5 by default. In other words, if there is more than a 50% chance that a case belongs to the positive class, assign it to the positive class. We can alter this threshold, however, in situations where we need to be *really* sure before classifying a case as belonging to the positive class. For example, if we're using the model to predict whether a patient needs high-risk surgery, we want to be really sure before going ahead with the procedure!

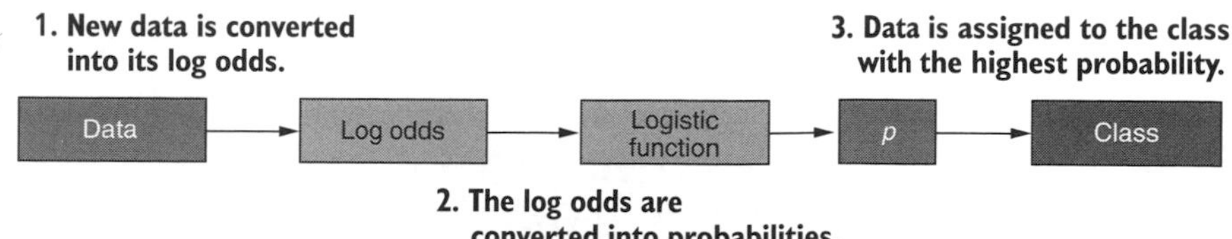
1. New data is converted into its log odds.
3. Data is assigned to the class with the highest probability.
Data
Log odds
Logistic function
p
Class
2. The log odds are converted into probabilities.

Figure 4.6 Summary of how logistic regression models predict class membership. Data is converted into log odds (logits), which are converted into odds and then into the probability of belonging to the "positive" class. Cases are assigned to the positive class if their probability exceeds a threshold probability (0.5 by default).

You will often see the model

$$log\ odds = y\text{-}intercept + slope * copper$$

rewritten as in equation 4.5.

$$\ln\left(\frac{p}{1-p}\right) = \beta_0 + \beta_{copper}x_{copper} \qquad \textbf{Equation 4.5}$$

Don't be scared by this! Look at equation 4.5 again. This is the way statisticians represent models that predict straight lines, and it is exactly the same as the equation describing log odds. The logistic regression model predicts the log odds (on the left of the equals) by adding the y-intercept (β_0) and the slope of the line (β_{copper}) multiplied by the value of copper (x_{copper}).

You may be wondering: why are you showing me equations when you promised me you wouldn't? Well, in most situations, we won't have a single predictor; we'll have many. By representing the model in this way, you can see how it can be used to combine multiple predictors together *linearly*: in other words, by adding their effects together.

Let's say we also include the amount of the metal lead as a predictor for whether a painting is an original or not. The model will instead look like this:

$$\ln\left(\frac{p}{1-p}\right) = \beta_0 + \beta_{copper}x_{copper} + \beta_{lead}x_{lead} \qquad \textbf{Equation 4.6}$$

An example of what this model might look like is shown in figure 4.7. With two predictor variables, we can represent the model as a plane, with the log odds shown on the vertical axis. The same principle applies for more than two predictors, but it's difficult to visualize on a 2D surface.

Now, for any painting we pass into our model, the model does the following:

1. Multiplies its copper content by the slope for copper
2. Multiplies the lead content by the slope for lead
3. Adds these two values and the y-intercept together to get the log odds of that painting being an original

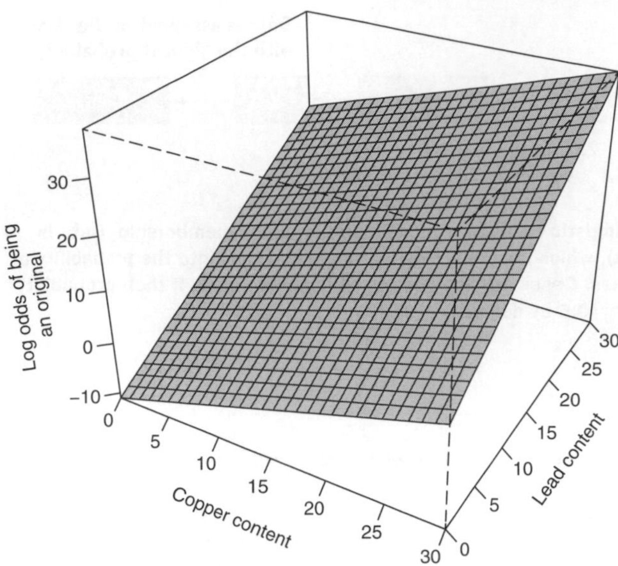

Figure 4.7 Visualizing a logistic regression model with two predictors. Copper content and lead content are plotted on the x- and z-axes, respectively. Log odds are plotted on the y-axis. The plane shown inside the plot represents the linear model that combines the intercept and the slopes of copper content and lead content to predict log odds.

4. Converts the log odds into a probability
5. Classifies the painting as an original if the probability is > 0.5, or classifies the painting as a forgery if the probability is < 0.5

We can extend the model to include as many predictor variables as we want:

$$\ln\left(\frac{p}{1-p}\right) = \beta_0 + \beta_1 x_1 + \beta_2 x_2 \ldots \beta_k x_k \qquad \textbf{Equation 4.7}$$

where k is the number of predictor variables in the dataset and the … represents all the variables in between.

TIP Remember in chapter 3, when I explained the difference between parameters and hyperparameters? Well, β_0, β_1, and so on are model parameters, because they are learned by the algorithm from the data.

The whole procedure for classifying new paintings is summarized in figure 4.8. First, we convert the copper and lead values of our new data into their log odds (logits) by using the linear model learned by the algorithm. Next, we convert the log odds into their probabilities using the logistic function. Finally, if the probability is > 0.5, we classify the painting as an original; and if its probability is < 0.5, we classify it as a forgery.

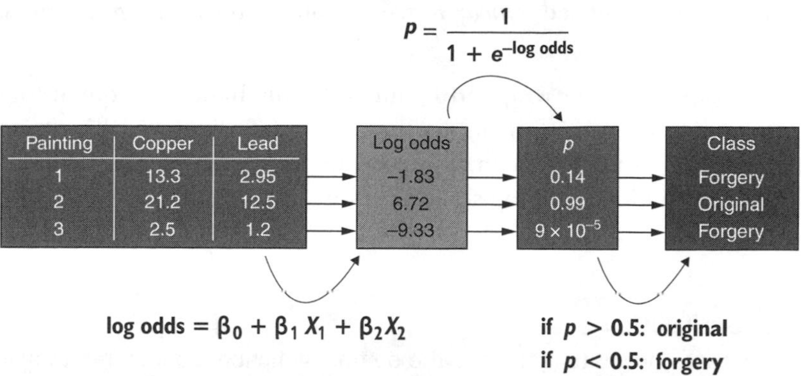

Figure 4.8 The process of classifying new paintings. The predictor variable values of three paintings are converted into log odds based on the learned model parameters (intercept and slopes). The log odds are converted into probabilities (p), and if $p >$ 0.5, the case is classified as the "positive" class.

NOTE Although the first and third paintings in figure 4.8 were both classified as forgeries, they had very different probabilities. As the probability of the third painting is much smaller than the probability of the first, we can be more confident that painting 3 is a forgery than we are confident that painting 1 is a forgery.

4.1.2 What if we have more than two classes?

The previous scenario is an example of binomial logistic regression. In other words, the decision about which class to assign to new data can take on only one of two named categories (*bi* and *nomos* from Latin and Greek, respectively). But we can use a variant of logistic regression to predict one of multiple classes. This is called *multinomial logistic regression,* because there are now multiple possible categories to choose from.

In multinomial logistic regression, instead of estimating a single logit for each case, the model estimates a logit for each case *for each of the output classes.* These logits are then passed into an equation called the *softmax function* which turns these logits into probabilities for each class, that sum to 1 (see figure 4.9). Then whichever class has the largest probability is selected as the output class.

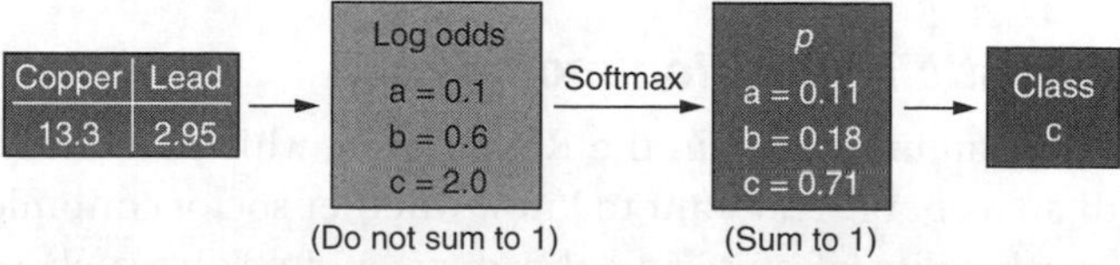

Figure 4.9 Summary of the softmax function. In the binomial case, only one logit is needed per case (the logit for the positive class). Where there are multiple classes (a, b, and c in this example), the model estimates one logit per class for each case. The softmax function maps these logits to probabilities that sum to one. The case is assigned to the class with the largest probability.

TIP You will sometimes see *softmax regression* and *multinomial logistic regression* used interchangeably.

The `classif.logreg` learner wrapped by mlr will only handle binomial logistic regression. There isn't currently an implementation of ordinary multinomial logistic regression wrapped by mlr. We can, however, use the `classif.LiblineaRL1LogReg` learner to perform multinomial logistic regression (although it has some differences I won't discuss).

The softmax function

It isn't necessary for you to memorize the softmax function, so feel free to skip this, but the softmax function is defined as

$$p_a = \frac{e^{logit_a}}{e^{logit_a} + e^{logit_b} + e^{logit_c}}$$

where p_a is the probability of a case belonging to class a, e is Euler's number (a fixed constant ~ 2.718), and $logit_a$, $logit_b$, and $logit_c$ are the logits for this case for being in classes a, b, and c, respectively.

If you're a math buff, this can be generalized to any number of classes using the equation

$$p_j = \frac{e^{logit_j}}{\sum_{k=1}^{K} e^{logit_k}}$$

where p_j is the probability of being in class j, and $\sum_{k=1}^{K}$ means to sum the e^{logits} from class 1 to class K (where there are K classes in total).

Write your own implementation of the softmax function in R, and try plugging other vectors of numbers into it. You'll find that it always maps the input to an output where all the elements sum to 1.

Now that you know how logistic regression works, you're going to build your first binomial logistic regression model.

4.2 Building your first logistic regression model

Imagine that you're a historian interested in the RMS *Titanic*, which famously sank in 1912 after colliding with an iceberg. You want to know whether socioeconomic factors influenced a person's probability of surviving the disaster. Luckily, such socioeconomic data is publicly available!

Your aim is to build a binomial logistic regression model to predict whether a passenger would survive the *Titanic* disaster, based on data such as their gender and how much they paid for their ticket. You're also going to interpret the model to decide which variables were important in influencing the probability of a passenger surviving. Let's start by loading the mlr and tidyverse packages:

```
library(mlr)
library(tidyverse)
```

4.2.1 Loading and exploring the Titanic dataset

Now let's load the data, which is built into the `titanic` package, convert it into a tibble (with `as_tibble()`), and explore it a little. We have a tibble containing 891 cases and 12 variables of passengers of the *Titanic*. Our goal is to train a model that can use the information in these variables to predict whether a passenger would survive the disaster.

Listing 4.1 Loading and exploring the *Titanic* dataset

```
install.packages("titanic")

data(titanic_train, package = "titanic")

titanicTib <- as_tibble(titanic_train)

titanicTib

# A tibble: 891 x 12
   PassengerId Survived Pclass Name  Sex     Age SibSp Parch Ticket
         <int>    <int>  <int> <chr> <chr> <dbl> <int> <int> <chr>
 1           1        0      3 Brau… male     22     1     0 A/5 2…
 2           2        1      1 Cumi… fema…    38     1     0 PC 17…
 3           3        1      3 Heik… fema…    26     0     0 STON/…
 4           4        1      1 Futr… fema…    35     1     0 113803
 5           5        0      3 Alle… male     35     0     0 373450
 6           6        0      3 Mora… male     NA     0     0 330877
 7           7        0      1 McCa… male     54     0     0 17463
 8           8        0      3 Pals… male      2     3     1 349909
 9           9        1      3 John… fema…    27     0     2 347742
10          10        1      2 Nass… fema…    14     1     0 237736
# … with 881 more rows, and 3 more variables: Fare <dbl>,
#   Cabin <chr>, Embarked <chr>
```

The tibble contains the following variables:

- `PassengerId`—An arbitrary number unique to each passenger
- `Survived`—An integer denoting survival (1 = survived, 0 = died)
- `Pclass`—Whether the passenger was housed in first, second, or third class
- `Name`—A character vector of the passengers' names
- `Sex`—A character vector containing "male" and "female"
- `Age`—The age of the passenger
- `SibSp`—The combined number of siblings and spouses on board
- `Parch`—The combined number of parents and children on board
- `Ticket`—A character vector with each passenger's ticket number

- `Fare`—The amount of money each passenger paid for their ticket
- `Cabin`—A character vector of each passenger's cabin number
- `Embarked`—A character vector of which port passengers embarked from

The first thing we're going to do is use tidyverse tools to clean and prepare the data for modeling.

4.2.2 Making the most of the data: Feature engineering and feature selection

Rarely will you be working with a dataset that is ready for modeling straight away. Typically, we need to perform some cleaning first to ensure that we get the most from the data. This includes steps such as converting data to the correct types, correcting mistakes, and removing irrelevant data. The `titanicTib` tibble is no exception; we need to clean it up before we can pass it to the logistic regression algorithm. We'll perform three tasks:

1. Convert the `Survived`, `Sex`, and `Pclass` variables into factors.
2. Create a new variable called `FamSize` by adding `SibSp` and `Parch` together.
3. Select the variables we believe to be of predictive value for our model.

If a variable should be a factor, it's important to let R know it's a factor, so that R treats it appropriately. We can see from the output of `titanicTib` in listing 4.1 that `Survived` and `Pclass` are both integer vectors (`<int>` is shown above their columns in the output) and that `Sex` is a character vector (`<chr>` above the column). Each of these variables should be treated as a factor because it represents discrete differences between cases that are repeated throughout the dataset.

We might hypothesize that the number of family members a passenger has on board might impact their survival. For example, people with many family members may be reluctant to board a lifeboat that doesn't have enough room for their whole family. While the `SibSp` and `Parch` variables contain this information separated by siblings and spouses, and parents and children, respectively, it may be more informative to combine these into a single variable containing overall family size.

This is an extremely important machine learning task called *feature engineering*: the modification of variables in your dataset to improve their predictive value. Feature engineering comes in two flavors:

- *Feature extraction*—Predictive information is held in a variable, but in a format that is not useful. For example, let's say you have a variable that contains the year, month, day, and time of day of certain events occurring. The time of day has important predictive value, but the year, month, and day do not. For this variable to be useful in your model, you would need to extract only the time-of-day information as a new variable.
- *Feature creation*—Existing variables are combined to create new ones. Merging the `SibSp` and `Parch` variables to create `FamSize` is an example.

Using feature extraction and feature creation allows us to extract predictive information present in our dataset but not currently in a format that maximizes its usefulness.

Finally, we will often have variables in our data that have no predictive value. For example, does knowing the passenger's name or cabin number help us predict survival? Possibly not, so let's remove them. Including variables with little or no predictive value adds noise to the data and will negatively impact how our models perform, so it's best to remove them.

This is another extremely important machine learning task called *feature selection*, and it is pretty much what it sounds like: keeping variables that add predictive value, and removing those that don't. Sometimes it's obvious to us as humans whether variables are useful predictors or not. Passenger name, for example, would not be useful because every passenger has a different name! In these situations, it's common sense to remove such variables. Often, however, it's not so obvious, and there are more sophisticated ways we can automate the feature-selection process. We'll explore this in later chapters.

All three of these tasks (converting to factors, feature engineering, and feature selection) are performed in listing 4.2. I've made our lives easier by defining a vector of the variables we wish to convert into factors, and then using the `mutate_at()` function to turn them all into factors. The `mutate_at()` function is like the `mutate()` function, but it allows us to mutate multiple columns at once. We supply the existing variables as a character vector to the `.vars` argument and tell it what we want to do to those variables using the `.funs` argument. In this case, we supply the vector of variables we defined, and the "factor" function to convert them into factors. We pipe the result of this into a `mutate()` function call that defines a new variable, `FamSize`, which is the sum of `SibSp` and `Parch`. Finally, we pipe the result of this into a `select()` function call, to select only the variables we believe may have some predictive value for our model.

Listing 4.2 Cleaning the *Titanic* data, ready for modeling

```
fctrs <- c("Survived", "Sex", "Pclass")

titanicClean <- titanicTib %>%
  mutate_at(.vars = fctrs, .funs = factor) %>%
  mutate(FamSize = SibSp + Parch) %>%
  select(Survived, Pclass, Sex, Age, Fare, FamSize)

titanicClean

# A tibble: 891 x 6
   Survived Pclass Sex      Age  Fare FamSize
   <fct>    <fct>  <fct>  <dbl> <dbl>   <int>
 1 0        3      male      22  7.25       1
 2 1        1      female    38 71.3        1
 3 1        3      female    26  7.92       0
 4 1        1      female    35 53.1        1
 5 0        3      male      35  8.05       0
 6 0        3      male      NA  8.46       0
 7 0        1      male      54 51.9        0
```

```
 8 0          3        male         2 21.1      4
 9 1          3        female      27 11.1      2
10 1          2        female      14 30.1      1
# ... with 881 more rows
```

When we print our new tibble, we can see that `Survived`, `Pclass`, and `Sex` are now factors (`<fct>` shown above their columns in the output); we have our new variable, `FamSize`; and we have removed irrelevant variables.

> **NOTE** Have I been too hasty in removing the `Name` variable from the tibble? Hidden in this variable are the salutations for each passenger (Miss, Mrs., Mr., Master, and so on), which may have predictive value. Using this information would require feature extraction.

4.2.3 Plotting the data

Now that we've cleaned our data a little, let's plot it to get better insight into the relationships in the data. Here's a little trick to simplify plotting multiple variables together using ggplot2. Let's convert the data into an untidy format, such that each of the predictor variable names is held in one column, and its values are held in another column, using the `gather()` function (refresh your memory of this by looking at the end of chapter 2).

> **NOTE** The `gather()` function will warn that "attributes are not identical across measure variables; they will be dropped." This is simply warning you that the variables you are gathering together don't have the same factor levels. Ordinarily this might mean you've collapsed variables you didn't mean to, but in this case we can safely ignore the warning.

Listing 4.3 Creating an untidy tibble for plotting

```
titanicUntidy <- gather(titanicClean, key = "Variable", value = "Value",
                        -Survived)
titanicUntidy

# A tibble: 4,455 x 3
   Survived Variable Value
   <fct>    <chr>    <chr>
 1 0        Pclass   3
 2 1        Pclass   1
 3 1        Pclass   3
 4 1        Pclass   1
 5 0        Pclass   3
 6 0        Pclass   3
 7 0        Pclass   1
 8 0        Pclass   3
 9 1        Pclass   3
10 1        Pclass   2
# ... with 4,445 more rows
```

We now have an untidy tibble with three columns: one containing the `Survived` factor, one containing the names of the predictor variables, and one containing their values.

NOTE Note that the value column is a character vector (`<chr>`). This is because it contains "male" and "female" from the `Sex` variable. As a column can only hold data of a single type, all the numerical data is also converted into characters.

You may be wondering why we're doing this. Well, it allows us to use ggplot2's *faceting* system to plot our different variables together. In listing 4.4, I take the `titanicUntidy` tibble, filter for the rows that *do not* contain the `Pclass` or `Sex` variables (as these are factors, we'll plot them separately), and pipe this data into a `ggplot()` call.

Listing 4.4 Creating subplots for each continuous variable

```
titanicUntidy %>%
  filter(Variable != "Pclass" & Variable != "Sex") %>%
  ggplot(aes(Survived, as.numeric(Value))) +
  facet_wrap(~ Variable, scales = "free_y") +
  geom_violin(draw_quantiles = c(0.25, 0.5, 0.75)) +
  theme_bw()
```

In the `ggplot()` function call, we supply `Survived` as the x aesthetic and `Value` as the y aesthetic (coercing it into a numeric vector with `as.numeric()` because it was converted into a character by our `gather()` function call earlier). Next—and here's the cool bit—we ask ggplot2 to *facet* by the `Variable` column, using the `facet_wrap()` function, and allow the y-axis to vary between the facets. Faceting allows us to draw subplots of our data, indexed by some faceting variable. Finally, we add a violin geometric object, which is similar to a box plot but also shows the density of data along the y-axis. The resulting plot is shown in figure 4.10.

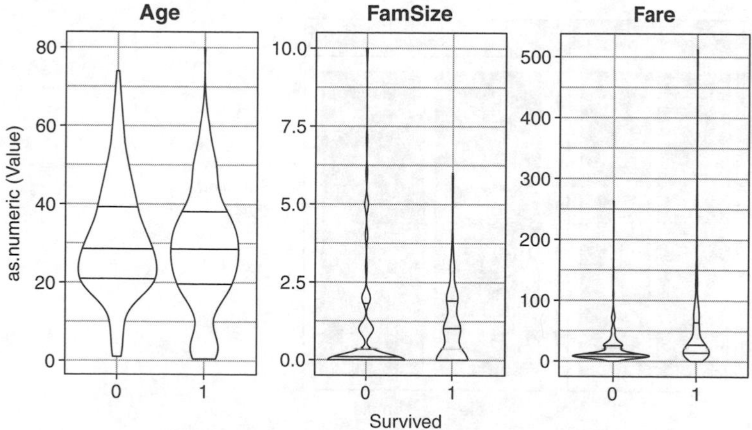

Figure 4.10 Faceted plot of `Survived` against `FamSize` and `Fare`. Violin plots show the density of data along the y-axis. The lines on each violin represent the first quartile, median, and third quartile (from lowest to highest).

Can you see how the faceting worked? Rows in the data with different values of `Variable` are plotted on different subplots! This is why we needed to gather the data into an untidy format: so we could supply a single variable for ggplot2 to facet by.

> **Exercise 1**
> Redraw the plot in figure 4.10, but add a `geom_point()` layer, setting the `alpha` argument to 0.05 and the `size` argument to 3. Does this make the violin plot make more sense?

Now let's do the same thing for the factors in our dataset by filtering the data for rows that contain *only* the `Pclass` and `Sex` variables. This time, we want to see what proportion of passengers in each level of the factors survived. To do so, we plot the factor levels on the x-axis by supplying `Value` as the x aesthetic mapping; and we want to use different colors to denote survival versus non-survival, so we supply `Survived` as the fill aesthetic. We facet by `Variable` as before and add a bar geometric object with the argument `position = "fill"`, which stacks the data for survivors and non-survivors such that they sum to 1 to show us the proportion of each. The resulting plot is shown in figure 4.11.

Listing 4.5 Creating subplots for each categorical variable

```
titanicUntidy %>%
  filter(Variable == "Pclass" | Variable == "Sex") %>%
  ggplot(aes(Value, fill = Survived)) +
  facet_wrap(~ Variable, scales = "free_x") +
  geom_bar(position = "fill") +
  theme_bw()
```

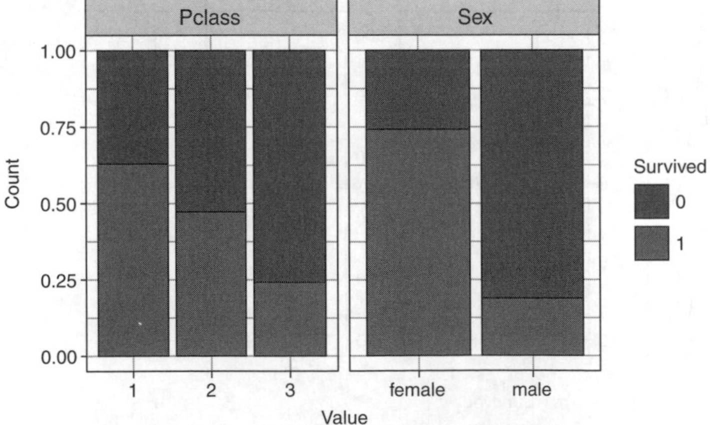

Figure 4.11 Faceted plot of `Survived` against `Pclass` and `Sex`. Filled bars represent the proportion of passengers at each level of the factors that survived (1 = survival).

NOTE In the `filter()` function calls in listings 4.4 and 4.5, I used the `&` and `|` operators to mean "and" and "or," respectively.

So it seems like passengers who survived tended to have slightly more family members on board (perhaps contradicting our hypothesis), although passengers with very large families on board tended not to survive. Age doesn't seem to have had an obvious impact on survival, but being female meant you would be much more likely to survive. Paying more for your fare increased your probability of survival, as did being in a higher class (though the two probably correlate).

Exercise 2

Redraw the plot in figure 4.11, but change the `geom_bar()` argument `position` equal to `"dodge"`. Do this again, but make the `position` argument equal to `"stack"`. Can you see the difference between the three methods?

4.2.4 Training the model

Now that we have our cleaned data, let's create a task, learner, and model with mlr (specifying `"classif.logreg"` to use logistic regression as our learner). By setting the argument `predict.type = "prob"`, the trained model will output the estimated probabilities of each class when making predictions on new data, rather than just the predicted class membership.

Listing 4.6 Creating a task and learner, and training a model

```
titanicTask <- makeClassifTask(data = titanicClean, target = "Survived")

logReg <- makeLearner("classif.logreg", predict.type = "prob")

logRegModel <- train(logReg, titanicTask)

Error in checkLearnerBeforeTrain(task, learner, weights) :
  Task 'titanicClean' has missing values in 'Age', but learner 'classif.logre
     g' does not support that!
```

Whoops! Something went wrong. What does the error message say? Hmm, it seems we have some missing data from the `Age` variable, and the logistic regression algorithm doesn't know how to handle that. Let's have a look at this variable. (I'm only displaying the first 60 elements to save room, but you can print the entire vector.)

Listing 4.7 Counting missing values in the `Age` variable

```
titanicClean$Age[1:60]
 [1] 22.0 38.0 26.0 35.0 35.0   NA 54.0  2.0 27.0 14.0  4.0 58.0 20.0
[14] 39.0 14.0 55.0  2.0   NA 31.0   NA 35.0 34.0 15.0 28.0  8.0 38.0
[27]   NA 19.0   NA   NA 40.0   NA   NA 66.0 28.0 42.0   NA 21.0 18.0
[40] 14.0 40.0 27.0   NA  3.0 19.0   NA   NA   NA   NA 18.0  7.0 21.0
[53] 49.0 29.0 65.0   NA 21.0 28.5  5.0 11.0
```

```
sum(is.na(titanicClean$Age))
[1] 177
```

Ah, we have lots of NAs (177 in fact!), which is R's way of labeling missing data.

4.2.5 Dealing with missing data

There are two ways to handle missing data:

- Simply exclude cases with missing data from the analysis
- Apply an *imputation* mechanism to fill in the gaps

The first option may be valid when the ratio of cases with missing values to complete cases is very small. In that case, omitting cases with missing data is unlikely to have a large impact on the performance of our model. It is a simple, if not elegant, solution to the problem.

The second option, missing value imputation, is the process by which we use some algorithm to estimate what those missing values would have been, replace the NAs with these estimates, and use this imputed dataset to train our model. There are many different ways of estimating the values of missing data, and we'll use more sophisticated ones throughout the book, but for now, we'll employ mean imputation, where we simply take the mean of the variable with missing data and replace missing values with that.

In listing 4.8, I use mlr's `impute()` function to replace the missing data. The first argument is the name of the data, and the `cols` argument asks us which columns we want to impute and what method we want to apply. We supply the `cols` argument as a list of the column names, separated by commas if we have more than one. Each column listed should be followed by an = sign and the imputation method (`imputeMean()` uses the mean of the variable to replace NAs). I save the imputed data structure as an object, `imp`, and use `sum(is.na())` to count the number of missing values from the data.

Listing 4.8 Imputing missing values in the `Age` variable

```
imp <- impute(titanicClean, cols = list(Age = imputeMean()))

sum(is.na(titanicClean$Age))
[1] 177

sum(is.na(imp$data$Age))
[1] 0
```

We can see that those 177 missing values have all been imputed!

4.2.6 Training the model (take two)

Okay, we've imputed those pesky missing values with the mean and created the new object `imp`. Now let's try again by creating a task using the imputed data. The `imp` object contains both the imputed data and a description for the imputation process we used. To extract the data, we simply use `imp$data`.

Listing 4.9 Training a model on imputed data

```
titanicTask <- makeClassifTask(data = imp$data, target = "Survived")

logRegModel <- train(logReg, titanicTask)
```

This time, no error messages. Next, let's cross-validate our model to estimate how it will perform.

4.3 Cross-validating the logistic regression model

Remember that when we cross-validate, we should cross-validate our entire model-building procedure. This should include any data-dependent preprocessing steps, such as missing value imputation. In chapter 3, we used a wrapper function to wrap together our learner and our hyperparameter tuning procedure. This time, we're going to create a wrapper for our learner and our missing value imputation.

4.3.1 Including missing value imputation in cross-validation

The `makeImputeWrapper()` function wraps together a learner (given as the first argument) and an imputation method. Notice how we specify the imputation method in exactly the same way as for the `impute()` function in listing 4.8, by supplying a list of columns and their imputation method.

Listing 4.10 Wrapping together the learner and the imputation method

```
logRegWrapper <- makeImputeWrapper("classif.logreg",
                                   cols = list(Age = imputeMean()))
```

Now let's apply stratified, 10-fold cross-validation, repeated 50 times, to our wrapped learner.

> **NOTE** Remember that we first define our resampling method using `make-ResampleDesc()` and then use `resample()` to run the cross-validation.

Because we're supplying our wrapped learner to the `resample()` function, for each fold of the cross-validation, the mean of the `Age` variable in the training set will be used to impute any missing values.

Listing 4.11 Cross-validating our model-building process

```
kFold <- makeResampleDesc(method = "RepCV", folds = 10, reps = 50,
                          stratify = TRUE)

logRegwithImpute <- resample(logRegWrapper, titanicTask,
                             resampling = kFold,
                             measures = list(acc, fpr, fnr))

logRegwithImpute
```

```
Resample Result
Task: imp$data
Learner: classif.logreg.imputed
Aggr perf: acc.test.mean=0.7961500,fpr.test.mean=0.2992605,fnr.test.mean=0.14
    44175
Runtime: 10.6986
```

As this is a two-class classification problem, we have access to a few extra performance metrics, such as the false positive rate (`fpr`) and false negative rate (`fnr`). In the cross-validation procedure in listing 4.11, we ask for accuracy, false positive rate, and false negative rate to be reported as performance metrics. We can see that although on average across the repeats our model correctly classified 79.6% of passengers, it incorrectly classified 29.9% of passengers who died as having survived (false positives), and incorrectly classified 14.4% of passengers who survived as having died (false negatives).

4.3.2 Accuracy is the most important performance metric, right?

You might think that the accuracy of a model's predictions is the defining metric of its performance. Often, this is the case, but sometimes, it's not.

Imagine that you work for a bank as a data scientist in the fraud-detection department. It's your job to build a model that predicts whether credit card transactions are legitimate or fraudulent. Let's say that out of 100,000 credit card transactions, only 1 is fraudulent. Because fraud is relatively rare, (and because they're serving pizza for lunch today), you decide to build a model that simply classifies all transactions as legitimate.

The model accuracy is 99.999%. Pretty good? Of course not! The model isn't able to identify *any* fraudulent transactions and has a false negative rate of 100%!

The lesson here is that you should evaluate model performance *in the context of your particular problem.* Another example could be building a model that will guide doctors to use an unpleasant treatment, or not, for a patient. In the context of this problem, it may be acceptable to incorrectly *not* give a patient the unpleasant treatment, but it is imperative that you don't incorrectly give a patient the treatment if they don't need it!

If positive events are rare (as in our fraudulent credit card example), or if it is particularly important that you don't misclassify positive cases as negative, you should favor models that have a low false negative rate. If negative events are rare, or if it is particularly important that you don't misclassify negative cases as positive (as in our medical treatment example), you should favor models that have a low false positive rate.

Take a look at https://mlr.mlr-org.com/articles/tutorial/measures.html to see all the performance measures currently wrapped by mlr and the situations in which they can be used.

4.4 Interpreting the model: The odds ratio

I mentioned at the start of the chapter that logistic regression is very popular because of how interpretable the model parameters (the y-intercept, and the slopes for each of the predictors) are. To extract the model parameters, we must first turn our mlr model object, `logRegModel`, into an R model object using the `getLearnerModel()`

function. Next, we pass this R model object as the argument to the `coef()` function, which stands for *coefficients* (another term for parameters), so this function returns the model parameters.

Listing 4.12 Extracting model parameters

```
logRegModelData <- getLearnerModel(logRegModel)

coef(logRegModelData)

 (Intercept)      Pclass2      Pclass3      Sexmale          Age
 3.809661697 -1.000344806 -2.132428850 -2.775928255 -0.038822458
        Fare      FamSize
 0.003218432 -0.243029114
```

The intercept is the log odds of surviving the *Titanic* disaster when all continuous variables are 0 and the factors are at their reference levels. We tend to be more interested in the slopes than the y-intercept, but these values are in log odds units, which are difficult to interpret. Instead, people commonly convert them into *odds ratios*.

An odds ratio is, well, a ratio of odds. For example, if the odds of surviving the *Titanic* if you're female are about 7 to 10, and the odds of surviving if you're male are 2 to 10, then the odds ratio for surviving if you're female is 3.5. In other words, if you were female, you would have been 3.5 times more likely to survive than if you were male. Odds ratios are a very popular way of interpreting the impact of predictors on an outcome, because they are easily understood.

4.4.1 Converting model parameters into odds ratios

How do we get from log odds to odds ratios? By taking their exponent ($e^{\text{log odds}}$). We can also calculate 95% confidence intervals using the `confint()` function, to help us decide how strong the evidence is that each variable has predictive value.

Listing 4.13 Converting model parameters into odds ratios

```
exp(cbind(Odds_Ratio = coef(logRegModelData), confint(logRegModelData)))

Waiting for profiling to be done...
             Odds_Ratio       2.5 %       97.5 %
(Intercept) 45.13516691 19.14718874 109.72483921
Pclass2      0.36775262  0.20650392   0.65220841
Pclass3      0.11854901  0.06700311   0.20885220
Sexmale      0.06229163  0.04182164   0.09116657
Age          0.96192148  0.94700049   0.97652950
Fare         1.00322362  0.99872001   1.00863263
FamSize      0.78424868  0.68315465   0.89110044
```

Most of these odds ratios are less than 1. An odds ratio less than 1 means an event is *less* likely to occur. It's usually easier to interpret these if you divide 1 by them. For example, the odds ratio for surviving if you were male is 0.06, and 1 divided by 0.06 = 16.7.

This means that, holding all other variables constant, men were 16.7 times *less* likely to survive than women.

For continuous variables, we interpret the odds ratio as how much more likely a passenger is to survive for every one-unit increase in the variable. For example, for every additional family member, a passenger was 1/0.78 = 1.28 times less likely to survive.

For factors, we interpret the odds ratio as how much more likely a passenger is to survive, compared to the reference level for that variable. For example, we have odds ratios for `Pclass2` and `Pclass3`, which are how many more times passengers in classes 2 and 3 are likely to survive compared to those in class 1, respectively.

The 95% confidence intervals indicate the strength of the evidence that each variable has predictive value. An odds ratio of 1 means the odds are equal and the variable has no impact on prediction. Therefore, if the 95% confidence intervals include the value 1, such as those for the `Fare` variable, then this *may* suggest that this variable isn't contributing anything.

4.4.2 When a one-unit increase doesn't make sense

A one-unit increase often isn't easily interpretable. Say you get an odds ratio that says for every additional ant in an anthill, that anthill is 1.000005 times more likely to survive a termite attack. How can you comprehend the importance of such a small odds ratio?

When it doesn't make sense to think in one-unit increases, a popular technique is to $\log_2$ transform the continuous variables instead, before training the model with them. This won't impact the predictions made by the model, but now the odds ratio can be interpreted this way: every time the number of ants *doubles*, the anthill is *x* times more likely to survive. This will give much larger and much more interpretable odds ratios.

4.5 Using our model to make predictions

We've built, cross-validated, and interpreted our model, and now it would be nice to use the model to make predictions on new data. This scenario is a little unusual in that we've built a model based on a historical event, so (hopefully!) we won't be using it to predict survival of another Titanic disaster. Nevertheless, I want to illustrate to you how to make predictions with a logistic regression model, the same as you can for any other supervised algorithm. Let's load some unlabeled passenger data, clean it ready for prediction, and pass it through our model.

Listing 4.14 Using our model to make predictions on new data

```
data(titanic_test, package = "titanic")

titanicNew <- as_tibble(titanic_test)

titanicNewClean <- titanicNew %>%
  mutate_at(.vars = c("Sex", "Pclass"), .funs = factor) %>%
```

```
  mutate(FamSize = SibSp + Parch) %>%
  select(Pclass, Sex, Age, Fare, FamSize)

predict(logRegModel, newdata = titanicNewClean)

Prediction: 418 observations
predict.type: prob
threshold: 0=0.50,1=0.50
time: 0.00
     prob.0     prob.1 response
1 0.9178036 0.08219636        0
2 0.5909570 0.40904305        0
3 0.9123303 0.08766974        0
4 0.8927383 0.10726167        0
5 0.4069407 0.59305933        1
6 0.8337609 0.16623907        0
... (#rows: 418, #cols: 3)
```

4.6 Strengths and weaknesses of logistic regression

While it often isn't easy to tell which algorithms will perform well for a given task, here are some strengths and weaknesses that will help you decide whether logistic regression will perform well for you.

The strengths of the logistic regression algorithm are as follows:

- It can handle both continuous and categorical predictors.
- The model parameters are very interpretable.
- Predictor variables are *not* assumed to be normally distributed.

The weaknesses of the logistic regression algorithm are these:

- It won't work when there is complete separation between classes.
- It assumes that the classes are *linearly separable*. In other words, it assumes that a flat surface in *n*-dimensional space (where *n* is the number of predictors) can be used to separate the classes. If a curved surface is required to separate the classes, logistic regression will underperform compared to some other algorithms.
- It assumes a linear relationship between each predictor and the log odds. If, for example, cases with low and high values of a predictor belong to one class, but cases with medium values of the predictor belong to another class, this linearity will break down.

Exercise 3

Repeat the model-building process, but omit the `Fare` variable. Does it make a difference to model performance as estimated by cross-validation? Why?

Exercise 4

Extract the salutations from the `Name` variable, and convert any that aren't `"Mr"`, `"Dr"`, `"Master"`, `"Miss"`, `"Mrs"`, or `"Rev"` to `"Other"`. Look at the following code for a hint as to how to extract the salutations with the `str_split()` function from the stringr tidyverse package:

```
names <- c("Mrs. Pool", "Mr. Johnson")

str_split(names, pattern = "\\.")
[[1]]
[1] "Mrs"   " Pool"

[[2]]
[1] "Mr"        " Johnson"
```

Exercise 5

Build a model that includes `Salutation` as another predictor, and cross-validate it. Does this improve model performance?

Summary

- Logistic regression is a supervised learning algorithm that classifies new data by calculating the probabilities of the data belonging to each class.
- Logistic regression can handle continuous and categorical predictors, and models a linear relationship between the predictors and the log odds of belonging to the positive class.
- Feature engineering is the process by which we extract information from, or create new variables from, existing variables to maximize their predictive value.
- Feature selection is the process of choosing which variables in a dataset have predictive value for machine learning models.
- Imputation is a strategy for dealing with missing data, where some algorithm is used to estimate what the missing values would have been. You learned how to apply mean imputation for the *Titanic* dataset.
- Odds ratios are an informative way of interpreting the impact each of our predictors has on the odds of a case belonging to the positive class. They can be calculated by taking the exponent of the model slopes ($e^{\text{log odds}}$).

Solutions to exercises

1. Redraw the violin plots, adding a `geom_point()` layer with transparency:

```
titanicUntidy %>%
  filter(Variable != "Pclass" & Variable != "Sex") %>%
  ggplot(aes(Survived, as.numeric(Value))) +
  facet_wrap(~ Variable, scales = "free_y") +
```

```
  geom_violin(draw_quantiles = c(0.25, 0.5, 0.75)) +
  geom_point(alpha = 0.05, size = 3) +
  theme_bw()
```

2 Redraw the bar plots, but use the `"dodge"` and `"stack"` position arguments:

```
titanicUntidy %>%
  filter(Variable == "Pclass" | Variable == "Sex") %>%
  ggplot(aes(Value, fill = Survived)) +
  facet_wrap(~ Variable, scales = "free_x") +
  geom_bar(position = "dodge") +
  theme_bw()

titanicUntidy %>%
  filter(Variable == "Pclass" | Variable == "Sex") %>%
  ggplot(aes(Value, fill = Survived)) +
  facet_wrap(~ Variable, scales = "free_x") +
  geom_bar(position = "stack") +
  theme_bw()
```

3 Build the model, but omit the `Fare` variable:

```
titanicNoFare <- select(titanicClean, -Fare)

titanicNoFareTask <- makeClassifTask(data = titanicNoFare,
                                     target = "Survived")

logRegNoFare <- resample(logRegWrapper, titanicNoFareTask,
                         resampling = kFold,
                         measures = list(acc, fpr, fnr))

logRegNoFare
```

Omitting the `Fare` variable makes little difference to model performance, because it has no additional predictive value to the `Pclass` variable (look at the odds ratio and confidence interval for `Fare` in listing 4.13).

4 Extract salutations from the `Name` variable (there are many ways of doing this, so don't worry if your way is different than mine):

```
surnames <- map_chr(str_split(titanicTib$Name, "\\."), 1)

salutations <- map_chr(str_split(surnames, ", "), 2)

salutations[!(salutations %in% c("Mr", "Dr", "Master",
                                 "Miss", "Mrs", "Rev"))] <- "Other"
```

5 Build a model using `Salutation` as a predictor:

```
fctrsInclSals <- c("Survived", "Sex", "Pclass", "Salutation")

titanicWithSals <- titanicTib %>%
  mutate(FamSize = SibSp + Parch, Salutation = salutations) %>%
```

```
  mutate_at(.vars = fctrsInclSals, .funs = factor) %>%
  select(Survived, Pclass, Sex, Age, Fare, FamSize, Salutation)

titanicTaskWithSals <- makeClassifTask(data = titanicWithSals,
                                       target = "Survived")

logRegWrapper <- makeImputeWrapper("classif.logreg",
                                   cols = list(Age = imputeMean()))

kFold <- makeResampleDesc(method = "RepCV", folds = 10, reps = 50,
                          stratify = TRUE)

logRegWithSals <- resample(logRegWrapper, titanicTaskWithSals,
                           resampling = kFold,
                           measures = list(acc, fpr, fnr))
logRegWithSals
```

The feature extraction paid off! Including `Salutation` as a predictor improved model performance.

5 Classifying by maximizing separation with discriminant analysis

This chapter covers

- Understanding linear and quadratic discriminant analysis
- Building discriminant analysis classifiers to predict wines

Discriminant analysis is an umbrella term for multiple algorithms that solve classification problems (where we wish to predict a categorical variable) in a similar way. While there are various discriminant analysis algorithms that learn slightly differently, they all find a new representation of the original data that maximizes the separation between the classes.

Recall from chapter 1 that predictor variables are the variables we hope contain the information needed to make predictions on new data. Discriminant function analysis algorithms find a new representation of the predictor variables (which must be continuous) by combining them together into new variables that best *discriminate* the classes. This combination of predictor variables often has the handy benefit of reducing the number of predictors to a much smaller number. Because of this, despite discriminant analysis algorithms being classification algorithms, they are similar to some of the dimension-reduction algorithms we'll encounter in part 4 of the book.

NOTE *Dimension reduction* is the process of learning how the information in a set of variables can be condensed into a smaller number of variables, with as little information loss as possible.

5.1 What is discriminant analysis?

In this section, you'll learn why discriminant analysis is useful and how it works. Imagine that you want to find out if you can predict how patients will respond to a drug based on their gene expression. You measure the expression level of 1,000 genes and record whether they respond positively, negatively, or not at all to the drug (a three-class classification problem).

A dataset that has as many predictor variables as this (and it isn't rare to find datasets this large) presents a few problems:

- The data is very difficult to explore and plot manually.
- There may be many predictor variables that contain no or very little predictive information.
- We have the *curse of dimensionality* to contend with (a problem algorithms encounter when trying to learn patterns in high-dimensional data).

In our gene expression example, it would be nearly impossible to plot all 1,000 genes in such a way that we could interpret the similarities/differences between the classes. Instead, we could use discriminant analysis to take all that information and condense it into a manageable number of *discriminant functions*, each of which is a combination of the original variables. Put another way, discriminant analysis takes the predictor variables as input and finds a new, lower-dimensional representation of those variables that maximizes the separation between the classes. Therefore, while discriminant analysis is a classification technique, it employs dimension reduction to achieve its goal. This is illustrated in figure 5.1.

NOTE Due to their dimensionality reduction, discriminant analysis algorithms are popular techniques for classification problems where you have many continuous predictor variables.

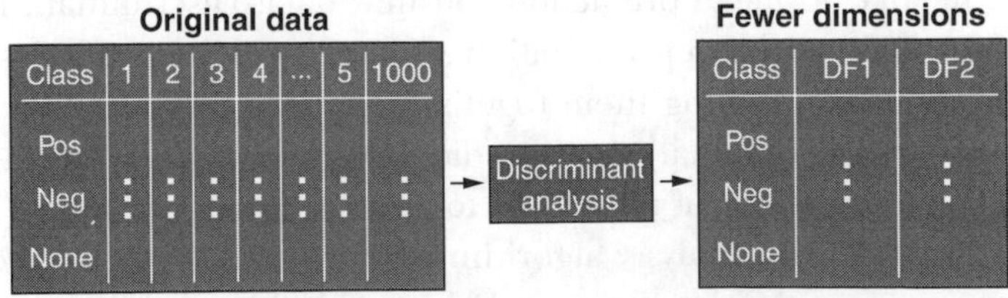

Figure 5.1 Discriminant analysis algorithms take the original data and combine continuous predictor variables together into new variables that maximize the separation of the classes.

The number of these discriminant functions will be the smaller of these:

- The number of classes minus 1
- The number of predictor variables

In the gene expression example, the information contained in those 1,000 predictor variables would be condensed into just 2 variables (three classes minus 1). We could now easily plot these two new variables against each other to see how separable our three classes are!

As you learned in chapter 4, including predictor variables that contain little or no predictive value adds noise, which can negatively impact how the learned model performs. When discriminant analysis algorithms learn their discriminant functions, greater weight or importance is given to predictors that better discriminate the classes. Predictors that contain little or no predictive value are given less weight and contribute less to the final model. To a degree, this lower weighting of uninformative predictors mitigates their impact on model performance.

> **NOTE** Despite mitigating the impact of weak predictors, a discriminant analysis model will still tend to perform better after performing feature selection (removing weakly predictive predictors).

The curse of dimensionality is a terrifying-sounding phenomenon that causes problems when working with high-dimensional data (data with many predictor variables). As the *feature space* (the set of all possible combinations of predictor variables) increases, the data in that space becomes more *sparse*. Put more plainly, for the same number of cases in a dataset, if you increase the feature space, the cases get further apart from each other, and there is more empty space between them. This is demonstrated in figure 5.2 by going from a one-feature space to a three-feature space.

The consequence of this increase in dimensionality is that an area of the feature space may have very few cases occupying it, so an algorithm is more likely to learn

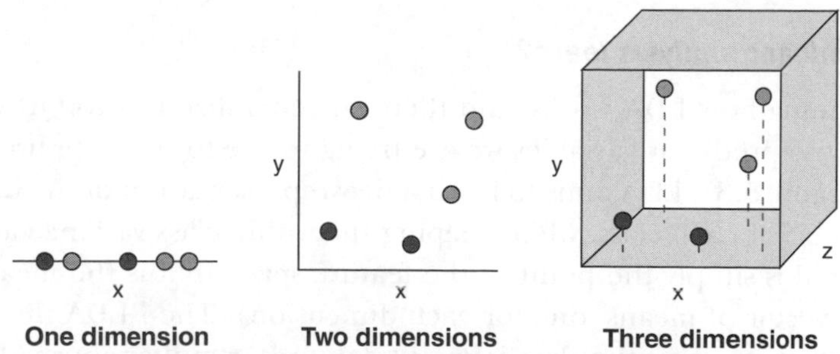

Figure 5.2 Data becomes more sparse as the number of dimensions increases. Two classes are shown in one-, two-, and three-dimensional feature spaces. The dotted lines in the three-dimensional representation are to clarify the position of the points along the z-axis. Note the increasing empty space with increased dimensions.

from "exceptional" cases in the data. When algorithms learn from exceptional cases, this results in models that are overfit and have a lot of variance in their predictions. This is the curse of dimensionality.

> **NOTE** As the number of predictor variables increases linearly, the number of cases would need to increase exponentially to maintain the same density in the feature space.

This isn't to say that having more variables is bad, however! For most problems, adding predictors with valuable information improves the predictive accuracy of a model . . . until it doesn't (until we get diminishing returns). So how do we guard against overfitting due to the curse of dimensionality? By performing feature selection (as we did in chapter 4) to include only variables that have predictive value, and/or by performing dimension reduction. You will learn about a number of specific dimension-reduction algorithms in part 4 of this book, but discriminant analysis actually performs dimension reduction as part of its learning procedure.

> **NOTE** The phenomenon of the predictive power of a model increasing as the number of predictor variables increases, but then decreasing again as we continue to add more predictors, is called the *Hughes phenomenon*, after the statistician G. Hughes.

Discriminant analysis isn't one algorithm but instead comes in many flavors. I'm going to teach you the two most fundamental and commonly used algorithms:

- Linear discriminant analysis (LDA)
- Quadratic discriminant analysis (QDA)

In the next section, you'll learn how these algorithms work and how they differ. For now, suffice it to say that LDA and QDA learn linear (straight-line) and curved decision boundaries between classes, respectively.

5.1.1 How does discriminant analysis learn?

I'll start by explaining how LDA works, and then I'll generalize this to QDA. Imagine that we have two predictor variables we are trying to use to separate two classes in our data (see figure 5.3). LDA aims to learn a new representation of the data that separates the *centroid* of each class, while keeping the within-class variance as low as possible. A centroid is simply the point in the feature space that is the mean of all the predictors (a vector of means, one for each dimension). Then LDA finds a line through the origin that, when the data is *projected* onto it, simultaneously does the following:

- Maximizes the difference between the class centroids along the line
- Minimizes the within-class variance along the line

To choose this line, the algorithm maximizes the expression in equation 5.1 over all possible axes:

$$\frac{(\bar{x}_1 - \bar{x}_2)^2}{s_1^2 + s_2^2}$$ **Equation 5.1**

The numerator is the difference between the class means ($\bar{x}_1$ and $\bar{x}_2$ for the means of class 1 and class 2, respectively), squared to ensure that the value is positive (because we don't know which will be bigger). The denominator is the sum of variances of each class along the line (s_1^2 and s_2^2 for the variances of class 1 and class 2, respectively). The intuition behind this is that we want the means of the classes to be as separated as possible, with the scatter/variance within each class to be as small as possible.

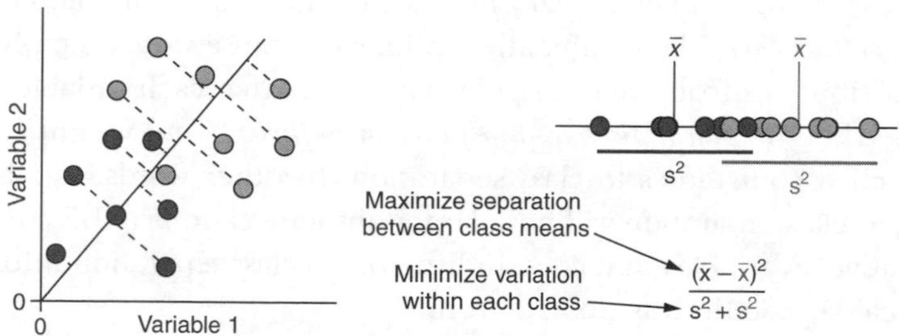

Figure 5.3 Learning a discriminant function in two dimensions. LDA learns a new axis such that, when the data is projected onto it (dashed lines), it maximizes the difference between class means while minimizing intra-class variance. $\bar{x}$ and s^2 are the mean and variance of each class along the new axis, respectively.

Why not simply find the line that maximizes the separation of the centroids? Because the line that best separates the centroids doesn't guarantee the best separation of the cases in the different classes. This is illustrated in figure 5.4. In the example on the

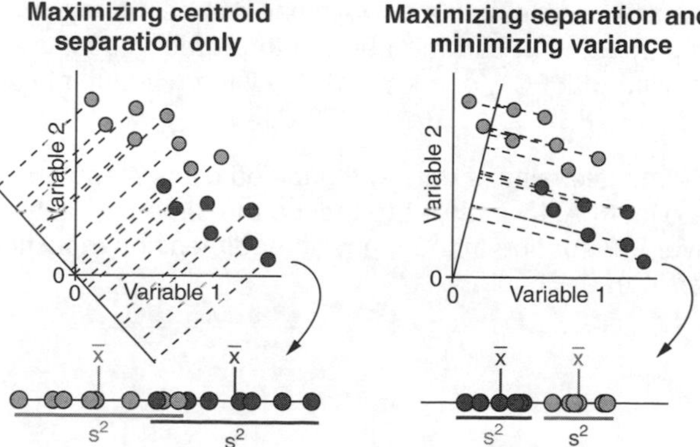

Figure 5.4 Constructing a new axis that only maximizes class centroid separation doesn't fully resolve the classes (left example). Constructing a new axis that maximizes centroid separation while also minimizing variance within each class results in better separation of the classes (right). $\bar{x}$ and s^2 are the mean and variance of each class along the new axis, respectively.

left, a new axis is drawn that simply maximizes the separation of the centroids of the two classes. When we project the data onto this new axis, the classes are not fully resolved because the relatively high variance means they overlap with each other. In the example on the right, however, the new axis tries to maximize centroid separation while minimizing the variance of each class along that axis. This results in centroids that are slightly closer together, but much smaller variances, such that the cases from the two classes are fully separated.

This new axis is called a *discriminant function*, and it is a linear combination of the original variables. For example, a discriminant function could be described by this equation:

$$DF = -0.5 \times var_1 + 1.2 \times var_2 + 0.85 \times var_3$$

In this way, the discriminant function (DF) in this equation is a linear combination of variables var_1, var_2 and var_3. The combination is linear because we are simply adding together the contributions from each variable. The values that each variable is multiplied by are called the *canonical discriminant function coefficients* and weight each variable by how much it contributes to class separation. In other words, variables that contribute most to class separation will have larger absolute canonical DF coefficients (positive or negative). Variables that contain little or no class-separation information will have canonical DF coefficients closer to zero.

Linear discriminant analysis vs. principal component analysis

If you've come across principal component analysis (PCA) before, you might be wondering how it differs from linear discriminant analysis (LDA). PCA is an unsupervised learning algorithm for dimension reduction, meaning that, unlike LDA, it doesn't rely on labeled data.

While both algorithms can be used to reduce the dimensionality of the dataset, they do so in different ways and to achieve different goals. Whereas LDA creates new axes that maximize class separation, so that we can classify new data using these new axes, PCA creates new axes that maximize the variance of the data projected onto them. Rather than classification, the goal of PCA is to explain as much of the variation and information in the data as possible, using only a small number of new axes. This new, lower-dimensional representation can then be fed into other machine learning algorithms. (If you're unfamiliar with PCA, don't worry! You'll learn about it in depth in chapter 13.)

If you want to reduce the dimensionality of data with labeled class membership, you should typically favor LDA over PCA. If you want to reduce the dimensionality of unlabeled data, you should favor PCA (or one of the many other dimension-reduction algorithms we'll discuss in part 4 of the book).

5.1.2 What if we have more than two classes?

Discriminant analysis can handle classification problems with more than two classes. But how does it learn the best axis in this situation? Instead of trying to maximize the separation between class centroids, it maximizes the separation between each class centroid and the *grand centroid* of the data (the centroid of all the data, ignoring class membership). This is illustrated in figure 5.5, where we have two continuous measurements made on cases from three classes. The class centroids are shown with triangles, and the grand centroid is indicated by a cross.

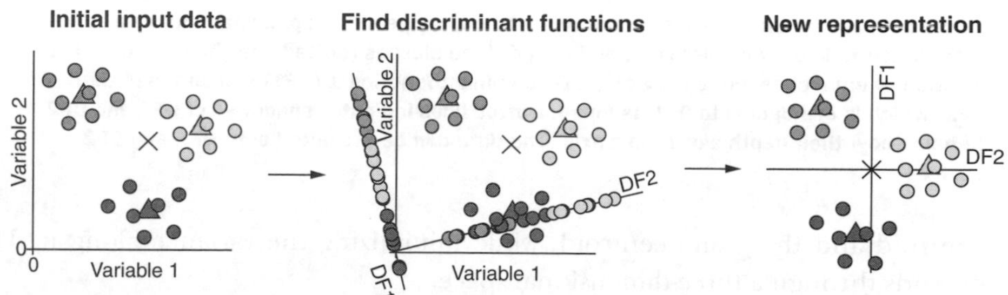

Figure 5.5 When there are more than two classes, LDA maximizes the distance between each class centroid (triangles) and the grand centroid (cross) while minimizing intra-class variance. Once the first discriminant function is found, a second is constructed that is orthogonal to it. The original data can be plotted against these functions.

LDA first finds the axis that best separates the class centroids from the grand centroid that minimizes the variance of each class along it. Then, LDA constructs a second DF that is *orthogonal* to the first. This simply means the second DF must be perpendicular to the first (at a right angle in this 2D example).

> **NOTE** The number of DFs will be whichever is smaller: (number of classes) minus 1, or the number of predictor variables.

The data is then projected onto these new axes such that each case gets a *discriminant score* for each function (its value along the new axis). These discriminant scores can be plotted against each other to form a new representation of the original data.

But what's the big deal? We've gone from having two predictor variables to having . . . two predictor variables! In fact, can you see that all we've done is center and scale the data, and rotate it around zero? When we only have two variables, discriminant analysis cannot perform any dimension reduction because the number of DFs is the smaller of the number of classes minus 1 and the number of variables (and we only have two variables).

But what about when we have more than two predictor variables? Figure 5.6 shows an example where we have three predictor variables (*x*, *y*, and *z*) and three classes. Just as in figure 5.5, LDA finds the DF that maximizes the separation between each class

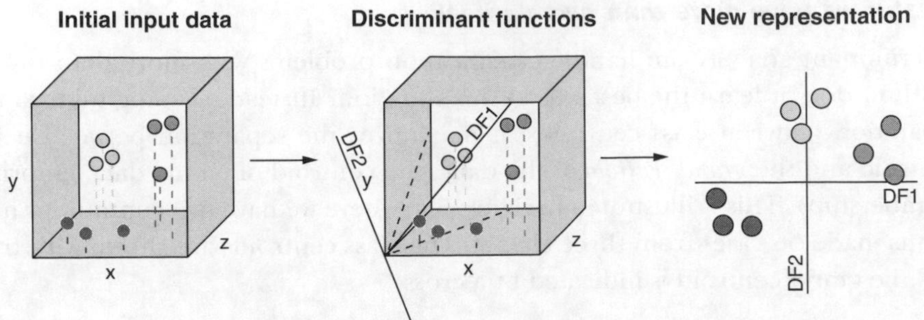

Figure 5.6 When there are more than two predictors, the cube represents a feature space with three predictor variables (*x*, *y*, and *z*) and three classes (dotted lines help indicate the position of each case along the z-axis). Discriminant function 1 (DF1) is found, and then DF2, which is orthogonal to DF1, is found. Dotted lines indicate "shadows" of DF1 and DF2 to help show their depth along the z-axis. The data can be projected onto DF1 and DF2.

centroid and the grand centroid, while minimizing the variance along it. This line extends through a three-dimensional space.

Next, LDA finds the second DF (which is orthogonal to the first), which also tries to maximize separation while minimizing variance. Because we only have three classes (and the number of DFs is the smaller of the number of classes minus 1 or the number of predictors), we stop at two DFs. By taking the discriminant scores of each case in the data (the values of each case along the two DFs), we can plot our data in only two dimensions.

NOTE The first DF always does the best job at separating the classes, followed by the second, the third, and so on.

LDA has taken a three-dimensional dataset and combined the information in those three variables into two new variables that maximize the separation between the classes. That's pretty cool—but if instead of just three predictor variables we had 1,000 (as in the example I used earlier), LDA would *still* condense all this information into only 2 variables! That's super cool.

5.1.3 Learning curves instead of straight lines: QDA

LDA performs well if the data within each class is normally distributed across all the predictor variables, and the classes have similar *covariances*. Covariance simply means how much one variable increases/decreases when another variable increases/decreases. So LDA assumes that for each class in the dataset, the predictor variables *covary* with each other the same amount.

This often isn't the case, and classes have different covariances. In this situation, QDA tends to perform better than LDA because it doesn't make this assumption (though it still assumes the data is normally distributed). Instead of learning straight lines that separate the classes, QDA learns curved lines. It is also well suited, therefore,

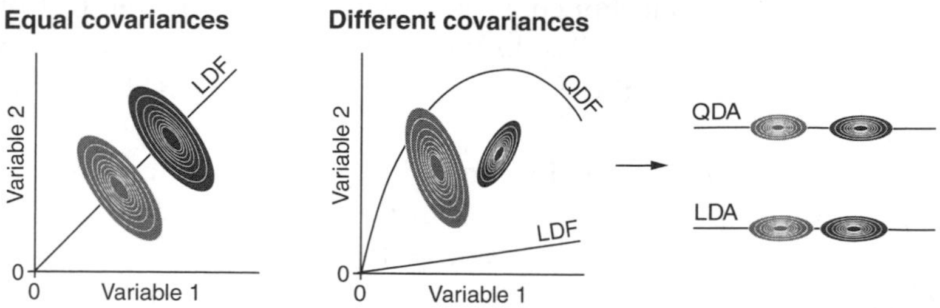

Figure 5.7 Examples of two classes which have equal covariance (the relationship between variable 1 and 2 is the same for both classes) and different covariances. Ovals represent distributions of data within each class. Quadratic and linear DFs (QDF and LDF) are shown. The projection of the classes with different covariances onto each DF is shown.

to situations in which classes are best separated by a nonlinear decision boundary. This is illustrated in figure 5.7.

In the example on the left in the figure, the two classes are normally distributed across both variables and have equal covariances. We can see that the covariances are equal because, for both classes, as variable 1 increases, variable 2 decreases by the same amount. In this situation, LDA and QDA will find similar DFs, although LDA is slightly less prone to overfitting than QDA because it is less flexible.

In the example on the right in the figure, the two classes are normally distributed, but their covariances are different. In this situation, QDA will find a curved DF that, when the data is projected onto it, will tend to do a better job of separating the classes than a linear DF.

5.1.4 How do LDA and QDA make predictions?

Whichever method you've chosen, the DFs have been constructed, and you've reduced your high-dimensional data into a small number of discriminants. How do LDA and QDA use this information to classify new observations? They use an extremely important statistical theorem called *Bayes' rule.*

Bayes' rule provides us with a way of answering the following question: given the values of the predictor variables for any case in our data, what is the probability of that case belonging to class k? This is written as $p(k|x)$, where k represents membership in class k, and x represents the values of the predictor variables. We would read this as "the probability of belonging to class k, given the data, x." This is given by Bayes' rule:

$$p(k|x) = \frac{p(x|k) \times p(k)}{p(x)} \qquad \textbf{Equation 5.2}$$

Don't be scared by this! There are only four terms in the equation, and I'm going to walk you through them. You already know $p(k|x)$ is the probability of a case belonging to class k given the data. This is called the *posterior probability.*

p(x|k) is the same thing, but flipped around: what is the probability of observing this data, given the case belongs to class k? Put another way: if this case *was* in class k, what is the *likelihood* of it having these values of the predictor variables? This is called the *likelihood.*

p(k) is called the *prior probability* and is simply the probability of any case belonging to class k. This is the proportion of all cases in the data that belong to class *k*. For example, if 30% of cases were in class k, *p(k)* would equal 0.3.

Finally, *p(x)* is the probability of observing a case with exactly these predictor values in the dataset. This is called the *evidence.* Estimating the evidence is often very difficult (because each case in the dataset may have a unique combination of predictor values), and it only serves to make all the posterior probabilities sum to 1. Therefore, we can omit the evidence from the equation and say that

$$p(k|x) \propto p(x|k) \times p(k)$$ **Equation 5.3**

where the ∝ symbol means the values on either side of it are *proportional* to each other instead of *equal* to each other. In a more digestible way,

$$posterior \propto likelihood \times prior$$

The prior probability for a case (*p(k)*) is easy to work out: it's the proportion of cases in the dataset that belong to class *k*. But how do we calculate the likelihood (*p(x|k)*)? The likelihood is calculated by projecting the data onto its DFs and estimating its *probability density.* The probability density is the relative probability of observing a case with a particular combination of discriminant scores.

Discriminant analysis assumes that the data is normally distributed, so it estimates the probability density by fitting a normal distribution to each class across each DF. The center of each normal distribution is the class centroid, and its standard deviation is one unit on the discriminant axis. This is illustrated in figure 5.8 for a single DF and for two DFs (the same thing happens in more than two dimensions but is difficult to visualize). You can see that cases near the class centroid along the discriminant axes have a high probability density for that class, and cases far away have a lower probability density.

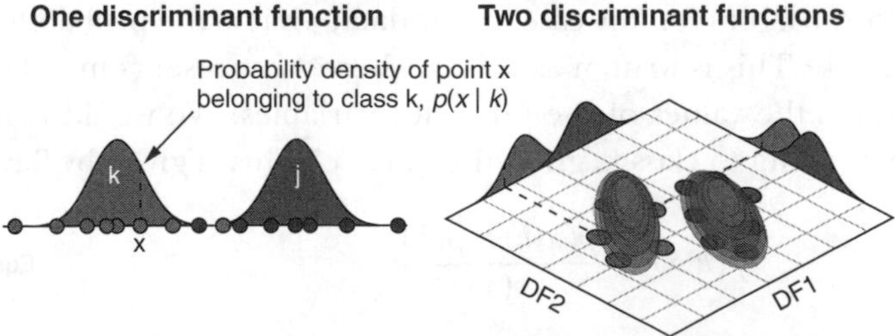

Figure 5.8 The probability density of each class is assumed to be normally distributed, where the center of each distribution is the centroid of the class. This is shown for one DF (for classes k and j) and for two.

Once the probability density is estimated for a case for a given class, it can be passed into the equation:

$$posterior = likelihood \times prior$$

The posterior probability is estimated for each class, and the class that has the highest probability is what the case is classified as.

NOTE The prior probability (proportion of cases in that class) is important because if the classes are severely imbalanced, despite a case being far from the centroid of a class, the case could be more likely to belong to that class simply because there are so many more cases in it.

Bayes' rule is very important in statistics and machine learning. Don't worry if you don't quite understand it yet; that's by design. I want to introduce you to it gently now, and we'll cover it in more depth in chapter 6.

5.2 Building your first linear and quadratic discriminant models

Now that you know how discriminant analysis works, you're going to build your first LDA model. If you haven't already, load the mlr and tidyverse packages:

```
library(mlr)
library(tidyverse)
```

5.2.1 Loading and exploring the wine dataset

In this section, you'll learn how to build and evaluate the performance of linear and quadratic discriminant analysis models. Imagine that you're a detective in a murder mystery. A local wine producer, Ronald Fisher, was poisoned at a dinner party when someone replaced the wine in the carafe with wine poisoned with arsenic.

Three other (rival) wine producers were at the party and are your prime suspects. If you can trace the wine to one of those three vineyards, you'll find your murderer. As luck would have it, you have access to some previous chemical analysis of the wines from each of the vineyards, and you order an analysis of the poisoned carafe at the scene of the crime. Your task is to build a model that will tell you which vineyard the wine with the arsenic came from and, therefore, the guilty party.

Let's load the wine data built into the HDclassif package (after installing it), convert it into a tibble, and explore it a little. We have a tibble containing 178 cases and 14 variables of measurements made on various wine bottles.

Listing 5.1 Loading and exploring the wine dataset

```
install.packages("HDclassif")

data(wine, package = "HDclassif")

wineTib <- as_tibble(wine)
```

```
wineTib

# A tibble: 178 x 14
   class    V1    V2    V3    V4    V5    V6    V7    V8    V9
   <int> <dbl> <dbl> <dbl> <dbl> <int> <dbl> <dbl> <dbl> <dbl>
 1     1  14.2  1.71  2.43  15.6   127  2.8   3.06 0.28   2.29
 2     1  13.2  1.78  2.14  11.2   100  2.65  2.76 0.26   1.28
 3     1  13.2  2.36  2.67  18.6   101  2.8   3.24 0.3    2.81
 4     1  14.4  1.95  2.5   16.8   113  3.85  3.49 0.24   2.18
 5     1  13.2  2.59  2.87  21     118  2.8   2.69 0.39   1.82
 6     1  14.2  1.76  2.45  15.2   112  3.27  3.39 0.34   1.97
 7     1  14.4  1.87  2.45  14.6    96  2.5   2.52 0.3    1.98
 8     1  14.1  2.15  2.61  17.6   121  2.6   2.51 0.31   1.25
 9     1  14.8  1.64  2.17  14      97  2.8   2.98 0.290  1.98
10     1  13.9  1.35  2.27  16      98  2.98  3.15 0.22   1.85
# ... with 168 more rows, and 4 more variables: V10 <dbl>,
#   V11 <dbl>, V12 <dbl>, V13 <int>
```

Often, as data scientists, we receive data that is messy or not well curated. In this case, the names of the variables are missing! We could continue working with `V1`, `V2`, and so on, but it would be hard to keep track of which variable is which. So we're going to manually add the variable names. Who said the life of a data scientist was glamorous? Then, we'll convert the `class` variable to a factor.

Listing 5.2 Cleaning the dataset

```
names(wineTib) <- c("Class", "Alco", "Malic", "Ash", "Alk", "Mag",
                    "Phe", "Flav", "Non_flav", "Proan", "Col", "Hue",
                    "OD", "Prol")

wineTib$Class <- as.factor(wineTib$Class)

wineTib

# A tibble: 178 x 14
   Class  Alco Malic   Ash   Alk   Mag   Phe  Flav Non_flav Proan
   <fct> <dbl> <dbl> <dbl> <dbl> <int> <dbl> <dbl>    <dbl> <dbl>
 1 1      14.2  1.71  2.43  15.6   127  2.8   3.06    0.28   2.29
 2 1      13.2  1.78  2.14  11.2   100  2.65  2.76    0.26   1.28
 3 1      13.2  2.36  2.67  18.6   101  2.8   3.24    0.3    2.81
 4 1      14.4  1.95  2.5   16.8   113  3.85  3.49    0.24   2.18
 5 1      13.2  2.59  2.87  21     118  2.8   2.69    0.39   1.82
 6 1      14.2  1.76  2.45  15.2   112  3.27  3.39    0.34   1.97
 7 1      14.4  1.87  2.45  14.6    96  2.5   2.52    0.3    1.98
 8 1      14.1  2.15  2.61  17.6   121  2.6   2.51    0.31   1.25
 9 1      14.8  1.64  2.17  14      97  2.8   2.98    0.290  1.98
10 1      13.9  1.35  2.27  16      98  2.98  3.15    0.22   1.85
# ... with 168 more rows, and 4 more variables: Col <dbl>,
#   Hue <dbl>, OD <dbl>, Prol <int>
```

That's much better. We can see that we have 13 continuous measurements made on 178 bottles of wine, where each measurement is the amount of a different compound/

element in the wine. We also have a single categorical variable, `Class`, which tells us which vineyard the bottle comes from.

NOTE Lots of people consider it good form to keep variable names lowercase. I don't mind so much so long as my style is consistent. Therefore, notice that I changed the name of the grouping variable `class` to `Class`.

5.2.2 Plotting the data

Let's plot the data to get an idea of how the compounds vary between the vineyards. As for the *Titanic* dataset in chapter 4, we're going to gather the data into an untidy format so we can facet by each of the variables.

Listing 5.3 Creating an untidy tibble for plotting

```
wineUntidy <- gather(wineTib, "Variable", "Value", -Class)

ggplot(wineUntidy, aes(Class, Value)) +
  facet_wrap(~ Variable, scales = "free_y") +
  geom_boxplot() +
  theme_bw()
```

The resulting plot is shown in figure 5.9.

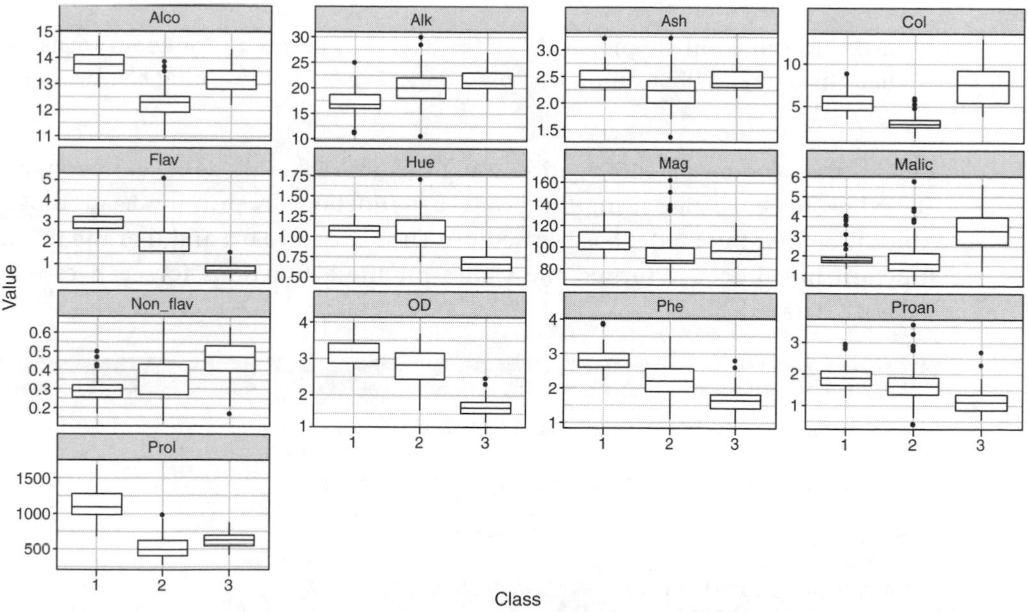

Figure 5.9 Box and whiskers plots of each continuous variable in the data against vineyard number. For the box and whiskers, the thick horizontal line represents the median, the box represents the interquartile range (IQR), the whiskers represent the Tukey range (1.5 times the IQR above and below the quartiles), and the dots represent data outside of the Tukey range.

A data scientist (and detective working the case) looking at this data would jump for joy! Look at how many obvious differences there are between wines from the three different vineyards. We should easily be able to build a well-performing classification model because the classes are so separable.

5.2.3 Training the models

Let's define our task and learner, and build a model as usual. This time, we supply `"classif.lda"` as the argument to `makeLearner()` to specify that we're going to use LDA.

> **TIP** LDA and QDA have no hyperparameters to tune and are therefore said to have a *closed-form solution*. In other words, all the information that LDA and QDA need is in the data. Their performance is also unaffected by variables on different scales. They will give the same result whether the data is scaled or not!

Listing 5.4 Creating the task and learner, and training the model

```
wineTask <- makeClassifTask(data = wineTib, target = "Class")

lda <- makeLearner("classif.lda")

ldaModel <- train(lda, wineTask)
```

> **NOTE** Recall from chapter 3 that the `makeClassifTask()` function warns us that our data is a tibble and not a pure `data.frame`. This warning can be safely ignored.

Let's extract the model information using the `getLearnerModel()` function, and get DF values for each case using the `predict()` function. By printing `head(ldaPreds)`, we can see that the model has learned two DFs, `LD1` and `LD2`, and that the `predict()` function has indeed returned the values for these functions for each case in our `wineTib` dataset.

Listing 5.5 Extracting DF values for each case

```
ldaModelData <- getLearnerModel(ldaModel)

ldaPreds <- predict(ldaModelData)$x

head(ldaPreds)
        LD1       LD2
1 -4.700244 1.9791383
2 -4.301958 1.1704129
3 -3.420720 1.4291014
4 -4.205754 4.0028715
5 -1.509982 0.4512239
6 -4.518689 3.2131376
```

To visualize how well these two learned DFs separate the bottles of wine from the three vineyards, let's plot them against each other. We start by piping the `wineTib` dataset into a `mutate()` call where we create a new column for each of the DFs. We pipe this mutated tibble into a `ggplot()` call and set `LD1`, `LD2`, and `Class` as the x, y, and color aesthetics, respectively. Finally, we add a `geom_point()` layer to add dots, and a `stat_ellipse()` layer to draw 95% confidence ellipses around each class.

Listing 5.6 Plotting the DF values against each other

```
wineTib %>%
  mutate(LD1 = ldaPreds[, 1],
         LD2 = ldaPreds[, 2]) %>%
  ggplot(aes(LD1, LD2, col = Class)) +
  geom_point() +
  stat_ellipse() +
  theme_bw()
```

The resulting plot is shown in figure 5.10.

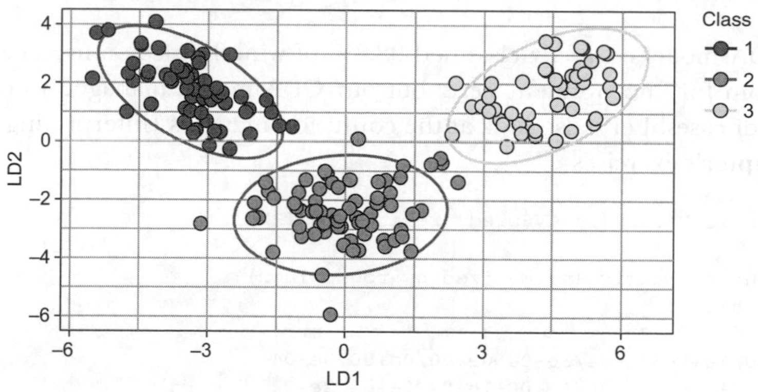

Figure 5.10 Plotting the DFs against each other. The values for `LD1` and `LD2` for each case are plotted against each other, shaded by their class.

Looking good. Can you see that LDA has reduced our 13 predictor variables into just two DFs that do an excellent job of separating the wines from each of the vineyards?

Next, let's use exactly the same procedure to build a QDA model.

Listing 5.7 Plotting the DF values against each other

```
qda <- makeLearner("classif.qda")

qdaModel <- train(qda, wineTask)
```

NOTE Sadly, it isn't easy to extract the DFs from the implementation of QDA that mlr uses, to plot them as we did for LDA.

Now, let's cross-validate our LDA and QDA models together to estimate how they'll perform on new data.

Listing 5.8 Cross-validating the LDA and QDA models

```
kFold <- makeResampleDesc(method = "RepCV", folds = 10, reps = 50,
                          stratify = TRUE)

ldaCV <- resample(learner = lda, task = wineTask, resampling = kFold,
                  measures = list(mmce, acc))

qdaCV <- resample(learner = qda, task = wineTask, resampling = kFold,
                  measures = list(mmce, acc))

ldaCV$aggr
mmce.test.mean  acc.test.mean
    0.01177012     0.98822988

qdaCV$aggr
mmce.test.mean  acc.test.mean
   0.007977296    0.992022704
```

Great! Our LDA model correctly classified 98.8% of wine bottles on average. There isn't much room for improvement here, but our QDA model managed to correctly classify 99.2% of cases! Let's also look at the confusion matrices (interpreting them is part of the chapter's exercises):

```
calculateConfusionMatrix(ldaCV$pred, relative = TRUE)

Relative confusion matrix (normalized by row/column):
        predicted
true     1           2           3           -err.-
  1      1e+00/1e+00 3e-04/3e-04 0e+00/0e+00 3e-04
  2      8e-03/1e-02 1e+00/1e+00 1e-02/2e-02 2e-02
  3      0e+00/0e+00 1e-02/7e-03 1e+00/1e+00 1e-02
  -err.-       0.010       0.007       0.021 0.01


Absolute confusion matrix:
        predicted
true        1    2    3 -err.-
  1      2949    1    0      1
  2        29 3470   51     80
  3         0   23 2377     23
  -err.-   29   24   51    104

calculateConfusionMatrix(qdaCV$pred, relative = TRUE)

Relative confusion matrix (normalized by row/column):
        predicted
true     1           2           3           -err.-
  1      0.993/0.984 0.007/0.006 0.000/0.000 0.007
```

```
  2       0.014/0.016 0.986/0.991 0.000/0.000 0.014
  3       0.000/0.000 0.005/0.003 0.995/1.000 0.005
  -err.-        0.016       0.009       0.000 0.009


Absolute confusion matrix:
        predicted
true         1    2    3 -err.-
  1       2930   20    0     20
  2         49 3501    0     49
  3          0   12 2388     12
  -err.-    49   32    0     81
```

Now, detective, the chemical analysis of the poisoned wine is in. Let's use our QDA model to predict which vineyard it came from:

```
poisoned <- tibble(Alco = 13, Malic = 2, Ash = 2.2, Alk = 19, Mag = 100,
                   Phe = 2.3, Flav = 2.5, Non_flav = 0.35, Proan = 1.7,
                   Col = 4, Hue = 1.1, OD = 3, Prol = 750)

predict(qdaModel, newdata = poisoned)

Prediction: 1 observations
predict.type: response
threshold:
time: 0.00
  response
1        1
```

The model predicts that the poisoned bottle came from vineyard 1. Time to go and make an arrest!

Ronald Fisher

You may be happy to know that, in the real world, Ronald Fisher wasn't poisoned at a dinner party. This is, perhaps, fortunate for you, because Sir Ronald Fisher (1890-1962) was a famous biostatistician who went on to be called the father of statistics. Fisher developed many statistical tools and concepts we use today, including discriminant analysis. In fact, linear discriminant analysis is commonly confused with *Fisher's discriminant analysis*, the original form of discriminant analysis that Fisher developed (but which is slightly different).

However, Fisher was also a proponent of eugenics, the belief that some races are superior to others. In fact, he shared his opinions in a 1952 UNESCO statement called "The Race Question," in which he said that "the groups of mankind differ profoundly in their innate capacity for intellectual and emotional development" (https://unesdoc.unesco.org/ark:/48223/pf0000073351). Perhaps now you don't feel so sorry for our murder mystery victim.

5.3 Strengths and weaknesses of LDA and QDA

While it often isn't easy to tell which algorithms will perform well for a given task, here are some strengths and weaknesses that will help you decide whether LDA and QDA will perform well for you.

The strengths of the LDA and QDA algorithms are as follows:

- They can reduce a high-dimensional feature space into a much more manageable number.
- They can be used for classification or as a preprocessing (dimension reduction) technique for other classification algorithms that may perform better on the dataset.
- QDA can learn curved decision boundaries between classes (this isn't the case for LDA).

The weaknesses of the LDA and QDA algorithms are these:

- They can only handle continuous predictors (although recoding a categorical variable as numeric *may* help in some cases).
- They assume the data is normally distributed across the predictors. If the data is not, performance will suffer.
- LDA can only learn linear decision boundaries between classes (this isn't the case for QDA).
- LDA assumes equal covariances of the classes, and performance will suffer if this isn't the case (this isn't the case for QDA).
- QDA is more flexible than LDA and so can be more prone to overfitting.

Exercise 1

Interpret the confusion matrices shown in the previous section.

a. Which model is better at identifying wines from vineyard 3?
b. Does our LDA model misclassify more wines from vineyard 2 as being from vineyard 1 or vineyard 3?

Exercise 2

Extract the discriminant scores from our LDA model, and use only these as the predictors for a kNN model (including tuning *k*). Experiment with your own cross-validation strategy. Look back at chapter 3 if you need a refresher on training a kNN model.

Summary

- Discriminant analysis is a supervised learning algorithm that projects the data onto a lower-dimensional representation to create discriminant functions.
- Discriminant functions are linear combinations of the original (continuous) variables that maximize the separation of class centroids while minimizing the variance of each class along them.
- Discriminant analysis comes in many flavors, the most fundamental of which are LDA and QDA.
- LDA learns linear decision boundaries between classes and assumes that classes are normally distributed and have equal covariances.
- QDA can learn curved decision boundaries between classes and assumes that each class is normally distributed, but does *not* assume equal covariances.
- The number of discriminant functions is the smaller of the number of classes minus 1, or the number of predictor variables.
- Class prediction uses Bayes' rule to estimate the posterior probability of a case belonging to each of the classes.

Solutions to exercises

1. Interpret the confusion matrices:
   a. Our QDA model is better at identifying wines from vineyard 3. It misclassified 12 as from vineyard 2, whereas the LDA model misclassified 23.
   b. Our LDA model misclassifies more cases from vineyard 2 as from vineyard 3 than as from vineyard 1.
2. Use the discriminant scores from the LDA as predictors in a kNN model:

```
# CREATE TASK ----
wineDiscr <- wineTib %>%
  mutate(LD1 = ldaPreds[, 1], LD2 = ldaPreds[, 2]) %>%
  select(Class, LD1, LD2)

wineDiscrTask <- makeClassifTask(data = wineDiscr, target = "Class")

# TUNE K ----
knnParamSpace <- makeParamSet(makeDiscreteParam("k", values = 1:10))
gridSearch <- makeTuneControlGrid()
cvForTuning <- makeResampleDesc("RepCV", folds = 10, reps = 20)
tunedK <- tuneParams("classif.knn", task = wineDiscrTask,
                     resampling = cvForTuning,
                     par.set = knnParamSpace,
                     control = gridSearch)

knnTuningData <- generateHyperParsEffectData(tunedK)
plotHyperParsEffect(knnTuningData, x = "k", y = "mmce.test.mean",
                    plot.type = "line") +
    theme_bw()
```

```
# CROSS-VALIDATE MODEL-BUILDING PROCESS ----
inner <- makeResampleDesc("CV")
outer <- makeResampleDesc("CV", iters = 10)
knnWrapper <- makeTuneWrapper("classif.knn", resampling = inner,
                              par.set = knnParamSpace,
                              control = gridSearch)

cvWithTuning <- resample(knnWrapper, wineDiscrTask, resampling = outer)
cvWithTuning

# TRAINING FINAL MODEL WITH TUNED K ----
tunedKnn <-
 setHyperPars(makeLearner("classif.knn"), par.vals = tunedK$x)

tunedKnnModel <- train(tunedKnn, wineDiscrTask)
```

6 Classifying with naive Bayes and support vector machines

This chapter covers

- Working with the naive Bayes algorithm
- Understanding the support vector machine algorithm
- Tuning many hyperparameters simultaneously with a random search

The naive Bayes and support vector machine (SVM) algorithms are supervised learning algorithms for classification. Each algorithm learns in a different way. The naive Bayes algorithm uses *Bayes' rule*, which you learned about in chapter 5, to estimate the probability of new data belonging to one of the classes in the dataset. The case is then assigned to the class with the highest probability. The SVM algorithm looks for a *hyperplane* (a surface that has one less dimension than there are predictor variables) that separates the classes. The position and direction of this hyperplane depend on *support vectors*: cases that lie closest to the boundary between the classes.

NOTE While commonly used for classification, the SVM algorithm can also be used for regression problems. I won't discuss how here, but if you're interested (and want to explore SVMs in more depth generally), see *Support Vector Machines* by Andreas Christmann and Ingo Steinwart (Springer, 2008).

The naive Bayes and SVM algorithms have different properties that make each suitable in different circumstances. For example, naive Bayes can mix both continuous and categorical predictors natively, while for SVMs, categorical variables must first be recoded into a numerical format. On the other hand, SVMs are excellent at finding decision boundaries between classes that are not linearly separable, by adding a new dimension to the data that reveals a linear boundary. The naive Bayes algorithm will rarely outperform an SVM trained on the same problem, but naive Bayes tends to perform well for problems like spam detection and text classification.

Models trained using naive Bayes also have a probabilistic interpretation. For each case on which the model makes predictions, the model outputs the probability of that case belonging to one class over another, giving us a measure of certainty in our prediction. This is useful for situations in which we may want to further scrutinize cases with probabilities close to 50%. Conversely, models trained using the SVM algorithm typically don't output easily interpretable probabilities, but have a *geometric* interpretation. In other words, they partition the feature space and classify cases based on which partition they fall within. SVMs are more computationally expensive to train than naive Bayes models, so if a naive Bayes model performs well for your problem, there may be no reason to choose a model that is more computationally expensive to train.

By the end of this chapter, you'll know how the naive Bayes and SVM algorithms work and how to apply them to your data. You will also have learned how to tune several hyperparameters simultaneously, because the SVM algorithm has many of them. And you will understand how to apply the more pragmatic approach of using a *random search*—instead of the grid search we applied in chapter 3—to find the combination of hyperparameters that performs best.

6.1 What is the naive Bayes algorithm?

In the last chapter, I introduced you to Bayes' rule (named after the mathematician Thomas Bayes). I showed how discriminant analysis algorithms use Bayes' rule to predict the probability of a case belonging to each of the classes, based on its discriminant function values. The naive Bayes algorithm works in exactly the same way, except that it doesn't perform dimension reduction as discriminant analysis does, and it can handle categorical, as well as continuous, predictors. In this section, I hope to convey a deeper understanding of how Bayes' rule works with a few examples.

Imagine that 0.2% of the population have unicorn disease (symptoms include obsession with glitter and compulsive rainbow drawing). The test for unicorn disease has a true positive rate of 90% (if you have the disease, the test will detect it 90% of the time). When tested, 5% of the whole population get a positive result from the test. Based on this information, if you get a positive result from the test, what is the probability you have unicorn disease?

Many people's instinct is to say 90%, but this doesn't account for how prevalent the disease is and the proportion of tests that are positive (which also includes false positives). So how do we estimate the probability of having the disease, given a positive test result? Well, we use Bayes' rule. Let's remind ourselves of what Bayes' rule is:

$$p(k|x) = \frac{p(x|k) \times p(k)}{p(x)}$$

Where

- $p(k|x)$ is the probability of having the disease (k) given a positive test result (x). This is called the *posterior probability*.
- $p(x|k)$ is the probability of getting a positive test result if you *do* have the disease. This is called the *likelihood*.
- $p(k)$ is the probability of having the disease regardless of any test. This is the proportion of people in the population with the disease and is called the *prior probability*.
- $p(x)$ is the probability of getting a positive test result and includes the true positives and false positives. This is called the *evidence*.

We can rewrite this in plain English:

$$\text{posterior} = \frac{\text{likelihood} \times \text{prior}}{\text{evidence}}$$

So our likelihood (the probability of getting a positive test result if we do have unicorn disease) is 90%, or 0.9 expressed as a decimal. Our prior probability (the proportion of people with unicorn disease) is 0.2%, or 0.002 as a decimal. Finally, our evidence (the probability of getting a positive test result) is 5%, or 0.05 as a decimal. You can see all these values illustrated in figure 6.1. Now we simply substitute in these values into Bayes' rule:

$$\text{posterior} = \frac{0.9 \times 0.002}{0.05} = 0.036$$

Phew! After taking into account the prevalence of the disease and the proportion of tests that are positive (including false positives), a positive test means we have only a 3.6% chance of actually having the disease—much better than 90%! This is the power of Bayes' rule: it allows you to incorporate prior information to get a more accurate estimation of *conditional probabilities* (the probability of something, given the data).

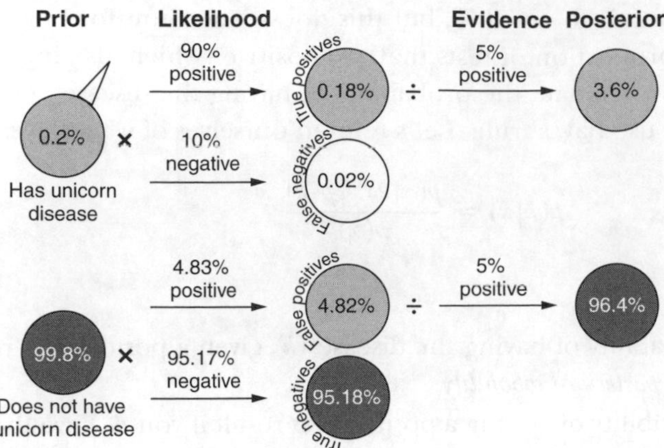

Figure 6.1 Using Bayes' rule to calculate the posterior probability of having unicorn disease, given a positive test result. The priors are the proportion of people with or without the disease. The likelihoods are the probabilities of getting positive or negative test results for each disease status. The evidence is the probability of getting a positive test result (true positives plus the false positives).

6.1.1 Using naive Bayes for classification

Let's take another, more machine learning–focused, example. Imagine that you have a database of tweets from the social media platform Twitter, and you want to build a model that automatically classifies each tweet into a topic. The topics are

- Politics
- Sports
- Movies
- Other

You create four categorical predictor variables:

- Whether the word *opinion* is present
- Whether the word *score* is present
- Whether the word *game* is present
- Whether the word *cinema* is present

> **NOTE** I'm keeping things simple for this example. If we were really trying to build a model to predict tweet topics, we would need to include many more words than this!

For each of our four topics, we can express the probability of a case belonging to that topic as

$$p(\text{topic}|\text{words}) = \frac{p(\text{words}|\text{topic}) \times p(\text{topic})}{p(\text{words})}$$

Now that we have more than one predictor variable, *p*(words|topic) is the likelihood of a tweet having that exact combination of words present, given the tweet is in that topic. We estimate this by finding the likelihood of having this combination of values of each predictor variable *individually*, given that the tweet belongs to that topic, and multiply them together. This looks like this:

$$p(\text{topic}|\text{words}) =$$

$$\frac{p(\text{opinion}|\text{topic}) \times p(\text{score}|\text{topic}) \times p(\text{game}|\text{topic}) \times p(\text{cinema}|\text{topic}) \times p(\text{topic})}{p(\text{opinion}) \times p(\text{score}) \times p(\text{game}) \times p(\text{cinema})}$$

For example, if a tweet contains the words *opinion*, *score*, and *game*, but not *cinema*, then the likelihood would be as follows for any particular topic:

$$p(\text{words}|\text{topic}) =$$

$$p(\text{opinion}_{\text{yes}}|\text{topic}) \times p(\text{score}_{\text{yes}}|\text{topic}) \times p(\text{game}_{\text{yes}}|\text{topic}) \times p(\text{cinema}_{\text{no}}|\text{topic})$$

Now, the likelihood of a tweet containing a certain word if it's in a particular topic is simply the proportion of tweets from that topic that contain that word. Multiplying the likelihoods together from each predictor variable gives us the likelihood of observing this *combination* of predictor variable values (this combination of words), given a particular class.

This is what makes naive Bayes "naive." By estimating the likelihood for each predictor variable individually and then multiplying them, we are making the very strong assumption that the predictor variables are *independent*. In other words, we are assuming that the value of one variable has no relationship to the value of another one. In the majority of cases, this assumption is not true. For example, if a tweet contains the word *score*, it may be more likely to also include the word *game*.

In spite of this naive assumption being wrong quite often, naive Bayes tends to perform well even in the presence of non-independent predictors. Having said this, strongly dependent predictor variables will impact performance.

So the likelihood and prior probabilities are fairly simple to compute and are the parameters learned by the algorithm; but what about the evidence (*p*(words))? In practice, because the values of the predictor variables are usually reasonably unique to each case in the data, calculating the evidence (the probability of observing that combination of values) is very difficult. As the evidence is really just a normalizing constant that makes all the posterior probabilities sum to 1, we can discard it and simply multiply the likelihood and prior probability:

$$\textit{posterior} \propto \textit{likelihood} \times \textit{prior}$$

Note that instead of an = sign, I use ∝ to mean "proportional to," because without the evidence to normalize the equation, the posterior is no longer equal to the likelihood times the prior. This is okay, though, because proportionality is good enough to find the most likely class. Now, for each tweet, we calculate the relative posterior probability for each of the topics:

$$p(politics|words) \propto p(words|politics) \times p(politics)$$
$$p(sports|words) \propto p(words|sports) \times p(sports)$$
$$p(movies|words) \propto p(words|movies) \times p(movies)$$
$$p(other|words) \propto p(words|other) \times p(other)$$

Then we assign the tweet to the topic with the highest relative posterior probability.

6.1.2 Calculating the likelihood for categorical and continuous predictors

When we have a categorical predictor (such as whether a word is present or not), naive Bayes uses that proportion of training cases in that particular class, with that value of the predictor. When we have a continuous variable, naive Bayes (typically) assumes that the data within each group is normally distributed. The probability density of each case based on this fitted normal distribution is then used to estimate the likelihood of observing this value of the predictor in that class. In this way, cases near the mean of the normal distribution for a particular class will have high probability density for that class, and cases far away from the mean will have a low probability density. This is the same way you saw discriminant analysis calculate the likelihood in figure 5.7 in chapter 5.

When your data has a mixture of categorical and continuous predictors, because naive Bayes assumes independence between data values, it simply uses the appropriate method for estimating the likelihood, depending on whether each predictor is categorical or continuous.

6.2 Building your first naive Bayes model

In this section, I'll teach you how to build and evaluate the performance of a naive Bayes model to predict political party affiliation. Imagine that you're a political scientist. You're looking for common voting patterns in the mid-1980s that would predict whether a US congressperson was a Democrat or Republican. You have the voting record of each member of the House of Representatives in 1984, and you identify 16 key votes that you believe most strongly split the two political parties. Your job is to train a naive Bayes model to predict whether a congressperson was a Democrat or a Republican, based on how they voted throughout the year. Let's start by loading the mlr and tidyverse packages:

```
library(mlr)
library(tidyverse)
```

6.2.1 Loading and exploring the HouseVotes84 dataset

Now let's load the data, which is built into the mlbench package, convert it into a tibble (with `as_tibble()`), and explore it.

> **NOTE** Remember that a tibble is just a tidyverse version of a data frame that helps make our lives a little easier.

We have a tibble containing 435 cases and 17 variables of members of the House Representatives in 1984. The `Class` variable is a factor indicating political party membership, and the other 16 variables are factors indicating how the individuals voted on each of the 16 votes. A value of `y` means they voted in favor, a value of `n` means they voted against, and a missing value (`NA`) means the individual either abstained or did not vote. Our goal is to train a model that can use the information in these variables to predict whether a congressperson was a Democrat or Republican, based on how they voted.

Listing 6.1 Loading and exploring the `HouseVotes84` dataset

```
data(HouseVotes84, package = "mlbench")

votesTib <- as_tibble(HouseVotes84)

votesTib

# A tibble: 435 x 17
   Class V1    V2    V3    V4    V5    V6    V7    V8    V9    V10
   <fct> <fct> <fct> <fct> <fct> <fct> <fct> <fct> <fct> <fct> <fct>
 1 repu… n     y     n     y     y     y     n     n     n     y
 2 repu… n     y     n     y     y     y     n     n     n     n
 3 demo… NA    y     y     NA    y     y     n     n     n     n
 4 demo… n     y     y     n     NA    y     n     n     n     n
 5 demo… y     y     y     n     y     y     n     n     n     n
 6 demo… n     y     y     n     y     y     n     n     n     n
 7 demo… n     y     n     y     y     y     n     n     n     n
 8 repu… n     y     n     y     y     y     n     n     n     n
 9 repu… n     y     n     y     y     y     n     n     n     n
10 demo… y     y     y     n     n     n     y     y     y     n
# … with 425 more rows, and 6 more variables: V11 <fct>, V12 <fct>,
#   V13 <fct>, V14 <fct>, V15 <fct>, V16 <fct>
```

> **NOTE** Ordinarily I would manually give names to unnamed columns to make it clearer what I'm working with. In this example, the variable names are the names of votes and are a little cumbersome, so we'll stick with V1, V2, and so on. If you want to see what issue each vote was for, run `?mlbench::HouseVotes84`.

It looks like we have a few missing values (`NA`s) in our tibble. Let's summarize the number of missing values in each variable using the `map_dbl()` function. Recall from chapter 2 that `map_dbl()` iterates a function over every element of a vector/list (or, in this case, every column of a tibble), applies a function to that element, and returns a vector containing the function output.

The first argument to the `map_dbl()` function is the name of the data we're going to apply the function to, and the second argument is the function we want to apply. I've chosen to use an anonymous function (using the ~ symbol as shorthand for `function(.)`.

NOTE Recall from chapter 2 that an *anonymous* function is a function that we define on the fly instead of predefining a function and assigning it to an object.

Our function passes each vector to `sum(is.na(.))` to count the number of missing values in that vector. This function is applied to each column of the tibble and returns the number of missing values for each.

Listing 6.2 Using the `map_dbl()` function to show missing values

```
map_dbl(votesTib, ~sum(is.na(.)))

Class    V1    V2    V3    V4    V5    V6    V7    V8    V9   V10
    0    12    48    11    11    15    11    14    15    22     7
  V11   V12   V13   V14   V15   V16
   21    31    25    17    28   104
```

Every column in our tibble has missing values except the `Class` variable! Luckily, the naive Bayes algorithm can handle missing data in two ways:

- By omitting the variables with missing values for a particular case, but still using that case to train the model
- By omitting that case entirely from the training set

By default, the naive Bayes implementation that mlr uses is to keep cases and drop variables. This usually works fine if the ratio of missing to complete values for the majority of cases is quite small. However, if you have a small number of variables and a large proportion of missing values, you may wish to omit the cases instead (and, more broadly, consider whether your dataset is sufficient for training).

Exercise 1

Use the `map_dbl()` function as we did in listing 6.2 to count the number of `y` values in each column of `votesTib`. Hint: Use `which(. == "y")` to return the rows in each column that equal `y`.

6.2.2 *Plotting the data*

Let's plot our data to get a better understanding of the relationships between political party and votes. Once again, we'll use our trick to gather the data into an untidy format so we can facet across the predictors. Because we're plotting categorical variables against each other, we set the position argument of the geom_bar() function to "fill", which creates stacked bars for y, n, and NA responses that sum to 1.

Listing 6.3 Plotting the HouseVotes84 dataset

```
votesUntidy <- gather(votesTib, "Variable", "Value", -Class)

ggplot(votesUntidy, aes(Class, fill = Value)) +
  facet_wrap(~ Variable, scales = "free_y") +
  geom_bar(position = "fill") +
  theme_bw()
```

The resulting plot is shown in figure 6.2. We can see there are some very clear differences in opinion between Democrats and Republicans!

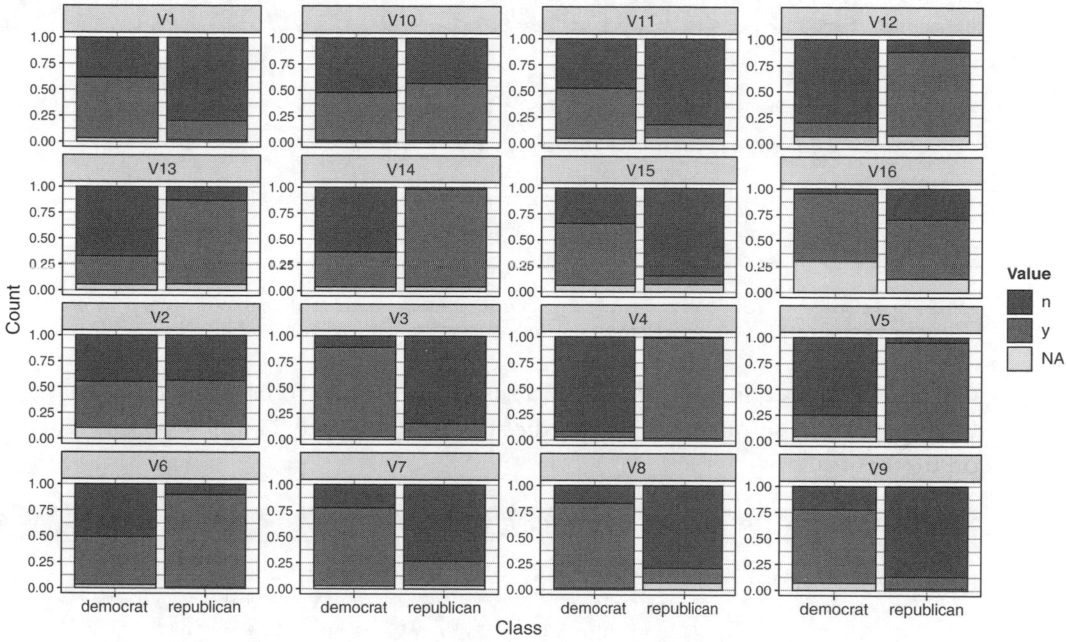

Figure 6.2 Filled bar charts showing the proportion of Democrats and Republicans that voted for (y) or against (n) or abstained (NA) on 16 different votes.

6.2.3 Training the model

Now let's create our task and learner, and build our model. We set the Class variable as the classification target of the makeClassifTask() function, and the algorithm we supply to the makeLearner() function is "classif.naiveBayes".

Listing 6.4 Creating the task and learner, and training the model

```
votesTask <- makeClassifTask(data = votesTib, target = "Class")

bayes <- makeLearner("classif.naiveBayes")

bayesModel <- train(bayes, votesTask)
```

The model training completes with no errors because naive Bayes can handle missing data.

Next, we'll use 10-fold cross-validation repeated 50 times to evaluate the performance of our model-building procedure. Again, because this is a two-class classification problem, we have access to the false positive rate and false negative rate, and so we ask for these as well in the `measures` argument to the `resample()` function.

Listing 6.5 Cross-validating the naive Bayes model

```
kFold <- makeResampleDesc(method = "RepCV", folds = 10, reps = 50,
                          stratify = TRUE)

bayesCV <- resample(learner = bayes, task = votesTask,
                    resampling = kFold,
                    measures = list(mmce, acc, fpr, fnr))

bayesCV$aggr

mmce.test.mean  acc.test.mean  fpr.test.mean  fnr.test.mean
    0.09820658     0.90179342     0.08223529     0.10819658
```

Our model correctly predicts 90% of test set cases in our cross-validation. That's not bad! Now let's use our model to predict the political party of a new politician, based on their votes.

Listing 6.6 Using the model to make predictions

```
politician <- tibble(V1 = "n", V2 = "n", V3 = "y", V4 = "n", V5 = "n",
                     V6 = "y", V7 = "y", V8 = "y", V9 = "y", V10 = "y",
                     V11 = "n", V12 = "y", V13 = "n", V14 = "n",
                     V15 = "y", V16 = "n")

politicianPred <- predict(bayesModel, newdata = politician)

getPredictionResponse(politicianPred)

[1] democrat
Levels: democrat republican
[source]
```

Our model predicts that the new politician is a Democrat.

Exercise 2

Wrap your naive Bayes model inside the `getLearnerModel()` function. Can you identify the prior probabilities and the likelihoods for each vote?

6.3 Strengths and weaknesses of naive Bayes

While it often isn't easy to tell which algorithms will perform well for a given task, here are some strengths and weaknesses that will help you decide whether naive Bayes will perform well for your task.

The strengths of naive Bayes are as follows:

- It can handle both continuous and categorical predictor variables.
- It's computationally inexpensive to train.
- It commonly performs well on topic classification problems where we want to classify documents based on the words they contain.
- It has no hyperparameters to tune.
- It is probabilistic and outputs the probabilities of new data belonging to each class.
- It can handle cases with missing data.

The weaknesses of naive Bayes are these:

- It assumes that continuous predictor variables are normally distributed (typically), and performance will suffer if they're not.
- It assumes that predictor variables are independent of each other, which usually isn't true. Performance will suffer if this assumption is severely violated.

6.4 What is the support vector machine (SVM) algorithm?

In this section, you'll learn how the SVM algorithm works and how it can add an extra dimension to data to make the classes linearly separable. Imagine that you would like to predict whether your boss will be in a good mood or not (a very important machine learning application). Over a couple of weeks, you record the number of hours you spend playing games at your desk and how much money you make the company each day. You also record your boss's mood the next day as good or bad (they're very binary). You decide to use the SVM algorithm to build a classifier that will help you decide whether you need to avoid your boss on a particular day. The SVM algorithm will learn a linear hyperplane that separates the days your boss is in a good mood from the days they are in a bad mood. The SVM algorithm is also able to add an extra dimension to the data to find the best hyperplane.

6.4.1 *SVMs for linearly separable data*

Take a look at the data shown in figure 6.3. The plots show the data you recorded on the mood of your boss, based on how hard you're working and how much money you're making the company.

The SVM algorithm finds an optimal linear hyperplane that separates the classes. A hyperplane is a surface that has one less dimension than there are variables in the dataset. For a two-dimensional feature space, such as in the example in figure 6.3, a hyperplane is simply a straight line. For a three-dimensional feature space, a hyperplane is a surface. It's hard to picture hyperplanes in a four or more dimensional feature space, but the principle is the same: they are surfaces that cut through the feature space.

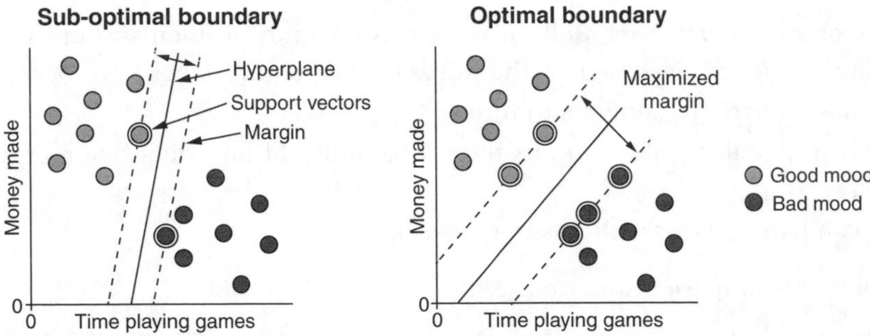

Figure 6.3 The SVM algorithm finds a hyperplane (solid line) that passes through the feature space. An optimal hyperplane is one that maximizes the margin around itself (dotted lines). The margin is a region around the hyperplane that touches the fewest cases. Support vectors are shown with double circles.

For problems where the classes are fully, linearly separable, there may be many different hyperplanes that do just as good a job at separating the classes in the training data. To find an optimal hyperplane (which will, hopefully, generalize better to unseen data), the algorithm finds the hyperplane that maximizes the *margin* around itself. The margin is a distance around the hyperplane that touches the fewest training cases. The cases in the data that touch the margin are called *support vectors* because they support the position of the hyperplane (hence, the name of the algorithm).

The support vectors are the most important cases in the training set because they define the boundary between the classes. Not only this, but the hyperplane that the algorithm learns is entirely dependent on the position of the support vectors and none of the other cases in the training set. Take a look at figure 6.4. If we move the position of one of the support vectors, then we move the position of the hyperplane. If, however, we move a non-support vector case, there is no influence on the hyperplane at all!

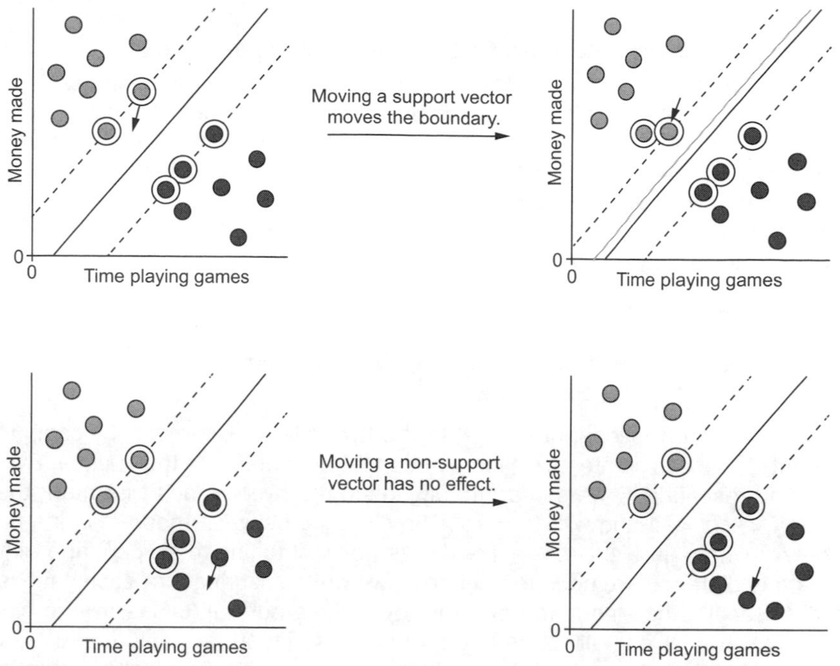

Figure 6.4 The position of the hyperplane is entirely dependent on the position of support vectors. Moving a support vector moves the hyperplane from its original position (dotted line) to a new position (top two plots). Moving a non-support vector has no impact on the hyperplane (bottom two plots).

SVMs are extremely popular right now. That's mainly for three reasons:

- They are good at finding ways of separating non-linearly separable classes.
- They tend to perform well for a wide variety of tasks.
- We now have the computational power to apply them to larger, more complex datasets.

This last point is important because it highlights a potential downside of SVMs: they tend to be more computationally expensive to train than many other classification algorithms. For this reason, if you have a very large dataset, and computational power is limited, it may be economical for you to try cheaper algorithms first and see how they perform.

TIP Usually, we favor predictive performance over speed. But a computationally cheap algorithm that performs well enough for your problem may be preferable to you than one that is very expensive. Therefore, I may try cheaper algorithms before trying the expensive ones.

How does the SVM algorithm find the optimal hyperplane?

The math underpinning how SVMs work is complex, but if you're interested, here are some of the basics of how the hyperplane is learned. Recall from chapter 4 that the equation for a straight line can be written as $y = ax + b$, where a and b are the slope and y-intercept of the line, respectively. We could rearrange this equation to be $y - ax - b = 0$ by shifting all the terms onto one side of the equals sign. Using this formulation, we can say that any point that falls on the line is one that satisfies this equation (the expression will equal zero).

You'll often see the equation for a hyperplane given as $wx + b = 0$, where w is the vector $(-b \;\; -a \;\; 1)$, x is the vector $(1 \;\; x \;\; y)$, and b is still the intercept. In the same way that any point that lies on a straight line satisfies $y - ax - b = 0$, any point that falls on a hyperplane satisfies the equation $wx + b = 0$.

The vector w is orthogonal or *normal* to the hyperplane. Therefore, by changing the intercept, b, we can create new hyperplanes that are parallel to the original. By changing b (and rescaling w) we can arbitrarily define the hyperplanes that mark the margins as $wx + b = -1$ and $wx + b = +1$. The distance between these margins is given by $2/||w||$, where $||w||$ is $\sqrt{-b^2 + -a^2 + 1^2}$. As we want to find the hyperplane that maximizes this distance, we need to minimize $||w||$ while ensuring that each case is classified correctly. The algorithm does this by making sure all cases in one class lie below $wx + b = -1$ and all cases in the other class lie above $wx + b = +1$. A simple way of doing this is to multiply the predicted value of each case by its corresponding label (–1 or +1), making all outputs positive. This creates the constraint that the margins must satisfy $y_i(wx_i + b) \geq 1$. The SVM algorithm therefore tries to solve the following minimization problem:

minimize $||w||$ subject to $y_i(wx_i + b) \geq 1$ for $i = 1 \ldots N$.

6.4.2 What if the classes aren't fully separable?

In the illustrations I've shown you so far, the classes have been fully separable. This is so I could clearly show you how the positioning of the hyperplane is chosen to maximize the margin. But what about situations where the classes are *not* completely separable? How can the algorithm find a hyperplane when there is no margin that won't have cases *inside* it?

The original formulation of SVMs uses what is often referred to as a *hard margin.* If an SVM uses a hard margin, then no cases are allowed to fall within the margin. This means that, if the classes are not fully separable, the algorithm will fail. This is, of course, a massive problem, because it relegates *hard-margin SVM* to handling only "easy" classification problems where the training set can be clearly partitioned into its component classes. As a result, an extension to the SVM algorithm called *soft-margin SVM* is much more commonly used. In soft-margin SVM, the algorithm still learns a hyperplane that best separates the classes, but it allows cases to fall inside its margin.

The soft-margin SVM algorithm still tries to find the hyperplane that best separates the classes, but it is penalized for having cases inside its margin. How severe the penalty is for having a case inside the margin is controlled by a hyperparameter that controls how "hard" or "soft" the margin is (we'll discuss this hyperparameter and how it affects the position of the hyperplane later in the chapter). The harder the margin is, the fewer cases will be inside it; the hyperplane will depend on a smaller number of support vectors. The softer the margin is, the more cases will be inside it; the hyperplane will depend on a larger number of support vectors. This has consequences for the bias-variance trade-off: if our margin is too hard, we might overfit the noise near the decision boundary, whereas if our margin is too soft, we might underfit the data and learn a decision boundary that does a bad job of separating the classes.

6.4.3 SVMs for non-linearly separable data

Great! So far the SVM algorithm seems quite simple—and for linearly separable classes like in our boss-mood example, it is. But I mentioned that one of the strengths of the SVM algorithm is that it can learn decision boundaries between classes that are *not* linearly separable. I've told you that the algorithm learns linear hyperplanes, so this seems like a contradiction. Well, here's what makes the SVM algorithm so powerful: it can add an extra dimension to your data to find a linear way to separate nonlinear data.

Take a look at the example in figure 6.5. The classes are not linearly separable using the two predictor variables. The SVM algorithm adds an extra dimension to the

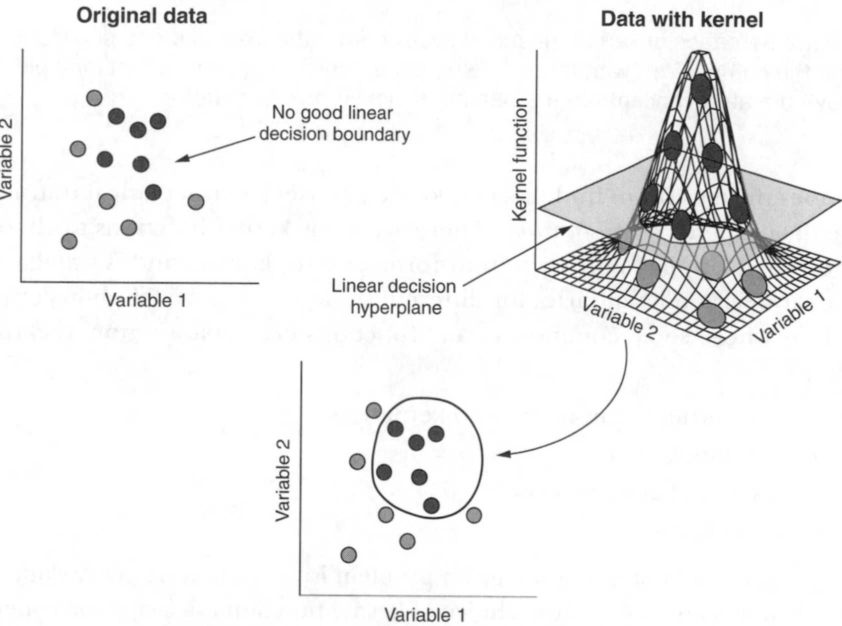

Figure 6.5 The SVM algorithm adds an extra dimension to linearly separate the data. The classes in the original data are not linearly separable. The SVM algorithm adds an extra dimension that, in a two-dimensional feature space, can be illustrated as a "stretching" of the data into a third dimension. This additional dimension allows the data to be linearly separated. When this hyperplane is projected back onto the original two dimensions, it appears as a curved decision boundary.

data, such that a linear hyperplane can separate the classes in this new, higher-dimensional space. We can visualize this as a sort of deformation or stretching of the feature space. The extra dimension is called a *kernel*.

NOTE Recall from chapter 5 that discriminant analysis condenses the information from the predictor variables into a smaller number of variables. Contrast this to the SVM algorithm, which expands the information from the predictor variables into an extra variable!

Why is it called a kernel?

The word *kernel* may confuse you (it certainly confuses me). It has nothing to do with the kernel in computing (the bit of your operating system that directly interfaces with the computer hardware), or kernels in corn or fruit.

The truth is that the reason they are called kernels is murky. In 1904, a German mathematician named David Hilbert published *Grundzüge einer allgemeinen theorie der linearen integralgleichungen* (*Principles of a general theory of linear integral equations*). In this book, Hilbert uses the word *kern* to mean the *core* of an integral equation. In 1909, an American mathematician called Maxime Bôcher published *An introduction to the study of integral equations* in which he translates Hilbert's use of the word *kern* to *kernel*.

The mathematics of kernel functions evolved from the work in these publications and took the name *kernel* with them. The extremely confusing thing is that multiple, seemingly unrelated concepts in mathematics include the word *kernel*!

How does the algorithm find this new kernel? It uses a mathematical transformation of the data called a *kernel function*. There are many kernel functions to choose from, each of which applies a different transformation to the data and is suitable for finding linear decision boundaries for different situations. Figure 6.6 shows examples of situations where some common kernel functions can separate non-linearly separable data:

- Linear kernel (equivalent to no kernel)
- Polynomial kernel
- Gaussian radial basis kernel
- Sigmoid kernel

The type of kernel function for a given problem isn't learned from the data—we have to specify it. Because of this, the choice of kernel function is a *categorical* hyperparameter (a hyperparameter that takes discrete, not continuous values). Therefore, the best approach for choosing the best-performing kernel is with hyperparameter tuning.

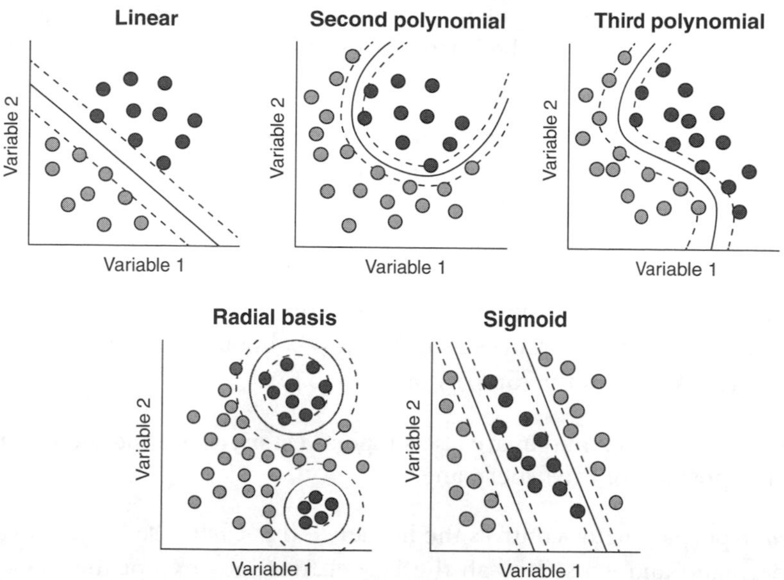

Figure 6.6 Examples of kernel functions. For each example, the solid line indicates the decision boundary (projected back onto the original feature space), and the dashed lines indicate the margin. With the exception of the linear kernel, imagine that the cases of one of the groups are raised off the page in a third dimension.

6.4.4 Hyperparameters of the SVM algorithm

This is where SVMs become fun/difficult/painful, depending on your problem, computational budget, and sense of humor. We need to tune quite a lot of hyperparameters when building an SVM. This, coupled with the fact that training a single model can be moderately expensive, can make training an optimally performing SVM take quite a long time. You'll see this in the worked example in section 6.5.2.

So the SVM algorithm has quite a few hyperparameters to tune, but the most important ones to consider are as follows:

- The *kernel* hyperparameter (shown in figure 6.6)
- The *degree* hyperparameter, which controls how "bendy" the decision boundary will be for the polynomial kernel (shown in figure 6.6)
- The *cost* or *C* hyperparameter, which controls how "hard" or "soft" the margin is (shown in figure 6.7)
- The *gamma* hyperparameter, which controls how much influence individual cases have on the position of the decision boundary (shown in figure 6.7)

The effects of the kernel function and *degree* hyperparameter are shown in figure 6.6. Note the difference in the shape of the decision boundary between the second- and third-degree polynomials.

NOTE The higher the degree of the polynomial, the more bendy and complex a decision boundary can be learned, but this has the potential to overfit the training set.

The *cost* (also called *C*) hyperparameter in soft-margin SVMs assigns a cost or penalty to having cases inside the margin or, put another way, tells the algorithm how bad it is to have cases inside the margin. A low cost tells the algorithm that it's acceptable to have more cases inside the margin and will result in wider margins that are less influenced by local differences near the class boundary. A high cost imposes a harsher penalty on having cases inside the boundary and will result in narrower margins that are more influenced by local differences near the class boundary. The effect of *cost* is illustrated for a linear kernel in the top part of figure 6.6.

NOTE Cases inside the margin are also support vectors, as moving them would change the position of the hyperplane.

The *gamma* hyperparameter controls the influence that each case has on the position of the hyperplane and is used by all the kernel functions except the linear kernel. Think of each case in the training set jumping up and down shouting, "Me! Me! Classify me correctly!" The larger *gamma* is, the more attention-seeking each case is, and the more granular the decision boundary will be (potentially leading to overfitting). The smaller *gamma* is, the less attention-seeking each case will be, and the less granular the decision boundary will be (potentially leading to underfitting). The effect of *gamma* is illustrated for a Gaussian radial basis kernel in the bottom part of figure 6.7.

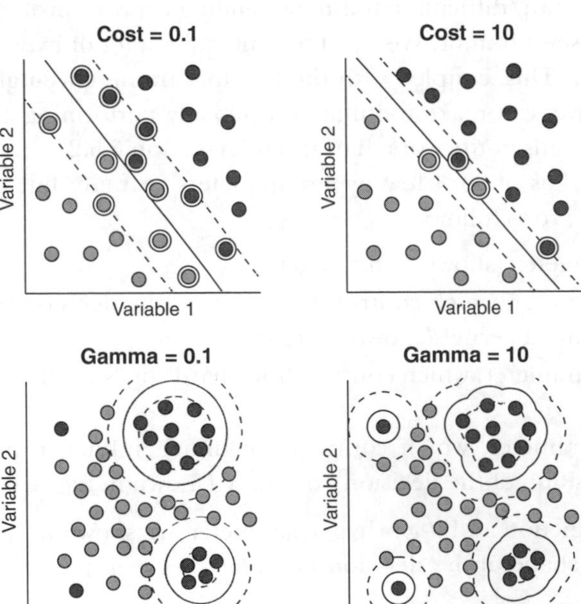

Figure 6.7 The impact of the *cost* and *gamma* hyperparameters. Larger values of the *cost* hyperparameter give greater penalization for having cases inside the margin. Larger values of the *gamma* hyperparameter mean individual cases have greater influence on the position of the decision boundary, leading to more complex decision boundaries.

So the SVM algorithm has multiple hyperparameters to tune! I'll show you how we can tune these simultaneously using mlr in section 6.5.2.

6.4.5 What if we have more than two classes?

So far, I've only shown you examples of two-class classification problems. This is because the SVM algorithm is inherently geared toward separating two classes. But can we use it for multiclass problems (where we're trying to predict more than two classes)? Absolutely! When there are more than two classes, instead of creating a single SVM, we make multiple models and let them fight it out to predict the most likely class for new data. There are two ways of doing this:

- One-versus-all
- One-versus-one

In the one-versus-all (also called *one versus rest*) approach, we create as many SVM models as there are classes. Each SVM model describes a hyperplane that best separates one class from *all the other classes.* Hence the name, one-versus-all. When we classify new, unseen cases, the models play a game of *winner takes all.* Put simply, the model that puts the new case on the "correct" side of its hyperplane (the side with the class it separates from all the others) wins. The case is then assigned to the class that the model was trying to separate from the others. This is illustrated in the plot on the left in figure 6.8.

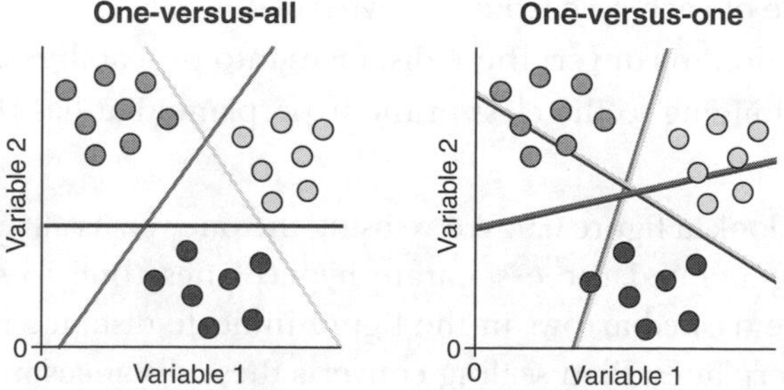

Figure 6.8 One-versus-all and one-versus-one approaches to multiclass SVMs. In the one-versus-all approach, a hyperplane is learned per class, separating it from all the other cases. In the one-versus-one approach, a hyperplane is learned for every pair of classes, separating them while ignoring the data from the other classes.

In the one-versus-one approach, we create an SVM model for every pair of classes. Each SVM model describes a hyperplane that best separates one class from *one other class,* ignoring data from the other classes. Hence, the name, one-versus-one. When we classify new, unseen cases, each model casts a vote. For example, if one model separates classes A and B, and the new data falls on the B side of the decision boundary, that model will vote for B. This continues for all the models, and the majority class vote wins. This is illustrated in the plot on the right in figure 6.8.

Which do we choose? Well in practice, there is usually little difference in the performance of the two methods. Despite training more models (for more than three classes), one-versus-one is sometimes less computationally expensive than one-versus-all. This is because, although we're training more models, the training sets are smaller (because of the ignored cases). The implementation of the SVM algorithm called by mlr uses the one-versus-one approach.

There is, however, a problem with these approaches. There will often be regions of the feature space in which none of the models gives a clear winning class. Can you see the triangular space between the hyperplanes on the left in figure 6.8? If a new case appeared inside this triangle, none of the three models would clearly win outright. This is a sort of classification no-man's land. Though not as obvious in figure 6.8, this also occurs with the one-versus-one approach.

If there is no outright winner when predicting a new case, a technique called *Platt scaling* is used (named after computer scientist John Platt). Platt scaling takes the distances of the cases from each hyperplane and converts them into probabilities using the logistic function. Recall from chapter 4 that the logistic function maps a continuous variable to probabilities between 0 and 1. Using Platt scaling to make predictions proceeds like this:

1. For every hyperplane (whether we use one-versus-all or one-versus-one):
   a. Measure the distance of each case from the hyperplane.
   b. Use the logistic function to convert these distances into probabilities.
2. Classify new data as belonging to the class of the hyperplane that has the highest probability.

If this seems confusing, take a look at figure 6.9. We're using the one-versus-all approach in the figure, and we have generated three separate hyperplanes (one to separate each class from the rest). The dashed arrows in the figure indicate distance in either direction, away from the hyperplanes. Platt scaling converts these distances into probabilities using the logistic function (the class each hyperplane separates from the rest has positive distance).

When we classify new, unseen data, the distance of the new data is converted into a probability using each of the three S-shaped curves, and the case is classified as the one that gives the highest probability. Handily, all of this is taken care of for us in the implementation of SVM called by mlr. If we supply a three-class classification task, we will get a one-versus-one SVM model with Platt scaling without having to change our code.

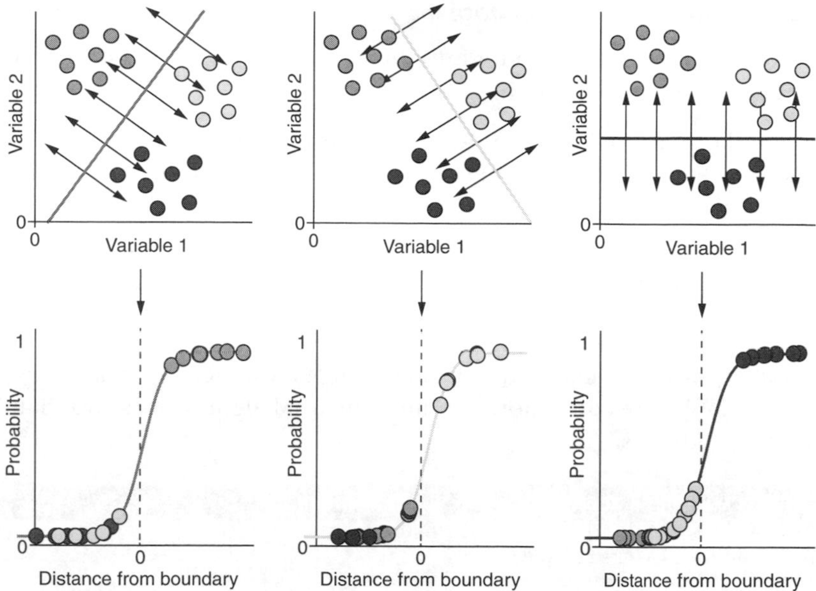

Figure 6.9 How Platt scaling is used to get probabilities for each hyperplane. This example shows a one-versus-all approach (it also applies to one-versus-one). For each hyperplane, the distance of each case from the hyperplane is recorded (indicated by double-headed arrows). These distances are converted into probabilities using the logistic function.

6.5 Building your first SVM model

In this section, I'll teach you how to build an SVM model and tune multiple hyperparameters simultaneously. Imagine that you're sick and tired of receiving so many spam emails (maybe you don't need to imagine!). It's difficult for you to be productive because you get so many emails requesting your bank details for a mysterious Ugandan inheritance, and trying to sell you Viagra.

You decide to perform a feature extraction on the emails you receive over a few months, which you manually class as spam or not spam. These features include things like the number of exclamation marks and the frequency of certain words. With this data, you want to make an SVM that you can use as a spam filter, which will classify new emails as spam or not spam.

In this section, you'll learn how to train an SVM model and tune multiple hyperparameters simultaneously. Let's start by loading the mlr and tidyverse packages:

```
library(mlr)
library(tidyverse)
```

6.5.1 *Loading and exploring the spam dataset*

Now let's load the data, which is built into the kernlab package, convert it into a tibble (with `as_tibble()`), and explore it.

> **NOTE** The kernlab package should have been installed along with mlr as a suggested package. If you get an error when trying to load the data, you may need to install it with `install.packages("kernlab")`.

We have a tibble containing 4,601 emails and 58 variables extracted from emails. Our goal is to train a model that can use the information in these variables to predict whether a new email is spam or not.

> **NOTE** Except for the factor `type`, which denotes whether an email is spam, all of the variables are continuous, because the SVM algorithm cannot handle categorical predictors.

Listing 6.7 Loading and exploring the spam dataset

```
data(spam, package = "kernlab")

spamTib <- as_tibble(spam)

spamTib

# A tibble: 4,601 x 58
    make address   all num3d   our  over remove internet order  mail
   <dbl>   <dbl> <dbl> <dbl> <dbl> <dbl>  <dbl>    <dbl> <dbl> <dbl>
 1 0        0.64 0.64      0 0.32  0      0         0    0     0
 2 0.21     0.28 0.5       0 0.14  0.28   0.21      0.07 0     0.94
 3 0.06     0    0.71      0 1.23  0.19   0.19      0.12 0.64  0.25
 4 0        0    0         0 0.63  0      0.31      0.63 0.31  0.63
 5 0        0    0         0 0.63  0      0.31      0.63 0.31  0.63
 6 0        0    0         0 1.85  0      0         1.85 0     0
 7 0        0    0         0 1.92  0      0         0    0     0.64
 8 0        0    0         0 1.88  0      0         1.88 0     0
 9 0.15     0    0.46      0 0.61  0      0.3       0    0.92  0.76
10 0.06     0.12 0.77      0 0.19  0.32   0.38      0    0.06  0
# ... with 4,591 more rows, and 48 more variables...
```

> **TIP** This dataset has a lot of features! I'm not going to discuss the meaning of each one, but you can see a description of what they mean by running `?kernlab::spam`.

6.5.2 *Tuning our hyperparameters*

Let's define our task and learner. This time, we supply `"classif.svm"` as the argument to `makeLearner()` to specify that we're going to use SVM.

Listing 6.8 Creating the task and learner

```
spamTask <- makeClassifTask(data = spamTib, target = "type")

svm <- makeLearner("classif.svm")
```

Before we train our model, we need to tune our hyperparameters. To find out which hyperparameters are available for tuning for an algorithm, we simply pass the name of the algorithm in quotes to `getParamSet()`. For example, listing 6.9 shows how to print the hyperparameters for the SVM algorithm. I've removed some rows and columns of the output to make it fit, but the most important columns are there:

- The row name is the name of the hyperparameter.
- `Type` is whether the hyperparameter takes numeric, integer, discrete, or logical values.
- `Def` is the default value (the value that will be used if you don't tune the hyperparameter).
- `Constr` defines the constraints for the hyperparameter: either a set of specific values or a range of acceptable values.
- `Req` defines whether the hyperparameter is required by the learner.
- `Tunable` is logical and defines whether that hyperparameter can be tuned (some algorithms have options that cannot be tuned but can be set by the user).

Listing 6.9 Printing available SVM hyperparameters

```
getParamSet("classif.svm")

                 Type      Def              Constr  Req  Tunable
cost          numeric        1            0 to Inf    Y     TRUE
kernel       discrete   radial  [lin,poly,rad,sig]    -     TRUE
degree        integer        3            1 to Inf    Y     TRUE
gamma         numeric        -            0 to Inf    Y     TRUE
scale   logicalvector     TRUE                   -    -     TRUE
```

The SVM algorithm is sensitive to variables being on different scales, so it's usually a good idea to scale the predictors first. Notice the scale hyperparameter: it tells us that the algorithm will scale the data for us by default.

Extracting the possible values for a hyperparameter

While the `getParamSet()` function is useful, I don't find it particularly simple to extract information from. If you call `str(getParamSet("classif.svm"))`, you'll see that it has a reasonably complex structure.

To extract information about a particular hyperparameter, you need to call `getParamSet("classif.svm")$pars$[HYPERPAR]` (where `[HYPERPAR]` is replaced by the hyperparameter you're interested in). To extract the possible values for that hyperparameter, you append `$values` to the call. For example, the following extracts the possible kernel functions:

```
getParamSet("classif.svm")$pars$kernel$values

$linear
[1] "linear"
```

(continued)

```
$polynomial
[1] "polynomial"

$radial
[1] "radial"

$sigmoid
[1] "sigmoid"
```

These are the most important hyperparameters for us to tune:

- *Kernel*
- *Cost*
- *Degree*
- *Gamma*

Listing 6.10 defines the hyperparameters we want to tune. We're going to start by defining a vector of kernel functions we wish to tune.

TIP Notice that I omit the linear kernel. This is because the linear kernel is the same as the polynomial kernel with *degree* = 1, so we'll just make sure we include 1 as a possible value for the *degree* hyperparameter. Including the linear kernel *and* the first-degree polynomial kernel is simply a waste of computing time.

Next, we use the `makeParamSet()` function to define the hyperparameter space we wish to tune over. To the `makeParamSet()` function, we supply the information needed to define each hyperparameter we wish to tune, separated by commas. Let's break this down line by line:

- The *kernel* hyperparameter takes discrete values (the name of the kernel function), so we use the `makeDiscreteParam()` function to define its values as the vector of kernels we created.
- The *degree* hyperparameter takes integer values (whole numbers), so we use the `makeIntegerParam()` function and define the lower and upper values we wish to tune over.
- The *cost* and *gamma* hyperparameters take numeric values (any number between zero and infinity), so we use the `makeNumericParam()` function to define the lower and upper values we wish to tune over.

For each of these functions, the first argument is the name of the hyperparameter given by `getParamSet("classif.svm")`, in quotes.

Listing 6.10 Defining the hyperparameter space for tuning

```
kernels <- c("polynomial", "radial", "sigmoid")

svmParamSpace <- makeParamSet(
  makeDiscreteParam("kernel", values = kernels),
  makeIntegerParam("degree", lower = 1, upper = 3),
  makeNumericParam("cost", lower = 0.1, upper = 10),
  makeNumericParam("gamma", lower = 0.1, 10))
```

Cast your mind back to chapter 3, when we tuned *k* for the kNN algorithm. We used the grid search procedure during tuning to try every value of *k* that we defined. This is what the grid search method does: it tries every combination of the hyperparameter space you define and finds the best-performing combination.

Grid search is great because, provided you specify a sensible hyperparameter space to search over, it will always find the best-performing hyperparameters. But look at the hyperparameter space we defined for our SVM. Let's say we wanted to try values for the *cost* and *gamma* hyperparameters from 0.1 to 10, in steps of 0.1 (that's 100 values of each). We're trying three kernel functions and three values of the *degree* hyperparameter. To perform a grid search over this parameter space would require training a model 90,000 times! In such a situation, if you have the time, patience, and computational budget for such a grid search, then good for you. I, for one, have better things I could be doing with my computer!

Instead, we can employ a technique called *random search*. Rather than trying every possible combination of parameters, random search proceeds as follows:

1 Randomly select a combination of hyperparameter values.
2 Use cross-validation to train and evaluate a model using those hyperparameter values.
3 Record the performance metric of the model (usually mean misclassification error for classification tasks).
4 Repeat (iterate) steps 1 to 3 as many times as your computational budget allows.
5 Select the combination of hyperparameter values that gave you the best-performing model.

Unlike grid search, random search isn't guaranteed to find the best set of hyperparameter values. However, with enough iterations, it can usually find a good combination that performs well. By using random search, we can run 500 combinations of hyperparameter values, instead of all 90,000 combinations.

Let's define our random search using the `makeTuneControlRandom()` function. We use the `maxit` argument to tell the function how many iterations of the random search procedure we want to use. You should try to set this as high as your computational budget allows, but in this example we'll stick to 20 to prevent the example from taking too long. Next, we describe our cross-validation procedure. Remember I said in chapter 3 that I prefer k-fold cross-validation unless the process is computationally expensive. Well, this is computationally expensive, so we're compromising by using holdout cross-validation instead.

Listing 6.11 Defining the random search

```
randSearch <- makeTuneControlRandom(maxit = 20)

cvForTuning <- makeResampleDesc("Holdout", split = 2/3)
```

There's something else we can do to speed up this process. R, as a language, doesn't make that much use of multithreading (using multiple CPUs simultaneously to accomplish a task). However, one of the benefits of the mlr package is that it allows multithreading to be used with its functions. This helps you use multiple cores/CPUs on your computer to accomplish tasks such as hyperparameter tuning and cross-validation much more quickly.

> **TIP** If you don't know how many cores your computer has, you can find out in R by running `parallel::detectCores()`. (If your computer only has one core, the 90s called—they want their computer back.)

To run an mlr process in parallel, we place its code between the `parallelStartSocket()` and `parallelStop()` functions from the parallelMap package. To start our hyperparameter tuning process, we call the `tuneParams()` function and supply the following as arguments:

- First argument = name of the learner
- `task` = name of our task
- `resampling` = cross-validation procedure (defined in listing 6.11)
- `par.set` = hyperparameter space (defined in listing 6.10)
- `control` = search procedure (random search, defined in listing 6.11)

This code between the `parallelStartSocket()` and `parallelStop()` functions is shown in listing 6.12. Notice that the downside of running cross-validation processes in parallel is that we no longer get a running update of how far we've got.

> **WARNING** The computer I'm writing this on has four cores, and this code takes nearly a minute to run on it. It is of the utmost importance that you go make a cup of tea while it runs. Milk and no sugar, please.

Listing 6.12 Performing hyperparameter tuning

```
library(parallelMap)
library(parallel)

parallelStartSocket(cpus = detectCores())

tunedSvmPars <- tuneParams("classif.svm", task = spamTask,
                     resampling = cvForTuning,
```

```
                      par.set = svmParamSpace,
                      control = randSearch)

parallelStop()
```

TIP The *degree* hyperparameter only applies to the polynomial kernel function, and the *gamma* hyperparameter doesn't apply to the linear kernel. Does this create errors when the random search selects combinations that don't make sense? Nope. If the random search selects the sigmoid kernel, for example, it simply ignores the value of the *degree* hyperparameter.

Welcome back after our interlude! You can print the best-performing hyperparameter values and the performance of the model built with them by calling `tunedSvm`, or extract just the named values (so you can train a new model using them) by calling `tunedSvm$x`. Looking at the following listing, we can see that the first-degree polynomial kernel function (equivalent to the linear kernel function) gave the model that performs the best, with a *cost* of 5.8 and *gamma* of 1.56.

Listing 6.13 Extracting the winning hyperparameter values from tuning

```
tunedSvmPars

Tune result:
Op. pars: kernel=polynomial; degree=1; cost=5.82; gamma=1.56
mmce.test.mean=0.0645372

tunedSvmPars$x
$kernel
[1] "polynomial"

$degree
[1] 1

$cost
[1] 5.816232

$gamma
[1] 1.561584
```

Your values are probably different than mine. This is the nature of the random search: it may find different winning combinations of hyperparameter values each time it's run. To reduce this variance, we should commit to increasing the number of iterations the search makes.

6.5.3 Training the model with the tuned hyperparameters

Now that we've tuned our hyperparameters, let's build our model using the best-performing combination. Recall from chapter 3 that we use the `setHyperPars()` function to combine a learner with a set of predefined hyperparameter values. The first argument is the learner we want to use, and the `par.vals` argument is the object containing our tuned hyperparameter values. We then train a model using our `tunedSvm` learner with the `train()` function.

Listing 6.14 Training the model with tuned hyperparameters

```
tunedSvm <- setHyperPars(makeLearner("classif.svm"),
                         par.vals = tunedSvmPars$x)

tunedSvmModel <- train(tunedSvm, spamTask)
```

> **TIP** Because we already defined our learner in listing 6.8, we could simply have run `setHyperPars(svm, par.vals = tunedSvmPars$x)` to achieve the same result.

6.6 Cross-validating our SVM model

We've built a model using tuned hyperparameters. In this section, we'll cross-validate the model to estimate how it will perform on new, unseen data.

Recall from chapter 3 that it's important to cross-validate *the entire model-building process*. This means any *data-dependent* steps in our model-building process (such as hyperparameter tuning) need to be included in our cross-validation. If we don't include them, our cross-validation is likely to give an overoptimistic estimate (a *biased* estimate) of how well the model will perform.

> **TIP** What counts as a data-*independent* step in model building? Things like removing nonsense variables by hand, changing variable names and types, and replacing a missing value code with `NA`. These steps are data-independent because they would be the same regardless of the values in the data.

Recall also that to include hyperparameter tuning in our cross-validation, we need to use a *wrapper function* that wraps together our learner and hyperparameter tuning process. The cross-validation process is shown in listing 6.15.

Because mlr will use nested cross-validation (where hyperparameter tuning is performed in the inner loop, and the winning combination of values is passed to the outer loop), we first define our outer cross-validation strategy using the `makeResamplDesc()` function. In this example, I've chosen 3-fold cross-validation for the outer loop. For the inner loop, we'll use the `cvForTuning` resampling description defined in listing 6.11 (holdout cross-validation with a 2/3 split).

Next, we make our wrapped learner using the `makeTuneWrapper()` function. The arguments are as follows:

- First argument = name of the learner
- `resampling` = inner loop cross-validation strategy
- `par.set` = hyperparameter space (defined in listing 6.10)
- `control` = search procedure (defined in listing 6.11)

As the cross-validation will take a while, it's prudent to start parallelization with the `parallelStartSocket()` function. Now, to run our nested cross-validation, we call the `resample()` function, where the first argument is our wrapped learner, the second argument is our task, and the third argument is our outer cross-validation strategy.

> **WARNING** This takes a little over a minute on my four-core computer. In the meantime, you know what to do. Milk and no sugar, please. Do you have any cake?

Listing 6.15 Cross-validating the model-building process

```
outer <- makeResampleDesc("CV", iters = 3)

svmWrapper <- makeTuneWrapper("classif.svm", resampling = cvForTuning,
                              par.set = svmParamSpace,
                              control = randSearch)

parallelStartSocket(cpus = detectCores())

cvWithTuning <- resample(svmWrapper, spamTask, resampling = outer)

parallelStop()
```

Now let's take a look at the result of our cross-validation procedure by printing the contents of the `cvWithTuning` object.

Listing 6.16 Extracting the cross-validation result

```
cvWithTuning

Resample Result
Task: spamTib
Learner: classif.svm.tuned
Aggr perf: mmce.test.mean=0.0988956
Runtime: 73.89
```

We're correctly classifying 1 – 0.099 = 0.901 = 90.1% of emails as spam or not spam. Not bad for a first attempt!

6.7 Strengths and weaknesses of the SVM algorithm

While it often isn't easy to tell which algorithms will perform well for a given task, here are some strengths and weaknesses that will help you decide whether the SVM algorithm will perform well for your case.

The strengths of the SVM algorithm are as follows:

- It's very good at learning complex nonlinear decision boundaries.
- It performs very well on a wide variety of tasks.
- It makes no assumptions about the distribution of the predictor variables.

The weaknesses of the SVM algorithm are these:

- It is one of the most computationally expensive algorithms to train.
- It has multiple hyperparameters that need to be tuned simultaneously.
- It can only handle continuous predictor variables (although recoding a categorical variable as numeric *may* help in some cases).

Exercise 3

The `NA` values in `votesTib` include when politicians abstained from voting, so recode these values into the value `"a"` and cross-validate a naive Bayes model including them. Does this improve performance?

Exercise 4

Perform another random search for the best SVM hyperparameters using nested cross-validation. This time, limit your search to the linear kernel (so no need to tune *degree* or *gamma*), search over the range 0.1 and 100 for the *cost* hyperparameter, and increase the number of iterations to 100. Warning: This took nearly 12 minutes to complete on my machine!

Summary

- The naive Bayes and support vector machine (SVM) algorithms are supervised learners for classification problems.
- Naive Bayes uses Bayes' rule (defined in chapter 5) to estimate the probability of new data belonging to each of the possible output classes.
- The SVM algorithm finds a hyperplane (a surface with one less dimension than there are predictors) that best separates the classes.
- While naive Bayes can handle both continuous and categorical predictor variables, the SVM algorithm can only handle continuous predictors.
- Naive Bayes is computationally cheap, while the SVM algorithm is one of the most expensive algorithms.
- The SVM algorithm can use kernel functions to add an extra dimension to the data that helps find a linear decision boundary.
- The SVM algorithm is sensitive to the values of its hyperparameters, which must be tuned to maximize performance.
- The mlr package allows parallelization of intensive processes, such as hyperparameter tuning, by using the parallelMap package.

Solutions to exercises

1 Use the `map_dbl()` function to count the number of `y` values in each column of `votesTib`:

```
map_dbl(votesTib, ~ length(which(. == "y")))
```

2 Extract the prior probabilities and likelihoods from your naive Bayes model:

```
getLearnerModel(bayesModel)

# The prior probabilities are 0.61 for democrat and
# 0.39 for republican (at the time these data were collected!).

# The likelihoods are shown in 2x2 tables for each vote.
```

3 Recode the `NA` values from the `votesTib` tibble, and cross-validate a model including these values:

```
votesTib[] <- map(votesTib, as.character)

votesTib[is.na(votesTib)] <- "a"

votesTib[] <- map(votesTib, as.factor)

votesTask <- makeClassifTask(data = votesTib, target = "Class")

bayes <- makeLearner("classif.naiveBayes")

kFold <- makeResampleDesc(method = "RepCV", folds = 10, reps = 50,
                          stratify = TRUE)

bayesCV <- resample(learner = bayes, task = votesTask, resampling = kFold,
                    measures = list(mmce, acc, fpr, fnr))

bayesCV$aggr

# Only a very slight increase in accuracy
```

4 Perform a random search restricted to the linear kernel, tuning over a larger range of values for the *cost* hyperparameter:

```
svmParamSpace <- makeParamSet(
  makeDiscreteParam("kernel", values = "linear"),
  makeNumericParam("cost", lower = 0.1, upper = 100))

randSearch <- makeTuneControlRandom(maxit = 100)

cvForTuning <- makeResampleDesc("Holdout", split = 2/3)

outer <- makeResampleDesc("CV", iters = 3)
```

```
svmWrapper <- makeTuneWrapper("classif.svm", resampling = cvForTuning,
                              par.set = svmParamSpace,
                              control = randSearch)

parallelStartSocket(cpus = detectCores())

cvWithTuning <-
resample(svmWrapper, spamTask, resampling = outer) # ~1 min

parallelStop()

cvWithTuning
```

7 Classifying with decision trees

This chapter covers

- Working with decision trees
- Using the recursive partitioning algorithm
- An important weakness of decision trees

There's nothing like the great outdoors. I live in the countryside, and when I walk my dog in the woods, I'm reminded just how much we rely on trees. Trees produce the atmosphere we breathe, create habitats for wildlife, provide us with food, and are surprisingly good at making predictions. Yes, you read that right: trees are good at making predictions. But before you go asking the birch in your back garden for next week's lottery numbers, I should clarify that I'm referring to several supervised learning algorithms that use a branching tree structure. This family of algorithms can be used to solve both classification and regression tasks, can handle continuous and categorical predictors, and are naturally suited to solving multiclass classification problems.

NOTE Remember that a predictor variable is a variable we believe may contain information about the value of our outcome variable. Continuous predictors can have any numeric value on their measurement scale, while categorical variables can have only finite, discrete values/categories.

The basic premise of all tree-based classification algorithms is that they learn a sequence of questions that separates cases into different classes. Each question has a binary answer, and cases will be sent down the left or right branch depending on which criteria they meet. There can be branches within branches; and once the model is learned, it can be graphically represented as a tree. Have you ever played the game 20 Questions, where you have to guess what object someone is thinking of by asking yes-or-no questions? What about the game Guess Who, where you have to guess the other player's character by asking questions about their appearance? These are examples of tree-based classifiers.

By the end of this chapter, you'll see how such simple, interpretable models can be used to make predictions. We'll finish the chapter by highlighting an important weakness of decision trees, which you'll learn how to overcome in the next chapter.

7.1 What is the recursive partitioning algorithm?

In this section, you'll learn how decision tree algorithms—and specifically, the *recursive partitioning* (rpart) algorithm—work to learn a tree structure. Imagine that you want to create a model to represent the way people commute to work, given features of the vehicle. You gather information on the vehicles, such as how many wheels they have, whether they have an engine, and their weight. You could formulate your classification process as a series of sequential questions. Every vehicle is evaluated at each question and moves either left or right in the model depending on how its features satisfy the question. An example of such a model is shown in figure 7.1.

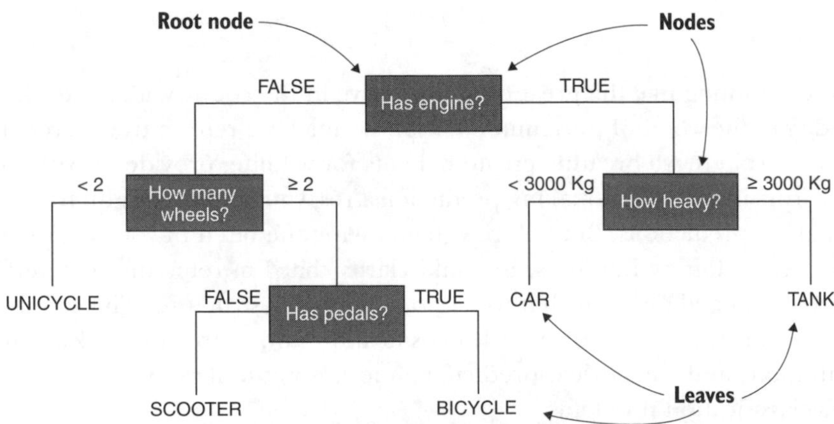

Figure 7.1 The structure of a decision tree. The root node is the node that contains all the data prior to splitting. Nodes are split by a splitting criterion into two branches, each of which leads to another node. Nodes that do not split any further are called *leaves*.

Notice that our model has a branching, tree-like structure, where each question splits the data into two branches. Each branch can lead to additional questions, which have branches of their own. The question parts of the tree are called *nodes*, and the very first question/node is called the *root node*. Nodes have one branch leading to them and two branches leading away from them. Nodes at the end of a series of questions are called *leaf nodes* or *leaves*. Leaf nodes have a single branch leading to them but no branches leading away from them. When a case finds its way down the tree into a leaf node, it progresses no further and is classified as the majority class within that leaf. It may seem strange to you (it does to me, anyway) that the root is at the top and the leaves are at the bottom, but this is the way tree-based models are usually represented.

NOTE Although not shown in this small example, it is perfectly fine (and common) to have questions about the same feature in different parts of the tree.

This all seems simple so far. But in the previous simplistic example, we could have constructed this ourselves by hand. (In fact, I did!) So tree-based models aren't necessarily learned by machine learning. A decision tree could be an established HR process for dealing with disciplinary action, for example. You could have a tree-based approach to deciding which flight to buy (is the price above your budget, is the airline reliable, is the food terrible, and so on). So how can we learn the structure of a decision tree automatically for complex datasets with many features? Enter the rpart algorithm.

NOTE Tree-based models can be used for both classification *and* regression tasks, so you may see them described as *classification and regression trees* (CART). However, CART is a trademarked algorithm whose code is proprietary. The rpart algorithm is simply an open source implementation of CART. You'll learn how to use trees for regression tasks in chapter 12.

At each stage of the tree-building process, the rpart algorithm considers all of the predictor variables and selects the predictor that does the best job of discriminating the classes. It starts at the root and then, at each branch, looks again for the next feature that will best discriminate the classes of the cases that took that branch. But how does rpart decide on the best feature at each split? This can be done a few different ways, and rpart offers two approaches: the difference in *entropy* (called the *information gain*) and the difference in *Gini index* (called the *Gini gain*). The two methods usually give very similar results; but the Gini index (named after the sociologist and statistician Corrado Gini) is slightly faster to compute, so we'll focus on it.

TIP The Gini index is the default method rpart uses to decide how to split the tree. If you're concerned that you're missing the best-performing model, you can always compare Gini index and entropy during hyperparameter tuning.

7.1.1 Using Gini gain to split the tree

In this section, I'll show you how Gini gain is calculated to find the best split for a particular node when growing a decision tree. Entropy and the Gini index are two ways of trying to measure the same thing: *impurity*. Impurity is a measure of how heterogeneous the classes are within a node.

NOTE If a node contains only a single class (which would make it a leaf), it would be said to be *pure*.

By estimating the impurity (with whichever method you choose) that would result from using each predictor variable for the next split, the algorithm can choose the feature that will result in the smallest impurity. Put another way, the algorithm chooses the feature that will result in subsequent nodes that are as homogeneous as possible.

So what does the Gini index look like? Figure 7.2 shows an example split. We have 20 cases in a parent node belonging to two classes, A and B. We split the node into two leaves based on some criterion. In the left leaf, we have 11 cases from class A and 3 from class B. In the right leaf, we have 5 from class B and 1 from class A.

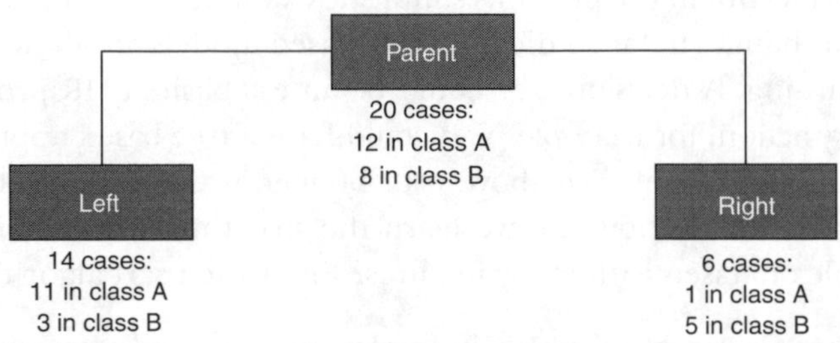

Figure 7.2 An example decision tree split for 20 cases belonging to classes A and B

We want to know the *Gini gain* of this split. The Gini gain is the difference between the Gini index of the parent node and the Gini index of the split. Looking at our example in figure 7.2, the Gini index for any node is calculated as

$$\text{Gini index} = 1 - (p(A)^2 + p(B)^2)$$

where $p(A)$ and $p(B)$ are the proportions of cases belonging to classes A and B, respectively. So the Gini indices for the parent node and the left and right leaves are shown in figure 7.3.

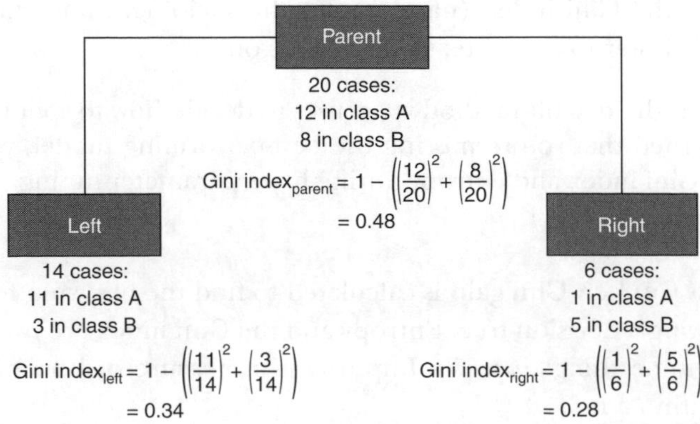

Figure 7.3 Calculating the Gini index of the parent node and the left and right leaves

Now that we have the Gini indices for the left and right leaves, we can calculate the Gini index for the split as a whole. The Gini index of the split is the sum of the left and right Gini indices multiplied by the proportion of cases they accepted from the parent node:

$$\text{Gini index}_{\text{split}} = p(\text{left}) \times \text{Gini index}_{\text{left}} + p(\text{right}) \times \text{Gini index}_{\text{right}}$$

$$\text{Gini index}_{\text{split}} = \frac{14}{20} \times 0.34 + \frac{6}{20} \times 0.28 = 0.32$$

And the Gini gain (the difference between the Gini indices of the parent node and the split) is simply

$$\text{Gini gain} = 0.48 - 0.32 = 0.16$$

where 0.48 is the Gini index of the parent, as calculated in figure 7.3.

The Gini gain at a particular node is calculated for each predictor variable, and the predictor that generates the largest Gini gain is used to split that node. This process is repeated for every node as the tree grows.

Generalizing the Gini index to any number of classes

In this example, we've considered only two classes, but the Gini index of a node is easily calculable for problems that have many classes. In that situation, the equation for Gini index generalizes to

$$\text{Gini index} = 1 - \sum_{k=1}^{K} p(\text{class}_{k)})^2$$

which is just a fancy way of saying that we calculate $p(class_k)^2$ for each class from 1 to *K* (the number of classes), add them all up, and subtract this value from 1.

If you're interested, the equation for entropy is

$$\text{entropy} = \sum_{k=1}^{K} - p(\text{class}_k) \times \log_2 p(\text{class}_k)$$

which is just a fancy way of saying that we calculate $-p(class) \times \log_2 p(class)$ for each class from 1 to *K* (the number of classes) and add them all up (which becomes a subtraction because the first term is negative). As for Gini gain, the information gain is calculated as the entropy of the parent minus the entropy of the split (which is calculated exactly the same way as the Gini index for the split).

7.1.2 What about continuous and multilevel categorical predictors?

In this section, I'll show you how the splits are chosen for continuous and categorical predictor variables. When a predictor variable is *dichotomous* (has only two levels), it's quite obvious how to use it for a split: cases with one value go left, and cases with the other value go right. Decision trees can also split the cases using continuous variables, but what value is chosen as the split point? Have a look at the example in figure 7.4. We have cases from three classes plotted against two continuous variables. The feature space is split into rectangles by each node. At the first node, the cases are split into those with a value of variable 2, greater than or less than 20. The cases that make it to the second node are further split into those with a value of variable 1, greater than or less than 10,000.

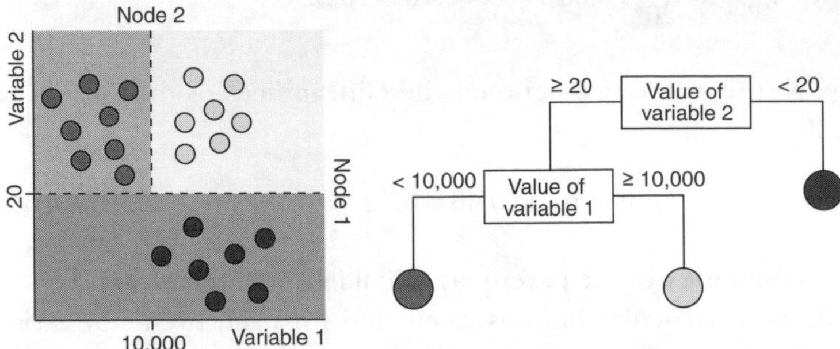

Figure 7.4 How splitting is performed for continuous predictors. Cases belonging to three classes are plotted against two continuous variables. The first node splits the feature space into rectangles based on the value of variable 2. The second node further splits the variable 2 ≥ 20 feature space into rectangles based on the value of variable 1.

> **NOTE** Notice that the variables are on vastly different scales. The rpart algorithm isn't sensitive to variables being on different scales, so there's no need to scale and center your predictors!

But how is the exact split point chosen for a continuous predictor? Well, the cases in the training set are arranged in order of the continuous variable, and the Gini gain is evaluated for the midpoint between each adjacent pair of cases. If the greatest Gini gain among all predictor variables is one of these midpoints, then this is chosen as the split for that node. This is illustrated in figure 7.5.

A similar procedure is used for categorical predictors with more than two levels. First, the Gini index is computed for each level of the predictor (using the proportion of each class that has that value of the predictor). The factor levels are arranged in order of their Gini indices, and the Gini gain is evaluated for a split between each adjacent pair of levels. Take a look at the example in figure 7.6. We have a factor with three levels (A, B, and C): we evaluate the Gini index of each and find that their values are B < A < C. Now we evaluate the Gini gain for the splits B versus A and C, and C versus B and A.

In this way, we can create a binary split from categorical variables with many predictors without having to try every single possible combination of level splits (2^{m-1}, where *m* is the number of levels of the variable). If the split B versus A and C is found

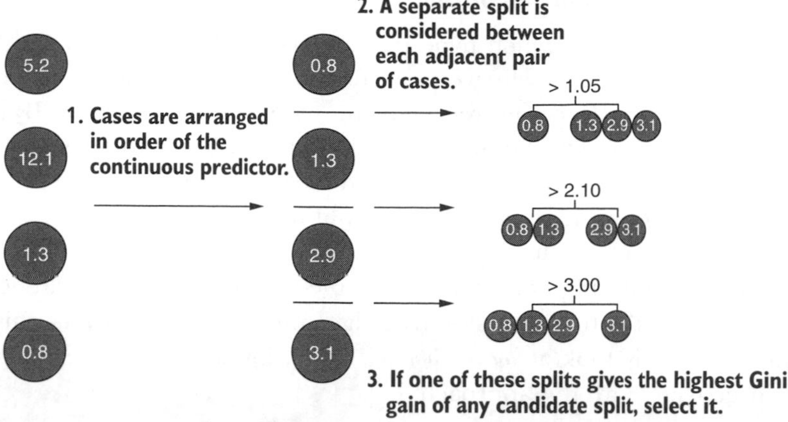

Figure 7.5 How the split point is chosen for continuous predictors. Cases (circles) are arranged in order of their value of the continuous predictor. The midpoint between each adjacent pair of cases is considered as a candidate split, and the Gini gain is calculated for each. If one of these splits has the highest Gini gain of any candidate split, it will be used to split the tree at this node.

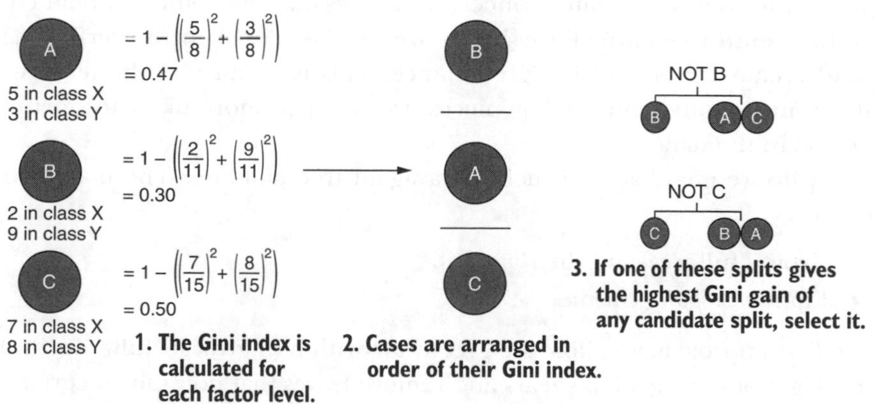

Figure 7.6 How the split point is chosen for categorical predictors. The Gini index of each factor level is calculated using the proportion of cases from each class with that factor level. The factor levels are arranged in order of their Gini indices, and the Gini gain is evaluated for each split between adjacent levels.

to have the greatest Gini gain, then cases reaching this node will go down one branch if they have a value of B for this variable, and will go down the other branch if they have a value of A or C.

7.1.3 Hyperparameters of the rpart algorithm

In this section, I'll show you which hyperparameters need to be tuned for the rpart algorithm, what they do, and why we need to tune them in order to get the best-performing tree possible. Decision tree algorithms are described as *greedy*. By greedy, I don't mean they take an extra helping at the buffet line; I mean they search for the split that will perform best *at the current node*, rather than the one that will produce the best result globally. For example, a particular split might discriminate the classes best at the current node but result in poor separation further down that branch. Conversely, a split that results in poor separation at the current node may yield better separation further down the tree. Decision tree algorithms would never pick this second split because they only look at *locally optimal* splits, instead of *globally optimal* ones. There are three issues with this approach:

- The algorithm isn't guaranteed to learn a globally optimal model.
- If left unchecked, the tree will continue to grow deeper until all the leaves are pure (of only one class).
- For large datasets, growing extremely deep trees becomes computationally expensive.

While it's true that rpart isn't guaranteed to learn a globally optimal model, the depth of the tree is of greater concern to us. Besides the computational cost, growing a full-depth tree until all the leaves are pure is very likely to overfit the training set and create a model with high variance. This is because as the feature space is split up into smaller and smaller pieces, we're much more likely to start modeling the noise in the data.

How do we guard against such extravagant tree building? There are two ways of doing it:

- Grow a full tree, and then *prune* it.
- Employ *stopping criteria.*

In the first approach, we allow the greedy algorithm to grow its full, overfit tree, and then we get out our garden shears and remove leaves that don't meet certain criteria. This process is imaginatively named *pruning*, because we end up removing branches and leaves from our tree. This is sometimes called *bottom-up* pruning because we start from the leaves and prune up toward the root.

In the second approach, we include conditions during tree building that will force splitting to stop if certain criteria aren't met. This is sometimes called *top-down* pruning because we are pruning the tree as it grows down from the root.

Both approaches may yield comparable results in practice, but there is a slight computational edge to top-down pruning because we don't need to grow full trees and then prune them back. For this reason, we will use the stopping criteria approach.

The stopping criteria we can apply at each stage of the tree-building process are as follows:

- Minimum number of cases in a node before splitting
- Maximum depth of the tree
- Minimum improvement in performance for a split
- Minimum number of cases in a leaf

These criteria are illustrated in figure 7.7. For each candidate split during tree building, each of these criteria is evaluated and must be passed for the node to be split further.

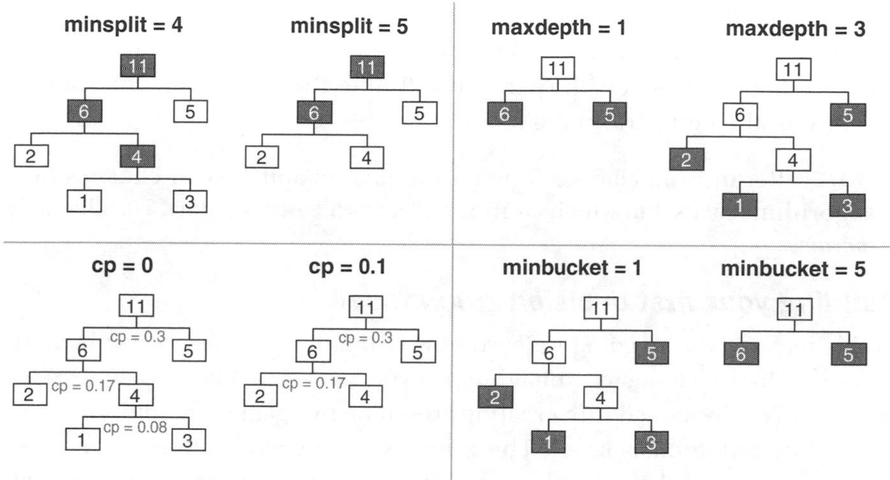

Figure 7.7 Hyperparameters of rpart. Important nodes are highlighted in each example, and the numbers in each node represent the number of cases. The *minsplit*, *maxdepth*, *cp*, and *minbucket* hyperparameters all simultaneously constrain the splitting of each node.

The minimum number of cases needed to split a node is called *minsplit* by rpart. If a node has fewer than the specified number, the node will not be split further. The maximum depth of the tree is called *maxdepth* by rpart. If a node is already at this depth, it will not be split further. The minimum improvement in performance is, confusingly, not the Gini gain of a split. Instead, a statistic called the *complexity parameter* (*cp* in rpart) is calculated for each level of depth of the tree. If the *cp* value of a depth is less than the chosen threshold value, the nodes at this level will not be split further. In other words, if adding another layer to the tree doesn't improve the performance of the model by *cp*, don't split the nodes. The *cp* value is calculated as

$$cp = \frac{p(\text{incorrect}_{l+1}) - p(\text{incorrect}_l)}{n(\text{splits}_l) - n(\text{splits}_{l+1})}$$

where $p(\text{incorrect})$ is the proportion of incorrectly classified cases at a particular depth of the tree, and $n(\text{splits})$ is the number of splits at that depth. The indices l and $l + 1$ indicate the current depth (l) and one depth above ($l + 1$). This reduces to the difference in incorrectly classified cases in one depth compared to the depth above it, divided by the number of new splits added to the tree. If this seems a bit abstract at the moment, we'll work through an example when we build our own decision tree in section 7.7.

Finally, the minimum number of cases in a leaf is called *minbucket* by rpart. If splitting a node would result in leaves containing fewer cases than *minbucket*, the node will not be split.

These four criteria combined can make for very stringent and complicated stopping criteria. Because the values of these criteria cannot be learned directly from the data, they are hyperparameters. What do we do with hyperparameters? Tune them! So when we build a model with rpart, we will tune these stopping criteria to get values that give us the best-performing model.

> **NOTE** Recall from chapter 3 that a variable or option than controls how an algorithm learns, but which cannot be learned from the data, is called a *hyperparameter*.

7.2 Building your first decision tree model

In this section, you're going to learn how to build a decision tree with rpart and how to tune its hyperparameters. Imagine that you work in public engagement at a wildlife sanctuary. You're tasked with creating an interactive game for children, to teach them about different animal classes. The game asks the children to think of any animal in the sanctuary, and then asks them questions about the physical characteristics of that animal. Based on the responses the child gives, the model should tell the child what class their animal belongs to (mammal, bird, reptile, and so on). It's important for your model to be general enough that it can be used at other wildlife sanctuaries. Let's start by loading the mlr and tidyverse packages:

```
library(mlr)
library(tidyverse)
```

7.3 Loading and exploring the zoo dataset

Let's load the zoo dataset that is built into the mlbench package, convert it into a tibble, and explore it. We have a tibble containing 101 cases and 17 variables of observations made on various animals; 16 of these variables are logical, indicating the presence or absence of some characteristic, and the type variable is a factor containing the animal classes we wish to predict.

Listing 7.1 Loading and exploring the zoo dataset

```
data(Zoo, package = "mlbench")

zooTib <- as_tibble(Zoo)

zooTib
```

```
# A tibble: 101 x 17
   hair  feathers eggs  milk  airborne aquatic predator toothed backbone
   <lgl> <lgl>    <lgl> <lgl> <lgl>    <lgl>   <lgl>    <lgl>   <lgl>
 1 TRUE  FALSE    FALSE TRUE  FALSE    FALSE   TRUE     TRUE    TRUE
 2 TRUE  FALSE    FALSE TRUE  FALSE    FALSE   FALSE    TRUE    TRUE
 3 FALSE FALSE    TRUE  FALSE FALSE    TRUE    TRUE     TRUE    TRUE
 4 TRUE  FALSE    FALSE TRUE  FALSE    FALSE   TRUE     TRUE    TRUE
 5 TRUE  FALSE    FALSE TRUE  FALSE    FALSE   TRUE     TRUE    TRUE
 6 TRUE  FALSE    FALSE TRUE  FALSE    FALSE   FALSE    TRUE    TRUE
 7 TRUE  FALSE    FALSE TRUE  FALSE    FALSE   FALSE    TRUE    TRUE
 8 FALSE FALSE    TRUE  FALSE FALSE    TRUE    FALSE    TRUE    TRUE
 9 FALSE FALSE    TRUE  FALSE FALSE    TRUE    TRUE     TRUE    TRUE
10 TRUE  FALSE    FALSE TRUE  FALSE    FALSE   FALSE    TRUE    TRUE
# ... with 91 more rows, and 8 more variables: breathes <lgl>, venomous <lgl>,
#   fins <lgl>, legs <int>, tail <lgl>, domestic <lgl>, catsize <lgl>,
#   type <fct>
```

Unfortunately, mlr won't let us create a task with logical predictors, so let's convert them into factors instead. There are a few ways to do this, but dplyr's `mutate_if()` function comes in handy here. This function takes the data as the first argument (or we could have piped this in with `%>%`). The second argument is our criterion for selecting columns, so here I've used `is.logical` to consider only the logical columns. The final argument is what to do with those columns, so I've used `as.factor` to convert the logical columns into factors. This will leave the existing factor `type` untouched.

Listing 7.2 Converting logical variables to factors

```
zooTib <- mutate_if(zooTib, is.logical, as.factor)
```

TIP Alternatively, I could have used `mutate_all(zooTib, as.factor)`, because the `type` column is already a factor.

7.4 Training the decision tree model

In this section, I'll walk you through training a decision tree model using the rpart algorithm. We'll tune the algorithm's hyperparameters and train a model using the optimal hyperparameter combination.

Let's define our task and learner, and build a model as usual. This time, we supply `"classif.rpart"` as the argument to `makeLearner()` to specify that we're going to use rpart.

Listing 7.3 Creating the task and learner

```
zooTask <- makeClassifTask(data = zooTib, target = "type")

tree <- makeLearner("classif.rpart")
```

Next, we need to perform hyperparameter tuning. Recall that the first step is to define a hyperparameter space over which we want to search. Let's look at the hyperparameters available to us for the rpart algorithm, in listing 7.4. We've already discussed the most important hyperparameters for tuning: *minsplit, minbucket, cp,* and *maxdepth.* There are a few others you may find useful to know about.

The *maxcompete* hyperparameter controls how many candidate splits can be displayed for each node in the model summary. The model summary shows the candidate splits in order of how much they improved the model (Gini gain). It may be useful to understand what the next-best split was after the one that was actually used, but tuning *maxcompete* doesn't affect model performance, only its summary.

The *maxsurrogate* hyperparameter is similar to *maxcompete* but controls how many *surrogate splits* are shown. A surrogate split is a split used if a particular case is missing data for the actual split. In this way, rpart can handle missing data as it learns which splits can be used in place of missing variables. The *maxsurrogate* hyperparameter controls how many of these surrogates to retain in the model (if a case is missing a value for the main split, it is passed to the first surrogate split, then to the second surrogate if it is also missing a value for the first surrogate, and so on). Although we don't have any missing data in our dataset, future cases we wish to predict might. We *could* set this to zero to save some computation time, which is equivalent to not using surrogate variables, but doing so might reduce the accuracy of predictions made on future cases with missing data. The default value of 5 is usually fine.

> **TIP** Recall from chapter 6 that we can quickly count the number of missing values per column of a data.frame or tibble by running `map_dbl(zooTib, ~sum(is.na(.)))`.

The *usesurrogate* hyperparameter controls how the algorithm uses surrogate splits. A value of zero means surrogates will not be used, and cases with missing data will not be classified. A value of 1 means surrogates will be used, but if a case is missing data for the actual split *and* for all the surrogate splits, that case will not be classified. The default value of 2 means surrogates will be used, but a case with missing data for the actual split and for all the surrogate splits will be sent down the branch that contained the most cases. The default value of 2 is usually appropriate.

> **NOTE** If you have cases that are missing data for the actual split *and* all the surrogate splits for a node, you should probably consider the impact missing data is having on the quality of your dataset!

Listing 7.4 Printing available rpart hyperparameters

```
getParamSet(tree)

                   Type len  Def    Constr Req Tunable Trafo
minsplit        integer   -   20 1 to Inf   -    TRUE     -
minbucket       integer   -    - 1 to Inf   -    TRUE     -
cp              numeric   - 0.01   0 to 1   -    TRUE     -
maxcompete      integer   -    4 0 to Inf   -    TRUE     -
maxsurrogate    integer   -    5 0 to Inf   -    TRUE     -
```

```
usesurrogate   discrete      -    2     0,1,2    -    TRUE      -
surrogatestyle discrete      -    0       0,1    -    TRUE      -
maxdepth        integer      -   30   1 to 30    -    TRUE      -
xval            integer      -   10 0 to Inf     -   FALSE      -
parms           untyped      -    -         -    -    TRUE      -
```

Now, let's define the hyperparameter space we want to search over. We're going to tune the values of *minsplit* (an integer), *minbucket* (an integer), *cp* (a numeric), and *maxdepth* (an integer).

NOTE Remember that we use `makeIntegerParam()` and `makeNumericParam()` to define the search spaces for integer and numeric hyperparameters, respectively.

Listing 7.5 Defining the hyperparameter space for tuning

```
treeParamSpace <- makeParamSet(
  makeIntegerParam("minsplit", lower = 5, upper = 20),
  makeIntegerParam("minbucket", lower = 3, upper = 10),
  makeNumericParam("cp", lower = 0.01, upper = 0.1),
  makeIntegerParam("maxdepth", lower = 3, upper = 10))
```

Next, we can define how we're going to search the hyperparameter space we defined in listing 7.5. Because the hyperparameter space is quite large, we're going to use a random search rather than a grid search. Recall from chapter 6 that a random search is not exhaustive (will not try every hyperparameter combination) but will randomly select combinations as many times (iterations) as we tell it to. We're going to use 200 iterations.

In listing 7.6 we also define our cross-validation strategy for tuning. Here, I'm going to use ordinary 5-fold cross-validation. Recall from chapter 3 that this will split the data into five folds and use each fold as the test set once. For each test set, a model will be trained on the rest of the data (the training set). This will be performed for each combination of hyperparameter values tried by the random search.

NOTE Ordinarily, if classes are imbalanced, I would use stratified sampling. Here, though, because we have very few cases in some of the classes, there are not enough cases to stratify (try it: you'll get an error). For this example, we won't stratify; but in situations where you have very few cases in a class, you should consider whether there is enough data to justify keeping that class in the model.

Listing 7.6 Defining the random search

```
randSearch <- makeTuneControlRandom(maxit = 200)

cvForTuning <- makeResampleDesc("CV", iters = 5)
```

Finally, let's perform our hyperparameter tuning!

Listing 7.7 Performing hyperparameter tuning

```
library(parallel)
library(parallelMap)

parallelStartSocket(cpus = detectCores())

tunedTreePars <- tuneParams(tree, task = zooTask,
                            resampling = cvForTuning,
                            par.set = treeParamSpace,
                            control = randSearch)

parallelStop()

tunedTreePars

Tune result:
Op. pars: minsplit=10; minbucket=4; cp=0.0133; maxdepth=9
mmce.test.mean=0.0698
```

To speed things up, we first start parallelization by running `parallelStartSocket()`, setting the number of CPUs equal to the number we have available.

> **TIP** If you want to use your computers for other things while tuning occurs, you may wish to set the number of CPUs used to fewer than the maximum available to you.

Then we use the `tuneParams()` function to start the tuning process. The arguments are the same as we've used previously: the first is the learner, the second is the task, `resampling` is the cross-validation method, `par.set` is the hyperparameter space, and `control` is the search method. Once it's completed, we stop parallelization and print our tuning results.

> **WARNING** This takes about 30 seconds to run on my four-core machine.

The rpart algorithm isn't nearly as computationally expensive as the support vector machine (SVM) algorithm we used for classification in chapter 6. Therefore, despite tuning four hyperparameters, the tuning process doesn't take as long (which means we can perform more search iterations).

7.4.1 Training the model with the tuned hyperparameters

Now that we've tuned our hyperparameters, we can train our final model using them. Just like in the previous chapter, we use the `setHyperPars()` function to create a learner using the tuned hyperparameters, which we access using `tunedTreePars$x`. We can then train the final model using the `train()` function, as usual.

Listing 7.8 Training the final tuned model

```
tunedTree <- setHyperPars(tree, par.vals = tunedTreePars$x)

tunedTreeModel <- train(tunedTree, zooTask)
```

One of the wonderful things about decision trees is how interpretable they are. The easiest way to interpret the model is to draw a graphical representation of the tree. There are a few ways of plotting decision tree models in R, but my favorite is the `rpart.plot()` function from the package of the same name. Let's install the rpart.plot package first and then extract the model data using the `getLearnerModel()` function.

Listing 7.9 Plotting the decision tree

```
install.packages("rpart.plot")

library(rpart.plot)

treeModelData <- getLearnerModel(tunedTreeModel)

rpart.plot(treeModelData, roundint = FALSE,
           box.palette = "BuBn",
           type = 5)
```

The first argument of the `rpart.plot()` function is the model data. Because we trained this model using mlr, the function will give us a warning that it cannot find the data used to train the model. We can safely ignore this warning, but if it irritates you as much as it irritates me, you can prevent it by supplying the argument `roundint = FALSE`. The function will also complain if we have more classes that its default color palette (neediest function ever!). Either ignore this or ask for a different palette by setting the `box.palette` argument equal to one of the predefined palettes (run `?rpart.plot` for a list of available palettes). The `type` argument changes how the tree is displayed. I quite like the simplicity of option 5, but check `?rpart.plot` to experiment with the other options.

The plot generated by listing 7.9 is shown in figure 7.8. Can you see how simple and interpretable the tree is? When predicting the classes of new cases, they start at the top (the root) and follow the branches based on the splitting criterion at each node.

The first node asks whether the animal produces milk or not. This split was chosen because it has the highest Gini gain of all candidate splits (it immediately discriminates mammals, which make up 41% of the training set from the other classes). The leaf nodes tell us which class is classified by that node and the proportions of each class in that node. For example, the leaf node that classifies cases as mollusc.et.al contains 83% mollusc.et.al cases and 17% insect cases. The percentage at the bottom of each leaf indicates the percentage of cases in the training set in this leaf.

To inspect the *cp* values for each split, we can use the `printcp()` function. This function takes the model data as the first argument and an optional `digits` argument specifying how many decimal places to print in the output. There is some useful information in the output, such as the variables actually used for splitting the data and the root node error (the error before any splits). Finally, the output includes a table of the *cp* values for each split.

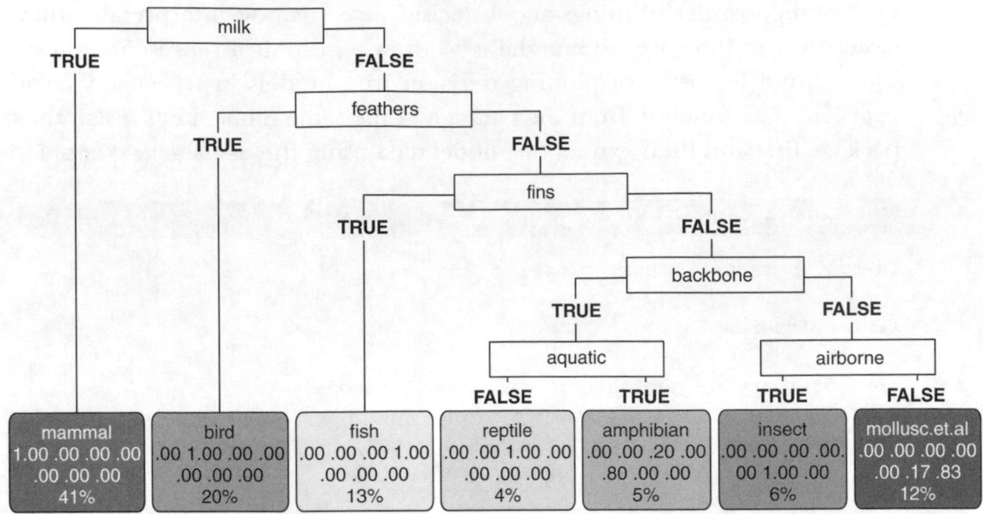

Figure 7.8 Graphical representation of our decision tree model. The splitting criterion is shown for each node. Each leaf node shows the predicted class, the proportion of each of the classes in that leaf, and the proportion of all cases in that leaf.

Listing 7.10 Exploring the model

```
printcp(treeModelData, digits = 3)

Classification tree:
rpart::rpart(formula = f, data = d, xval = 0, minsplit = 7, minbucket = 3,
    cp = 0.0248179216007702, maxdepth = 5)

Variables actually used in tree construction:
[1] airborne aquatic  backbone feathers fins     milk

Root node error: 60/101 = 0.594

n= 101

      CP nsplit rel error
1 0.3333      0     1.000
2 0.2167      1     0.667
3 0.1667      2     0.450
4 0.0917      3     0.283
5 0.0500      5     0.100
6 0.0248      6     0.050
```

Remember that in section 7.1.3, I showed you how the *cp* values were calculated:

$$cp = \frac{p(\text{incorrect}_{l+1}) - p(\text{incorrect}_l)}{n(\text{splits}_l) - n(\text{splits}_{l+1})}$$

So that you can get a better understanding of what the *cp* value means, let's work through how the *cp* values were calculated in the table in listing 7.10.

The *cp* value for the first split is

$$cp = \frac{1.00 - 0.667}{1 - 0} = 0.333$$

The *cp* value for the second split is

$$cp = \frac{0.667 \quad 0.450}{2 - 1} = 0.217$$

and so on. If any candidate split would yield a *cp* value lower than the threshold set by tuning, the node is not split further.

> **TIP** For a detailed summary of the model, run `summary(treeModelData)`. The output is quite long (and gets longer the deeper your tree goes), so I won't print it here. It includes the *cp* table, orders the predictors by their importance, and displays the primary and surrogate splits for each node.

7.5 Cross-validating our decision tree model

In this section, we'll cross-validate our model-building process, including hyperparameter tuning. We've done this a few times already now, but it's so important that I'm going to reiterate: you *must* include data-dependent preprocessing in your cross-validation. This includes the hyperparameter tuning we performed in listing 7.7.

First, we define our outer cross-validation strategy. This time I'm using 5-fold cross-validation as my outer cross-validation loop. We'll use the `cvForTuning` resampling description we made in listing 7.6 for the inner loop.

Next, we create our wrapper by "wrapping together" our learner and hyperparameter tuning process. We supply our inner cross-validation strategy, hyperparameter space, and search method to the `makeTuneWrapper()` function.

Finally, we can start parallelization with the `parallelStartSocket()` function, and start the cross-validation process with the `resample()` function. The `resample()` function takes our wrapped learner, task, and outer cross-validation strategy as arguments.

> **WARNING** This takes about 2 minutes on my four-core machine.

Listing 7.11 Cross-validating the model-building process

```
outer <- makeResampleDesc("CV", iters = 5)

treeWrapper <- makeTuneWrapper("classif.rpart", resampling = cvForTuning,
                               par.set = treeParamSpace,
                               control = randSearch)

parallelStartSocket(cpus = detectCores())
```

```
cvWithTuning <- resample(treeWrapper, zooTask, resampling = outer)

parallelStop()
```

Now let's look at the cross-validation result and see how our model-building process performed.

Listing 7.12 Extracting the cross-validation result

```
cvWithTuning

Resample Result
Task: zooTib
Learner: classif.rpart.tuned
Aggr perf: mmce.test.mean=0.1200
Runtime: 112.196
```

Hmm, that's a little disappointing, isn't it? During hyperparameter tuning, the best hyperparameter combination gave us a mean misclassification error (MMCE) of 0.0698 (you likely got a different value). But our cross-validated estimate of model performance gives us an MMCE of 0.12. Quite a large difference! What's going on? Well, this is an example of overfitting. Our model is performing better during hyperparameter tuning than during cross-validation. This is also a good example of why it's important to include hyperparameter tuning inside our cross-validation procedure.

We've just discovered the main problem with the rpart algorithm (and decision trees in general): they tend to produce models that are overfit. How do we overcome this problem? The answer is to use an *ensemble method*, an approach where we use multiple models to make predictions for a single task. In the next chapter, I'll show you how ensemble methods work, and we'll use them to vastly improve our decision tree model. I suggest that you save your .R file, as we're going to continue using the same dataset and task in the next chapter. This is so I can highlight for you how much better these ensemble techniques are, compared to ordinary decision trees.

7.6 Strengths and weaknesses of tree-based algorithms

While it often isn't easy to tell which algorithms will perform well for a given task, here are some strengths and weaknesses that will help you decide whether decision trees will perform well for you.

The strengths of tree-based algorithms are as follows:

- The intuition behind tree-building is quite simple, and each individual tree is very interpretable.
- It can handle categorical and continuous predictor variables.
- It makes no assumptions about the distribution of the predictor variables.
- It can handle missing values in sensible ways.
- It can handle continuous variables on different scales.

The weakness of tree-based algorithms is this:

- Individual trees are very susceptible to overfitting—so much so that they are rarely used.

Summary

- The rpart algorithm is a supervised learner for both classification and regression problems.
- Tree-based learners start with all the cases in the root node and find sequential binary splits until cases find themselves in leaf nodes.
- Tree construction is a greedy process and can be limited by setting stopping criteria (such as the minimum number of cases required in a node before it can be split).
- The Gini gain is a criterion used to decide which predictor variable will result in the best split at a particular node.
- Decision trees have a tendency to overfit the training set.

8 Improving decision trees with random forests and boosting

This chapter covers

- Understanding ensemble methods
- Using bagging, boosting, and stacking
- Using the random forest and XGBoost algorithms
- Benchmarking multiple algorithms against the same task

In the last chapter, I showed you how we can use the recursive partitioning algorithm to train decision trees that are very interpretable. We finished by highlighting an important limitation of decision trees: they have a tendency to overfit the training set. This results in models that generalize poorly to new data. As a result, individual decision trees are rarely used, but they can become extremely powerful predictors when many trees are combined together.

By the end of this chapter, you'll understand the difference between ordinary decision trees and *ensemble methods,* such as *random forest* and *gradient boosting,* which combine multiple trees to make predictions. Finally, as this is the last chapter in the classification part of the book, you'll learn what *benchmarking* is and how to use it to find the best-performing algorithm for a particular problem. Benchmarking is the process of letting a bunch of different learning algorithms fight it out to select the one that performs best for a particular problem.

We will continue to work with the zoo dataset we were using in the previous chapter. If you no longer have the `zooTib`, `zooTask`, and `tunedTree` objects defined in your global environment (run `ls()` to find out), just rerun listings 7.1 through 7.8 from the previous chapter.

8.1 Ensemble techniques: Bagging, boosting, and stacking

In this section, I'll show you what ensemble methods are and how they can be used to improve the performance of tree-based models. Imagine that you wanted to know what a country's views were on a particular issue. What would you consider to be a better barometer of public opinion: the opinion of a single person you ask on the street, or the collective vote of many people at the ballot box? In this scenario, the decision tree is the single person on the street. You create a single model, pass it new data, and ask its opinion as to what the predicted output should be. Ensemble methods, on the other hand, are the collective vote.

The idea behind ensemble methods is that instead of training a single model, you train multiple models (sometimes hundreds or even thousands of models). Next, you ask the opinion of each of those models as to what the predicted output should be for new data. You then consider the votes from all the models when making the final prediction. The idea is that predictions informed by a majority vote will have less variance than predictions made by a lone model.

There are three different ensemble methods:

- Bootstrap aggregating
- Boosting
- Stacking

Let's discuss each of these in more detail.

8.1.1 Training models on sampled data: Bootstrap aggregating

In this section, I'll explain the principle of the bootstrap aggregating ensemble technique, and how this is used in an algorithm called *random forest.* Machine learning algorithms can be sensitive to noise resulting from outliers and measurement error. If noisy data exists in our training set, then our models are more likely to have high variance when making predictions on future data. How can we train a learner that makes use of all the data available to us, but can look past this noisy data and reduce prediction variance? The answer is to use *b*ootstrap *agg*regat*ing* (or *bagging* for short).

The premise of bagging is quite simple:

1. Decide how many sub-models you're going to train.
2. For each sub-model, randomly sample cases from the training set, with replacement, until you have a sample the same size as the original training set.
3. Train a sub-model on each sample of cases.

4 Pass new data through each sub-model, and let them vote on the prediction.
5 The *modal* prediction (the most frequent prediction) from all the sub-models is used as the predicted output.

The most critical part of bagging is the random sampling of the cases. Imagine that you're playing Scrabble and have the bag of 100 letter tiles. Now imagine that you put your hand into the bag, blindly rummage around a little, pull out a tile, and write down what letter you got. This is taking a random sample. Then, crucially, you put the tile back. This is called *replacement*, and sampling with replacement simply means putting the values back after you've drawn them. This means the same value could be drawn again. You continue to do this until you have drawn 100 random samples, the same number as are in the bag to begin with. This process is called *bootstrapping* and is an important technique in statistics and machine learning. Your bootstrap sample of 100 tiles should do a reasonable job of reflecting the frequencies of each letter in the original bag.

So why does training sub-models on bootstrap samples of the training set help us? Imagine that cases are distributed over their feature space. Each time we take a bootstrap sample, because we are sampling with replacement, we are more likely to select a case near the center of that distribution than a case that lies near the extremes of the distribution. Some of the bootstrap samples may contain many extreme values and make poor predictions on their own, but here's the second crucial part of bagging: we *aggregate* the predictions of all these models. This simply means we let them all make their predictions and then take the majority vote. The effect of this is a sort of averaging out of all the models, which reduces the impact of noisy data and reduces overfitting. Bagging for decision trees is illustrated in figure 8.1.

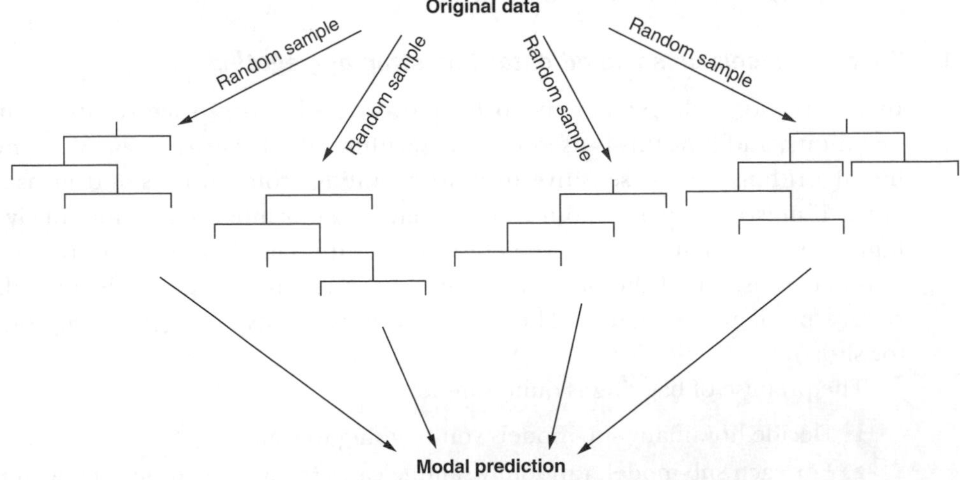

Figure 8.1 Bootstrap aggregating (bagging) with decision trees. Multiple decision trees are learned in parallel, each one trained on a bootstrap sample of cases from the training set. When predicting new data, each tree makes a prediction, and the modal (most frequent) prediction wins.

Bagging (and, as you'll learn, boosting and stacking) is a technique that can be applied to any supervised machine learning algorithm. Having said this, it works best on algorithms that tend to create low-bias, high-variance models, such as decision trees. In fact, there is a famous and very popular implementation of bagging for decision trees called *random forest.* Why is it called random forest? Well, it uses many random samples from the training set to train a decision tree. What do many trees make? A forest!

TIP Although the "no free lunch" theorem still applies (as mentioned in chapter 1), individual decision trees seldom perform better than their random forest counterparts. For this reason, I may build a decision tree to get a broad understanding of the relationships in my data, but I tend to jump straight in with an ensemble technique for predictive modeling.

So the random forest algorithm uses bagging to create a large number of trees. These trees are saved as part of the model; when we pass the model new data, each tree makes its own prediction, and the modal prediction is returned. The random forest algorithm has one extra trick up its sleeve, however. At each node of a particular tree, the algorithm randomly selects a proportion of the predictor variables it will consider for that split. At the next node, the algorithm makes another random selection of predictor variables it will consider for that split, and so on. While this may seem counterintuitive, the result of randomly sampling cases *and* randomly sampling features is to create individual trees that are highly *uncorrelated.*

NOTE If some variables in the data are highly predictive of the outcome, then these variables will be selected as split criteria for many of the trees. Trees that contain the same splits as each other don't contribute any more information. This is why it's desirable to have uncorrelated trees, so that different trees contribute different predictive information. Randomly sampling *cases* reduces the impact that noise and outlying cases have on the model.

8.1.2 Learning from the previous models' mistakes: Boosting

In this section, I'll explain the principle of the boosting ensemble technique and how it is used in algorithms called *AdaBoost, XGBoost,* and others. With bagging, the individual models are trained in parallel. In contrast, boosting is an ensemble technique that, again, trains many individual models, but builds them sequentially. Each additional model seeks to correct the mistakes of the previous ensemble of models.

Just like bagging, boosting can be applied to any supervised machine learning algorithm. However, boosting is most beneficial when using *weak learners* as the submodels. By *weak learner,* I don't mean someone who keeps failing their driving test; I mean a model that only does a little better at making predictions than a random guess. For this reason, boosting has been traditionally applied to shallow decision trees. By *shallow,* I mean a decision tree that doesn't have many levels of depth, or may have only a single split.

NOTE Decision trees with only one split are imaginatively called *decision stumps.* You can see an example of a decision stump if you look back at figure 7.2.

The function of boosting is to combine many weak learners together to form one strong ensemble learner. The reason we use weak learners is that there is no improvement in model performance when boosting with strong learners versus weak learners. So why waste computational resources training hundreds of strong, probably more complex learners, when we can get the same performance by training weak, less complex ones?

There are two methods of boosting, which differ in the way they correct the mistakes of the previous set of models:

- Adaptive boosting
- Gradient boosting

WEIGHTING INCORRECTLY PREDICTED CASES: ADAPTIVE BOOSTING

There is only one well-known adaptive boosting algorithm, which is the famous AdaBoost algorithm published in 1997. AdaBoost works as follows. Initially, all cases in the training set have the same importance, or *weight*. An initial model is trained on a bootstrap sample of the training set where the probability of a case being sampled is proportional to its weight (all equal at this point). The cases that this initial model incorrectly classifies are given more weight/importance, while cases that it correctly classifies are given less weight/importance.

The next model takes another bootstrap sample from the training set, but the weights are no longer equal. Remember that the probability of a case being sampled is proportional to its weight. So, a case with twice as much weight as another case is twice as likely to be sampled (and more likely to be sampled repeatedly). This ensures that cases incorrectly classified by the previous model are more likely to be featured in the bootstrap for the subsequent model. The subsequent model is therefore more likely to learn rules that will correctly classify these cases.

Once we have at least two models, the data are classified based on an aggregated vote, just like in bagging. Cases that are incorrectly classified by the majority vote are then given more weight, and cases that are correctly classified by the majority vote are given less weight. Perhaps slightly confusingly, the models themselves also have a weight. This model weight is based on how many mistakes a particular model makes (more mistakes, less weight). If you only have two models in an ensemble, one of which predicts group A and the other of which predicts group B, the model with the higher weight wins the vote.

This process continues: a new model is added to the ensemble, all the models vote, weights are updated, and the next model samples the data based on the new weights. Once we reach the maximum number of predefined trees, the process stops, and we get our final ensemble model. This is illustrated in figure 8.2. Think about the impact this is having: new models are correcting the mistakes of the previous set of models. This is why boosting is an excellent way of reducing bias. However, just like bagging, it also reduces variance, because we're also taking bootstrap samples! When unseen cases are passed to the final model for prediction, each tree votes individually (like in bagging), but each vote is weighted by the model weight.

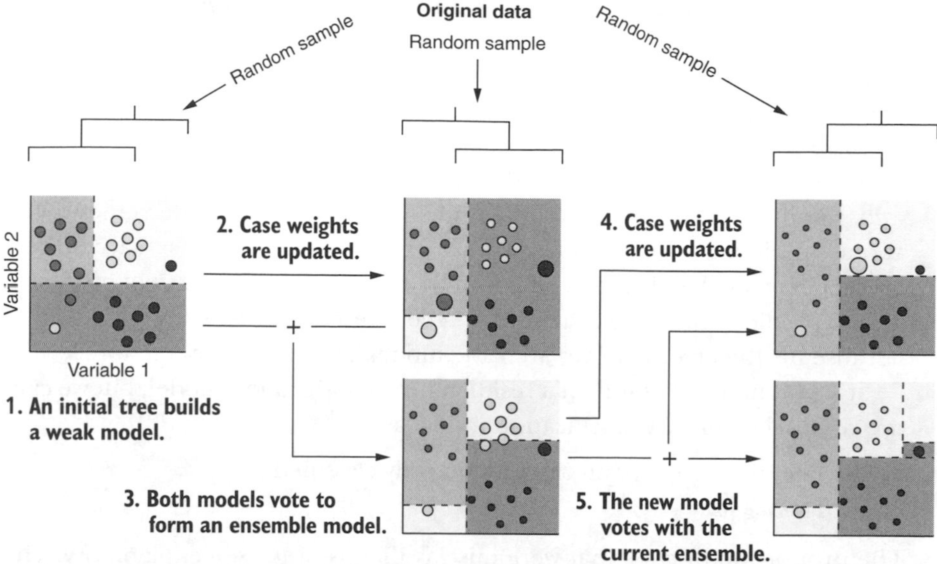

Figure 8.2 Adaptive boosting with decision trees. An initial model is trained on a random sample of the training set. Correctly classified cases get lower weights, while incorrectly classified cases get higher weights (indicated by data point size). The probability of subsequent models sampling each case is proportional to the case's weight. As trees are added, they vote to form an ensemble model, the predictions of which are used to update the weights at every iteration.

How are the model weights and case weights calculated?

The model weight is calculated as

$$\text{model weight} = 0.5 \times \ln\left(\frac{1 - p(\text{incorrect})}{p(\text{incorrect})}\right)$$

where ln is the natural logarithm and *p*(incorrect) is the proportion of incorrectly classified cases.

The case weights are calculated as

$$\text{case weight} = \begin{cases} \text{initial weight} \times e^{-\text{model weight}}; \text{ if correctly classified} \\ \text{initial weight} \times e^{\text{model weight}}; \text{ if incorrectly classified} \end{cases}$$

This notation simply means that for cases correctly classified, we use the formula on the top; and for cases incorrectly classified, we use the formula on the bottom. The only subtle difference is that the model weight is negative for cases that were correctly classified. Plug some numbers into these formulas: you'll find that the formula for correctly classified cases decreases their weight, while the formula for incorrectly classified cases increases it.

LEARNING FROM THE PREVIOUS MODELS' RESIDUALS: GRADIENT BOOSTING

Gradient boosting is very similar to adaptive boosting, only differing in the way it corrects the mistakes of the previous models. Rather than weighting the cases differently depending on the accuracy of their classification, subsequent models try to predict the *residuals* of the previous ensemble of models.

A *residual*, or residual error, is the difference between the true value (the "observed" value) and the value predicted by a model. This is easier to understand when thinking about predicting a continuous variable (regression). Imagine that you're trying to predict how much debt a person has. If an individual has a real debt of $2,500, but our model predicts they have a debt of $2,100, the residual is $400. It's called a residual because it's the error left over after the model has made its prediction.

It's a bit harder to think of a residual for a classification model, but we can quantify the residual error of a classification model as

- The proportion of all cases incorrectly classified
- The *log loss*

The proportion of cases that were misclassified is pretty self-explanatory. The log loss is similar but more greatly penalizes a model that makes incorrect classifications *confidently*. If your friend tells you with "absolute certainty" that Helsinki is the capital of Sweden (it's not), you'd think less of them than if they said they "think it might be" the capital. This is how log loss treats misclassification error. For either method, models that give the correct classifications will have a lower error than those that make lots of misclassifications. Which method is better? Once again it depends, so we'll let hyperparameter tuning choose the best one.

> **NOTE** Using the proportion of misclassified cases as the residual error tends to result in models that are a little more tolerant of a small number of misclassified cases than using the log loss. These measures of residual error that are minimized at each iteration are called *loss functions*.

So in gradient boosting, subsequent models are chosen that minimize the residual error of the previous ensemble of models. By minimizing the residual error, subsequent models will, in effect, favor the correct classification of cases that were previously misclassified (thereby modeling the residuals).

Calculating log loss

It isn't necessary for you to know the formula for log loss, but for math buffs who are interested, it is calculated as

$$\text{log loss} = -\frac{1}{N}\sum_{i=1}^{N}\sum_{k=1}^{K} y_{ik}\ln(p_{ik})$$

where N is the number of cases, K is the number of classes, ln is the natural logarithm, y_{ik} is an indicator as to whether label k is the correct classification for case i, and p_{ik} is the proportion of cases belonging to the same class as case *i* that were correctly classified. We can read this as follows:

1. For every case in the training set:
   a. Take the proportion of cases belonging to the same class as that case that were correctly classified.
   b. Take the natural logarithm of these proportions.
2. Sum these logs.
3. Multiply by –1 / *N*.

Gradient boosting doesn't necessarily train sub-models on samples of the training set. If we choose to sample the training set, the process is called *stochastic gradient boosting* (*stochastic* just means "random," but it is a good word to impress your friends with). Sampling in stochastic gradient descent is usually *without replacement*, which means it isn't a bootstrap sample. We don't need to replace each case during sampling because it's not important to sample cases based on their weights (like in AdaBoost) and there is little impact on performance. Just like for AdaBoost and random forest, it's a good idea to sample the training set, because doing so reduces variance. The proportion of cases we sample from the training set can be tuned as a hyperparameter.

There are a number of gradient boosting algorithms around, but probably the best known is the XGBoost (extreme gradient boosting) algorithm. Published in 2014, XGBoost is an extremely popular classification and regression algorithm. Its popularity is due to how well it performs on a wide range of tasks, as it tends to outperform most other supervised learning algorithms. Many Kaggle (an online community that runs machine learning competitions) data science competitions have been won using XGBoost, and it has become the supervised learning algorithm many data scientists try before anything else.

While XGBoost is an implementation of gradient boosting, it has a few tricks up its sleeve:

- It can build different branches of each tree *in parallel*, speeding up model building.
- It can handle missing data.
- It employs *regularization*. You'll learn more about this in chapter 11, but it prevents individual predictors from having too large of an impact on predictions (this helps to prevent overfitting).

TIP There are even more recent gradient boosting algorithms available, such as LightGBM and CatBoost. These are not currently wrapped by the mlr package, so we'll stick with XGBoost, but feel free to explore them yourself!

8.1.3 Learning from predictions made by other models: Stacking

In this section, I'll explain the principle of the stacking ensemble technique and how it is used to combine predictions from multiple algorithms. Stacking is an ensemble technique that, while valuable, isn't as commonly used as bagging and boosting. For this reason, I won't discuss it in a lot of detail, but if you're interested in learning more, I recommend *Ensemble Methods: Foundations and Algorithms* by Zhi-Hua Zhou (Chapman and Hall/CRC, 2012).

In bagging and boosting, the learners are often (but don't always have to be) *homogeneous.* Put another way, all of the sub-models were learned by the same algorithm (decision trees). Stacking explicitly uses different algorithms to learn the sub-models. For example, we may choose to use the kNN algorithm (from chapter 3), logistic regression algorithm (from chapter 4), and the SVM algorithm (from chapter 6) to build three independent *base models.*

The idea behind stacking is that we create base models that are good at learning different patterns in the feature space. One model may then be good at predicting in one area of the feature space but makes mistakes in another area. One of the other models may do a good job of predicting values in an area of the feature space where the others do poorly. So here's the key in stacking: the predictions made by the base models are used as predictor variables (along with all the original predictors) by another model: the *stacked model.* This stacked model is then able to learn from the predictions made by the base models to make more accurate predictions of its own. Stacking can be tedious and complicated to implement, but it usually results in improved model performance if you use base learners that are different enough from each other.

I hope I've conveyed a basic understanding of ensemble techniques, in particular the random forest and XGBoost algorithms. In the next section, we'll use these two algorithms to train models on our zoo task and see which performs the best!

NOTE Ensemble methods like bagging, boosting, and stacking are not strictly machine learning algorithms in their own right. They are algorithms that can be *applied* to other machine learning algorithms. For example, I've described bagging and boosting here as being applied to decision trees. This is because ensembling is most commonly applied to tree-based learners; but we could just as easily apply bagging and boosting to other machine learning algorithms, such as kNN and linear regression.

8.2 Building your first random forest model

In this section, I'll show you how to build a random forest model (using bootstrapping to train many trees and aggregating their predictions) and how to tune its hyperparameters. There are four important hyperparameters for us to consider:

- *ntree*—The number of individual trees in the forest
- *mtry*—The number of features to randomly sample at each node

- *nodesize*—The minimum number of cases allowed in a leaf (the same as *minbucket* in rpart)
- *maxnodes*—The maximum number of leaves allowed

Because we're aggregating the votes of many trees in random forest, the more trees we have, the better. There is no downside to having more trees aside from computational cost: at some point, we get diminishing returns. Rather than tuning this value, I usually fix it to a number of trees I know fits my computational budget, generally several hundred to the low thousands. Later in this section, I'll show you how to tell if you've used enough trees, or if you can reduce your tree number to speed up training times.

The other three hyperparameters—*mtry*, *nodesize*, and *maxnodes*—will need tuning, though, so let's get started. We'll continue with our `zooTask` that we defined in the last chapter (if you no longer have `zooTask` defined in your global environment, just rerun listings 7.1, 7.2, and 7.3). The first thing to do is create a learner with the `makeLearner()` function. This time, our learner is `"classif.randomForest"`:

```
forest <- makeLearner("classif.randomForest")
```

Next, we'll create the hyperparameter space we're going to tune over. To begin with, we want to fix the number of trees at 300, so we simply specify `lower = 300` and `upper = 300` in its `makeIntegerParam()` call. We have 16 predictor variables in our dataset, so let's search for an optimal value of *mtry* between 6 and 12. Because some of our groups are very small (probably too small), we'll need to allow our leaves to have a small number of cases in them, so we'll tune *nodesize* between 1 and 5. Finally, we don't want to constrain the tree size too much, so we'll search for a *maxnodes* value between 5 and 20.

Listing 8.1 Tuning the random forest hyperparameters

```
forestParamSpace <- makeParamSet(                              # Creates the hyperparameter tuning space
  makeIntegerParam("ntree", lower = 300, upper = 300),
  makeIntegerParam("mtry", lower = 6, upper = 12),
  makeIntegerParam("nodesize", lower = 1, upper = 5),
  makeIntegerParam("maxnodes", lower = 5, upper = 20))

randSearch <- makeTuneControlRandom(maxit = 100)               # Defines a random search method with 100 iterations

cvForTuning <- makeResampleDesc("CV", iters = 5)               # Defines a 5-fold cross-validation strategy

parallelStartSocket(cpus = detectCores())

tunedForestPars <- tuneParams(forest, task = zooTask,          # Tunes the hyperparameters
                              resampling = cvForTuning,
                              par.set = forestParamSpace,
                              control = randSearch)

parallelStop()

tunedForestPars                                                # Prints the tuning results
```

```
Tune result:
Op. pars: ntree=300; mtry=11; nodesize=1; maxnodes=13
mmce.test.mean=0.0100
```

Now let's train a final model by using `setHyperPars()` to make a learner with our tuned hyperparameters, and then passing it to the `train()` function:

```
tunedForest <- setHyperPars(forest, par.vals = tunedForestPars$x)

tunedForestModel <- train(tunedForest, zooTask)
```

How do we know if we've included enough trees in our forest? We can plot the mean *out-of-bag* error against the tree number. When building a random forest, remember that we take a bootstrap sample of cases for each tree. The out-of-bag error is the mean prediction error for each case, by trees that *did not* include that case in their bootstrap. Out-of-bag error estimation is specific to algorithms that use bagging and allows us to estimate the performance of the forest as it grows.

The first thing we need to do is extract the model information using the `getLearnerModel()` function. Then we can simply call `plot()` on this model data object (specifying what colors and linetypes to use for each class). Let's add a legend using the `legend()` function so we know what we're looking at.

Listing 8.2 Plotting the out-of-bag error

```
forestModelData <- getLearnerModel(tunedForestModel)

species <- colnames(forestModelData$err.rate)

plot(forestModelData, col = 1:length(species), lty = 1:length(species))

legend("topright", species,
       col = 1:length(species),
       lty = 1:length(species))
```

The resulting plot is shown in figure 8.3. You won't be able to see the line color in the print version of the book, but you will in the ebook or if you reproduce the plot yourself in R. The plot shows the mean out-of-bag error for each class (separate lines and a line for the mean) against different numbers of trees in the forest. Can you see that once we have at least 100 trees in the forest, our error estimates stabilize? This indicates that we have enough trees in our forest (and could even use fewer). If you train a model and the mean out-of-bag error doesn't stabilize, you should add more trees!

Okay, so we're happy there are enough trees in our forest. Now let's properly cross-validate our model-building procedure, including hyperparameter tuning. We'll start by defining our outer cross-validation strategy as ordinary 5-fold cross-validation.

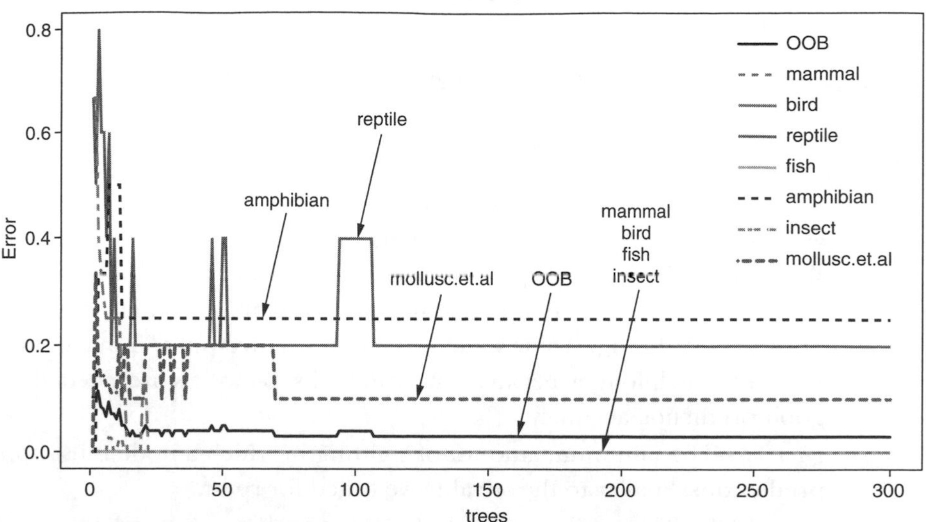

Figure 8.3 Plotting the mean out-of-bag error against tree number. For a given forest size during training, the mean out-of-bag error is plotted on the y-axis for each class (different lines) and for the overall out of bag (OOB) error. The out-of-bag error is the mean prediction error for each case, by trees that *did not* include that case in their bootstrap sample. The y-axis shows the mean out-of-bag error across all cases.

Listing 8.3 Cross-validating the model-building process

```
outer <- makeResampleDesc("CV", iters = 5)

forestWrapper <- makeTuneWrapper("classif.randomForest",
                                 resampling = cvForTuning,
                                 par.set = forestParamSpace,
                                 control = randSearch)

parallelStartSocket(cpus = detectCores())

cvWithTuning <- resample(forestWrapper, zooTask, resampling = outer)

parallelStop()

cvWithTuning

Resample Result
Task: zooTib
Learner: classif.randomForest.tuned
Aggr perf: mmce.test.mean=0.0400
Runtime: 66.1805
```

Wow! Look how much better our random forest model performs compared to our original decision tree (remind yourself by looking at listing 7.12 in the last chapter)!

Bagging has greatly improved our classification accuracy. Next, let's see if XGBoost can do even better.

8.3 Building your first XGBoost model

In this section, I'll show you how to build an XGBoost model and how to tune its hyperparameters. There are eight (!) important hyperparameters for us to consider:

- *eta*—Known as the *learning rate*. This is a number between 0 and 1, which model weights are multiplied by to give their final weight. Setting this value below 1 slows down the learning process because it "shrinks" the improvements made by each additional model. Preventing the ensemble from learning too quickly prevents overfitting. A low value is generally better but will make model training take much longer because many model sub-models are needed to achieve good prediction accuracy.
- *gamma*—The minimum amount of splitting by which a node must improve the predictions. Similar to the *cp* value we tuned for rpart.
- *max_depth*—The maximum levels deep that each tree can grow.
- *min_child_weight*—The minimum degree of impurity needed in a node before attempting to split it (if a node is pure enough, don't try to split it again).
- *subsample*—The proportion of cases to be randomly sampled (without replacement) for each tree. Setting this to 1 uses all the cases in the training set.
- *colsample_bytree*—The proportion of predictor variables sampled for each tree. We could also tune *colsample_bylevel* and *colsample_bynode*, which instead sample predictors for each level of depth in a tree and at each node, respectively.
- *nrounds*—The number of sequentially built trees in the model.
- *eval_metric*—The type of residual error/loss function we're going to use. For multiclass classification, this will either be the proportion of cases that were incorrectly classified (called *merror* by XGBoost) or the log loss (called *mlogloss* by XGBoost).

The first thing to do is create a learner with the `makeLearner()` function. This time, our learner is `"classif.xgboost"`:

```
xgb <- makeLearner("classif.xgboost")
```

Irritatingly, XGBoost only likes to play with numerical predictor variables. Our predictors are currently factors, so we'll need to mutate them into numerics and then define a new task with this mutated tibble. I've used the `mutate_at()` function to convert all the variables except `type` (by setting `.vars = vars(-type)`) into numerics (by setting `.funs = as.numeric`).

Listing 8.4 Converting factors into numerics

```
zooXgb <- mutate_at(zooTib, .vars = vars(-type), .funs = as.numeric)

xgbTask <- makeClassifTask(data = zooXgb, target = "type")
```

NOTE In our example, it doesn't make a difference that our predictors are all numeric. This is because most of our predictors are binary except *legs*, which makes sense as a numeric variable. However, if we have a factor with many discrete levels, does it make sense to treat it as numeric? In theory, no; but in practice, it can work quite well. We simply recode each level of the factor as an arbitrary integer and let the decision tree find the best split for us. This is called *numerical encoding* (and is what we've done to the variables in our dataset). You may have heard of another method of encoding categorical features called *one-hot encoding*. While I won't discuss one-hot encoding here, I want to mention that one-hot encoding factors for tree based models often results in *poor performance*.

Now we can define our hyperparameter space for tuning.

WARNING This takes about 3 minutes on my four-core machine.

Listing 8.5 Tuning XGBoost hyperparameters

```
xgbParamSpace <- makeParamSet(
  makeNumericParam("eta", lower = 0, upper = 1),
  makeNumericParam("gamma", lower = 0, upper = 5),
  makeIntegerParam("max_depth", lower = 1, upper = 5),
  makeNumericParam("min_child_weight", lower = 1, upper = 10),
  makeNumericParam("subsample", lower = 0.5, upper = 1),
  makeNumericParam("colsample_bytree", lower = 0.5, upper = 1),
  makeIntegerParam("nrounds", lower = 20, upper = 20),
  makeDiscreteParam("eval_metric", values = c("merror", "mlogloss")))

randSearch <- makeTuneControlRandom(maxit = 1000)

cvForTuning <- makeResampleDesc("CV", iters = 5)

tunedXgbPars <- tuneParams(xgb, task = xgbTask,
                           resampling = cvForTuning,
                           par.set = xgbParamSpace,
                           control = randSearch)

tunedXgbPars

Tune result:
Op. pars: eta=0.669; gamma=0.368; max_depth=1; min_child_weight=1.26;
subsample=0.993; colsample_bytree=0.847; nrounds=10;
eval_metric=mlogloss; mmce.test.mean=0.0190
```

Because more trees are usually better until we stop seeing a benefit, I don't usually tune the *nrounds* hyperparameter but set it based on my computational budget to start with (here I've set it to 20 by making the `lower` and `upper` arguments the same). Once we've built the model, we can check if the error flattens out after a certain number of trees and decide if we need more or can use fewer (just like we did for the random forest model).

Once we've defined our hyperparameter space, we define our search method as a random search with 1,000 iterations. I like to set the number of iterations as high as I can, especially as we're tuning so many hyperparameters simultaneously. We define our cross-validation strategy as ordinary 5-fold cross-validation and then run the tuning procedure. Because XGBoost will use all of our cores to parallelize the building of each tree (take a look at your CPU usage during hyperparameter tuning), we won't parallelize the tuning procedure as well.

Now let's train our final XGBoost model using our tuned hyperparameters. You should be starting to get familiar with this now. We first use `setHyperPars()` to make a learner, and then pass it to the `train()` function.

Listing 8.6 Training the final tuned model

```
tunedXgb <- setHyperPars(xgb, par.vals = tunedXgbPars$x)

tunedXgbModel <- train(tunedXgb, xgbTask)
```

Let's plot the loss function against the iteration number to get an idea of whether we included enough trees.

Listing 8.7 Plotting iteration number against log loss

```
xgbModelData <- getLearnerModel(tunedXgbModel)

ggplot(xgbModelData$evaluation_log, aes(iter, train_mlogloss)) +
  geom_line() +
  geom_point()
```

First, we extract the model data using `getLearnerModel()`. Next, we can extract a data frame containing the loss function data for each iteration with the `$evaluation_log` component of the model data. This contains the columns `iter` (iteration number) and `train_mlogloss` (the log loss for that iteration). We can plot these against each other to see if the loss has flattened out (indicating that we have trained enough trees).

> **NOTE** My hyperparameter tuning selected log loss as the best loss function. If yours selected classification error, you will need to use `$train_merror` here instead of `$train_mlogloss`.

The resulting plot from listing 8.7 is shown in figure 8.4. Can you see that the log loss flattens out after around 15 iterations? This means we've trained enough trees and aren't wasting computational resources by training too many.

It's also possible to plot the individual trees in the ensemble, which is a nice way of interpreting the model-building process (unless you have a huge number of trees). For this, we need to install the DiagrammeR package first and then pass the model data object as an argument to the XGBoost package function `xgb.plot.tree()`. We can also specify which trees to plot with the `trees` argument.

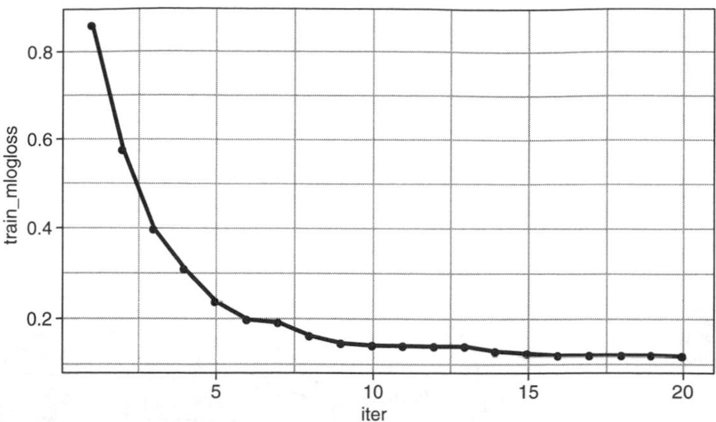

Figure 8.4 Plotting log loss against the number of trees during model building. The curve flattens out after 15 trees, suggesting there is no benefit to adding more trees to the model.

Listing 8.8 Plotting individual decision trees

```
install.packages("DiagrammeR")
xgboost::xgb.plot.tree(model = xgbModelData, trees = 1:5)
```

The resulting graphic is shown in figure 8.5. Notice that the trees we're using are shallow, and some are decision stumps (tree 2 doesn't even have a split).

> **TIP** I won't discuss the information shown in each node in figure 8.5, but for a better understanding you can run `?xgboost::xgb.plot.tree`. You can also represent the final ensemble as a single tree structure by using `xgboost::xgb.plot.multi.trees(xgbModelData)`; this helps you to interpret your model as a whole.

Finally, let's cross-validate our model-building process exactly as we did for our random forest and rpart models.

> **WARNING** This takes nearly 15 minutes on my four-core machine! I strongly suggest you do something else during this time.

Listing 8.9 Plotting individual decision trees

```
outer <- makeResampleDesc("CV", iters = 3)

xgbWrapper <- makeTuneWrapper("classif.xgboost",
                              resampling = cvForTuning,
                              par.set = xgbParamSpace,
                              control = randSearch)

cvWithTuning <- resample(xgbWrapper, xgbTask, resampling = outer)

cvWithTuning
```

```
Resample Result
Task: zooXgb
Learner: classif.xgboost.tuned
Aggr perf: mmce.test.mean=0.0390
Runtime: 890.29
```

Phenomenal! The cross-validation estimates that our model has an accuracy of 1 – 0.039 = 0.961 = 96.1%! Go XGBoost!

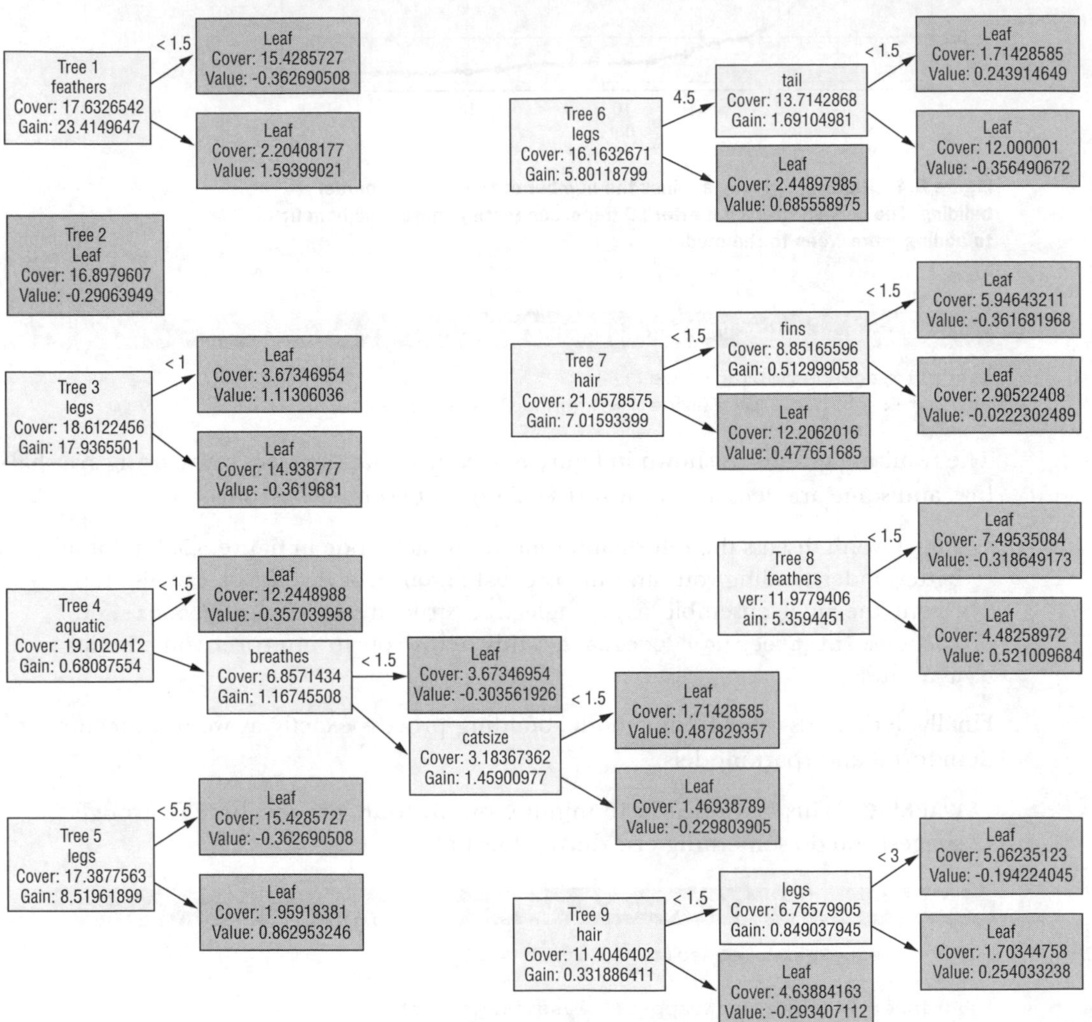

Figure 8.5 Plotting individual trees from our XGBoost model

8.4 Strengths and weaknesses of tree-based algorithms

While it often isn't easy to tell which algorithms will perform well for a given task, here are some strengths and weaknesses that will help you decide whether random forest or XGBoost will perform well for you.

The strengths of the random forest and XGBoost algorithms are as follows:

- They can handle categorical and continuous predictor variables (though XGBoost requires some numerical encoding).
- They make no assumptions about the distribution of the predictor variables.
- They can handle missing values in sensible ways.
- They can handle continuous variables on different scales.
- Ensemble techniques can drastically improve model performance over individual trees. XGBoost in particular is excellent at reducing both bias and variance.

The weaknesses of tree-based algorithms are these:

- Random forest reduces variance compared to rpart but does not reduce bias (XGBoost reduces both).
- XGBoost can be computationally expensive to tune because it has many hyperparameters and grows trees sequentially.

8.5 Benchmarking algorithms against each other

In this section, I'll teach you what *benchmarking* is, and we'll use it to compare the performance of several algorithms on a particular task. The classification drawer of your toolbox has lots of algorithms in it now! Experience is a great way to choose an algorithm for a particular task. But remember, we are always subject to the "no free lunch" theorem. You may find yourself surprised sometimes that a simpler algorithm outperforms a more complex one for a particular task. A good way of deciding which algorithm will perform best on a particular task is to perform a *benchmarking* experiment.

Benchmarking is simple. You create a list of learners you're interested in trying, and let them fight it out to find the one that learns the best-performing model. Let's do this with `xgbTask`.

Listing 8.10 Plotting individual decision trees

```
learners = list(makeLearner("classif.knn"),
                makeLearner("classif.LiblineaRL1LogReg"),
                makeLearner("classif.svm"),
                tunedTree,
                tunedForest,
                tunedXgb)

benchCV <- makeResampleDesc("RepCV", folds = 10, reps = 5)

bench <- benchmark(learners, xgbTask, benchCV)
```

```
bench

  task.id                  learner.id mmce.test.mean
1  zooXgb                 classif.knn        0.03182
2  zooXgb classif.LiblineaRL1LogReg        0.09091
3  zooXgb                 classif.svm        0.07109
4  zooXgb               classif.rpart        0.09891
5  zooXgb        classif.randomForest        0.03200
6  zooXgb             classif.xgboost        0.04564
```

First, we create a list of learner algorithms including k-nearest neighbors (`"classif.knn"`), multinomial logistic regression (`"classif.LiblineaRL1LogReg"`), support vector machine (`"classif.svm"`), our `tunedTree` model that we trained in the previous chapter, and the `tunedForest` and `tunedXgb` models that we trained in this chapter. If you no longer have the `tunedTree` model defined in your global environment, rerun listings 7.1 through 7.8.

> **NOTE** This isn't quite a fair comparison, because the first three learners will be trained using default hyperparameters, whereas the tree-based models have been tuned.

We define our cross-validation method using `makeResampleDesc()`. This time, I've opted for 10-fold cross-validation repeated 5 times. It's important to note that mlr is clever here: while the data is partitioned randomly into folds for each repeat, *the same partitioning* is used for every learner. Put more plainly, for each cross-validation repeat, each learner in the benchmark gets exactly the same training set and test set.

Finally, we use the `benchmark()` function to run the benchmark experiment. The first argument is the list of learners, the second argument is the name of the task, and the third argument is the cross-validation method.

What did I tell you about no free lunches? The humble k-nearest neighbors is performing better on this task than the mighty XGBoost algorithm—even though we didn't tune it!

Summary

- The random forest and XGBoost algorithms are supervised learners for both classification and regression problems.
- Ensemble techniques construct multiple sub-models to result in a model that performs better than any one of its components alone.
- Bagging is an ensemble technique that trains multiple sub-models in parallel on bootstrap samples of the training set. Each sub-model then votes on the prediction for new cases. Random forest is an example of a bagging algorithm.
- Boosting is an ensemble technique that trains multiple sub-models sequentially, where each subsequent sub-model focuses on the mistakes of the previous set of sub-models. AdaBoost and XGBoost are examples of boosting algorithms.
- Benchmarking allows us to compare the performance of multiple algorithms/models on a single task.

Part 3

Regression

Take a moment to look back on what you've learned so far. Assuming you've completed parts 1 and 2 of this book, you now possess the skills you need to tackle a large range of classification problems. In this part of the book, we'll shift our focus from predicting categorical variables to predicting continuous ones.

As you learned in chapter 1, we use the term *regression* for supervised machine learning that predicts a continuous outcome variable. In chapters 9 through 12, you're going to learn a variety of regression algorithms that will help you deal with different data situations. Some of them are suited to situations in which there are linear relationships between predictor variables and your outcome, and are highly interpretable. Others are able to model nonlinear relationships but may not be quite so interpretable.

We'll start by covering linear regression—which, as you'll learn, is closely related to the logistic regression we worked with in chapter 4. In fact, if you're already familiar with linear regression, you may be wondering why I've waited until now to cover linear regression, when the theory of logistic regression is built on it. It's because to make your learning more simple and enjoyable, I wanted to cover classification, regression, dimension reduction, and clustering separately, so each of these topics is distinct in your mind. But I hope the theory we'll cover in this next part will solidify your understanding of logistic regression.

Regression

9 Linear regression

This chapter covers

- Working with linear regression
- Performance metrics for regression tasks
- Using machine learning algorithms to impute missing values
- Performing feature selection algorithmically
- Combining preprocessing wrappers in mlr

Our first stop in part 3, "Regression," brings us to *linear regression.* A classical and commonly used statistical method, linear regression builds predictive models by estimating the strength of the relationship between our predictor variables and our outcome variable. Linear regression is so named because it assumes the relationships between the predictor variables with the outcome variable are linear. Linear regression can handle both continuous and categorical predictor variables, and I'll show you how in this chapter.

By the end of this chapter, I hope you'll understand a general approach to regression problems with mlr, and how this differs from classification. In particular, you'll understand the different performance metrics we use for regression tasks, because mean misclassification error (MMCE) is no longer meaningful. I'll also show you, as I promised in chapter 4, more sophisticated approaches to missing value imputation and feature selection. Finally, I'll cover how to combine as many preprocessing steps as we like using sequential wrappers, so we can include them in our cross-validation.

9.1 What is linear regression?

In this section, you'll learn what linear regression is and how it uses the equation of a straight line to make predictions. Imagine that you want to predict the pH of batches of cider, based on the amount of apple content in each batch (in kilograms). An example of what this relationship might look like is shown in figure 9.1.

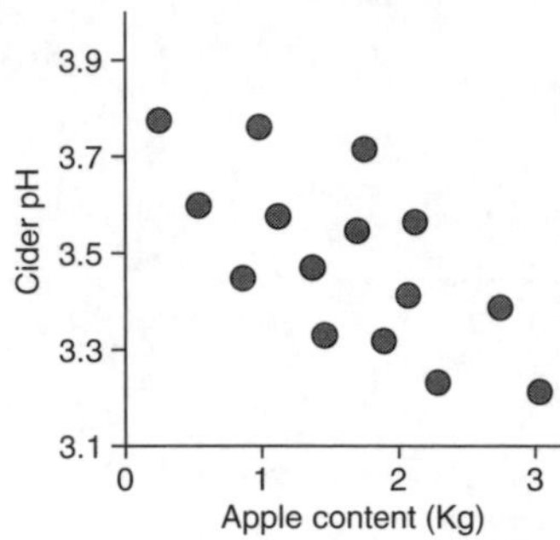

Figure 9.1 Imaginary data of how the pH of cider batches changes with apple content

> **NOTE** Recall from high school chemistry that the lower the pH, the more acidic a substance is.

The relationship between apple weight and cider pH appears linear, and we could model this relationship using a straight line. Recall from chapter 1 that the only parameters needed to describe a straight line are the slope and intercept:

$$y = \text{intercept} + \text{slope} \times x$$

y is the outcome variable, x is the predictor variable, the intercept is the value of y when x is zero (where the line crosses the y-axis), and the slope is how much y changes when x increases by one unit.

> **NOTE** Interpreting the slope is useful because it tells us about how the outcome variable changes with the predictor(s), but interpreting the intercept is usually not so straightforward (or useful). For example, a model that predicts a spring's tension from its length might have a positive intercept, suggesting that a spring of zero length has tension! If all the variables are centered to have a mean of zero, then the intercept can be interpreted as the value of y at the mean of x (which is often more useful information). Centering your variables like this doesn't affect the slopes because the relationships between variables remain the same. Therefore, predictions made by linear regression models are unaffected by centering and scaling your data.

If you were to read this out loud in plain English, you would say: "For any particular case, the value of the outcome variable, *y*, is the model intercept, plus the value of the predictor variable, *x*, times its slope."

Statisticians write this equation as

$$y = \beta_0 + \beta_1 x_1 + \varepsilon$$

where β_0 is the intercept, β_1 is the slope for variable x_1, and ε is the unobserved error unaccounted for by the model.

> **NOTE** The parameters (also called *coefficients*) of a linear regression model are only estimates of the true values. This is because we are typically only working with a finite sample from the wider population. The only way to derive the true parameter values would be to measure the entire population, something that is usually impossible.

So to learn a model that can predict pH from apple weight, we need a way to estimate the intercept and slope of a straight line that best represents this relationship.

Linear regression isn't technically an algorithm. Rather, it's the approach to modeling relationships using the straight-line equation. We could use a few different algorithms to estimate the intercept and slope of a straight line. For simple situations like our cider pH problem, the most common algorithm is *ordinary least squares* (OLS).

The job of OLS is to learn the combination of values for the intercept and slope that minimizes the *residual sum of squares.* We came across the concept of a residual in chapter 7 as the amount of information left unexplained by a model. In linear regression, we can visualize this as the vertical distance (along the y-axis) between a case and the straight line. But OLS doesn't just consider the raw distances between each case and the line: it squares them first and then adds them all up (hence, *sum* of *squares*). This is illustrated for our cider example in figure 9.2.

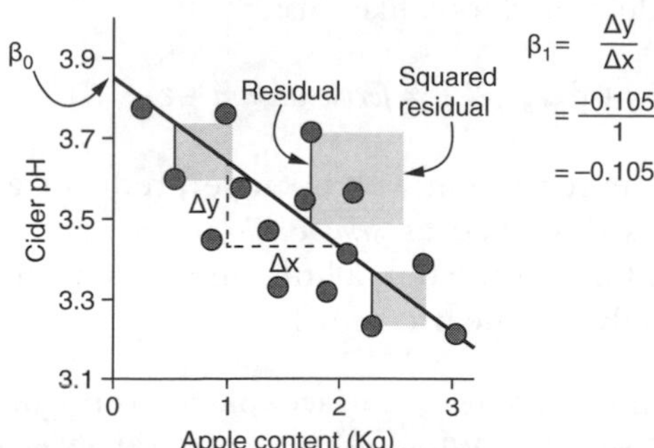

Figure 9.2 Finding the least squares line through the data. Residuals are the vertical distances between the cases and the line. The area of the boxes represents the squared residuals for three of the cases. The intercept (β_0) is where the line hits the y-axis when x = 0. The slope is the change in y (Δy) divided by the change in x (Δx).

Why does OLS square the distances? You may read that this is because it makes any negative residuals (for cases that lie below the line) positive, so they contribute to the sum of squares rather than subtract from it. This is certainly a handy by-product of squaring, but if that was true, we would simply use |*residual*| to denote the *absolute* value (removing the negative sign). We use the squared residuals so that we disproportionately penalize cases that are far away from their predicted value.

9.1.1 What if we have multiple predictors?

OLS finds the combination of slope and intercept that minimizes the sum of squares, and the line learned in this way will be the one that best fits the data. But regression problems are rarely as simplistic as trying to predict an outcome with a single predictor; what about when we have multiple predictor variables? Let's add another variable to our cider pH problem: fermentation time (see figure 9.3).

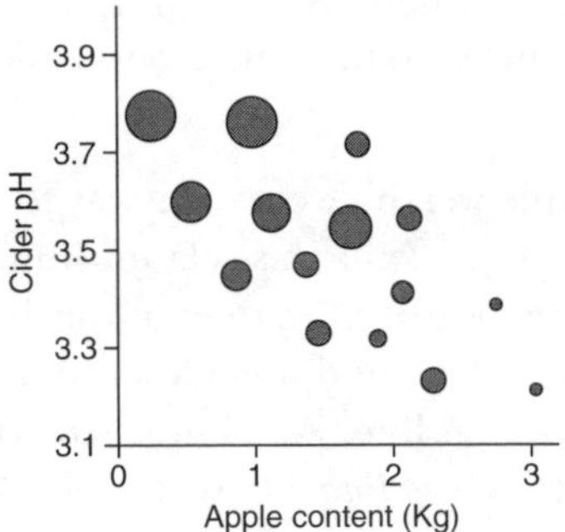

Figure 9.3 Adding an additional variable: the size of each dot corresponds to the fermentation time of each cider batch.

When we have multiple predictors, a slope is estimated for each (using OLS), and the contributions of each variable are added together linearly, along with the model intercept (which is now the value of y when each predictor equals zero). The slopes in linear regression tell us how the outcome variable changes for a one-unit increase in each predictor *while holding all other predictors constant.* In other words, the slopes tell us how the outcome changes when we change the predictor variables, one at a time. For example, our two-predictor cider model would look like this:

$$y = \beta_0 + \beta_{apples} \times apples + \beta_{fermentation} \times fermentation + \varepsilon$$

NOTE You will sometimes see linear regression with a single predictor and regression with multiple predictors described as *simple linear regression* and *multiple regression*, respectively. I find this distinction a little unnecessary, however, because we rarely work with only a single predictor.

When we have two predictors, our line becomes a surface/plane. You can see this illustrated for our cider example in figure 9.4. When we have more than two predictors, our plane becomes a hyperplane. Indeed, our straight-line equation can be generalized to any number of predictors

$$y = \beta_0 + \beta_1 x_1 + \beta_2 x_2 \ldots \beta_k x_k + \varepsilon$$

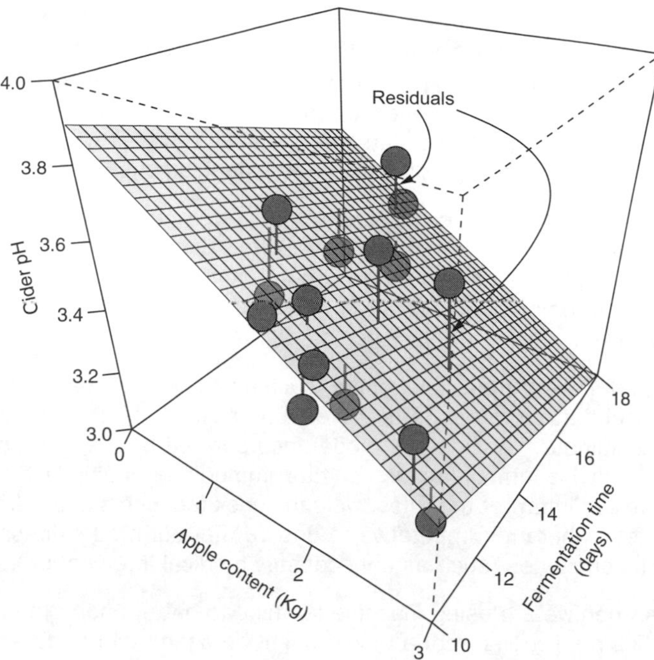

Figure 9.4 Representing a linear model with two predictors. Combining apple content and fermentation time in our linear model can be represented as a surface. The solid lines show the residual error for each case (its vertical distance from the surface).

where there are *k* predictors in the model. This is called the *general linear model*, and it is the central equation of all linear models. If you're coming from a traditional statistical modeling background, you may be familiar with *t* tests and analysis of variance. These approaches all use the general linear model to represent the relationships between the predictor variables and the outcome.

> **NOTE** The general linear model is not quite the same as the *generalized linear model*, which refers to a class of models that allow different distributions for the outcome variable. I'll talk about the generalized linear model soon.

Do you recognize the general linear model? You saw something similar to it when we covered logistic regression in chapter 4. In fact, everything on the right side of the equation is identical. The only difference is what was on the left side of the equals sign. Recall that in logistic regression, we predict the log odds of a case belonging to a particular class. In linear regression, we simply predict the case's value of the outcome variable.

When interpretability is as or more important than performance

While another regression algorithm may perform better for a particular task, models formulated using the general linear model are often favored for how interpretable they are. The slopes tell you how much the outcome variable changes with a one-unit increase of each predictor variable, holding all other variables constant.

There are other algorithms that may learn models that perform better on a particular task but aren't as interpretable. Such models are often described as being black boxes, where the model takes input and gives output, but it's not easy to see and/or interpret the rules inside the model that led to that particular output. Random forest, XGBoost, and SVMs are examples of black-box models.

So when would we prefer an interpretable model (such as a linear regression model), over a black-box model that performs better? Well, one example is if our model has the potential to discriminate. Imagine if a model incorporated bias against women during training. It might be difficult to detect this immediately using a black-box model, whereas if we can interpret the rules, we can check for such biases. A similar consideration is safety, where it's imperative to ensure that our model doesn't give potentially dangerous outcomes (such as unnecessary medical intervention).

Another example is when we are using machine learning to better understand a system or nature. Getting predictions from a model might be useful, but understanding those rules to deepen our understanding and stimulate further research may be of more importance. Black boxes can make this difficult.

Finally, understanding the rules of our model allows us to make changes in the way we do things. Imagine that a business uses a linear regression model to predict demand for a particular product, based on things like its cost and how much the company spends on advertising. Not only can the company predict future demand, but it also can control it, by interpreting the rules of how the predictor variables impact the outcome.

When modeling our data with the general linear model, we make the assumption that our residuals are normally distributed and *homoscedastic*. Homoscedastic is a ridiculous-sounding word (impress your friends with it) that simply means the variance of the outcome variable doesn't increase as the predicted value of the outcome increases.

TIP The opposite of homoscedastic is *heteroscedastic*.

We also make the assumption that there is a linear relationship between each predictor variable and the outcome, and that the effects of the predictor variables on the response variable are additive (rather than multiplicative).

When these assumptions are valid, our model will make more accurate and unbiased predictions. However, the general linear model can be extended to handle situations in which the assumption of normally distributed residuals is violated (logistic regression is one such example).

NOTE I'll show you how we can check the validity of these assumptions when we build our own linear regression model later in the chapter.

In situations such as this, we turn to the *generalized linear model*. The generalized linear model is the same as the general linear model (in fact, the latter is a special case of the former), except that it uses various transformations called *link functions* to map the outcome variable to the linear predictions made by the right-hand side of the equals sign. For example, count data is rarely normally distributed, but by building a generalized model with an appropriate link function, we can transform linear predictions made by the model back into counts. I don't intend to talk any further about generalized linear models here, but a good resource on this topic (if a little heavy) is *Generalized Linear Models With Examples in R* by Peter K. Dunn and Gordon K. Smyth (Springer, 2018).

TIP If the residuals are heteroscedastic, it sometimes helps to build a model that predicts some transformation of the outcome variable instead. For example, predicting the $\log_{10}$ of the response variable is a common choice. Predictions made by such a model can then be transformed back onto the original scale for interpretation. When the effect of multiple predictors on the outcome is not additive, we can add *interaction* terms to our model that state the effect of one predictor variable has on the outcome when the other predictor variable changes.

9.1.2 What if our predictors are categorical?

So far, we've only considered the situation where our predictors are continuous. Because the general linear model is essentially the equation of a straight line, and we use it to find the slopes between variables, how can we find the slope of a categorical variable? Does this even make sense? Well, it turns out we can cheat by recoding categorical variables into *dummy variables*. Dummy variables are new representations of categorical variables that map the categories to 0 and 1.

Imagine that we want to predict the acidity of cider batches based on the type of apple: Gala or Braeburn. We want to find the intercept and slope that describes the relationship between these two apple types and acidity, but how do we do that? Remember earlier that the slope is how much y increases when x increases by one unit. If we recode our apple type variable such that Gala = 0 and Braeburn = 1, we can treat apple type as a continuous variable and find how much acidity changes as we go from 0 to 1. Take a look at figure 9.5: the intercept is the value of y when x is 0, which is the mean acidity when apple type = Gala. Gala is therefore said to be our *reference level*. The slope is the change in y with a one-unit increase in x, which is the difference between the mean acidity for Gala and the mean acidity with Braeburn. This may feel like cheating, but it works, and the slope with the least squares will be the one that connects the means of the categories.

NOTE Which category you choose as the reference level makes no difference to the predictions made by a model and is the first level of the factor (the first alphabetically by default).

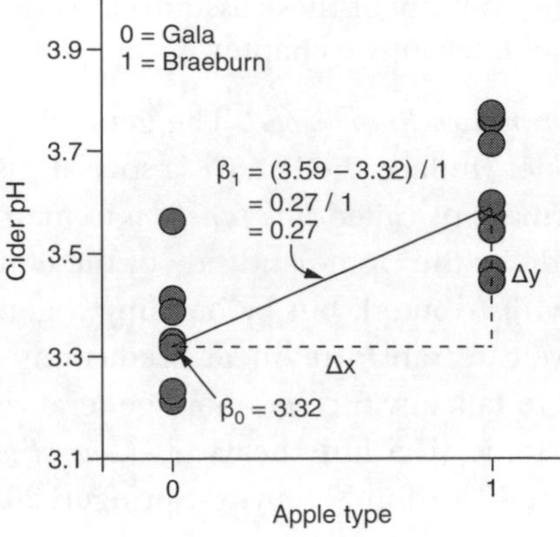

Figure 9.5 Finding the slope between two levels of a categorical variable using a dummy variable. The apple types are recoded as 0 and 1 and treated as a continuous variable. The slope now represents the difference in means between the two apple types, and the intercept represents the mean of the reference category (Gala).

Recoding dichotomous (two-level) factors into a single dummy variable with values of 0 and 1 makes sense, but what if we have a *polytomous* factor (a factor with more than two levels)? Do we code them as 1, 2, 3, 4, and so on, and treat this as a single continuous predictor? Well, this wouldn't work because it's unlikely that a single straight line would connect the means of the categories. Instead, we create $k - 1$ dummy variables, where k is the number of levels of the factor.

Take a look at the example in figure 9.6. We have four types of apples (Granny Smith is my favorite) and would like to predict pH based on the apple type used to make a particular batch of cider. To convert our four-level factor into dummy variables, we do the following:

1. Create a table of three columns, where each column represents a dummy variable.
2. Choose a reference level (Gala, in this case).
3. Set the value of each dummy variable to 0 for the reference level.
4. Set the value of each dummy variable to 1 for a particular factor level.

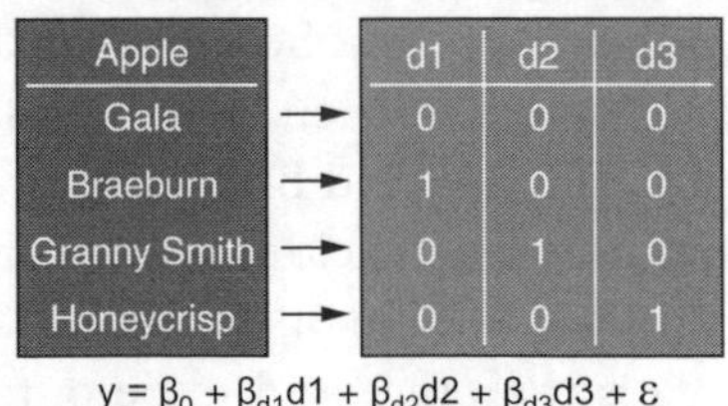

Figure 9.6 Recoding a polytomous categorical variable into $k - 1$ dummy variables. A four-level factor can be represented using three ($k - 1$) dummy variables. The reference level (Gala) has a value of 0 for each dummy variable. The other levels have a value of 1 for a particular dummy variable. A slope is estimated for each dummy.

We've now turned our single variable of four levels into three distinct dummy variables that each take a value of 1 or 0. But how does this help us? Well, each dummy variable acts as a flag in the model formula to denote which level a particular case belongs to. The full model as shown in figure 9.6 is

$$y = \beta_0 + \beta_{d1}\, d1 + \beta_{d2}\, d2 + \beta_{d3}\, d3 + \varepsilon$$

Now, because the intercept (β_0) represents acidity when all predictors are equal to 0, this is now the mean of the reference level, Gala. The slopes in the model β_{d1}, β_{d2}, and so on) represent the difference between the mean of the reference level and the means of each of the other levels. If a batch of cider was made with a particular type of apple, its dummy variables will "switch on" the slope between that type of apple and the reference class, and "switch off" the others. For example, let's say a particular batch was made with Braeburn apples. The model would look like this:

$$y = \beta_0 + \beta_{d1} \times 1 + \beta_{d2} \times 0 + \beta_{d3} \times 0 + \varepsilon$$

The slopes of the other apple types are still in the model, but because their dummy variables are set to 0, they make no contribution to the predicted value!

Models we build using the general linear model can mix both continuous and categorical predictors together. When we use our model to make predictions on new data, we simply do the following:

1. Take the values of each of the predictor variables for that data.
2. Multiply these values with the relevant slopes learned by the model.
3. Add these values together.
4. Add the intercept.

The result is our predicted value for that data.

I hope by now you have a basic understanding of linear regression, so let's turn this knowledge into skills by building your first linear regression model!

9.2 Building your first linear regression model

In this section, I'll teach you how to build, evaluate, and interpret a linear regression model to predict daily air pollution. I'll also show other ways of imputing missing data and selecting relevant features, and how to bundle as many preprocessing steps into your cross-validation as you like.

Imagine that you're an environmental scientist interested in predicting daily levels of atmospheric ozone pollution in Los Angeles. Recall from high school chemistry that ozone is an *allotrope* (a fancy way of saying "another form") of oxygen molecule that has three oxygen atoms instead of two (as in the dioxygen that you're breathing right now). While ozone in the stratosphere protects us from the sun's UV rays, products from burning fossil fuels can be converted into ozone at ground level, where it is toxic. Your job is to build a regression model that can predict ozone pollution levels based on the time of year and meteorological readings, such as humidity and temperature. Let's start by loading the mlr and tidyverse packages:

```
library(mlr)

library(tidyverse)
```

9.2.1 Loading and exploring the Ozone dataset

Now let's load the data, which is built into the mlbench package (I like the data examples in this package), convert it into a tibble (with `as_tibble()`), and explore it. We're also going to give more readable names to the variables. We have a tibble containing 366 cases and 13 variables of daily meteorological and ozone readings.

Listing 9.1 Loading and exploring the `Ozone` dataset

```
data(Ozone, package = "mlbench")

ozoneTib <- as_tibble(Ozone)

names(ozoneTib) <- c("Month", "Date", "Day", "Ozone", "Press_height",
                     "Wind", "Humid", "Temp_Sand", "Temp_Monte",
                     "Inv_height", "Press_grad", "Inv_temp", "Visib")

ozoneTib

# A tibble: 366 x 13
   Month Date  Day   Ozone Press_height  Wind Humid Temp_Sand Temp_Monte
   <fct> <fct> <fct> <dbl>        <dbl> <dbl> <dbl>     <dbl>      <dbl>
 1 1     1     4         3         5480     8    20        NA       NA
 2 1     2     5         3         5660     6    NA        38       NA
 3 1     3     6         3         5710     4    28        40       NA
 4 1     4     7         5         5700     3    37        45       NA
 5 1     5     1         5         5760     3    51        54       45.3
 6 1     6     2         6         5720     4    69        35       49.6
 7 1     7     3         4         5790     6    19        45       46.4
 8 1     8     4         4         5790     3    25        55       52.7
 9 1     9     5         6         5700     3    73        41       48.0
10 1     10    6         7         5700     3    59        44       NA
# ... with 356 more rows, and 4 more variables: Inv_height <dbl>,
#   Press_grad <dbl>, Inv_temp <dbl>, Visib <dbl>
```

At present, the `Month`, `Day`, and `Date` variables are factors. Arguably this may make sense, but we're going to treat them as numerics for this exercise. To do this, we use the handy `mutate_all()` function, which takes the data as the first argument and a transformation/function as the second argument. Here, we use `as.numeric` to convert all the variables into the numeric class.

NOTE The `mutate_all()` function doesn't alter the names of the variables, it just transforms them in place.

Next, we have some missing data in this dataset (use `map_dbl(ozoneTib, ~sum(is.na(.)))` to see how many). Missing data is okay in our predictor variables (we'll deal with this later using imputation), but missing data for the variable we're trying to predict is not okay. Therefore, we remove the cases without any ozone measurement by piping the result of the `mutate_all()` call into the `filter()` function, where we remove cases with an `NA` value for `Ozone`.

Listing 9.2 Cleaning the data

```
ozoneClean <- mutate_all(ozoneTib, as.numeric) %>%
  filter(is.na(Ozone) == FALSE)

ozoneClean

# A tibble: 361 x 13
   Month  Date   Day Ozone Press_height  Wind Humid Temp_Sand Temp_Monte
   <dbl> <dbl> <dbl> <dbl>        <dbl> <dbl> <dbl>     <dbl>      <dbl>
 1     1     1     4     3         5480     8    20        NA         NA
 2     1     2     5     3         5660     6    NA        38         NA
 3     1     3     6     3         5710     4    28        40         NA
 4     1     4     7     5         5700     3    37        45         NA
 5     1     5     1     5         5760     3    51        54       45.3
# ... with 356 more rows, and 4 more variables: Inv_height <dbl>,
#   Press_grad <dbl>, Inv_temp <dbl>, Visib <dbl>
```

NOTE Could we have imputed missing data in our target variable? Yes we could, but this has the potential to introduce bias into our model. This is because we'll be training a model to predict values that were themselves generated by a model.

Let's plot each of our predictor variables against `Ozone` to get an idea of the relationships in the data. We start with our usual trick of gathering the variables with the `gather()` function so we can plot them on separate facets.

Listing 9.3 Plotting the data

```
ozoneUntidy <- gather(ozoneClean, key = "Variable",
                      value = "Value", -Ozone)

ggplot(ozoneUntidy, aes(Value, Ozone)) +
  facet_wrap(~ Variable, scale = "free_x") +
  geom_point() +
  geom_smooth() +
  geom_smooth(method = "lm", col = "red") +
  theme_bw()
```

NOTE Remember we have to use `-Ozone` to prevent the `Ozone` variable from being gathered with the others.

In our `ggplot()` call, we facet by `Variable` and allow the x-axes of the facets to vary by setting the `scale` argument equal to `"free_x"`. Then, along with a `geom_point` layer, we add two `geom_smooth` layers. The first `geom_smooth` is given no arguments and so uses the default settings. By default, `geom_smooth` will draw a LOESS curve to the data (a curvy, local regression line) if there are fewer than 1,000 cases, or a GAM curve if there are 1,000 or more cases. Either will give us an idea of the shape of the relationships. The second `geom_smooth` layer specifically asks for the `lm` method (linear model), which draws a linear regression line that best fits the data. Drawing both of these will help us identify if there are relationships in the data that are nonlinear.

The resulting plot is shown in figure 9.7. Hmm, some of the predictors have a linear relationship with ozone levels, some have a nonlinear relationship, and some seem to have no relationship at all!

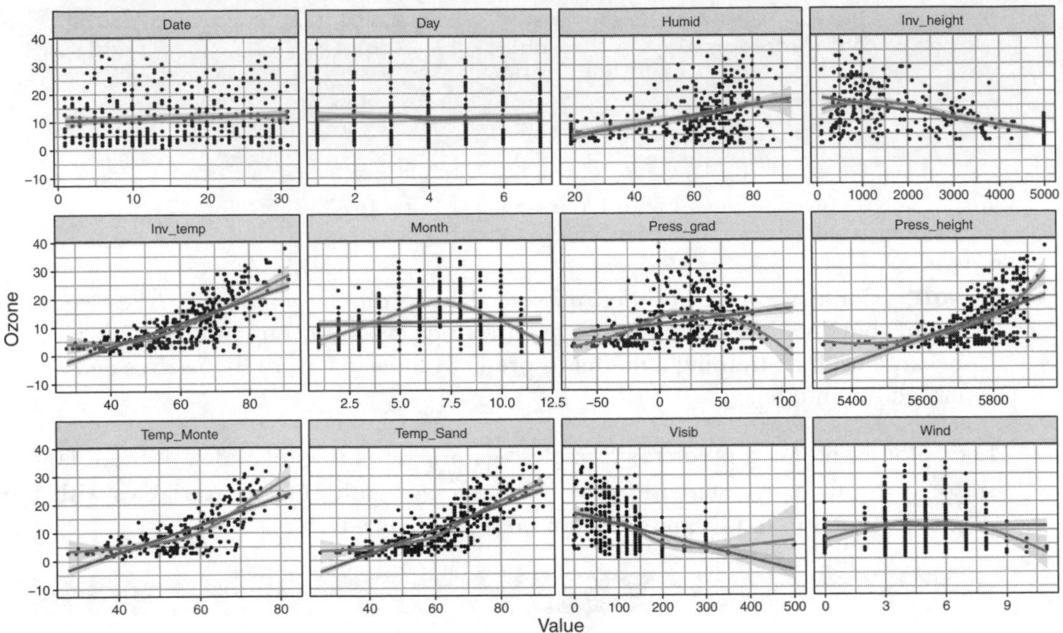

Figure 9.7 Plotting each predictor variable in the `Ozone` dataset against the `Ozone` variable. The straight lines represent linear regression lines, and the curved lines represent GAM lines.

9.2.2 *Imputing missing values*

Linear regression can't handle missing values. Therefore, to avoid having to throw away a large portion of our dataset, we're going to use imputation to fill in the gaps. In chapter 4, we used mean imputation to replace missing values (`NA`s) with the mean of the variable. While this may work, it only uses the information within that single variable to predict missing values, and all missing values within a single variable will take the same value, potentially biasing the model. Instead, we can actually use machine learning algorithms to predict the value of a missing observation, using all of the other variables in the dataset! In this section, I'm going to show you how we can do this with mlr.

If you run `?imputations`, you'll be able to see the imputation methods that come packaged with mlr. These include methods such as `imputeMean()`, `imputeMedian()`, and `imputeMode()` (for replacing missing values with the mean, median, and mode of each variable, respectively). But the most important method is the one last on the list:

`imputeLearner()`. The `imputeLearner()` function lets us specify a supervised machine learning algorithm to predict what the missing values would have been, based on the information held in all the other variables. For example, if we want to impute missing values of a continuous variable, the process proceeds as follows:

1. Split the dataset into cases with and without missing values for this particular variable.
2. Decide on a regression algorithm to predict what the missing values would have been.
3. Considering only the cases *without* missing values, use the algorithm to predict the values of the variable with missing values, using the other variables in the dataset (including the dependent variable you're trying to predict in your final model).
4. Considering only the cases *with* missing values, use the model learned in step 3 to predict the missing values based on the values of the other predictors.

We employ the same strategy when imputing categorical variables, except that we choose a classification algorithm instead of a regression one. So we end up using a supervised learning algorithm to fill in the blanks so that we can use another algorithm to train our final model!

So how do we choose an imputation algorithm? There are a few practical considerations, but as always it depends somewhat and it may pay off to try different methods and see which one gives you the best performance. We can at least initially whittle it down to either a classification or regression algorithm, depending on whether the variable with missing values is continuous or categorical. Next, whether we have missing values in one or multiple variables makes a difference because if it's the latter, we will need to choose an algorithm that can itself handle missing values. For example, let's say we try to use logistic regression to impute missing values of a categorical variable. We'll get to step 3 in the previous procedure and stop because the other variables in the data (that the algorithm is trying to use to predict the categorical variable) also contain missing values. Logistic regression can't handle that and will throw an error. If the only variable with missing values was the one we were trying to impute, this wouldn't have been a problem. Finally, the only other consideration is computational budget. If the algorithm you're using to learn your final model is already computationally expensive, using a computationally expensive algorithm to impute your missing values is added expense. Within these constraints, it's often best to experiment with different imputation learners and see which one works best for the task at hand.

When doing any form of missing-value imputation, it's extremely important to ensure that the data is either *missing at random* (MAR) or *missing completely at random* (MCAR), and not *missing not at random* (MNAR). If data is MCAR, it means the likelihood of a missing value is not related to any variable in the dataset. If data is MAR, it means the likelihood of a missing value is related only to the value of the other variables in the dataset. For example, someone might be less likely to fill in their salary on a form because of their age. In either of these situations, we can still build models that are unbiased due to the presence of missing data. But consider the situation where someone is less likely to fill in their salary on a form because their salary is low. This is an example of data *missing not at random* (MNAR), where the likelihood of a missing value depends on the value of the variable itself. In such a situation, you would likely build a model that is biased to overestimate the salaries of the people in your survey.

How do we tell if our data is MCAR, MAR, or MNAR? Not easily. There are methods for distinguishing MCAR and MAR. For example, you could build a classification model that predicts whether a case has a missing value for a particular variable. If the model does better at predicting missing values than a random guess, then the data is MAR. If the model can't do much better than a random guess, then the data is probably MCAR. Is there a way to tell whether data is MNAR? Unfortunately not. Being confident that your data is not MNAR depends on good experiment design and thoughtful examination of your predictor variables.

> **TIP** There is a more powerful imputation technique called *multiple imputation*. The premise of multiple imputation is that you create many new datasets, replacing missing data with sensible values in each one. You then train a model on each of these imputed datasets and return the average model. While this is probably the most widely used imputation technique, sadly, it isn't implemented yet in mlr, so we won't use it here. However, I strongly suggest you read the documentation for the mice package in R.

For our ozone data, we have missing values across several variables, and they're all continuous variables. Therefore, I'm going to choose a regression algorithm that can handle missing data: rpart. Yep, you heard me right: we're going to impute the missing values with the rpart decision tree algorithm. When we covered tree-based learners in chapter 7, we only considered them for classification problems; but decision trees can be used to predict continuous variables, too. I'll show you how this works in detail in chapter 12; but for now, we'll let rpart do its thing and impute our missing values for us.

Listing 9.4 Using rpart to impute missing values

```
imputeMethod <- imputeLearner("regr.rpart")

ozoneImp <- impute(as.data.frame(ozoneClean),
                   classes = list(numeric = imputeMethod))
```

We first use the `imputeLearner()` function to define what algorithm we're going to use to impute the missing values. The only argument we supply to this function is the name of the learner, which in this case is `"regr.rpart"`.

> **TIP** There is an additional, optional argument, `features`, that lets us specify which variables in the dataset to use in the prediction of missing values. The default is to use all the other variables, but you can use this to specify variables

without any missing values, allowing you to use algorithms that can't themselves handle missing data. See ?imputeLearner for more detail.

Next, we use the `impute()` function to create the imputed dataset, to which the first argument is the data. We've wrapped our tibble inside the `as.data.frame()` function just to prevent repeated warnings about the data being a tibble and not a data frame (these can be safely ignored). We can specify different imputation techniques for different columns by supplying a named list to the `cols` argument. For example, we could say `cols = list(var1 = imputeMean(), var2 = imputeLearner("regr.lm"))`. We can also specify different imputation techniques for different classes of variable (one technique for numeric variables, another for factors) using the `classes` argument in the same way. In the following listing, we use the `classes` argument to impute all the variables (they are all numeric) using the `imputeMethod` we defined.

This results in a dataset we can access using `ozoneImp$data`, whose missing values have been replaced with predictions from a model learned by the rpart algorithm. Now we can define our task and learner using the imputed dataset. By supplying `"regr.lm"` as an argument to the `makeLearner()` function, we're telling mlr that we want to use linear regression.

Listing 9.5 Defining our task and learner

```
ozoneTask <- makeRegrTask(data = ozoneImp$data, target = "Ozone")

lin <- makeLearner("regr.lm")
```

NOTE In part 2 of this book, we were used to defining learners as `classif.[ALGORITHM]`. In this part of the book, instead of `classif.`, the prefix will be `regr.`. This is important because the same algorithm can sometimes be used for classification *and* regression, so the prefix tells mlr which task we want to use the algorithm for.

9.2.3 Automating feature selection

Sometimes it may be obvious which variables have no predictive value and can be removed from the analysis. Domain knowledge is also very important here, where we include variables in the model that we, as experts, believe to have some predictive value for the outcome we're studying. But it's often better to take a less subjective approach to feature selection, and allow an algorithm to choose the relevant features for us. In this section, I'll show you how we can implement this in mlr.

There are two methods for automating feature selection:

- *Filter methods*—Filter methods compare each of the predictors against the outcome variable, and calculate a metric of how much the outcome varies with the predictor. This metric could be a correlation: for example, if both variables are continuous. The predictor variables are ranked in order of this metric (which, in theory, ranks them in order of how much information they can contribute to the model), and we can choose to drop a certain number or proportion of the worst-performing variables from our model. The number or proportion of variables we drop can be tuned as a hyperparameter during model building.

- *Wrapper methods*—With wrapper methods, rather than using a single, out-of-model statistic to estimate feature importance, we iteratively train our model with different predictor variables. Eventually, the combination of predictors that gives us the best performing model is chosen.

  There are different ways of doing this, but one such example is *sequential forward selection.* In sequential forward selection, we start with no predictors and then add predictors one by one. At each step of the algorithm, the feature that results in the best model performance is chosen. Finally, when the addition of any more predictors doesn't result in an improvement in performance, feature addition stops, and the final model is trained on the selected predictors.

Which method should we choose? It boils down to this: wrapper methods may result in models that perform better, because we are actually using the model we're training to estimate predictor importance. However, because we're training a fresh model at each iteration of the selection process (and each step may include other preprocessing steps such as imputation), wrapper methods tend to be computationally expensive. Filter methods, on the other hand, may or may not select the best-performing set of predictors but are much less computationally expensive.

THE FILTER METHOD FOR FEATURE SELECTION

I'm going to show you both methods for our ozone example, starting with the filter method. There are a number of metrics we can use to estimate predictor importance. To see the list of the available filter methods built into mlr, run `listFilterMethods()`. There are too many to describe in full, but common choices include these:

- *Linear correlation*—When both predictor and outcome are continuous
- *ANOVA*—When the predictor is categorical and the outcome is continuous
- *Chi-squared*—When both the predictor and outcome are continuous
- *Random forest importance*—Can be used whether the predictors and outcomes are categorical or continuous (the default)

TIP Feel free to experiment with the methods implemented in mlr. Many of them require you to first install the FSelector package: `install.packages ("FSelector")`.

The default method used by mlr (because it doesn't depend on whether the variables are categorical or continuous) is to build a random forest to predict the outcome, and return the variables that contributed most to model predictions (using the out-of-bag error we discussed in chapter 8). In this example, because both the predictors and outcome variable are continuous, we'll use linear correlation to estimate variable importance (it's a little more interpretable than random forest importance).

First, we use the `generateFilterValuesData()` function (longest function name ever!) to generate an importance metric for each predictor. The first argument is the task, which contains our dataset and lets the function know that `Ozone` is our target variable. The second, optional argument is `method`, to which we can supply one of the methods listed by `listFilterMethods()`. In this example, I've used `"linear.correlation"`. By extracting the `$data` component of this object, we get the table of predictors with their Pearson correlation coefficients.

Listing 9.6 Using a filter method for feature selection

```
filterVals <- generateFilterValuesData(ozoneTask,
                                       method = "linear.correlation")

filterVals$data

           name    type linear.correlation
1         Month numeric           0.053714
2          Date numeric           0.082051
3           Day numeric           0.041514
4  Press_height numeric           0.587524
5          Wind numeric           0.004681
6         Humid numeric           0.451481
7     Temp_Sand numeric           0.769777
8    Temp_Monte numeric           0.741590
9    Inv_height numeric           0.575634
10   Press_grad numeric           0.233318
11     Inv_temp numeric           0.727127
12        Visib numeric           0.414715

plotFilterValues(filterVals) + theme_bw()
```

It's easier to interpret this information as a plot, which we can generate with the `plotFilterValues()` function, giving the object we saved the filter values to as its argument. The resulting plot is shown in figure 9.8.

Exercise 1

Generate and plot filter values for `ozoneTask`, but using the default method `randomForestSRC_importance` (don't overwrite the `filterVals` object). Are the variables ranked in the same order of importance between the two methods?

Now that we have a way of ranking our predictors in order of their estimated importance, we can decide how to "skim off" the least informative ones. We do this using the `filterFeatures()` function, which takes the task as the first argument, our `filterVals` object as the `fval` argument, and either the `abs`, `per`, or `threshold` argument. The `abs` argument allows us to specify the absolute number of best predictors to retain. The `per` argument allows us to specify a top percentage of best predictors to

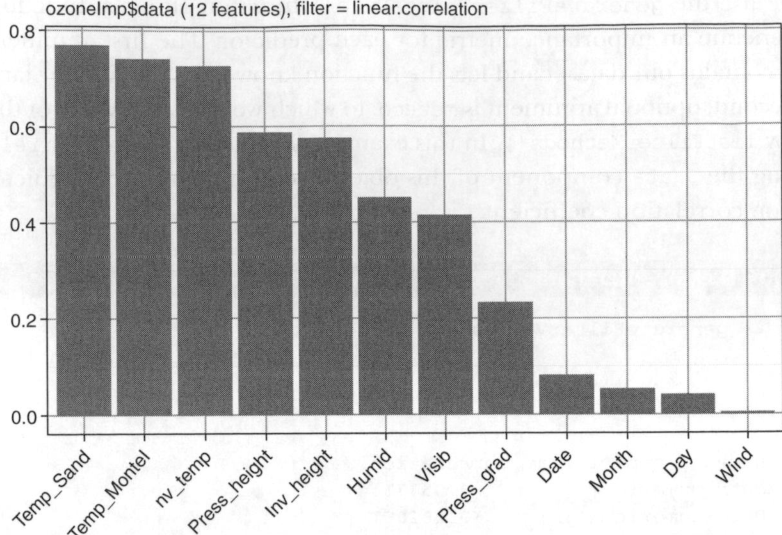

Figure 9.8 Plotting the correlation of each predictor against the ozone level using `plotFilterValues()`

retain. The `threshold` argument allows us to specify a value of our filtering metric (in this case, correlation coefficient) that a predictor must exceed in order to be retained. We *could* manually filter our predictors using one of these three methods. This is shown in the following listing, but I've commented the lines out because we're not going to do this. Instead, we can wrap together our learner (linear regression) and the filter method so that we can treat any of `abs`, `per`, and `threshold` as hyperparameters and tune them.

Listing 9.7 Manually selecting which features to drop

```
#ozoneFiltTask <- filterFeatures(ozoneTask,
#                                fval = filterVals, abs = 6)
#ozoneFiltTask <- filterFeatures(ozoneTask,
#                                fval = filterVals, per = 0.25)
#ozoneFiltTask <- filterFeatures(ozoneTask,
#                                fval = filterVals, threshold = 0.2)
```

To wrap together our learner and filter method, we use the `makeFilterWrapper()` function, supplying the linear regression learner we defined as the `learner` argument and our filter metric as the `fw.method` argument.

Listing 9.8 Creating a filter wrapper

```
filterWrapper = makeFilterWrapper(learner = lin,
                                  fw.method = "linear.correlation")
```

WARNING Confusing terminology alert! We are still using the *filter method* for feature selection. It's unfortunately confusing that we are making a *filter wrapper*, but this is not the *wrapper method* for feature selection. We will cover this shortly.

When we wrap together a learner and a preprocessing step, the hyperparameters for both become available for tuning as part of our wrapped learner. In this situation, it means we can tune the *abs*, *per*, or *threshold* hyperparameter using cross-validation, to select the best-performing features. In this example, we're going to tune the absolute number of features to retain.

Listing 9.9 Tuning the number of predictors to retain

```
lmParamSpace <- makeParamSet(
  makeIntegerParam("fw.abs", lower = 1, upper = 12)
)

gridSearch <- makeTuneControlGrid()

kFold <- makeResampleDesc("CV", iters = 10)

tunedFeats <- tuneParams(filterWrapper, task = ozoneTask, resampling = kFold,
                         par.set = lmParamSpace, control = gridSearch)

tunedFeats

Tune result:
Op. pars: fw.abs=10
mse.test.mean=20.8834
```

TIP If you run `getParamSet(filterWrapper)`, you'll see that the hyperparameter names for *abs*, *per*, and *threshold* have become *fw.abs*, *fw.per*, and *fw.threshold*, now that we've wrapped the filter method. Another useful hyperparameter, *fw.mandatory.feat*, allows you to force certain variables to be included regardless of their scores.

First, we define the hyperparameter space, as usual, with `makeParamSet()`, and define *fw.abs* as an integer between 1 and 12 (the minimum and maximum number of features we're going to retain). Next, we define our old friend, the grid search, using `makeTuneControlGrid()`. This will try every value of our hyperparameter. We define an ordinary 10-fold cross-validation strategy using `makeResampleDesc()` and then perform the tuning with `tuneParams()`. The first argument is our wrapped learner, and then we supply our task, cross-validation method, hyperparameter space, and search procedure.

Our tuning procedure picks the 10 predictors with the highest correlation with ozone as the best-performing combination. But what's `mse.test.mean`? You haven't seen this performance metric before. Well, the performance metrics we used for classification, such as mean misclassification error, don't make sense when we're predicting continuous variables. For regression problems, there are three commonly used performance metrics:

- *Mean absolute error (MAE)*—Finds the absolute residual between each case and the model, adds them all up, and divides by the number of cases. We can interpret this as the mean absolute distance of the cases from the model.
- *Mean square error (MSE)*—Similar to MAE but *squares* the residuals before finding their mean. This means MSE is more sensitive to outliers than MAE, because the size of the squared residual grows quadratically, the further from the model prediction it is.

  MSE is the default performance metric for regression learners in mlr. The choice of MSE or MAE depends on how you want to treat outliers in your data: if you want your model to be able to predict such cases, use MSE; otherwise, if you want your model to be less sensitive to outliers, use MAE.
- *Root mean square error (RMSE)*—Because MSE squares the residual, its value isn't on the same scale as the outcome variable. Instead, if we take the square root of the MSE, we get the RMSE.

  When tuning hyperparameters and comparing models, MSE and RMSE will always select the same models (because RMSE is simply a transformation of MSE), but RMSE has the benefit of being on the same scale as our outcome variable and so is more interpretable.

TIP Other regression performance metrics are available to us, such as the percentage versions of MAE and MSE. If you're interested in reading about more of the performance metrics available in mlr (and there are a lot of them), run `?measures`.

Exercise 2

Repeat the feature-filtering process in listings 9.8 and 9.9, but use the default `fw.method` argument (`randomForestSRC_importance`, or just don't supply it). Does this select the same number of predictors as when we used linear correlation? Which method was faster?

Using the MSE performance metric, our tuned filter method has concluded that retaining the 10 features with the highest correlation with the ozone level results in the best-performing model. We can now train a final model that includes only these top 10 features in the task.

Listing 9.10 Training the model with filtered features

```
filteredTask <- filterFeatures(ozoneTask, fval = filterVals,
                               abs = unlist(tunedFeats$x))

filteredModel <- train(lin, filteredTask)
```

First, we create a new task that includes only the filtered features, using the `filterFeatures()` function. To this function, we supply the name of the existing task, the `filterVals` object we defined in listing 9.6, and the number of features to retain as the argument to `abs`. This value can be accessed as the `$x` component of `tunedFeats` and needs to be wrapped in `unlist()`; otherwise, the function will throw an error. This creates a new task that contains only the filtered predictors and retains `Ozone` as the target variable. Finally, we train the linear model using this task.

THE WRAPPER METHOD FOR FEATURE SELECTION

With the filter method, we generate univariate statistics describing how each predictor relates to the outcome variable. This may result in selecting the most informative predictors, but it isn't guaranteed to. Instead, we can use the actual model we're trying to train to determine which features help it make the best predictions. This has the potential to select a better-performing combination of predictors, but it is computationally more expensive as we're training a fresh model for every permutation of predictor variables.

Let's start by defining how we're going to search for the best combination of predictors. We have four options:

- *Exhaustive search*—This is basically a grid search. It will try every possible combination of predictor variables in your dataset and select the one that performs the best. This is guaranteed to find the best combination but can be prohibitively slow. For example, in our 12-predictor dataset, exhaustive search would need to try more than 1.3×10^9 different variable combinations!
- *Random search*—This is just like random search in hyperparameter tuning. We define a number of iterations and randomly select feature combinations. The best combination after the final iteration wins. This is usually less intensive (depending on how many iterations you choose), but it isn't guaranteed to find the best combination of features.
- *Sequential search*—From a particular starting point, we either add or remove features at each step that improve performance. This can be one of the following:
  - *Forward search*—We start with an empty model and sequentially add the feature that improves the model most until additional features no longer improve the performance.
  - *Backward search*—We start with all the features and remove the feature whose removal improves the model the most until additional removals no longer improve the performance.
  - *Floating forward search*—Starting from an empty model, we either add one variable or remove one variable at each step, whichever improves the model the most, until neither an addition nor a removal improves model performance.
  - *Floating backward search*—The same as floating forward, except we start with a full model.
- *Genetic algorithm*—This method, inspired by Darwinian evolution, finds pairs of feature combinations that act as "parents" to "offspring" variable combinations,

which inherit the best-performing features. This method is very cool but can be computationally expensive as the feature space grows.

Wow! With so many options to choose from, where do we start? Well, I find the exhaustive and genetic searches prohibitively slow for a large feature space. While the random search can alleviate this problem, I find a sequential search to be a good compromise between computational cost and probability of finding the best-performing feature combination. Of its different variants, you may want to experiment with the various options to see which results in the best-performing model. I like the floating versions because they consider both addition and removal at each step, so for this example we're going to use floating backward selection.

First, we define the search method using the `makeFeatSelControlSequential()` function (wow, the mlr authors really do love their long function names). We use `"sfbs"` as the method argument to use a sequential floating backward selection. Then, we use the `selectFeatures()` function to perform the feature selection. To this function we supply the learner, task, cross-validation strategy defined in listing 9.9, and search method. It's as easy as that. When we run the function, every permutation of predictor variables is cross-validated using our `kFold` strategy to get an estimate of its performance. By printing the result of this process, we can see the algorithm selected six predictors that had a slightly lower MSE value than the predictors selected by our filter method in listing 9.9.

TIP To see all of the available wrapper methods and how to use them, run `?FeatSelControl`.

Now I need to warn you about a frustrating bug with regard to the sequential floating forward search. As of this writing, using `"sffs"` as the feature-selection method will throw this error in some circumstances: `Error in sum(x) : invalid 'type' (list) of argument`. If you try to use `"sffs"` as the search method in this example, you may get such an error. Therefore, while this is very frustrating, I've opted to use sequential floating *backward* search (`"sfbs"`) instead.

Listing 9.11 Using a wrapper method for feature selection

```
featSelControl <- makeFeatSelControlSequential(method = "sfbs")

selFeats <- selectFeatures(learner = lin, task = ozoneTask,
                           resampling = kFold, control = featSelControl)

selFeats

FeatSel result:
Features (6): Month, Press_height, Humid, Temp_Sand, Temp_Monte, Inv_height
mse.test.mean=20.4038
```

Now, just as we did for the filter method, we can create a new task using the imputed data that contains only those selected predictors, and train a model on it.

Listing 9.12 Using a wrapper method for feature selection

```
ozoneSelFeat <- ozoneImp$data[, c("Ozone", selFeats$x)]

ozoneSelFeatTask <- makeRegrTask(data = ozoneSelFeat, target = "Ozone")

wrapperModel <- train(lin, ozoneSelFeatTask)
```

9.2.4 Including imputation and feature selection in cross-validation

I've said it many times before, but I'm going to say it again: include all data-dependent preprocessing steps in your cross-validation! But up to this point, we've only needed to consider a single preprocessing step. How do we combine more than one? Well, mlr makes this process extremely simple. When we wrap together a learner and a preprocessing step, we have essentially created a new learner algorithm that includes that preprocessing. So to include an additional preprocessing step, we simply wrap the wrapped learner! I've illustrated this for our example in figure 9.9. This results in a sort of Matryoshka doll of wrappers, where one is encapsulated by another, which is encapsulated by another, and so on.

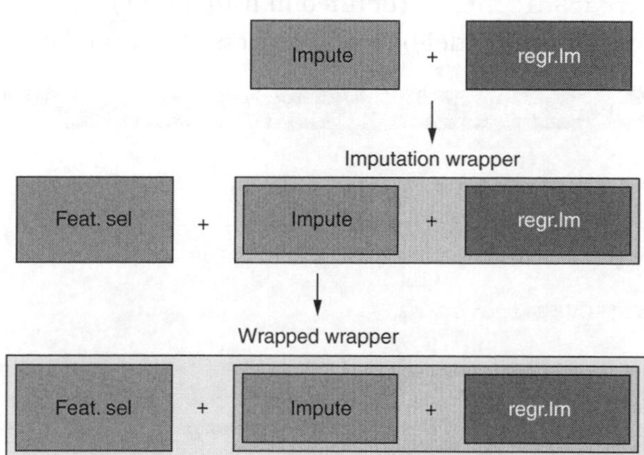

Figure 9.9 Combining multiple preprocessing wrappers. Once a learner and preprocessing step (such as imputation) have been combined in a wrapper, this wrapper can be used as the learner in another wrapper.

Using this strategy, we can combine as many preprocessing steps as we like to create a pipeline. The innermost wrapper will always be used first, then the next innermost, and so on.

> **NOTE** Because the innermost wrapper is used first, through to the outermost, it's important to think carefully about the order you wish the preprocessing steps to take.

Let's reinforce this in your mind by actually doing it. We're going to make an impute wrapper and then pass it as the learner to a feature-selection wrapper.

Listing 9.13 Combining imputation and feature selection wrappers

```
imputeMethod <- imputeLearner("regr.rpart")

imputeWrapper <- makeImputeWrapper(lin,
                                   classes = list(numeric = imputeMethod))

featSelWrapper <- makeFeatSelWrapper(learner = imputeWrapper,
                                     resampling = kFold,
                                     control = featSelControl)
```

First, we redefine our imputation method using the `imputeLearner()` function (first defined in listing 9.4). Then, we create an imputation wrapper using the `makeImputeWrapper()` function, which takes the learner as the first argument. We use `list(numeric = imputeMethod)` as the `classes` argument to apply this imputation strategy to all of our numeric predictors (all of them, duh).

Now here comes the neat bit: we create a feature-selection wrapper using `makeFeatSelWrapper()`, and supply the imputation wrapper we created as the learner. This is the crucial step because we're creating a wrapper with another wrapper! We set the cross-validation method as `kFold` (defined in listing 9.9) and the method of searching feature combinations as `featSelControl` (defined in listing 9.11).

Now, let's cross-validate our entire model-building process like good data scientists.

Listing 9.14 Cross-validating the model-building process

```
library(parallel)
library(parallelMap)

ozoneTaskWithNAs <- makeRegrTask(data = ozoneClean, target = "Ozone")

kFold3 <- makeResampleDesc("CV", iters = 3)

parallelStartSocket(cpus = detectCores())

lmCV <- resample(featSelWrapper, ozoneTaskWithNAs, resampling = kFold3)

parallelStop()

lmCV

Resample Result
Task: ozoneClean
Learner: regr.lm.imputed.featsel
Aggr perf: mse.test.mean=20.5394
Runtime: 86.7071
```

After loading our friends the parallel and parallelMap packages, we define a task using the `ozoneClean` tibble, which still contains missing data. Next, we define an ordinary 3-fold cross-validation strategy for our cross-validation procedure. Finally, we start parallelization with `parallelStartSocket()` and start the cross-validation procedure by supplying the learner (the wrapped wrapper), task, and cross-validation strategy to the `resample()` function. This took nearly 90 seconds on my four-core machine, so I suggest you start the process and then read on for a summary of what the code is doing.

The cross-validation process proceeds like this:

1. Split the data into three folds.
2. For each fold:
   a. Use the rpart algorithm to impute the missing values.
   b. Perform feature selection: Update template to support more than two levels of nested ordered lists.
   c. Use a selection method (such as backward search) to select combinations of features to train models on.
   d. Use 10-fold cross-validation to evaluate the performance of each model.
3. Return the best-performing model for each of the three outer folds.
4. Return the mean MSE to give us our estimate of performance.

We can see that our model-building process gives us a mean MSE of 20.54, suggesting a mean residual error of 4.53 on the original ozone scale (taking the square root of 20.54).

9.2.5 *Interpreting the model*

Due to their simple structure, linear models are usually quite simple to interpret, because we can look at the slopes for each predictor to infer how much the outcome variable is affected by each. However, whether these interpretations are justified or not depends on whether some model assumptions have been met, so in this section I'll show you how to interpret the model output and generate some diagnostic plots.

First, we need to extract the model information from our model object using the `getLearnerModel()` function. By calling `summary()` on the model data, we get an output with lots of information about our model. Take a look at the following listing.

Listing 9.15 Interpreting the model

```
wrapperModelData <- getLearnerModel(wrapperModel)

summary(wrapperModelData)

Call:
stats::lm(formula = f, data = d)

Residuals:
    Min       1Q   Median       3Q      Max
-13.934   -2.950   -0.284    2.722   13.829
```

```
Coefficients:
              Estimate Std. Error t value Pr(>|t|)
(Intercept)  41.796670  27.800562    1.50  0.13362
Month        -0.296659   0.078272   -3.79  0.00018
Press_height -0.010353   0.005161   -2.01  0.04562
Wind         -0.122521   0.128593   -0.95  0.34136
Humid         0.076434   0.014982    5.10  5.5e-07
Temp_Sand     0.227055   0.043397    5.23  2.9e-07
Temp_Monte    0.266534   0.063619    4.19  3.5e-05
Inv_height   -0.000474   0.000185   -2.56  0.01099
Visib        -0.005226   0.003558   -1.47  0.14275

Residual standard error: 4.46 on 352 degrees of freedom
Multiple R-squared:  0.689, Adjusted R-squared:  0.682
F-statistic: 97.7 on 8 and 352 DF,  p-value: <2e-16
```

The `Call` component would normally tell us the formula we used to create the model (which variables, and whether we added more complex relationships between them). Because we built this model using mlr, we unfortunately don't get that information here; but the model formula is all of the selected predictors combined linearly together.

The `Residuals` component gives us some summary statistics about the model residuals. Here we're looking to see if the median is approximately 0 and that the first and third quartiles are approximately the same. If they aren't, this might suggest the residuals are either not normally distributed, or heteroscedastic. In both situations, not only could this negatively impact model performance, but it could make our interpretation of the slopes incorrect.

The `Coefficients` component shows us a table of model parameters and their standard errors. The intercept is 41.8, which is the estimate of the ozone level when all other variables are 0. In this particular case it doesn't really make sense for some of our variables to be 0 (`month`, for example) so we won't draw too much interpretation from this. The estimates for the predictors are their slopes. For example, our model estimates that for a one-unit increase in the `Temp_Sand` variable, `Ozone` increases by 0.227 (holding all other variables constant). The `Pr(>|t|)` column contains the *p* values that, in theory, represent the probability of seeing a slope this large if the population slope was actually 0. Use the *p* values to guide your model-building process, by all means; but there are some problems associated with *p* values, so don't put too much faith in them.

Finally, `Residual standard error` is the same as RMSE, `Multiple R-squared` is an estimate of the proportion of variance in the data accounted for by our model (68.9%), and `F-statistic` is the ratio of variance explained by our model to the variance not explained by the model. The *p* value here is an estimate of the probability that our model is better than just using the mean of `Ozone` to make predictions.

NOTE Notice the residual standard error value is close to but not the same as the RMSE estimated for the model-building process by cross-validation. This difference is because we cross-validated the model-building procedure, not this particular model itself.

We can very quickly and easily print diagnostic plots for linear models in R by supplying the model data as the argument to `plot()`. Ordinarily, this will prompt you to press Enter to cycle through the plots. I find this irritating and so prefer to split the plotting device into four parts using the `mfrow` argument to the `par()` function. This means when we create our diagnostic plots (there will be four of them), they will be tiled in the same plotting window. These plots may help us identify flaws in our model that impact predictive performance.

TIP I change this back again with the `par()` function afterward.

Listing 9.16 Creating diagnostic plots of the model

```
par(mfrow = c(2, 2))
plot(wrapperModelData)
par(mfrow = c(1, 1))
```

The resulting plot is shown in figure 9.10. The Residuals vs. Fitted plot shows the predicted ozone level on the x-axis and the residual on the y-axis for each case. We *hope* that there are no patterns in this plot. In other words, the amount of error shouldn't depend on the predicted value. In this situation, we have a curved relationship. This indicates that we have nonlinear relationships between predictors and ozone, and/or heteroscedasticity.

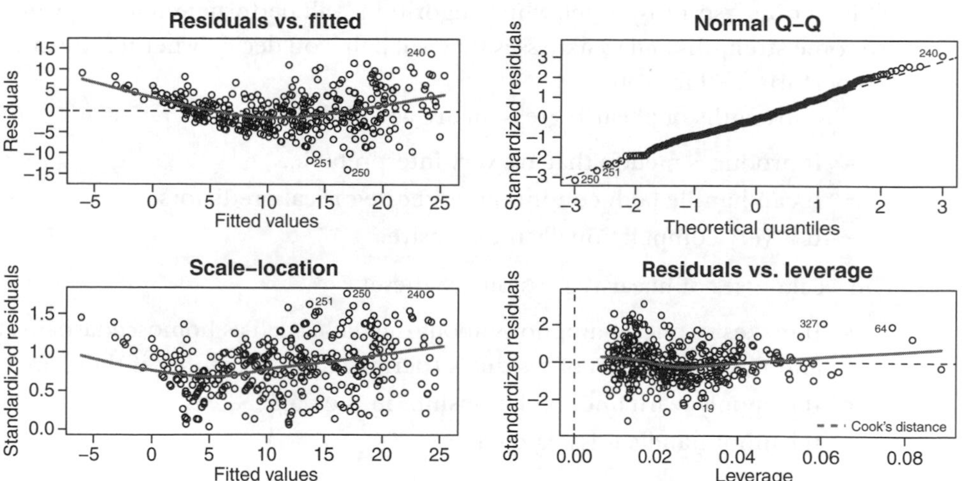

Figure 9.10 Plotting diagnostic plots for our linear model. The Residuals vs. Fitted and Scale-Location plots help identify patterns that suggest nonlinearity and heteroscedasticity. The Normal Q-Q plot helps identify non-normality of residuals, and the Residuals vs. Leverage plot helps identify influential outliers.

The Normal Q-Q (quantile-quantile) plot shows the quantiles of the model residuals plotted against their quantiles if they were drawn from a theoretical normal distribution.

If the data deviates considerably from a 1:1 diagonal line, this suggests the residuals are not normally distributed. This doesn't seem to be a problem for this model: the residuals line up nicely on the diagonal.

The Scale-Location plot helps us identify heteroscedasticity of the residuals. There should be no patterns here, but it looks like the residuals are increasingly varied with larger predicted values, suggesting heteroscedasticity.

Finally, the Residuals vs. Leverage plot helps us to identify cases that have excessive influence on the model parameters (potential outliers). Cases that fall inside a dotted region of the plot called *Cook's distance* may be outliers whose inclusion or exclusion makes a large difference to the model. Because we can't even see Cook's distance here (it is beyond the axis limits), we have no worries about outliers.

These diagnostic plots (particularly the Residuals vs. Fitted plot) indicate the presence of nonlinear relationships between the predictor variables and the outcome variable. We may, therefore, be able to get better predictive performance from a model that doesn't assume linearity. In the next chapter, I'll show you how *generalized additive models* work, and we'll train one to improve our model performance. I suggest you save your .R file, because we're going to continue using the same dataset and task in the next chapter. This is so I can highlight to you how much nonlinearity can impact the performance of linear regression.

9.3 Strengths and weaknesses of linear regression

While it often isn't easy to tell which algorithms will perform well for a given task, here are some strengths and weaknesses that will help you decide whether linear regression will perform well for you.

The strengths of linear regression are as follows:

- It produces models that are very interpretable.
- It can handle both continuous and categorical predictors.
- It is very computationally inexpensive.

The weaknesses of linear regression are these:

- It makes strong assumptions about the data, such as homoscedasticity, linearity, and the distribution of residuals (performance may suffer if these are violated).
- It can only learn linear relationships in the data.
- It cannot handle missing data.

Exercise 3

Instead of using a wrapper method, cross-validate the process of building our model using a filter method. Are the estimated MSE values similar? Which method is faster? Tips:

a First, create a filter wrapper using our `imputeWrapper` as the learner.

b Define a hyperparameter space to tune `"fw.abs"` using `makeParamSet()`.

c Define a tuning wrapper that takes the filter wrapper as a learner and performs a grid search.
d Use `resample()` to perform cross-validation, using the tuning wrapper as the learner.

Summary

- Linear regression can handle continuous and categorical predictors.
- Linear regression uses the equation of a straight line to model relationships in the data as straight lines.
- Missing values can be imputed using supervised learning algorithms that use the information from all the other variables.
- Automated feature selection takes two forms: filter methods and wrapper methods.
- Filter methods of feature selection calculate univariate statistics outside of a model, to estimate how related predictors are to the outcome.
- Wrapper methods actively train models on different permutations of the predictors to select the best-performing combination.
- Preprocessing steps can be combined together in mlr by sequential wrapping of wrapper functions.

Solutions to exercises

1 Generate filter values using the default `randomForestSRC_importance` method:

```
filterValsForest <- generateFilterValuesData(ozoneTask,
                              method = "randomForestSRC_importance")

filterValsForest$data

plotFilterValues(filterValsForest) + theme_bw()

# The randomForestSRC_importance method ranks variables
# in a different order of importance.
```

2 Repeat feature filtering using the default filter statistic:

```
filterWrapperDefault <- makeFilterWrapper(learner = lin)

tunedFeats <- tuneParams(filterWrapperDefault, task = ozoneTask,
                         resampling = kFold, par.set = lmParamSpace,
                         control = gridSearch)

tunedFeats

# The default filter statistic (randomForestSRC) tends to select fewer
# predictors in this case, but the linear.correlation statistic was faster.
```

3 Cross-validate building a linear regression model, but using a filter method:

```
filterWrapperImp <- makeFilterWrapper(learner = imputeWrapper,
                                      fw.method = "linear.correlation")

filterParam <- makeParamSet(
  makeIntegerParam("fw.abs", lower = 1, upper = 12)
)

tuneWrapper <- makeTuneWrapper(learner = filterWrapperImp,
                               resampling = kFold,
                               par.set = filterParam,
                               control = gridSearch)

filterCV <- resample(tuneWrapper, ozoneTask, resampling = kFold)

filterCV

# We have a similar MSE estimate for the filter method
# but it is considerably faster than the wrapper method. No free lunch!
```

10 Nonlinear regression with generalized additive models

This chapter covers

- Including polynomial terms in linear regression
- Using splines in regression
- Using generalized additive models (GAMs) for nonlinear regression

In chapter 9, I showed you how linear regression can be used to create very interpretable regression models. One of the strongest assumptions made by linear regression is that there is a linear relationship between each predictor variable and the outcome. This is often not the case, so in this chapter I'll introduce you to a class of models that allows us to model nonlinear relationships in the data.

We'll start by discussing how we can include *polynomial* terms in linear regression to model nonlinear relationships, and the advantages and disadvantages of doing this. We'll then move on to the more sophisticated *generalized additive models*, which give us considerably more flexibility to model complex nonlinear relationships. I'll also show you how these generalized additive models can handle both continuous and categorical variables, just like in linear regression.

By the end of this chapter, I hope you'll understand how to create nonlinear regression models that are still surprisingly interpretable. We will continue to work with the ozone dataset we were using in the previous chapter. If you no longer have the `ozoneClean` object defined in your global environment, just rerun listings 9.1 and 9.2 from chapter 9.

10.1 Making linear regression nonlinear with polynomial terms

In this section, I'll show you how we can take the general linear model we discussed in the previous chapter and extend it to include nonlinear, polynomial relationships between predictor variables and the outcome variable. Linear regression makes the strong assumption that there is a linear relationship between predictor variables and the outcome. Sometimes real-world variables have linear relationships, or can be sufficiently approximated by one, but often they do not. Surely the general linear model falls down when faced with nonlinear relationships, right? After all, it's called the general *linear* model and uses the equation of a straight line. Well, it turns out that the general linear model is surprisingly flexible, and we can use it to model *polynomial* relationships.

Recall from high school math that a polynomial equation is just an equation with multiple terms (single numbers or variables). If all the terms in the equation are raised to the power of 1 (an *exponent* of 1)—in other words, they are all equal to themselves—the equation is a *first-degree polynomial*. If the highest exponent in the equation is 2—in other words, one or some of the terms are squared but there are no higher exponents—the equation is a *second-degree polynomial* or *quadratic* polynomial. If the highest exponent is 3, the equation is a *cubic* polynomial; and if the highest exponent is 4, the equation is a *quartic* polynomial.

> **TIP** Although there are names for higher-degree polynomials, people usually just call them *n*th-degree polynomials (for example, a fifth-degree polynomial). This is, of course, unless you want to sound super-precocious!

Let's have a look at some examples of *n*th-degree polynomials:

- $y = x^1$ (linear)
- $y = x^2$ (quadratic)
- $y = x^3$ (cubic)
- $y = x^4$ (quartic)

The shape of these functions is shown for values of x between –30 and 30 in figure 10.1. When the exponent is 1, the function is a straight line; but when the exponent is greater than 1, the function is curvy.

We can use this to our advantage: if the relationships between our predictor variables and our outcome variable have a curved relationship, we might be able to model this relationship by including *n*th-degree polynomials in our model definition. Think back to our cider example in chapter 9. Imagine that instead of a linear relationship between apple content and cider batch pH, we have a downward curvilinear relationship like the

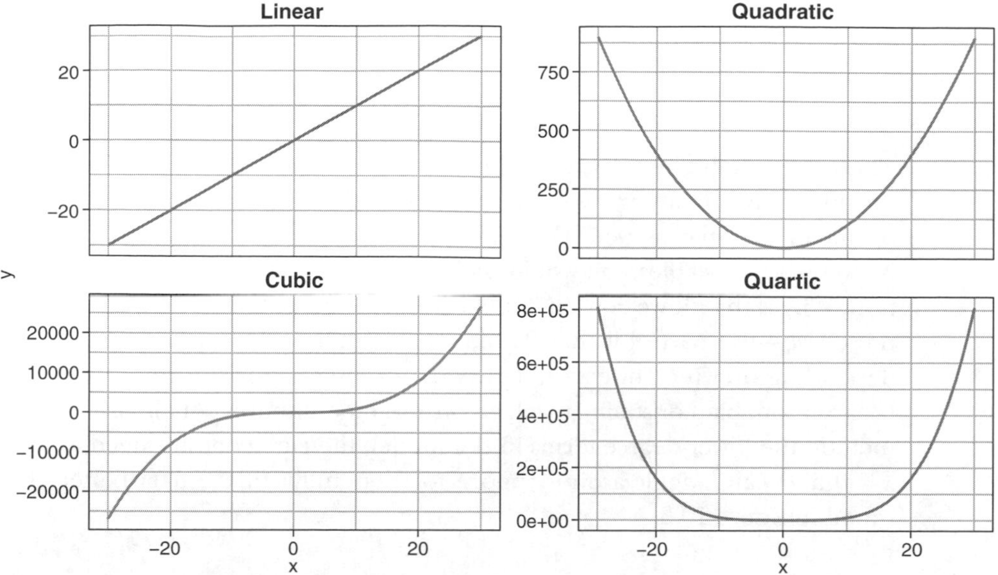

Figure 10.1 Shapes of polynomial functions from the first to the fourth degree. When the *x* variable is raised to the first power, the equation models a straight line. As we increase the power that *x* is raised to, the equations model lines with varying degrees of flexibility.

one illustrated in figure 10.2. A straight line no longer models this relationship very well, and predictions made by such a model are likely to have high bias. Instead, we can better model this relationship by including a quadratic term in the model definition.

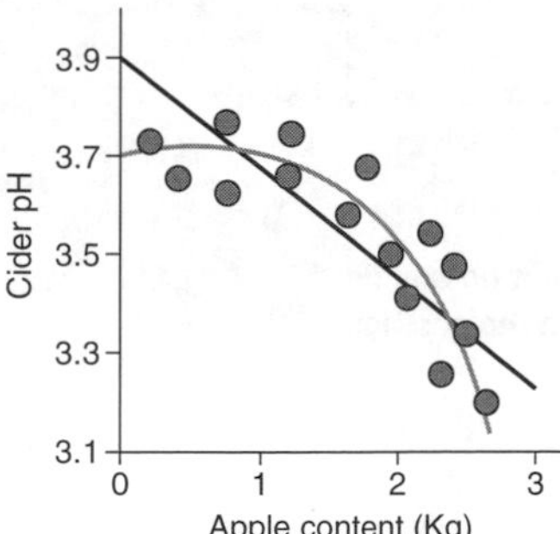

Figure 10.2 Comparing linear and quadratic fits to an imaginary nonlinear relationship between apple content and cider acidity

The formula for the model shown in figure 10.2 would be

$$y = \beta_{apples} \times apples + \beta_{apples^2} \times apples^2 + \varepsilon$$

where β_{apples^2} is the *slope* for the $apples^2$ term, which is more easily understood as how much the line curves as apple content increases (larger absolute values result in a more extreme curve). For a single predictor variable, we can generalize this for any *n*th-degree polynomial relationship as

$$y = \beta_0 + \beta_1 x + \beta_1 x^2 + \ldots \beta_n x^n + \varepsilon$$

where n is the highest degree of polynomial you're modeling. Notice that when performing polynomial regression, it's usual to include all the lower-degree terms for that predictor variable as well. For example, if you're modeling a quartic relationship between two variables, you would include x, x^2, x^3, *and* x^4 terms in your model definition. Why is this? If we don't include the lower-degree terms in the model, the *vertex* of the curve—the part of it that flattens out (either at the top or bottom of the curve, depending on which direction it curves)—is forced to pass through $x = 0$. This might be a reasonable constraint to place on the model, but it usually isn't. Instead, if we include the lower-degree terms in the model, the curve doesn't need to pass through $x = 0$ and can "wiggle around" more to (hopefully) fit the data better. This is illustrated in figure 10.3.

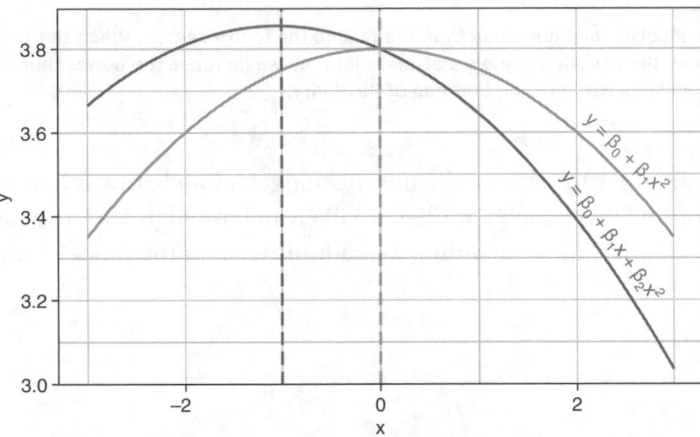

Figure 10.3 Comparing the shape of polynomial functions that do and do not include the first-degree term. Vertical dotted lines indicate the position of each function's vertex on the x-axis.

Just as we saw in chapter 9, when the model is given new data, it multiplies the values of the predictor variables (including the specified exponents) by their slopes and then adds them all together with the intercept to get the predicted value. The model we're using is still the general linear model, because we're *linearly* combining the model terms (adding them together).

10.2 More flexibility: Splines and generalized additive models

When using polynomial terms in linear regression, the higher the degree of polynomial we use, the more flexible our model will be. High-degree polynomials allow us to capture complicated nonlinear relationships in the data but are therefore more likely to overfit the training set. Sometimes, increasing the degree of the polynomials doesn't help anyway, because the relationship between the predictor variable and outcome variable may not be the same across the range of the predictor variable. In such situations, instead of using high-degree polynomials, we can use *splines*. In this section, I'll explain what splines are and how to use them, and how they relate to polynomials and a set of models called *generalized additive models* (GAMs).

A spline is a *piecewise* polynomial function. This means it splits the predictor variable into regions and fits a separate polynomial within each region, which regions connect to each other via knots. A *knot* is a position along the predictor variable that divides the regions within which the separate polynomials are fit. The polynomial curves in each region of the predictor pass through the knots that delimit that region. This allows us to model complex nonlinear relationships that are not constant across the range of the predictor variable. This is illustrated in figure 10.4 using our cider example.

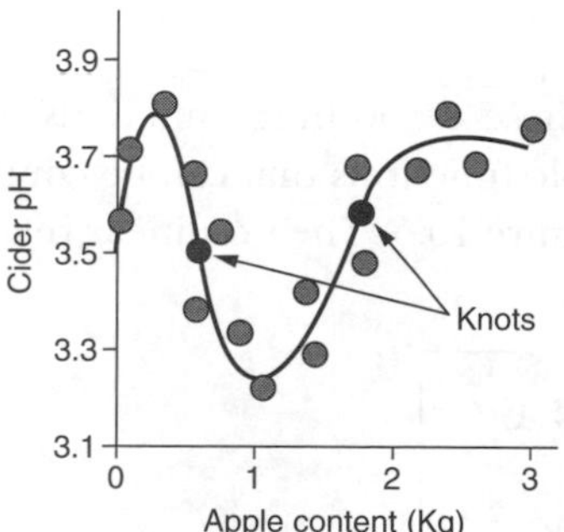

Figure 10.4 Fitting a spline to a nonlinear relationship. The solid dots indicate the knots. Individual polynomial functions fit the data between the knots and connect to each other through them.

Using splines is a great way of modeling complicated relationships such as the one shown in figure 10.4, but this approach has some limitations:

- The position and number of the knots need to be chosen manually. Both choices can make a big impact on the shape of the spline. The choice of knot position is typically either at obvious regions of change in the data or at regular intervals across the predictor, such as at the quartiles.
- The degree of the polynomials between knots needs to be chosen. We generally use cubic splines or higher, because these ensure that the polynomials connect with each other smoothly through the knots (quadratic polynomials may leave the spline disconnected at the knots).
- It can become difficult to combine splines of different predictors.

So, can we do better than simple spline regression? Absolutely. The solution is GAMs. GAMs extend the general linear model such that instead of

$$y = \beta_0 + \beta_1 x + \beta_2 x_2 + \ldots \beta_2 x_2 + \varepsilon$$

they take the form

$$y = \beta_0 + f_1(x_1) + f_2(x_2) + \ldots f_k(x_k) + \varepsilon$$

where each $f(x)$ represents a function of a particular predictor variable. These functions can be any sort of smoothing function but will typically be a combination of multiple splines.

> **NOTE** Can you see that the general linear model is a special case of the generalized additive model, where the function for each predictor variable is the *identity function* ($f(x) = x$)? We can go one step further then and say that the *generalized linear* model is a special case of the *generalized additive* model. This is because we can also use different link functions with GAMs that allow us to use them to predict categorical variables (as in logistic regression) or count variables.

10.2.1 How GAMs learn their smoothing functions

The most common method of constructing these smoothing functions is to use splines as *basis functions.* Basis functions are simple functions that can be combined to form a more complex function. Take a look at figure 10.5. The nonlinear relationship

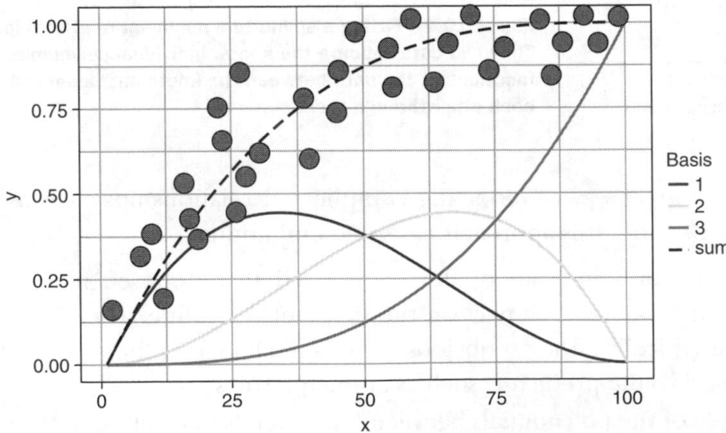

Figure 10.5 Smoothing functions for continuous variables in GAMs are commonly the sum of a series of basis functions, which are often splines. Three spline basis functions are summed at each value of *x* to predict the value of *y*. The dotted line shows the sum of the three basis functions, which models the nonlinear relationship in the data.

between the *x* and *y* variables is modeled as a weighted sum of three splines. In other words, at each value of *x*, we sum the contributions from each of these basis functions to give us the function that models the relationship (the dotted line). The overall function is a *weighted* sum because each basis function has a corresponding weight, determining how much it contributes to the final function.

Let's take another look at the GAM formula:

$$y = \beta_0 + f_1(x_1) + f_2(x_2) + \ldots f_k(x_k) + \varepsilon$$

So each $f_k(x_k)$ is a smoothing function of that particular variable. When these smoothing functions use splines as basis functions, the function can be expressed as

$$f(x_i) = a_1 b_1(x_i) + a_2 b_2(x_i) + \ldots + a_n b_n(x_i)$$

where $b_1(x_i)$ is the value of the first basis function evaluated at a particular value of *x*, and a_1 is the weight of the first basis function. GAMs estimate the weights of these basis functions in order to minimize the residual square error of the model.

GAMs automatically learn a nonlinear relationship between each predictor variable and the outcome variable, and then add these effects together linearly, along with the intercept. GAMs overcome the limitations of simply using splines in the general linear model by doing the following:

- Automatically selecting the knots for spline functions
- Automatically selecting the degree of flexibility of the smoothing functions by controlling the weights of the basis functions
- Allowing us to combine splines of multiple predictor variables simultaneously

TIP If I want to use linear modeling and the relationship between my predictors and outcome variable is nonlinear, GAMs are my go-to model. This is because of their flexibility and their ability to overcome the limitations of polynomial regression. The exception is if I have a theoretical reason to believe there is a specific polynomial relationship (say, quadratic) in the data. In such a situation, using linear regression with a polynomial term may result in a simpler model, where a GAM might overfit.

10.2.2 How GAMs handle categorical variables

So far, I've shown you that GAMs learn nonlinear relationships between our predictor variables and our outcome. But what about when our predictor variables are categorical? Well, GAMs can handle categorical variables in two different ways.

One method is to treat categorical variables exactly the same way we do for the general linear model, and create $k - 1$ dummy variables that encode the effect of each level of the predictor on the outcome. When we use this method, the predicted value of a case is simply the sum of all of the smoothing functions, plus the contribution from the categorical variable effects. This method assumes independence between the categorical variable and the continuous variables (in other words, the smoothing functions are the same across each level of the categorical variable).

The other method is to model a separate smoothing function for each level of the categorical variable. This is important in situations where there are distinct nonlinear relationships between continuous variables and the outcome at each level of a categorical variable.

> **NOTE** When specifying a GAM as our learner through mlr, the default method is the first approach.

GAMs are extraordinarily flexible and powerful for a huge range of machine learning problems. If you would like to delve deeper into the nuts and bolts of GAMs, I recommend *Generalized Additive Models: An Introduction with R* by Simon Wood (Chapman and Hall/CRC, 2017).

I hope by now you have a basic understanding of polynomial regression and GAMs, so let's turn this knowledge into skills by building your first nonlinear regression model!

10.3 Building your first GAM

We finished chapter 9 by interrogating the diagnostic plots of our linear regression model, and deciding it looked as though we have nonlinear relationships in the data. Therefore, in this section I'm going to show you how to model the data using a GAM, to account for the nonlinear relationships between the predictors and outcome.

I'll start with some feature engineering. From figure 9.7 in chapter 9, it looks like there's a curved relationship between `Month` and `Ozone`, peaking in summer and declining in winter. Because we also have access to the day of the month, let's see if we can get a more predictive value by combining the two. Put another way, instead of getting month-of-the-year resolution, let's get day-of-the-year resolution from our data.

To achieve this, we mutate a new column called `DayOfYear`. We use the `interaction()` function to generate a variable that contains the information from both the `Date` and `Month` variables. Because the `interaction()` function returns a factor, we wrap it inside the `as.numeric()` function to convert it into a numeric vector that represents the days of the year.

> **Exercise 1**
>
> To get a better idea of what `interaction()` is doing, run the following:
>
> ```
> interaction(1:4, c("a", "b", "c", "d"))
> ```

Because the new variable contains the information from the `Date` and `Month` variables, we remove them from the data using the `select()` function—they are now redundant. We then plot our new variable to see how it relates to `Ozone`.

Listing 10.1 Creating an interaction between `Date` and `Month`

```
ozoneForGam <- mutate(ozoneClean,
                      DayOfYear = as.numeric(interaction(Date, Month))) %>%
               select(c(-"Date", -"Month"))

ggplot(ozoneForGam, aes(DayOfYear, Ozone)) +
  geom_point() +
  geom_smooth() +
  theme_bw()
```

The resulting plot is shown in figure 10.6. Aha! The relationship between ozone levels and the time of year is even clearer if we use day, instead of month, resolution.

> **Exercise 2**
>
> Add another `geom_smooth()` layer to the plot, using these arguments to fit a quadratic polynomial line to the data:
>
> - `method = "lm"`
> - `formula = "y ~ x + I(x^2)"`
> - `col = "red"`
>
> Does this polynomial relationship fit the data well?

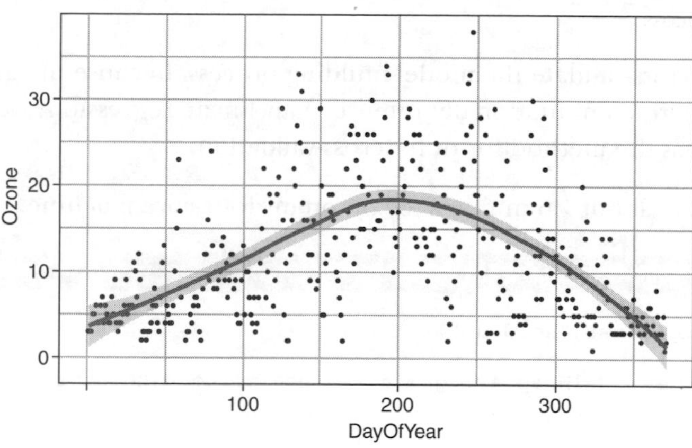

Figure 10.6 Plotting the `DayOfYear` variable against ozone levels

Now let's define our task, imputation wrapper, and feature-selection wrapper, just as we did for our linear regression model. Sadly, there isn't yet an implementation of ordinary GAMs wrapped by mlr (such as from the mgcv package). Instead, however, we have access to the gamboost algorithm, which uses boosting (as you learned about in chapter 8) to learn an ensemble of GAM models. Therefore, for this exercise, we'll use the `regr.gamboost` learner. Other than the different learner (`regr.gamboost` instead of `regr.lm`), we create our imputation and feature selection wrappers exactly the same way as in listing 9.13.

Listing 10.2 Defining the task and wrappers

```
gamTask <- makeRegrTask(data = ozoneForGam, target = "Ozone")

imputeMethod <- imputeLearner("regr.rpart")

gamImputeWrapper <- makeImputeWrapper("regr.gamboost",
                                      classes = list(numeric = imputeMethod))

gamFeatSelControl <- makeFeatSelControlSequential(method = "sfbs")

kFold <- makeResampleDesc("CV", iters = 10)

gamFeatSelWrapper <- makeFeatSelWrapper(learner = gamImputeWrapper,
                                        resampling = kFold,
                                        control = gamFeatSelControl)
```

NOTE The authors of mlr wrote it to allow the incorporation of virtually any machine learning algorithm. If there is an algorithm from a package you want to use that isn't yet wrapped by mlr, you can implement it yourself so that you can use mlr's functionality with it. While doing so isn't super-complicated, it does take a bit of explaining. Therefore, if you want to do this, I recommend following the mlr tutorial at http://mng.bz/gV5x, which does a good job of explaining the process.

All that's left to do is cross-validate the model-building process. Because the gamboost algorithm is much more computationally intense than linear regression, we're only going to use `holdout` as the method for outer cross-validation.

WARNING This takes about 1.5 minutes to run on my four-core machine.

Listing 10.3 Cross-validating the GAM model-building process

```
holdout <- makeResampleDesc("Holdout")

gamCV <- resample(gamFeatSelWrapper, gamTask, resampling = holdout)

gamCV

Resample Result
Task: ozoneForGam
Learner: regr.gamboost.imputed.featsel
Aggr perf: mse.test.mean=16.4009
Runtime: 147.441
```

Great! Our cross-validation suggests that modeling the data using the gamboost algorithm will outperform a model learned by linear regression (the latter gave us a mean MSE of 22.8 in the previous chapter).

Now let's actually build a model so I can show you how to interrogate your GAM models to understand the nonlinear functions they've learned for your predictor variables.

WARNING This takes about 3 minutes to run on my four-core machine.

Listing 10.4 Training a GAM

```
library(parallel)
library(parallelMap)

parallelStartSocket(cpus = detectCores())

gamModel <- train(gamFeatSelWrapper, gamTask)

parallelStop()

gamModelData <- getLearnerModel(gamModel, more.unwrap = TRUE)
```

First, we train a boosted GAM using our `gamTask`. We can just use `gamFeatSelWrapper` as our learner, because this performs imputation and feature selection for us. To speed things along, we can parallelize the feature selection by running the `parallelStartSocket()` function before running the `train()` function to actually train the model.

We then extract the model information using the `getLearnerModel()` function. This time, because our learner is a wrapper function, we need to supply an additional argument, `more.unwrap = TRUE`, to tell mlr that it needs to go all the way down through the wrappers to extract the base model information.

Now, let's understand our model a little better by plotting the functions it learned for each of the predictor variables. This is as easy as calling `plot()` on our model information. We can also look at the residuals from the model by extracting them with the `resid()` function. This allows us to plot the predicted values (by extracting the `$fitted()` component) against their residuals to look for patterns that suggest a poor fit. We can also plot the quantiles of the residuals against the quantiles of a theoretical normal distribution, using `qqnorm()` and `qqline()`, to see if they are normally distributed.

Listing 10.5 Plotting our GAM

```
par(mfrow = c(3, 3))

plot(gamModelData, type = "l")

plot(gamModelData$fitted(), resid(gamModelData))

qqnorm(resid(gamModelData))

qqline(resid(gamModelData))

par(mfrow = c(1, 1))
```

TIP Because we're about to create a subplot for every predictor, and two for the residuals, we first divide the plotting device into nine parts using the `mfrow` argument of the `par()` function. We set this back again using the same function. You may have a different number of predictors than I do, as returned from your feature selection.

The resulting plot is shown in figure 10.7. For each predictor, we get a plot of its value against how much that predictor contributes to the ozone estimate across its values. Lines show the shape of the functions learned by the algorithm, and we can see that they are all nonlinear.

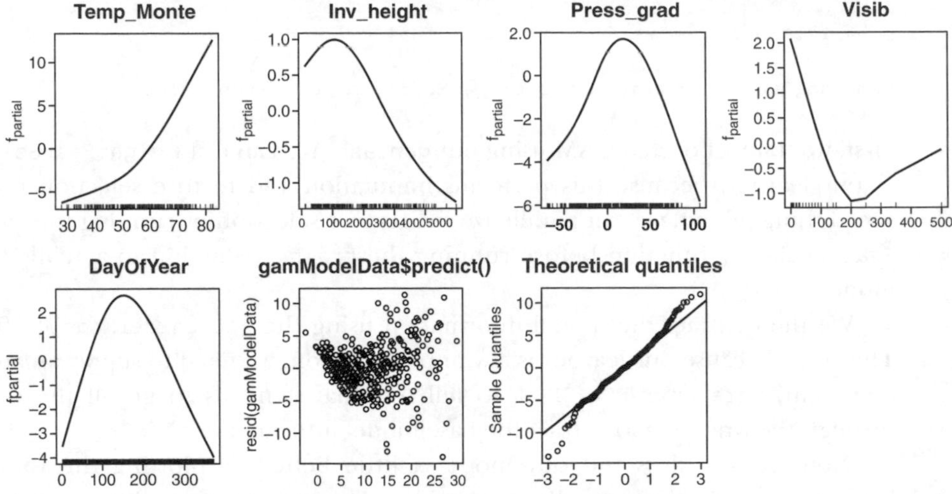

Figure 10.7 Plotting the nonlinear relationships learned by our GAM. The rug at the base of each plot shows the position of each case along the x-axis. The residual vs. fitted plot (middle panel of the second row) shows a pattern suggestive of heteroscedasticity, and the normal Q-Q plot (right panel of the second row) shows the residuals are normally distributed.

TIP The "rug" of tick marks at the base of each plot indicates the position of training cases. This helps us identify regions of each variable that have few cases, such as at the top end of the `Visib` variable. GAMs have the potential to overfit in regions with few cases.

Finally, looking at the residual plots, we can still see a pattern, which may indicate heteroscedasticity in the data. We could try training a model on a transformed `Ozone` variable (such as $\log_{10}$) to see if this helps, or use a model that doesn't make this assumption. The quantile plot shows that most of the residuals lie close to the diagonal line, indicating that they approximate a normal distribution, with some deviation at the tails (which isn't uncommon).

10.4 Strengths and weaknesses of GAMs

While it often isn't easy to tell which algorithms will perform well for a given task, here are some strengths and weaknesses that will help you decide whether GAMs will perform well for you.

The strengths of GAMs are as follows:

- They produce models that are very interpretable, despite being nonlinear.
- They can handle both continuous and categorical predictors.
- They can automatically learn nonlinear relationships in the data.

The weaknesses of GAMs are these:

- They still make strong assumptions about the data, such as homoscedasticity and the distribution of residuals (performance may suffer if these are violated).
- GAMs have a propensity to overfit the training set.
- GAMs can be particularly poor at predicting data outside the range of values of the training set.
- They cannot handle missing data.

Exercise 3

Just as in exercise 3 in chapter 9, instead of using a wrapper method, cross-validate the process of building our GAM using a filter method. Are the estimated MSE values similar? Which method is faster? Tips:

a. First, create a filter wrapper, using `gamImputeWrapper` as the learner.
b. Define a hyperparameter space to tune `"fw.abs"` using `makeParamSet()`.
c. Create a grid search definition using `makeTuneControlGrid()`.
d. Define a tune wrapper that takes the filter wrapper as a learner and performs a grid search.
e. Use `resample()` to perform cross-validation, using the tune wrapper as the learner.

Summary

- Polynomial terms can be included in linear regression to model nonlinear relationships between the predictor variables and the outcome.
- Generalized additive models (GAMs) are supervised learners for regression problems that can handle continuous and categorical predictors.
- GAMs use the equation of a straight line, but allow nonlinear relationships between the predictor variables and the outcome.
- The nonlinear functions learned by GAMs are often splines created from the sum of a series of basis functions.

Solutions to exercises

1 Experiment with the interaction() function:

```
interaction(1:4, c("a", "b", "c", "d"))
```

2 Add a geom_smooth() layer, fitting a quadratic relationship to the data:

```
ggplot(ozoneForGam, aes(DayOfYear, Ozone)) +
  geom_point() +
  geom_smooth() +
  geom_smooth(method = "lm", formula = "y ~ x + I(x^2)", col = "red") +
  theme_bw()

# The quadratic polynomial does a pretty good job of modeling the
# relationship between the variables.
```

3 Cross-validate building a GAM but using a filter method:

```
filterWrapperImp <- makeFilterWrapper(learner = gamImputeWrapper,
                                      fw.method = "linear.correlation")

filterParam <- makeParamSet(
  makeIntegerParam("fw.abs", lower = 1, upper = 12)
)

gridSearch <- makeTuneControlGrid()

tuneWrapper <- makeTuneWrapper(learner = filterWrapperImp,
                               resampling = kFold,
                               par.set = filterParam,
                               control = gridSearch)

filterGamCV <- resample(tuneWrapper, gamTask, resampling = holdout)

filterGamCV
```

11 Preventing overfitting with ridge regression, LASSO, and elastic net

This chapter covers

- Managing overfitting in regression problems
- Understanding regularization
- Using the L1 and L2 norms to shrink parameters

Our societies are full of checks and balances. In our political systems, parties balance each other (in theory) to find solutions that are at neither extreme of each other's views. Professional areas, such as financial services, have regulatory bodies to prevent them from doing wrong and ensure that the things they say and do are truthful and correct. When it comes to machine learning, it turns out we can apply our own form of regulation to the learning process to prevent the algorithms from overfitting the training set. We call this regulation in machine learning *regularization*.

11.1 What is regularization?

In this section, I'll explain what regularization is and why it's useful. Regularization (also sometimes called *shrinkage*) is a technique that prevents the parameters of a model from becoming too large and "shrinks" them toward 0. The result of regularization is models that, when making predictions on new data, have less variance.

NOTE Recall that when we say a model has "less variance," we mean it makes less-variable predictions on new data, because it is not as sensitive to the noise in the training set.

While we can apply regularization to most machine learning problems, it is most commonly used in linear modeling, where it shrinks the slope parameter of each predictor toward 0. Three particularly well-known and commonly used regularization techniques for linear models are as follows:

- Ridge regression
- Least absolute shrinkage and selection operator (LASSO)
- Elastic net

These three techniques can be thought of as extensions to linear models that reduce overfitting. Because they shrink model parameters toward 0, they can also automatically perform feature selection by forcing predictors with little information to have no or negligible impact on predictions.

NOTE When I say "linear modeling," I'm referring to the modeling of data using the general linear model, generalized linear model, or generalized additive model that I showed you in chapters 9 and 10.

By the end of this chapter, I hope you'll have an intuitive understanding of what regularization is, how it works, and why it's important. You'll understand how ridge regression and LASSO work and how they're useful, and how elastic net is a mixture of them both. Finally, you'll build ridge regression, LASSO, and elastic net models, and use benchmarking to compare them to each other and to a linear regression model with no regularization.

11.2 What is ridge regression?

In this section, I'll show you what ridge regression is, how it works, and why it's useful. Take a look at the example in figure 11.1, which I've reproduced from chapter 3. I used this figure in chapter 3 to show you what underfitting and overfitting look like for classification problems. When we underfit the problem, we partition the feature space in a way that doesn't do a good job of capturing local differences near the

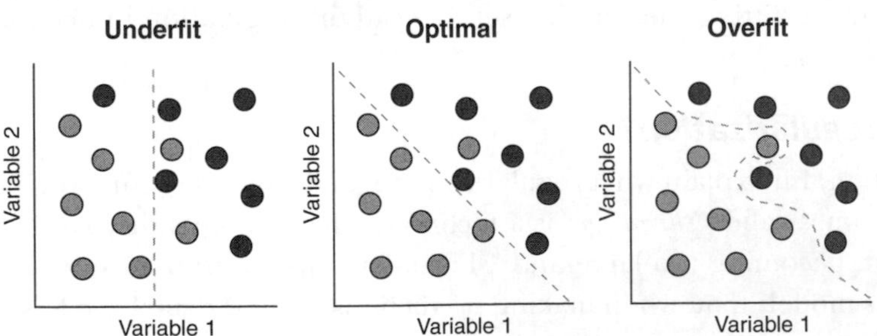

Figure 11.1 Examples of underfitting, optimal fitting, and overfitting for a two-class classification problem. The dotted line represents a decision boundary.

decision boundary. When we overfit, we place too much importance on these local differences and end up with a decision boundary that captures much of the noise in the training set, resulting in an overly complex decision boundary.

Now take a look at figure 11.2, which shows an example of what underfitting and overfitting look like for regression problems. When we underfit the data, we miss local differences in the relationship and produce a model that has high bias (makes inaccurate predictions). When we overfit the data, our model is too sensitive to local differences in the relationship and has high variance (will make very variable predictions on new data).

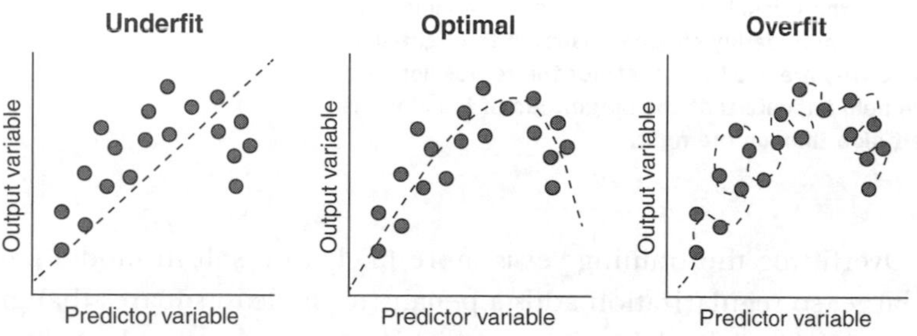

Figure 11.2 Examples of underfitting, optimal fitting, and overfitting for a single-predictor regression problem. The dotted line represents the regression line.

> **NOTE** The example I've used to labor this point is of a nonlinear relationship, but the sample applies to models of linear relationships too.

The principal job of regularization is to prevent algorithms from learning models that are overfit, by discouraging complexity. This is achieved by penalizing model parameters that are large, shrinking them toward 0. This might sound counterintuitive: surely the model parameters learned by ordinary least squares (OLS from chapter 9) are the best, as they minimize the residual error. The problem is that this is only necessarily true for the training set, and not the test set.

Consider the example in figure 11.3. In the left-side plot, imagine that we only measured the two more darkly shaded cases. OLS would learn a line that passes through both cases, because this will minimize the sum of squares. We collect more cases in our study, and when we plot them on the right-side plot, we can see that the first model we trained doesn't generalize well to the new data. This is due to *sampling error*, which is the difference between the distribution of data in our sample of cases and the distribution of data in the wider population we're trying to make predictions on. In this (slightly contrived) case, because we only measured two cases, the sample doesn't do a good job of representing the wider population, and we learned a model that overfit the training set.

This is where regularization comes in. While OLS will learn the model that best fits the training set, the training set probably isn't perfectly representative of the wider

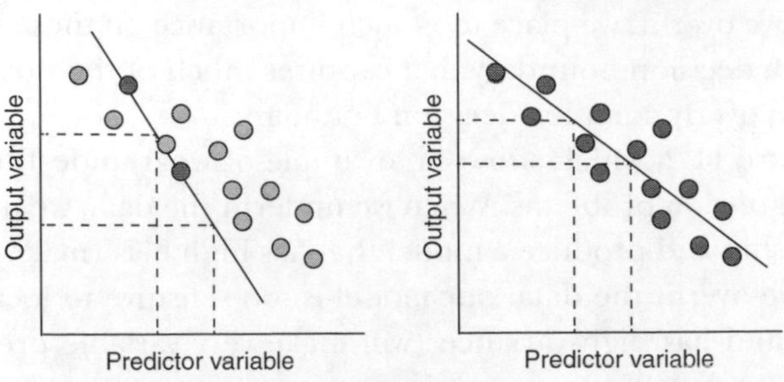

Figure 11.3 Sampling error leads to models that don't generalize well to new data. In the left-side example, a regression line is fit, considering only the more darkly shaded cases. In the right-side example, all the cases are used to construct the regression line. The dotted lines help indicate that the magnitude of the slope is larger on the left side than on the right.

population. Overfitting the training set is more likely to result in model parameters that are too large, so regularization adds a penalty to the least squares that grows bigger with larger estimated model parameters. This process usually adds a little bias to the model, because we're intentionally underfitting the training set, but the reduction in model variance often results in a better model anyway. This is especially true in situations where the ratio of predictors to cases is large.

NOTE How representative your dataset is of the wider population depends on carefully planning your data acquisition, avoiding introducing bias with experimental design (or identifying and correcting for it if the data already exists), and ensuring that your datasets are sufficiently large to learn real patterns. If your dataset poorly represents the wider population, no machine learning technique, including cross-validation, will be able to help you!

So regularization can help prevent overfitting due to sampling error, but perhaps a more important use of regularization is in preventing the inclusion of spurious predictors. If we add predictors to an existing linear regression model, we're likely to get better predictions on the training set. This might lead us (falsely) to believe we are creating a better model by including more predictors. This is sometimes called *kitchen-sink regression* (because everything goes in, including the kitchen sink). For example, imagine that you want to predict the number of people in a park on a given day, and you include the value of the FTSE 100 that day as a predictor. It's unlikely (unless the park was near the London Stock Exchange, perhaps) that the value of the FTSE 100 has an influence on the number of people. Retaining this spurious predictor in the model has the potential to result in overfitting the training set. Because regularization will shrink this parameter, it will reduce the degree to which the model overfits the training set.

Regularization can also help in situations that are *ill-posed*. An ill-posed problem in mathematics is one that does not satisfy these three conditions: having a solution, having a unique solution, and having a solution that depends on the initial conditions. In statistical modeling, a common ill-posed problem is when there is not one optimal parameter value, often encountered when the number of parameters is higher than the number of cases. In situations like this, regularization can make estimating the parameters a more stable problem.

What does this penalty look like that we add to the least squares estimate? Two penalties are frequently used: the L1 norm and the L2 norm. I'll start by showing you what the L2 norm is and how it works, because this is the regularization method used in ridge regression. Then I'll extend this to show you how LASSO uses the L1 norm method, and how elastic net combines both the L1 and L2 norms.

11.3 What is the L2 norm, and how does ridge regression use it?

In this section, I'll show you a mathematical and graphical explanation of the L2 norm, how ridge regression uses it, and why you would use it. Imagine that you want to predict how busy your local park will be, depending on the temperature that day. An example of what this data might look like is shown in figure 11.4.

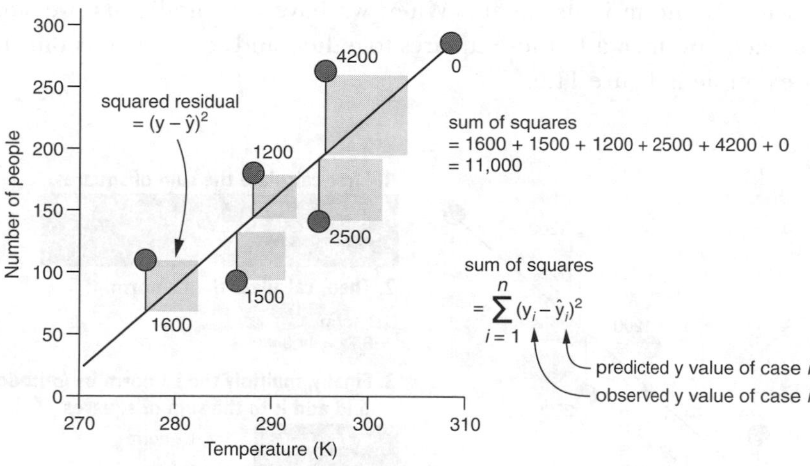

Figure 11.4 Calculating the sum of squares from a model that predicts the number of people in a park based on the temperature

> **NOTE** I realize that people may be reading this who are from countries that use Fahrenheit or Celsius to measure temperature, so I've shown the scale in Kelvin to irritate everyone equally.

When using OLS, the residuals for a particular combination of intercept and slope are calculated for each case and squared. These squared residuals are then all added up to give the sum of squares. We can represent this in mathematical notation as in equation 11.1.

$$\text{sum of squares} = \sum_{i=1}^{n} (y_i - \hat{y}_i)^2 \qquad \textbf{Equation 11.1}$$

y_i is the value of the outcome variable for case i, and $\hat{y}_i$ is its value predicted by the model. This is the vertical distance of each case from the line. The Greek sigma ($\sum_{i=1}^{n}$) simply means that we calculate this vertical distance and square it for every case from the first one ($i = 1$) to the last one (n) and then add up all these values.

Mathematical functions that are minimized by machine learning algorithms to select the best combinations of parameters are called *loss functions*. Therefore, least squares is the loss function for the OLS algorithm.

Ridge regression modifies the least squares loss function slightly to include a term that makes the function's value larger, the larger the parameter estimates are. As a result, the algorithm now has to balance selecting the model parameters that minimize the sum of squares, and selecting parameters than minimize this new penalty. In ridge regression, this penalty is called the *L2 norm*, and it is very easy to calculate: we simply square all of the model parameters and add them up (all except the intercept). When we have only one continuous predictor, we have only one parameter (the slope), so the L2 norm is its square. When we have two predictors, we square the slopes for each and then add these squares together, and so on. This is illustrated for our park example in figure 11.5.

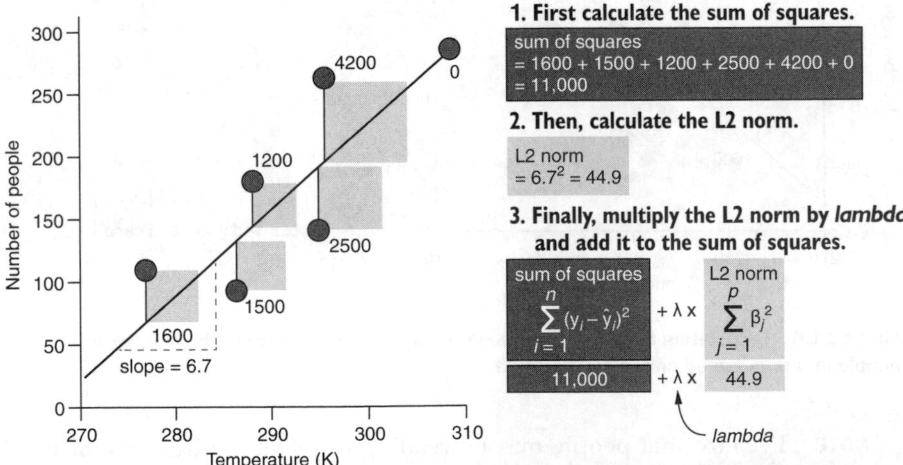

Figure 11.5 Calculating the sum of squares and the L2 norm for the slope between temperature and the number of people at the park.

NOTE Can you see that, in general, the more predictors a model has, the larger its L2 norm will be, because we are adding their squares together? Ridge regularization therefore penalizes models that are too complex (because they have too many predictors).

So that we can control how much we want to penalize model complexity, we multiply the L2 norm by a value called *lambda* (λ, because Greek letters always sound cool). *Lambda* can be any value from 0 to infinity and acts as a volume knob: large values of *lambda* strongly penalize model complexity, while small values of *lambda* weakly penalize model complexity. *Lambda* cannot be estimated from the data, so it is a hyperparameter that we need to tune to achieve the best performance by cross-validation. Once we calculate the L2 norm and multiply it by *lambda*, we then add this product to the sum of squares to get our penalized least squares loss function.

NOTE If we set *lambda* to 0, this removes the L2 norm penalty from the equation and we get back to the OLS loss function. If we set *lambda* to a very large value, all the slopes will shrink close to 0.

If we're mathematically minded, then we can represent this in mathematical notation as in equation 11.2. Can you see that this is the same as the sum of squares as in equation 11.1, but we've added the *lambda* and L2 norm terms?

$$\text{loss function}_{L2} = \sum_{i=1}^{n} (y_i - \hat{y}_i) + \lambda \sum_{j=1}^{p} \beta_j^2 \qquad \textbf{Equation 11.2}$$

So ridge regression learns a combination of model parameters that minimize this new loss function. Imagine a situation where we have many predictors. OLS might estimate a combination of model parameters that do a great job of minimizing the least squares loss function, but the L2 norm of this combination might be huge. In this situation, ridge regression would estimate a combination of parameters that have a slightly higher least squares value but a considerably lower L2 norm. Because the L2 norm gets smaller when model parameters are smaller, the slopes estimated by ridge regression will probably be smaller than those estimated by OLS.

IMPORTANT When using L2- or L1-penalized loss functions, it's critical that the predictor variables are scaled first (divided by their standard deviation to put them on the same scale). This is because we are adding the squared slopes (in the case of L2 regularization), and this value is going to be considerably larger for predictors on larger scales (millimeters versus kilometers, for example). If we don't scale the predictors first, they won't all be given equal importance.

If you prefer a more graphical explanation of the L2-penalized loss function (I know I do), take a look at figure 11.6. The x- and y-axes show values for two slope parameters, (β_1 and β_2). The shaded contour lines represent different sum of squares values for different combinations of the two parameters, where the combination resulting in the smallest sum of squares is at the center of the contours. The dashed circles centered at

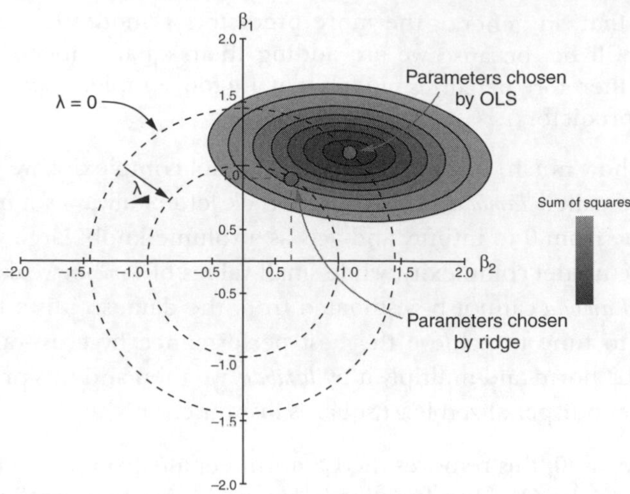

Figure 11.6 A graphical representation of the ridge regression penalty. The x- and y-axes represent the values of two model parameters. The solid, concentric circles represent the sum of squares value for different combinations of the parameters. The dashed circles represent the L2 norm multiplied by *lambda*.

0 represent the L2 norm multiplied by different values of *lambda*, for the combinations of β_1 and β_2 the dashed lines pass through.

Notice that when *lambda* = 0, the circle passes through the combination of β_1 and β_2 that minimizes the sum of squares. When *lambda* is increased, the circle shrinks symmetrically toward 0. Now the combination of parameters that minimizes the penalized loss function is the combination with the smallest sum of squares *that lies on the circle.* Put another way, the optimal solution when using ridge regression is always at the intersection of the circle and the ellipse around the OLS estimate. Can you see then that as we increase *lambda*, the circle shrinks and the selected combination of model parameters gets sucked toward 0?

NOTE In this example, I've illustrated L2 regularization for two slope parameters. If we had only one slope, we would represent the same process on a number line. If we had three parameters, the same would apply in a three-dimensional space, and the penalty circle would become a penalty sphere. This continues in as many dimensions as you have non-intercept parameters (where the penalty becomes a hypersphere).

So, by using the L2-penalized loss function to learn the slope parameters, ridge regression prevents us from training models that overfit the training data.

NOTE The intercept isn't included when calculating the L2 norm because it is defined as the value of the outcome variable when all the slope parameters are equal to 0.

11.4 What is the L1 norm, and how does LASSO use it?

Now that you know about ridge regression, learning how LASSO works will be a simple extension of what you've already learned. In this section, I'll show you what the L1 norm is, how it differs from the L2 norm, and how the least absolute shrinkage and selection operator (LASSO) uses it to shrink parameter estimates.

Let's remind ourselves what the L2 norm looks like, in equation 11.3. Recall that we square the value of each of the slope parameters and add them all up. We then multiply this L2 norm by *lambda* to get the penalty we add to the sum of squares loss function.

$$\text{L2 norm} = \sum_{j=1}^{p} \beta_j^2$$ **Equation 11.3**

The L1 norm is only slightly different than the L2 norm. Instead of squaring the parameter values, we take their absolute value instead and *then* sum them. This is shown in equation 11.4 by the vertical lines around β_j.

$$\text{L1 norm} = \sum_{j=1}^{p} |\beta_j|$$ **Equation 11.4**

We then create the loss function for LASSO (the L1-penalized loss function) in exactly the same way we did for ridge regression: we multiply the L1 norm by *lambda* (which has the same meaning) and add it to the sum of squares. The L1-penalized loss function is shown in equation 11.5. Notice that the only difference between this equation and equation 11.2 is that we take the absolute value of the parameters before summing them, instead of squaring them. Say we had three slopes, one of which was negative: 2.2, –3.1, 0.8. The L1 norm of these three slopes would be 2.2 + 3.1 + 0.8 = 6.1.

$$\text{loss function}_{\text{L1}} = \sum_{i=1}^{n} (y_i - \hat{y}_i) + \lambda \sum_{j=1}^{p} |\beta_j|$$ **Equation 11.5**

I can already hear you thinking, "So what? What's the benefit/difference of using the L1 norm instead of the L2 norm?" Well, ridge regression can shrink parameter estimates toward 0, but they will never actually *be* 0 (unless the OLS estimate is 0 to begin with). So if you have a machine learning task where you believe all the variables should have some degree of predictive value, ridge regression is great because it won't remove any variables. But what if you have a large number of variables and/or you want an algorithm that will perform feature selection for you? LASSO is helpful here because unlike ridge regression, LASSO *is* able to shrink small parameter values to 0, effectively removing that predictor from the model.

Let's represent this graphically the same way we did for ridge regression. Figure 11.7 shows the contours of the sum of squares for the same two imaginary parameters as in

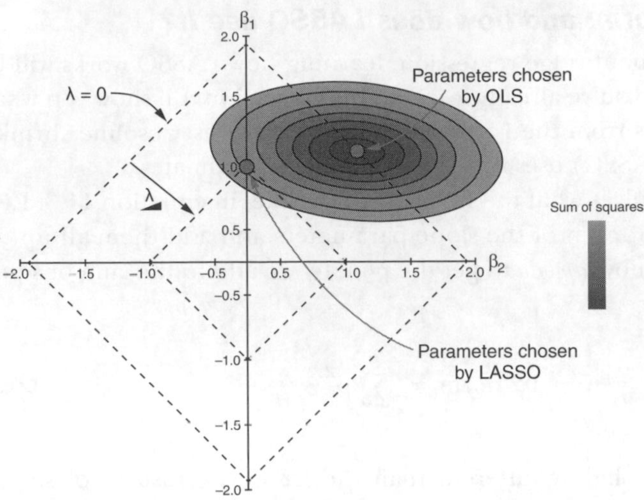

Figure 11.7 A graphical representation of the LASSO penalty. The x- and y-axes represent the values of two model parameters. The solid, concentric circles represent the sum of squares value for different combinations of the parameters. The dashed diamonds represent the L2 norm multiplied by *lambda*.

figure 11.6. Instead of forming a circle, the LASSO penalty forms a square, rotated 45° such that its vertices lie along the axes (I guess you could call this a diamond). Can you see that, for the same *lambda* as in our ridge regression example, the combination of parameters with the smallest sum of squares that touches the diamond is one where parameter β_2 is 0? This means the predictor represented by this parameter has been removed from the model.

> **NOTE** If we had three parameters, we could represent the LASSO penalty as a cube (with its vertices aligned with the axes). It's hard to visualize this in more than three dimensions, but the LASSO penalty would be a hypercube.

Just to make this extra clear, I've overlaid the LASSO and ridge penalties in figure 11.8, including dotted lines that highlight the parameter values chosen by each method.

11.5 What is elastic net?

In this section, I'll show you what elastic net is and how it mixes L2 and L1 regularization to find a compromise between ridge regression and LASSO parameter estimates. Sometimes you may have a prior justification for why you wish to use ridge regression or LASSO. If it's important that you include all your predictors in the model, however small their contribution, use ridge regression. If you want the algorithm to perform feature selection for you by shrinking uninformative slopes to 0, use LASSO. More often than not, though, the decision between ridge regression and LASSO isn't a clear one. In such situations, *don't* choose between them: use elastic net, instead.

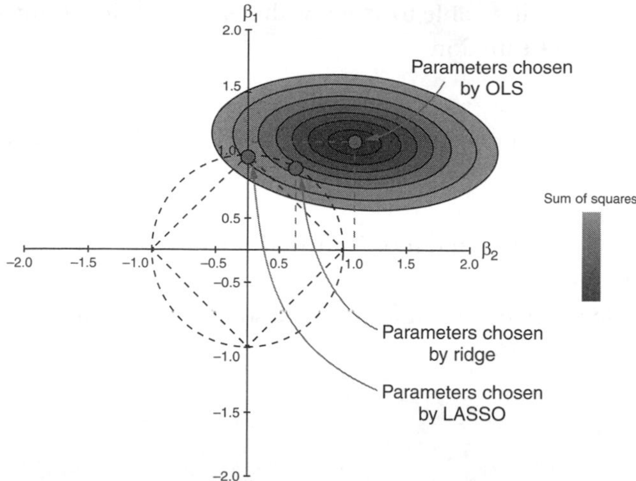

Figure 11.8 Comparing the ridge regression and LASSO penalties

NOTE One important limitation of LASSO is that if you have more predictors than cases, it will select at most a number of predictors equal to the number of cases in the data. Put another way, if your dataset contains 100 predictors and 50 cases, LASSO will set the slopes of at least 50 predictors to 0!

Elastic net is an extension of linear modeling that includes both L2 *and* L1 regularization in its loss function. It finds a combination of parameter estimates somewhere between those found by ridge regression and LASSO. We're also able to control just how much importance we place on the L2 versus the L1 norms using the hyperparameter *alpha*.

Take a look at equation 11.6. We multiply the L2 norm by $1 - \alpha$, multiply the L1 norm by α, and add up these values. We multiply this value by *lambda* and add it to the sum of squares. *Alpha* here can take any value between 0 and 1:

- When *alpha* is 0, the L1 norm becomes 0, and we get ridge regression.
- When *alpha* is 1, the L2 norm becomes 0, and we get LASSO.
- When *alpha* is between 0 and 1, we get a mixture of ridge regression and LASSO.

How do we choose *alpha*? We don't! We tune it as a hyperparameter and let cross-validation choose the best-performing value for us.

$$\text{loss function}_{\text{elastic}} = SS + \lambda\left((1 - \alpha) \times L2\ norm + \alpha \times L1\ norm\right) \quad \textbf{Equation 11.6}$$

If you're more mathematically inclined, the full elastic net loss function is shown in equation 11.7. If you're not mathematically inclined, feel free to skip over this; but if you look carefully, I'm sure you'll be able to see how the elastic net loss function combines the ridge and LASSO loss functions.

$$\text{loss function}_{\text{elastic}} = \sum_{i=1}^{n} (y_i - \hat{y}_i) + \lambda\left((1-\alpha)\sum_{j=1}^{p} \beta_j^2 + \alpha \sum_{j=1}^{p} |\beta_j|\right) \quad \text{Equation 11.7}$$

Prefer a graphical explanation? Yep, me too. Figure 11.9 compares the shapes of the ridge, LASSO, and elastic net penalties. Because the elastic net penalty is somewhere between the ridge and LASSO penalties, it looks like a square with rounded sides.

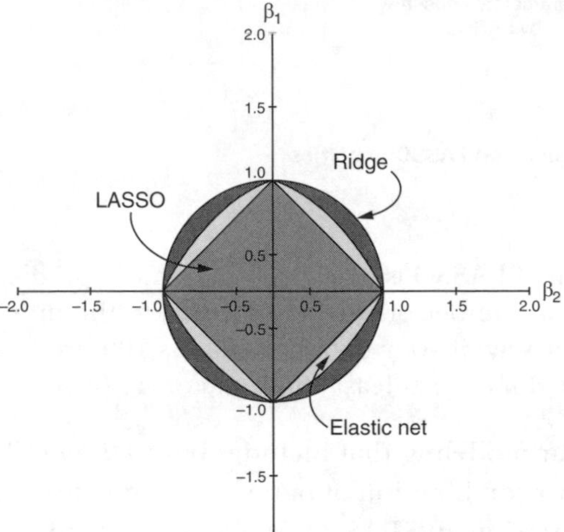

Figure 11.9 Comparing the shape of the ridge regression, LASSO, and elastic net penalties

So why might we prefer elastic net over ridge regression or LASSO? Well, elastic net can shrink parameter estimates to 0, allowing it to perform feature selection like LASSO. But it also circumvents LASSO's limitation of not being able to select more variables than there are cases. Another limitation of LASSO is that if there is a group of predictors that are correlated with each other, LASSO will only select one of the predictors. Elastic net, on the other hand, is able to retain the group of predictors.

For these reasons, I usually dive straight in with elastic net as my regularization method of choice. Even if pure ridge or LASSO will result in the best-performing model, the ability to tune *alpha* as a hyperparameter still allows the possibility of selecting ridge or LASSO, although the optimal solution is usually somewhere between them. An exception to this is when we have prior knowledge about the effect of the predictors we've included in our model. If we have very strong domain knowledge that predictors ought to be included in the model, then we may have a preference for ridge regression. Conversely, if we have a strong prior belief that there are variables that probably don't contribute anything (but we don't know which), we may prefer LASSO.

I hope I've conveyed how regularization can be used to extend linear models to avoid overfitting. You should now also have a conceptual understanding of ridge regression, LASSO, and elastic net, so let's turn concepts into experience by training a model of each!

11.6 Building your first ridge, LASSO, and elastic net models

In this section, we're going to build ridge, LASSO, and elastic net models on the same dataset, and use benchmarking to compare how they perform against each other and against a vanilla (unregularized) linear model. Imagine that you're trying to estimate the market price of wheat for the coming year in Iowa. The market price depends on the yield for that particular year, so you're trying to predict the yield of wheat from rain and temperature measurements. Let's start by loading the mlr and tidyverse packages:

```
library(mlr)

library(tidyverse)
```

11.6.1 Loading and exploring the Iowa dataset

Now let's load the data, which is built into the lasso2 package, convert it into a tibble (with `as_tibble()`), and explore it.

> **NOTE** You may need to install the lasso2 package first with `install.packages ("lasso2")`.

We have a tibble containing only 33 cases and 10 variables of various rainfall and temperature measurements, the year, and the wheat yield.

Listing 11.1 Loading and exploring the `Iowa` dataset

```
data(Iowa, package = "lasso2")

iowaTib <- as_tibble(Iowa)

iowaTib

# A tibble: 33 x 10
    Year Rain0 Temp1 Rain1 Temp2 Rain2 Temp3 Rain3 Temp4 Yield
   <int> <dbl> <dbl> <dbl> <dbl> <dbl> <dbl> <dbl> <dbl> <dbl>
 1  1930  17.8  60.2  5.83  69    1.49  77.9  2.42  74.4  34
 2  1931  14.8  57.5  3.83  75    2.72  77.2  3.3   72.6  32.9
 3  1932  28.0  62.3  5.17  72    3.12  75.8  7.1   72.2  43
 4  1933  16.8  60.5  1.64  77.8  3.45  76.4  3.01  70.5  40
 5  1934  11.4  69.5  3.49  77.2  3.85  79.7  2.84  73.4  23
 6  1935  22.7  55    7     65.9  3.35  79.4  2.42  73.6  38.4
 7  1936  17.9  66.2  2.85  70.1  0.51  83.4  3.48  79.2  20
 8  1937  23.3  61.8  3.8   69    2.63  75.9  3.99  77.8  44.6
 9  1938  18.5  59.5  4.67  69.2  4.24  76.5  3.82  75.7  46.3
10  1939  18.6  66.4  5.32  71.4  3.15  76.2  4.72  70.7  52.2
# ... with 23 more rows
```

Let's plot the data to get a better understanding of the relationships within it. We'll use our usual trick of gathering the data so we can facet by each variable, supplying `"free_x"` as the `scales` argument to allow the x-axis to vary between facets. To get an indication as to any linear relationships with `Yield`, I also applied a `geom_smooth` layer, using `"lm"` as the argument to `method` to get linear fits.

Listing 11.2 Plotting the data

```
iowaUntidy <- gather(iowaTib, "Variable", "Value", -Yield)

ggplot(iowaUntidy, aes(Value, Yield)) +
  facet_wrap(~ Variable, scales = "free_x") +
  geom_point() +
  geom_smooth(method = "lm") +
  theme_bw()
```

The resulting plot is shown in figure 11.10. It looks like some of the variables correlate with `Yield`; but notice that because we don't have a large number of cases, the slopes of some of these relationships could drastically change if we only removed a couple of cases near the extremes of the x-axis. For example, would the slope between `Rain2` and `Yield` be nearly as steep if we hadn't measured those three cases with the highest rainfall? We're going to need regularization to prevent overfitting for this dataset.

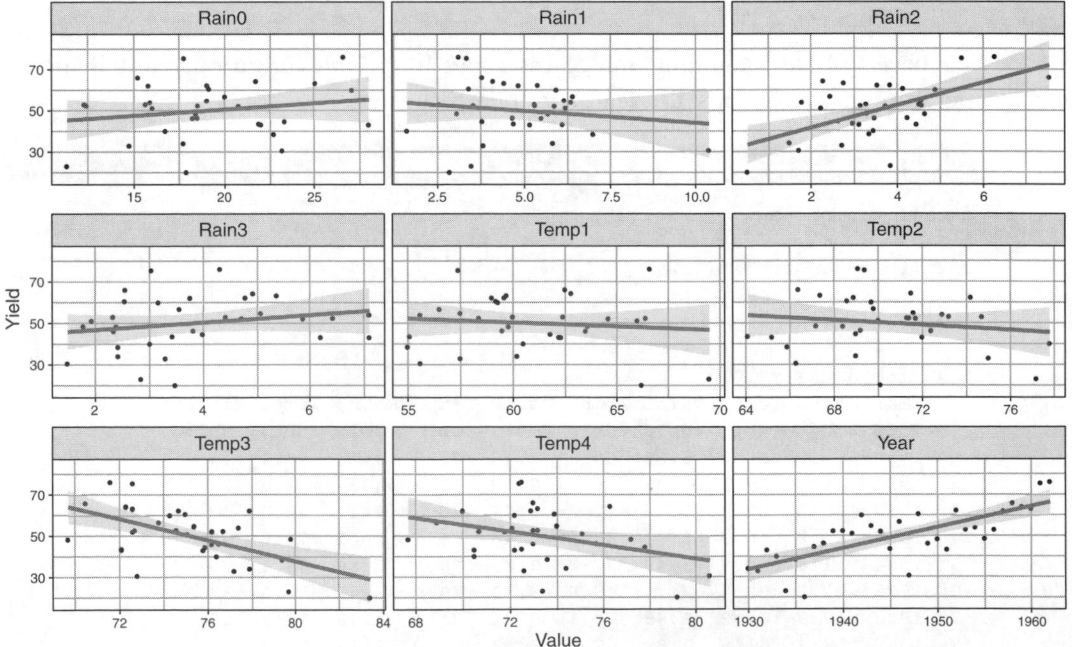

Figure 11.10 Plotting each of the predictors against wheat yield for the `Iowa` dataset. Lines represent linear model fits between each predictor and yield.

11.6.2 Training the ridge regression model

In this section, I'll walk you through training a ridge regression model to predict `Yield` from our `Iowa` dataset. We'll tune the *lambda* hyperparameter and train a model using its optimal value.

Let's define our task and learner, this time supplying `"regr.glmnet"` as the argument to `makeLearner()`. Handily, the `glmnet` function (from the package of the same name) allows us to create ridge, LASSO, and elastic net models using the same function. Notice that we set the value of *alpha* equal to 0 here. This is how we specify that we want to use pure ridge regression with the `glmnet` function. We also supply an argument that you haven't seen before: `id`. The `id` argument just lets us supply a unique name to every learner. The reason we need this now is that later in the chapter, we're going to benchmark our ridge, LASSO, and elastic net learners against each other. Because we create each of these with the same `glmnet` function, we'll get an error because they won't each have a unique identifier.

Listing 11.3 Creating the task and learner

```
iowaTask <- makeRegrTask(data = iowaTib, target = "Yield")

ridge <- makeLearner("regr.glmnet", alpha = 0, id = "ridge")
```

Let's get an idea of how much each predictor would contribute to a model's ability to predict `Yield`. We can use the `generateFilterValuesData()` and `plotFilterValues()` functions we used in chapter 9 when performing feature selection using the filter method.

Listing 11.4 Generating and plotting filter values

```
filterVals <- generateFilterValuesData(iowaTask)

plotFilterValues(filterVals) + theme_bw()
```

The resulting plot is shown in figure 11.11. We can see that `Year` contains the most predictive information about `Yield`; `Rain3`, `Rain1`, and `Rain0` seem to contribute very little; and `Temp1` seems to make a negative contribution, suggesting that including it in the model will be to the detriment of predictive accuracy.

But we're not going to perform feature selection. Instead, we're going to enter all the predictors and let the algorithm shrink the ones that contribute less to the model. The first thing we need to do is tune the *lambda* hyperparameter that controls just how big a penalty to apply to the parameter estimates.

NOTE Remember that when *lambda* equals 0, we are applying no penalty and get the OLS parameter estimates. The larger *lambda* is, the more the parameters are shrunk toward 0.

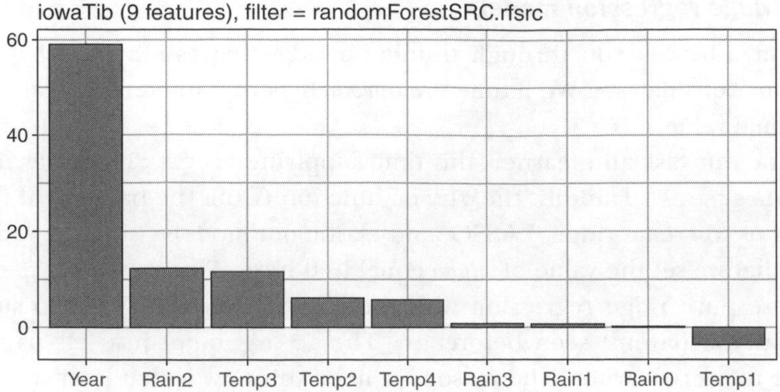

Figure 11.11 Plotting the result of `generateFilterValuesData()`. Bar height represents how much information each predictor contains about wheat yield.

We'll start by defining the hyperparameter space we're going to search to find the optimal value of *lambda*. Recall that to do this, we use the `makeParamSet()` function, supplying each of our hyperparameters to search, separated by commas. Because we only have one hyperparameter to tune, and because *lambda* can take any numeric value between 0 and infinity, we use the `makeNumericParam()` function to specify that we want to search for numeric values of *lambda* between 0 and 15.

NOTE Notice that I've called the hyperparameter `"s"` instead of `"lambda"`. If you run `getParamSet(ridge)`, you will indeed see a tunable hyperparameter called *lambda*, so what's with the `"s"`? The authors of glmnet helpfully wrote it so that it will build models for a range of *lambda*s for us. Then we can plot the *lambda*s to see which one gives the best cross-validated performance. This is handy, but seeing as we're using mlr as a universal interface to many machine learning packages, it makes sense for us to tune *lambda* ourselves the way we're used to. The glmnet *lambda* hyperparameter is used for specifying a *sequence* of *lambda* values to try, and the authors specifically recommend *not* supplying a single value for this hyperparameter. Instead, the *s* hyperparameter is used to train a model with a single, specific *lambda*, so this is what we will tune when using mlr. For more information, I suggest reading the documentation for glmnet by running `?glmnet::glmnet`.

Next, let's define our search method as a random search with 200 iterations using `makeTuneControlRandom()`, and define our cross-validation method as 3-fold cross-validation repeated 5 times, using `makeResampleDesc()`. Finally, we run our hyperparameter tuning process with the `tuneParams()` function. To speed things up a little, let's use `parallelStartSocket()` to parallelize the search.

WARNING This takes about 30 seconds on my four-core machine.

Listing 11.5 Tuning the *lambda* (s) hyperparameter

```
ridgeParamSpace <- makeParamSet(
  makeNumericParam("s", lower = 0, upper = 15))

randSearch <- makeTuneControlRandom(maxit = 200)

cvForTuning <- makeResampleDesc("RepCV", folds = 3, reps = 10)

library(parallel)
library(parallelMap)

parallelStartSocket(cpus = detectCores())

tunedRidgePars <- tuneParams(ridge, task = iowaTask,
                             resampling = cvForTuning,
                             par.set = ridgeParamSpace,
                             control = randSearch)

parallelStop()

tunedRidgePars

Tune result:
Op. pars: s=6.04
mse.test.mean=96.8360
```

Our tuning process selected 6.04 as the best-performing *lambda* (yours might be a little different due to the random search). But how can we be sure we searched over a large enough range of *lambdas*? Let's plot each value of *lambda* against the mean MSE of its models and see if it looks like there may be a better value outside of our search space (greater than 15).

First, we extract the *lambda* and mean MSE values for each iteration of the random search by supplying our tuning object as the argument to the `generateHyperParsEffectData()` function. Then, we supply this data as the first argument of the `plotHyperParsEffect()` function and tell it we want to plot the values of *s* on the x-axis and the mean MSE (`"mse.test.mean"`) on the y-axis, and that we want a line that connects the data points.

Listing 11.6 Plotting the hyperparameter tuning process

```
ridgeTuningData <- generateHyperParsEffectData(tunedRidgePars)

plotHyperParsEffect(ridgeTuningData, x = "s", y = "mse.test.mean",
                    plot.type = "line") +
  theme_bw()
```

The resulting plot is shown in figure 11.12. We can see that the MSE is minimized for *lambdas* between 5 and 6, and it seems that increasing *lambda* beyond 6 results in models that perform worse. If the MSE seemed to be still decreasing at the edge of our search

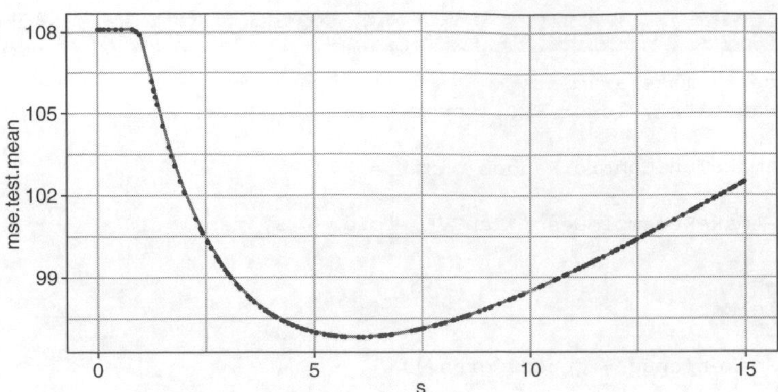

Figure 11.12 Plotting the ridge regression *lambda*-tuning process. The x-axis represents *lambda*, and the y-axis represents the mean MSE. Dots represent values of *lambda* sampled by the random search. The line connects the dots.

space, we would need to expand the search in case we're missing better hyperparameter values. Because we appear to be at the minimum, we're going to stop our search here.

NOTE Maybe I've been too hasty, because it's possible we are only in a *local minimum*, the smallest MSE value compared to the values of *lambda* around it. When searching a hyperparameter space, there may be many local minima (plural of *minimum*); but we really want to find the *global minimum*, which is the lowest MSE value across all possible hyperparameter values. For example, imagine that if we keep increasing *lambda*, the MSE gets higher but then starts to come down again, forming a hill. It's possible that this hill continues to decrease even more than the minimum shown in figure 11.12. Therefore, it's a good idea to really search your hyperparameter space well to try to find that global minimum.

Exercise 1

Repeat the tuning process, but this time expand the search space to include values of s between 0 and 50 (don't overwrite anything). Did our original search find a local minimum or the global minimum?

Okay, now that we think we've selected the best-performing value of *lambda*, let's train a model using that value. First, we use the `setHyperPars()` function to define a new learner using our tuned *lambda* value. Then, we use the `train()` function to train the model on our `iowaTask`.

Listing 11.7 Training a ridge regression model using the tuned *lambda*

```
tunedRidge <- setHyperPars(ridge, par.vals = tunedRidgePars$x)

tunedRidgeModel <- train(tunedRidge, iowaTask)
```

One of the main motivations for using linear models is that we can interpret the slopes to get an idea of how much the outcome variable changes with each predictor. So let's extract the parameter estimates from our ridge regression model. First, we extract the model data using the `getLearnerModel()` function. Then, we use the `coef()` function (short for *coefficients*) to extract the parameter estimates. Note that because of the way glmnet works, we need to supply the value of *lambda* to get the parameters for that model.

When we print `ridgeCoefs`, we get a matrix containing the name of each parameter and its slope. The intercept is the estimated `Yield` when all the predictors are 0. Of course, it doesn't make much sense to have negative wheat yield, but because it doesn't make sense for all the predictors to be 0 (such as the year), we won't interpret this. We're more interested in interpreting the slopes, which are reported on the predictor's original scale. We can see that for every additional year, wheat yield increased by 0.533 bushels per acre. For a one-inch increase in `Rain1`, wheat yield *decreased* by 0.703, and so on.

NOTE Recall that I mentioned how important it is to scale our predictors so that they are weighted equally when calculating the L1 and/or L2 norms. Well, glmnet does this for us by default, using its `standardize = TRUE` argument. This is handy, but it's important to remember that the parameter estimates are transformed back onto the variables' original scale.

Listing 11.8 Extracting the model parameters

```
ridgeModelData <- getLearnerModel(tunedRidgeModel)

ridgeCoefs <- coef(ridgeModelData, s = tunedRidgePars$x$s)

ridgeCoefs

10 x 1 sparse Matrix of class "dgCMatrix"
                      1
(Intercept) -908.45834
Year           0.53278
Rain0          0.34269
Temp1         -0.23601
Rain1         -0.70286
Temp2          0.03184
Rain2          1.91915
Temp3         -0.57963
Rain3          0.63953
Temp4         -0.47821
```

Let's plot these parameter estimates against the estimates from unregularized linear regression, so you can see the effect of parameter shrinkage. First, we need to train a linear model using OLS. We could do this with mlr, but as we're not going to do anything fancy with this model, we can create one quickly using the `lm()` function. The first argument to `lm()` is the formula `Yield ~ .`, which means `Yield` is our outcome variable, and we want to model it (~) using all other variables in the data (`.`). We tell the function where to find the data, and wrap the whole `lm()` function inside the `coef()` function to extract its parameter estimates.

Next, we create a tibble containing three variables:

- The parameter names
- The ridge regression parameter values
- The `lm` parameter values

Because we want to exclude the intercepts, we use `[-1]` to subset all the parameters except the first one (the intercept).

So that we can facet by model, we `gather()` the data and then plot it using `ggplot()`. Because it's nice to see things in ascending or descending order, we supply `reorder(Coef, Beta)`, which will use the `Coef` variable as the x aesthetic ordered by the `Beta` variable. By default, `geom_bar()` tries to plot frequencies, but because we want bars to represent the actual value of each parameter, we set the `stat = "identity"` argument.

Listing 11.9 Plotting the model parameters

```
lmCoefs <- coef(lm(Yield ~ ., data = iowaTib))

coefTib <- tibble(Coef = rownames(ridgeCoefs)[-1],
                  Ridge = as.vector(ridgeCoefs)[-1],
                  Lm = as.vector(lmCoefs)[-1])

coefUntidy <- gather(coefTib, key = Model, value = Beta, -Coef)

ggplot(coefUntidy, aes(reorder(Coef, Beta), Beta, fill = Model)) +
  geom_bar(stat = "identity", col = "black") +
  facet_wrap(~Model) +
  theme_bw()  +
  theme(legend.position = "none")
```

The resulting plot is shown in figure 11.13. In the left facet, we have the parameter estimates for the unregularized model; and in the right facet, we have the estimates for our ridge regression model. Can you see that most of the ridge regression parameters (though not all) are smaller than those for the unregularized model? This is the effect of regularization.

Exercise 2

Create another plot exactly the same as in figure 11.13, but this time *include* the intercepts. Are they the same between the two models? Why?

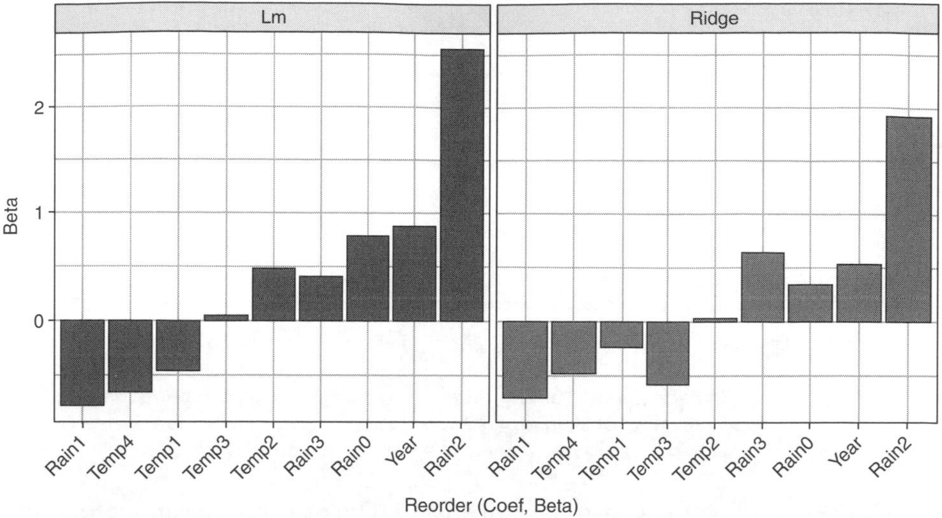

Figure 11.13 Comparing the parameter estimates of our ridge regression model to our OLS regression model

11.6.3 Training the LASSO model

In this section, we'll repeat the model-building process of the previous section, but using LASSO instead. Once we've trained our model, we'll add to our figure, so we can compare parameter estimates between the models, to give you a better understanding of how the techniques differ.

We start by defining the LASSO learner, this time setting *alpha* equal to 1 (to make it pure LASSO). And we give the learner an ID, which we'll use when we benchmark the models later:

```
lasso <- makeLearner("regr.glmnet", alpha = 1, id = "lasso")
```

Now, let's tune *lambda* as we did before for ridge regression.

WARNING This takes about 30 seconds on my four-core machine.

Listing 11.10 Tuning *lambda* for LASSO

```
lassoParamSpace <- makeParamSet(
  makeNumericParam("s", lower = 0, upper = 15))

parallelStartSocket(cpus = detectCores())

tunedLassoPars <- tuneParams(lasso, task = iowaTask,
                             resampling = cvForTuning,
                             par.set = lassoParamSpace,
                             control = randSearch)
```

```
parallelStop()

tunedLassoPars

Tune result:
Op. pars: s=1.37
mse.test.mean=87.0126
```

Now we plot the tuning process to see if we need to expand our search.

Listing 11.11 Plotting the hyperparameter tuning process

```
lassoTuningData <- generateHyperParsEffectData(tunedLassoPars)

plotHyperParsEffect(lassoTuningData, x = "s", y = "mse.test.mean",
                    plot.type = "line") +
  theme_bw()
```

The resulting plot is shown in figure 11.14. Once again, we can see that the selected value of *lambda* falls at the bottom of the valley of mean MSE values. Notice that the mean MSE flat-lines after *lambda* values of 10: this is because the penalty is so large here that all the predictors have been removed from the model, and we get the mean MSE of an intercept-only model.

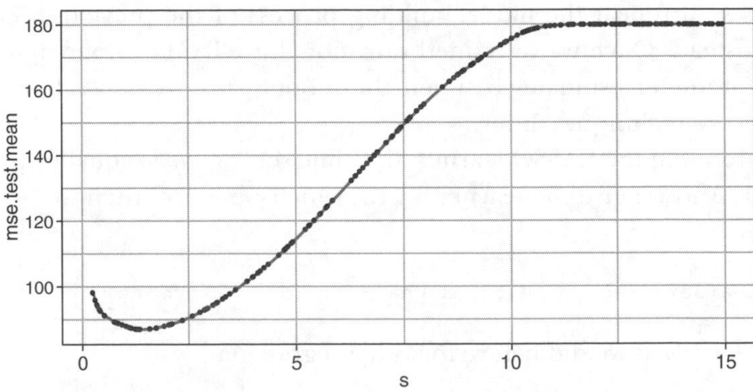

Figure 11.14 Plotting the LASSO *lambda*-tuning process. The x-axis represents *lambda*, and the y-axis represents the mean MSE. Dots represent values of *lambda* sampled by the random search. The line connects the dots.

Let's train a LASSO model using our tuned value of *lambda*.

Listing 11.12 Training a LASSO model using the tuned *lambda*

```
tunedLasso <- setHyperPars(lasso, par.vals = tunedLassoPars$x)

tunedLassoModel <- train(tunedLasso, iowaTask)
```

Now let's look at the parameter estimates from our tuned LASSO model and see how they compare to the ridge and OLS estimates. Once again, we use the `getLearnerModel()` function to extract the model data and then the `coef()` function to extract the parameter estimates. Notice something unusual? Three of our parameter estimates are just dots. Well, those dots actually represent 0.0. Zilch. Nada. Nothing. The slopes of these parameters in the dataset have been set to exactly 0. This means they have been removed from the model completely. This is how LASSO can be used for performing feature selection.

Listing 11.13 Extracting the model parameters

```
lassoModelData <- getLearnerModel(tunedLassoModel)

lassoCoefs <- coef(lassoModelData, s = tunedLassoPars$x$s)

lassoCoefs

10 x 1 sparse Matrix of class "dgCMatrix"
                    1
(Intercept) -1.361e+03
Year         7.389e-01
Rain0        2.217e-01
Temp1        .
Rain1        .
Temp2        .
Rain2        2.005e+00
Temp3       -4.065e-02
Rain3        1.669e-01
Temp4       -4.829e-01
```

Let's plot these parameter estimates alongside those from our ridge and OLS models to give a more graphical comparison. To do this, we simply add a new column to our `coefTib` tibble using `$LASSO`; it contains the parameter estimates from our LASSO model (excluding the intercept). We then gather this data so we can facet by model, and plot it as before using `ggplot()`.

Listing 11.14 Plotting the model parameters

```
coefTib$LASSO <- as.vector(lassoCoefs)[-1]

coefUntidy <- gather(coefTib, key = Model, value = Beta, -Coef)

ggplot(coefUntidy, aes(reorder(Coef, Beta), Beta, fill = Model)) +
  geom_bar(stat = "identity", col = "black") +
  facet_wrap(~ Model) +
  theme_bw() +
  theme(legend.position = "none")
```

The resulting plot is shown in figure 11.15. The plot nicely highlights the difference between ridge, which shrinks parameters toward 0 (but never actually to 0), and LASSO, which can shrink parameters to exactly 0.

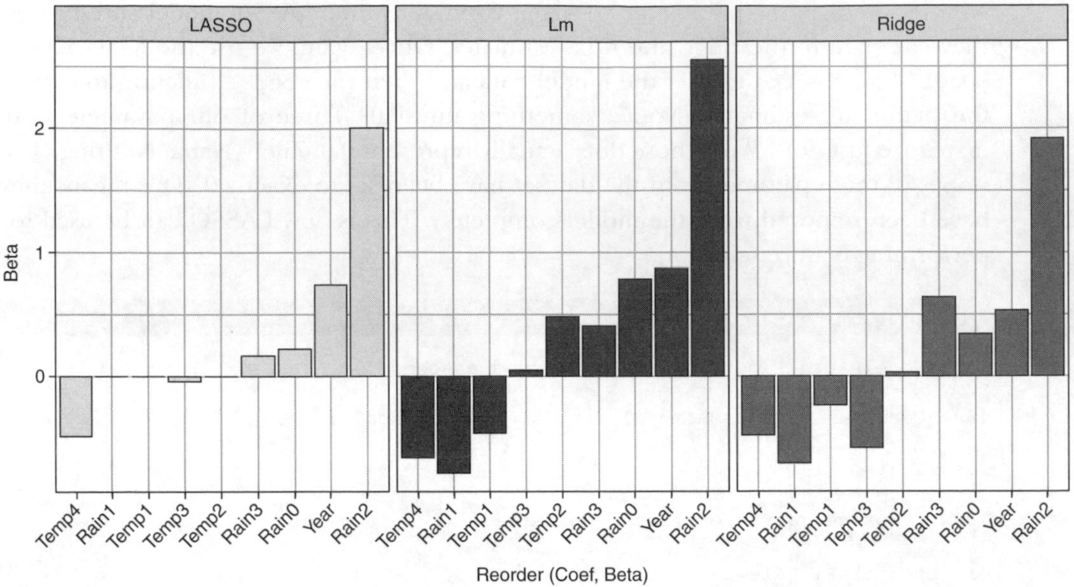

Figure 11.15 Comparing the parameter estimates of our ridge regression model, LASSO model, and OLS regression model

11.6.4 Training the elastic net model

This section is going to look a lot like the previous two, but I'll show you how to train an elastic net model by tuning both *lambda* and *alpha*. We'll start by creating an elastic net learner; this time we won't supply a value of *alpha*, because we're going to tune it to find the best trade-off between L1 and L2 regularization. We also give it an ID that we can use later when benchmarking:

```
elastic <- makeLearner("regr.glmnet", id = "elastic")
```

Now let's define the hyperparameter space we're going to tune over, this time including *alpha* as a numeric hyperparameter bounded between 0 and 1. Because we're now tuning two hyperparameters, let's increase the number of iterations of our random search to get a little more coverage of the search space. Finally, we run the tuning process as before and print the optimal result.

WARNING This takes about a minute on my four-core machine.

Listing 11.15 Tuning *lambda* and *alpha* for elastic net

```
elasticParamSpace <- makeParamSet(
  makeNumericParam("s", lower = 0, upper = 10),
  makeNumericParam("alpha", lower = 0, upper = 1))
```

```
randSearchElastic <- makeTuneControlRandom(maxit = 400)

parallelStartSocket(cpus = detectCores())

tunedElasticPars <- tuneParams(elastic, task = iowaTask,
                               resampling = cvForTuning,
                               par.set = elasticParamSpace,
                               control = randSearchElastic)

parallelStop()

tunedElasticPars

Tune result:
Op. pars: s=1.24; alpha=0.981
mse.test.mean=84.7701
```

Now let's plot our tuning process to confirm that our search space was large enough. This time, because we are tuning two hyperparameters simultaneously, we supply *lambda* and *alpha* as the x- and y-axes, and mean MSE (`"mse.test.mean"`) as the z-axis. Setting the `plot.type` argument equal to `"heatmap"` will draw a heatmap where the color is mapped to whatever we set as the z-axis. For this to work, though, we need to fill in the gaps between our 1,000 search iterations. To do this, we supply the name of any regression algorithm to the `interpolate` argument. Here, I've used `"regr.kknn"`, which uses k-nearest neighbors to fill in the gaps based on the MSE values of the nearest search iterations. We add a single `geom_point` to the plot to indicate the combination of *lambda* and *alpha* that were selected by our tuning process.

> **NOTE** This interpolation is for visualization only, so while choosing different interpolation learners may change the tuning plot, it won't affect our selected hyperparameters.

Listing 11.16 Plotting the tuning process

```
elasticTuningData <- generateHyperParsEffectData(tunedElasticPars)

plotHyperParsEffect(elasticTuningData, x = "s", y = "alpha",
                    z = "mse.test.mean", interpolate = "regr.kknn",
                    plot.type = "heatmap") +
  scale_fill_gradientn(colours = terrain.colors(5)) +
  geom_point(x = tunedElasticPars$x$s, y = tunedElasticPars$x$alpha,
             col = "white") +
  theme_bw()
```

The resulting plot is shown in figure 11.16. Beautiful! You could hang this on your wall and call it art. Notice that the selected combination of *lambda* and *alpha* (the white dot) falls in a valley of mean MSE values, suggesting our hyperparameter search space was wide enough.

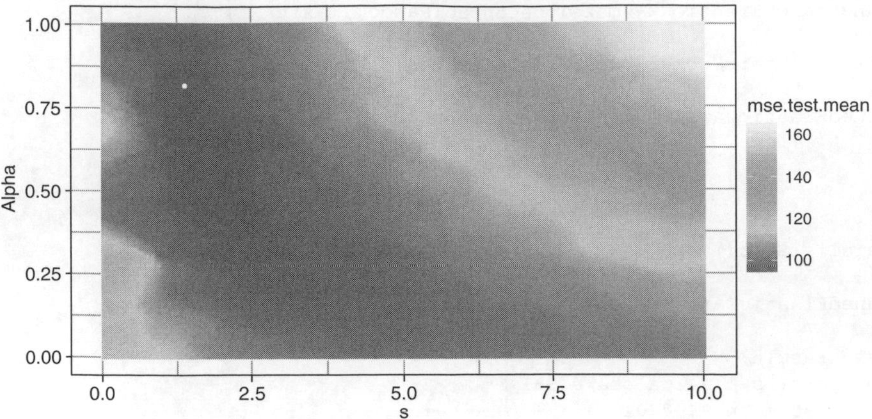

Figure 11.16 Plotting the hyperparameter tuning process for our elastic net model. The x-axis represents *lambda*, the y-axis represents *alpha*, and the shading represents mean MSE. The white dot represents the combination of hyperparameters chosen by our tuning process.

> **Exercise 3**
>
> Let's experiment with the `plotHyperParsEffect()` function. Change the `plot.type` argument to `"contour"`, add the argument `show.experiments = TRUE`, and redraw the plot. Next, change `plot.type` to `"scatter"`, remove the `interpolate` and `show.experiments` arguments, and remove the `scale_fill_gradientn()` layer.

Now let's train the final elastic net model using our tuned hyperparameters.

Listing 11.17 Training an elastic net model using tuned hyperparameters

```
tunedElastic <- setHyperPars(elastic, par.vals = tunedElasticPars$x)

tunedElasticModel <- train(tunedElastic, iowaTask)
```

Next, we can extract the model parameters and plot them alongside the other three models, as we did in listings 11.9 and 11.14.

Listing 11.18 Plotting the model parameters

```
elasticModelData <- getLearnerModel(tunedElasticModel)

elasticCoefs <- coef(elasticModelData, s = tunedElasticPars$x$s)

coefTib$Elastic <- as.vector(elasticCoefs)[-1]

coefUntidy <- gather(coefTib, key = Model, value = Beta, -Coef)

ggplot(coefUntidy, aes(reorder(Coef, Beta), Beta, fill = Model)) +
  geom_bar(stat = "identity", position = "dodge", col = "black") +
```

```
facet_wrap(~ Model) +
theme_bw()
```

The resulting plot is shown in figure 11.17. Notice that our elastic net model's parameter estimates are something of a compromise between those estimated by ridge regression and those estimated by LASSO. The elastic net model's parameters are more similar to those estimated by pure LASSO, however, because our tuned value of *alpha* was close to 1 (remember that when *alpha* equals 1, we get pure LASSO).

> **Exercise 4**
>
> Redraw the plot in figure 11.17, but remove the `facet_wrap()` layer and set the position argument of `geom_bar()` equal to `"dodge"`. Which visualization do you prefer?

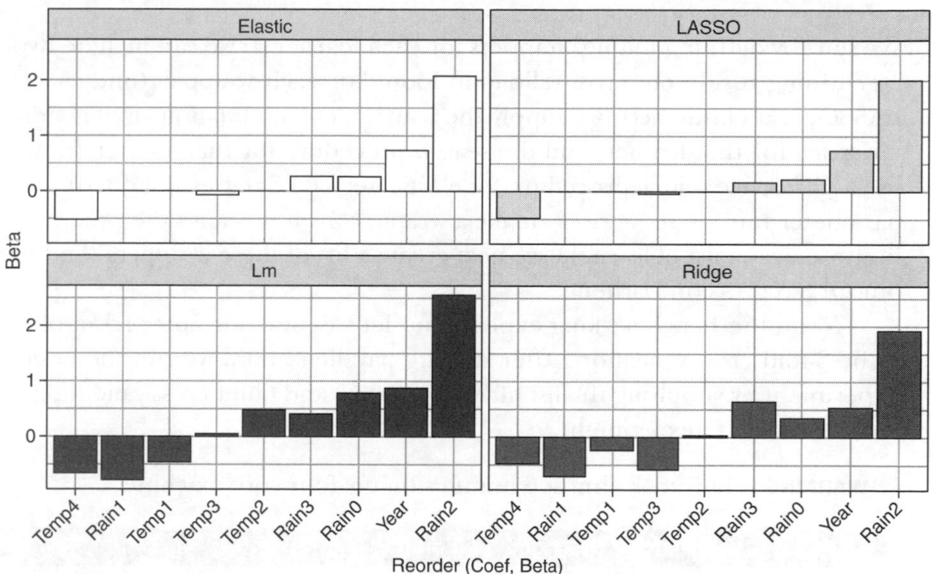

Figure 11.17 Comparing the parameter estimates of our ridge regression model, LASSO model, elastic net model, and OLS regression model

11.7 Benchmarking ridge, LASSO, elastic net, and OLS against each other

Let's use benchmarking to simultaneously cross-validate and compare the performance of our ridge, LASSO, elastic net, and OLS modeling processes. Recall from chapter 8 that benchmarking takes a list of learners, a task, and a cross-validation procedure. Then, for each iteration/fold of the cross-validation process, a model is trained using each learner on the same training set, and evaluated on the same test set. Once the entire cross-validation process is complete, we get the mean performance metric (MSE, in this case) for each learner, allowing us to compare which would perform best.

Listing 11.19 Plotting the model parameters

```
ridgeWrapper <- makeTuneWrapper(ridge, resampling = cvForTuning,
                                par.set = ridgeParamSpace,
                                control = randSearch)

lassoWrapper <- makeTuneWrapper(lasso, resampling = cvForTuning,
                                par.set = lassoParamSpace,
                                control = randSearch)

elasticWrapper <- makeTuneWrapper(elastic, resampling = cvForTuning,
                                  par.set = elasticParamSpace,
                                  control = randSearchElastic)

learners = list(ridgeWrapper, lassoWrapper, elasticWrapper, "regr.lm")
```

We start by defining tuning wrappers for each learner so we can include hyperparameter tuning inside our cross-validation loop. For each wrapper (one each for ridge, LASSO, and elastic net), we supply the learner, cross-validation strategy, the parameter space for that learner, and the search procedure for that learner (notice that we use a difference search procedure for elastic net). OLS regression doesn't need hyperparameter tuning, so we don't make a wrapper for it. Because the `benchmark()` function requires a list of learners, we next create a list of these wrappers (and `"regr.lm"`, our OLS regression learner).

To run the benchmarking experiment, let's define our outer resampling strategy to be 3-fold cross-validation. After starting parallelization, we run the benchmarking experiment by supplying the list of learners, task, and outer cross-validation strategy to the `benchmark()` experiment.

WARNING This took almost 6 minutes on my four-core machine.

Listing 11.20 Plotting the model parameters

```
library(parallel)
library(parallelMap)

kFold3 <- makeResampleDesc("CV", iters = 3)

parallelStartSocket(cpus = detectCores())

bench <- benchmark(learners, iowaTask, kFold3)

parallelStop()

bench

  task.id     learner.id mse.test.mean
1 iowaTib   ridge.tuned           95.48
2 iowaTib   lasso.tuned           93.98
```

```
3 iowaTib elastic.tuned          99.19
4 iowaTib       regr.lm         120.37
```

Perhaps surprisingly, ridge and LASSO regression both outperformed elastic net, although all three regularization techniques outperformed OLS regression. Because elastic net has the potential to select both pure ridge or pure LASSO (based on the value of the *alpha* hyperparameter), increasing the number of iterations of the random search could end up putting elastic net on top.

11.8 Strengths and weaknesses of ridge, LASSO, and elastic net

While it often isn't easy to tell which algorithms will perform well for a given task, here are some strengths and weaknesses that will help you decide whether ridge regression, LASSO, and elastic net will perform well for you.

The strengths of ridge, LASSO, and elastic net are as follows:

- They produce models that are very interpretable.
- They can handle both continuous and categorical predictors.
- They are computationally inexpensive.
- They often outperform OLS regression.
- LASSO and elastic net can perform feature selection by setting the slopes of uninformative predictors equal to 0.
- They can also be applied to generalized linear models (such as logistic regression).

The weaknesses of ridge, LASSO, and elastic net are these:

- They make strong assumptions about the data, such as homoscedasticity (constant variance) and the distribution of residuals (performance may suffer if these are violated).
- Ridge regression cannot perform feature selection automatically.
- LASSO cannot estimate more parameters than cases in the training set.
- They cannot handle missing data.

Exercise 5

Create a new tibble that contains only the `Yield` variable, and make a new regression task using this data, with `Yield` set as the target.

- a Train an ordinary OLS model on this data (a model with no predictors).
- b Train a LASSO model on the original `iowaTask` with a *lambda* value of 500.
- c Cross-validate both models using leave-one-out cross-validation (`makeResampleDesc("LOO")`).
- d How do the mean MSE values of both models compare? Why?

Exercise 6

Calling `plot()` on a `glmnet` model object doesn't plot model residuals. Install the plotmo package and use its `plotres()` function, passing the model data objects for the ridge, LASSO, and elastic net models as arguments.

Summary

- Regularization is a set of techniques that prevents overfitting by shrinking model parameter estimates.
- There are three regularization techniques for linear models: ridge regression, LASSO, and elastic net.
- Ridge regression uses the L2 norm to shrink parameter estimates toward 0 (but never exactly to 0, unless they were 0 to begin with).
- LASSO uses the L1 norm to shrink parameter estimates toward 0 (and possibly exactly to 0, resulting in feature selection).
- Elastic net combines both L2 and L1 regularization, the ratio of which is controlled by the *alpha* hyperparameter.
- For all three, the *lambda* hyperparameter controls the strength of shrinkage.

Solutions to exercises

1 Expand the search space to include values of *lambda* from 0 to 50:

```
ridgeParamSpaceExtended <- makeParamSet(
  makeNumericParam("s", lower = 0, upper = 50))

parallelStartSocket(cpus = detectCores())

tunedRidgeParsExtended <- tuneParams(ridge, task = iowaTask, # ~30 sec
                              resampling = cvForTuning,
                              par.set = ridgeParamSpaceExtended,
                              control = randSearch)

parallelStop()

ridgeTuningDataExtended <- generateHyperParsEffectData(
                                   tunedRidgeParsExtended)

plotHyperParsEffect(ridgeTuningDataExtended, x = "s", y = "mse.test.mean",
                    plot.type = "line") +
  theme_bw()

# The previous value of s was not just a local minimum,
# but the global minimum.
```

2 Plot the intercepts for the ridge and LASSO models:

```
coefTibInts <- tibble(Coef = rownames(ridgeCoefs),
                      Ridge = as.vector(ridgeCoefs),
                      Lm = as.vector(lmCoefs))
```

```
coefUntidyInts <- gather(coefTibInts, key = Model, value = Beta, -Coef)

ggplot(coefUntidyInts, aes(reorder(Coef, Beta), Beta, fill = Model)) +
  geom_bar(stat = "identity", col = "black") +
  facet_wrap(~Model) +
  theme_bw()  +
  theme(legend.position = "none")

# The intercepts are different. The intercept isn't included when
# calculating the L2 norm, but is the value of the outcome when all
# the predictors are zero. Because ridge regression changes the parameter
# estimates of the predictors, the intercept changes as a result.
```

3 Experiment with different ways of plotting the hyperparameter tuning process:

```
plotHyperParsEffect(elasticTuningData, x = "s", y = "alpha",
                    z = "mse.test.mean", interpolate = "regr.kknn",
                    plot.type = "contour", show.experiments = TRUE) +
  scale_fill_gradientn(colours = terrain.colors(5)) +
  geom_point(x = tunedElasticPars$x$s, y = tunedElasticPars$x$alpha) +
  theme_bw()

plotHyperParsEffect(elasticTuningData, x = "s", y = "alpha",
                    z = "mse.test.mean", plot.type = "scatter") +
  theme_bw()
```

4 Plot the model coefficients using horizontally dodged bars instead of facets:

```
ggplot(coefUntidy, aes(reorder(Coef, Beta), Beta, fill = Model)) +
  geom_bar(stat = "identity", position = "dodge", col = "black") +
  theme_bw()
```

5 Compare the performance of a LASSO model with a high *lambda*, and an OLS model with no predictors:

```
yieldOnly <- select(iowaTib, Yield)

yieldOnlyTask <- makeRegrTask(data = yieldOnly, target = "Yield")

lassoStrict <- makeLearner("regr.glmnet", lambda = 500)

loo <- makeResampleDesc("LOO")

resample("regr.lm", yieldOnlyTask, loo)

Resample Result
Task: yieldOnly
Learner: regr.lm
Aggr perf: mse.test.mean=179.3428
Runtime: 0.11691

resample(lassoStrict, iowaTask, loo)

Resample Result
Task: iowaTib
```

```
Learner: regr.glmnet
Aggr perf: mse.test.mean=179.3428
Runtime: 0.316366

# The MSE values are identical. This is because when lambda is high
# enough, all predictors will be removed from the model, just as if
# we trained a model with no predictors.
```

6 Use the `plotres()` function to plot model diagnostics for glmnet models:

```
install.packages("plotmo")

library(plotmo)

plotres(ridgeModelData)

plotres(lassoModelData)

plotres(elasticModelData)

# The first plot shows the estimated slope for each parameter for
# different values of (log) lambda. Notice the different shape
# between ridge and LASSO.
```

12 Regression with kNN, random forest, and XGBoost

This chapter covers

- Using the k-nearest neighbors algorithm for regression
- Using tree-based algorithms for regression
- Comparing k-nearest neighbors, random forest, and XGBoost models

You're going to find this chapter a breeze. This is because you've done everything in it before (sort of). In chapter 3, I introduced you to the k-nearest neighbors (kNN) algorithm as a tool for classification. In chapter 7, I introduced you to decision trees and then expanded on this in chapter 8 to cover random forest and XGBoost for classification. Well, conveniently, these algorithms can also be used to predict continuous variables. So in this chapter, I'll help you extend these skills to solve regression problems.

By the end of this chapter, I hope you'll understand how kNN and tree-based algorithms can be extended to predict continuous variables. As you learned in chapter 7, decision trees suffer from a tendency to overfit their training data and so are often vastly improved by using ensemble techniques. Therefore, in this chapter, you'll train a random forest model and an XGBoost model, and benchmark their performance against the kNN algorithm.

NOTE Recall from chapter 8 that random forest and XGBoost are two tree-based learners that create an ensemble of many trees to improve prediction accuracy. Random forest trains many trees in parallel on different bootstrap samples from the data, and XGBoost trains sequential trees that prioritize misclassified cases.

12.1 Using k-nearest neighbors to predict a continuous variable

In this section, I'll show you how you can use the kNN algorithm for regression, graphically and intuitively. Imagine that you're not a morning person (perhaps, like me, you don't have to imagine very hard), and you like to spend as much time in bed as possible. To maximize the amount of time you spend sleeping, you decide to train a machine learning model to predict how long it takes you to commute to work, based on the time you leave the house. It takes you 40 minutes to get ready in the morning, so you hope this model will tell you what time you need to leave the house to get to work on time, and therefore what time you need to wake up.

Every day for two weeks, you record the time you leave the house and how long your journey takes. Your journey time is affected by the traffic (which varies across the morning), so your journey length changes, depending on when you leave. An example of what the relationship between departure time and journey length might look like is shown in figure 12.1.

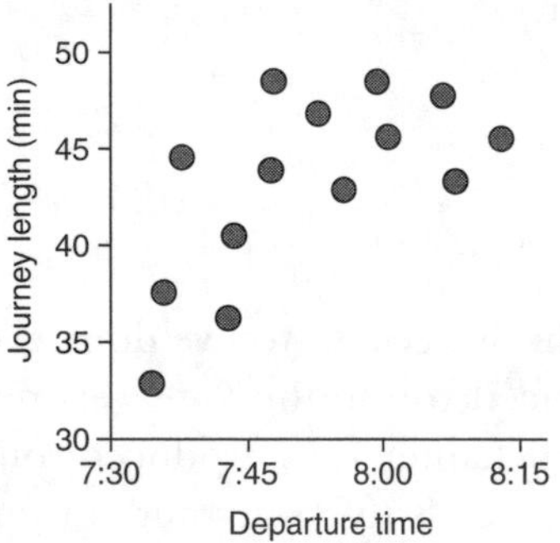

Figure 12.1 An example relationship for how long your commute to work takes, depending on what time you leave the house

Recall from chapter 3 that the kNN algorithm is a lazy learner. In other words, it doesn't do any work during model training (instead, it just stores the training data); it does all of its work when it makes predictions. When making predictions, the kNN algorithm looks in the training set for the *k* cases most similar to each of the new, unlabeled data values. Each of those *k* most similar cases votes on the predicted value of the new data. When using kNN for classification, these votes are for class membership, and the winning vote selects the class the model outputs for the new data. To remind you how this process works, I've reproduced a modified version of figure 3.4 from chapter 3, in figure 12.2.

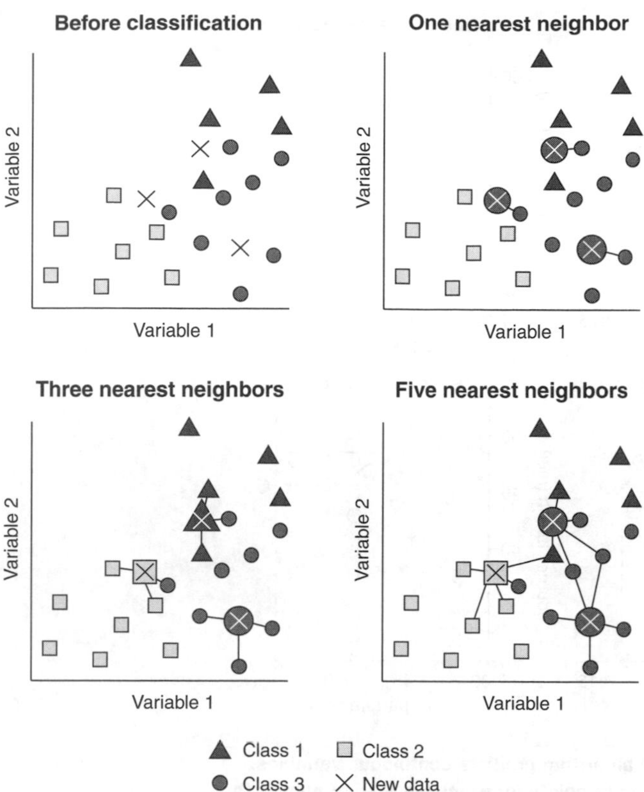

Figure 12.2 The kNN algorithm for classification: identifying the *k* nearest neighbors and taking the majority vote. Lines connect the unlabeled data with their one, three, and five nearest neighbors. The majority vote in each scenario is indicated by the shape drawn under each cross.

The voting process when using kNN for regression is very similar, except that we take the mean of these *k* votes as the predicted value for the new data.

This process is illustrated for our commuting example in figure 12.3. The crosses on the x-axis represent new data: times we left the house and for which we want to predict journey length. If we train a one-nearest neighbor model, the model finds the single case from the training set that is closest to the departure time of each of the new data points, and uses that value as the predicted journey length. If we train a three-nearest neighbor model, the model finds the three training cases with departure times most similar to each of the new data points, takes the mean journey length of those nearest cases, and outputs this as the predicted value for the new data. The same applies to any number of *k* we use to train the model.

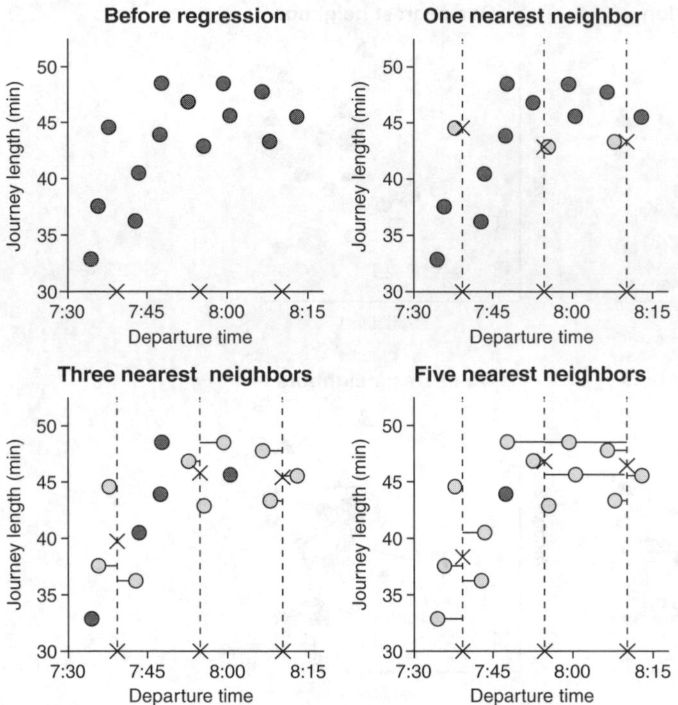

Figure 12.3 How the kNN algorithm predicts continuous variables. The crosses represent new data points for which we wish to predict the journey length. For the one-, three-, and five-nearest neighbor models, the nearest neighbors to each new data point are highlighted in a lighter shade. In each case, the predicted value is the mean journey length of the nearest neighbors.

NOTE Just like when we used kNN for classification, selecting the best-performing value of *k* is critical to model performance. If we select a *k* that is too low, we may produce a model that is overfitted and makes predictions with high variance. If we select a *k* that is too high, we may produce a model that is underfitted and makes predictions with high bias.

12.2 Using tree-based learners to predict a continuous variable

In this section, I'll show you how you can use tree-based algorithms to predict a continuous outcome variable. Back in chapter 7, I showed you how tree-based algorithms (such as the rpart algorithm) split a feature space into separate regions, one binary split at a time. The algorithm tries to partition the feature space such that each region contains only cases from a particular class. Put another way, the algorithm tries to learn binary splits that result in regions that are as pure as possible.

NOTE Remember that the *feature space* refers to all possible combinations of predictor variable values, and that *purity* refers to how homogeneous the cases are within a single region.

To refresh your memory, I've reproduced figure 7.4 in figure 12.4, showing how a feature space of two predictor variables can be partitioned to predict the membership of three classes.

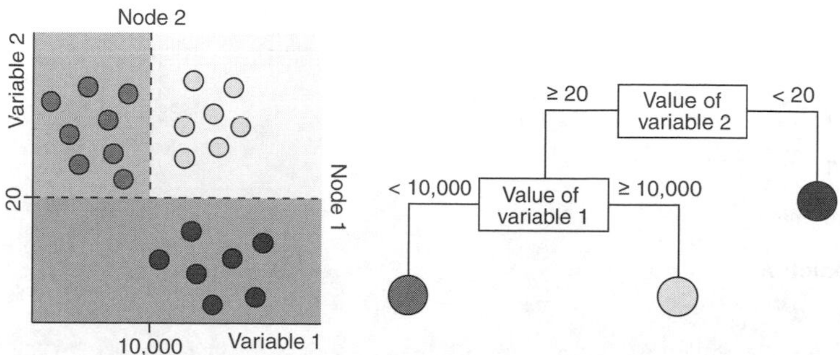

Figure 12.4 How splitting is performed for classification problems. Cases belonging to three classes are plotted against two continuous variables. The first node splits the feature space into rectangles based on the value of variable 2. The second node further splits the variable 2 ≥ 20 feature space into rectangles based on the value of variable 1.

Classification with tree-based algorithms is a bit like herding animals into their pens on a farm. It's quite obvious that we want one pen for the chickens, one for the cows, and one for the alpacas (I don't think you see many alpacas on farms, but I'm particularly fond of them). So conceptually, it's quite easy for us to picture splitting regions of the feature space into different pens for different categories. But perhaps it's not so easy to picture splitting the feature space to predict a continuous variable.

So how does this partitioning work for regression problems? In exactly the same way: the only difference is that instead of each region representing a class, it represents a value of the continuous outcome variable. Take a look at figure 12.5, where we're creating a regression tree using our journey length example. The nodes of the regression tree split the feature space (departure time) into distinct regions. Each region represents the mean of the outcome variable of the cases inside it. When making predictions on new data, the model will predict the value of the region the new data falls into. The leaves of the tree are no longer classes, but numbers. This is illustrated for situations with one and two predictor variables in figure 12.5, but it extends to any number of predictors.

Just as for classification, regression trees can handle both continuous and categorical predictor variables (with the exception of XGBoost, which requires categorical variables to be numerically encoded). The way splits are decided for continuous and

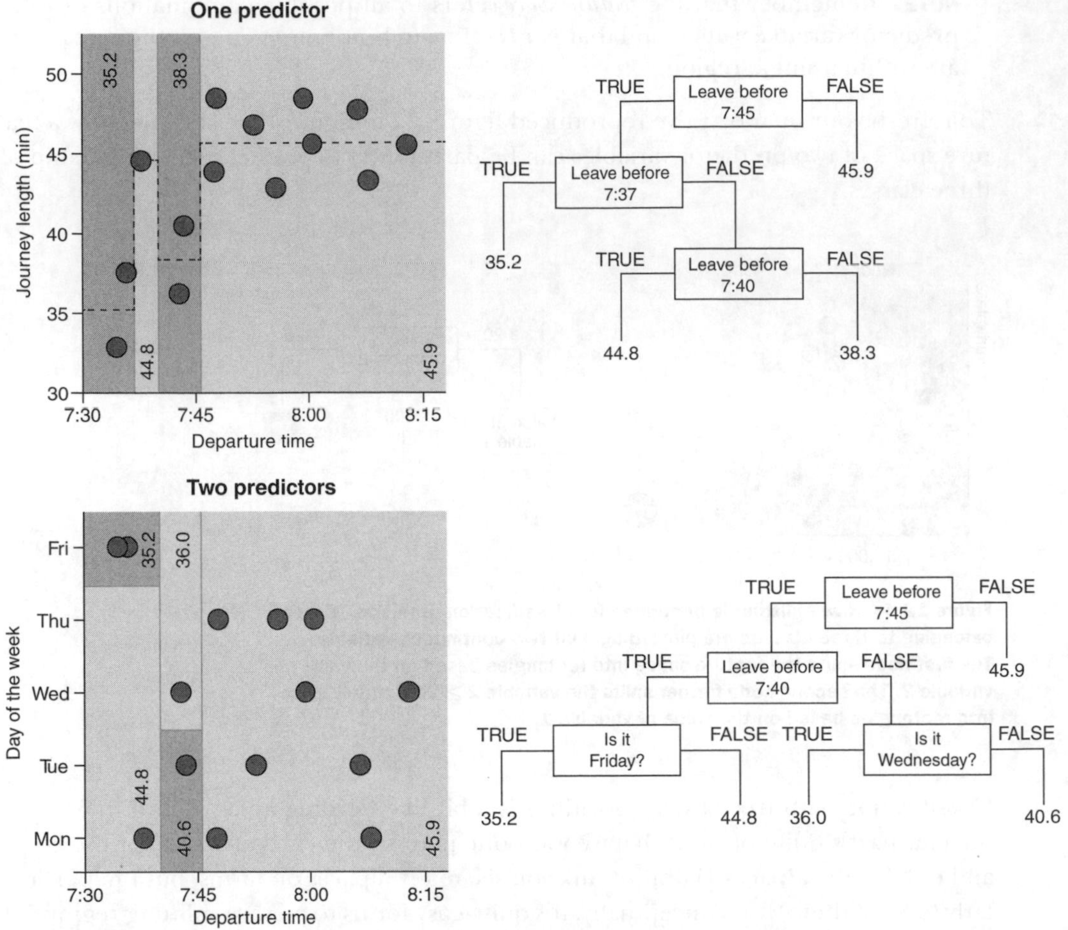

Figure 12.5 How splitting is performed for regression problems. The feature space is split into shaded regions based on the nodes of the tree next to each plot. The predicted journey length is shown inside each region. The dashed line in the top plot demonstrates how journey length is predicted from departure time based on the tree. The bottom plot shows a two-predictor situation.

categorical variables is the same as for classification trees, except that instead of finding the split that has the highest Gini gain, the algorithm looks for the split with the lowest sum of squares.

> **NOTE** Recall from chapter 7 that the Gini gain is the difference between the Gini indices of the parent node and of the split. The Gini index is a measure of impurity and is equal to $1 - (p(A)^2 + p(B)^2)$, where $p(A)$ and $p(B)$ are the proportions of cases belonging to classes A and B, respectively.

For each candidate split, the algorithm calculates the sum of squared residuals for the left and right split, and adds them together to form the sum of squared residuals for

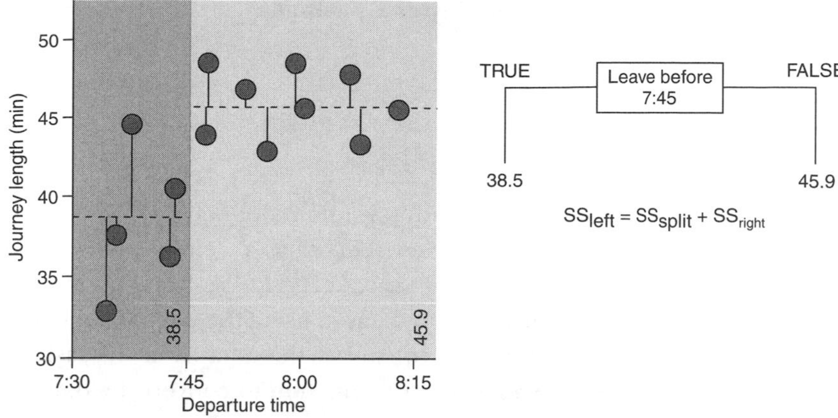

Figure 12.6 How candidate splits are chosen for regression problems. The measure of purity is the sum of squares for the split, which is the combined sums of squares for the left and right nodes. Each sum of squares is the vertical distance between each case and the predicted value for the leaf it belongs to.

the split as a whole. In figure 12.6, the algorithm is considering the candidate split of a departure time before 7:45. For each case where the departure time was before 7:45, the algorithm calculates the mean journey length, finds the residual error (the difference between each case's journey length and the mean), and squares it. The same is done for the cases where you left the house after 7:45, with their respective mean. These two sums of squared residual values are added together to give the sum of squares for the split. If you prefer to see this in mathematical notation, it's shown in equation 12.1.

$$SS_{split} = \sum_{i \in \text{left}} (y_i - \hat{y}_{\text{left}})^2 + \sum_{i \in \text{right}} (y_i - \hat{y}_{\text{right}})^2 \qquad \textbf{Equation 12.1}$$

where $i \in$ *left* and $i \in$ *right* indicate cases belonging to the left and right splits, respectively.

The candidate split with the lowest sum of squares is chosen as the split for any particular point in the tree. So, for regression trees, *purity* refers to how spread the data are around the mean of the node.

12.3 Building your first kNN regression model

In this section, I'll teach you how to define a kNN learner for regression, tune the *k* hyperparameter, and train a model so you can use it to predict a continuous variable. Imagine that you're a chemical engineer trying to predict the amount of heat released by various batches of fuel, based on measurements you made on each batch. We're first going to train a kNN model on this task and then compare how it performs to a random forest and an XGBoost model, later in the chapter.

Let's start by loading the mlr and tidyverse packages:

```
library(mlr)

library(tidyverse)
```

12.3.1 Loading and exploring the fuel dataset

The mlr package, conveniently, comes with several predefined tasks to help you experiment with different learners and processes. The dataset we're going to work with in this chapter is contained inside mlr's `fuelsubset.task`. We load this task into our R session the same way we would any built-in dataset: using the `data()` function. We can then use mlr's `getTaskData()` function to extract the data from the task, so we can explore it. As always, we use the `as_tibble()` function to convert the data frame into a tibble.

Listing 12.1 Loading and exploring the fuel dataset

```
data("fuelsubset.task")

fuel <- getTaskData(fuelsubset.task)

fuelTib <- as_tibble(fuel)

fuelTib

# A tibble: 129 x 367
   heatan   h20 UVVIS.UVVIS.1 UVVIS.UVVIS.2 UVVIS.UVVIS.3 UVVIS.UVVIS.4
    <dbl> <dbl>         <dbl>         <dbl>         <dbl>         <dbl>
 1   26.8  2.3         0.874          0.748        0.774          0.747
 2   27.5  3          -0.855         -1.29        -0.833         -0.976
 3   23.8  2.00       -0.0847        -0.294       -0.202         -0.262
 4   18.2  1.85       -0.582         -0.485       -0.328         -0.539
 5   17.5  2.39       -0.644         -1.12        -0.665         -0.791
 6   20.2  2.43       -0.504         -0.890       -0.662         -0.744
 7   15.1  1.92       -0.569         -0.507       -0.454         -0.576
 8   20.4  3.61        0.158          0.186        0.0303         0.183
 9   26.7  2.5         0.334          0.191        0.0777         0.0410
10   24.9  1.28        0.0766         0.266        0.0808        -0.0733
# … with 119 more rows, and 361 more variables
```

We have a tibble containing 129 different batches of fuel and 367 variables/features! In fact, there are so many variables that I've truncated the printout of the tibble to remove the names of the variables that didn't fit on my console.

> **TIP** Run `names(fuelTib)` to return the names of all the variables in the dataset. This is useful when working with large datasets with too many columns to visualize on the console.

The `heatan` variable is the amount of energy released by a certain quantity of fuel when it is combusted (measured in megajoules). The `h20` variable is the percentage of humidity in the fuel's container. The remaining variables show how much ultraviolet or near-infrared light of a particular wavelength each batch of fuel absorbs (each variable represents a different wavelength).

TIP To see all the tasks that come built into mlr, use `data(package = "mlr")`.

Let's plot the data to get an idea of how the `heatan` variable correlates with the `absorbance` variable at various wavelengths of ultraviolet and near-infrared light. We'll up our tidyverse game by doing some more-complicated operations, so let me take you step by step through the process in listing 12.2:

1. Because we want to plot a separate `geom_smooth()` line for every case in the data, we first pipe the data into a `mutate()` function call, where we create an `id` variable that just acts as a row index. We use `nrow(.)` to specify the number of rows in the data object piped into `mutate()`.
2. We pipe the result of step 1 into a `gather()` function to create a key-value pair of variables containing the spectral information (`wavelength` as the key, `absorbance` at that wavelength as the value). We omit the `heatan`, `h20`, and `id` variables from the gathering process (`c(-heatan, -h20, -id)`).
3. We pipe the result of step 2 into another `mutate()` function to create two new variables:
   a. A character vector that indicates whether the row shows absorbance of ultraviolet or near-infrared spectra
   b. A numeric vector that indicates the wavelength of that particular spectrum

I've introduced two functions here from the stringr tidyverse package: `str_sub()` and `str_extract()`. The `str_sub()` function splits a character string into its individual alphanumeric characters and symbols, and returns the ones that are between the `start` and `end` arguments. For example, `str_sub("UVVIS.UVVIS.1", 1, 3)` returns `"UVV"`. We use this function to mutate a column with the value `"UVV"` when the spectrum is ultraviolet and `"NIR"` when the spectrum is near-infrared.

The `str_extract()` function looks for a particular pattern in a character string, and returns that pattern. In the example in listing 12.2, we asked the function to look for any numerical digits, using `\\d`. The `+` after `\\d` tells the function that the pattern may be matched more than once. For example, compare the output of `str_extract ("hello123", "\\d")` and `str_extract("hello123", "\\d+")`.

Listing 12.2 Preparing the data for plotting

```
fuelUntidy <- fuelTib %>%
  mutate(id = 1:nrow(.)) %>%
  gather(key = "variable", value = "absorbance",
  c(-heatan, -h20, -id)) %>%
  mutate(spectrum = str_sub(variable, 1, 3),
         wavelength = as.numeric(str_extract(variable, "(\\d)+")))

fuelUntidy
```

```
# A tibble: 47,085 x 7
   heatan   h20    id variable        absorbance spectrum wavelength
    <dbl> <dbl> <int> <chr>                <dbl> <chr>         <dbl>
 1   26.8  2.3      1 UVVIS.UVVIS.1     0.874  UVV               1
 2   27.5  3        2 UVVIS.UVVIS.1    -0.855  UVV               1
 3   23.8  2.00     3 UVVIS.UVVIS.1    -0.0847 UVV               1
 4   18.2  1.85     4 UVVIS.UVVIS.1    -0.582  UVV               1
 5   17.5  2.39     5 UVVIS.UVVIS.1    -0.644  UVV               1
 6   20.2  2.43     6 UVVIS.UVVIS.1    -0.504  UVV               1
 7   15.1  1.92     7 UVVIS.UVVIS.1    -0.569  UVV               1
 8   20.4  3.61     8 UVVIS.UVVIS.1     0.158  UVV               1
 9   26.7  2.5      9 UVVIS.UVVIS.1     0.334  UVV               1
10   24.9  1.28    10 UVVIS.UVVIS.1     0.0766 UVV               1
# ... with 47,075 more rows
```

This was some reasonably complex data manipulation, so run the code and take a look at the resulting tibble, and make sure you understand how we created it.

> **TIP** We search for patterns in character vectors by specifying *regular expressions,* such as `"\\d+"` in listing 12.2. A regular expression is a special text string for describing a search pattern. Regular expressions are very useful tools for extracting (sometimes-complex) patterns from character strings. If I've piqued your interest in regular expressions, you can learn more about how to use them in R by running `?regex`.

Now that we've formatted our data for plotting, we're going to draw three plots:

- `absorbance` versus `heatan`, with a separate curve for every wavelength
- `wavelength` versus `absorbance`, with a separate curve for every case
- Humidity (`h20`) versus `heatan`

In the plot for `absorbance` versus `heatan`, we wrap `wavelength` inside the `as.factor()` function, so that each wavelength will be drawn with a discrete color (rather than a gradient of colors from low to high wavelengths). To prevent the `ggplot()` function from drawing a huge legend showing the color of each of the lines, we suppress the legend by adding `theme(legend.position = "none")`. We facet by spectrum to create subplots for the ultraviolet and near-infrared spectra, allowing the x-axis to vary between subplots using the `scales = "free_x"` argument.

I don't know about you, but I was always told in school to add titles to my plots. We can do this in ggplot2 using the `ggtitle()` function, supplying the title we want in quotes.

> **TIP** The `theme()` function allows you to customize almost anything about the appearance of your ggplots, including font sizes and the presence/absence of grid lines. I won't discuss this in depth, but I recommend taking a look at the help page using `?theme` to find out what you can do.

In the plot for `wavelength` versus `absorbance`, we set the `group` aesthetic equal to the `id` variable we created, so that the `geom_smooth()` layer will draw a separate curve for each batch of fuel.

Listing 12.3 Plotting the data

```
fuelUntidy %>%
  ggplot(aes(absorbance, heatan, col = as.factor(wavelength))) +
  facet_wrap(~ spectrum, scales = "free_x") +
  geom_smooth(se = FALSE, size = 0.2) +
  ggtitle("Absorbance vs heatan for each wavelength") +
  theme_bw() +
  theme(legend.position = "none")

fuelUntidy %>%
  ggplot(aes(wavelength, absorbance, group = id, col = heatan)) +
  facet_wrap(~ spectrum, scales = "free_x") +
  geom_smooth(se = FALSE, size = 0.2) +
  ggtitle("Wavelength vs absorbance for each batch") +
  theme_bw()

fuelUntidy %>%
  ggplot(aes(h20, heatan)) +
  geom_smooth(se = FALSE) +
  ggtitle("Humidity vs heatan") +
  theme_bw()
```

The resulting plots are shown in figure 12.7 (I've combined them into a single figure to save space). Data really is beautiful sometimes, isn't it? In the plots of `absorbance` against `heatan`, each line corresponds to a particular wavelength. The relationship between each predictor variable and the outcome variable is complex and nonlinear. There is also a nonlinear relationship between `h20` and `heatan`.

In the plots of `wavelength` against `absorbance`, each line corresponds to a particular batch of fuel, and the lines show its `absorbance` of ultraviolet and near-infrared light. The shading of the line corresponds to the `heatan` value of that batch. It's difficult to identify patterns in these plots, but certain `absorbance` profiles seem to correlate with higher and lower `heatan` values.

TIP While you can certainly overfit your data, you can never over-plot it. When starting an exploratory analysis, I will plot my dataset in multiple different ways to get a better understanding of it from different angles/perspectives.

Exercise 1

Add an additional `geom_smooth()` layer to the plot of `absorbance` versus `heatan` with these arguments:

- `group = 1`
- `col = "blue"`

Using the argument `group = 1`, create a single smoothing line that models *all* of the data, ignoring groups.

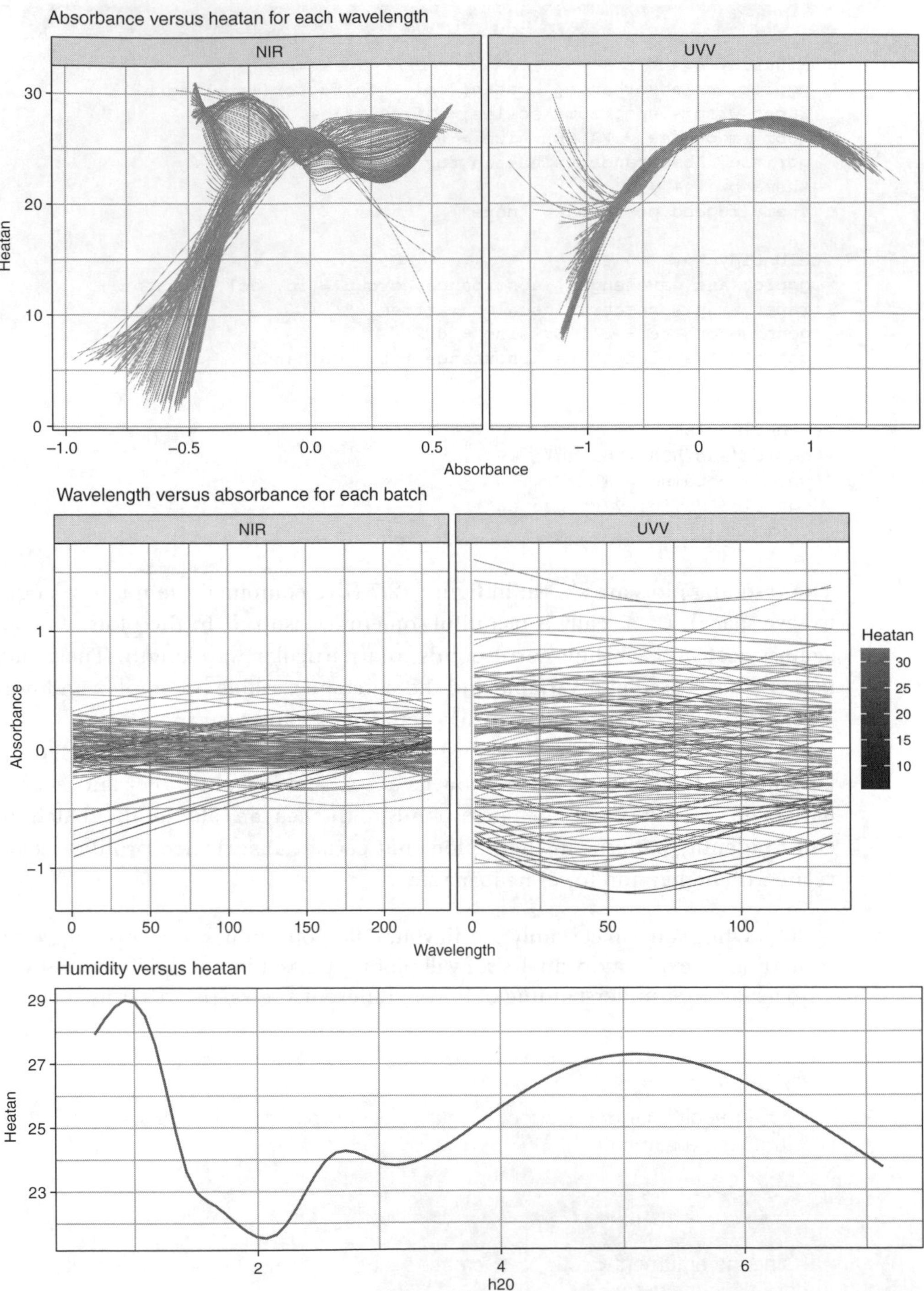

Figure 12.7 Plotting the relationships in the fuelTib dataset. The topmost plots show `absorbance` against `heatan` with separate lines drawn for each `wavelength`, faceted by near-infrared (NIR) or ultraviolet (UVV) light. The middle plots show `wavelength` against `absorbance` shaded by `heatan` with separate lines drawn for each batch of fuel, faceted by NIR or UVV light. The bottom plot shows `h20` against `heatan`.

Modeling spectral data

The dataset we're working with is an example of *spectral data*. Spectral data contains observations made across a range of (usually) wavelengths. For example, we might measure how much a substance absorbs light from a range of different colors.

Statisticians and data scientists call this kind of data *functional data*, where there are many dimensions in the dataset (the wavelengths we measure across) and there is a particular order to those dimensions (starting by measuring the absorbance at the lowest wavelength and working our way to the highest wavelength).

A branch of statistics called *functional data analysis* is dedicated to modeling data like this. In functional data analysis, each predictor variable is turned into a function (for example, a function that describes how absorbance changes over ultraviolet and near-infrared wavelengths). That function is then used in the model as a predictor, to predict the outcome variable. We won't apply this kind of technique to this data, but if you're interested in functional data analysis, check out *Functional Data Analysis* by James Ramsay (Springer, 2005).

Because the predefined `fuelsubset.task` defines the ultraviolet and near-infrared spectra as functional variables, we're going to define our own task, treating each wavelength as a separate predictor. We do this, as usual, with the `makeRegrTask()` function, setting the `heatan` variable as our target. We then define our kNN learner using the `makeLearner()` function.

Listing 12.4 Defining the task and kNN learner

```
fuelTask <- makeRegrTask(data = fuelTib, target = "heatan")

kknn <- makeLearner("regr.kknn")
```

NOTE Notice that for regression, the name of the learner is `"regr.kknn"` with two k's, rather than the `"classif.knn"` we used in chapter 3. This is because this function is taken from the kknn package, which allows us to perform *kernel k-nearest neighbors*, where we use a kernel function (just like with SVMs in chapter 6) to find a linear decision boundary between classes.

12.3.2 Tuning the k hyperparameter

In this section, we're going to tune *k* to get the best-performing kNN model possible. Remember that for regression, the value of *k* determines how many of the nearest neighbors' outcome values to average when making predictions on new cases. We first define the hyperparameter search space using the `makeParamSet()` function, and define *k* as a discrete hyperparameter with possible values 1 through 12. Then we define our search procedure as a grid search (so that we will try every value in the search space), and define a 10-fold cross-validation strategy.

As we've done many times before, we run the tuning process using the `tuneParams()` function, supplying the learner, task, cross-validation method, hyperparameter space, and search procedure as arguments.

Listing 12.5 Tuning *k*

```
kknnParamSpace <- makeParamSet(makeDiscreteParam("k", values = 1:12))

gridSearch <- makeTuneControlGrid()

kFold <- makeResampleDesc("CV", iters = 10)

tunedK <- tuneParams(kknn, task = fuelTask,
                     resampling = kFold,
                     par.set = kknnParamSpace,
                     control = gridSearch)

tunedK

Tune result:
Op. pars: k=7
mse.test.mean=10.7413
```

We can plot the hyperparameter tuning process by extracting the tuning data with the `generateHyperParsEffectData()` function and passing this to the `plotHyperParsEffect()` function, supplying our hyperparameter (`"k"`) as the x-axis and MSE (`"mse.test.mean"`) as the y-axis. Setting the `plot.type` argument equal to `"line"` connects the samples with a line.

Listing 12.6 Plotting the tuning process

```
knnTuningData <- generateHyperParsEffectData(tunedK)

plotHyperParsEffect(knnTuningData, x = "k", y = "mse.test.mean",
                    plot.type = "line") +
  theme_bw()
```

The resulting plot is shown in figure 12.8. We can see that the mean MSE starts to rise as *k* increases beyond 7, so it looks like our search space was appropriate.

> **Exercise 2**
>
> Let's make sure our search space was large enough. Repeat the tuning process, but search values of *k* from 1 to 50. Plot this tuning process just like we did in figure 12.8. Was our original search space large enough?

Now that we have our tuned value of *k*, we can define a learner using that value, with the `setHyperPars()` function, and train a model using it.

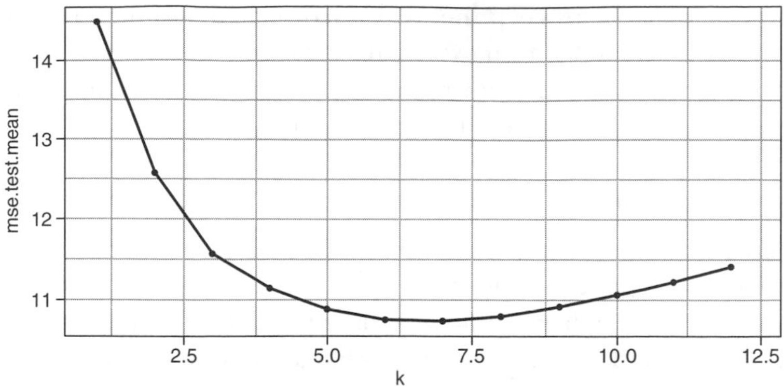

Figure 12.8 Plotting our hyperparameter tuning process. The average MSE (`mse.test.mean`) is shown for each value of *k*.

Listing 12.7 Training the final, tuned kNN model

```
tunedKnn <- setHyperPars(makeLearner("regr.kknn"), par.vals = tunedK$x)

tunedKnnModel <- train(tunedKnn, fuelTask)
```

12.4 Building your first random forest regression model

In this section, I'll teach you how to define a random forest learner for regression, tune its many hyperparameters, and train a model for our fuel task.

> **NOTE** We can also use the rpart algorithm to build a regression tree, but as it is almost always outperformed by bagged and boosted learners, we're going to skip over it and dive straight in with random forest and XGBoost. Recall that bagged (bootstrap-aggregated) learners train multiple models on bootstrap samples of the data, and return the majority vote. Boosted learners train models sequentially, putting more emphasis on correcting the mistakes of the previous ensemble of models.

We'll start by defining our random forest learner. Notice that rather than `"classif.randomForest"` as in chapter 8, the regression equivalent is `"regr.randomForest"`:

```
forest <- makeLearner("regr.randomForest")
```

Next, we're going to tune the hyperparameters of our random forest learner: `ntree`, `mtry`, `nodesize`, and `maxnodes`. I first defined what these hyperparameters do in chapter 8, but let's recap each one here:

- `ntree` controls the number of individual trees to train. More trees is usually better until adding more doesn't improve performance further.
- `mtry` controls the number of predictor variables that are randomly sampled for each individual tree. Training each individual tree on a random selection of

predictor variables helps keep the trees uncorrelated and therefore helps prevent the ensemble model from overfitting the training set.

- `nodesize` defines the minimum number of cases allowed in a leaf node. For example, setting `nodesize` equal to 1 would allow each case in the training set to have its own leaf.
- `maxnodes` defines the maximum number of nodes in each individual tree.

As usual, we create our hyperparameter search space using the `makeParamSet()` function, defining each hyperparameter as an integer with sensible lower and upper bounds.

We define a random search with 100 iterations and start the tuning procedure with our forest learner, fuel task, and `holdout` cross-validation strategy.

> **WARNING** This tuning process takes a little while, so let's use our good friends the parallel and parallelMap packages. Using parallelization, this takes 2 minutes on my four-core machine.

Listing 12.8 Hyperparameter tuning for random forest

```
forestParamSpace <- makeParamSet(
  makeIntegerParam("ntree", lower = 50, upper = 50),
  makeIntegerParam("mtry", lower = 100, upper = 367),
  makeIntegerParam("nodesize", lower = 1, upper = 10),
  makeIntegerParam("maxnodes", lower = 5, upper = 30))

randSearch <- makeTuneControlRandom(maxit = 100)

library(parallel)

library(parallelMap)

parallelStartSocket(cpus = detectCores())

tunedForestPars <- tuneParams(forest, task = fuelTask,
                              resampling = kFold,
                              par.set = forestParamSpace,
                              control = randSearch)

parallelStop()

tunedForestPars

Tune result:
Op. pars: ntree=50; mtry=244; nodesize=6; maxnodes=25
mse.test.mean=6.3293
```

Next, let's train the random forest model using our tuned hyperparameters. Once we've trained the model, it's a good idea to extract the model information and pass this to the `plot()` function to plot the out-of-bag error. Recall from chapter 8 that the out-of-bag error is the mean prediction error for each case by trees that *did not* include that case in their bootstrap sample. The only difference between the out-of-bag error for classification and regression random forests is that in classification, the error was the proportion of cases that were misclassified; but in regression, the error is the mean squared error.

Listing 12.9 Training the model and plotting the out-of-bag error

```
tunedForest <- setHyperPars(forest, par.vals = tunedForestPars$x)

tunedForestModel <- train(tunedForest, fuelTask)

forestModelData <- getLearnerModel(tunedForestModel)

plot(forestModelData)
```

The resulting plot is shown in figure 12.9. It looks like the out-of-bag error stabilizes after 30–40 bagged trees, so we can be satisfied that we have included enough trees in our forest.

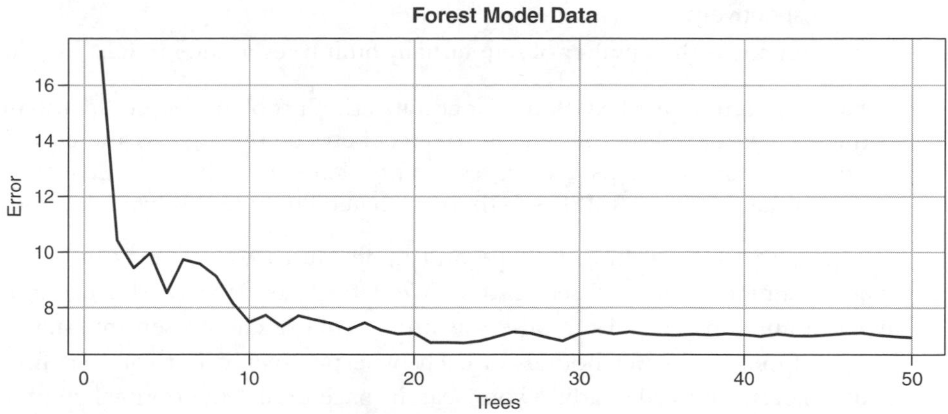

Figure 12.9 Plotting the out-of-bag error for our random forest model. The Error y-axis shows the mean square error for all cases, predicted by trees that didn't include that case in the training set. This is shown for varying numbers of trees in the ensemble. The flattening out of the line suggests we have included enough individual trees in the forest.

12.5 Building your first XGBoost regression model

In this section, I'll teach you how to define an XGBoost learner for regression, tune its many hyperparameters, and train a model for our fuel task. We'll start by defining our XGBoost learner. Just like for the kNN and random forest learners, instead of using `"classif.xgboost"` as in chapter 8, the regression equivalent is `"regr.xgboost"`:

```
xgb <- makeLearner("regr.xgboost")
```

Next, we're going to tune the hyperparameters of our XGBoost learner: `eta`, `gamma`, `max_depth`, `min_child_weight`, `subsample`, `colsample_bytree`, and `nrounds`. I first defined what these hyperparameters do in chapter 8, but again, let's recap each one here:

- eta is known as the *learning rate*. It takes a value between 0 and 1, which is multiplied by the model weight of each tree to slow down the learning process to prevent overfitting.
- gamma is the minimum amount of splitting by which a node must improve the loss function (MSE in the case of regression).
- max_depth is the maximum number of levels deep that each tree can grow.
- min_child_weight is the minimum degree of impurity needed in a node before attempting to split it (if a node is pure enough, don't try to split it again).
- subsample is the proportion of cases to be randomly sampled (without replacement) for each tree. Setting this to 1 uses all the cases in the training set.
- colsample_bytree is the proportion of predictor variables sampled for each tree. We could also tune colsample_bylevel and colsample_bynode, which instead sample predictors for each level of depth in a tree and at each node, respectively.
- nrounds is the number of sequentially built trees in the model.

NOTE When we used XGBoost for classification problems, we could also tune the eval_metric hyperparameter to select between the log loss and classification error loss functions. For regression problems, we only have one loss function available to us—RMSE—so there is no need to tune this hyperparameter.

In listing 12.10, we define the type and upper and lower bounds of each of these hyperparameters that we'll search over. We define max_depth and nrounds as integer hyperparameters, and all the others as numerics. I've chosen sensible starting values for the upper and lower bounds of each hyperparameter, but you may find in your own projects you need to adjust your search space to find the optimal combination of values. I usually fix the nrounds hyperparameter as a single value that fits my computational budget to start with, and then plot the loss function (RMSE) against the tree number to see if the model error has flattened out. If it hasn't, I increase the nrounds hyperparameter until it does. We'll perform this in listing 12.11.

Once the search space is defined, we start the tuning process just like we have the previous two times in this chapter.

WARNING This takes around 1.5 minutes on my four-core machine.

Listing 12.10 Hyperparameter tuning for XGBoost

```
xgbParamSpace <- makeParamSet(
  makeNumericParam("eta", lower = 0, upper = 1),
  makeNumericParam("gamma", lower = 0, upper = 10),
  makeIntegerParam("max_depth", lower = 1, upper = 20),
  makeNumericParam("min_child_weight", lower = 1, upper = 10),
  makeNumericParam("subsample", lower = 0.5, upper = 1),
```

```
  makeNumericParam("colsample_bytree", lower = 0.5, upper = 1),
  makeIntegerParam("nrounds", lower = 30, upper = 30))

tunedXgbPars <- tuneParams(xgb, task = fuelTask,
                           resampling = kFold,
                           par.set = xgbParamSpace,
                           control = randSearch)

tunedXgbPars

Tune result:
Op. pars: eta=0.188; gamma=6.44; max_depth=11; min_child_weight=1.55; subsamp
     le=0.96; colsample_bytree=0.7; nrounds=30
mse.test.mean=6.2830
```

Now that we have our tuned combination of hyperparameters, let's train the final model using this combination. Once we've done this, we can extract the model information and use it to plot the iteration number (tree number) against the RMSE to see if we included enough trees in our ensemble. The RMSE information for each tree number is contained in the `$evaluation_log` component of the model information, so we use this as the data argument for the `ggplot()` function, specifying `iter` and `train_rmse` to plot the tree number and its RMSE as the x and y aesthetics, respectively.

Listing 12.11 Training the model and plotting RMSE against tree number

```
tunedXgb <- setHyperPars(xgb, par.vals = tunedXgbPars$x)

tunedXgbModel <- train(tunedXgb, fuelTask)

xgbModelData <- getLearnerModel(tunedXgbModel)

ggplot(xgbModelData$evaluation_log, aes(iter, train_rmse)) +
  geom_line() +
  geom_point() +
  theme_bw()
```

The resulting plot is shown in figure 12.10. We can see that 30 iterations/trees is just about enough for the RMSE to have flattened out (including more iterations won't result in a better model).

12.6 Benchmarking the kNN, random forest, and XGBoost model-building processes

I love a bit of healthy competition. In this section, we're going to benchmark the kNN, random forest, and XGBoost model-building processes against each other. We start by creating tuning wrappers that wrap together each learner with its hyperparameter tuning process. Then we create a list of these wrapper learners to pass into `benchmark()`. As this process will take some time, we're going to define and use a `holdout`

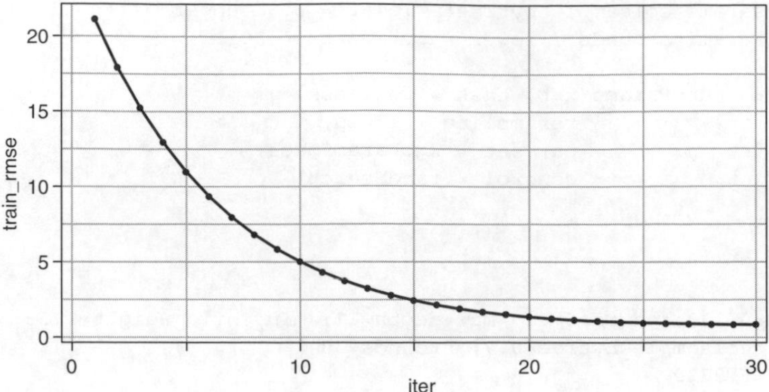

Figure 12.10 Plotting the average root mean square error (`train_rmse`) against the iteration of the boosting process. The curve flattens out just before 30 iterations, suggesting that we have included enough trees in our ensemble.

cross-validation procedure to evaluate the performance of each wrapper (ideally we would use k-fold or repeated k-fold).

> **WARNING** It's tea and cake time! This takes around 7 minutes to run on my four-core machine. Using the parallelMap package won't help because we're training XGBoost models as part of the benchmark, and XGBoost works fastest if you allow it to perform its own internal parallelization.

Listing 12.12 Benchmarking kNN, random forest, and XGBoost

```
kknnWrapper <- makeTuneWrapper(kknn, resampling = kFold,
                                  par.set = kknnParamSpace,
                                  control = gridSearch)

forestWrapper <- makeTuneWrapper(forest, resampling = kFold,
                                  par.set = forestParamSpace,
                                  control = randSearch)

xgbWrapper <- makeTuneWrapper(xgb, resampling = kFold,
                                 par.set = xgbParamSpace,
                                 control = randSearch)

learners = list(kknnWrapper, forestWrapper, xgbWrapper)

holdout <- makeResampleDesc("Holdout")

bench <- benchmark(learners, fuelTask, holdout)

bench

  task.id                learner.id mse.test.mean
1 fuelTib          regr.kknn.tuned        10.403
2 fuelTib regr.randomForest.tuned         6.174
3 fuelTib       regr.xgboost.tuned         8.043
```

According to this benchmark result, the random forest algorithm is likely to give us the best-performing model, with a mean prediction error of 2.485 (the square root of 6.174).

12.7 Strengths and weaknesses of kNN, random forest, and XGBoost

The strengths and weaknesses of the kNN, random forest, and XGBoost algorithms are the same for regression as they were for classification.

Exercise 3

Get a more accurate estimate of each of our model-building processes by rerunning the benchmark experiment, changing our `holdout` cross-validation object to our `kFold` object. Warning: This took nearly an hour on my four-core machine! Save the benchmark result to an object, and pass that object as the only argument to the `plotBMRBoxplots()` function.

Exercise 4

Cross-validate the model-building process of the model that won the benchmark in exercise 3, but perform 2,000 iterations of the random search during hyperparameter tuning. Use `holdout` as the inner cross-validation loop and 10-fold cross-validation as the outer loop. Warning: I'd suggest you use parallelization and leave this running during lunch or overnight.

Summary

- The k-nearest neighbors (kNN) and tree-based algorithms can be used for regression as well as classification.
- When predicting a continuous outcome variable, the predictions made by kNN are the mean outcome values of the k-nearest neighbors.
- When predicting a continuous outcome variable, the leaves of tree-based algorithms are the mean of the cases within that leaf.
- Out-of-bag error and RMSE can still be used to identify whether random forest and XGBoost ensembles have enough trees, respectively, in regression problems.

Solutions to exercises

1 Plot `absorbance` versus `heatan` with an additional `geom_smooth()` layer that models the whole dataset:

```
fuelUntidy %>%
  ggplot(aes(absorbance, heatan, col = as.factor(wavelength))) +
  facet_wrap(~ spectrum, scales = "free_x") +
  geom_smooth(se = FALSE, size = 0.2) +
  geom_smooth(group = 1, col = "blue") +
```

```
  ggtitle("Absorbance vs heatan for each wavelength") +
  theme_bw() +
  theme(legend.position = "none")
```

2 Expand the kNN search space to include values between 1 and 50:

```
kknnParamSpace50 <- makeParamSet(makeDiscreteParam("k", values = 1:50))

tunedK50 <- tuneParams(kknn, task = fuelTask,
                       resampling = kFold,
                       par.set = kknnParamSpace50,
                       control = gridSearch)

tunedK50

knnTuningData50 <- generateHyperParsEffectData(tunedK50)

plotHyperParsEffect(knnTuningData50, x = "k", y = "mse.test.mean",
                    plot.type = "line") +
  theme_bw()

# Our original search space was large enough.
```

3 Use 10-fold cross-validation as the outer cross-validation loop for the benchmark experiment:

```
benchKFold <- benchmark(learners, fuelTask, kFold)

plotBMRBoxplots(benchKFold)
```

4 Cross-validate the model-building process for the algorithm that won the benchmark, performing 2,000 iterations of the random search and using `holdout` as the inner cross-validation strategy (inside the tuning wrapper):

```
holdout <- makeResampleDesc("Holdout")

randSearch2000 <- makeTuneControlRandom(maxit = 2000)

forestWrapper2000 <- makeTuneWrapper(forest, resampling = holdout,
                                     par.set = forestParamSpace,
                                     control = randSearch2000)

parallelStartSocket(cpus = detectCores())

cvWithTuning <- resample(forestWrapper2000, fuelTask, resampling = kFold)

parallelStop()
```

Part 4

Dimension reduction

You're now on your way to becoming a supervised machine learning virtuoso! So far, your toolbox of machine learning algorithms gives you the skills to tackle many real-world classification and regression problems. We're now going to move into the realm of unsupervised learning, where we are no longer relying on labeled data to learn patterns from the data. Because we no longer have a ground truth to compare to, validating the performance of unsupervised learners can be challenging, but I'll show practical ways to ensure the best performance possible.

Recall from chapter 1 that unsupervised learning can be divided into two goals: dimension reduction and clustering. In chapters 13, 14, and 15, I'll introduce you to several dimension-reduction algorithms you can use to turn a large number of variables into a smaller, more manageable number. Our motivations for doing this might be to simplify the process of visualizing patterns in data with many dimensions; or as a preprocessing step before passing our data into a supervised algorithm, to mitigate the curse of dimensionality.

13 Maximizing variance with principal component analysis

This chapter covers

- Understanding dimension reduction
- Dealing with high dimensionality and collinearity
- Using principal component analysis to reduce dimensionality

Dimension reduction comprises a number of approaches that turn a set of (potentially many) variables into a smaller number of variables that retain as much of the original, multidimensional information as possible. We sometimes want to reduce the number of dimensions we're working with in a dataset, to help us visualize the relationships in the data or to avoid the strange phenomena that occur in high dimensions. So dimension reduction is a critical skill to add to your machine learning toolbox!

Our first stop in dimension reduction brings us to a very well-known and useful technique: *principal component analysis* (*PCA*). PCA, which has been around since the turn of the twentieth century, creates new variables that are linear combinations of the original variables. In this way, PCA is similar to discriminant analysis, which we encountered in chapter 5; but instead of constructing new variables that separate classes, PCA constructs new variables that explain most of the variation/

information in the data. In fact, there are no labels for PCA, because it is unsupervised and learns patterns in the data itself without a ground truth. We can then use the two or three of these new variables that capture most of the information as inputs to regression, classification, or clustering algorithms, as well as use them to better understand how the variables in our data are related to each other.

> **NOTE** The first historical example of dimension reduction was a map with two dimensions. Another form of dimension reduction that we encounter in our daily lives is the compression of audio into formats like .mp3 and .flac.

The mlr package doesn't have a dimension-reduction class of tasks, and it doesn't have a class of dimension-reduction learners (something like `dimred.[ALGORITHM]`, I suppose). PCA is the only dimension-reduction algorithm wrapped by mlr that we can include as a preprocessing step (like imputation or feature selection). In view of this, we're going to leave the safety of the mlr package for the time being.

By the end of this chapter, I hope you'll understand what dimension reduction is and why we sometimes need it. I will show you how the PCA algorithm works and how you can use it to reduce the dimensions of a dataset to help identify counterfeit banknotes.

13.1 Why dimension reduction?

In this section, I'll show you the main reasons for applying dimension reduction:

- Making it easier to visualize a dataset with many variables
- Mitigating the curse of dimensionality
- Mitigating the effects of collinearity

I'll expand on what the curse of dimensionality and collinearity are and why they cause problems for machine learning, as well as why dimension reduction can reduce the impact of both when we're searching for patterns in data.

13.1.1 Visualizing high-dimensional data

When starting an exploratory analysis, one of the first things you should always do is plot your data. It's important that we, as data scientists, have an intuitive understanding of the structure of our data, the relationships between variables, and how the data is distributed. But what if we have a dataset containing thousands of variables? Where do we even start? Plotting each of these variables against each other isn't really an option anymore, so how can we get a feel for the overall structure in our data? Well, we can reduce the dimensions down to a more manageable number, and plot these instead. We won't get all the information of the original dataset when doing this, but it will help us identify patterns in our data, like clusters of cases that might suggest a grouping structure in the data.

13.1.2 Consequences of the curse of dimensionality

In chapter 5, I discussed the curse of dimensionality. This slightly dramatic-sounding phenomenon describes a set of challenges we encounter when trying to identify patterns in a dataset with many variables. One aspect of the curse of dimensionality is that for a fixed number of cases, as we increase the number of dimensions in the dataset (increase the feature space), the cases get further and further apart. To reiterate this point in figure 13.1, I've reproduced figure 5.2 from chapter 5. In this situation, the data is said to become *sparse*. Many machine learning algorithms struggle to learn patterns from sparse data and may start to learn from the noise in the dataset instead.

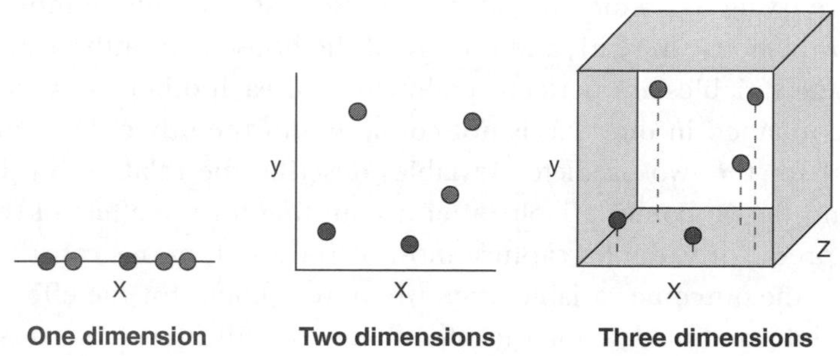

Figure 13.1 Data becomes more sparse as the number of dimensions increases. Two classes are shown in one-, two-, and three-dimensional feature spaces. The dotted lines in the three-dimensional representation are to clarify the position of the points along the z-axis. Note the increasing empty space with increased dimensions.

Another aspect of the curse of dimensionality is that as the number of dimensions increases, the distances between the cases begin to converge to a single value. Put another way, for a particular case, the ratio between the distance to its nearest neighbor and its furthest neighbor tends toward 1 in high dimensions. This presents a challenge to algorithms that rely on measuring distances (particularly Euclidean distance), such as k-nearest neighbors, because distance starts to become meaningless.

Finally, it's quite common to encounter situations in which we have many more variables than we have cases in the data. This is referred to as the *p >> n problem*, where *p* is the number of variables and *n* is the number of cases. This, again, results in sparse regions of the feature space, making it difficult for many algorithms to converge on an optimal solution.

13.1.3 Consequences of collinearity

Variables in a dataset often have varying degrees of correlation with each other. Sometimes we may have two variables that correlate very highly with each other, such that one basically contains the information of the other (say, with a Pearson correlation coefficient > 0.9). In such situations, these variables are said to be *collinear* or exhibit *collinearity*. An example of two variables that might be collinear are annual income and the maximum amount of money a bank is willing to loan someone; you could probably predict one from the other with a high degree of accuracy.

TIP When more than two variables are collinear, we say we have *multicollinearity* in our dataset. When one variable can be *perfectly* predicted from another variable or combination of variables, we are said to have *perfect collinearity*.

So what's the problem with collinearity? Well, it depends on the goal of your analysis and what algorithms you are using. The most commonly encountered negative impact of collinearity is on the parameter estimates of linear regression models.

Let's say you're trying to predict the value of houses based on the number of bedrooms, the age of the house in years, and the age of the house in months, using linear regression. The age variables are perfectly collinear with each other, because there's no information contained in one that is not contained in the other. The parameter estimates (slopes) for the two predictor variables describe the relationship between each predictor and the outcome variable, after accounting for the effect of the other variable. If both predictor variables capture most of (or all of, in this case) the same information about the outcome variable, then when we account for the effect of one, there will be no information left for the other one to contribute. As a result, the parameter estimates for both predictors will be smaller than they should be (because each was estimated after accounting for the effect of the other).

So collinearity makes the parameter estimates more variable and more sensitive to small changes in the data. This is mostly a problem if you're interested in interpreting and making inferences about the parameter estimates. If all you care about is predictive accuracy, and not interpreting the model parameters, then collinearity may not be a problem for you at all.

It's worth mentioning, however, that collinearity is particularly problematic when working with the naive Bayes algorithm you learned about in chapter 6. Recall that the "naive" in naive Bayes refers to the fact that this algorithm assumes independence between predictors. This assumption is often invalid in the real world, but naive Bayes is usually resistant to small correlations between predictor variables. When predictors are highly correlated, however, the predictive performance of naive Bayes will suffer considerably, though this is usually easy to identify when you cross-validate your model.

13.1.4 Mitigating the curse of dimensionality and collinearity by using dimension reduction

How can you mitigate the impacts of the curse of dimensionality and/or collinearity on the predictive performance of your models? Why, with dimension reduction, of course! If you can compress most of the information from 100 variables into just 2 or 3, then the problems of data sparsity and near-equal distances disappear. If you turn two collinear variables into one new variable that captures all the information of both, then the problem of dependence between the variables disappears.

But we've already encountered another set of techniques that can mitigate the curse of dimensionality and collinearity: regularization. As we saw in chapter 11, regularization can be used to shrink the parameter estimates and even completely remove weakly contributing predictors. Regularization can therefore reduce sparsity resulting from the curse of dimensionality, and remove variables that are collinear with others.

NOTE For most people, tackling the curse of dimensionality is a more important use of dimension reduction than reducing collinearity.

13.2 What is principal component analysis?

In this section, I'll show you what PCA is, how it works, and why it's useful. Imagine that we measure two variables on seven people, and we want to compress this information down into a single variable using PCA. The first thing we need to do is center the variables by subtracting each variable's mean from its corresponding value for each case.

In addition to centering our variables, we can also scale them by dividing each variable by its standard deviation. This is important if the variables are measured on different scales—otherwise, those on large scales will be weighted more heavily. If our variables are on similar scales, this standardization step isn't necessary.

With our centered and (possibly) scaled data, PCA now finds a new axis that satisfies two conditions:

- The axis passes through the origin.
- The axis maximizes the variance of the data along itself.

The new axis that satisfies these conditions is called the first *principal axis*. When the data is projected onto this principal axis (moved at a right angle onto the nearest point on the axis), this new variable is called the first *principal component*, often abbreviated PC1. This process of centering the data and finding PC1 is shown in figure 13.2.

The first principal axis is the line through the origin of the data that, once the data is projected onto it, has the greatest variance along it and is said to "maximize the

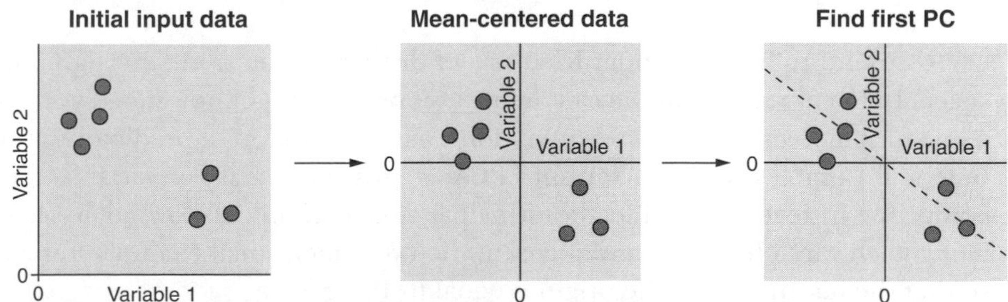

Figure 13.2 The first thing we do before applying the PCA algorithm is (usually) to center the data by subtracting the mean of each variable for each case. This places the origin at the center of the data. The first principal axis is then found: it is the axis that passes through the origin and maximizes the variance of the data when projected onto it.

variance." This is illustrated in figure 13.3. This axis is chosen because if this is the line that accounts for the majority of the variance in the data, then it is also the line that accounts for the majority of the information in the data.

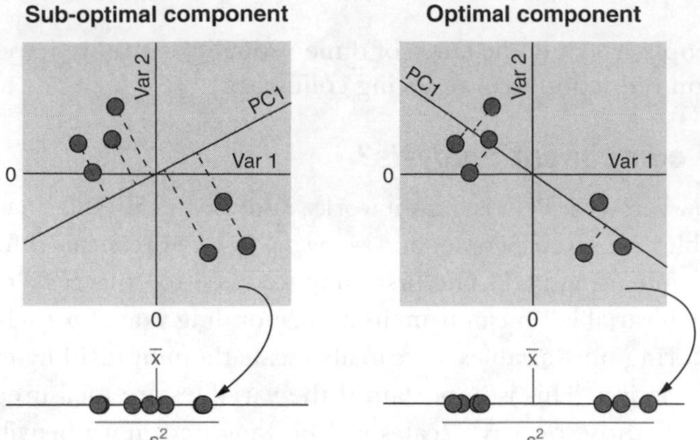

Figure 13.3 What it means for the first principal axis to "maximize the variance." The left-side plot shows a sub-optimal candidate principal axis. The right-side plot shows the optimal candidate principal axis. The data is shown projected onto each principal axis below the respective plots. The variance of the data along the axis is greatest on the right side.

This new principal axis is actually a linear combination of the predictor variables. Look again at figure 13.3. The first principal axis extends through the two clusters of cases to form a negative slope between var 1 and var 2. Just like in linear regression, we can express this line in terms of how one variable changes when the other variable changes (as the line passes through the origin, the intercept is 0). Take a look at figure 13.4, where I've highlighted how much var 2 changes when var 1 increases by two units along the principal axis. For every two-unit change in var 1, var 2 decreases by 0.68 units.

It's useful to have a standardized way of describing the slope through our feature space. In linear regression, we can define a slope in terms of how much y changes with a one-unit increase in x. But we often don't have any notion of predictor variables and outcome variables when performing PCA: we just have a set of variables we wish to compress. Instead, we define the principal axis in terms of how far we need to go along each variable (the x- and y-axes in the two-dimensional example in figure 13.4) so that the distance from the origin is equal to 1.

Have another look at figure 13.4. We're trying to calculate the length of sides a and b of the triangle when length c is equal to 1. This will then tell us how far along var 1 and var 2 we need to go, to be one unit away from the origin along the principal axis. How do we calculate the length of c? Why, our good friend Pythagoras's theorem can

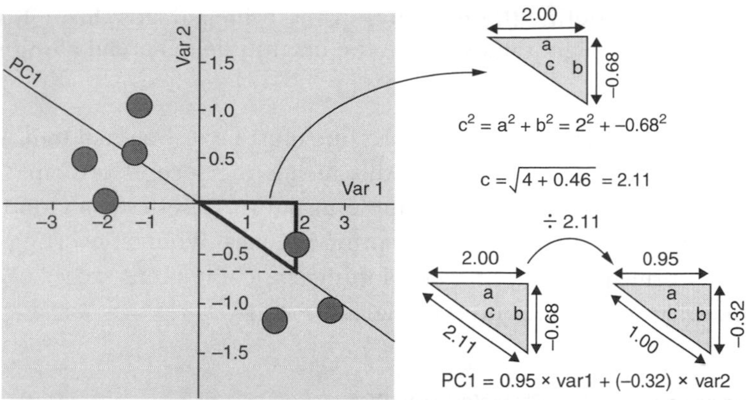

Figure 13.4 Calculating the eigenvector for a principal component. The distances along each variable are scaled so that they mark a point that is one unit along the principal axis away from the origin. We can illustrate this graphically by taking a triangle defined by the change in one variable over the change in the other variable, and using Pythagoras's theorem to find the distance from the origin to divide by.

help! By applying $c^2 = a^2 + b^2$, we can work out that if we go along var 1 2.00 units and along var 2 –0.68 units, the length of c is equal to 2.11. To normalize this such that the length of c is equal to 1, we simply divide all three sides of the triangle by 2.11. We now define our principal axis as follows: for every 0.95 unit increase in var 1, we decrease along var 2 by 0.32.

Note that this transformation doesn't change the direction of the line; all it does is normalize everything so that the distance from the origin is 1. These normalized distances along each variable that define a principal axis are called an *eigenvector*. The formula for the principal component that results from the principal axis is therefore

$$PC1 = 0.95 \times \text{var } 1 + (-0.32) \times \text{var } 2$$ **Equation 13.1**

So for any particular case, we center it (subtract the mean of each variable), take its value of var 1 and multiply by 0.95, and then add the result to the value of var 2 multiplied by –0.32, to get this case's value of PC1. The value of a principal component for a case is called its *component score*.

Once we've found the first principal axis, we need to find the next one. PCA will find as many principal axes as there are variables or one less than the number of cases in the dataset, whichever is smaller. So the first principal component is always the one that explains most of the variance in the data. Concretely, if we calculate the variance of the cases along each principal component, PC1 will have the largest value. The variance of the data along a particular principal component is called its *eigenvalue*.

NOTE If eigenvectors define the direction of the principal axis through the original feature space, eigenvalues define the magnitude of spread along the principal axis.

Once the first principal axis is found, the next one must be orthogonal to it. When we have only two dimensions in our dataset, this means the second principal axis will form a right angle with the first. The example in figure 13.5 shows a cloud of cases being projected onto their first and second principal axes. When converting only two variables into two principal components, plotting the component scores of the data amounts to rotating the data around the origin.

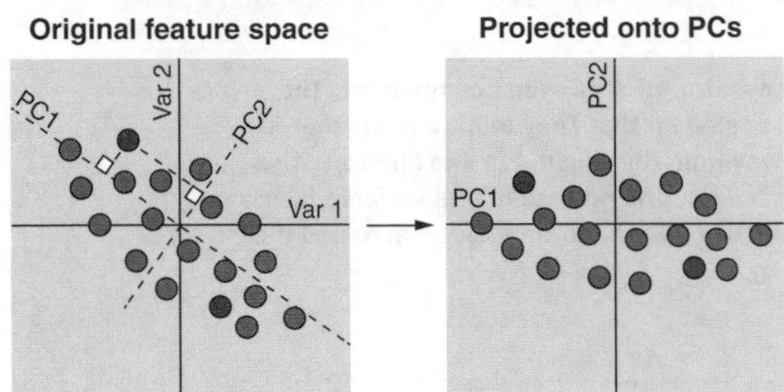

Figure 13.5 In a two-dimensional feature space, the first principal axis is the one that maximizes the variance (as it always is), and the second principal axis is orthogonal (at a right angle) to the first. In this situation, plotting the principal components simply results in a rotation of the data.

NOTE This imposed orthogonality is one of the reasons PCA is good at removing collinearity between variables: it can turn a set of correlated variables into a set of uncorrelated (orthogonal) variables.

After rotating the data in figure 13.5, the majority of the variance in the data is explained by PC1, and PC2 is orthogonal to it. But PCA is usually used to *reduce dimensions,* not just rotate bivariate data, so how are the principal axes calculated when we have a higher-dimensional space? Take a look at figure 13.6. We have a cloud of data in three dimensions that is closest to us at the bottom right of the feature space and gets further from us at the top left (notice that the points get smaller). The first principal axis is still the one that explains most of the variance in the data, but this time it extends through three-dimensional space (from front right to top left). The same process occurs in a feature space that has more than three dimensions, but it's difficult to visualize that!

The second principal axis is still orthogonal to the first, but as we now have three dimensions to play around with, it is free to rotate around the first in a plane that still maintains a right angle between them. I've illustrated this rotational freedom with a circle around the origin that gets fainter, the further away from us it is. The second principal axis is the one that is orthogonal to the first but explains the majority of the remaining variance in the data. The third principal axis must be orthogonal to the preceding axes (at right angles to both of them) and therefore has no freedom to move. The first principal component always explains the most variance, followed by the second, the third, and so on.

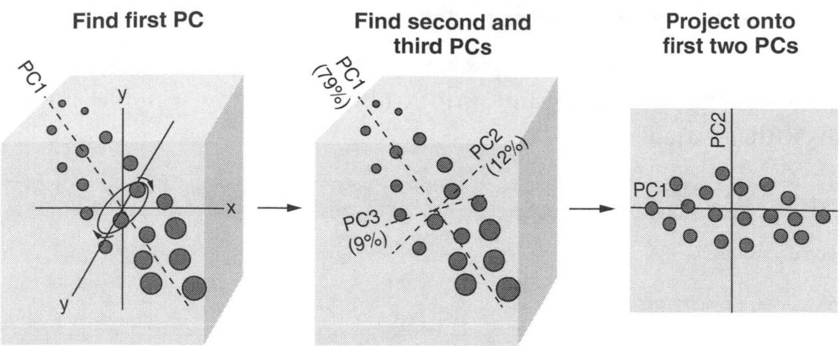

Figure 13.6 In a three-dimensional feature space, the second principal axis is still orthogonal to the first principal axis, but it has freedom to rotate around the first (indicated by the ellipse with arrows in the left-side plot) until it maximizes the remaining variance. The third principal axis is orthogonal to the first and second principal axes and so has no freedom to rotate; it explains the least amount of variance.

At this point you might be asking, if PCA calculates principal components for the smaller of the number of variables or the number of cases minus one, how exactly does it reduce the number of dimensions? Well, simply calculating the principal components isn't dimension reduction at all! Dimension reduction comes into it regarding *how many of the principal components we decide to keep in the remainder of our analysis.* In the example in figure 13.6, we have three principal components, but the first two account for 79% + 12% = 91% of the variation in the dataset. If these two principal components capture enough of the information in the original dataset to make the dimension reduction worthwhile (perhaps we get better results from a clustering or classification algorithm), then we can happily discard the remaining 9% of the information. Later in the chapter, I'll show you some ways to decide how many principal components to keep.

13.3 Building your first PCA model

In this section, we'll turn the PCA theory we just covered into skills by reducing the dimensions of a dataset, using PCA. Imagine that you work for the Swiss Federal Department of Finance (due to your love of money, chocolate, cheese, and political neutrality). The department believes that a large number of counterfeit Swiss bankotes are in circulation, and it's your job to find a way of identifying them. Nobody has looked into this before, and there is no labeled data to go on. So you ask 200 of your colleagues to each give you a banknote (you promise to give them back), and you measure the dimensions of each note. You hope that there will be some discrepancies between genuine notes and counterfeit ones that you may be able to identify using PCA.

In this section, we'll tackle this problem by

1. Exploring and plotting the original dataset before PCA
2. Using the `prcomp()` function to learn the principal components from the data
3. Exploring and plotting the result of the PCA model

13.3.1 Loading and exploring the banknote dataset

We'll start by loading the tidyverse packages, loading the data from the mclust package, and converting the data frame into a tibble. We have a tibble containing 200 banknotes with 7 variables.

Listing 13.1 Loading the banknote dataset

```
library(tidyverse)

data(banknote, package = "mclust")

swissTib <- as_tibble(banknote)

swissTib

# A tibble: 200 x 7
   Status  Length  Left Right Bottom   Top Diagonal
   <fct>    <dbl> <dbl> <dbl>  <dbl> <dbl>    <dbl>
 1 genuine   215.  131   131.    9     9.7      141
 2 genuine   215.  130.  130.    8.1   9.5      142.
 3 genuine   215.  130.  130.    8.7   9.6      142.
 4 genuine   215.  130.  130.    7.5  10.4      142
 5 genuine   215   130.  130.   10.4   7.7      142.
 6 genuine   216.  131.  130.    9    10.1      141.
 7 genuine   216.  130.  130.    7.9   9.6      142.
 8 genuine   214.  130.  129.    7.2  10.7      142.
 9 genuine   215.  129.  130.    8.2  11        142.
10 genuine   215.  130.  130.    9.2  10        141.
# ... with 190 more rows
```

The keen-eyed among you may have noticed that this tibble is, in fact, labeled. We have the variable `Status` telling us whether each note is genuine or counterfeit. This is purely for teaching purposes; we're going to exclude it from the PCA analysis but map the labels onto the final principal components later, to see whether the PCA model separates the classes.

In situations where I have a clear outcome variable, I often plot each of my predictor variables against the outcome (as we've done in previous chapters). In unsupervised learning situations, we don't have an outcome variable, so I prefer to plot all variables against each other (provided I don't have so many variables as to prohibit doing so). We can do this easily using the `ggpairs()` function from the GGally package, which you may need to install first. We pass our tibble as the first argument to the `ggpairs()` function, and then we supply any additional aesthetic mappings by passing ggplot2's `aes()` function to the mapping argument. Finally, we add a `theme_bw()` layer to add the black-and-white theme.

Listing 13.2 Plotting the data with `ggpairs()`

```
install.packages("GGally")

library(GGally)
```

```
ggpairs(swissTib, mapping = aes(col = Status)) +
  theme_bw()
```

The resulting plot is shown in figure 13.7. The output from `ggpairs()` takes a little getting used to, but it draws a different kind of plot for each combination of variable types. For example, along the top row of facets are box plots showing the distribution of each continuous variable against the categorical variable. We get the same thing in histogram form down the left column of facets. The diagonal facets show the distributions of values for each variable, ignoring all others. Finally, dot plots shown the bivariate relationships between pairs of continuous variables.

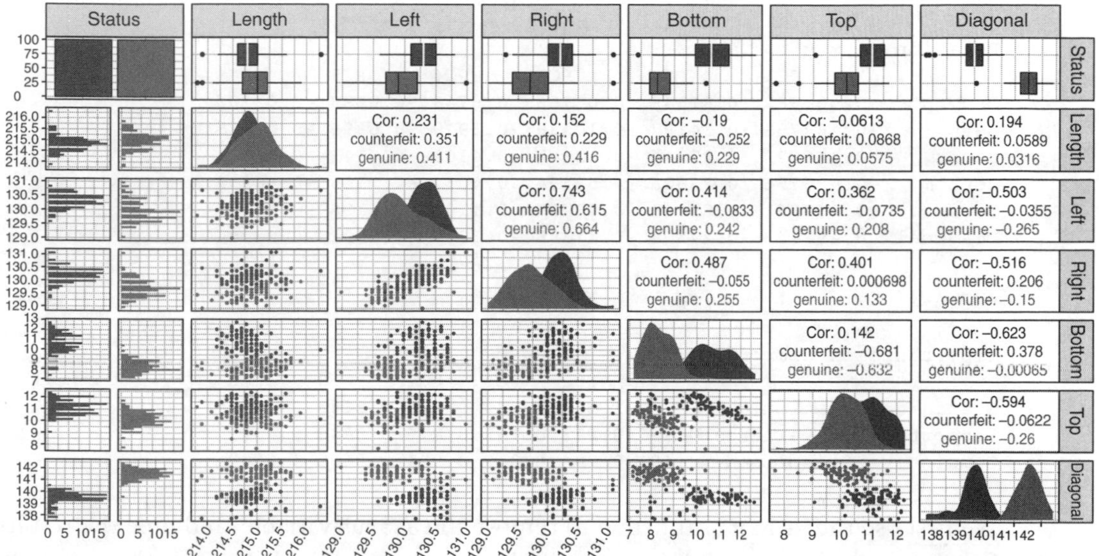

Figure 13.7 The result of calling the `ggpairs()` function on our banknote dataset. Each variable is plotted against every other variable, with different plot types drawn depending on the combination of variable types.

Looking at the plots, we can see that some of the variables seem to differentiate between the genuine and counterfeit banknotes, such as the `Diagonal` variable. The `Length` variable, however, contains little information that discriminates the two classes of banknotes.

> **NOTE** You see that if we had many more variables, visualizing them against each other in this way would start to become difficult!

13.3.2 Performing PCA

In this section, we're going to use the PCA algorithm to learn the principal components of our banknote dataset. To do this, I'll introduce you to the `prcomp()` function from the stats package that comes with your base R installation. Once we've done this, we'll inspect the output of this function to interpret the component scores of the principal components. I'll then show you how to extract and interpret *variable loadings* from the principal components, which tell us how much each original variable correlates with each principal component.

Listing 13.3 Performing the PCA

```
pca <- select(swissTib, -Status) %>%
  prcomp(center = TRUE, scale = TRUE)

pca

Standard deviations (1, .., p=6):
[1] 1.7163 1.1305 0.9322 0.6706 0.5183 0.4346

Rotation (n x k) = (6 x 6):
              PC1      PC2      PC3     PC4     PC5      PC6
Length   0.006987 -0.81549  0.01768  0.5746 -0.0588  0.03106
Left    -0.467758 -0.34197 -0.10338 -0.3949  0.6395 -0.29775
Right   -0.486679 -0.25246 -0.12347 -0.4303 -0.6141  0.34915
Bottom  -0.406758  0.26623 -0.58354  0.4037 -0.2155 -0.46235
Top     -0.367891  0.09149  0.78757  0.1102 -0.2198 -0.41897
Diagonal 0.493458 -0.27394 -0.11388 -0.3919 -0.3402 -0.63180

summary(pca)

Importance of components:
                         PC1   PC2   PC3   PC4    PC5    PC6
Standard deviation     1.716 1.131 0.932 0.671 0.5183 0.4346
Proportion of Variance 0.491 0.213 0.145 0.075 0.0448 0.0315
Cumulative Proportion  0.491 0.704 0.849 0.924 0.9685 1.0000
```

We first use the `select()` function to remove the `Status` variable, and pipe the resulting data into the `prcomp()` function. There are two additional important arguments to the `prcomp()` function: `center` and `scale`. The `center` argument controls whether the data is mean-centered before applying PCA, and its default value is `TRUE`. We should always center the data before applying PCA because this removes the intercept and forces the principal axes to pass through the origin.

The `scale` argument controls whether the variables are divided by their standard deviations to put them all on the same scale as each other, and its default value is `FALSE`. There isn't a clear consensus on whether you should standardize your variables before running PCA. A common rule of thumb is that if your original variables are measured on a similar scale, standardization isn't necessary; but if you have one variable measuring grams and another measuring kilograms, you should standardize them by setting `scale = TRUE` to put them on the same scale. This is important because if you have one variable measured on a much larger scale, this variable will dominate the eigenvectors, and the other variables will contribute much less information to the principal components. In this example, we'll set `scale = TRUE`, but one of the exercises for this chapter is to set `scale = FALSE` and compare the results.

NOTE In this example, we're not interested in including the `Status` variable in our dimension-reduction model; but even if we were, PCA cannot handle categorical variables. If you have categorical variables, your options are to encode them as numeric (which may or may not work), use a different approach for dimension reduction (there are some that handle categorical variables that I won't discuss here), or extract the principal components from the continuous variables and then recombine these with the categorical variables in the final dataset.

When we print the `pca` object, we get a printout of some information from our model. The `Standard deviations` component is a vector of the standard deviations of the data along each of the principal components. Because the variance is the square of the standard deviation, to convert these standard deviations into the eigenvalues for the principal components, we can simply square them. Notice that the values get smaller from left to right? This is because the principal components explain sequentially less of the variance in the data.

The `Rotation` component contains the six eigenvectors. Remember that these eigenvectors describe how far along each original variable we go, so that we're one unit along the principal axis away from the origin. These eigenvectors describe the direction of the principal axes.

If we pass our PCA results to the `summary()` function, we get a breakdown of the importance of each of the principal components. The `Standard deviation` row is the same as we saw a moment ago and contains the square root of the eigenvalues. The `Proportion of Variance` row tells us how much of the total variance is accounted for by each principal component. This is calculated by dividing each eigenvalue by the sum of the eigenvalues. The `Cumulative Proportion` row tells us how much variance is accounted for by the principal components so far. For example, we can see that PC1 and PC2 account for 49.1% and 21.3% of the total variance, respectively; cumulatively, they both account for 70.4%. This information is useful when we're deciding how many principal components to retain for our downstream analysis.

If we're interested in interpreting our principal components, it's useful to extract the *variable loadings*. The variable loadings tell us how much each of the original variables correlates with each of the principal components. The formula for calculating the variable loadings for a particular principal component is

$$\text{variable loadings} = \text{eigenvector} \times \sqrt{\text{eigenvalue}} \quad \textbf{Equation 13.2}$$

We can calculate all of the variable loadings simultaneously for all principal components and return them as a tibble using the `map_dfc()` function.

Listing 13.4 Calculating variable loadings

```
map_dfc(1:6, ~pca$rotation[, .] * sqrt(pca$sdev ^ 2)[.])

# A tibble: 6 x 6
      V1        V2          V3          V4         V5          V6
```

```
     <dbl>  <dbl>   <dbl>   <dbl>   <dbl>    <dbl>
1  0.0120 -0.922  0.0165  0.385  -0.0305  0.0135
2 -0.803  -0.387 -0.0964 -0.265   0.331  -0.129
3 -0.835  -0.285 -0.115  -0.289  -0.318   0.152
4 -0.698   0.301 -0.544   0.271  -0.112  -0.201
5 -0.631   0.103  0.734   0.0739 -0.114  -0.182
6  0.847  -0.310 -0.106  -0.263  -0.176  -0.275
```

We can interpret these values as Pearson correlation coefficients, so we can see that the `Length` variable has very little correlation with PC1 (0.012) but a very strong negative correlation with PC2 (–0.922). This helps us conclude that, on average, cases with a small component score for PC2 have a larger `Length`.

13.3.3 Plotting the result of our PCA

Next, let's plot the results of our PCA model to better understand the relationships in the data by seeing if the model has revealed any patterns. There are some nice plotting functions for PCA results in the factoextra package, so let's install and load this package and play with it (see listing 13.5). Once you've loaded the package, use the `get_pca()` function to grab the information from our PCA model so we can apply factoextra functions to it.

TIP Although we manually calculated the variable loadings in listing 13.4, an easier way of extracting this information is by printing the `$coord` component of the `pcaDat` object we create in listing 13.5.

The `fviz_pca_biplot()` function draws a *biplot*. A biplot is a common method of simultaneously plotting the component scores, and the variable loadings for the first two principal components. You can see the biplot in the top left of figure 13.8. The dots show the component scores for each of the banknotes against the first two principal components, and the arrows indicate the variable loadings of each variable. This plot helps us identify that we seem to have two distinct clusters of banknotes, and the arrows help us to see which variables tend to correlate with each of the clusters. For example, the rightmost cluster in this plot tends to have higher values for the `Diagonal` variable.

TIP The `label = "var"` argument tells the function to only label the variables; otherwise, it labels each case with its row number, and this makes me go cross-eyed.

The `fviz_pca_var()` function draws a *variable loading plot*. You can see the variable loading plot at top right in figure 13.8. Notice that this shows the same variable loading arrows as in the biplot, but now the axes represent the correlation of each of the variables with each principal component. If you look again at the variable loadings calculated in listing 13.4, you'll see that this plot is showing the same information: how much each original variable correlates with the first two principal components.

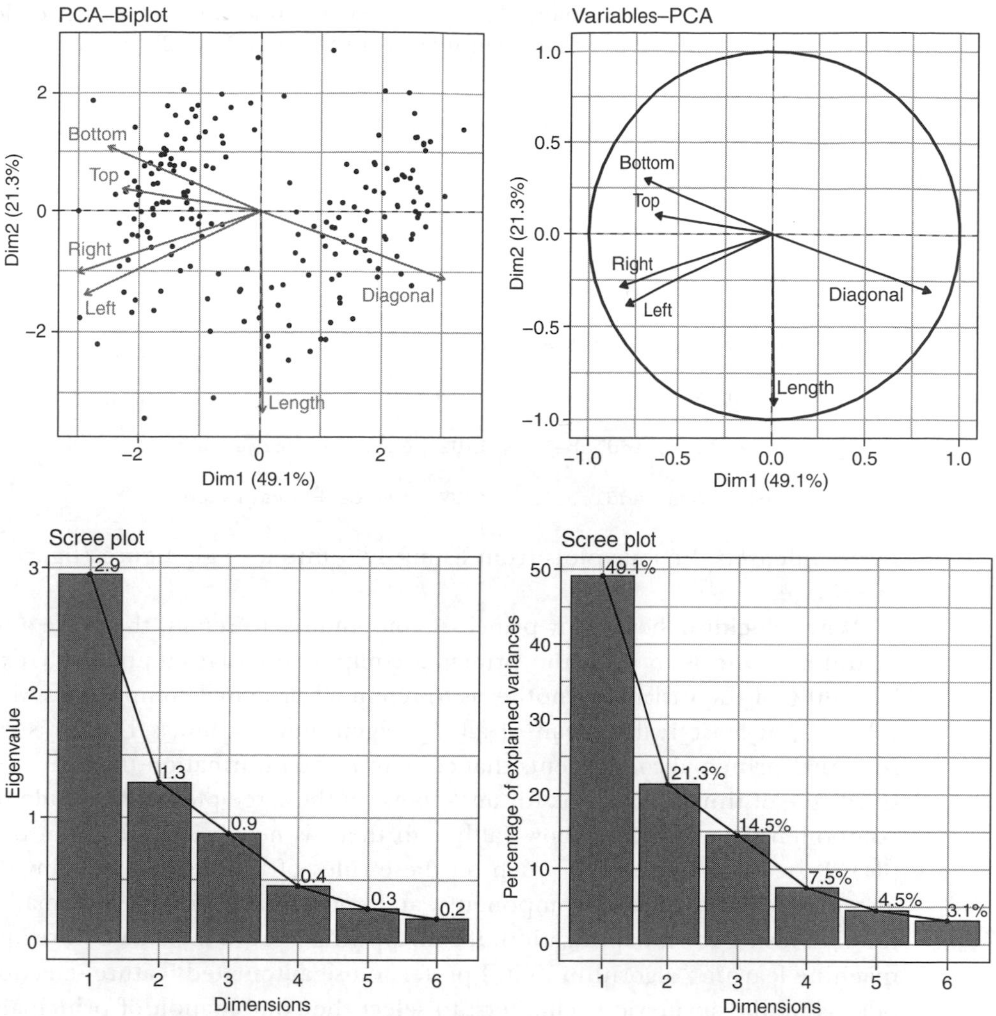

Figure 13.8 Typical exploratory plots for PCA analysis as supplied by the factoextra package. The top-left plot shows a biplot, combining each case's component scores with arrows to show the variable loadings. The top-right plot shows the variable loading plot with a correlation circle (the boundary within which the variable loadings must lie). The bottom scree plots show the eigenvalue (left) and percentage explained variance (right).

The `fviz_screeplot()` function draws a *scree plot.* A scree plot is a common way of plotting the principal components against the amount of variance they explain in the data, as a graphical way to help identify how many principal components to retain. The function allows us to plot either the eigenvalue or the percentage variance accounted for by each principal component, using the `choice` argument. You can see scree plots with these two different y-axes in the bottom two plots in figure 13.8.

NOTE Scree plots are so named because they resemble a *scree slope*, the collection of rocks and rubble that accumulates at the foot of a cliff due to weathering and erosion.

Listing 13.5 Plotting the PCA results

```
install.packages("factoextra")

library(factoextra)

pcaDat <- get_pca(pca)

fviz_pca_biplot(pca, label = "var")

fviz_pca_var(pca)

fviz_screeplot(pca, addlabels = TRUE, choice = "eigenvalue")

fviz_screeplot(pca, addlabels = TRUE, choice = "variance")
```

I've condensed the four plots from listing 13.5 into a single figure (figure 13.8) to save space.

When deciding how many principal components to retain, there are a few rules of thumb. One is to keep the principal components that cumulatively explain at least 80% of the variance. Another is to retain all principal components with eigenvalues of at least 1; the mean of all the eigenvalues is always 1, so this results in retaining principal components that contain more information than the average. A third rule of thumb is to look for an "elbow" in the scree plot and exclude principal components beyond the elbow (although there is no obvious elbow in our example). Instead of relying too much on these rules of thumb, I look at my data projected onto the principal components, and consider how much information I can tolerate losing for my application. If I'm applying PCA to my data before applying a machine learning algorithm to it, I prefer to use automated feature-selection methods, as we did in previous chapters, to select the combination of principal components that results in the best performance.

Finally, let's plot our first two principal components against each other and see how well they're able to separate the genuine and counterfeit banknotes. We first mutate the original dataset to include a column of component scores for PC1and PC2 (extracted from our `pca` object using `$x`). We then plot the principal components against each other and add a color aesthetic for the `Status` variable.

Listing 13.6 Mapping genuine and counterfeit labels

```
swissPca <- swissTib %>%
  mutate(PCA1 = pca$x[, 1], PCA2 = pca$x[, 2])

ggplot(swissPca, aes(PCA1, PCA2, col = Status)) +
  geom_point() +
  theme_bw()
```

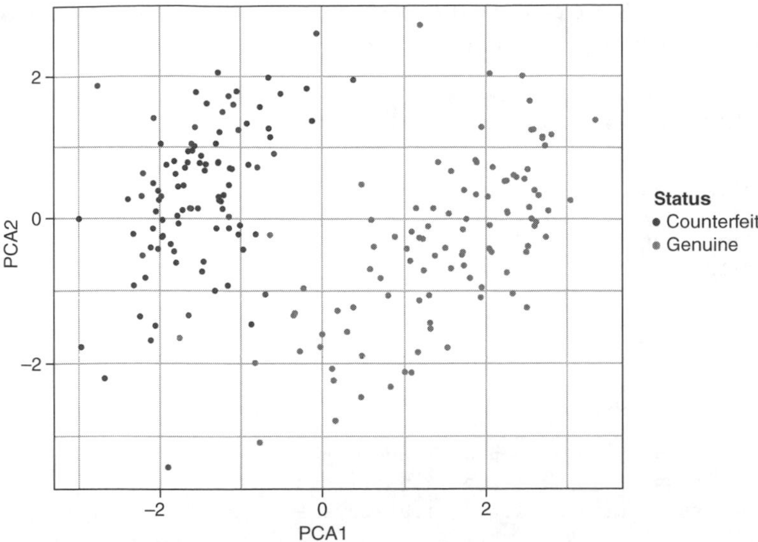

Figure 13.9 The PCA component scores are plotted for each case, shaded by whether they were genuine or counterfeit.

The resulting plot is shown in figure 13.9. We started with six continuous variables and condensed most of that information into just two principal components that contain enough information to separate the two clusters of banknotes! If we didn't have labels, having identified different clusters of data, we would now try to understand what those two clusters were, and perhaps come up with a way of discriminating genuine banknotes from counterfeits.

> **Exercise 1**
> Add a `stat_ellipse()` layer to the plot in figure 13.9 to add 95% confidence ellipses to each class of banknote.

13.3.4 Computing the component scores of new data

We have our PCA model, but what do we do when we get new data? Well, because the eigenvectors describe exactly how much each variable contributes to the value of each principal component, we can simply calculate the component scores of new data (including centering and scaling, if we performed this as part of the model).

Let's generate some new data to see how this works in practice. In listing 13.7, we first define a tibble consisting of two new cases, and all the same variables entered into our PCA model. To calculate the component scores of these new cases, we simply use the `predict()` function, passing the model as the first argument and the new data as the second argument. As we can see, the `predict()` function returns both cases' component scores for each of the principal components.

Listing 13.7 Computing the component scores of new data

```
newBanknotes <- tibble(
  Length = c(214, 216),
  Left = c(130, 128),
  Right = c(132, 129),
  Bottom = c(12, 7),
  Top = c(12, 8),
  Diagonal = c(138, 142)
)

predict(pca, newBanknotes)

        PC1     PC2     PC3    PC4    PC5   PC6
[1,] -4.729  1.9989 -0.1058 -1.659 -3.203 1.623
[2,]  6.466 -0.8918 -0.8215  3.469 -1.838 2.339
```

You've learned how to apply PCA to your data and interpret the information it provides. In the next chapter, I'll introduce two *nonlinear* dimension-reduction techniques. I suggest that you save your .R file, because we're going to continue using the same dataset in the next chapter. This is so we can compare the performance of these nonlinear algorithms to the representation we created here using PCA.

13.4 Strengths and weaknesses of PCA

While it often isn't easy to tell which algorithms will perform well for a given task, here are some strengths and weaknesses that will help you decide whether PCA will perform well for you.

The strengths of PCA are as follows:

- PCA creates new axes that are directly interpretable in terms of the original variables.
- New data can be projected onto the principal axes.
- PCA is really a mathematical transformation and so is computationally inexpensive.

The weaknesses of PCA are these:

- Mapping from high dimensions to low dimensions cannot be nonlinear.
- It cannot handle categorical variables natively.
- The final number of principal components to retain must be decided by us for the application at hand.

Exercise 2

Rerun the PCA on our Swiss banknote dataset, but this time set the `scale` argument to `FALSE`. Compare the following to the PCA we trained on scaled data:

- a Eigenvalues
- b Eigenvectors
- c Biplot
- d Variable loading plot
- e Scree plot

Exercise 3

Do the same as in exercise 2 again, but this time set the arguments `center = FALSE` and `scale = TRUE`.

Summary

- Dimension reduction is a class of unsupervised learning that learns a low-dimensional representation of a high-dimensional dataset while retaining as much information as possible.
- PCA is a linear dimension-reduction technique that finds new axes that maximize the variance in the data. The first of these principal axes maximizes the most variance, followed by the second, and the third, and so on, which are all orthogonal to the previously computed axes.
- When data is projected onto these principal axes, the new variables are called principal components.
- In PCA, eigenvalues represent the variance along a principal component, and the eigenvector represents the direction of the principal axis through the original feature space.

Solutions to exercises

1 Add 95% confidence ellipses to the plot of PCA1 versus PCA2:

```
ggplot(swissPca, aes(PCA1, PCA2, col = Status)) +
  geom_point() +
  stat_ellipse() +
  theme_bw()
```

2 Compare the PCA results when `scale = FALSE`:

```
pcaUnscaled <- select(swissTib, -Status) %>%
  prcomp(center = TRUE, scale = FALSE)

pcaUnscaled
```

```
fviz_pca_biplot(pcaUnscaled, label = "var")

fviz_pca_var(pcaUnscaled)

fviz_screeplot(pcaUnscaled, addlabels = TRUE, choice = "variance")
```

3 Compare the PCA results when `center = FALSE` and `scale = TRUE`:

```
pcaUncentered <- select(swissTib, -Status) %>%
  prcomp(center = FALSE, scale = TRUE)

pcaUncentered

fviz_pca_biplot(pcaUncentered, label = "var")

fviz_pca_var(pcaUncentered)

fviz_screeplot(pcaUncentered, addlabels = TRUE, choice = "variance")
```

14 Maximizing similarity with t-SNE and UMAP

This chapter covers

- Understanding nonlinear dimension reduction
- Using t-distributed stochastic neighbor embedding
- Using uniform manifold approximation and projection

In the last chapter, I introduced you to PCA as our first dimension-reduction technique. While PCA is a linear dimension-reduction algorithm (it finds linear combinations of the original variables), sometimes the information in a set of variables can't be extracted as a linear combination of these variables. In such situations, there are a number of nonlinear dimension-reduction algorithms we can turn to, such as *t-distributed stochastic neighbor embedding* (t-SNE), and *uniform manifold approximation and projection* (UMAP).

t-SNE is one of the most popular nonlinear dimension-reduction algorithms. It measures the distance between each observation in the dataset and every other observation, and then randomizes the observations across (usually) two new axes. The observations are then iteratively shuffled around these new axes until their distances to each other in this two-dimensional space are as similar to the distances in the original high-dimensional space as possible.

UMAP is another nonlinear dimension-reduction algorithm that overcomes some of the limitations of t-SNE. It works similarly to t-SNE (finds distances in a feature space with many variables and then tries to reproduce these distances in low-dimensional space), but differs in the way it measures distances.

By the end of this chapter, I hope you'll understand what nonlinear dimension reduction is and why it can be beneficial compared to linear dimension reduction. I will show you how the t-SNE and UMAP algorithms work and how they're different from each other, and we'll apply each of them to our banknote dataset from chapter 13 so we can compare their performance with PCA. If you no longer have the `swissTib` and `newBanknotes` objects defined in your global environment, just rerun listings 13.1 and 13.7.

14.1 What is t-SNE?

In this section, I'll show you what t-distributed stochastic neighbor embedding is, how it works, and why it's useful. t-distributed stochastic neighbor embedding is such a mouthful—I'm glad people shorten it to t-SNE (usually pronounced "tee-snee," or occasionally "tiz-nee"), not least because when you hear someone say it, you can say "bless you," and everyone laughs (at least the first few times).

Whereas PCA is a linear dimension-reduction algorithm (because it finds new axes that are linear combinations of the original variables), t-SNE is a nonlinear dimension-reduction algorithm. It is nonlinear because instead of finding new axes that are logical combinations of the original variables, it focuses on the similarities between nearby cases in a dataset and tries to reproduce these similarities in a lower-dimensional space. The main benefit of this approach is that t-SNE will almost always do a better job than PCA of highlighting patterns in the data (such as clusters). One of the downsides of this approach is that the axes are no longer interpretable, because they don't represent logical combinations of the original variables.

The first step in the t-SNE algorithm is to compute the distance between each case and every other case in the dataset. By default, this distance is the Euclidean distance, which is the straight-line distance between any two points in the feature space (but we can use other measures of distance instead). These distances are then converted into probabilities. This is illustrated in figure 14.1.

For a particular case in the dataset, the distance between this case and all other cases is measured. Then a normal distribution is centered on this case, and the distances are converted into probabilities by mapping them onto the probability density of the normal distribution. The standard deviation of this normal distribution is inversely related to the density of cases around the case in question. Put another way, if there are lots of cases nearby (more dense), then the standard deviation of the normal distribution is smaller; but if there are few cases nearby (less dense), then the standard deviation is larger.

After converting the distances to probabilities, the probabilities for each case are scaled by dividing them by their sum. This makes the probabilities sum to 1 for every

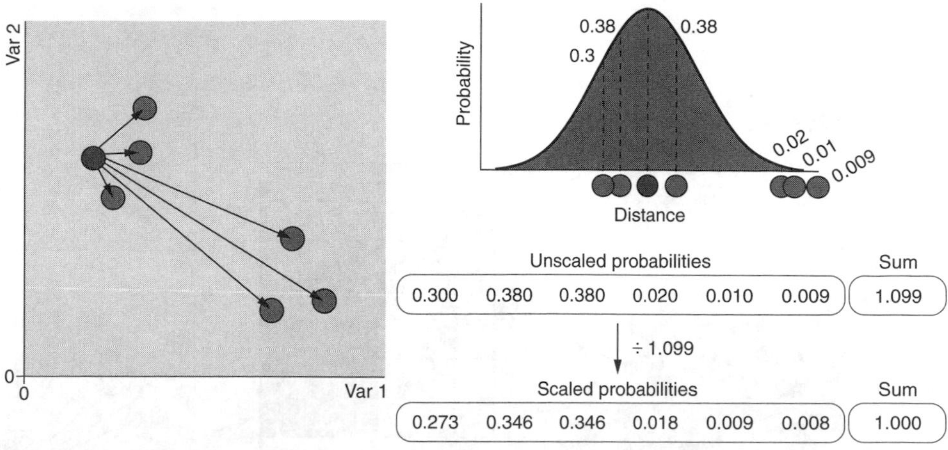

Figure 14.1 t-SNE measures the distance from each case to every other case, converted into a probability by fitting a normal distribution over the current case. These probabilities are scaled by dividing them by their sum, so that they add to 1.

case in the dataset. Using different standard deviations for different densities, and then normalizing the probabilities to 1 for every case, means if there are dense clusters and sparse clusters of cases in the dataset, t-SNE will expand the dense clusters and compress the sparse ones so they can be visualized more easily together. The exact relationship between data density and the standard deviation of the normal distribution depends on a hyperparameter called *perplexity*, which we'll discuss shortly.

Once the scaled probabilities have been calculated for each case in the dataset, we have a matrix of probabilities that describes how similar each case is to each of the other cases. This is visualized in figure 14.2 as a heatmap, which is a useful way of thinking about it.

Our matrix of probabilities is now our reference, or template, for how the data values relate to each other in the original, high-dimensional space. The next step in the t-SNE algorithm is to randomize the cases along (usually) two new axes (this is where the "stochastic" bit of the name comes from).

NOTE It doesn't need to be two axes, but it commonly is. This is because humans struggle to visualize data in more than two dimensions at once, and because, beyond three dimensions, the computational cost of t-SNE becomes more and more prohibitive.

t-SNE calculates the distances between the cases in this new, randomized, low-dimensional space and converts them into probabilities just like before. The only difference is that instead of using the normal distribution, it now uses Student's t distribution. The t distribution looks a bit like a normal distribution, except that it's not quite as tall in the middle, and its tails are flatter and extend further out (see figure 14.3). It's

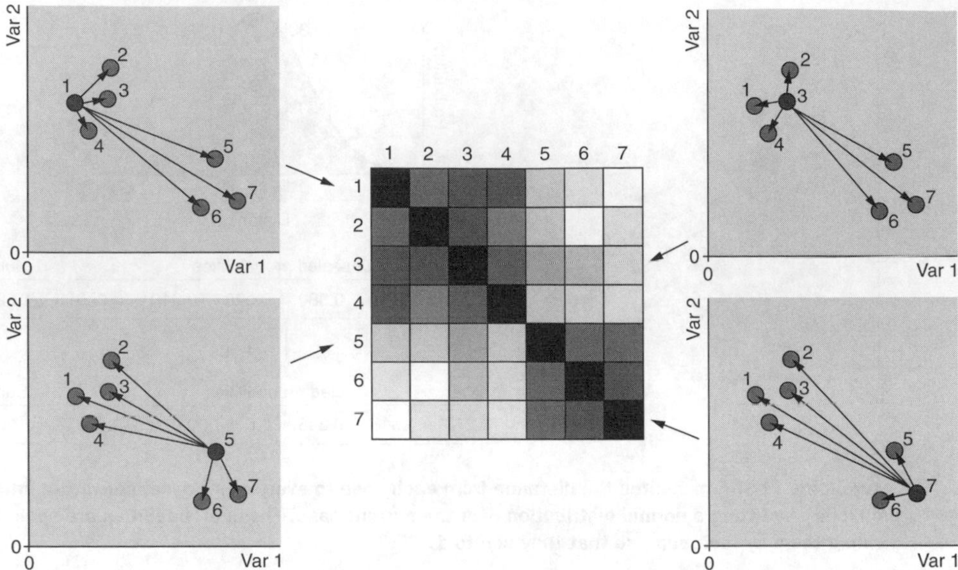

Figure 14.2 The scaled probabilities for each case are stored as a matrix of values. This is visualized here as a heatmap: the closer two cases are, the darker the box is that represents their distance in the heatmap.

a bit like if someone sat on a normal distribution and squashed it. This is where the "t" in t-SNE comes from. I'll explain why we use the t distribution momentarily.

The job for t-SNE now is to "shuffle" the data points around these new axes, step by step, to make the matrix of probabilities in the lower-dimensional space look as close as possible to the matrix of probabilities in the original, high-dimensional space. The intuition here is that if the matrices are as similar as possible, then the data each case

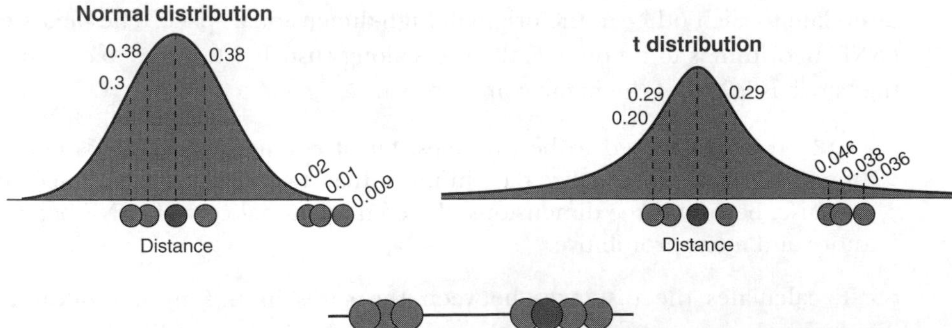

Figure 14.3 When converting distances in the lower-dimensional representation into probabilities, t-SNE fits a Student's t distribution over the current case instead of a normal distribution. The Student's t distribution has longer tails, meaning dissimilar cases are pushed further away to achieve the same probability as in the high-dimensional representation.

was close to in the original feature space will still be close by in the low-dimensional space. You can think of this as a game of attraction and repulsion.

To make the probability matrix in low-dimensional space look like the one in high-dimensional space, each case needs to move closer to cases that were close to it in the original data, and away from cases that were far away. So cases that should be nearby will pull their neighbor toward them, but cases that should be far away will push non-neighbors away from them. The balance of these attractive and repulsive forces causes each case in the dataset to move in a direction that makes the two probability matrices a little more similar. Now, in this new position, the low-dimensional probability matrix is calculated again, and the cases move again, making the low- and high-dimensional matrices look a little more similar again. This process continues until we reach a predetermined number of iterations, or until the *divergence* (difference) between the matrices stops improving. This whole process is illustrated in figure 14.4.

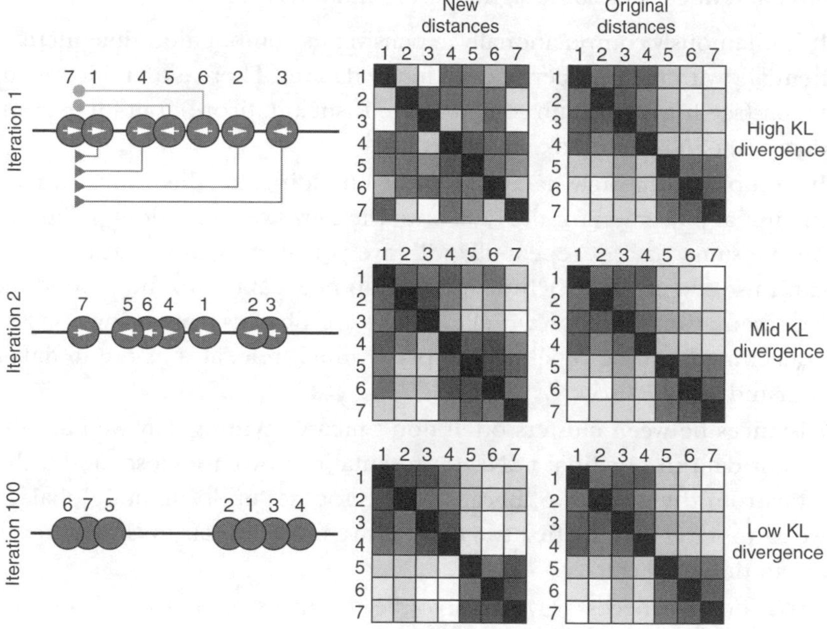

Figure 14.4 Cases are randomly initialized over the new axes (one axis is shown here). The probability matrix is computed for this axis, and the cases are shuffled around to make this matrix resemble the original, high-dimensional matrix by minimizing the Kullback-Leibler (KL) divergence. During shuffling, cases are attracted toward cases that are similar to them (lines with circles) and repulsed away from cases that are dissimilar (lines with triangles).

NOTE The difference between the two matrices is measured using a statistic called the *Kullback-Leibler divergence*, which is large when the matrices are very different and zero when the matrices are perfectly identical.

Why do we use the t distribution to convert distances into probabilities in the low-dimensional space? Well, notice again from figure 14.4 that the tails of the t distribution are wider than for the normal distribution. This means that, in order to get the same probability as from the normal distribution, dissimilar cases need to be pushed further away from the case the t distribution is centered over. This helps spread out clusters of data that might be present in the data, helping us to identify them more easily. A major consequence of this, however, is that t-SNE is often said to retain *local* structure in the low-dimensional representation, but it doesn't usually retain *global* structure. Practically, this means we can interpret cases that are close to each other in the final representation as being similar to each other, but we can't easily say which clusters of cases were more similar to other clusters of cases in the original data.

Once this iterative process has converged at a low KL divergence, we should have a low-dimensional representation of our original data that preserves the similarities between nearby cases. While t-SNE typically outperforms PCA for highlighting patterns in data, it does have some significant limitations:

- It is infamously computationally expensive: its computation time increases exponentially with the number of cases in the dataset. There is a multicore implementation (see https://github.com/RGLab/Rtsne.multicore), but for extremely large datasets, t-SNE could take hours to run.
- It cannot project new data onto the embedding. By this I mean that, because the initial placement of the data onto the new axes is random, rerunning t-SNE on the same dataset repeatedly will give you slightly different results. Thus we can't use the `predict()` function to map new data onto the lower-dimensional representation as we can with PCA. This prohibits us from using t-SNE as part of a machine learning pipeline and pretty much relegates its use to data exploration and visualization.
- Distances between clusters often don't mean anything. Say we have three clusters of data in our final t-SNE representation: two are close, and a third is far away from the other two. Because t-SNE focuses on local, not global, structure, we cannot say that the first two clusters are more similar to each other than they are to the third cluster.
- t-SNE doesn't necessarily preserve the distances or density of the data in the final representation, so passing the output of t-SNE into clustering algorithms that rely on distances or densities tends not to work as well as you might expect.
- We need to select sensible values for a number of hyperparameters, which can be difficult if the t-SNE algorithm takes minutes to hours to run on a dataset.

14.2 Building your first t-SNE embedding

In this section, I'm going to show you how to use the t-SNE algorithm to create a low-dimensional embedding of our Swiss banknote dataset, to see how it compares with the PCA model we created in the previous chapter. First, we'll install and load the Rtsne package in R, and then I'll explain the various hyperparameters that control how t-SNE learns. Then, we'll create a t-SNE embedding using the optimal combination of hyperparameters. Finally, we'll plot the new, lower-dimensional representation learned by the t-SNE algorithm, and compare it to the PCA representation we plotted in chapter 13.

14.2.1 Performing t-SNE

Let's start by installing and loading the Rtsne package:

```
install.packages("Rtsne")

library(Rtsne)
```

t-SNE has four important hyperparameters that can drastically change the resulting embedding:

- *perplexity*—Controls the width of the distributions used to convert distances into probabilities. High values place more focus on global structure, whereas small values place more focus on local structure. Typical values lie in the range 5 to 50. The default value is 30.
- *theta*—Controls the trade-off between speed and accuracy. Because t-SNE is slow, people commonly use an implementation called *Barnes-Hut* t-SNE, which allows us to perform the embedding much faster but with some loss of accuracy. The *theta* hyperparameter controls this trade-off, with 0 being "exact" t-SNE and 1 being the fastest but least accurate t-SNE. The default value is 0.5.
- *eta*—How far each data point moves at each iteration (also called the *learning rate*). Lower values need more iterations to reach convergence but may result in a more accurate embedding. The default value is 200, and this is usually fine.
- *max_iter*—The maximum iterations allowed before computation stops. This will depend on your computational budget, but it's important to have enough iterations to reach convergence. The default value is 1,000.

TIP The most important hyperparameters to tune are usually *perplexity* and *max_iter*.

Our approach to tuning hyperparameters thus far has been to allow an automated tuning process to choose the best combination for us, through either a grid search or random search. But due to its computational cost, most people will run t-SNE with its default hyperparameter values and change them if the embedding doesn't look sensible. If this sounds very subjective, that's because it is; but people are usually able to identify visually whether t-SNE is pulling apart clusters of observations nicely.

To give you a visual aid for how each of these hyperparameters affects the final embedding, I've run t-SNE on our Swiss banknote data using a grid of hyperparameter values. Figure 14.5 shows the final embeddings with different combinations of *theta* (rows) and *perplexity* (columns) using the default values of *eta* and *max_iter*. Notice that the clusters become tighter with larger values of *perplexity* and are lost with very low

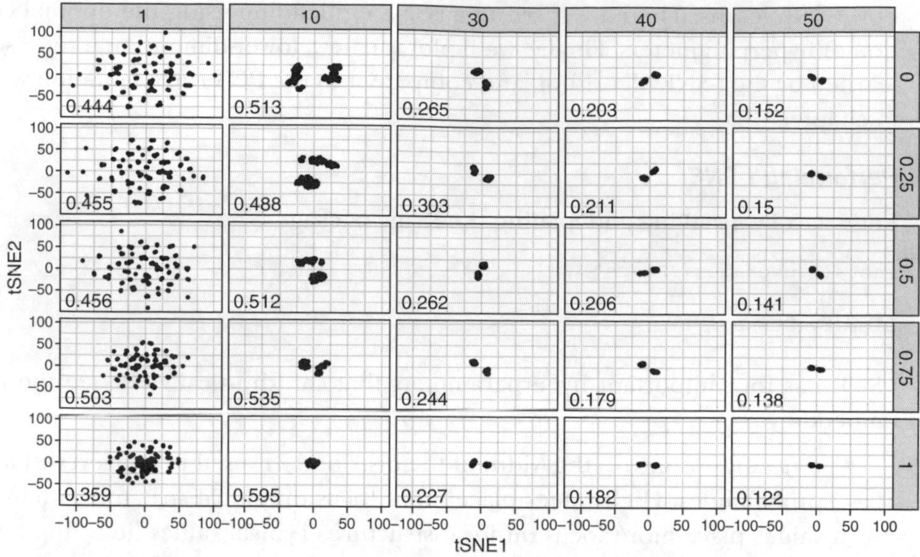

Figure 14.5 The effect on the final t-SNE embedding of the banknote dataset of changing *theta* (row facets) and *perplexity* (column facets) using the default values of *eta* and *max_iter*

values. Also notice that for reasonable values of *perplexity*, the clusters are best resolved when *theta* is set to 0 (exact t-SNE).

Figure 14.6 shows the final embeddings with different combinations of *max_iter* (rows) and *eta* (columns). The effect here is a little more subtle, but smaller values of

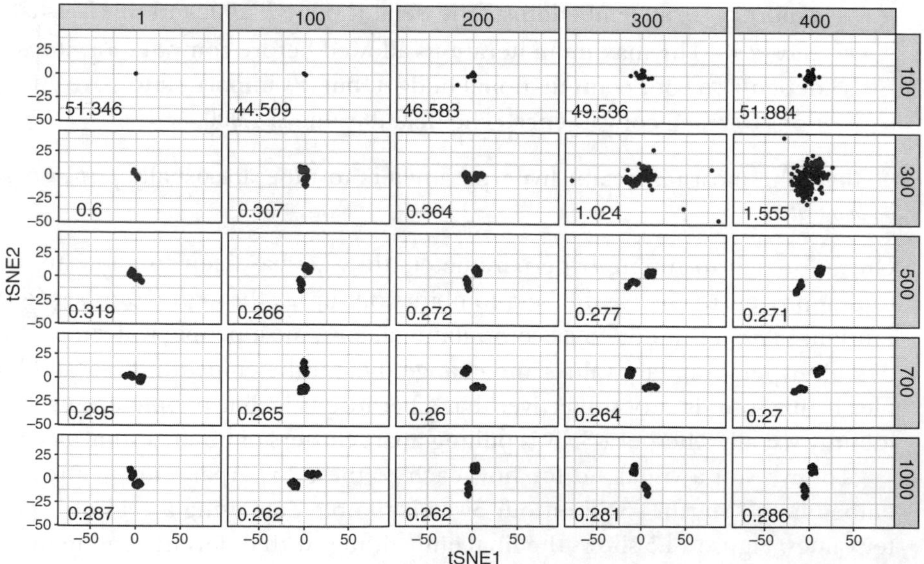

Figure 14.6 The effect on the final t-SNE embedding of the banknote dataset of changing *max_iter* (row facets) and *eta* (column facets) using the default values of *theta* and *perplexity*

eta need a larger number of iterations in order to converge (because the cases move in smaller steps at each iteration). For example, for an *eta* of 100, 1,000 iterations is sufficient to separate the clusters; but with an *eta* of 1, the clusters remain poorly resolved after 1,000 iterations. If you would like to see the code I used to generate these figures, the code for this chapter is available at www.manning.com/books/machine-learning-with-r-tidyverse-and-mlr.

Now that you're a little more tuned in to how t-SNE's hyperparameters affect its performance, let's run t-SNE on our Swiss banknote dataset. Just like for PCA, we first select all the columns except the categorical variable (t-SNE also cannot handle categorical variables) and pipe this data into the `Rtsne()` function. We manually set the values of the *perplexity*, *theta*, and *max_iter* hyperparameters (honestly, I rarely alter *eta*) and set the argument `verbose = TRUE` so the algorithm prints a running commentary on what the KL divergence is at each iteration.

Listing 14.1 Running t-SNE

```
swissTsne <- select(swissTib, -Status) %>%
  Rtsne(perplexity = 30, theta = 0, max_iter = 5000, verbose = TRUE)
```

TIP By default, the `Rtsne()` function reduces the dataset to two dimensions. If you want to return another number, you can set this using the `dims` argument.

That didn't take too long, did it? For a small dataset like this, t-SNE takes only a few seconds. But it quickly gets slow (see what I did there?) as the dataset increases in size.

14.2.2 Plotting the result of t-SNE

Next, let's plot the two t-SNE dimensions against each other to see how well they separated the genuine and counterfeit banknotes. Because we can't interpret the axes in terms of how much each variable correlates with them, it's common for people to color their t-SNE plots by the values of each of their original variables, to help identify which clusters have higher and lower values. To do this, we first use the `mutate_if()` function to center the numeric variables in our original dataset (by setting `.funs = scale` and `.predicate = is.numeric`). We include `scale = FALSE` to only center the variables, not divide by their standard deviations. The reason we center the variables is that we're going to shade by their value on the plots, and we don't want variables with larger values dominating the color scales (omit this line and see the difference in the final plot for yourself).

Next, we mutate two new columns that contain the t-SNE axes values for each case. Finally, we gather the data so that we can facet by each of the original variables. We plot this data, mapping the value of each original variable to the color aesthetic and the status of each banknote (genuine versus counterfeit) to the shape aesthetic, and facet by the original variables. We add a custom color scale gradient to make the color scale more readable in print.

Listing 14.2 Plotting the t-SNE embedding

```
swissTibTsne <- swissTib %>%
  mutate_if(.funs = scale, .predicate = is.numeric, scale = FALSE) %>%
  mutate(tSNE1 = swissTsne$Y[, 1], tSNE2 = swissTsne$Y[, 2]) %>%
  gather(key = "Variable", value = "Value", c(-tSNE1, -tSNE2, -Status))

ggplot(swissTibTsne, aes(tSNE1, tSNE2, col = Value, shape = Status)) +
  facet_wrap(~ Variable) +
  geom_point(size = 3) +
  scale_color_gradient(low = "dark blue", high = "cyan") +
  theme_bw()
```

The resulting plot is shown in figure 14.7. Wow! Notice how much better t-SNE does than PCA at representing the differences between the two clusters in a feature space with only two dimensions. The clusters are well resolved, although if you look closely, you can see a couple of cases that seem to be in the wrong cluster. Shading the points by the value of each variable also helps us identify that counterfeit notes tend to have lower values of the `Diagonal` variable and higher values of the `Bottom` and `Top` variables. It also seems as though there might be a small second cluster of counterfeit notes: this could be a set of notes made by a different counterfeiter, or an artifact

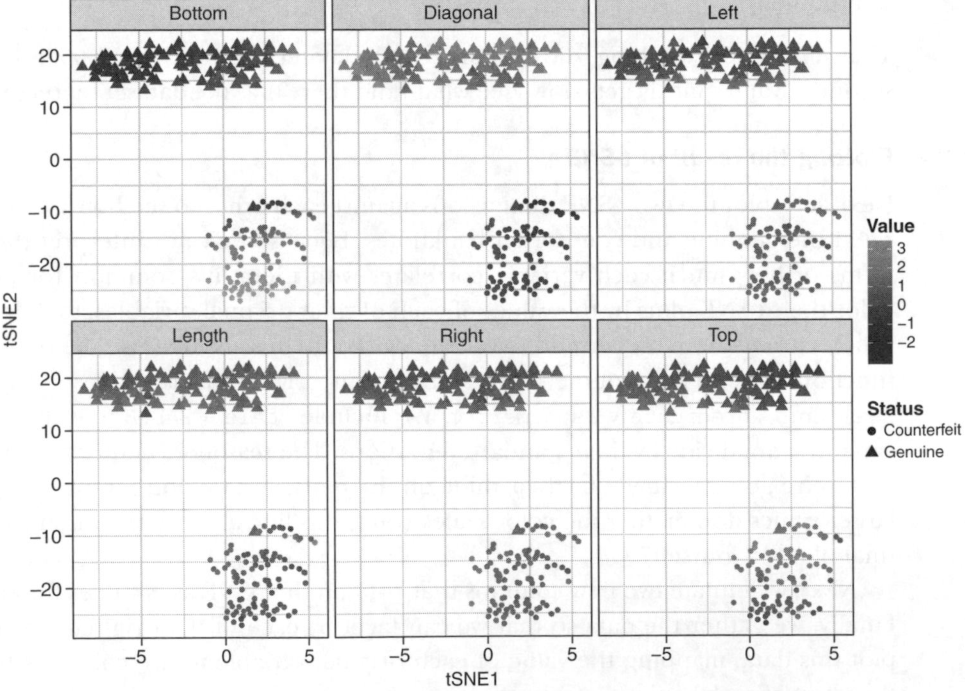

Figure 14.7 tSNE1 and tSNE2 axes plotted against each other, faceted and shaded by the original variables, and shaped by whether each case was a genuine or counterfeit banknote

of an imperfect combination of hyperparameters. More investigation would be needed to tell if these are actually a distinct cluster.

NOTE Do your plots look a little different than mine? Of course they do! Remember that the initial embedding is random (stochastic), so each time you run t-SNE on the same data and with the same hyperparameters, you'll get a slightly different embedding.

Exercise 1

Recreate the plot in figure 14.7, but this time don't center the variables before running t-SNE on them (just remove the `mutate_if()` layer). Can you see why scaling was necessary?

14.3 What is UMAP?

In this section, I'll show you what UMAP is, how it works, and why it's useful. Uniform manifold approximation and projection, fortunately shortened to UMAP, is a nonlinear dimension-reduction algorithm like t-SNE. UMAP is state of the art, having only been published in 2018, and it has a few benefits over the t-SNE algorithm.

First, it's considerably faster than t-SNE, where the length of time it takes to run increases less than the square of the number of cases in the dataset. To put this in perspective, a dataset that might take t-SNE hours to compress will take UMAP minutes.

The second benefit (and the main benefit, in my eyes) is that UMAP is a deterministic algorithm. In other words, given the same input, it will always give the same output. This means that, unlike with t-SNE, we can project new data onto the lower-dimensional representation, allowing us to incorporate UMAP into our machine learning pipelines.

The third benefit is that UMAP preserves both local *and* global structure. Practically, this means that not only can we interpret two cases close to each other in lower dimensions as being similar to each other in high dimensions, but we can also interpret two *clusters* of cases close to each other as being more similar to each other in high dimensions.

So how does UMAP work? Well, UMAP assumes the data is distributed along a *manifold*. A manifold is an *n*-dimensional smooth geometric shape where, for every point on this manifold, there exists a small neighborhood around that point that looks like a flat, two-dimensional plane. If that doesn't make sense to you, consider that the world is a three-dimensional manifold, any part of which can be mapped into a flat representation literally called a map. UMAP searches for a surface, or a space with many dimensions, along which the data is distributed. The distances between cases *along the manifold* can then be calculated, and a lower-dimensional representation of the data can be optimized iteratively to reproduce these distances.

Prefer a visual representation? Me too. Have a look at figure 14.8. I've drawn a question mark as a manifold and randomly seeded 15 cases around the manifold across 2 variables. UMAP's job is to learn the question mark manifold so that it can measure the distances between cases along the manifold instead of ordinary Euclidean distance, like t-SNE does. It achieves this by searching a region around each case, for another case. Where these regions encapsulate another case, the cases get connected by an edge. This is what I've done in the top row of figure 14.8—but can you see that the manifold is incomplete? There are gaps in my question mark. This is because the regions I searched around each case had the same radius, and the data wasn't uniformly distributed along the manifold. If the cases had been spaced out along the question mark at regular intervals, then this approach would have worked, provided I selected an appropriate radius for the search regions.

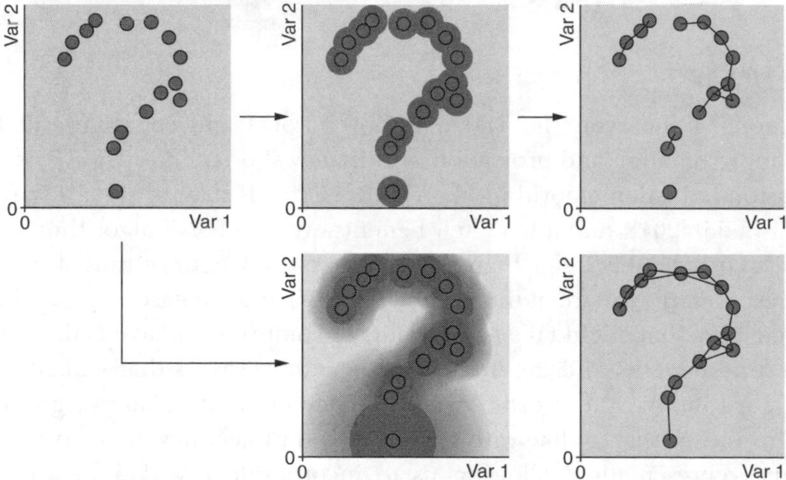

Figure 14.8 How UMAP learns a manifold. UMAP expands a search region around each case. A naive form of this is shown in the top row, where the radius of each search region is the same. When cases with overlapping search regions are connected by edges, there are gaps in the manifold. In the bottom row, the search region extends to the nearest neighbor and then extends outward in a fuzzy way, with a radius inversely related to the density of data in that region. This results in a complete manifold.

Real-world data is rarely evenly distributed, and UMAP solves this problem in two ways. First, it expands each search region for each case until it meets its nearest neighbor. This ensures that there are no orphan cases: while there can be multiple, disconnected manifolds in a dataset, every case must connect to at least one other case. Second, UMAP creates an additional search region that has a larger radius in lower-density areas and a smaller radius in high-density regions. These search regions are described as *fuzzy*, in that the further from the center another case finds itself, the lower the probability that an edge exists between those cases. This forces an artificial uniform distribution of the cases (and is where the "uniform" in UMAP comes from).

This process is represented in the lower row of figure 14.8; notice that we now get a more complete estimation of the underlying manifold.

The next step is to place the data onto a new manifold in (usually) two new dimensions. Then the algorithm iteratively shuffles this new manifold around until the distances between the cases along the manifold look like the distances between the cases along the original, high-dimensional manifold. This is similar to the optimization step of t-SNE, except that UMAP minimizes a different loss function called *cross-entropy* (whereas t-SNE minimizes KL divergence).

NOTE Just like for t-SNE, we can create more than two new dimensions if we want to.

Once UMAP has learned the lower-dimensional manifold, new data can be projected onto this manifold to get the values on the new axes for visualization or as input for another machine learning algorithm.

NOTE UMAP can also be used to perform *supervised dimension reduction*, which really just means that given high-dimensional, labeled data, it learns a manifold that can be used to classify cases into groups.

14.4 Building your first UMAP model

In this section, I'm going to show you how to use the UMAP algorithm to create a low-dimensional embedding of our Swiss banknote dataset. Remember that we're trying to see if we can find a lower-dimensional representation of this dataset to help us identify patterns, such as different types of banknotes. We'll start by installing and loading the umap package in R. Just as we did for t-SNE, we'll discuss UMAP's hyperparameters and how they affect the embedding. Then we'll train a UMAP model on the banknote dataset and plot it to see how it compares with our PCA model and t-SNE embedding.

14.4.1 Performing UMAP

In this section, we'll install and load the umap package and then tune and train our UMAP model. Let's start by installing and loading the umap package:

```
install.packages("umap")

library(umap)
```

Just like t-SNE, UMAP has four important hyperparameters that control the resulting embedding:

- *n_neighbors*—Controls the radius of the fuzzy search region. Larger values will include more neighboring cases, forcing the algorithm to focus on more global structure. Smaller values will include fewer neighbors, forcing the algorithm to focus on more local structure.

- *min_dist*—Defines the minimum distance apart that cases are allowed to be in the lower-dimensional representation. Low values result in "clumpy" embeddings, whereas larger values result in cases being spread further apart.
- *metric*—Defines which distance metric UMAP will use to measure distances along the manifold. By default, UMAP uses ordinary Euclidean distance, but other (sometimes crazy) distance metrics can be used instead. A common alternative to Euclidean distance is *Manhattan distance* (also called *taxi cab distance*): instead of measuring the distance between two points as a single (possibly diagonal) distance, it measures the distance between two points one variable at a time and adds up these little journeys, just like a taxi cab driving around blocks in a city.

  We can also apply t-SNE with distance metrics other than Euclidean, but we first need to manually calculate these distances ourselves. The UMAP implementation just lets us specify the distance we want, and it takes care of the rest.
- *n_epochs*—Defines the number of iterations of the optimization step.

Once again, to give you a visual aid of how each of these hyperparameters affects the final embedding, I've run UMAP on our Swiss banknote data using a grid of hyperparameter values. Figure 14.9 shows the final embeddings with different combinations of *n_neighbors* (rows) and *min_dist* (columns) using the default values of *metric* and *n_epochs*. Notice that the cases are more spread out for smaller values of *n_neighbors* and *min_dist* and that the clusters begin to break apart with low values for the *n_neighbors* hyperparameter.

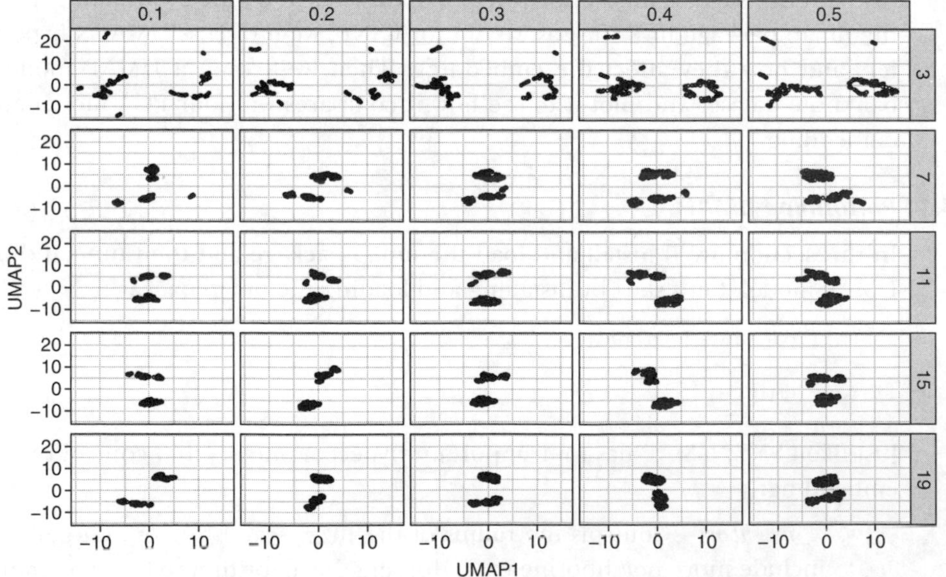

Figure 14.9 The effect on the final UMAP embedding of the banknote dataset of changing *n_neighbors* (row facets) and *min_dist* (column facets) using the default values of *metric* and *n_epochs*

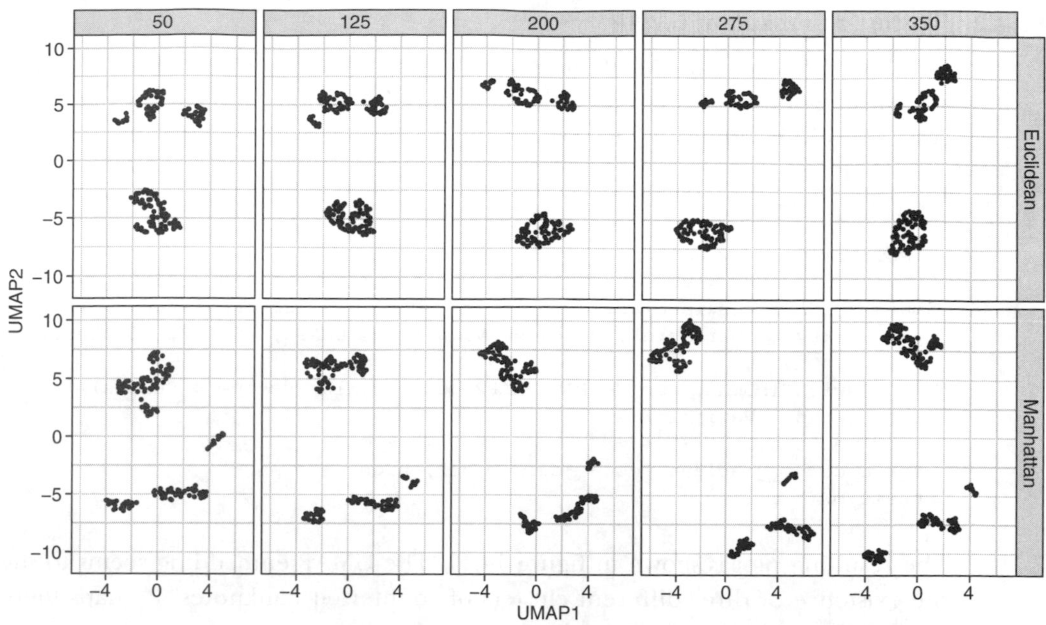

Figure 14.10 The effect on the final UMAP embedding of the swissTib dataset of changing *metric* (row facets) and *n_epochs* (column facets) using the default values of *n_neighbors* and *min_dist*

Figure 14.10 shows the final embeddings with different combinations of *metric* (rows) and *n_epochs* (columns). The effect here is a little more subtle, but the clusters tend to be farther apart with more iterations. It also looks as though Manhattan distance does a slightly better job of breaking up those three smaller clusters (which we've not seen before!). If you would like to see the code I used to generate these figures, the code for this chapter is available at www.manning.com/books/machine-learning-with-r-the-tidyverse-and-mlr.

I hope that demystifies UMAP's hyperparameters a little. Now let's run UMAP on our Swiss banknote dataset. Just like before, we first select all the columns except the categorical variable (UMAP cannot currently handle categorical variables, but this may change in the future) and pipe this data into the `as.matrix()` function (just to prevent an irritating warning message). This matrix is then piped into the `umap()` function, within which we manually set the values of all four hyperparameters and set the argument `verbose = TRUE` so the algorithm prints a running commentary on the number of epochs (iterations) that have passed.

Listing 14.3 Performing UMAP

```
swissUmap <- select(swissTib, -Status) %>%
             as.matrix() %>%
             umap(n_neighbors = 7, min_dist = 0.1,
                  metric = "manhattan", n_epochs = 200, verbose = TRUE)
```

14.4.2 Plotting the result of UMAP

Next, let's plot the two UMAP dimensions against each other to see how well they separated the genuine and counterfeit banknotes. We go through exactly the same process as we did in listing 14.2 to reshape the data so it's ready for plotting.

Listing 14.4 Plotting the UMAP embedding

```
swissTibUmap <- swissTib %>%
  mutate_if(.funs = scale, .predicate = is.numeric, scale = FALSE) %>%
  mutate(UMAP1 = swissUmap$layout[, 1], UMAP2 = swissUmap$layout[, 2]) %>%
  gather(key = "Variable", value = "Value", c(-UMAP1, -UMAP2, -Status))

ggplot(swissTibUmap, aes(UMAP1, UMAP2, col = Value, shape = Status)) +
  facet_wrap(~ Variable) +
  geom_point(size = 3) +
  scale_color_gradient(low = "dark blue", high = "cyan") +
  theme_bw()
```

The resulting plot is shown in figure 14.11. The UMAP embedding seems to suggest the existence of three different clusters of counterfeit banknotes! Perhaps there are three different counterfeiters at large.

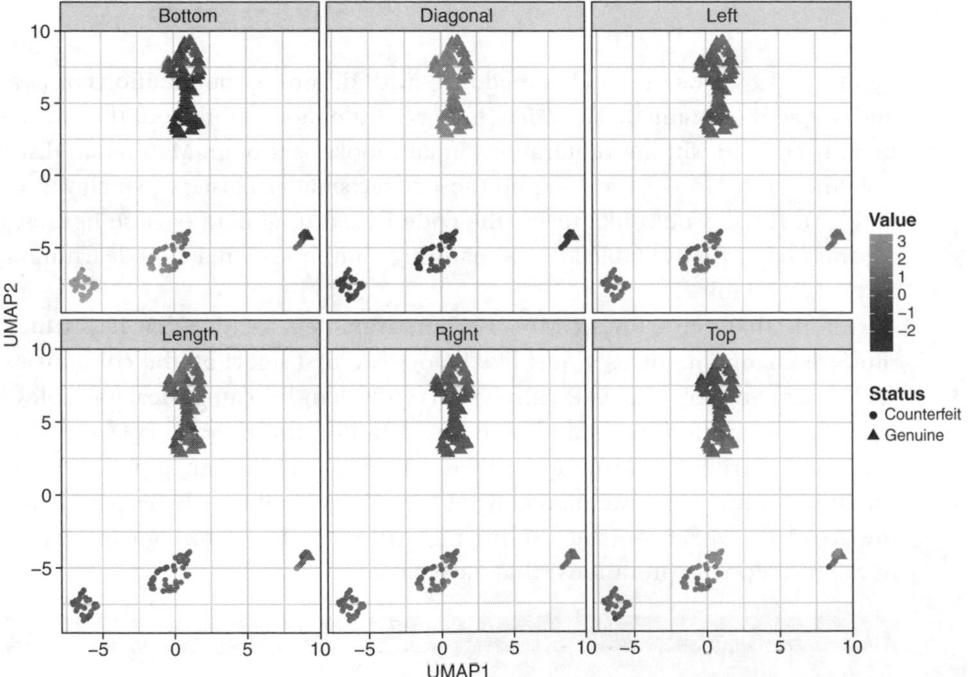

Figure 14.11 UMAP1 and UMAP2 axes plotted against each other, faceted and shaded by the original variables, and shaped by whether each case was a genuine or counterfeit banknote

14.4.3 Computing the UMAP embeddings of new data

Remember I said that, unlike t-SNE, new data can be projected reproducibly onto a UMAP embedding? Well, let's do this for the `newBanknotes` tibble we defined when predicting PCA component scores in chapter 13 (rerun listing 13.7 if you no longer have this defined). In fact, the process is exactly the same: we use the `predict()` function with the model as the first argument and the new data as the second argument. This outputs a matrix, where the rows represent the two cases and the columns represent the UMAP axes:

```
predict(swissUmap, newBanknotes)

      [,1]    [,2]
1 -6.9516 -7.777
2  0.1213  6.160
```

14.5 Strengths and weaknesses of t-SNE and UMAP

While it often isn't easy to tell which algorithms will perform well for a given task, here are some strengths and weaknesses that will help you decide whether t-SNE and UMAP will perform well for you.

The strengths of t-SNE and UMAP are as follows:

- They can learn nonlinear patterns in the data.
- They tend to separate clusters of cases better than PCA.
- UMAP can make predictions on new data.
- UMAP is computationally inexpensive.
- UMAP preserves both local *and* global distances.

The weaknesses of t-SNE and UMAP are these:

- The new axes of t-SNE and UMAP are not directly interpretable in terms of the original variables.
- t-SNE cannot make predictions on new data (different result each time).
- t-SNE is computationally expensive.
- t-SNE doesn't necessarily preserve global structure.
- They cannot handle categorical variables natively.

> **Exercise 2**
>
> Rerun UMAP on our Swiss banknote dataset, but this time include the argument `n_components = 3` (feel free to experiment by changing the values of the other hyperparameters). Pass the `$layout` component of the UMAP object to the `GGally::ggpairs()` function. (Tip: You'll need to wrap this object in `as.data.frame()`, or `ggpairs()` will have a hissy fit.)

Summary

- t-SNE and UMAP are nonlinear dimension-reduction algorithms.
- t-SNE converts the distances between all cases in the data into probabilities based on the normal distribution and then iteratively shuffles the cases around in a lower-dimensional space to reproduce these distances.
- In the lower-dimensional space, t-SNE uses Student's t distribution to convert distances to probabilities to better separate clusters of data.
- UMAP learns a manifold that the data are arranged along and then iteratively shuffles the data around in a lower-dimensional space to reproduce the distances between cases along the manifold.

Solutions to exercises

1 Recreate the plot of t-SNE1 versus t-SNE2 without scaling the variables first:

```
swissTib %>%
  mutate(tSNE1 = swissTsne$Y[, 1], tSNE2 = swissTsne$Y[, 2]) %>%
  gather(key = "Variable",
         value = "Value",
         c(-tSNE1, -tSNE2, -Status)) %>%
  ggplot(aes(tSNE1, tSNE2, col = Value, shape = Status)) +
  facet_wrap(~ Variable) +
  geom_point(size = 3) +
  scale_color_gradient(low = "dark blue", high = "cyan") +
  theme_bw()

# Scaling is necessary because the scales of the variables are different
# from each other.
```

2 Rerun UMAP, but output and plot three new axes instead of two:

```
umap3d <- select(swissTib, -Status) %>%
  as.matrix() %>%
  umap(n_neighbors = 7, min_dist = 0.1, n_components = 3,
       metric = "manhattan", n_epochs = 200, verbose = TRUE)

library(GGally)

ggpairs(as.data.frame(umap3d$layout), mapping = aes(col = swissTib$Status))
```

15 Self-organizing maps and locally linear embedding

This chapter covers

- Creating self-organizing maps to reduce dimensionality
- Creating locally linear embeddings of high-dimensional data

In this chapter, we're continuing with dimension reduction: the class of machine learning tasks focused on representing the information contained in a large number of variables, in a smaller number of variables. As you learned in chapters 13 and 14, there are multiple possible ways to reduce the dimensions of a dataset. Which dimension-reduction algorithm works best for you depends on the structure of your data and what you're trying to achieve. Therefore, in this chapter, I'm going to add two more nonlinear dimension-reduction algorithms to your ever-growing machine learning toolbox: self-organizing maps (SOMs) and locally linear embedding (LLE).

15.1 Prerequisites: Grids of nodes and manifolds

Both the SOM and LLE algorithms reduce a large dataset into a smaller, more manageable number of variables, but they work in very different ways. The SOM algorithm creates a two-dimensional grid of *nodes*, like grid references on a map. Each case in the data is placed into a node and then shuffled around the nodes so that cases that are more similar to each other in the original data are put close together on the map.

This is probably difficult to picture in your head, so let's look at an analogy. Imagine that you have a big jar of beads with your sewing kit. There are beads of different sizes and weights, and some are more elongated than others. It's raining, and there's nothing better to do, so you decide that you will organize your beads into sets to make it easier to find the beads you need in the future. You arrange a grid of bowls on the table and consider each bead in turn. You then place beads that are most similar to each other in the same bowl. You put beads that are similar, but not the same, in adjacent bowls, while beads that are very different go into bowls that are far away from each other. An example of what this might look like is shown in figure 15.1.

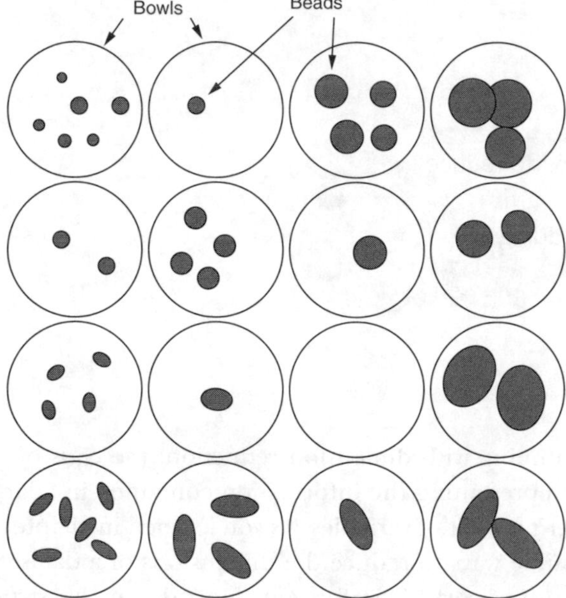

Figure 15.1 Placing beads into bowls based on their characteristics. Similar beads are placed in the same or nearby bowls, while dissimilar beads are placed in bowls far away from each other. One bowl didn't have any beads placed in it, but that's okay.

Once you've placed all the beads into bowls, you look at your grid and notice that a pattern has emerged. All the large, spherical beads congregate around the top-right corner of the grid. As you move from right to left, the beads get smaller; and as you move from top to bottom, the beads become more elongated. Your process of placing beads into bowls based on the similarities between them has revealed structure in the beads.

This is what self-organizing maps try to do. The "map" of a self-organizing map is equivalent to the grid of bowls, where each bowl is called a *node*.

The LLE algorithm, on the other hand, learns a manifold on which the data lies, similar to the UMAP algorithm you saw in chapter 14. Recall that a manifold is an *n*-dimensional smooth geometric shape that can be constructed from a series of linear "patches." Whereas UMAP tries to learn the manifold in one go, LLE looks for these local, linear patches of data around each case, and then combines these linear patches together to form the (potentially nonlinear) manifold.

If this is hard to picture, take a look at figure 15.2. A sphere is a smooth, three-dimensional manifold. We can approximate a sphere by breaking it up into a series of flat surfaces that combine together (the more of these surfaces we use, the more closely we can approximate the sphere). This is shown on the left side of figure 15.2. Imagine that someone gave you a flat sheet of paper and a pair of scissors, and asked you to create a sphere. You might cut the sheet into the kind of shape shown on the right side of figure 15.2. You could then fold this flat sheet of paper to approximate the sphere. Can you see that the flat, two-dimensional cutting is a lower-dimensional representation of the sphere? This is the general principle behind LLE, except that it tries to learn the manifold that represents the data, and represents it in fewer dimensions.

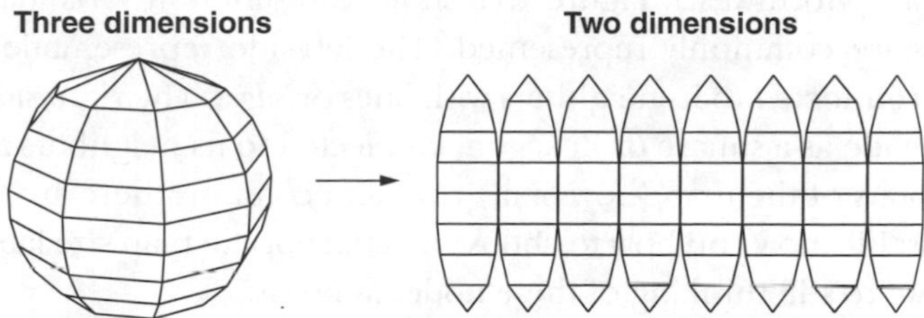

Figure 15.2 A sphere is a three-dimensional manifold. We can reconstruct a sphere as a series of linear patches that connect to one another. This three-dimensional manifold of a sphere can be represented in two dimensions by cutting a sheet of paper in a certain way.

In this chapter, I'll show you in more detail how the SOM and LLE algorithms work and how we can use them to reduce the dimensions of data collected on various flea beetles. I'll also show you a particularly fun example of how LLE can "unroll" some complex and unusually shaped data.

15.2 What are self-organizing maps?

In this section, I'll explain what SOMs are, how they work, and why they're useful for dimension reduction. Consider the purpose of a map. Maps conveniently represent the layout of a part of the globe (which is not flat) in two dimensions, such that areas of the planet that are close to each other are drawn close to each other on the map. This is a convoluted way of saying that you'll find India drawn closer to Sri Lanka than to Madagascar, because they are closer to each other in space.

The goal of a SOM is very similar; but instead of countries, towns, and cities, the SOM tries to represent a dataset in two dimensions, such that cases in the data that are more similar to each other are drawn close to each other. The first step of the algorithm is to create a grid of nodes in a two-dimensional lattice (like the grid of bowls in figure 15.1).

15.2.1 Creating the grid of nodes

In this section, I'll fully explain what I mean when I say the SOM algorithm creates a grid of nodes. Much like the grid of bowls we were sorting beads into in figure 15.1, the SOM algorithm starts by creating a grid of nodes. For now, you can just think of a node as a bowl into which we will eventually put cases from the dataset. I've used the word *grid* to help you picture the lattice structure of the nodes, but the word *map* is more commonly used, so we'll use this from now on.

The map can be made up of square/rectangular nodes, much like square grid references on a map; or hexagonal nodes, which fit together snugly like a honeycomb. When the map is made of square nodes, each node is connected to four of its neighbors (you could say they're its north, south, east, and west neighbors). When the map is made of hexagonal nodes, each node is connected to six of its neighbors (northeast, east, southeast, southwest, west, and northwest). Figure 15.3 shows two different ways that square and hexagonal SOMs are commonly represented. The left-side representation shows each node as a circle, connected to its neighbors with lines or *edges*. The right-side representation shows each node as a square or hexagon, connected to its neighbors across its flat sides. The dimensions of the map (how many rows and columns there are) need to be decided upon by us; I'll show you how to choose an appropriate map size later in the chapter. Remember, we're still thinking of these nodes as bowls.

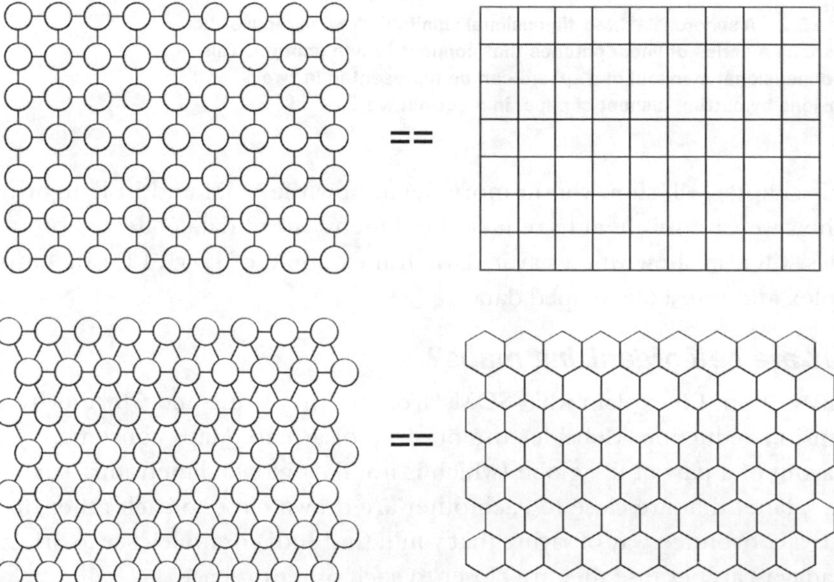

Figure 15.3 Common graphical representations of square and hexagonal self-organizing maps. The top two maps show a grid of rectangular nodes that are each connected to four neighbors. The bottom two maps show a grid of hexagonal nodes that are each connected to six neighbors.

NOTE SOMs were created by a Finnish computer scientist named Teuvo Kohonen, so you will sometimes see them called *Kohonen maps*. The SOM algorithm has been so popular that Professor Kohonen is the most frequently cited Finnish computer scientist of all time.

Once the map has been created, the next step is to randomly assign each node a set of *weights*.

15.2.2 Randomly assigning weights, and placing cases in nodes

In this section, I'll explain what I mean by the term *weights*, and what they relate to. I'll show you how these weights are randomly initialized for every node in the map.

Imagine that we have a dataset with three variables, and we want to distribute the cases of this dataset across the nodes of our map. Eventually, we hope the algorithm will place the cases in the nodes such that similar cases are in the same node or a nearby node, and dissimilar cases are placed in nodes far away from each other.

After the creation of the map, the next thing the algorithm does is randomly assign each node a set of weights: one weight for each variable in the dataset. So for our example, each node has three weights, because we have three variables. These weights are just random numbers, and you can think of them as guesses for the value of each of the variables. If this is hard to visualize, take a look at figure 15.4. We have a dataset containing three variables, and we are looking at three nodes from a map. Each node has three numbers written under it: one corresponding to each variable in the dataset. For example, the weights for node 1 are 3 (for var 1), 9 (for var 2), and 1 (for var 3). Remember, at this point these are just random guesses for the value of each variable.

Next, the algorithm chooses a case at random from the dataset and calculates which node's weights are the closest match to this case's values for each of the variables. For example, if there were a case in the dataset whose values for var 1, var 2, and var 3 were 3, 9, and 1, respectively, this case would perfectly match the weights of node 1. To find which node's weights are most similar to the case in question, the distance is calculated between each case and the weights of each node in the map. This distance is usually the squared Euclidean distance. Remember that Euclidean distance is just the straight-line distance between two points, so the squared Euclidean distance just omits the square root step to make the computation faster.

In figure 15.4, you can see the distances calculated between the first case and each of the node's weights. This case is most similar to the weights of node 1, because it has the smallest squared Euclidean distance to them (93.09).

NOTE The illustration in figure 15.4 shows only three nodes, for brevity, but the distance is calculated for every single node on the map.

Once the distances between a particular case and all of the nodes have been calculated, the node with the smallest distance (most similar to the case) is selected as that case's *best matching unit* (BMU). This is illustrated in figure 15.5. Just like when we put beads into bowls, the algorithm takes that case and places it inside its BMU.

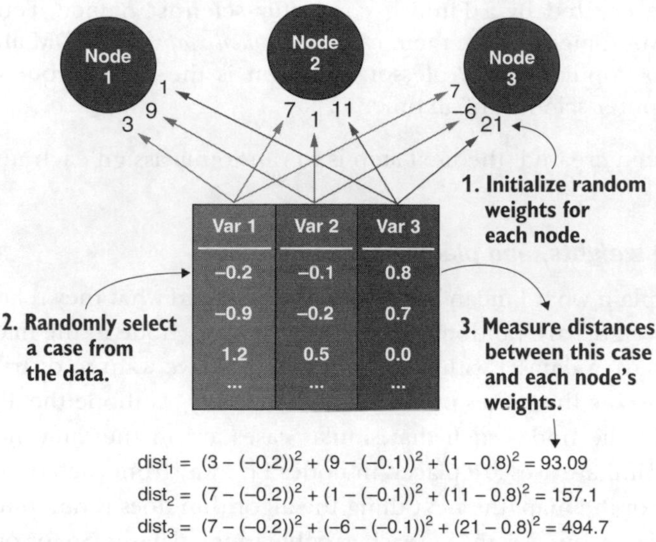

Figure 15.4 How distances between each case to each node are calculated. The arrows pointing from each variable to each node represent the weight for that variable on that particular node (for example, the weights of node 1 are 3, 9, and 1). Distance is calculated by finding the difference between a node's weights and a case's value for each variable, squaring these differences, and summing them.

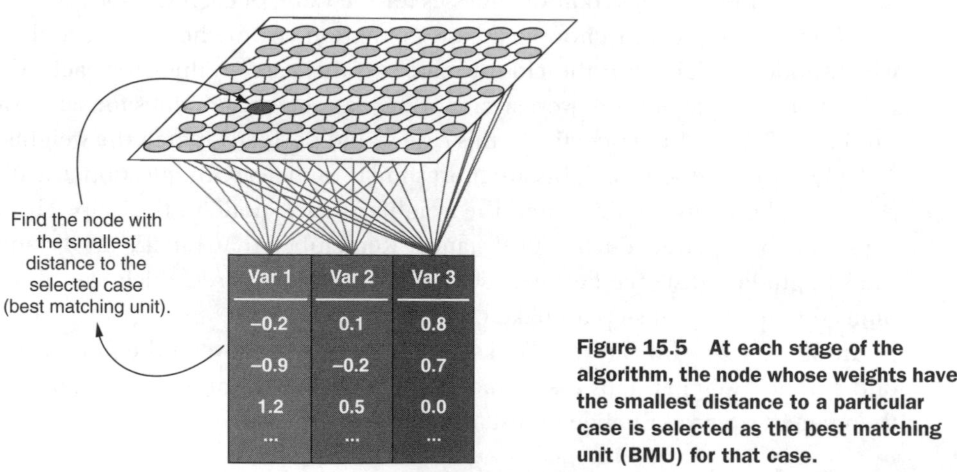

Figure 15.5 At each stage of the algorithm, the node whose weights have the smallest distance to a particular case is selected as the best matching unit (BMU) for that case.

15.2.3 Updating node weights to better match the cases inside them

In this section, I'll show you how the weights of a case's BMU and the weights of the surrounding nodes are updated to more closely match the data. First, though, let's summarize our knowledge of the SOM algorithm so far:

1 Create the map of nodes.
2 Randomly assign weights to each node (one for each variable in the dataset).
3 Select a case at random, and calculate its distance to the weights of every node in the map.
4 Put the case into the node whose weights have the smallest distance to the case (the case's BMU).

Now that the BMU has been selected, its weights are updated to be more similar to the case we placed inside it. However, it's not only the BMU's weights that are updated. Nodes in the *neighborhood* of the BMU also have their weights updated (nodes that are near to the BMU). We can define the neighborhood in a few different ways: a common way is to use the *bubble function*. With the bubble function, we simply define a radius (or bubble) around the BMU, and all nodes inside that radius have their weights updated to the same degree. Any nodes outside the radius are not updated at all. For the bubble function, a radius of 3 would include any node within three direct connections of the BMU.

Another popular choice is to update the node weights of the map based on how far they are from the BMU (the farther from the BMU, the less the node's weights are updated). This is most commonly done using the *Gaussian* function. You can picture this as though we fit a Gaussian distribution centered over the BMU, and the node weights around the BMU are updated proportionally to the density of the Gaussian over them. We still define a radius around the BMU that defines how broad or skinny the Gaussian is, but this time it's a soft radius that has no hard cutoff. The Gaussian function is popular, but it's a little more computationally expensive than the simple bubble function.

NOTE The bubble and Gaussian functions used to update the weights of the nodes in the neighborhood around the BMU are called *neighborhood functions*.

Our choice of neighborhood function is a hyperparameter, as it will affect the way our map updates its nodes but cannot be estimated from the data itself.

NOTE You will sometimes see the set of weights for a node referred to as its *codebook vector*.

Whichever neighborhood function we use, the benefit of updating node weights in a neighborhood around the BMU is that, over time, doing so creates neighborhoods of nodes that are similar to each other but still capture some variation in the data. Another trick the algorithm uses is that, as time goes on, both the radius of this neighborhood and the amount by which the weights are updated get smaller. This means the map is updated very rapidly initially and then makes smaller and smaller updates as the learning process continues. This helps the map converge to a solution that, hopefully, places similar cases in the same or nearby nodes. This process of updating node weights in the neighborhood of the BMU is illustrated in figure 15.6.

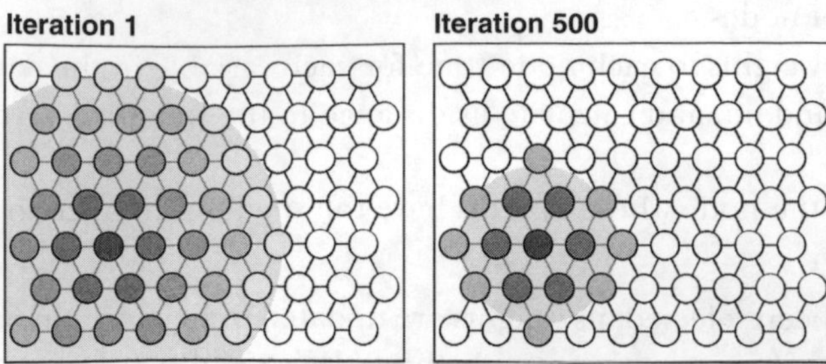

Figure 15.6 Between the first and last iteration of the algorithm, both the radius of the neighborhood around a BMU (the darkest node) and the amount by which neighboring node weights are updated get smaller. The radius of a Gaussian neighborhood function is shown as a translucent circle centered over the BMU, and the amount each neighboring node is updated is represented by how dark its shading is. If the bubble neighborhood function was shown, all nodes would be shaded the same (as they're updated by the same amount).

Now that we've determined the BMU for a particular case and updated its weights and the weights of its neighbors, we simply repeat the procedure for the next iteration, selecting another random case from the data. As this process continues, cases will likely be selected more than once and will move around the map as their BMU changes over time. To put it another way, cases will change nodes if the one they are currently in is no longer their BMU. Eventually, similar cases will converge to a particular region of the map.

The result is that over time, the nodes on the map start to fit the dataset better. And eventually, cases that are similar to each other in the original feature space will be placed either in the same node or in nearby nodes on the map.

NOTE Remember that the *feature space* refers to all possible combinations of predictor variable values.

Before we get our hands dirty by building our own SOM, let's recap the whole algorithm to make sure it sticks in your mind:

1. Create the map of nodes.
2. Randomly assign weights to each node (one for each variable in the dataset).
3. Select a case at random, and calculate its distance to the weights of every node in the map.
4. Put the case into the node whose weights have the smallest distance to the case (the case's BMU).
5. Update the weights of the BMU and the nodes in its neighborhood (depending on the neighborhood function) to more closely match the cases inside it.
6. Repeat steps 3-5 for the specified number of iterations.

15.3 Building your first SOM

In this section, I'll show you how to use the SOM algorithm to reduce the dimensions of a dataset into a two-dimensional map. By doing so, we hope to reveal some structure in the data by placing similar cases in the same or nearby nodes. For example, if a grouping structure is hidden in the data, we hope that different groups will separate to different regions of the map. I'll also show you the algorithm's hyperparameters and what they do.

> **NOTE** Remember that a hyperparameter is a variable that controls the performance/function of an algorithm but cannot be directly estimated from the data itself.

Imagine that you're the ringleader of a flea circus. You decide to take measurements for all of your fleas to see if different groups of fleas perform better at certain circus tasks. Let's start by loading the tidyverse and GGally packages:

```
library(tidyverse)

library(GGally)
```

15.3.1 Loading and exploring the flea dataset

Now let's load the data, which is built into the GGally package; convert it into a tibble (with `as_tibble()`); and plot it using the `ggpairs()` function we discovered in chapter 14.

Listing 15.1 Loading and exploring the flea dataset

```
data(flea)

fleaTib <- as_tibble(flea)

fleaTib

# A tibble: 74 x 7
   species  tars1 tars2  head aede1 aede2 aede3
   <fct>    <int> <int> <int> <int> <int> <int>
 1 Concinna   191   131    53   150    15   104
 2 Concinna   185   134    50   147    13   105
 3 Concinna   200   137    52   144    14   102
 4 Concinna   173   127    50   144    16    97
 5 Concinna   171   118    49   153    13   106
 6 Concinna   160   118    47   140    15    99
 7 Concinna   188   134    54   151    14    98
 8 Concinna   186   129    51   143    14   110
 9 Concinna   174   131    52   144    14   116
10 Concinna   163   115    47   142    15    95
# ... with 64 more rows

ggpairs(flea, mapping = aes(col = species)) +
  theme_bw()
```

We have a tibble containing 7 variables, measured on 74 different fleas. The `species` variable is a factor telling us the species each flea belongs to, while the others are continuous measurements made on various parts of the fleas' bodies. We're going to omit the `species` variable from our dimension reduction, but we'll use it later to see whether our SOM clusters together fleas from the same species.

The resulting plot is shown in figure 15.7. We can see that the three species of fleas can be discriminated between using different combinations of the continuous variables. Let's train a SOM to reduce these six continuous variables into a representation with only two dimensions, and see how well it separates the three species of fleas.

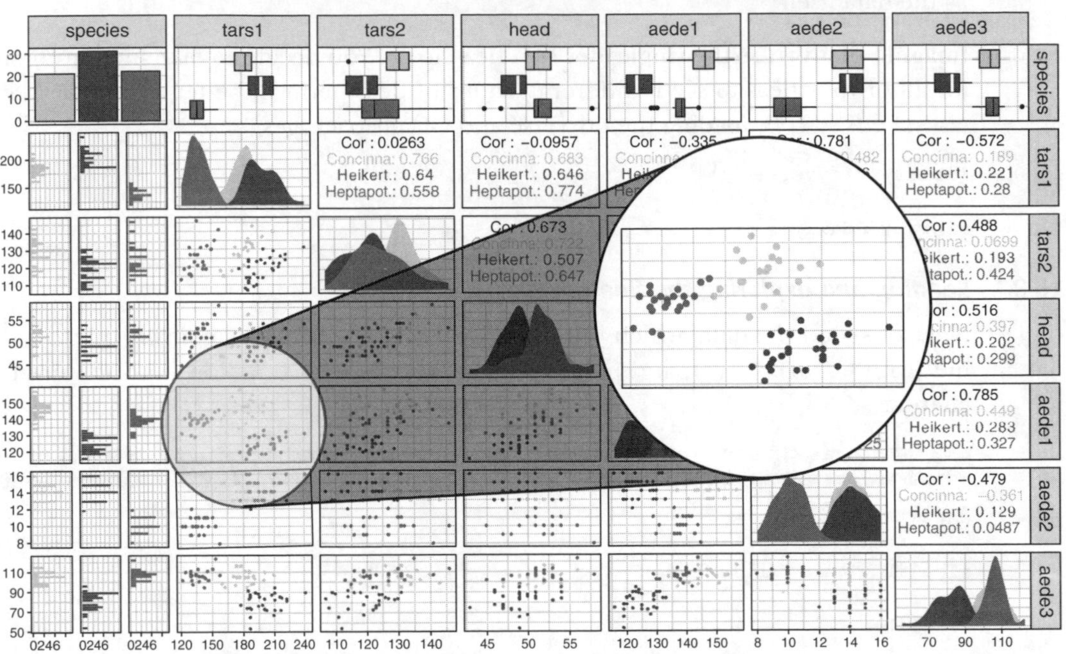

Figure 15.7 A matrix of plots created using the `ggpairs()` function, plotting all variables against each other from the flea dataset. Because the individual plots are quite small, I've manually zoomed in on one plot with a virtual magnifying glass (much like one you might need to use to see the fleas).

15.3.2 Training the SOM

Let's train our SOM to place fleas in nodes such that (hopefully) fleas of the same species are placed near each other and fleas of different species are separated. We start by installing and loading the kohonen package (named after Teuvo Kohonen, of course). The next thing we need to do is create a grid of nodes that will become our map. We do this using the `somgrid()` function (as shown in listing 15.2), and we have a few choices to make:

- The dimensions of the map
- Whether our map will be made of rectangular or hexagonal nodes

- Which neighborhood function to use
- How the edges of the map will behave

I've used the arguments of the `somgrid()` function to make these choices, but let's explore what they each mean and how they each affect the resulting map.

Listing 15.2 Loading the kohonen package and creating a SOM grid

```
install.packages("kohonen")

library(kohonen)

somGrid <- somgrid(xdim = 5, ydim = 5, topo = "hexagonal",
                   neighbourhood.fct = "bubble", toroidal = FALSE)
```

CHOOSING THE DIMENSIONS OF THE MAP

First, we need to choose the number of nodes in the x and y dimensions, using the `xdim` and `ydim` arguments, respectively. This is very important because it determines the size of the map and the granularity with which it will partition our cases. How do we choose the dimensions of our map? This, as it turns out, isn't an easy question to answer. Too few nodes, and all of our data will be piled up so that clusters of cases merge with each other. Too many nodes, and we could end up with nodes containing a single case, or even no cases at all, diluting any clusters and preventing interpretation.

The optimal dimensions of a SOM depend largely on the number of cases in the data. We want to aim to have cases in most of the nodes for a start, but really the optimal number of nodes in the SOM is whichever best reveals patterns in the data. We can also plot the *quality* of each node, which is a measure of the average difference between each case in a particular node and that node's final weights. We can then consider choosing a map size that gives us the best-quality nodes. In this example, we'll start by creating a 5 × 5 grid, but this subjectivity in selecting the dimensions of the map is arguably a weakness of SOMs.

> **TIP** The x and y dimensions of the grid don't need to be of equal length. If I find a grid dimensionality that reveals patterns reasonably well in a dataset, I may extend the map in one dimension to see if this further helps to separate clusters of cases. There is an implementation of the SOM algorithm called *growing SOM*, where the algorithm grows the size of the grid based on the data. After you finish this chapter, I suggest you have a look at the GrowingSOM package in R: https://github.com/alexhunziker/GrowingSOM.

CHOOSING WHETHER THE MAP HAS RECTANGULAR OR HEXAGONAL NODES

The next choice is to decide whether our grid is formed of rectangular or hexagonal nodes. Rectangular nodes are connected to four adjacent nodes, whereas hexagonal nodes are connected to six adjacent nodes. Thus when a node's weights are updated, a hexagonal node will update its six immediate neighbors the most, whereas a rectangular node will update its four immediate neighbors the most. While hexagonal nodes can potentially result in "smoother" maps in which clusters of data appear more rounded (whereas clusters of data in a grid of rectangular nodes may appear "blocky"), it depends on your data. In this example, we'll specify that we want a hexagonal topology by setting the `topo = "hexagonal"` argument.

> **TIP** I usually prefer the results I get from hexagonal nodes, both in terms of the patterns they reveal in my data and aesthetically.

Choosing a neighborhood function

Next, we need to choose which neighborhood function we're going to use, supplying our choice to the `neighbourhood.fct` argument (note the British spelling). The two options are `"bubble"` and `"gaussian"`, corresponding to the two neighborhood functions we discussed earlier. Our choice of neighborhood function is a hyperparameter, and we could tune it; but for this example we're just going to use the bubble neighborhood function, which is the default.

Choosing how the map edges behave

The final choice we need to make is whether we want our grid to be *toroidal* (another word to impress your friends with). If the grid is toroidal, nodes on the left edge of the map are connected to the nodes on the right edge (and the equivalent for nodes on the top and bottom edges). If you were to walk off the left edge of a toroidal map, you would reappear on the right! Because nodes on the edges have fewer connections to other nodes, their weights tend to be updated less than those of nodes in the middle of the map. Therefore, it may be beneficial to use a toroidal map to help prevent cases from "piling up" on the map edges, though toroidal maps tend to be harder to interpret. In this example, we will set the toroidal argument to `FALSE` to make the final map more interpretable.

Training the SOM with the som() function

Now that we've initialized our grid, we can pass our tibble into the `som()` function to train our map.

Listing 15.3 Training the SOM

```
fleaScaled <- fleaTib %>%
  select(-species) %>%
  scale()

fleaSom <- som(fleaScaled, grid = somGrid, rlen = 5000,
               alpha = c(0.05, 0.01))
```

We start by piping the tibble into the `select()` function to remove the `species` factor. Cases are assigned to the node with the most similar weights, so it's important to scale our variables so that variables on large scales aren't given more importance. To this end, we pipe the output of the `select()` function call into the `scale()` function to center and scale each variable.

To build the SOM, we use the `som()` function from the kohonen package, supplying the following:

- The data as the first argument
- The grid object created in listing 15.2 as the second argument
- The two hyperparameter arguments *rlen* and *alpha*

The *rlen* hyperparameter is simply the number of times the dataset is presented to the algorithm for sampling (the number of iterations); the default is 100. Just like in other algorithms we've seen, more iterations are usually better until we get diminishing returns. I'll show you soon how to assess whether you've included enough iterations.

The *alpha* hyperparameter is the learning rate and is a vector of two values. Remember that as the number of iterations increases, the amount by which the weights of each node is updated decreases. This is controlled by the two values of *alpha*. Iteration 1 uses the first value of *alpha*, which linearly declines to the second value of *alpha* at the last iteration.

The vector `c(0.05, 0.01)` is the default; but for larger SOMs, if you're concerned the SOM is doing a poor job of separating classes with subtle differences between them, you can experiment with reducing these values to make the learning rate even slower.

NOTE If you make the learning rate of an algorithm slower, you typically need to increase the number of iterations to help it converge to a stable result.

15.3.3 Plotting the SOM result

Now that we've trained our SOM, let's plot some diagnostic information about it. The kohonen package comes with plotting functions to draw SOMs, but it uses base R graphics rather than ggplot2. The syntax to plot a SOM object is `plot(x, type, shape)`, where x is our SOM object, type is the type of plot we want to draw, and `shape` lets us specify whether we want the nodes to be drawn as circles or with straight edges (squares if the grid is rectangular, hexagons if the grid is hexagonal).

Listing 15.4 Plotting SOM diagnostics

```
par(mfrow = c(2, 3))

plotTypes <- c("codes", "changes", "counts", "quality",
               "dist.neighbours", "mapping")

walk(plotTypes, ~plot(fleaSom, type = ., shape = "straight"))
```

NOTE I prefer to draw straight-edged plots, but the choice is aesthetic only. Experiment with setting the shape argument to `"round"` and `"straight"`.

There are six different diagnostic plots we can draw for our SOM, but rather than writing out the `plot()` function six times, we define a vector with the names of the plot types and use `walk()` to plot them all at once. We first split the plotting device into six regions by running `par(mfrow = c(2, 3))`.

We could achieve the same thing with `purrr::map()`, but `purrr::walk()` calls a function for its side effects (such as drawing a plot) and silently returns its input (which is useful if you want to plot an intermediate dataset in a series of operations that pipe into each other). The convenience here is that `purrr:::walk()` doesn't print any output to the console.

WARNING The kohonen package also contains a function called `map()`. If you have the kohonen package *and* the purrr package loaded, it's a good idea to include the package prefix in the function call (`kohonen::map()` and `purrr::map()`).

The resulting plots are shown in figure 15.8. The Codes plot is a fan plot representation of the weights for each node. Each segment of the fan represents the weight for a particular variable (as designated in the legend), and the distance the fan extends from the center represents the magnitude of its weight. For example, nodes in the top-left corner of my plot have the highest weights for the `tars2` variable. This plot can help us to identify regions of the map that are associated with higher or lower values of particular variables.

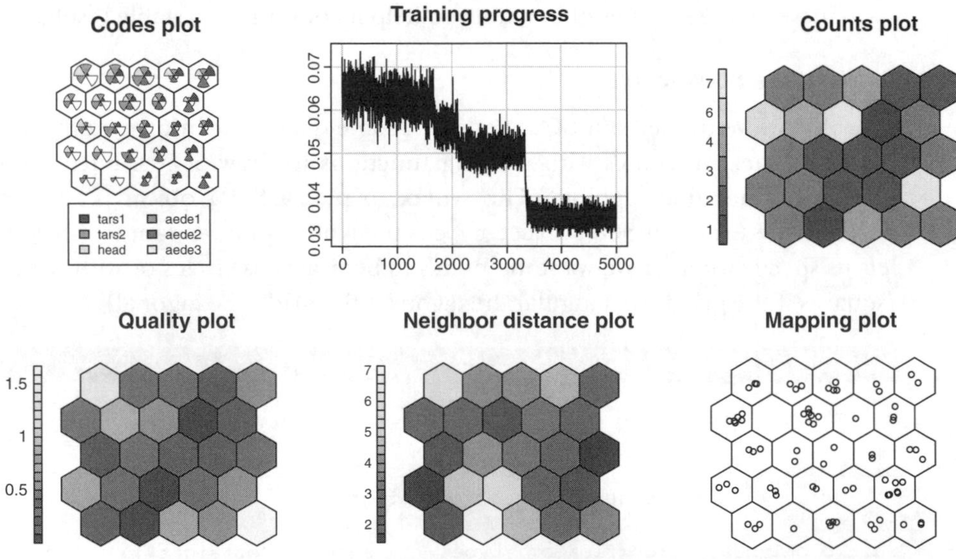

Figure 15.8 Diagnostic plots for our SOM. The Codes fan plot for each node indicates the weight for each variable. The Training Progress plot shows the mean distance between each case and its BMU for each iteration. The Counts plot shows the number of cases per node. The Quality plot shows the mean distance between each case and the weights of its BMU. The Neighbor Distance plot shows the sum of differences between cases in one node and cases in neighboring nodes. The Mapping plot draws the cases inside their assigned nodes.

NOTE Do your plots look a little different than mine? That's because the node weights are randomly initialized each time we run the algorithm. Arguably, this is a disadvantage of the SOM algorithm, as it may produce different results on the same data when run repeatedly. This disadvantage is mitigated by the fact that—unlike t-SNE, for example—we can map new data onto an existing SOM.

The Training Progress plot helps us to assess if we have included enough iterations while training the SOM. The x-axis shows the number of iterations (specified by the *rlen* argument), and the y-axis shows the mean distance between each case and its BMU at each iteration. We hope to see the profile of this plot flatten out before we reach our maximum number of iterations, which it seems to in this case. If we felt that the plot hadn't leveled out yet, we would increase the number of iterations.

The Counts plot is a heatmap showing the number of cases assigned to each node. In this plot, we're looking to be sure we don't have lots of empty nodes (suggesting the map is too big) and that we have a reasonably even distribution of cases across the map. If we had lots of cases piled up at the edges, we might consider increasing the map dimensions or training a toroidal map instead.

The Quality plot shows the mean distance between each case and the weights of its BMU. The lower this value is, the better.

The Neighbor Distance plot shows the sum of distances between cases in one node and cases in the neighboring nodes. You'll sometimes see this referred to as a *U matrix plot*, and it can be useful in identifying clusters of cases on the map. Because cases on the edge of a cluster of nodes have a greater distance to cases in an adjacent cluster of nodes, high-distance nodes tend to separate clusters. This often looks like dark regions of the map (potential clusters) separated by light regions. It's difficult to interpret a map as small as this, but it appears as though we may have clusters on the left and right edges, and possibly a cluster at the top center.

Finally, the Mapping plot shows the distribution of cases among the nodes. Note that the position of a case within a node doesn't mean anything—they are just *dodged* (moved a small, random distance) so that they don't all sit on top of each other.

The Codes plot is a useful way to visualize the weights of each node, but it becomes difficult to read when you have many variables, and it doesn't give an interpretable indication of magnitude. Instead, I prefer to create heatmaps: one for each variable. We use the `getCodes()` function to extract the weights for each node, where each row is a node and each column is a variable, and convert this into a tibble. The following listing shows how to then create a separate heatmap for each variable, this time using `iwalk()` to iterate over each of the columns.

Listing 15.5 Plotting heatmaps for each variable

```
getCodes(fleaSom) %>%
  as_tibble() %>%
  iwalk(~plot(fleaSom, type = "property", property = .,
             main = .y, shape = "straight"))
```

NOTE Recall from chapter 2 that each of the `map()` functions has an `i` equivalent (`imap()`, `imap_dbl()`, `iwalk()`, and so on) that allows us to pass the name/position of each element to the function. The `iwalk()` function is shorthand for `walk2(.x, .y = names(.x), .f)`, allowing us to access the name of each element by using `.y` inside our function.

We set the `type` argument equal to `"property"`, which allows us to color each node by some numerical property. We then use the `property` argument to tell the function exactly what property we want to plot. To set the title of each plot equal to the name of the variable it displays, we set the `main` argument equal to `.y` (this is why I chose to use `iwalk()` instead of `walk()`).

The resulting plot is shown in figure 15.9. The heatmaps show very different patterns of weights for each of the variables. Nodes on the right side of the map have higher weights for the `tars1` and `aede2` variables and lower weights for the `aede3` variable (which is lowest in the bottom-right corner of the map). Nodes in the upper-left corner of the map have higher weights for the `tars2`, `head`, and `aede1` variables. Because the variables were scaled before training the SOM, the heatmap scales are in standard deviation units for each variable.

Because we have some class information about our fleas, let's plot our SOM, coloring each case by its species.

Listing 15.6 Plotting flea species onto the SOM

```
par(mfrow = c(1, 2))

nodeCols <- c("cyan3", "yellow", "purple")

plot(fleaSom, type = "mapping", pch = 21,
     bg = nodeCols[as.numeric(fleaTib$species)],
     shape = "straight", bgcol = "lightgrey")
```

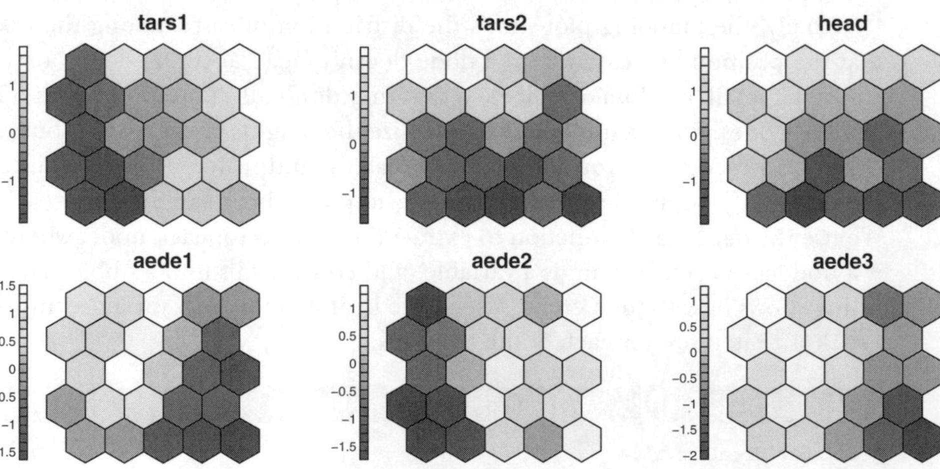

Figure 15.9 Separate heatmaps showing node weights for each original variable. The scales are in standard deviation units.

First, we define a vector of colors to use to distinguish the classes from each other. Then, we create a mapping plot using the `plot()` function, and using the `type = "mapping"` argument. We set the `pch = 21` argument to use a filled circle to indicate each case (so we can set a background color for each species). The `bg` argument sets the background color of the points. By converting the `species` variable into a numeric vector and using it to subset the color vector, each point will have a background color corresponding to its species. Finally, we use the `shape` argument to draw hexagons instead of circles, and set the background color (`bgcol`) equal to `"lightgrey"`.

The resulting plot is shown in figure 15.10. Can you see that the SOM has arranged itself such that fleas from the same species (that are more similar to each other than fleas from other species) are assigned to nodes near cases of the same species? I've created a plot on the right side of figure 15.10 that used a clustering algorithm to find clusters of nodes. I've colored the nodes by the cluster each node was assigned to, and added thick borders that separate the clusters. Because we haven't covered clustering yet, I don't want to explain how I did this (the code is available at www.manning.com/books/machine-learning-with-r-the-tidyverse-and-mlr), but I wanted to show you that the SOM managed to separate the different classes and that clustering can be performed on a SOM! We'll start covering clustering in the next chapter.

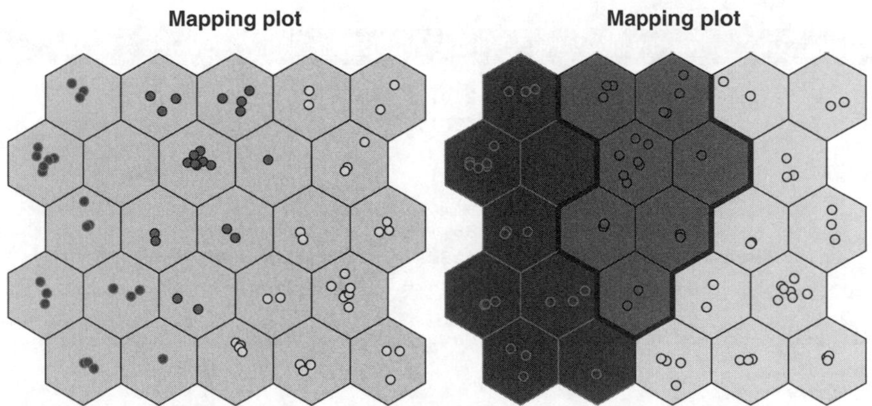

Figure 15.10 Showing class membership on the SOM. The left-side mapping plot shows cases drawn inside their assigned nodes, shaded by which flea species they belong to. The right-side plot shows the same information, but nodes are shaded by cluster membership after applying a clustering algorithm to the nodes. The solid black lines separate nodes assigned to different clusters.

NOTE SOMs are a little different than other dimension-reduction techniques, in that they don't really create new variables for which each case is given a value (for example, the principal components in PCA). SOMs reduce dimensionality by placing cases into nodes on a two-dimensional map, rather than creating new variables. So if we want to perform cluster analysis on the result of a SOM, we can use the weights to cluster the nodes. This essentially treats each node as a case in a new dataset. If our cluster analysis returns clusters of nodes, we can assign cases from the original dataset to the cluster that their node belongs to.

Exercise 1

Create another map using the `somgrid()` function, but this time set the arguments as follows:

- `topo = rectangular`
- `toroidal = TRUE`

Train a SOM using this map, and create its mapping plot, as in figure 15.10. Notice how each node is now connected with four of its neighbors. Can you see how the `toroidal` argument affects the final map? If not, set this argument to `FALSE`, but keep everything else the same, and see the difference.

15.3.4 Mapping new data onto the SOM

In this section, I'll show you how we can take new data and map it onto our trained SOM. Let's create two new cases with all of the continuous variables in the data we used to train the SOM.

Listing 15.7 Plotting flea species onto the SOM

```
newData <- tibble(tars1 = c(120, 200),
                  tars2 = c(125, 120),
                  head = c(52, 48),
                  aede1 = c(140, 128),
                  aede2 = c(12, 14),
                  aede3 = c(100, 85)) %>%
           scale(center = attr(fleaScaled, "scaled:center"),
                 scale = attr(fleaScaled, "scaled:scale"))

predicted <- predict(fleaSom, newData)

par(mfrow = c(1, 1))

plot(fleaSom, type = "mapping", classif = predicted, shape = "round")
```

Once we define the tibble, we pipe it into the `scale()` function, because we trained the SOM on scaled data. But here's the really important part: a common mistake is to scale the new data by subtracting its own mean and dividing by its own standard deviation. This will likely lead to an incorrect mapping, because we need to subtract the mean and divide by the standard deviation *of the training set*. Fortunately, these values are stored as attributes of the scaled dataset, and we can access them using the `attr()` function.

TIP If you're not quite sure what the `attr()` function is retrieving, run `attributes(fleaScaled)` to see the full list of attributes of the `fleaScaled` object.

We use the `predict()` function with the SOM object as the first argument and the new, scaled data as the second argument, to map the new data onto our SOM. We can then plot the position of the new data on the map using the `plot()` function, supplying the `type = "mapping"` argument. The `classif` argument allows us to specify an object returned by the `predict()` function, to draw only the new data. This time, we use the argument `shape = "round"` to show what the circular nodes look like.

The resulting plot is shown in figure 15.11. Each case is placed in a separate node whose weights best represent the case's variable values. Look back at figures 15.9 and 15.10 and see what you can infer about these two cases based on their position on the map.

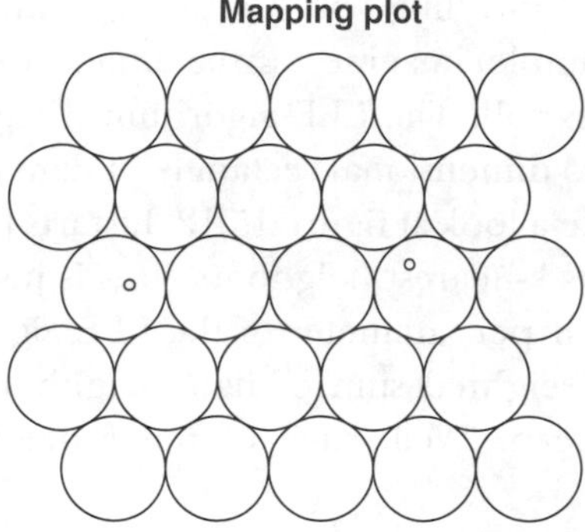

Figure 15.11 New data can be mapped onto an existing SOM. This mapping plot shows a graphical representation of the nodes to which the two new cases are assigned.

Using SOMs for supervised learning

We're concentrating on SOMs for their use as unsupervised learners for dimension reduction. This is probably the most common use for SOMs, but they can also be used for both regression and classification, making SOMs very unusual among machine learning algorithms.

In a supervised setting, SOMs actually create two maps: let's call them the x and y maps. The x map is the same as what you've learned so far; the weights of its nodes are iteratively updated such that similar cases are placed in nearby nodes and dissimilar cases are placed in distant nodes, using only the predictor variables in the dataset. Once the cases are placed into their respective nodes on the x map, they don't move. The weights of the y map's nodes represent values of the outcome variable. The algorithm now randomly selects cases again and iteratively updates the weights of each y map node to better match the values of the outcome variable of the cases in that node. The weights could represent a continuous outcome variable (in the case of regression) or a set of class probabilities (in the case of classification).

We can train a supervised SOM using the `xyf()` function from the kohonen package. Use `?xyf()` to learn more.

15.4 What is locally linear embedding?

In this section, I'll explain what LLE is, how it works, why it's useful, and how it differs from SOMs. Just like UMAP, the LLE algorithm tries to identify an underlying manifold that the data lies on. But LLE does this in a slightly different way: instead of trying to learn the manifold all at once, it learns local, linear patches of data around each case and then combines these linear patches to form the (potentially nonlinear) manifold.

> **NOTE** An oft-quoted mantra of the LLE algorithm is to "think globally, fit locally": the algorithm looks at small, local patches around each case and uses these patches to construct the wider manifold.

The LLE algorithm is particularly good at "unrolling" or "unfurling" data that is rolled or twisted into unusual shapes. For example, imagine a three-dimensional dataset where the cases are rolled up into a Swiss roll. The LLE algorithm is capable of unrolling the data and representing it as a two-dimensional rectangle of data points.

So how does the LLE algorithm work? Take a look at figure 15.12. It starts by selecting a case from the dataset and calculating its k-nearest neighbors (this is just like in the kNN algorithm from chapter 3, so k is a hyperparameter of the LLE algorithm). LLE then represents this case as a linear, weighted sum of its k neighbors. I can already hear you asking: what does that mean? Well, each of the k neighbors is

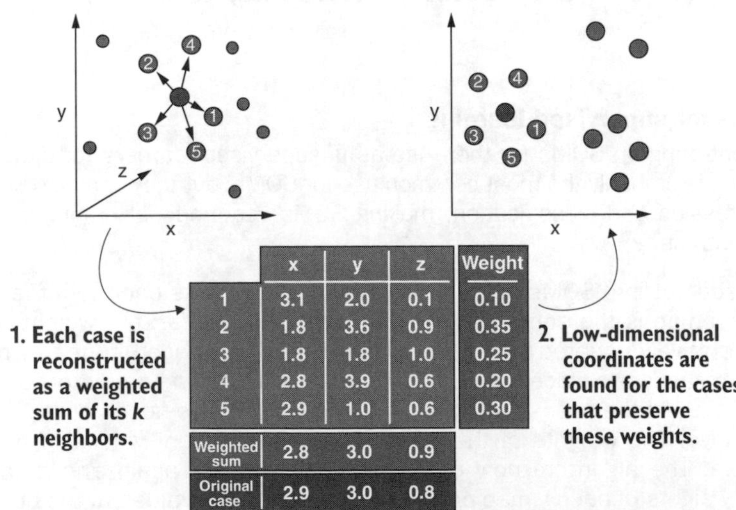

y
z
x
y
x
1. Each case is reconstructed as a weighted sum of its k neighbors.
2. Low-dimensional coordinates are found for the cases that preserve these weights.
x | y | z | Weight
1 | 3.1 | 2.0 | 0.1 | 0.10
2 | 1.8 | 3.6 | 0.9 | 0.35
3 | 1.8 | 1.8 | 1.0 | 0.25
4 | 2.8 | 3.9 | 0.6 | 0.20
5 | 2.9 | 1.0 | 0.6 | 0.30
Weighted sum | 2.8 | 3.0 | 0.9
Original case | 2.9 | 3.0 | 0.8

Figure 15.12 The distance between each case and every other case is calculated, and their k-nearest neighbors are assigned (distance along the z-axis in the top-left plot is indicated by the size of the circle). For each case, the algorithm learns a set of weights, one for each nearest neighbor, that sum to 1. Each neighbor's variable values are multiplied by its weight (so row 1 becomes x = 3.1 × 0.1, y = 2.0 × 0.1, z = 0.1 × 0.1). The weighted values of each neighbor are summed (the columns are summed) to approximate the original values of the selected case.

assigned a weight: a value between 0 and 1, such that the weights for all the k-nearest neighbors sum to 1. The variable values of a particular neighbor are multiplied by its weight (so the weighted values are a fraction of the original values).

> **NOTE** Because the LLE algorithm relies on measuring the distance between cases to calculate the nearest neighbors, it is sensitive to differences between the scales of the variables. It's often a good idea to scale the data before embedding it.

When the weighted values for each variable are added up across the k-nearest neighbors, this new weighted sum should approximate the variable values of the case for which we calculated the k-nearest neighbors in the first place. Therefore, the LLE algorithm learns a weight for each nearest neighbor such that, when we multiply each neighbor by its weight and add these values together, we get the original case (or an approximation). This is what I mean when I say LLE represents each case as a linear, weighted sum of its neighbors.

This process is repeated for each case in the dataset: its k-nearest neighbors are calculated, and then weights are learned that can be used to reconstruct it. Because the weights are combined linearly (summed), the algorithm is essentially learning a linear "patch" around each case. But how does it combine these patches to learn the manifold? Well, the data is placed into a low-dimensional space, typically two or three dimensions, such that the coordinates in this new space preserve the weights learned in the previous step. Put another way, the data is placed in this new feature space such that each case can *still* be calculated from the weighted sum of its neighbors.

15.5 Building your first LLE

In this section, I'll show you how to use the LLE algorithm to reduce the dimensions of a dataset into a two-dimensional map. We'll start with an unusual example that really shows off the power of LLE as a nonlinear dimension-reduction algorithm. This example is unusual because it represents data shaped in a three-dimensional *S* that is unlike something we're likely to encounter in the real world. Then we'll use LLE to create a two-dimensional embedding of our flea circus data to see how it compares to the SOM we created earlier.

15.5.1 Loading and exploring the S-curve dataset

Let's start by installing and loading the lle package:

```
install.packages("lle")

library(lle)
```

Next, let's load the lle_scurve_data dataset from the lle package, give names to its variables, and convert it into a tibble. We have a tibble containing 800 cases and 3 variables.

Listing 15.8 Loading the S-curve dataset

```
data(lle_scurve_data)

colnames(lle_scurve_data) <- c("x", "y", "z")

sTib <- as_tibble(lle_scurve_data)

sTib

# A tibble: 800 x 3
        x     y      z
    <dbl> <dbl>  <dbl>
 1  0.955 4.95  -0.174
 2 -0.660 3.27  -0.773
 3 -0.983 1.26  -0.296
 4  0.954 1.68  -0.180
 5  0.958 0.186 -0.161
 6  0.852 0.558 -0.471
 7  0.168 1.62  -0.978
 8  0.948 2.32   0.215
 9 -0.931 1.51  -0.430
10  0.355 4.06   0.926
# … with 790 more rows
```

This dataset consists of cases that are folded into the shape of the letter *S* in three dimensions. Let's create a three-dimensional plot to visualize this, using the plot3D and plot3Drgl packages (starting with their installation).

Listing 15.9 Plotting the S-curve dataset in three dimensions

```
install.packages(c("plot3D", "plot3Drgl"))

library(plot3D)

scatter3D(x = sTib$x, y = sTib$y, z = sTib$z, pch = 19,
          bty = "b2", colkey = FALSE, theta = 35, phi = 10,
          col = ramp.col(c("darkred", "lightblue")))

plot3Drgl::plotrgl()
```

The `scatter3D()` function allows us to create a three-dimensional plot, and the `plotrgl()` function lets us rotate it interactively. Here is a summary of the arguments to `scatter3D()`:

- `x`, `y`, and `z`—Which variables to plot on their respective axes.
- `pch`—The shape of the points we wish to draw (`19` draws filled circles).
- `bty`—The box type that's drawn around the data (`"b2"` draws a white box with gridlines; use `?scatter3D` to see the alternatives).
- `colkey`—Whether we want a legend for the coloring of each point.
- `theta` and `phi`—The viewing angle of the plot.

- col—The color palette we want to use to indicate the value of the z variable. Here, we use the ramp.col() function to specify the start and end colors of a color gradient.

Once we've created our static plot, we can turn it into an interactive plot that we can rotate by clicking and rotating it with our mouse, by simply calling the plotrgl() function with no arguments.

TIP You can use your mouse scroll wheel to zoom in and out of this interactive plot.

The resulting plot is shown in figure 15.13. Can you see that the data forms a three-dimensional *S*? This is an unusual dataset for sure, but one which I hope demonstrates the power of LLE for learning the manifold that underlies a dataset.

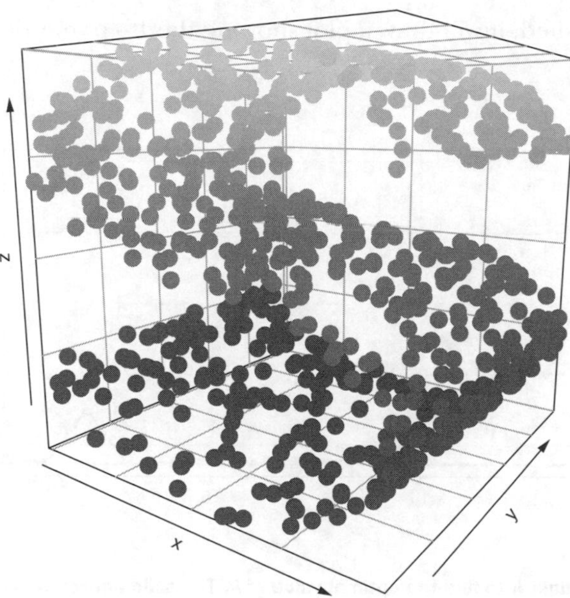

Figure 15.13 The S-curve dataset plotted in three dimensions using the scatter3D() function. The shading of the points is mapped to the z variable.

15.5.2 Training the LLE

Aside from the number of dimensions to which we want to reduce our dataset (usually two or three), *k* is the only hyperparameter we need to select. We can choose the best-performing value of *k* by using the calc_k() function. This function applies the LLE algorithm to our data, using different values of *k* in a range we specify. For each embedding that uses a different *k*, calc_k() calculates the distances between cases in the original data and in the low-dimensional representation. The correlation coefficient between these distances is calculated (ρ, or "rho") and used to calculate a metric (1 – ρ ^ 2) that can be used to select *k*. The value of *k* with the smallest value for this metric is the one that best preserves the distances between cases in the high- and low-dimensional representations.

Here is a summary of the arguments of `calc_k()`:

- The first argument is the dataset.
- The `m` argument is the number of dimensions we want to reduce our dataset into.
- The `kmin` and `kmax` arguments specify the minimum and maximum values of the range of *k* values the function will use.
- The `cpus` argument lets us specify the number of cores we want to use for parallelization (I used `parallel::detectCores()` to use all of them).

NOTE Because we're calculating an embedding for each value of *k*, if our range of values is large and/or our dataset contains many cases, I recommend parallelizing this function by setting the `parallel` argument to `TRUE`.

When this function has finished, it will draw a plot showing the $1 - \rho^2$ metric for each value of *k* (see figure 15.14).

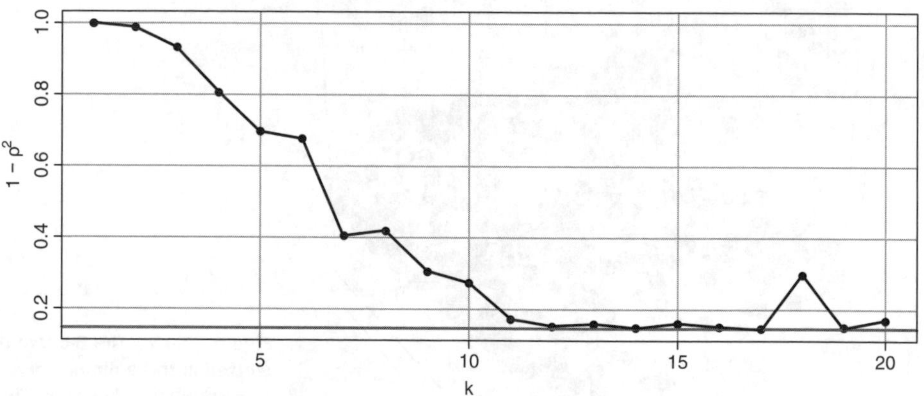

Figure 15.14 Plotting $1 - \rho^2$ against *k* to find the optimal value of *k*. The solid horizontal line indicates the value of *k* with the lowest $1 - \rho^2$.

The `calc_k()` function also returns a `data.frame` containing the $1 - \rho^2$ metric for each value of *k*. We use the `filter()` function to select the row containing the lowest value of the `rho` column. We will use the value of *k* that corresponds to this smallest value, to train our final LLE. In this example, the optimal value of *k* is 17 neighbors.

NOTE This is a little confusing because, actually, we want the highest value of rho (ρ), which gives us the smallest value of $1 - \rho^2$. Despite this column being called `rho`, it contains the values of $1 - \rho^2$, and so we want the smallest of these values.

Finally, we run the LLE algorithm using the `lle()` function, supplying the following:

- The data as the first argument
- The number of dimensions we want to embed into as the `m` argument
- The value of the *k* hyperparameter

Listing 15.10 Calculating *k* and performing the LLE

```
lleK <- calc_k(lle_scurve_data, m = 2, kmin = 1, kmax = 20,
               parallel = TRUE, cpus = parallel::detectCores())

lleBestK <- filter(lleK, rho == min(lleK$rho))

lleBestK

   k    rho
1 17 0.1469

lleCurve <- lle(lle_scurve_data, m = 2, k = lleBestK$k)
```

15.5.3 Plotting the LLE result

Now that we've performed our embedding, let's extract the two new LLE axes and plot the data onto them. This will allow us to visualize our data in this new, two-dimensional space to see if the algorithm has revealed a grouping structure.

Listing 15.11 Plotting the LLE

```
sTib <- sTib %>%
  mutate(LLE1 = lleCurve$Y[, 1],
         LLE2 = lleCurve$Y[, 2])

ggplot(sTib, aes(LLE1, LLE2, col = z)) +
  geom_point() +
  scale_color_gradient(low = "darkred", high = "lightblue") +
  theme_bw()
```

We start by mutating two new columns onto our original tibble, each containing the values of one of the new LLE axes. We then use the `ggplot()` function to plot the two LLE axes against each other, mapping the *z* variable to the color aesthetic. We add a `geom_point()` layer and a `scale_color_gradient()` layer that specifies the extreme colors of a color scale that will be mapped to the *z* variable. This will allow us to directly compare the position of each case in our new, two-dimensional representation to its position in the three-dimensional plot in figure 15.13.

The resulting plot is shown in figure 15.15. Can you see that LLE has flattened out the *S* shape into a flat, two-dimensional rectangle of points? If not, take a look back at figure 15.13 and try to relate the two figures. It's almost as if the data had been drawn onto a folded piece of paper, and LLE straightened it out! This is the power of manifold-learning algorithms for dimension reduction.

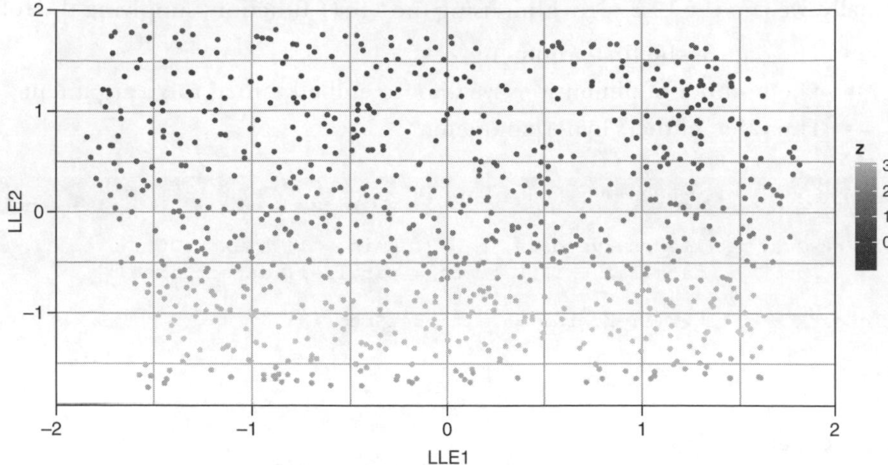

Figure 15.15 Plotting the two-dimensional embedding of the S-curve data. The shading of the points is mapped to the z variable, the same as in figure 15.11.

15.6 Building an LLE of our flea data

One criticism that is sometimes leveled at LLE is that it is designed to handle "toy data"—in other words, data that is constructed to form interesting and unusual shapes, but which rarely (if ever) manifests in real-world datasets. The S-curve data we worked on in the previous section is an example of toy data that was generated to test algorithms that learn a manifold that the data lies on. So in this section, we're going to see how well LLE performs on our flea circus dataset, and whether it can identify the clusters of fleas like our SOM could.

We're going to follow the same procedure as for the S-curve dataset:

1. Use the `calc_k()` function to calculate the best-performing value of *k*.
2. Perform the embedding in two dimensions.
3. Plot the two new LLE axes against each other.

This time, let's map the `species` variable to the color aesthetic, to see how well our LLE embedding separates the clusters.

Listing 15.12 Performing and plotting LLE on the flea dataset

```
lleFleaK <- calc_k(fleaScaled, m = 2, kmin = 1, kmax = 20,
                   parallel = TRUE, cpus = parallel::detectCores())

lleBestFleaK <- filter(lleFleaK, rho == min(lleFleaK$rho))

lleBestFleaK

   k    rho
1 12 0.2482

lleFlea <- lle(fleaScaled, m = 2, k = lleBestFleaK$k)
```

```
fleaTib <- fleaTib %>%
  mutate(LLE1 = lleFlea$Y[, 1],
         LLE2 = lleFlea$Y[, 2])

ggplot(fleaTib, aes(LLE1, LLE2, col = species)) +
  geom_point() +
  theme_bw()
```

The resulting plots are shown in figure 15.16 (I combined the plots into a single figure to save room). LLE seems to do a decent job of separating the different species of fleas, though the result isn't quite as impressive as the way LLE was able to unravel the S-curve dataset.

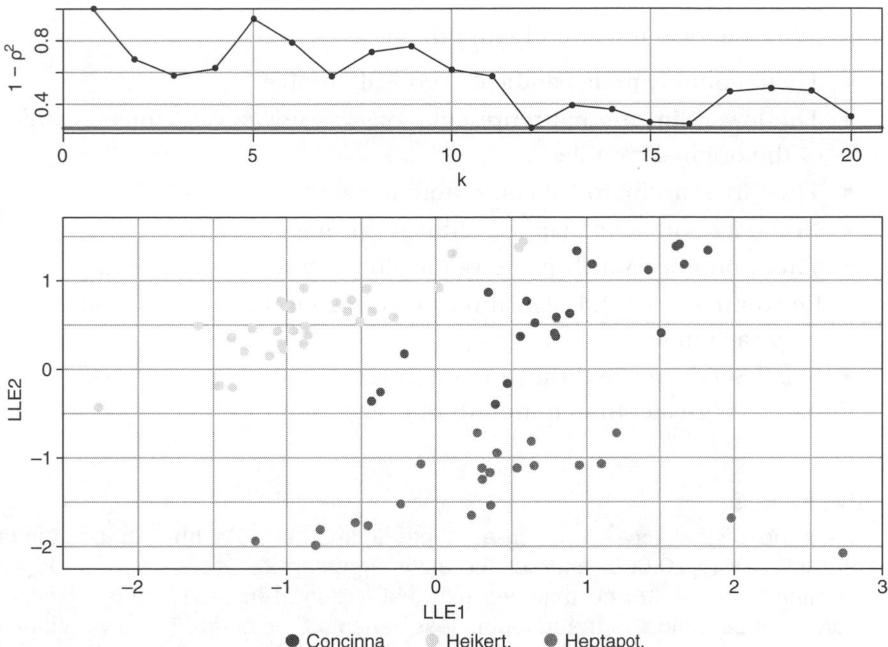

Figure 15.16 Plotting the output of listing 15.12. The top plot shows $1 - \rho^2$ for different values of *k*. The lower plot shows the two-dimensional embedding of the flea data, shaded by species.

> **NOTE** Sadly, because each case is reconstructed as a weighted sum of its neighbors, new data cannot be projected onto an LLE map. For this reason, LLE cannot be easily used as a preprocessing step for other machine learning algorithms, as new data can't be passed through it.

Exercise 2

Add 95% confidence ellipses for each flea species to the lower plot shown in figure 15.16.

15.7 Strengths and weaknesses of SOMs and LLE

While it often isn't easy to tell which algorithms will perform well for a given task, here are some strengths and weaknesses that will help you decide whether the SOM or LLE will perform well for you.

The strengths of SOMs and LLE are as follows:

- They are both nonlinear dimension-reduction algorithms, and so can reveal patterns in the data where linear algorithms (like PCA) may fail.
- New data can be mapped onto an existing SOM.
- They are reasonably inexpensive to train.
- Rerunning the LLE algorithm on the same dataset with the same value of *k* will always produce the same embedding.

The weaknesses of SOMs and LLE are these:

- They cannot natively handle categorical variables.
- The lower-dimensional representations are not directly interpretable in terms of the original variables.
- They are sensitive to data on different scales.
- New data cannot be mapped onto an existing LLE.
- They don't necessarily preserve the global structure of the data.
- Rerunning the SOM algorithm on the same dataset will produce a different map each time.
- Small SOMs can be difficult to interpret, so the algorithm works best with large datasets (greater than hundreds of cases).

Exercise 3

Using the original `somGrid` we created, create another SOM, but increase the number of iterations to 10,000, and set the *alpha* argument to `c(0.1, 0.001)` to slow the learning rate. Create the mapping plot just like in exercise 1. Retrain and plot the SOM multiple times. Is the mapping less variable than before? Can you think why?

Exercise 4

Repeat our LLE embedding, but embed in three dimensions instead of two. Plot this new embedding using the `scatter3()` function, coloring the points by species.

Exercise 5

Repeat our LLE embedding (in two dimensions), but this time use the unscaled variables. Plot the two LLE axes against each other, and map the `species` variable to the color aesthetic. Compare this embedding to the result using scaled variables.

Summary

- SOMs create a grid/map of nodes to which cases in the dataset are assigned.
- SOMs learn patterns in the data by updating the weights of each node until the map converges to a set of weights that preserves similarities among the cases.
- New data can be mapped onto an existing SOM, and SOM nodes can be clustered based on their weights.
- LLE reconstructs each case as a linear weighted sum of its neighbors.
- LLE then embeds the data in a lower-dimensional feature space that preserves the weights.
- LLE is excellent at learning complex manifolds that underlie a set of data, but new data cannot be mapped onto an existing embedding.

Solutions to exercises

1 Train a rectangular, toroidal SOM:

```
somGridRect <- somgrid(xdim = 5, ydim = 5, topo = "rectangular",
                       toroidal = TRUE)

fleaSomRect <- som(fleaScaled, grid = somGridRect, rlen = 5000,
                   alpha = c(0.05, 0.01))

plot(fleaSomRect, type = "mapping", pch = 21,
     bg = nodeCols[as.numeric(fleaTib$species)],
     shape = "straight", bgcol = "lightgrey")

# Making the map toroidal means that nodes on one edge are connected to
# adjacent nodes on the opposite side of the map.
```

2 Add 95% confidence ellipses for each flea species to the plot of LLE1 versus LLE2:

```
ggplot(fleaTib, aes(LLE1, LLE2, col = species)) +
  geom_point() +
  stat_ellipse() +
  theme_bw()
```

3 Train a SOM with more iterations, but a slower learning rate:

```
fleaSomAlpha <- som(fleaScaled, grid = somGrid, rlen = 10000,
                    alpha = c(0.01, 0.001))

plot(fleaSomAlpha, type = "mapping", pch = 21,
     bg = nodeCols[as.numeric(fleaTib$species)],
     shape = "straight", bgcol = "lightgrey")

# While the positions of the groups change between repeats, there is less
# variation in how well cases from the same species cluster together.
# This is because the learning rate is slower and there are more iterations.
```

4 Train an LLE in three dimensions:

```
lleFlea3 <- lle(fleaScaled, m = 3, k = lleBestFleaK$k)

fleaTib <- fleaTib %>%
  mutate(LLE1 = lleFlea3$Y[, 1],
         LLE2 = lleFlea3$Y[, 2],
         LLE3 = lleFlea3$Y[, 3])

scatter3D(x = fleaTib$LLE1, y = fleaTib$LLE2, z = fleaTib$LLE3, pch = 19,
          bty = "b2", colkey = FALSE, theta = 35, phi = 10, cex = 2,
          col = c("red", "blue", "green")[as.integer(fleaTib$species)],
          ticktype = "detailed")

plot3Drgl::plotrgl()
```

5 Train an LLE on the unscaled flea data:

```
lleFleaUnscaled <- lle(dplyr::select(fleaTib, -species),
                       m = 2, k = lleBestFleaK$k)

fleaTib <- fleaTib %>%
  mutate(LLE1 = lleFleaUnscaled$Y[, 1],
         LLE2 = lleFleaUnscaled$Y[, 2])

ggplot(fleaTib, aes(LLE1, LLE2, col = species)) +
  geom_point() +
  theme_bw()

# As we can see, the embedding is different depending on
# whether the variables are scaled or not.
```

Part 5

Clustering

Our next stop in unsupervised learning is clustering. Clustering covers a range of techniques used to identify clusters of cases in a dataset. A *cluster* is a set of cases that are more similar to each other than they are to cases in other clusters.

Conceptually, clustering can be considered similar to classification, in that we are trying to assign a discrete value to each case. The difference is that while classification uses labeled cases to learn patterns in the data that separate the classes, we use clustering when we don't have any prior knowledge about class membership or whether there are distinct classes in the data. Clustering therefore describes a set of algorithms that try to identify a grouping structure within a dataset.

In chapters 16 through 19, I'll arm you with different clustering techniques that can handle a range of clustering problems. Validating the performance of a clustering algorithm can be a challenge, and there may not always be an obvious or even a "correct" answer, but I'll teach you skills to help maximize the information you get from these approaches.

16 Clustering by finding centers with k-means

This chapter covers

- Understanding the need for clustering
- Understanding over- and underfitting for clustering
- Validating the performance of a clustering algorithm

Our first stop in clustering brings us to a very commonly used technique: *k-means clustering*. I've used the word *technique* here rather than *algorithm* because k-means describes a particular *approach* to clustering that multiple algorithms follow. I'll talk about these individual algorithms later in the chapter.

NOTE Don't confuse k-means with k-nearest neighbors! K-means is for unsupervised learning, whereas k-nearest neighbors is a supervised algorithm for classification.

K-means clustering attempts to learn a grouping structure in a dataset. The k-means approach starts with us defining how many clusters we believe there are in the dataset. This is what the *k* stands for; if we set *k* to 3, we will identify three clusters (whether these represent a real grouping structure or not). Arguably, this is a weakness for k-means, because we may not have any prior knowledge as to how many clusters to search for, but I'll show you ways to select a sensible value of *k*.

Once we have defined how many clusters, *k*, we want to search for, k-means will initialize (usually randomly) *k* centers or *centroids* in the dataset. Each centroid may not be an actual case from the data but has a random value for every variable in the data. Each of these centroids represents a cluster, and cases are assigned to the cluster of the centroid closest to them. Iteratively, the centroids move around the feature space in a way that attempts to minimize the variance of the data within each cluster but maximizes the separation of different clusters. At each iteration, cases are assigned to the cluster of the centroid that is closest to them.

By the end of this chapter, I hope you'll understand a general approach to clustering and what over- and underfitting look like for clustering tasks. I'll show you how to apply k-means clustering to a dataset and ways of evaluating clustering performance.

16.1 What is k-means clustering?

In this section, I'll show you how the general procedure for k-means clustering works and then explain the various algorithms that implement it and how they differ. K-means algorithms partition cases in a dataset into *k* clusters, where *k* is an integer defined by us. The clusters returned by k-means algorithms tend to be *n*-dimensionally spherical (where *n* is the number of dimensions of the feature space). This means the clusters tend to form a circle in two dimensions, a sphere in three dimensions, and a hypersphere in more than three dimensions. K-means clusters also tend to have a similar diameter. These are traits that may not be true of the underlying structure in the data.

There are a number of k-means algorithms, but some commonly used ones are as follows:

- Lloyd algorithm (also called Lloyd-Forgy algorithm)
- MacQueen algorithm
- Hartigan-Wong algorithm

The Lloyd, MacQueen, and Hartigan-Wong algorithms are conceptually quite similar but have some differences that affect both their computational cost and their performance on a particular problem. Let's go through each algorithm to explain how it works.

16.1.1 Lloyd's algorithm

In this section, I'll show you the easiest of these three algorithms to understand: Lloyd's algorithm. Imagine that you're a sports scientist, interested in the biophysical differences among runners. You measure the resting heart rate and maximum oxygen consumption of a cohort of runners, and you want to use k-means to identify clusters of runners that might benefit from different training regimens.

Let's say you have prior reason to believe there may be three distinct clusters of athletes in the dataset. The first step in Lloyd's algorithm is to randomly initialize *k* (three in this case) centroids in the data (see figure 16.1). Next, the distance between each case and each centroid is calculated. This distance is commonly the Euclidean distance (straight-line distance) but can be other distance metrics, such as the Manhattan distance (taxi cab distance).

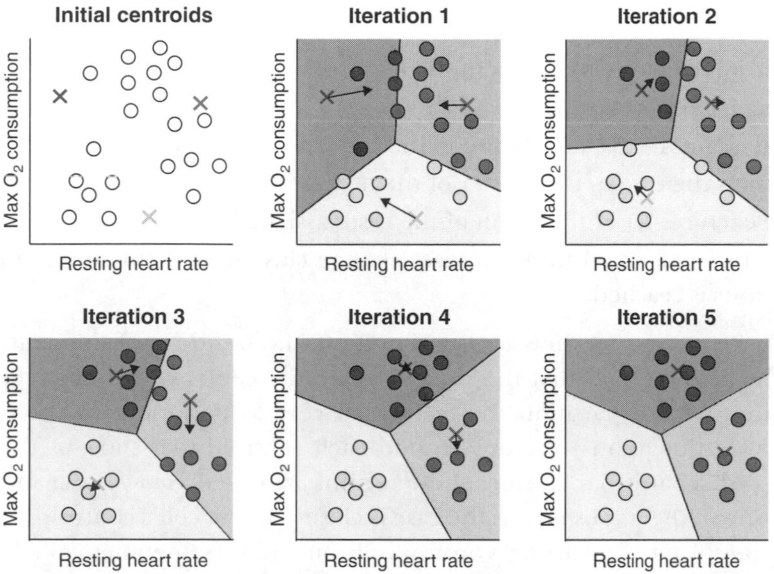

Figure 16.1 Five iterations of k-means clustering. In the top-left plot, three initial centers are randomly generated in the feature space (crosses). Cases are assigned to the cluster of their nearest center. At each iteration, each center moves to the mean of the cases in its cluster (indicated by arrows). The feature space can be partitioned up into Voronoi cells (I'll discuss these shortly), indicated by the shaded regions, that show regions of the feature space closest to a particular centroid.

> **NOTE** Because k-means relies on a distance metric, it's important to scale variables if they are measured on different scales; otherwise, variables on larger scales will disproportionately influence the result.

Each case is assigned to the cluster represented by its nearest centroid. In this way, each centroid serves as a *prototype* case for its cluster. Next, the centroids are moved, such that they are placed at the mean of the cases that were assigned to their cluster in the previous step (this is why the approach is called *k-means*).

The process now repeats itself: the distance between each case and each centroid is calculated, and cases are assigned to the cluster of the nearest centroid. Can you see that, because the centroids update and move around the feature space, the centroid nearest to a particular case may change over time? This process continues until no cases change clusters from one iteration to the next, or until a maximum number of iterations is reached. Notice that between iterations 4 and 5 in figure 16.1, no cases change clusters, so the algorithm stops.

NOTE Because the initial centers are usually randomly selected, it's important that we repeat the procedure several times, with new random initial centers each time. We can then use the centers that start with the lowest within-cluster sum of squared error.

Let's summarize the steps of Lloyd's algorithm:

1. Select *k*.
2. Randomly initialize *k* centers in the feature space.
3. For each case:
   a. Calculate the distance between the case and each center.
   b. Assign the case to the cluster of the nearest centroid.
4. Place each center at the mean of the cases assigned to its cluster.
5. Repeat steps 3 and 4 until no cases change clusters or a maximum number of iterations is reached.

In figure 16.1, can you see how at each iteration, the positions of the centroids are updated (the arrows) such that they move toward the center of genuine clusters? At each iteration, we can partition the feature space into polygonal (or polytopal, in more than two dimensions) regions around each centroid that show us the regions that "belong" to a particular cluster. These regions are called *Voronoi cells*; and if a case falls inside one of them, this means the case is closest to that cell's centroid and will be assigned to its cluster. Visualizing Voronoi cells on a plot (sometimes called a *Voronoi map*) is a useful way of visualizing how a clustering algorithm has partitioned the feature space.

16.1.2 MacQueen's algorithm

MacQueen's algorithm is extremely similar to Lloyd's algorithm, varying just subtly in when the centroids get updated. Lloyd's algorithm is called a *batch* or *offline* algorithm, meaning it updates the centroids together at the end of an iteration. MacQueen's algorithm, on the other hand, updates the centroids each time a case changes clusters and once the algorithm has passed through all the cases in the data.

NOTE Whereas Lloyd's algorithm is said to be a batch or offline algorithm, MacQueen's is said to be an *incremental* or *online* algorithm, because it updates the centroids each time a case moves clusters, rather than after a pass through all the data.

Just like with Lloyd's algorithm, MacQueen's algorithm initializes *k* centers, assigns each case to the cluster of the nearest centroid, and updates the position of the centroid to match the mean of its nearest cases. Then the algorithm considers each case in turn and calculates its distance to each centroid. If the case changes clusters (because it's now closer to a different centroid), both the new and old centroid positions are updated. The algorithm continues through the dataset, considering each case in turn. Once all cases have been considered, the centroid positions are updated again. If no cases change clusters, the algorithm stops; otherwise, it will perform another pass.

A benefit of MacQueen's algorithm over Lloyd's algorithm is that it tends to converge more quickly to an optimal solution. However, it may be slightly more computationally expensive for very large datasets.

Let's summarize the steps of MacQueen's algorithm:

1. Select *k*.
2. Randomly initialize *k* centers in the feature space.
3. Assign each case to the cluster of its nearest center.
4. Place each center at the mean of the cases assigned to its cluster.
5. For each case:
   a. Calculate the distance between the case and each centroid.
   b. Assign the case to the cluster of the nearest centroid.
   c. If the case changed clusters, update the position of the new and old centroids.
6. Once all cases have been considered, update all centroids.
7. If no cases change clusters, stop; otherwise, repeat step 5.

16.1.3 Hartigan-Wong algorithm

The third k-means algorithm is a little different from the Lloyd and MacQueen algorithms. The Hartigan-Wong algorithm starts by initializing *k* random centers and assigning each case to the cluster of its nearest center, just as we saw in the other two algorithms. Here's the different bit: for each case in the dataset, the algorithm calculates the sum of squared error of that case's current cluster *if that case was removed*, and the sum of squared error of each of the other clusters *if that case was included in those clusters*. Recall from previous chapters that the sum of squared error (or simply the sum of squares) is the difference between each case's values and its predicted values (in this context, its centroid), squared and summed across all the cases. If you prefer this in mathematical notation, have a look at equation 16.1.

$$SS = \sum_{i \in k} (x_i - c_k)^2 \qquad \textbf{Equation 16.1}$$

where $i \in k$ is the *i*th case belonging to cluster *k*, and c_k is the centroid of cluster *k*.

The cluster with the smallest sum of squared error (when including the case currently under consideration) is assigned as the cluster for that case. If a case changed clusters, then the centroids of the old and new clusters are updated to the mean of the cases in their cluster. The algorithm continues until no cases change clusters. As a result, a case could be assigned to a particular cluster (because it reduces the sum of squared error) even though it is closer to the centroid of another cluster.

Let's summarize the steps of the Hartigan-Wong algorithm:

1. Select *k*.
2. Randomly initialize *k* centers in the feature space.

3. Assign each case to the cluster of its nearest center.
4. Place each center at the mean of the cases assigned to its cluster.
5. For each case:
   a. Calculate the sum of squared error for its cluster, omitting the case under consideration.
   b. Calculate the sum of squared error for the other clusters, as if that case were included.
   c. Assign the case to the cluster with the smallest sum of squared error.
   d. If the case changed clusters, update the position of the new and old centroids.
6. If no cases change clusters, stop; otherwise, repeat step 5.

The Hartigan-Wong algorithm *tends* to find a better clustering structure than either the Lloyd or MacQueen algorithms, although we are always subject to the "no free lunch" theorem. Hartigan-Wong is also more computationally expensive than the other two algorithms, so it will be considerably slower for large datasets.

Which algorithm do we choose? Well, the choice is a discrete hyperparameter, so we can use hyperparameter tuning to help us choose the best-performing method and make sure we don't make the Wong choice!

16.2 Building your first k-means model

In this section, I'll show you how to build a k-means model in R, using the mlr package. I'll cover creating a cluster task and learner, and some methods we can use to evaluate the performance of a clustering algorithm.

Imagine that you're looking for clusters of white blood cells from patients with graft versus host disease (GvHD). GvHD is an unpleasant disease where residual white blood cells in transplanted tissue attack the body of the patient receiving the transplant. You take a biopsy from each patient and measure different proteins on the surface of each cell. You hope to create a clustering model that will help you identify different cell types from the biopsy, to help you better understand the disease. Let's start by loading the mlr and tidyverse packages:

```
library(mlr)

library(tidyverse)
```

16.2.1 Loading and exploring the GvHD dataset

Now let's load the data, which is built into the mclust package, convert it into a tibble (with `as_tibble()`), and explore it a little. We have a tibble containing 6,809 cases and 4 variables, each of which is a different protein measured on the surface of each cell.

Listing 16.1 Loading and exploring the GvHD dataset

```
data(GvHD, package = "mclust")

gvhdTib <- as_tibble(GvHD.control)
```

```
gvhdTib

# A tibble: 6,809 x 4
     CD4  CD8b   CD3   CD8
   <dbl> <dbl> <dbl> <dbl>
 1   199   420   132   226
 2   294   311   241   164
 3    85    79    14   218
 4    19     1   141   130
 5    35    29     6   135
 6   376   346   138   176
 7    97   329   527   406
 8   200   342   145   189
 9   422   433   163    47
10   391   390   147   190
# ... with 6,799 more rows
```

NOTE Calling `data(GvHD, package = "mclust")` actually loads two datasets: GvHD.control and GvHD.pos. We're going to work with the GvHD.control dataset, but at the end of this section, I'll get you to build a clustering model on the GvHD.pos dataset too.

Because k-means algorithms use a distance metric to assign cases to clusters, it's important that our variables are scaled so variables on different scales are given equal weight. All of our variables are continuous, so we can simply pipe our entire tibble into the `scale()` function. Remember that this will center and scale each variable by subtracting the mean and dividing by the standard deviation.

Listing 16.2 Scaling the GvHD dataset

```
gvhdScaled <- gvhdTib %>% scale()
```

Next, let's plot the data using our good friend `ggpairs()` from the GGally package. This time, we modify the way `ggpairs()` draws the facets. We use the `upper`, `lower`, and `diag` arguments to specify what kind of plots should be drawn above, below, and on the diagonal, respectively. Each of these arguments takes a list where each list element can be used to specify a different type of plot for continuous variables, discrete variables, and combinations of the two. Here, I've chosen to draw 2D density plots on the upper plots, scatterplots on the lower plots, and density plots on the diagonal.

To prevent overcrowding, we want to reduce the size of the points on the lower plots. To change any of the graphical options of the plots (such as size and color of the geoms), we just need to wrap the name of the plot type (literally) inside the `wrap()` function, along with the options we're changing. Here, we use `wrap("points", size = 0.5)` to draw scatterplots on the lower panels, with a smaller point size than the default.

NOTE Remember that *geom* stands for *geometric object*, referring to graphical elements like lines, dots, and bars on a plot.

Listing 16.3 Creating pairwise plots with ggpairs()

```
library(GGally)

ggpairs(GvHD.control,
        upper = list(continuous = "density"),
        lower = list(continuous = wrap("points", size = 0.5)),
        diag = list(continuous = "densityDiag")) +
  theme_bw()
```

> **NOTE** The default diagonal plot for continuous variables is a density plot. I explicitly defined it as such here anyway so you can see how you can control the upper, lower, and diagonal plots independently.

The resulting plot is shown in figure 16.2. Can you see different clusters of cases in the data? The human brain is pretty good at identifying clusters in two or even three dimensions, and it looks as though there are at least four clusters in the dataset. The density plots are useful to help us see dense regions of cases, which simply appear black in the scatterplots.

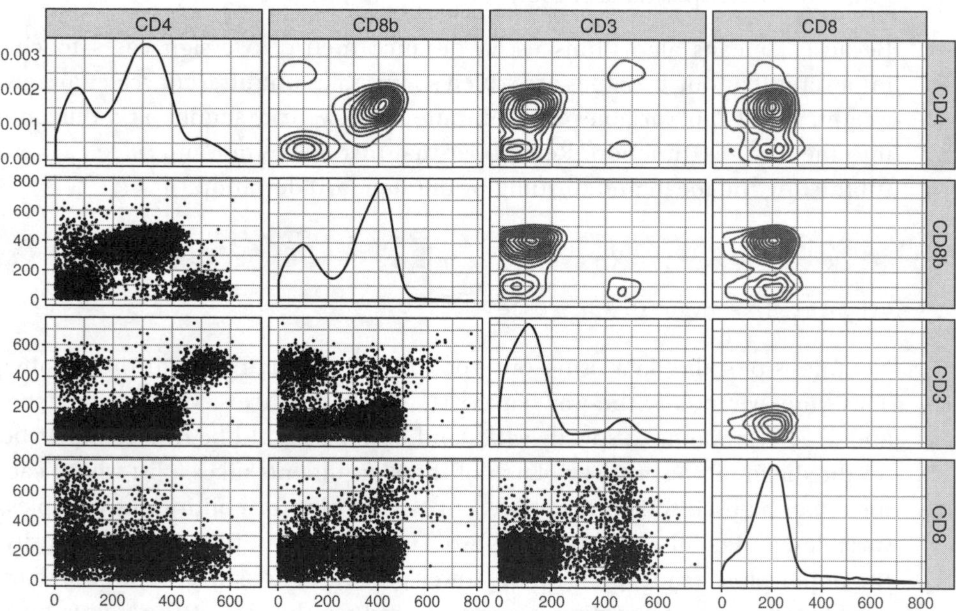

Figure 16.2 ggpairs() **plot of each variable against every other variable in our GvHD dataset. Scatterplots are shown below the diagonal, 2D density plots are shown above the diagonal, and 1D density plots are drawn on the diagonal. It appears as if there are multiple clusters in the data.**

16.2.2 Defining our task and learner

In this section, I'll show you how to define a clustering task and clustering learner. In mlr, we create a clustering task by using the `makeClusterTask()` function (no surprises there). We supply our scaled data (converted into a data frame) as the `data` argument.

IMPORTANT Notice that, unlike creating a supervised learning task (for classification or regression), we no longer need to supply the `target` argument. This is because in an unsupervised learning task, there is no labels variable to use as a target.

Let's use the `listLearners()` function that you learned about all the way back in chapter 3 to see what algorithms have been implemented by the mlr package so far. At the time of writing, only nine clustering algorithms are available to us. Admittedly, this is far fewer than the number of algorithms available for classification and regression, but mlr still provides some useful tools for clustering. If you want to use an algorithm that mlr doesn't currently wrap, you can always implement it yourself (visit the mlr website to see how: http://mng.bz/E1Pj).

Now let's define our k-means learner. We do this using the familiar `makeLearner()` function, this time supplying `"cluster.kmeans"` as the name of the learner. We use the `par.vals` argument to supply two arguments to the learner: `iter.max` and `nstart`.

NOTE Just as the prefixes for classification and regression learners were `classif.` and `regr.`, respectively, the prefix for clustering learners is `cluster.`.

Listing 16.4 Creating a cluster task and learner with mlr

```
gvhdTask <- makeClusterTask(data = as.data.frame(gvhdScaled))

listLearners("cluster")$class

[1] "cluster.cmeans"        "cluster.Cobweb"        "cluster.dbscan"
[4] "cluster.EM"            "cluster.FarthestFirst" "cluster.kkmeans"
[7] "cluster.kmeans"        "cluster.SimpleKMeans"  "cluster.XMeans"

kMeans <- makeLearner("cluster.kmeans",
                      par.vals = list(iter.max = 100, nstart = 10))
```

The `iter.max` argument sets an upper limit for the number of times the algorithm will cycle through the data (the default is 10). The k-means algorithms will all stop once cases stop moving clusters, but setting a maximum can be useful for large datasets that take a long time to converge. Later in this section, I'll show you how to tell if your clustering model has converged before reaching this limit.

The `nstart` argument controls how many times the function will randomly initialize the centers. Recall that the initial centers are usually randomly initialized somewhere in the feature space: this can have an impact on the final centroid positions and, therefore, the final cluster memberships. Setting the `nstart` argument higher than the default value of 1 will randomly initialize this number of centers. For each set of initial centers, the cases are assigned to the cluster of their nearest center in each set, and the set with the smallest within-cluster sum of squared error is then used for the rest of the clustering algorithm. In this way, the algorithm selects the set of centers that is already most similar to the real cluster centroids in the data. Increasing `nstart` is arguably more important than increasing the number of iterations.

TIP If you have a dataset with very clearly separable clusters, setting `nstart` higher than 1 might be a waste of computational resources. However, unless your dataset is very large, it's usually a good idea to set `nstart` > 1; in listing 16.4, I set mine to 10.

16.2.3 Choosing the number of clusters

In this section, I'll show you how we can sensibly choose the value of *k*, which defines the number of centers, and therefore clusters, that our model will identify. The need to choose *k* is often cited as a weakness of k-means clustering. This is because choosing *k* can be subjective. If you have prior domain knowledge as to how many clusters should theoretically be present in a dataset, then you should use this knowledge to guide your selection. If you're using clustering as a preprocessing step before a supervised learning algorithm (classification, for example), then the choice is quite easy: tune *k* as a hyperparameter of the whole model-building process, and compare the predictions of the final model against the original labels.

But what if we have no prior knowledge and no labeled data to compare against? And what happens if we get our selection wrong? Well, just like for classification and regression, clustering is subject to the bias-variance trade-off. If we want to generalize a clustering model to the wider population, it's important we neither overfit nor underfit the training data. Figure 16.3 illustrates what under- and overfitting might look like for a clustering problem. When we underfit, we fail to identify and separate real clusters in the data; but when we overfit, we split real clusters into smaller, nonsensical clusters that simply don't exist in the wider population.

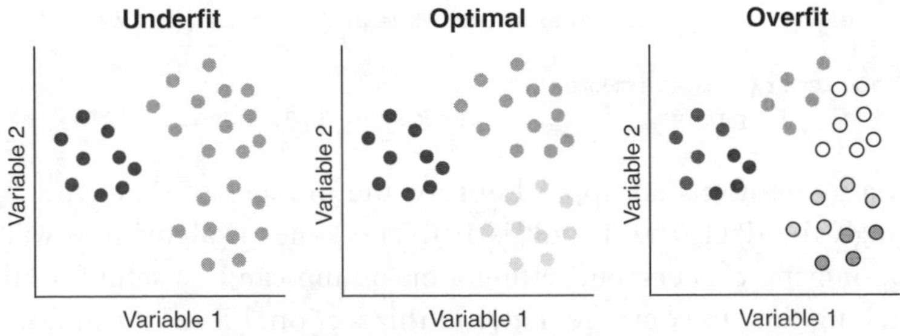

Figure 16.3 What under- and overfitting looks like for clustering tasks. In the left-side plot, the clusters are underfit (fewer clusters have been identified than actually exist). In the right-side plot, the clusters are overfit (real clusters are broken up into smaller clusters). In the center plot, an optimal clustering model has been found that faithfully represents the structure in the data.

Avoiding over- and underfitting clustering problems is not straightforward. People have proposed many different methods for avoiding over- and underfitting, and they won't all agree with one another for a particular problem. Many of these methods rely on the calculation of *internal cluster metrics*, which are statistics that aim to quantify the "quality" of a clustering result.

NOTE What constitutes "good-quality" clusters is poorly defined and somewhat subjective, but people typically mean that each cluster is as compact as possible, while the distances between clusters are as large as possible.

These metrics are "internal" because they are calculated from the clustered data itself rather than by comparing the result to any external label or ground truth. A common approach to selecting the number of clusters is to train multiple clustering models over a range of cluster numbers and compare the cluster metrics for each model to help choose the best-fitting one. Three commonly used internal cluster metrics are as follows:

- Davies-Bouldin index
- Dunn index
- Pseudo F statistic

Using the Davies-Bouldin index to evaluate clustering performance

The Davies-Bouldin index (named after its creators, David Davies and Donald Bouldin) quantifies the average separability of each cluster from its nearest counterpart. It does this by calculating the ratio of the within-cluster variance (also called the *scatter*) to the separation between cluster centroids (see figure 16.4).

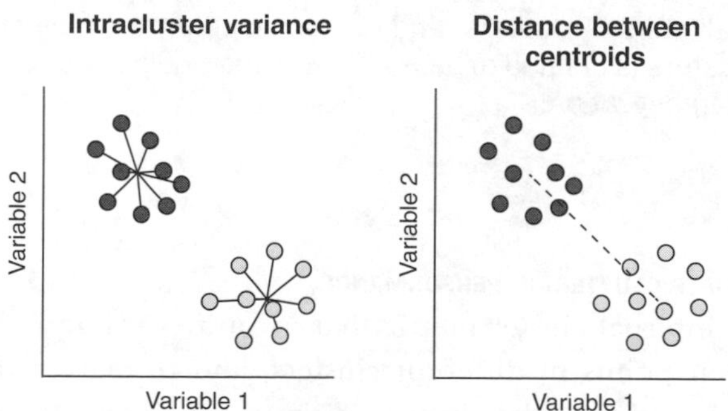

Figure 16.4 The Davies-Bouldin index calculates the intracluster (within-cluster) variance (left-side plot) and the distance between the centroids of each cluster (right-side plot). For each cluster, its nearest neighboring cluster is identified, and the sum of their intracluster variances is divided by the difference between their centroids. This value is calculated for each cluster, and the Davies-Bouldin index is the mean of these values.

If we fix the distance between clusters but make the cases within each cluster more spread out, the Davies-Bouldin index will get larger. Conversely, if we fix the within-cluster variance but move the clusters farther apart from each other, the index will get smaller. In theory, the smaller the value (which is bounded between zero and infinity), the better the separation between clusters. Boiled down into plain English, the Davies-Bouldin index quantifies the mean separability between each cluster and its most similar counterpart.

Calculating the Davies-Bouldin index

It's not necessary for you to memorize the formula for the Davies-Bouldin index (in fact, it's reasonably complex). If you are interested, we can define the scatter within clusters as

$$\text{scatter}_k = \left(\frac{1}{n_k} \sum_{i \in k}^{n_k} (x_i - c_k)^2\right)^{1/2}$$

where scatter_k is a measure of the scatter within cluster k, n_k is the number of cases in cluster k, x_i is the ith case in cluster k, and c_k is the centroid of cluster k.

The separation between clusters can be defined as

$$\text{separation}_{j,k} = \left(\sum_{1 \leq j \leq k}^{N} (c_j - c_k)^2\right)^{1/2}$$

where $\text{separation}_{j,k}$ is a measure of the separation between clusters j and k, c_j and c_k are their respective centroids, and N is the total number of clusters.

The ratio between the within-cluster scatter and the separation between two clusters is then calculated as

$$\text{ratio}_{j,k} = \frac{\text{scatter}_j + \text{scatter}_k}{\text{separation}_{j,k}}$$

This ratio is calculated for all pairs of clusters, and for each cluster, the largest ratio between it and the other clusters is defined to be R_k. The Davies-Bouldin index is then simply the mean of these largest ratios:

$$\text{DB} = \frac{1}{N} \sum_{k=1}^{N} R_k$$

USING THE DUNN INDEX TO EVALUATE CLUSTERING PERFORMANCE

The Dunn index is another internal cluster metric that quantifies the ratio between the smallest distance between points in different clusters, and the largest distance within any of the clusters, referred to as the cluster's *diameter* (see figure 16.5). These can be any distance metric but are commonly the Euclidean distance.

The intuition here is that if we maintain the same diameter of our clusters but move the closest pair apart, the Dunn index will get larger. Conversely, if we maintain

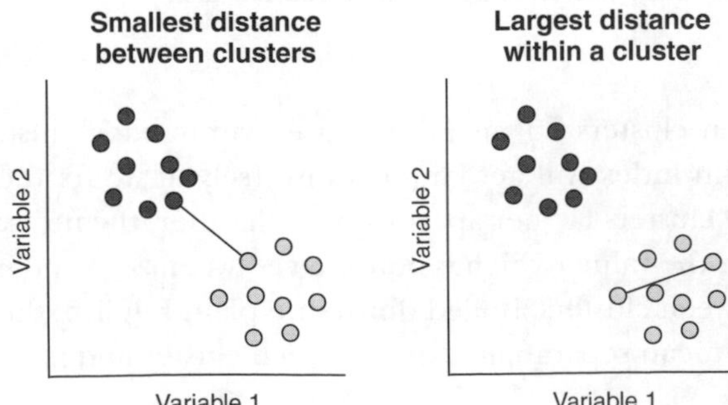

Figure 16.5 The Dunn index quantifies the ratio between the smallest distance between cases in different clusters (left-side plot) and the largest distance within a cluster (right-side plot).

the same distance between cluster centroids but shrink the diameter of the clusters (by making the clusters denser), the Dunn index will also increase. As such, the number of clusters resulting in the largest Dunn index is the one that results in the largest minimum distance between clusters and the smallest maximum distance between cases within a cluster.

> **Calculating the Dunn index**
>
> It's not necessary for you to memorize the formula for the Dunn index. If you are interested, we can define the Dunn index as
>
> $$\text{Dunn} = \min_{1 \leq i \leq k} \left\{ \min_{k} \left(\frac{\delta(c_i, c_j)}{\max\limits_{1 \leq i \neq i \leq k} \Delta(c_k)} \right) \right\}$$
>
> where $\delta(c_i,c_j)$ represents all pairwise differences between cases in clusters i and j, and $\delta(c_i)$ represents all pairwise differences between cases in cluster k.

USING THE PSEUDO F STATISTIC TO EVALUATE CLUSTERING PERFORMANCE

The pseudo F statistic is a ratio of the *between-cluster sum of squares* to the *within-cluster sum of squares* (see figure 16.6). The between-cluster sum of squares is the squared difference between each cluster centroid and the *grand centroid* (the centroid of the data as if it was all in one big cluster), weighted by the number of cases in that cluster, added up across each cluster. This is another way of measuring how separated the clusters are from each other (the farther the cluster centroids are from each other, the smaller the between sum of squares will be). The within-cluster sum of squares is the squared difference between each case and its cluster's centroid, added up across each cluster. This is another way of measuring the variance or dispersion within each cluster (the denser each cluster is, the smaller the within-cluster sum of squares will be).

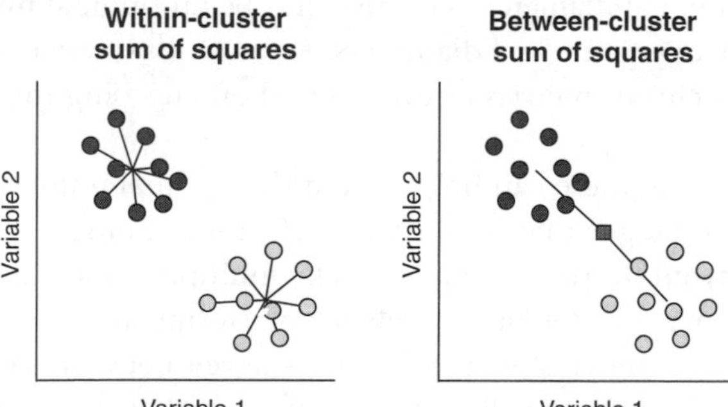

Figure 16.6 The pseudo F statistic is the ratio of the between-cluster sum of squares (right-side plot) to the within-cluster sum of squares (left-side plot). The grand centroid is shown as a square in the right-side plot.

Because the pseudo F statistic is also a ratio, if we maintain the same cluster variance but move the clusters farther apart, the pseudo F statistic will increase. Conversely, if we maintain the same separation between the cluster centroids but make the clusters more spread out, the pseudo F statistic will decrease. As such, the number of clusters that results in the largest pseudo F statistic is, in theory, the one that maximizes the separation of the clusters.

Calculating the pseudo F statistic

It's not necessary for you to memorize the formula for the pseudo F statistic. If you are interested, we can define the pseudo F statistic as

$$\text{Pseudo F} = \frac{SS_{between}/(k-1)}{SS_{within}/(n-k)}$$

where $SS_{between}$ and SS_{within} are calculated as

$$SS_{between} = \sum_{k}^{N} n_k (c_k - c_g)^2$$

$$SS_{within} = \sum_{k}^{N} \sum_{i \in k}^{n_k} (x_i - c_k)^2$$

where there are N clusters, n_k is the number of cases in cluster k, c_k is the centroid of cluster k, and c_g is the grand centroid of all the cases.

These are just three among the many commonly used internal cluster metrics, and at this point you might be wondering why there isn't just one metric that tells us how well separated our clusters are. The reason is that these metrics will tend to agree with each other when we have very clear, well-defined clusters, but will start to disagree with each other as the solution becomes more ambiguous, with some of the metrics performing better than others in certain circumstances. For example, internal cluster metrics that rely on calculating sums of squares may prefer to select a number of clusters that results in clusters of equal diameter. This may not be an optimal number of clusters if the real clusters have very unequal diameters. As such, it's often a good idea to consider multiple internal cluster metrics as evidence when choosing the number of clusters.

So internal cluster metrics like these can help us find the optimal number of clusters. But there is still always a danger that we might overfit the training data by *overclustering*. One approach to avoid overclustering is to take multiple bootstrap samples (sampling cases with replacement) of the data, apply the clustering algorithm to each sample, and compare how well the cluster memberships agree between samples. If there is high stability (in other words, the clustering result is *stable* between samples), then we have more confidence that we are not fitting the noise in the data.

For clustering algorithms that are able to predict the clusters of new data, like the k-means algorithms, another approach is to use a cross-validation-like procedure. This involves splitting the data into training and test sets (using k-fold, for example), training the clustering algorithm on the training set, predicting the cluster membership of the cases in the test set, and calculating internal cluster metrics for the predicted clusters. This approach has the benefit of allowing us both to test cluster stability and to calculate the metric on data the algorithm never saw. This is the approach we'll use to select the optimal number of clusters using k-means in this chapter.

NOTE With k-means clustering, new data can be projected onto an existing clustering model by simply assigning the new cases to the cluster of the nearest centroid.

16.2.4 Tuning k and the algorithm choice for our k-means model

In this section, I'll show you how we can tune *k* (the number of clusters) and our choice of k-means algorithm, using a cross-validation-like approach with internal cluster metrics applied to the predicted clusters. Let's start by defining our hyperparameter search space using the `makeParamSet()` function. We define two discrete hyperparameters over which to search for values: `centers`, which is the number of clusters the algorithm will search for (*k*), and `algorithm`, which specifies which of the three algorithms we will use to fit the model.

TIP Just as we've seen before, we can use `getParamSet(kMeans)` to find all the hyperparameters available to us.

We then define our search method as a grid search (to try every combination of hyperparameters) and define our cross-validation approach as 10-fold.

Listing 16.5 Defining how the hyperparameters will be tuned

```
kMeansParamSpace <- makeParamSet(
  makeDiscreteParam("centers", values = 3:8),
  makeDiscreteParam("algorithm",
                    values = c("Hartigan-Wong", "Lloyd", "MacQueen")))

gridSearch <- makeTuneControlGrid()

kFold <- makeResampleDesc("CV", iters = 10)
```

Now that we've defined our search space, let's perform the tuning. To use the Davies-Bouldin index and the pseudo F statistic performance measures, you'll first need to install the clusterSim package.

TIP Two other internal cluster metrics are implemented by mlr: silhouette and G2 (use `listMeasures("cluster")` to list the available metrics). Both metrics are more computationally expensive to compute, so we won't use them here, but they are additional metrics to help us decide on an appropriate number of clusters.

To perform tuning, we use the `tuneParams()` function. Because we didn't use this function during the dimension-reduction part of the book, let's refresh our memory of the arguments:

- The first argument is the name of the learner.
- The `task` argument is the name of our clustering task.
- The `resampling` argument is the name of our cross-validation strategy.
- The `par.set` argument is our hyperparameter search space.
- The `control` argument is our search method.
- The `measures` argument allows us to define which performance measures we want to calculate for each iteration of the search. Here, we ask for the Davies-Bouldin index (`db`), Dunn index (`dunn`), and pseudo F statistic (`G1`), in that order.

TIP We can supply a list of as many performance metrics as we want. All of them will be calculated for each iteration of the search, but the combination of hyperparameters that optimizes the value of the *first* metric in the list will always be returned from tuning. The mlr package also "knows" which metrics should be maximized and which ones should be minimized for best performance.

Just to reiterate: when we perform the tuning, for each combination of hyperparameters, the data will be split into 10 folds, and the k-means algorithm will be trained on the training set of each fold. The cases in each test set will be assigned to their nearest cluster centroid, and the internal cluster metric will be calculated on these test set clusters. Calling the result of the tuning shows us that Lloyd's algorithm with four clusters gave the lowest (most optimal) Davies-Bouldin index.

Listing 16.6 Performing the tuning experiment

```
install.packages("clusterSim")

tunedK <- tuneParams(kMeans, task = gvhdTask,
                     resampling = kFold,
                     par.set = kMeansParamSpace,
                     control = gridSearch,
                     measures = list(db, dunn, G1))

tunedK

Tune result:
Op. pars: centers=4; algorithm=Lloyd
db.test.mean=0.8010,dunn.test.mean=0.0489,G1.test.mean=489.5331
```

NOTE At the end of the tuning process, did you get the warning `did not converge in 100 iterations`? This is how to tell whether you've set the `iter.max` argument too low in your learner definition. Your choices are to either choose to accept the result as is, which may or may not be a near-optimal solution, or, if you have the computational budget, increase `iter.max`.

> **Exercise 1**
>
> Change our `kmeans` definition (created in listing 16.4) such that the value of `iter.max` is 200. Rerun the tuning procedure in listing 16.6. Does the error about not converging disappear?

To get a better understanding of how our three internal metrics vary with both cluster number and algorithm choice, let's plot the tuning process. Recall that to do this, we first need to extract the tuning data from our tuning result using the `generateHyperParsEffectData()` function. Call the `$data` component from the `kMeansTuningData` object so you can see how it's structured (I won't print it here, for the sake of space).

> **NOTE** Notice that we have a metric we didn't ask for: `exec.time`, which records how long it took to train a model with each combination of hyperparameters, in seconds.

Let's plot this data such that we have a different facet per performance metric and a different line per algorithm. To do this, we first need to gather the data such that the name of each performance metric is in one column and the value of the metric is in another column. We do this using the `gather()` function, naming the key column `"Metric"` and the value column `"Value"`. Because we only want *these* columns gathered, we supply a vector of columns we don't want to gather. Print the new, gathered dataset to make sure you understand what we did. Having the data in this format allows us to facet by algorithm and plot separate lines for each metric.

To plot the data, we use the `ggplot()` function, mapping `centers` (the number of clusters) and `Value` to the x and y aesthetics, respectively. By mapping `algorithm` to the `col` aesthetic, separate `geom_line()` and `geom_point()` layers will be drawn for each algorithm (with different colors). We use the `facet_wrap()` function to draw a separate subplot for each performance metric, setting the `scales = "free_y"` argument to allow different y-axes for each facet (as they have different scales). Finally, we add the `geom_line()` and `geom_point()` layers and a theme.

Listing 16.7 Plotting the tuning experiment

```
kMeansTuningData <- generateHyperParsEffectData(tunedK)

kMeansTuningData$data

gatheredTuningData <- gather(kMeansTuningData$data,
                             key = "Metric",
                             value = "Value",
                             c(-centers, -iteration, -algorithm))
```

```
ggplot(gatheredTuningData, aes(centers, Value, col = algorithm)) +
  facet_wrap(~ Metric, scales = "free_y") +
  geom_line() +
  geom_point() +
  theme_bw()
```

The resulting plot is shown in figure 16.7. Each facet shows a different performance metric, and each separate line shows one of the three algorithms. Notice that the clustering models with four clusters (centers), the Davies-Bouldin index is minimized, and the Dunn index and pseudo F statistic (G1) are maximized. Because lower values of the Davies-Bouldin index and higher values of the Dunn index and pseudo F statistic indicate (in theory) better-separated clusters, all three of the internal metrics agree with each other that four is the optimal number of clusters for this dataset. There is also very little disagreement between the different algorithms, particularly at the optimal value of four clusters.

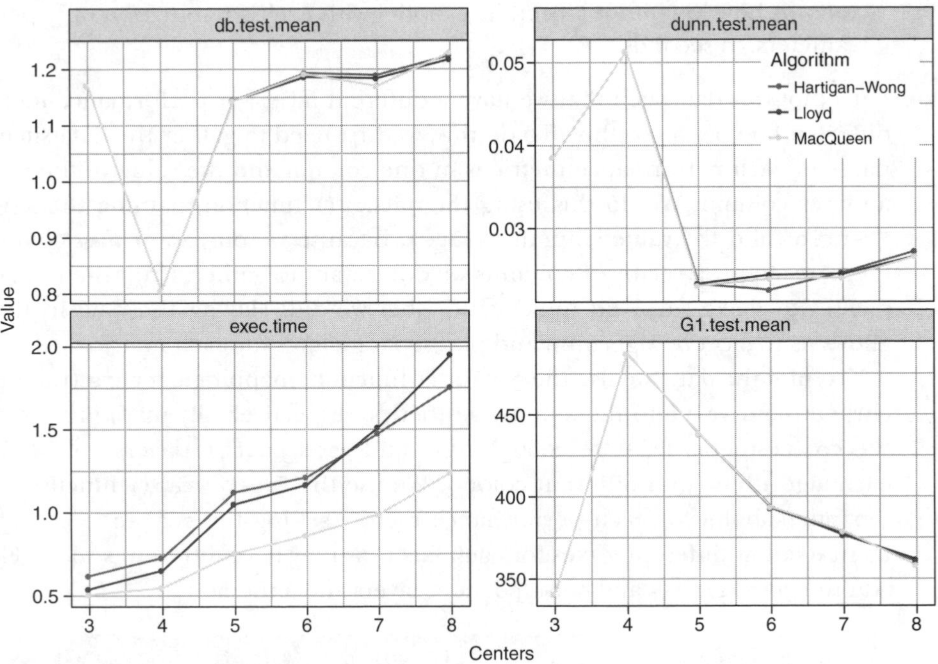

Figure 16.7 Plotting our tuning process. Each subplot shows the values of a different internal cluster metric. The different lines indicate the performance of each of the three different algorithms.

The greatest difference between the algorithms is their training time. Notice that MacQueen's algorithm is consistently faster than either of the others. This is due to the algorithm updating its centroids more frequently than Lloyd's and having to recompute distances less often than Hartigan-Wong. The Hartigan-Wong algorithm seems to be the most computationally intense at low cluster numbers but overtakes Lloyd's algorithm as the number of clusters increases beyond seven.

NOTE The tuning process selected Lloyd's algorithm because its Davis-Bouldin index was slightly smaller than for the other algorithms. For very large datasets, computation speed may be more important to you than a performance increase this small, in which case you might prefer to select MacQueen's algorithm due to its shorter training time.

16.2.5 Training the final, tuned k-means model

In this section, we'll use our tuned hyperparameters to train our final clustering model. You'll notice that we're *not* going to use nested cross-validation to cross-validate the whole model-building process. While the *k* means algorithm is able to predict cluster membership for new data, it isn't typically used as a predictive technique. Instead, we might use k-means to help us better define classes in our dataset, which we can later use to build classification models.

Let's start by creating a k-means learner that uses our tuned hyperparameter values, using the `setHyperPars()` function. We then train this tuned model on our `gvhdTask` using the `train()` function and use the `getLearnerModel()` function to extract the model data so we can plot the clusters. Print the model data by calling `kMeansModelData`, and examine the output; it contains a lot of useful information. By extracting the `$iter` component of the object, we can see that it took only three iterations for the algorithm to converge (far fewer than `iter.max`).

Listing 16.8 Training a model with the tuned hyperparameters

```
tunedKMeans <- setHyperPars(kMeans, par.vals = tunedK$x)

tunedKMeansModel <- train(tunedKMeans, gvhdTask)

kMeansModelData <- getLearnerModel(tunedKMeansModel)

kMeansModelData$iter

[1] 3
```

Finding the optimal number of clusters is not a well-defined problem; so, although internal metrics give evidence as to the correct number of clusters, you should still always try to validate your cluster model visually, to understand whether the result you're getting is sensible (at the very least). This may seem subjective, and it is, but it's much better for you to use your expert judgment than to rely solely on internal metrics. We can do this by plotting the data (as in figure 16.2) but coloring each case by its cluster membership.

TIP If the correct number of clusters is difficult for you to determine, it could be there simply aren't well-defined clusters in the data, or you may need to do further exploration, including generating more data. It may be worth trying a different clustering method: for example, one that doesn't find spherical clusters like k-means does, or one which can exclude outliers (like DBSCAN, which you'll meet in chapter 18).

To do this, we first add the cluster membership of each case as a new column in our `gvhdTib` tibble, using the `mutate()` function. We extract the vector of cluster memberships from the `$cluster` component of the model data and turn this into a factor using the `as.factor()` function, to ensure that a discrete color scheme is applied during plotting.

We then use `ggpairs()` to plot all variables against each other, mapping `kMeansCluster` to the color aesthetic. We use the upper argument to plot density plots on plots above the diagonal and apply the black-and-white theme.

Listing 16.9 Plotting the clusters using `ggpairs()`

```
gvhdTib <- mutate(gvhdTib,
                  kMeansCluster = as.factor(kMeansModelData$cluster))

ggpairs(gvhdTib, aes(col = kMeansCluster),
        upper = list(continuous = "density")) +
  theme_bw()
```

The resulting plot is shown in figure 16.8. To the eye, it looks like our k-means model does a pretty good job of capturing the structure in the data overall. But look at the plot of CD8 versus CD4: cluster three appears to be split. This suggests that either we

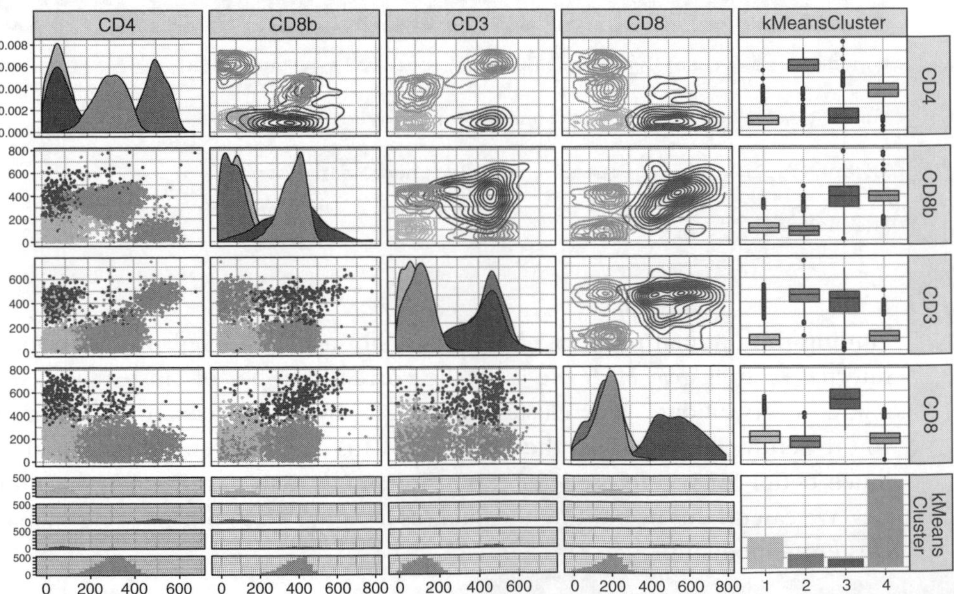

Figure 16.8 `ggpairs()` plot with the k-means cluster membership mapped to the color aesthetic. Box plots and histograms show how the values of the continuous variables vary between clusters.

have *underclustered* our data, or these cases have been assigned to the wrong cluster; or perhaps they are simply outlying cases, the importance of which is overstated by the density plot.

16.2.6 Using our model to predict clusters of new data

In this section, I'll show you how we can use an existing k-means model to predict cluster membership of new data. As I mentioned already, clustering techniques are not intended to be used for predicting classes of data—we have classification algorithms that excel at that. But the k-means algorithm *can* take new data and output the clusters to which the new cases are closest. This can be useful when you are still exploring and trying to understand the structure in your data, so let me demonstrate how.

Let's start by creating a tibble containing the data for a new case, including a value for each variable in the dataset on which we trained the model. Because we scaled the training data, we need to scale the values for this new case. Remember that it's important to scale new data we pass through a model according to the mean and standard deviation of the data used to train the model. The easiest way to do this is to use the `attr()` function to extract the `center` and `scale` attributes from the scaled data. Because the `scale()` function returns an object of class `matrix` (and the `predict()` function will throw an error if we give it a matrix), we need to pipe the scaled data into the `as_tibble()` function to turn it back into a tibble.

To predict which cluster the new case belongs to, we simply call the `predict()` function, supplying the model as the first argument and the new case as the `newdata` argument. We can see from the output that this new case is closest to the centroid of cluster 2.

Listing 16.10 Predicting cluster membership of new data

```
newCell <- tibble(CD4 = 510,
                  CD8b = 26,
                  CD3 = 500,
                  CD8 = 122) %>%
  scale(center = attr(gvhdScaled, "scaled:center"),
        scale = attr(gvhdScaled, "scaled:scale")) %>%
  as_tibble()

predict(tunedKMeansModel, newdata = newCell)

Prediction: 1 observations
predict.type: response
threshold:
time: 0.01
  response
1        2
```

You've now learned how to apply k-means clustering to your data. In the next chapter, I'll introduce *hierarchical clustering*, a set of clustering methods that help reveal a hierarchy in our data. I suggest that you save your .R file, because we're going to continue using the same dataset in the next chapter. This is so we can compare the performance of k-means and hierarchical clustering on the same dataset.

16.3 Strengths and weaknesses of k-means clustering

While it often isn't easy to tell which algorithms will perform well for a given task, here are some strengths and weaknesses that will help you decide whether k-means clustering will perform well for you.

The strengths of k-means clustering are as follows:

- Cases can move between clusters at each iteration until a stable result is found.
- It may be faster to compute than other algorithms when there are many variables.
- It is quite simple to implement.

The weaknesses of k-means clustering are these:

- It cannot natively handle categorical variables. This is because calculating the Euclidean distance on a categorical feature space isn't meaningful.
- It cannot select the optimal number of clusters.
- It is sensitive to data on different scales.
- Due to the randomness of the initial centroids, clusters may vary slightly between runs.
- It is sensitive to outliers.
- It preferentially finds spherical clusters of equal diameter, even if the underlying data doesn't fit this description.

Exercise 2

Cluster the GvHD.pos dataset in the same way we did with the GvHD.control dataset. Is the choice of cluster number as straightforward? You may need to manually supply a value for the `centers` argument, rather than rely on the output of the tuning procedure.

Summary

- Clustering is an unsupervised machine learning technique concerned with finding sets of cases in a dataset that are more similar to each other than to cases in other sets.
- K-means clustering involves the creation of randomly placed centroids that iteratively move toward the center of clusters in a dataset.
- The three most commonly used k-means algorithms are Lloyd's, Mac-Queen's, and Hartigan-Wong.
- The number of clusters for k-means needs to be selected by the user. This can be done graphically, and by combining internal cluster metrics with cross-validation and/or bootstrapping.

Solutions to exercises

1. Increase the `iter.max` of our k-means learner to 200:

```
kMeans <- makeLearner("cluster.kmeans",
                      par.vals = list(iter.max = 200, nstart = 10))

tunedK <- tuneParams(kMeans, task = gvhdTask,
                     resampling = kFold,
                     par.set = kMeansParamSpace,
                     control = gridSearch,
                     measures = list(db, dunn, G1))

# The error about not converging disappears when we set iter.max to 200.
```

2. Use k-means to cluster the GvHD.pos dataset:

```
gvhdPosTib <- as_tibble(GvHD.pos)

gvhdPosScaled <- scale(gvhdPosTib)

gvhdPosTask <- makeClusterTask(data = as.data.frame(gvhdPosScaled))

tunedKPos <- tuneParams(kMeans, task = gvhdPosTask,
                        resampling = kFold,
                        par.set = kMeansParamSpace,
                        control = gridSearch,
                        measures = list(db, dunn, G1))

kMeansTuningDataPos <- generateHyperParsEffectData(tunedKPos)

gatheredTuningDataPos <- gather(kMeansTuningDataPos$data,
                                key = "Metric",
                                value = "Value",
                                c(-centers, -iteration, -algorithm))

ggplot(gatheredTuningDataPos, aes(centers, Value, col = algorithm)) +
  facet_wrap(~ Metric, scales = "free_y") +
  geom_line() +
  geom_point() +
  theme_bw()

tunedKMeansPos <- setHyperPars(kMeans, par.vals = list("centers" = 4))

tunedKMeansModelPos <- train(tunedKMeansPos, gvhdPosTask)

kMeansModelDataPos <- getLearnerModel(tunedKMeansModelPos)

mutate(gvhdPosTib,
       kMeansCluster = as.factor(kMeansModelDataPos$cluster)) %>%
  ggpairs(mapping = aes(col = kMeansCluster),
          upper = list(continuous = "density")) +
  theme_bw()

# The optimal number of clusters is less clear than for GvHD.control.
```

17 Hierarchical clustering

This chapter covers

- Understanding hierarchical clustering
- Using linkage methods
- Measuring the stability of a clustering result

In the previous chapter, we saw how k-means clustering finds *k* centroids in the feature space and iteratively updates them to find a set of clusters. Hierarchical clustering takes a different approach and, as its name suggests, can learn a hierarchy of clusters in a dataset. Instead of getting a "flat" output of clusters, hierarchical clustering gives us a tree of clusters within clusters. As a result, hierarchical clustering provides more insight into complex grouping structures than flat clustering methods like k-means.

The tree of clusters is built iteratively by calculating the distance between each case or cluster, and every other case or cluster in the dataset at each step. Either the case/cluster pair that are most similar to each other are merged into a single cluster, or sets of cases/clusters that are most dissimilar from each other are split into separate clusters, depending on the algorithm. I'll introduce both approaches to you later in the chapter.

By the end of this chapter, I hope you'll understand how hierarchical clustering works. We'll apply this method to the GvHD data from the last chapter to help you understand how hierarchical clustering differs from k-means. If you no longer have the `gvhdScaled` object defined in your global environment, just rerun listings 16.1 and 16.2.

17.1 What is hierarchical clustering?

In this section, I'll give you a deeper understanding of what hierarchical clustering is and how it differs from k-means. I'll show you the two different approaches we can take to perform hierarchical clustering, how to interpret a graphical representation of the learned hierarchy, and how to choose the number of clusters to retain.

When we looked at k-means clustering in the last chapter, we only considered a single level of clustering. But sometimes, hierarchies exist in our dataset that clustering at a single, flat level is unable to highlight. For example, imagine that we were looking at clusters of instruments in an orchestra. At the highest level, we could place each instrument into one of four different clusters:

- Percussion
- Brass
- Woodwinds
- Strings

But we could then further split each of these clusters into sub-clusters based on the way they are played:

- Percussion
  - Played with a mallet
  - Played by hand
- Brass
  - Valve
  - Slide
- Woodwinds
  - Reeded
  - Non-reeded
- Strings
  - Plucked
  - Bowed

Next, we could further split this level of clusters into sub-clusters based on the sounds they make:

- Percussion
  - Played with a mallet
    - Timpani
    - Gong

  - Played by hand
    - Hand cymbals
    - Tambourine
- Brass
  - Valve
    - Trumpet
    - French horn
  - Slide
    - Trombone
- Woodwinds
  - Reeded
    - Clarinet
    - Bassoon
  - Non-reeded
    - Flute
    - Piccolo
- Strings
  - Plucked
    - Harp
  - Bowed
    - Violin
    - Cello

Notice that we have formed a hierarchy where there are clusters of instruments within other clusters, going all the way from a very high-level clustering down to each individual instrument. A common way to visualize hierarchies like this is with a graphical representation called a *dendrogram.* A possible dendrogram for our orchestra hierarchy is shown in figure 17.1.

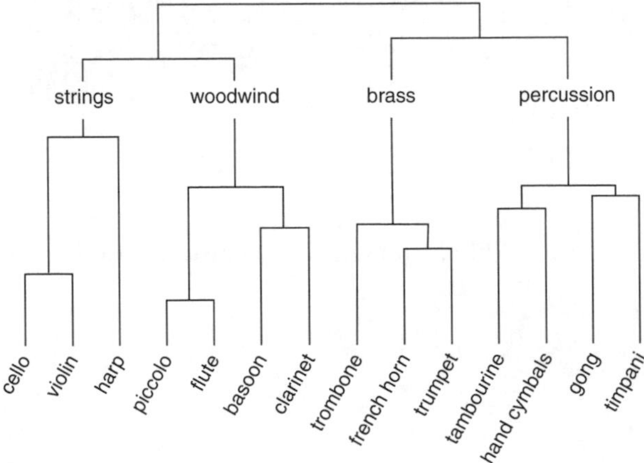

Figure 17.1 Dendrogram showing an imaginary clustering of instruments in an orchestra. Horizontal lines indicate the merging of separate clusters. The height of a merge indicates the similarity between the clusters (lower merge, higher similarity).

Notice that at the bottom of the dendrogram, each instrument is represented by its own vertical line, and at this level, each instrument is considered to be *in a cluster of its own*. As we move up the hierarchy, instruments in the same cluster are connected by a horizontal line. The height at which clusters merge like this is inversely proportional to how similar the clusters are to each other. For example, I have (subjectively) drawn this dendrogram to suggest that the piccolo and flute are more similar to each other than how similar the bassoon and clarinet are to each other.

Typically, when finding a hierarchy in data like this, one end of the dendrogram displays every case in its own cluster; these clusters merge upward until eventually, all the cases are placed into a single cluster. As such, I've indicated the position of our strings, woodwinds, brass, and percussion clusters, but I have continued clustering these clusters until there is only one cluster containing all the cases.

The purpose of hierarchical clustering algorithms, therefore, is to learn this hierarchy of clusters in a dataset. The main benefit of hierarchical clustering over k-means is that we get a much finer-grained understanding of the structure of our data, and this approach is often able to reconstruct real hierarchies in nature. For example, imagine that we sequence the genomes (all the DNA) of all breeds of dog. We can safely assume that the genome of a breed will be more similar to the genome of the breed(s) it was derived from than it is to the genomes of breeds it was not derived from. If we apply hierarchical clustering to this data, the hierarchy, which can be visualized as a dendrogram, can be directly interpreted as showing which breeds were derived from other breeds.

The hierarchy is very useful, but how do we partition the dendrogram into a finite set of clusters? Well, at any height on the dendrogram, we can *cut* the tree horizontally and take the number of clusters at that level. Another way of imagining it is that if we were to cut a slice through the dendrogram, however many individual branches would fall off is the number of clusters. Look back at figure 17.1. If we cut the tree where I've labeled the strings, woodwinds, brass, and percussion, we would get four individual clusters, and cases would be assigned to whichever of these four clusters they fell within. I'll show you how we can select a cut point later in this section.

NOTE If we cut the tree closer to the top, we get fewer clusters. If we cut the tree closer to the bottom, we get more clusters.

Okay, we have an understanding of *what* hierarchical clustering algorithms try to achieve. Now let's talk about *how* they achieve it. There are two approaches we can take while trying to learn hierarchies in data:

- Agglomerative
- Divisive

Agglomerative hierarchical clustering is where we start with every case isolated (and lonely) in its own cluster, and sequentially merge clusters until all the data resides within a single cluster. Divisive hierarchical clustering does the opposite: it starts with all the cases in a single cluster and recursively splits them into clusters until each case resides in its own cluster.

17.1.1 Agglomerative hierarchical clustering

In this section, I'll show you how agglomerative hierarchical clustering learns the structure in the data. The steps of the algorithm are quite simple:

1. Calculate some distance metric (defined by us) between each cluster and all other clusters.
2. Merge the most similar clusters together into a single cluster.
3. Repeat steps 1 and 2 until all cases reside in a single cluster.

An example of how this might look is shown in figure 17.2. We start with nine cases (and therefore nine clusters). The algorithm calculates a distance metric (more about this soon) between each of the clusters and merges the clusters that are most similar to each other. This continues until all the cases are gobbled up by the final supercluster.

So how do we calculate the distance between clusters? The first choice we need to make is what kind of distance we want to compute. As usual, the Euclidean and

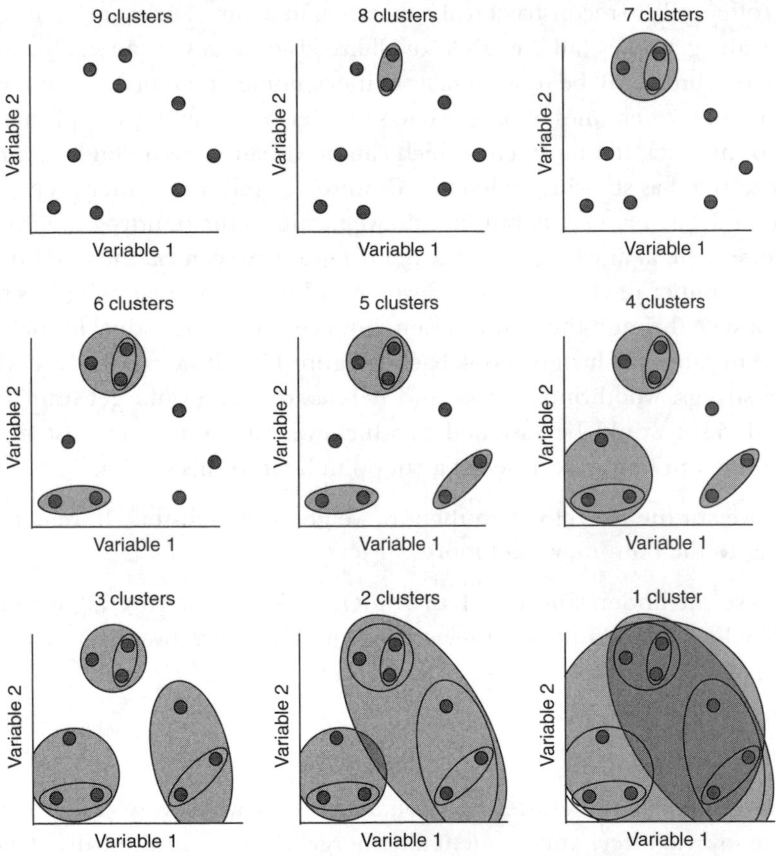

Figure 17.2 Agglomerative hierarchical clustering merges clusters that are closest to each other at each iteration. Ellipses indicate the formation of clusters at each iteration, going from top left to bottom right.

Manhattan distances are the most popular choices. The second choice is how to calculate this distance metric between clusters. Calculating the distance between two cases (two vectors) is reasonably obvious, but a *cluster* contains multiple cases; how do we calculate, say, Euclidean distance between two clusters? Well, we have a few options available to us, called *linkage methods*:

- Centroid linkage
- Single linkage
- Complete linkage
- Average linkage
- Ward's method

Each of these linkage methods is illustrated in figure 17.3. Centroid linkage calculates the distance (Euclidean or Manhattan, for example) between each cluster's centroid to every other cluster's centroid. Single linkage takes the distance between the *nearest* cases of two clusters, as the distance between those clusters. Complete linkage takes the distance between the *furthest* cases of two clusters, as the distance between those clusters. Average linkage takes the average distance between all the cases of two clusters, as the distance between those clusters.

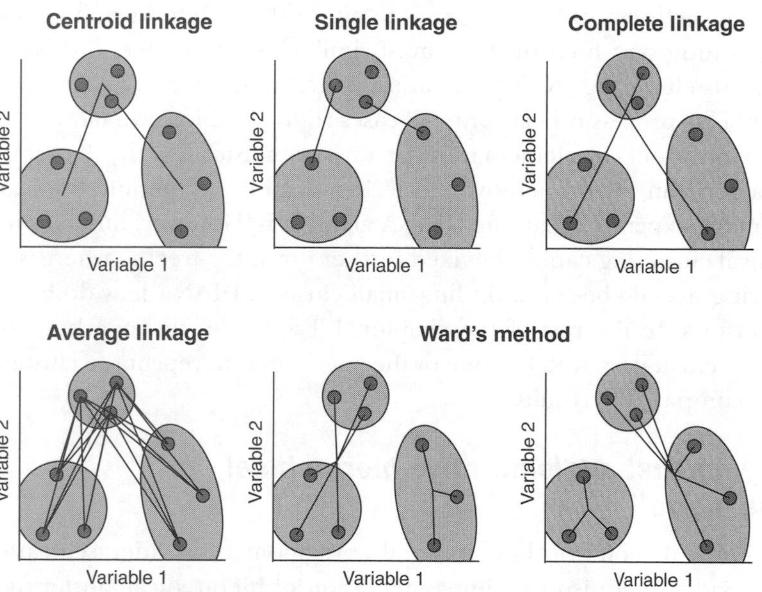

Figure 17.3 Different linkage methods to define the distance between clusters. Centroid linkage calculates the distance between cluster centroids. Single linkage calculates the smallest distance between clusters. Complete linkage calculates the largest distance between clusters. Average linkage calculates all pairwise distances between cases in two clusters and finds the mean. Ward's method calculates the within-cluster sum of squares for each candidate merge and chooses the one with the smallest value.

Ward's method is a little more complex. For every possible combination of clusters, Ward's method (sometimes called Ward's minimum variance method) calculates the within-cluster sum of squares. Take a look at the examples for Ward's method in figure 17.3. The algorithm has three clusters to consider merging. For each candidate merge, the algorithm calculates the sum of squared differences between each case and its cluster's centroid, and then adds these sums of squares together. The candidate merge that results in the smallest sum of squared differences is chosen at each step.

17.1.2 Divisive hierarchical clustering

In this section, I'll show you how divisive hierarchical clustering works. Unlike agglomerative clustering, divisive clustering starts with all cases in a single cluster and recursively divides this into smaller and smaller clusters, until each case resides in its own cluster. Finding the optimal split at each stage of clustering is a difficult task, so divisive clustering uses a heuristic approach.

At each stage of clustering, the cluster with the largest *diameter* is chosen. Recall from figure 16.5 that a cluster's diameter is the largest distance between any two cases within the cluster. The algorithm then finds the case in this cluster that has the largest average distance to all the other cases in the cluster. This most-dissimilar case starts its own *splinter group* (like a rebel without a cause). The algorithm then iterates through every case in the cluster and assigns cases to either the splinter group or the original cluster, depending on which they are most similar to. In essence, divisive clustering applies k-means clustering (with $k = 2$) at each level of the hierarchy, in order to split each cluster. This process repeats until all cases reside in their own cluster.

There is only one implementation of divisive clustering: the DIANA (DIvisive ANAlysis) algorithm. Agglomerative clustering is more commonly used and is less computationally expensive than the DIANA algorithm. However, mistakes made early in hierarchical clustering cannot be fixed further down the tree; so whereas agglomerative clustering may do better at finding small clusters, DIANA may do better at finding large clusters. In the rest of the chapter, I'll walk you through how to perform agglomerative clustering in R, but one of the exercises is to repeat the clustering using DIANA and compare the results.

17.2 Building your first agglomerative hierarchical clustering model

In this section, I'll show you how to build an agglomerative hierarchical clustering model in R. Sadly, there isn't an implementation of hierarchical clustering wrapped by the mlr package, so we're going to use the `hclust()` function from the built-in stats package.

The `hclust()` function that we'll use to perform agglomerative hierarchical clustering expects a *distance matrix* as input, rather than the raw data. A distance matrix contains the pairwise distances between each combination of elements. This distance can be any distance metric we specify, and in this situation, we'll use the Euclidean distance. Because computing the distances between cases is the first step of hierarchical clustering, you might expect `hclust()` to do this for us. But this two-step process of creating our own distance metric and then supplying it to `hclust()` does allow us the flexibility of using a variety of distance metrics.

We create a distance matrix in R using the `dist()` function, supplying the data we want to compute distances for as the first argument and the type of distance we want to use. Notice that we're using our scaled dataset, because hierarchical clustering is also sensitive to differences in scale between variables (as is any algorithm that relies on distance between continuous variables):

```
gvhdDist <- dist(gvhdScaled, method = "euclidean")
```

> **TIP** If you want a more visual example of what a distance matrix looks like, run `dist(c(4, 7, 11, 30, 16))`. *Don't* try to print the distance matrix we create in this section—it contains more than 2.3×10^7 elements!

Now that we have our distance matrix, we can run the algorithm to learn the hierarchy in our data. The first argument to the `hclust()` function is the distance matrix, and the `method` argument allows us to specify the linkage method we wish to use to define the distance between clusters. The options available are `"ward.D"`, `"ward.D2"`, `"single"`, `"complete"`, `"average"`, `"centroid"`, and a few less commonly used ones that I haven't defined (see `?hclust` if you're interested in these). Notice that there seem to be two options for Ward's method: the option `"ward.D2"` is the correct implementation of Ward's method, as I described earlier. In this example, we're going to start by using Ward's method (`"ward.D2"`), but I'll get you to compare the result of this to other methods as part of this chapter's exercises:

```
gvhdHclust <- hclust(gvhdDist, method = "ward.D2")
```

Now that `hclust()` has learned the hierarchical clustering structure of the data, let's represent this as a dendrogram. We can do this by simply calling `plot()` on our clustering model object, but the tree is a little clearer if we first convert our model into a dendrogram object and plot that. We can convert our clustering model into a dendrogram object using the `as.dendrogram()` function. To plot the dendrogram, we pass it to the `plot()` function. By default, the plot will draw a label for each case in the original data. Because we have such a large dataset, let's suppress these labels using the argument `leaflab = "none"`.

Listing 17.1 Plotting the dendrogram

```
gvhdDend <- as.dendrogram(gvhdHclust)

plot(gvhdDend, leaflab = "none")
```

The resulting plot is shown in figure 17.4. The y-axis here represents the distance between clusters, based on whatever linkage method (and distance metric) we used.

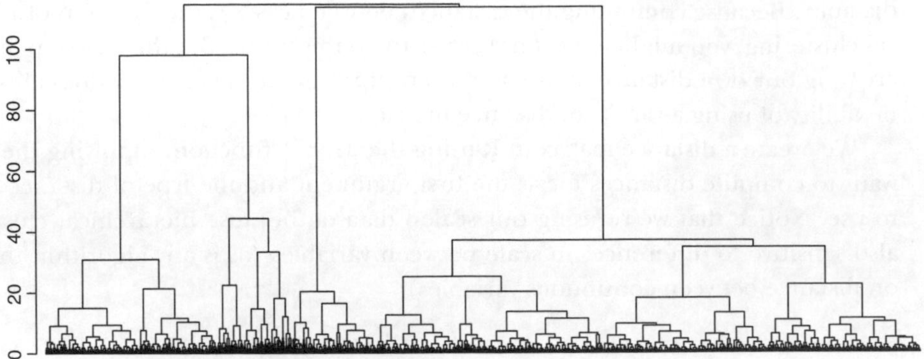

Figure 17.4 The resulting dendrogram representing our hierarchical clustering model. The y-axis represents the distances between cases. Horizontal lines indicate the positions at which cases/clusters merge with each other. The higher the merge, the less similar the clusters are to each other.

Because we used Ward's method, the values of this axis are the within-cluster sum of squares. When two clusters are merged together, they are connected by a horizontal line, the position of which along the y-axis corresponds to the distance between those clusters. Therefore, clusters of cases that merge lower down the tree (which is earlier in agglomerative clustering) are more similar to each other than clusters that merge further up the tree. The ordering of cases along the x-axis is optimized such that similar cases are drawn near each other to aid interpretation (otherwise, the branches would cross). As we can see, the dendrogram recursively joins clusters, from each case being in its own cluster to all the cases belonging to a supercluster.

> **Exercise 1**
>
> Repeat the clustering process, but this time specify `method = "manhattan"` when creating the distance matrix (don't overwrite any existing objects). Plot a dendrogram of the cluster hierarchy, and compare it to the dendrogram we got by using Euclidean distance.

The hierarchical clustering algorithm has done its job: it's learned the hierarchy, and what we do with it is up to us. We may want to directly interpret the structure of the tree to make some inference about a hierarchy that might exist in nature, though in our (large) dataset, that could be quite challenging.

Another common use of hierarchical clustering is to order the rows and columns of heatmaps, for example, for gene expression data. Ordering the rows and columns of a heatmap using hierarchical clustering helps researchers identify clusters of genes and clusters of patients simultaneously.

Finally, our primary motivation may be to identify a finite number of clusters within our dataset that are most interesting to us. This is what we will do with our clustering result.

17.2.1 Choosing the number of clusters

In this section, I'll show you ways of deciding how many clusters to extract from a hierarchy. Another way of thinking about this is that we're deciding what level of the hierarchy to use for clustering.

To define a finite number of clusters following hierarchical clustering, we need to define a cut point on our dendrogram. If we cut the tree near the top, we'll get fewer clusters; and if we cut the tree near the bottom, we'll get more clusters. So how do we choose a cut point? Well, our friends the Davies-Bouldin index, the Dunn index, and the pseudo F statistic can help us here. For k-means clustering, we performed a cross-validation-like procedure for estimating the performance of different numbers of clusters. Sadly, we can't use this approach for hierarchical clustering because, unlike k-means, hierarchical clustering *cannot predict cluster membership of new cases.*

> **NOTE** The hierarchical clustering algorithms themselves can't predict the cluster membership of new cases, but you *could* do something like assigning new data to the cluster with the nearest centroid. You could use this approach to create separate training and test sets to evaluate internal cluster metrics on.

Instead, we can make use of bootstrapping. Recall from chapter 8 that bootstrapping is the process of taking bootstrap samples, applying some computation to each sample, and returning a statistic(s). The mean of our bootstrapped statistic(s) tells us the most likely value, and the distribution gives us an indication as to the stability of the statistic(s).

> **NOTE** Remember that to get a bootstrap sample, we randomly select cases from a dataset, with replacement, to create a new sample the same size as the old. Sampling *with replacement* simply means that once we sample a particular case, we put it back, such that there is a possibility it will be drawn again.

In the context of hierarchical clustering, we can use bootstrapping to generate multiple samples from our data and generate a separate hierarchy for each sample. We can then select a range of cluster numbers from each hierarchy and calculate the internal cluster metrics for each. The advantage of using bootstrapping is that calculating the internal cluster metrics on the full dataset doesn't give us an indication of the stability of the estimate, whereas the bootstrap sample does. The bootstrap sample of cluster metrics will have some variation around its mean, so we can choose the number of clusters with the most optimal and stable metrics.

Let's start by defining our own function that takes our data and a vector of cluster memberships and returns our three familiar internal cluster metrics for the data: the Davies-Bouldin index, the Dunn index, and the pseudo F statistic. Because the function we'll use to calculate the Dunn index expects a distance matrix, we'll include an additional argument in our function to which we'll supply a precomputed distance matrix.

Listing 17.2 Defining the `cluster_metrics` function

```
cluster_metrics <- function(data, clusters, dist_matrix) {
  list(db       = clusterSim::index.DB(data, clusters)$DB,
       G1       = clusterSim::index.G1(data, clusters),
       dunn     = clValid::dunn(dist_matrix, clusters),
       clusters = length(unique(clusters))
  )
}
```

Follow the function body with me so what we're doing makes sense. We use the `function()` argument to define a function, assigning it to the name `cluster_metrics` (this will allow us to call the function using `cluster_metrics()`). We define three mandatory arguments for the function:

- `data`, to which we will pass the data we're clustering
- `clusters`, a vector containing the cluster membership of every case in `data`
- `dist_matrix`, to which we will pass the precomputed distance matrix for `data`

The *body* of the function (the instructions that tell the function what to do) is defined inside curly brackets (`{}`). Our function will return a list with four elements: the Davies-Bouldin index (`db`), the pseudo F statistic (`G1`), the Dunn index (`dunn`), and the number of clusters. Rather than define them from scratch, we're using predefined functions from other packages to compute the internal cluster metrics. The Davies-Bouldin index is computed using the `index.DB()` function from the clusterSim package, which takes the `data` and `clusters` arguments (the statistic itself is contained in the `$DB` component). The pseudo F statistic is computed using the `index.G1()` function, also from the clusterSim package, and takes the same arguments as `index.DB()`. The Dunn index is computed using the `dunn()` function from the clValid package, which takes the `dist_matrix` and `clusters` arguments.

Our motivation for defining this function is that we're going to take bootstrap samples from our dataset, learn the hierarchy in each, select a range of cluster numbers from each, and use our function to calculate these three metrics for each number of clusters within each bootstrap sample. So now, let's create our bootstrap samples. We'll create 10 bootstrap samples from our gvhdScaled dataset. We're using the `map()` function to repeat the sampling process 10 times, to return a list where each element is a different bootstrap sample.

Listing 17.3 Creating bootstrap samples

```
gvhdBoot <- map(1:10, ~ {
  gvhdScaled %>%
    as_tibble() %>%
    sample_n(size = nrow(.), replace = TRUE)
})
```

NOTE Remember that ~ is just shorthand for `function()`.

We're using the `sample_n()` function from the dplyr package to create the samples. This function randomly samples rows from a dataset. Because this function cannot handle matrices, we first need to pipe our gvhdScaled data into the `as_tibble()` function. By setting the argument `size = nrow(.)`, we're asking `sample_n()` to randomly draw a number of cases equal to the number of rows in the original dataset (the `.` is shorthand for "the dataset that was piped in"). By setting the `replace` argument equal to `TRUE`, we're telling the function to sample with replacement. Creating simple bootstrap samples really is as easy as this!

Now let's use our `cluster_metrics()` function to calculate those three internal metrics for a range of cluster numbers, for each bootstrap sample we just generated. Take a look at the following listing, and don't go cross-eyed! I'll take you through the code step by step.

Listing 17.4 Calculating performance metrics of our clustering model

```
metricsTib <- map_df(gvhdBoot, function(boot) {
  d <- dist(boot, method = "euclidean")
  cl <- hclust(d, method = "ward.D2")

  map_df(3:8, function(k) {
    cut <- cutree(cl, k = k)
    cluster_metrics(boot, clusters = cut, dist_matrix = d)
  })
})
```

TIP The `map_df()` function is just like `map()`, but instead of returning a list, it combines each element row-wise to return a data frame.

We start by calling the `map_df()` function so that we can apply a function to every element of our list of bootstrap samples. We define an anonymous function that takes `boot` (the current element being considered) as its only argument.

For each element in `gvhdBoot`, the anonymous function computes its Euclidean distance matrix, stores it as the object `d`, and performs hierarchical clustering using that matrix and Ward's method. Once we have the hierarchy for each bootstrap sample, we use another `map_df()` function call to select between three and eight clusters to partition the data into, and then calculate the three internal clustering methods on each result. We're going to use this process to see which number of clusters, between three and eight, gives us the best internal cluster metrics values.

Selecting the number of clusters to retain from a hierarchical clustering model is done using the `cutree()` function. We use this function to cut our dendrogram at a place that returns a number of clusters. We can do this either by specifying a height at which to cut, using the `h` argument, or by specifying a specific number of clusters to retain, using the `k` argument (as done here). The first argument is the result of calling the `hclust()` function. The output of the `cutree()` function is a vector indicating the cluster number assigned to each case in the dataset. Once we have this vector, we can call our `cluster_metrics()` function, supplying the bootstrap data, the vector of cluster membership, and the distance matrix.

> **WARNING** This took nearly 3 minutes to run on my machine!

If what we just did is a little unclear to you, print the `metricsTib` tibble to see what the output looks like. We have a tibble with one column for each of the internal cluster metrics, and a column indicating the number of clusters for which the metrics were calculated.

Let's plot the result of our bootstrapping experiment. We're going to create a separate subplot for each internal cluster metric (using faceting). Each subplot will show the number of clusters on the x-axis, the value of the internal cluster metric on the y-axis, a separate line for each individual bootstrap sample, and a line that connects the mean value across all bootstraps.

Listing 17.5 Transforming the data, ready for plotting

```
metricsTib <- metricsTib %>%
  mutate(bootstrap = factor(rep(1:10, each = 6))) %>%
  gather(key = "Metric", value = "Value", -clusters, -bootstrap)
```

We first need to mutate a new column, indicating the bootstrap sample each case belongs to. Because there are 10 bootstrap samples, evaluated for 6 different numbers of clusters each (3 to 8), we create this variable by using the `rep()` function to repeat each number from 1 to 10, six times. We wrap this inside the `factor()` function to ensure it isn't treated as a continuous variable when plotting. Next, we gather the data so that the choice of internal metric is contained within a single column and the value of that metric is held in another column. We specify `-clusters` and `-bootstrap` to tell the function *not* to gather these variables. Print this new tibble, and be sure you understand how we got there.

Now that our data is in this format, we can create the plot.

Listing 17.6 Calculating metrics

```
ggplot(metricsTib, aes(as.factor(clusters), Value)) +
  facet_wrap(~ Metric, scales = "free_y") +
  geom_line(size = 0.1, aes(group = bootstrap)) +
  geom_line(stat = "summary", fun.y = "mean", aes(group = 1)) +
  stat_summary(fun.data="mean_cl_boot",
               geom="crossbar", width = 0.5, fill = "white") +
  theme_bw()
```

We map the number of clusters (as a factor) to the x aesthetic and the value of the internal cluster metric to the y aesthetic. We add a `facet_wrap()` layer to facet by internal cluster metric, setting the `scales = "free_y"` argument because the metrics are on different scales. Next, we add a `geom_line()` layer, using the `size` argument to make these lines less prominent, and map the bootstrap sample number to the group aesthetic. This layer will therefore draw a separate, thin line for each bootstrap sample.

> **TIP** Notice that when you specify an aesthetic mapping inside the `ggplot()` function layer, the mapping is inherited by all additional layers that use that aesthetic. However, you can specify aesthetic mappings using the `aes()` function inside each geom function, and the mapping will apply to that layer only.

We then add another `geom_line()` layer that will connect the mean across all bootstrap samples. By default, the `geom_line()` function likes to connect individual values. If we want the function to connect a summary statistic (like a mean), we need to specify the `stat = "summary"` argument and then use the `fun.y` argument to tell the function what summary statistic we want to plot. Here we've used `"mean"`, but you can supply the name of any function that returns a single value of `y` for its input.

Finally, it would be nice to visualize the 95% confidence interval for the bootstrap sample. The 95% confidence intervals tell us that, if we were to repeat this experiment 100 times, 95 of the constructed confidence intervals would be expected to contain the true value of the metric. The more the estimates agree with each other between bootstrap samples, the smaller the confidence interval will be. We want to visualize the confidence intervals using the flexible `stat_summary()` function. This function can be used to visualize multiple summary statistics in many different ways. To draw the mean ± 95% confidence intervals, we use the `fun.data` argument to specify that we want `"mean_cl_boot"`. This will draw bootstrap confidence intervals (95% by default).

> **NOTE** The other option would be to use `"mean_cl_normal"` to construct the confidence intervals, but this assumes the data is normally distributed, and this may not be true.

Now that we've defined our summary statistics, let's specify the geom that we're going to use to represent them, using the `geom` argument. The geom `"crossbar"` draws what looks like the box part of a box and whiskers plot, where a solid line is drawn through the measure of central tendency that we specified (the mean, in this case) and the upper and lower limits of the box extend to the range of the measure of dispersion we asked for (95% confidence limits, in this case). Then, according to my preference, we set the width of the crossbars to 0.5 and the fill color to white.

The resulting plot is shown in figure 17.5. Take a moment to appreciate how beautiful the result is after all the hard work we just put in. Look back at listing 17.6 to make sure you understand how we created this plot (`stat_summary()` is probably the most confusing bit). It seems that the number of clusters resulting in the smallest mean Davies-Bouldin index and the largest mean Dunn index and mean pseudo F statistic is four. Take a look at the thin lines representing each individual bootstrap. Can you see that some of them might have led us to conclude that a different number of clusters was optimal? This is why bootstrapping these metrics is better than calculating each metric only once using a single dataset.

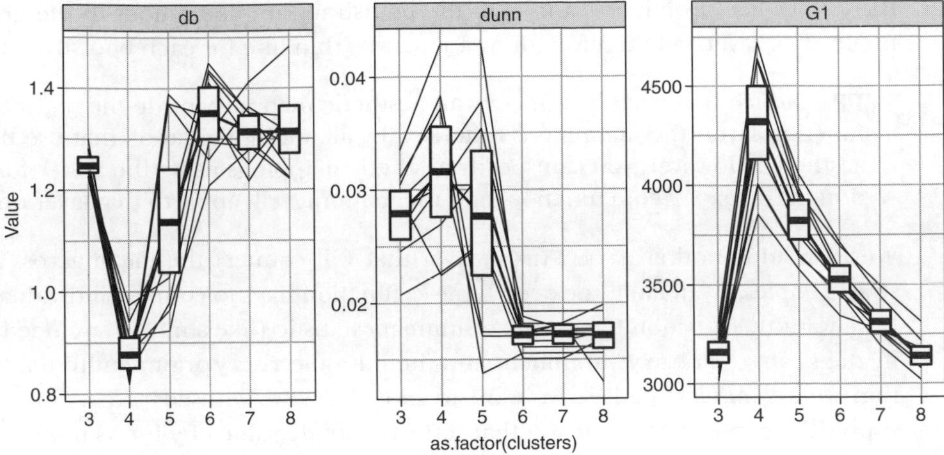

Figure 17.5 Plotting the result of our bootstrap experiment. Each subplot shows the result of a different internal cluster metric. The x-axis shows the cluster number, and the y-axis shows the value of each metric. Faint lines connect the results of each individual bootstrap sample, while the bold line connects the mean. The top and bottom of each crossbar indicate the 95% confidence interval for that particular value, and the horizontal line represents the mean.

> **Exercise 2**
>
> Let's experiment with another way we could visualize these results. Start with the following operations using dplyr (piping each step into the next):
>
> 1. Group the `metricsTib` object by `Metric`.
> 2. Use `mutate()` to replace the `Value` variable with `scale(Value)`.
> 3. Group by both `Metric` *and* `clusters`.
> 4. Mutate a new column, `Stdev`, equal to `sd(Value)`.
>
> Then pipe this tibble into a `ggplot()` call with the following aesthetic mappings:
>
> - `x = clusters`
> - `y = Metric`
> - `fill = Value`
> - `height = Stdev`
>
> Finally, add a `geom_tile()` layer. Look back at your code and make sure you understand how you created this plot and how to interpret it.

17.2.2 Cutting the tree to select a flat set of clusters

In this section, I'll show you how we can finally cut the dendrogram to return the cluster labels for our desired number of clusters. Our bootstrapping experiment has led us to conclude that four is the optimal number of clusters with which to represent the structure in our GvHD dataset. To extract a vector of cluster memberships representing these four clusters, we use the `cutree()` function, supplying our clustering model and `k` (the number of clusters we want to return). We can visualize how our dendrogram is cut to generate these four clusters by plotting the dendrogram as before and calling the `rect.hclust()` function with the same arguments we gave to `cutree()`.

Listing 17.7 Cutting the tree

```
gvhdCut <- cutree(gvhdHclust, k = 4)

plot(gvhdDend, leaflab = "none")

rect.hclust(gvhdHclust, k = 4)
```

This function draws rectangles on an existing dendrogram plot to show which branches are cut to result in the number of clusters we specified. The resulting plot is shown in figure 17.6.

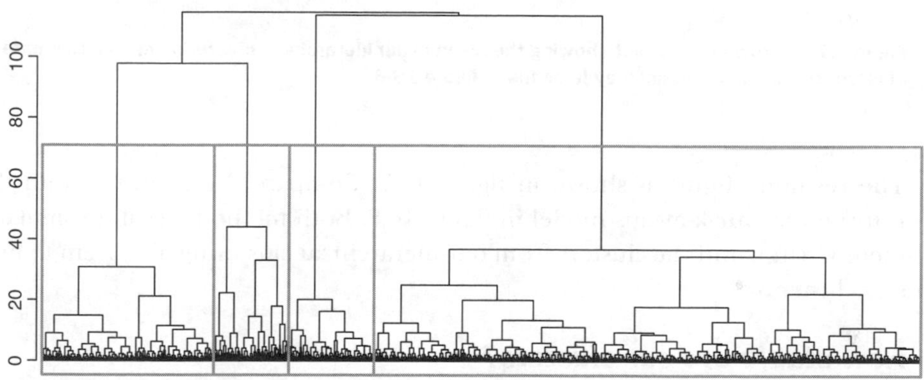

Figure 17.6 The same plot as in figure 17.4, but this time with rectangles indicating the clusters resulting from cutting the tree

Next, let's plot the clusters using `ggpairs()` like we did for our k-means model in chapter 16.

Listing 17.8 Plotting the clusters

```
gvhdTib <- mutate(gvhdTib, hclustCluster = as.factor(gvhdCut))

ggpairs(gvhdTib, aes(col = hclustCluster),
        upper = list(continuous = "density"),
        lower = list(continuous = wrap("points", size = 0.5))) +
  theme_bw()
```

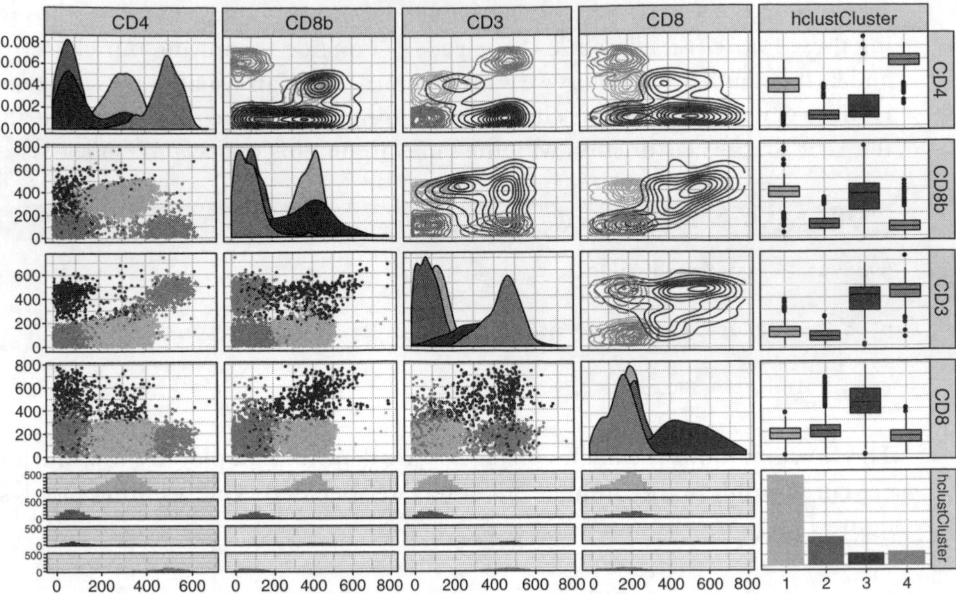

Figure 17.7 `ggpairs()` plot showing the result of our hierarchical clustering model. Compare these clusters to the ones obtained by k-means in figure 16.8.

The resulting figure is shown in figure 17.7. Compare these clusters with the ones returned by our k-means model in figure 16.8. Both methods result in similar cluster membership, and the clusters from our hierarchical clustering also seem to undercluster cluster 3.

17.3 How stable are our clusters?

In this section, I'll show you one more tool to evaluate the performance of our clustering model. In addition to calculating internal cluster metrics on each bootstrap sample in a bootstrapping experiment, we can also quantify how well the cluster memberships agree with each other between bootstrap samples. This agreement is called the cluster *stability*. A common way to quantify cluster stability is with a similarity metric called the *Jaccard index* (named after the botany professor who published it).

The Jaccard index quantifies the similarity between two sets of discrete variables. Its value can be interpreted as the percentage of the total values that are present in both sets, and it ranges from 0% (no common values) to 100% (all values common to both sets). The Jaccard index is defined in equation 17.1.

$$\text{Jaccard index} = \left(\frac{\text{number of values in both sets}}{\text{total number of unique values}}\right) \times 100 \qquad \textbf{Equation 17.1}$$

For example, if we have two sets

a = {3, 3, 5, 2, 8}

b = {1, 3, 5, 6}

then the Jaccard index is

$$\text{Jaccard index} = \left(\frac{2}{6}\right) \times 100 = 33.3\%$$

If we cluster on multiple bootstrap samples, we can calculate the Jaccard index between the "original" clusters (the clusters on all the data) and each of the bootstrap samples, and take the mean. If the mean Jaccard index is low, then cluster membership is changing considerably between bootstrap samples, indicating our clustering result is *unstable* and may not generalize well. If the mean Jaccard index is high, then cluster membership is changing very little, indicating a stable clustering result.

Luckily for us, the `clusterboot()` function from the fpc package has been written to do just this! Let's first load the fpc package into our R session. Because `clusterboot()` produces a series of base R plots as a side effect, let's split the plotting device into three rows and four columns to accommodate the output, using `par(mfrow = c(3, 4))`.

Listing 17.9 Using `clusterboot()` to calculate the Jaccard index

```
library(fpc)

par(mfrow = c(3, 4))

clustBoot <- clusterboot(gvhdDist, B = 10,
                         clustermethod = disthclustCBI,
                         k = 4, cut = "number", method = "ward.D2",
                         showplots = TRUE)

clustBoot

Number of resampling runs:  10

Number of clusters found in data:  4

 Clusterwise Jaccard bootstrap (omitting multiple points) mean:
[1] 0.9728 0.9208 0.8348 0.9624
```

The first argument to the `clusterboot()` function is the data. This argument will accept either the raw data or a distance matrix of class `dist` (it will handle either appropriately). The argument `B` is the number of bootstrap samples we wish to calculate, which

I've set to 10 for the sake of reducing running time. The `clustermethod` argument is where we specify which type of clustering model we wish to build (see `?clusterboot` for a list of available methods; many common methods are included). For hierarchical clustering, we set this argument equal to `disthclustCBI`. The `k` argument specifies the number of clusters we want to return, `method` lets us specify the distance metric to use for clustering, and `showplots` gives us the opportunity to suppress the printing of the plots if we wish. The function may take a couple of minutes to run.

I've truncated the output from printing the result of `clusterboot()` to show the most important information: the clusterwise Jaccard bootstrap means. These four values are the mean Jaccard indices for each cluster, between the original clusters and each bootstrap sample. We can see that all four clusters have good agreement (> 83%) across different bootstrap samples, suggesting high stability of the clusters.

The resulting plot is shown in figure 17.8. The first (top-left) and last (bottom-right) plots show the clustering on the original, full dataset. Each plot between these shows the clustering on a different bootstrap sample. This plot is a useful way of graphically evaluating the stability of the clusters.

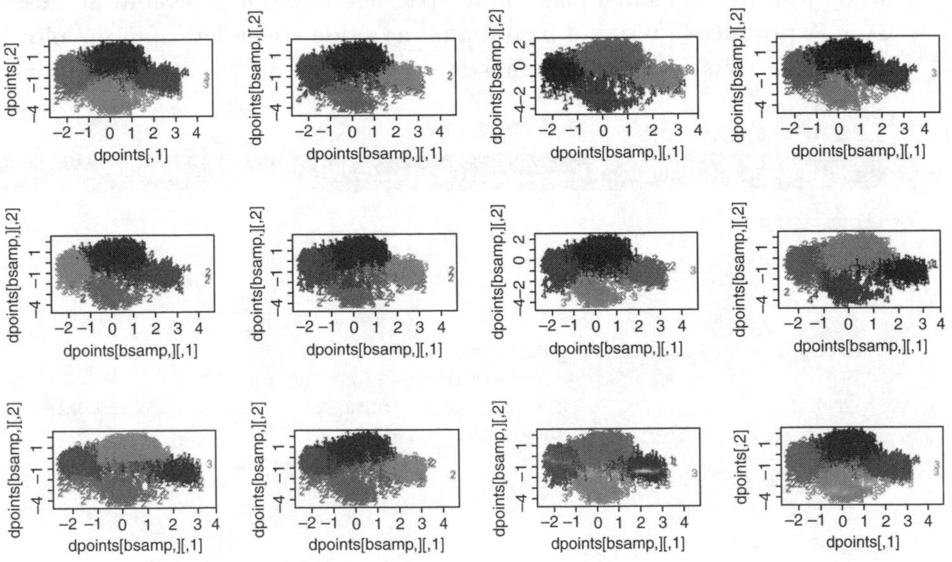

Figure 17.8 The graphical output of the `clusterboot()` function. The first and last plots show the full, original clusters of data, while the plots in between show the clusters on the bootstrap samples. The cluster membership of each case is indicated by a number. Notice the relatively high stability of the clusters.

17.4 Strengths and weaknesses of hierarchical clustering

While it often isn't easy to tell which algorithms will perform well for a given task, here are some strengths and weaknesses that will help you decide whether hierarchical clustering will perform well for you.

The strengths of hierarchical clustering are as follows:

- It learns a hierarchy that may in and of itself be interesting and interpretable.
- It is quite simple to implement.

The weaknesses of hierarchical clustering are these:

- It cannot natively handle categorical variables. This is because calculating the Euclidean distance on a categorical feature space isn't meaningful.
- It cannot select the optimal number of "flat" clusters.
- It is sensitive to data on different scales.
- It cannot predict cluster membership of new data.
- Once cases have been assigned to a cluster, they cannot be moved.
- It can become computationally expensive with large datasets.
- It is sensitive to outliers.

Exercise 3

Use the `clusterboot()` function to bootstrap the Jaccard index for k-means clustering (with four clusters), just like we did for hierarchical. This time, the `clustermethod` should be equal to `kmeansCBI` (to use k-means), and you should replace the `method` argument with `algorithm = "Lloyd"`. Which method results in more stable clusters: k-means or hierarchical clustering?

Exercise 4

Use the `diana()` function from the cluster package to perform divisive hierarchical clustering on the GvHD data. Save the output as an object, and plot the dendrogram by passing it into `as.dendrogram() %>% plot()`. Compare this to the dendrogram we got from agglomerative hierarchical clustering. Warning: this took nearly 15 minutes on my machine!

Exercise 5

Repeat our bootstrapping experiment with agglomerative hierarchical clustering, but this time fix the number of clusters to four and compare the different linkage methods on each bootstrap. Which linkage method performs the best?

Exercise 6

Recluster the data using `hclust()`, using the linkage method indicated as the best from exercise 5. Plot these clusters using `ggpairs()`, and compare them to those we generated using Ward's method. Does this new linkage method do a good job of finding clusters?

Summary

- Hierarchical clustering uses the distances between cases to learn a hierarchy of clusters.
- How these distances are calculated is controlled by our choice of linkage method.
- Hierarchical clustering can be bottom-up (agglomerative) or top-down (divisive).
- A flat set of clusters can be returned from a hierarchical clustering model by "cutting" the dendrogram at a particular height.
- Cluster stability can be measured by clustering on bootstrap samples and using the Jaccard index to quantify the agreement of cluster membership between samples.

Solutions to exercises

1 Create a hierarchical clustering model using the Manhattan distance, plot the dendrogram, and compare it:

```
gvhdDistMan <- dist(gvhdScaled, method = "manhattan")

gvhdHclustMan <- hclust(gvhdDistMan, method = "ward.D2")

gvhdDendMan <- as.dendrogram(gvhdHclustMan)

plot(gvhdDendMan, leaflab = "none")
```

2 Plot the bootstrap experiment in an alternate way:

```
group_by(metricsTib, Metric) %>%
  mutate(Value = scale(Value)) %>%
  group_by(Metric, clusters) %>%
  mutate(Stdev = sd(Value)) %>%

  ggplot(aes(as.factor(clusters), Metric, fill = Value, height = Stdev)) +
  geom_tile() +
  theme_bw() +
  theme(panel.grid = element_blank())
```

3 Use `clusterboot()` to evaluate the stability of our k-means model:

```
par(mfrow = c(3, 4))

clustBoot <- clusterboot(gvhdScaled,
                         B = 10,
```

```
                              clustermethod = kmeansCBI,
                              k = 4, algorithm = "Lloyd",
                              showplots = TRUE)

clustBoot

# k-means seems to give more stable clusters.
```

4 Cluster the data using the `diana()` function:

```
library(cluster)

gvhdDiana <- as_tibble(gvhdScaled) %>% diana()

as.dendrogram(gvhdDiana) %>% plot(leaflab = "none")
```

5 Repeat the bootstrap experiment, comparing different linkage methods:

```
cluster_metrics <- function(data, clusters, dist_matrix, linkage) {
  list(db    = clusterSim::index.DB(data, clusters)$DB,
       G1    = clusterSim::index.G1(data, clusters),
       dunn = clValid::dunn(dist_matrix, clusters),
       clusters = length(unique(clusters)),
       linkage = linkage
  )
}

metricsTib <- map_df(gvhdBoot, function(boot) {
  d <- dist(boot, method = "euclidean")
  linkage <- c("ward.D2", "single", "complete", "average", "centroid")

  map_df(linkage, function(linkage) {
    cl <- hclust(d, method = linkage)
    cut <- cutree(cl, k = 4)
    cluster_metrics(boot, clusters = cut, dist_matrix = d, linkage)
  })
})

metricsTib

metricsTib <- metricsTib %>%
  mutate(bootstrap = factor(rep(1:10, each = 5))) %>%
  gather(key = "Metric", value = "Value", -clusters, -bootstrap, -linkage)

ggplot(metricsTib, aes(linkage, Value)) +
  facet_wrap(~ Metric, scales = "free_y") +
  geom_line(size = 0.1, aes(group = bootstrap)) +
  geom_line(stat = "summary", fun.y = "mean", aes(group = 1)) +
  stat_summary(fun.data="mean_cl_boot",
               geom="crossbar", width = 0.5, fill = "white") +
  theme_bw()

# Single linkage seems the best, indicated by DB and Dunn,
# though pseudo F disagrees.
```

6 Cluster the data using the winning linkage method from exercise 5:

```
gvhdHclustSingle <- hclust(gvhdDist, method = "single")

gvhdCutSingle <- cutree(gvhdHclustSingle, k = 4)

gvhdTib <- mutate(gvhdTib, gvhdCutSingle = as.factor(gvhdCutSingle))

select(gvhdTib, -hclustCluster) %>%
  ggpairs(aes(col = gvhdCutSingle),
          upper = list(continuous = "density"),
          lower = list(continuous = wrap("points", size = 0.5))) +
  theme_bw()

# Using single linkage on this dataset does a terrible job of finding
# clusters! This is why visual evaluation of clusters is important:
# don't blindly rely on internal metrics only!
```

18 Clustering based on density: DBSCAN and OPTICS

This chapter covers

- Understanding density-based clustering
- Using the DBSCAN and OPTICS algorithms

Our penultimate stop in unsupervised learning techniques brings us to density-based clustering. Density-based clustering algorithms aim to achieve the same thing as k-means and hierarchical clustering: partitioning a dataset into a finite set of clusters that reveals a grouping structure in our data.

In the last two chapters, we saw how k-means and hierarchical clustering identify clusters using distance: distance between cases, and distance between cases and their centroids. Density-based clustering comprises a set of algorithms that, as the name suggests, uses the *density* of cases to assign cluster membership. There are multiple ways of measuring density, but we can define it as the number of cases per unit volume of our feature space. Areas of the feature space containing many cases packed closely together can be said to have high density, whereas areas of the feature space that contain few or no cases can be said to have low density. Our intuition here states that distinct clusters in a dataset will be represented by regions of high density, separated by regions of low density. Density-based clustering algorithms attempt to learn these distinct regions of high density and partition them into clusters. Density-based clustering algorithms have several nice properties that circumvent some of the limitations of k-means and hierarchical clustering.

By the end of this chapter, I hope you'll have a firm understanding of how two of the most commonly used density-based clustering algorithms work: DBSCAN and OPTICS. We'll also apply some of the skills you learned in the previous chapters to help us evaluate and compare the performance of different cluster models.

18.1 What is density-based clustering?

In this section, I'll show you how two of the most commonly used density-based clustering algorithms work:

- Density-based spatial clustering of applications with noise (DBSCAN)
- Ordering points to identify the clustering structure (OPTICS)

Aside from having names that were seemingly contrived to form interesting acronyms, DBSCAN and OPTICS both learn regions of high density, separated by regions of low density in a dataset. They achieve this in similar but slightly different ways, but both have a few advantages over k-means and hierarchical clustering:

- They are not biased to finding spherical clusters and can in fact find clusters of varying and complex shapes.
- They are not biased to finding clusters of equal diameter and can identify both very wide and very tight clusters in the same dataset.
- They are seemingly unique among clustering algorithms in that cases that do not fall within regions of high enough density are put into a separate "noise" cluster. This is often a desirable property, because it helps to prevent overfitting the data and allows us to focus on cases for which the evidence of cluster membership is stronger.

TIP If the separation of cases into a noise cluster isn't desirable for your application (but using DBSCAN or OPTICS is), you can use a heuristic method like classifying noise points based on their nearest cluster centroid, or adding them to the cluster of their k-nearest neighbors.

All three of these advantages can be seen in figure 18.1. The three subplots each show the same data, clustered using either DBSCAN, k-means (Hartigan-Wong algorithm), or hierarchical clustering (complete linkage). This dataset is certainly strange, and you might think you're unlikely to encounter real-world data like it, but it illustrates the advantages of density-based clustering over k-means and hierarchical clustering. The clusters in the data have very different shapes (that certainly aren't spherical) and diameters. While k-means and hierarchical clustering learn clusters that bisect and merge these real clusters, DBSCAN is able to faithfully find each shape as a distinct cluster. Additionally, notice that k-means and hierarchical clustering place every single case into a cluster. DBSCAN creates the cluster "0" into which it places any cases it considers to be noise. In this case, all cases outside of those geometrically shaped clusters

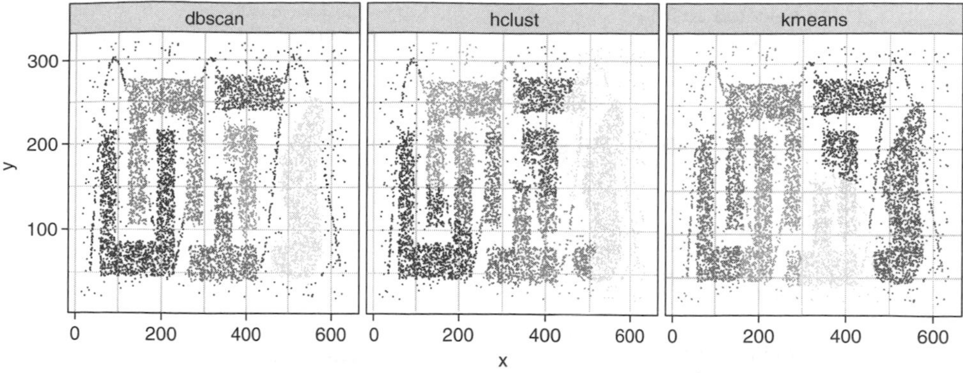

Figure 18.1 A challenging clustering problem. The dataset shown in each facet contains clusters of varying shapes and diameters, with cases that could be considered noise. The three subplots show the data clustered using DBSCAN, hierarchical clustering (complete linkage), and k-means (Hartigan-Wong). Of the three algorithms used, only DBSCAN is able to faithfully represent these shapes as distinct clusters.

are placed into the noise cluster. If you look carefully, though, you may notice a sine wave in the data that all three fail to identify as a cluster.

So how do density-based clustering algorithms work? Well the DBSCAN algorithm is a little easier to understand, so we'll start with it and build on it to understand OPTICS.

18.1.1 How does the DBSCAN algorithm learn?

In this section, I'll show you how the DBSCAN algorithm learns regions of high density in the data to identify clusters. In order to understand the DBSCAN algorithm, you first need to understand its two hyperparameters:

- *epsilon* (ε)
- *minPts*

The algorithm starts by selecting a case in the data and searching for other cases within a search radius. This radius is the *epsilon* hyperparameter. So *epsilon* is simply how far away from each case (in an *n*-dimensional sphere) the algorithm will search for other cases around a point. Epsilon is expressed in units of the feature space and will be the Euclidean distance by default. Larger values mean the algorithm will search further away from each case.

The *minPts* hyperparameter specifies the minimum number of points (cases) that a cluster must have in order for it to be a cluster. The *minPts* hyperparameter is therefore an integer. If a particular case has at least *minPts* cases inside its *epsilon* radius (including itself), that case is considered a *core point*.

Let's walk through the DBSCAN algorithm together by taking a look at figure 18.2. The first step of the algorithm is to select a case at random from the dataset. The

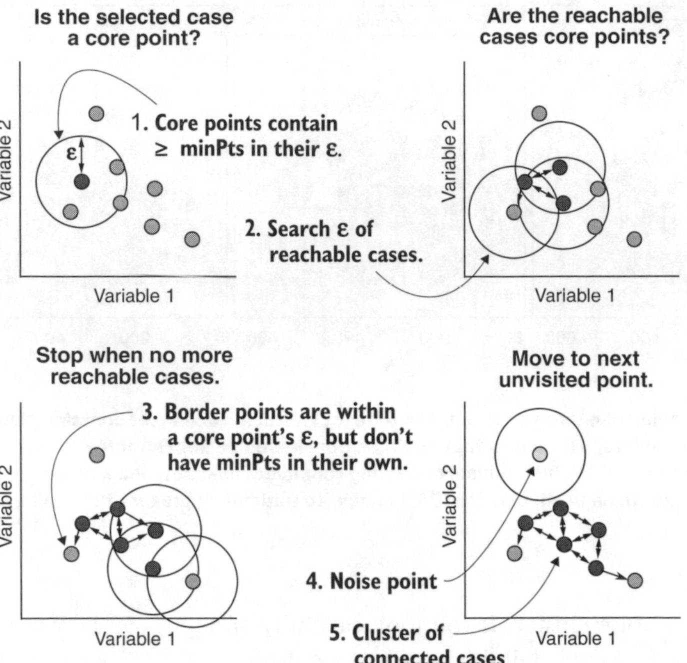

Figure 18.2 The DBSCAN algorithm. A case is selected at random, and if its *epsilon* radius (ε) contains *minPts* cases, it is considered a core point. Reachable cases of this core point are evaluated the same way until there are no more reachable cases. This network of density-connected cases is considered a cluster. Cases that are reachable from core points but are not themselves core points are border points. The algorithm moves on to the next unvisited case. Cases that are neither core nor border points are labeled as noise.

algorithm searches for other cases in an *n*-dimensional sphere (where *n* is the number of features in the dataset) with radius equal to *epsilon*. If this case contains at least *minPts* cases inside its search radius, it is marked as a core point. If the case does *not* contain *minPts* cases inside its search space, it is not a core point, and the algorithm moves on to another case.

Let's assume the algorithm picks a case and finds that it is a core point. The algorithm then visits each of the cases within *epsilon* of the core point and repeats the same task: looks to see if this case has *minPts* cases inside its own search radius. Two cases within each other's search radius are said to be *directly density connected* and *reachable* from each other. The search continues recursively, following all direct density connections from core points. If the algorithm finds a case that is reachable to a core point but does not itself have minPts-reachable cases, this case is considered a *border point*. The algorithm *only* searches the search space of core points, not border points.

Two cases are said to be *density connected* if they are not necessarily directly density connected but are connected to each other via a chain or series of directly density-connected cases. Once the search has been exhausted, and none of the visited cases have any more direct density connections left to explore, all cases that are density connected to each other are placed into the same cluster (including border points).

The algorithm now selects a different case in the dataset—one that it hasn't visited before—and the same process begins again. Once every case in the dataset has been visited, any lonesome cases that were neither core points nor border points are added to the noise cluster and are considered too far from regions of high density to confidently be clustered with the rest of the cases. So DBSCAN finds clusters by finding chains of cases in high-density regions of the feature space and throws out cases occupying sparse regions of the feature space.

NOTE Not searching outward from border points helps prevent the inclusion of noise events into clusters.

That was quite a lot of new terminology I just introduced! Let's have a quick recap to make these terms stick in your mind, because they're also important for the OPTICS algorithm:

- *Epsilon*—The radius of an *n*-dimensional sphere around a case, within which the algorithm searches for other cases
- *minPts*—The minimum number of cases allowed in a cluster, and the number of cases that must be within *epsilon* of a case for it to be a core point
- *Core point*—A case that has at least *minPts* reachable cases
- *Reachable/directly density connected*—When two cases are within *epsilon* of each other
- *Density connected*—When two cases are connected by a chain of directly density-connected cases but may not be directly density connected themselves
- *Border point*—A case that is reachable from a core point but is not itself a core point
- *Noise point*—A case that is neither a core point nor reachable from one

18.1.2 How does the OPTICS algorithm learn?

In this section, I'll show you how the OPTICS algorithm learns regions of high density in a dataset, how it's similar to DBSCAN, and how it differs. Technically speaking, OPTICS isn't actually a clustering algorithm. Instead, it creates an ordering of the cases in the data in such a way that we can extract clusters from it. That sounds a little abstract, so let's work through how OPTICS works.

The DBSCAN algorithm has one important drawback: it struggles to identify clusters that have different densities than each other. The OPTICS algorithm is an attempt to alleviate that drawback and identify clusters with varying densities. It does this by allowing the search radius around each case to expand dynamically instead of being fixed at a predetermined value.

In order to understand how OPTICS works, I need to introduce two new terms:

- Core distance
- Reachability distance

In OPTICS, the search radius around a case isn't fixed but expands until there are at least *minPts* cases within it. This means cases in dense regions of the feature space will have a small search radius, and cases in sparse regions will have a large search radius. The smallest distance away from a case that includes *minPts* other cases is called the *core distance*, sometimes abbreviated to ε'. In fact, the OPTICS algorithm only has one mandatory hyperparameter: *minPts*.

NOTE We can still supply *epsilon*, but it is mostly used to speed up the algorithm by acting as a maximum core distance. In other words, if the core distance reaches *epsilon*, just take *epsilon* as the core distance to prevent all cases in the dataset from being considered.

The *reachability distance* is the distance between a core point and another core point within its *epsilon*, but it cannot be less than the core distance. Put another way, if a case has a core point *inside* its core distance, the reachability distance between these cases *is* the core distance. If a case has a core point *outside* its core distance, then the reachability distance between these cases is simply the Euclidean distance between them.

NOTE In OPTICS, a case is a core point if there are *minPts* inside *epsilon*. If we don't specify *epsilon*, then all cases will be core points. The reachability distance between a case and a non-core point is undefined.

Take a look at the example in figure 18.3. You can see two circles centered around the darkly shaded case. The circle with the larger radius is *epsilon*, and the one with the smaller radius is the core distance (ε'). This example is showing the core distance for a *minPts* value of 4, because the core distance has expanded to include four cases (including the case in question). The arrows indicate the reachability distance between the core point and the other cases within its *epsilon*.

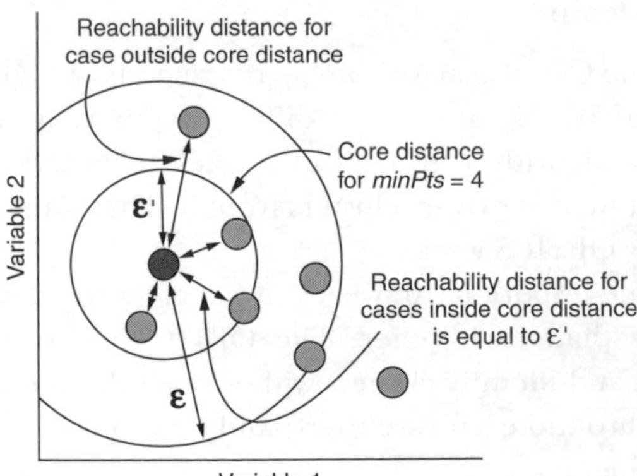

Figure 18.3 Defining the core distance and reachability distance. In OPTICS, *epsilon* (ε) is the maximum search distance. The core distance (ε') is the minimum search distance needed to include *minPts* cases (including the case in question). The reachability distance for a case is the larger of the core distance and the distance between the case in question, and another case inside its *epsilon* (maximum search distance).

Because the reachability distance is the distance between one core point and another core point within its *epsilon*, OPTICS needs to know which cases are core points. So the algorithm starts by visiting every case in the data and determining whether its core distance is less than *epsilon*. This is illustrated in figure 18.4. If a case's core distance is less than or equal to *epsilon*, the case is a core point. If a case's core distance is greater than *epsilon* (we need to expand out further than *epsilon* to find *minPts* cases), the case is *not* a core point. Examples of both are shown in figure 18.4.

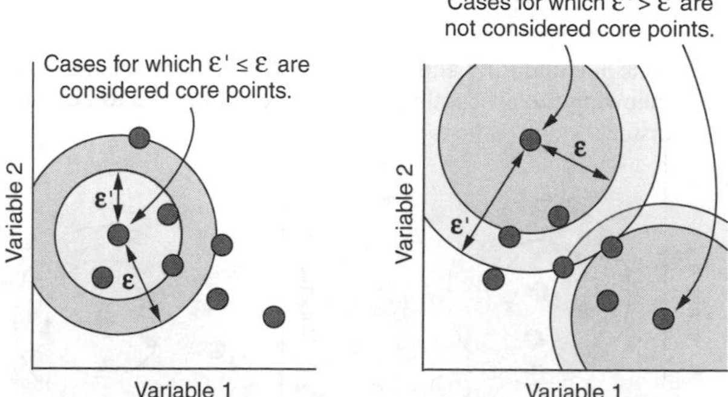

Figure 18.4 Defining core points in OPTICS. Cases for which the core distance (ε') is less than or equal to the maximum search distance (ε) are considered core points. Cases for which the core distance is greater than the maximum search distance are not considered core points.

Now that you understand the concepts of core distance and reachability distance, let's see how the OPTICS algorithm works. The first step is to visit each case in the data and mark it as a core point or not. The rest of the algorithm is illustrated in figure 18.5, so let's assume this has been done. OPTICS selects a case and calculates its core distance and its reachability distance to all cases inside its *epsilon* (the maximum search distance).

The algorithm does two things before moving on to the next case:

- Records the *reachability score* of the case
- Updates the processing order of cases

The reachability score of a case is different from a reachability distance (the terminology is unfortunately confusing). A case's reachability score is defined as the larger of its core distance or its smallest reachability distance. Let's rephrase: if a case doesn't have *minPts* cases inside *epsilon* (it isn't a core point), then its reachability score will be the reachability distance to its closest core point. If a case *does* have *minPts* cases inside *epsilon*, then its smallest reachability distance will be less than or equal to its core distance, so we just take the core distance as the case's reachability score.

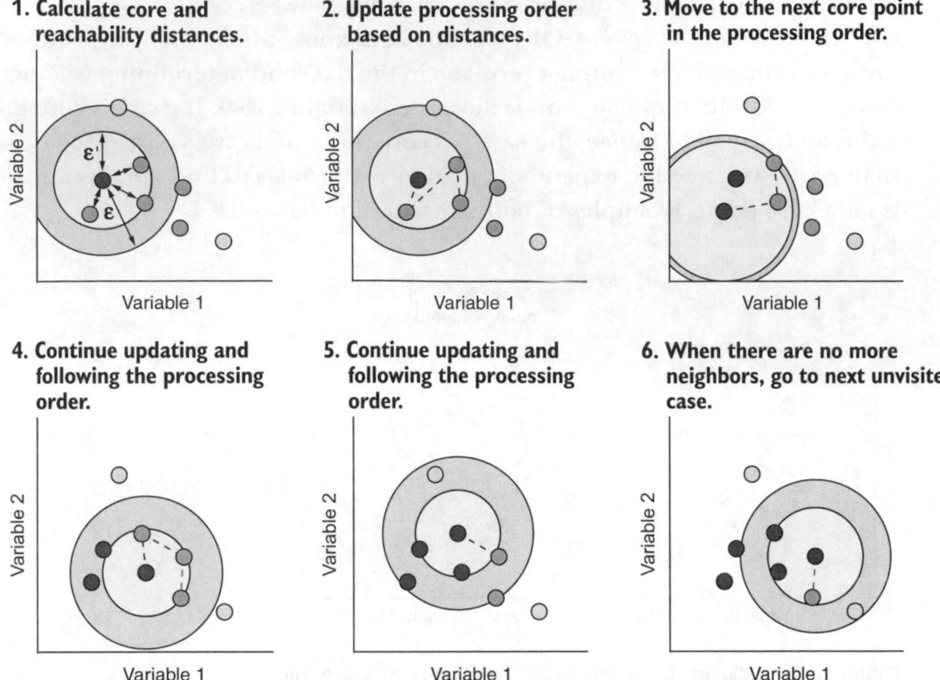

Figure 18.5 The OPTICS algorithm. A case is selected, and its core distance (ε') is measured. The reachability distance is calculated between this case and all the cases inside this case's maximum search distance (ε). The processing order of the dataset is updated such that the nearest case is visited next. The reachability score and the processing order are recorded for this case, and the algorithm moves on to the next one.

> **NOTE** Therefore, the reachability score of a case will never be less than its core distance, unless the core distance is greater than the maximum, *epsilon*, in which case *epsilon* will be the reachability score.

Once the reachability has been recorded for a particular case, the algorithm then updates the sequence of cases it's going to visit next (the processing order). It updates the processing order such that it will next visit the core point with the smallest reachability distance to the current case, then the one that is next-farthest away, and so on. This is illustrated in step 2 of figure 18.5.

The algorithm then visits the next case in the updated processing order and repeats the same process, likely changing the processing order once again. When there are no more reachable cases in the current chain, the algorithm moves on to the next unvisited core point in the dataset and repeats the process.

Once all cases have been visited, the algorithm returns both the processing order (the order in which each case was visited) and the reachability score of each case. If we plot processing order against reachability score, we get something like the top plot in figure 18.6. To generate this plot, I applied the OPTICS algorithm to a simulated

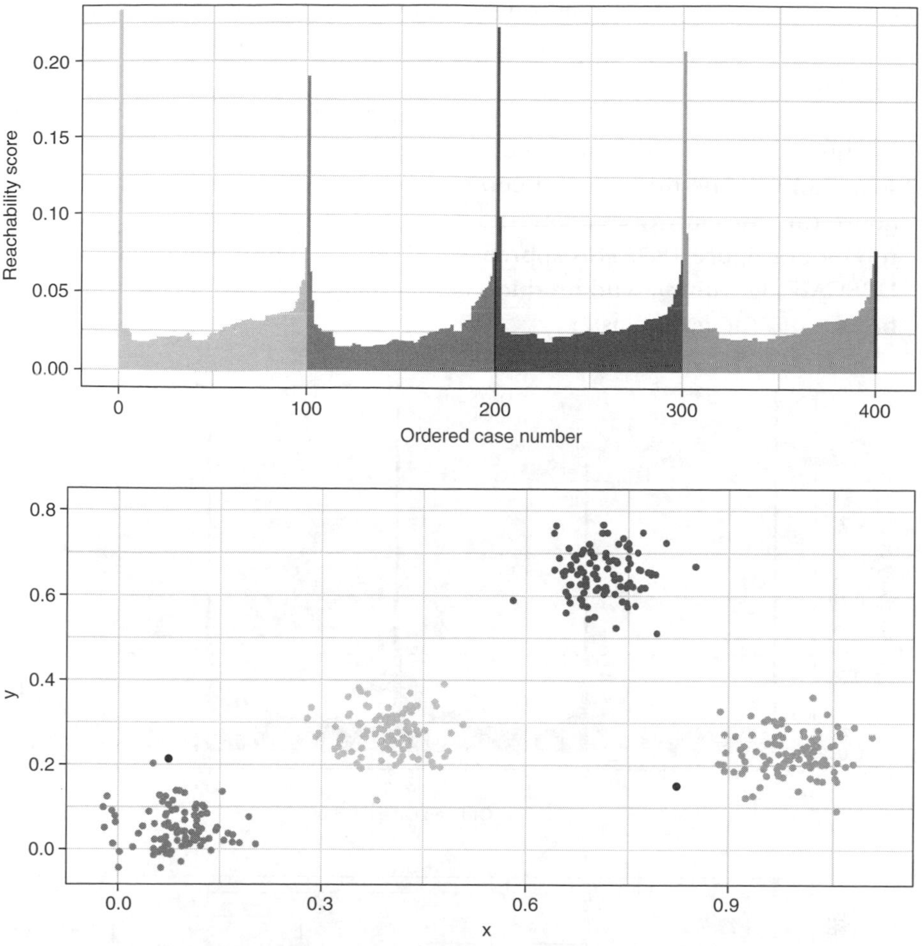

Figure 18.6 Reachability plot of a simulated dataset. The top plot shows the reachability plot learned by the OPTICS algorithm from the data shown in the bottom plot. The plots are shaded to indicate where each cluster in the feature space maps onto the reachability plot.

dataset with four clusters (you can find the code to reproduce this at www.manning.com/books/machine-learning-with-r-the-tidyverse-and-mlr). Notice that when we plot the processing order against the reachability score, we get four shallow troughs, each separated by spikes of high reachability. Each trough in the plot corresponds to a region of high density, while each spike indicates a separation of these regions by a region of low density.

NOTE The deeper the trough, the higher the density.

The OPTICS algorithm actually goes no further than this. Once it produces this plot, its work is done, and now it's our job to use the information contained in the plot to extract the cluster membership. This is why I said that OPTICS isn't technically a clustering algorithm but creates an ordering of the data that allows us to find clusters in the data.

So how do we extract clusters? We have a couple of options. One method would be to simply draw a horizontal line across the reachability plot, at some reachability score, and define the start and end of clusters as when the plot dips below and back above the line. Any cases above the line could be classified as noise, as shown in the top plot of figure 18.7. This approach will result in clustering very similar to what the DBSCAN algorithm would produce, except that some border points are more likely to be put into the noise cluster.

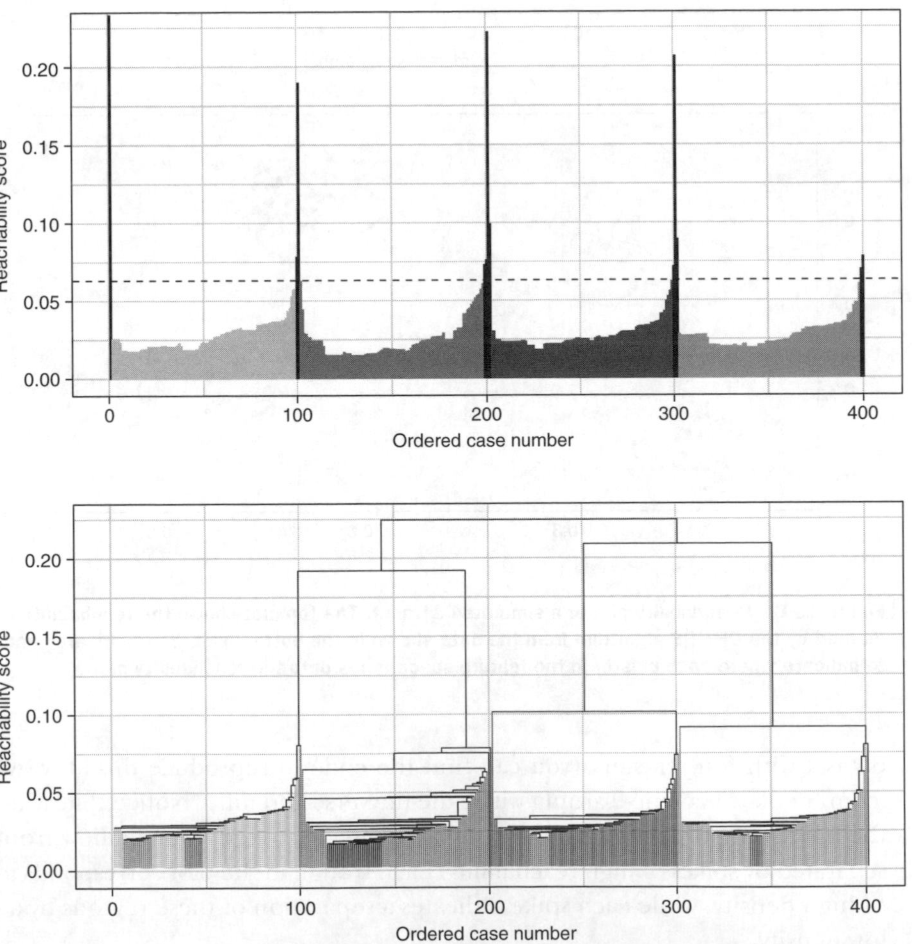

Figure 18.7 An illustration of different ways clusters can be extracted from a reachability plot. In the top plot, a single reachability score cut-off has been defined, and any troughs bordered by peaks above this cut-off are defined as clusters. In the bottom plot, a hierarchy of clusters is defined, based on the steepness of changes in reachability, allowing for clusters within clusters.

Another (usually more useful) method is to define a particular *steepness* in the reachability plot as indicative of the start and end of a cluster. We can define the start of a cluster as when we have a downward slope of at least this steepness, and its end as when we have an upward slope of at least this steepness. The method we'll use later defines the steepness as $1 - \xi$ (xi, pronounced "zy," "sigh," or "kzee," depending on your preference and mathematics teacher), where the reachability of two successive cases must change by a factor of $1 - \xi$. When we have a downward slope that meets this steepness criterion, the start of a cluster is defined; and when we have an upward slope that meets this steepness, the end of the cluster is defined.

NOTE Because ξ cannot be estimated from the data, it is a hyperparameter we must select/tune ourselves.

Using this method has two major benefits. First, it allows us to overcome DBSCAN's limitation of only finding clusters of equal density. Second, it allows us to find clusters within clusters, to form a hierarchy. Imagine that we have a downward slope that starts a cluster, and then we have *another* downward slope before the cluster ends: we have a cluster within a cluster. This hierarchical extraction of clusters from a reachability plot is shown in the bottom plot in figure 18.7.

NOTE Notice that neither of these methods works with the original data. They extract all the information to assign cluster memberships from the order and reachability scores generated by the OPTICS algorithm.

18.2 Building your first DBSCAN model

In this section, I'm going to show you how to use the DBSCAN algorithm to cluster a dataset. We'll then use some of the techniques you learned in chapter 17 to validate its performance and select the best-performing hyperparameter combination.

NOTE The mlr package does have a learner for the DBSCAN algorithm (`cluster.dbscan`), but we're not going to use it. There's nothing wrong with it; but as you'll see later, the presence of the noise cluster causes problems for our internal cluster metrics, so we're going to do our own performance validation outside of mlr.

18.2.1 Loading and exploring the banknote dataset

Let's start by loading the tidyverse and loading in the data, which is part of the mclust package. We're going to work with the Swiss banknote dataset to which we applied PCA, t-SNE, and UMAP in chapters 13 and 14. Once we've loaded in the data, we convert it into a tibble and create a separate tibble after scaling the data (because DBSCAN and OPTICS are sensitive to variable scales). Because we're going to imagine that we have no ground truth, we remove the `Status` variable, indicating which banknotes are genuine and which are counterfeit. Recall that the tibble contains 200 Swiss banknotes, with 6 measurements of their dimensions.

Listing 18.1 Loading the tidyverse packages and dataset

```
library(tidyverse)

data(banknote, package = "mclust")

swissTib <- select(banknote, -Status) %>%
  as_tibble()

swissTib

# A tibble: 200 x 6
   Length  Left Right Bottom   Top Diagonal
    <dbl> <dbl> <dbl>  <dbl> <dbl>    <dbl>
 1   215.  131   131.    9     9.7     141
 2   215.  130.  130.    8.1   9.5     142.
 3   215.  130.  130.    8.7   9.6     142.
 4   215.  130.  130.    7.5  10.4     142
 5   215   130.  130.   10.4   7.7     142.
 6   216.  131.  130.    9    10.1     141.
 7   216.  130.  130.    7.9   9.6     142.
 8   214.  130.  129.    7.2  10.7     142.
 9   215.  129.  130.    8.2  11       142.
10   215.  130.  130.    9.2  10       141.
# ... with 190 more rows

swissScaled <- swissTib %>% scale()
```

Let's plot the data using `ggpairs()` to remind ourselves of the structure of the data.

Listing 18.2 Plotting the data

```
library(GGally)

ggpairs(swissTib, upper = list(continuous = "density")) +
  theme_bw()
```

The resulting plot is shown in figure 18.8. It looks as though there are at least two regions of high density in the data, with a few scattered cases in lower-density regions.

18.2.2 Tuning the epsilon and minPts hyperparameters

In this section, I'll show you how to select sensible ranges of *epsilon* and *minPts* for DBSCAN, and how we can tune them manually to find the best-performing combination. Choosing the value of the *epsilon* hyperparameter is, perhaps, not obvious. How far away from each case should we search? Luckily, there is a heuristic method we can use to at least get in the right ballpark. This consists of calculating the distance from each point to its *k*th-nearest neighbor and then ordering the points in a plot based on this distance. In data with regions of high and low density, this tends to produce a plot containing a "knee" or "elbow" (depending on your preference). The optimal value of *epsilon* is in or near that knee/elbow. Because a core point in DBSCAN has *minPts* cases inside its

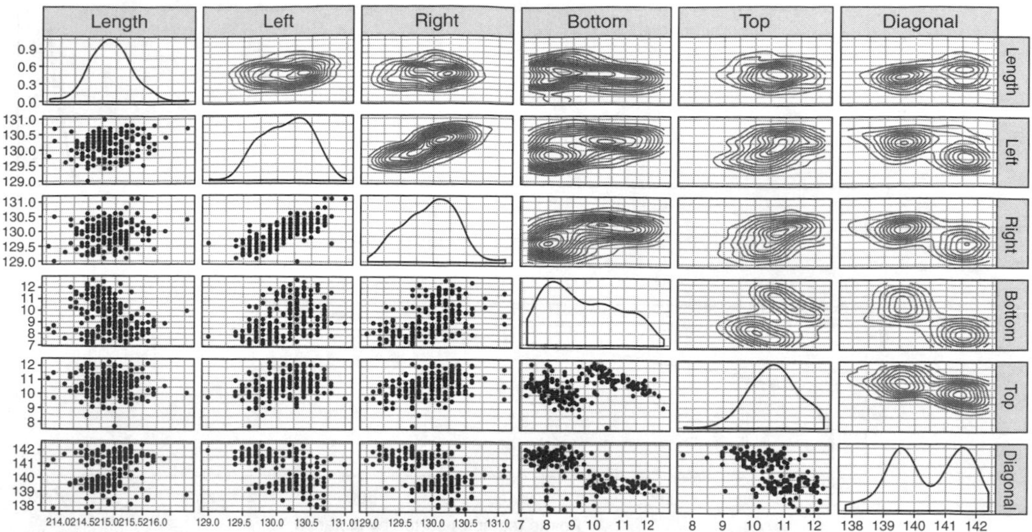

Figure 18.8 Plotting the Swiss banknote dataset with `ggpairs()`. 2D density plots are shown above the diagonal.

epsilon, choosing a value of *epsilon* at the knee of this plot means choosing a search distance that will result in cases in high-density regions being considered core points. We can create this plot using the `kNNdistplot()` function from the dbscan package.

Listing 18.3 Plotting the kNN distance plot

```
library(dbscan)

kNNdistplot(swissScaled, k = 5)

abline(h = c(1.2, 2.0))
```

We need to use the `k` argument to specify the number of nearest neighbors we want to calculate the distance to. But we don't yet know what our *minPts* argument should be, so how can we set `k`? I usually pick a sensible value that I believe is approximately correct (remember that *minPts* defines the minimum cluster size): here, I've selected 5. The position of the knee in the plot is relatively robust to changes in `k`.

The `kNNdistplot()` function will create a matrix with as many rows as there are cases in the dataset (200) and 5 columns, one for the distance between each case and each of its 5 nearest neighbors. Each of these 200 × 5 = 1,000 distances will be drawn on the plot.

We then use the `abline()` function to draw horizontal lines at the start and end of the knee, to help us identify the range of *epsilon* values we're going to tune over. The resulting plot is shown in figure 18.9. Notice that, reading the plot from left to right, after an initial sharp increase, the 5-nearest-neighbor distance increases only gradually, until it rapidly increases again. This region where the curve inflects upward is the

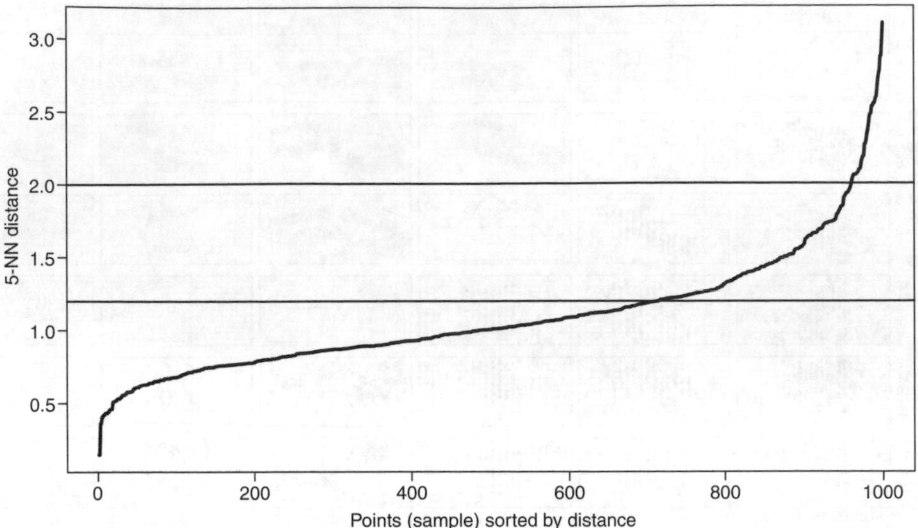

Figure 18.9 K-nearest neighbor distance plot with $k = 5$. Horizontal lines have been drawn using `abline()` to highlight the 5-NN distances at the start and end of the knee/elbow in the plot.

knee/elbow, and the optimal value of *epsilon* at this nearest-neighbor distance in this inflection. Using this method, we select 1.2 and 2.0 as the lower and upper limits over which to tune *epsilon.*

Let's manually define our hyperparameter search space for *epsilon* and *minPts.* We use the `expand.grid()` function to create a data frame containing every combination of the values of *epsilon* (`eps`) and *minPts* we want to search over. We're going to search across values of *epsilon* between 1.2 and 2.0, in steps of 0.1; and we're going to search across values of *minPts* between 1 and 9, in steps of 1.

Listing 18.4 Defining our hyperparameter search space

```
dbsParamSpace <- expand.grid(eps = seq(1.2, 2.0, 0.1),
                             minPts = seq(1, 9, 1))
```

Exercise 1

Print the `dbsParamSpace` object to give yourself a better intuition of what `expand.grid()` is doing.

Now that we've defined our hyperparameter search space, let's run the DBSCAN algorithm on each distinct combination of *epsilon* and *minPts.* To do this, we use the `pmap()` function from the purrr package to apply the `dbscan()` function to each row of the `dbsParamSpace` object.

Listing 18.5 Running DBSCAN on each combination of hyperparameters

```
swissDbs <- pmap(dbsParamSpace, dbscan, x = swissScaled)

swissDbs[[5]]

DBSCAN clustering for 200 objects.
Parameters: eps = 1.6, minPts = 1
The clustering contains 10 cluster(s) and 0 noise points.

  1   2   3   4   5   6   7   8   9  10
  1 189   1   1   1   3   1   1   1   1

Available fields: cluster, eps, minPts
```

We supply our scaled dataset as the argument to `dbscan()`'s argument, `x`. The output from `pmap()` is a list where each element is the result of running DBSCAN on that particular combination of *epsilon* and *minPts*. To view the output for a particular permutation, we simply subset the list.

The output, when printing the result of a `dbscan()` call, tells us the number of objects in the data, the values of *epsilon* and *minPts*, and the number of identified clusters and noise points. Perhaps the most important information is the number of cases within each cluster. In this example, we can see there are 189 cases in cluster 2, and just a single case in most of the other clusters. This is because this permutation was run with *minPts* equal to 1, which allows clusters to contain just a single case. This is rarely what we want and will result in a clustering model where no cases are identified as noise.

Now that we have our clustering result, we should visually inspect the clustering to see which (if any) of the permutations give a sensible result. To do this, we want to extract the vector of cluster membership from each permutation as a column and then add these columns to our original data.

The first step is to extract the cluster memberships as separate columns in a tibble. To do this, we use the `map_dfc()` function. We've encountered the `map_df()` function before: it applies a function to each element of a vector and returns the output as a tibble, where each output forms a different row of the tibble. This is actually the same as using `map_dfr()`, where the *r* means row-binding. If, instead, we want each output to form a different *column* of the tibble, we use `map_dfc()`.

NOTE I've truncated the output here for the sake of space.

Listing 18.6 Cluster memberships from DBSCAN permutations

```
clusterResults <- map_dfc(swissDbs, ~.$cluster)

clusterResults

# A tibble: 200 x 81
      V1    V2    V3    V4    V5    V6    V7    V8    V9   V10   V11
   <int> <int> <int> <int> <int> <int> <int> <int> <int> <int> <int>
```

```
 1    1    1    1    1    1    1    1    1    1    0    0
 2    2    2    2    2    2    2    2    2    2    1    1
 3    2    2    2    2    2    2    2    2    2    1    1
 4    2    2    2    2    2    2    2    2    2    1    1
 5    3    3    3    3    3    3    3    3    2    0    0
 6    4    4    4    4    4    2    2    2    2    0    0
 7    5    2    2    2    2    2    2    2    2    0    1
 8    2    2    2    2    2    2    2    2    2    1    1
 9    2    2    2    2    2    2    2    2    2    1    1
10    6    2    2    2    2    2    2    2    2    2    1
# ... with 190 more rows, and 70 more variables
```

Now that we have our tibble of cluster memberships, let's use the `bind_cols()` function to, well, bind the columns of our `swissTib` tibble and our tibble of cluster memberships. We call this new tibble `swissClusters`, which sounds like a breakfast cereal. Notice that we have our original variables, with additional columns containing the cluster membership output from each permutation.

NOTE Again, I've truncated the output slightly to save space.

Listing 18.7 Binding cluster memberships to the original data

```
swissClusters <- bind_cols(swissTib, clusterResults)

swissClusters

# A tibble: 200 x 87
    Length  Left Right Bottom   Top Diagonal    V1    V2    V3    V4
     <dbl> <dbl> <dbl>  <dbl> <dbl>    <dbl> <int> <int> <int> <int>
 1    215.   131  131.      9   9.7      141     1     1     1     1
 2    215.  130.  130.    8.1   9.5     142.     2     2     2     2
 3    215.  130.  130.    8.7   9.6     142.     2     2     2     2
 4    215.  130.  130.    7.5  10.4      142     2     2     2     2
 5    215   130.  130.   10.4   7.7     142.     3     3     3     3
 6    216.  131.  130.      9  10.1     141.     4     4     4     4
 7    216.  130.  130.    7.9   9.6     142.     5     2     2     2
 8    214.  130.  129.    7.2  10.7     142.     2     2     2     2
 9    215.  129.  130.    8.2  11       142.     2     2     2     2
10    215.  130.  130.    9.2  10       141.     6     2     2     2
# ... with 190 more rows, and 77 more variables
```

In order to plot the results, we would like to facet by permutation so we can draw a separate subplot for each combination of our hyperparameters. To do this, we need to `gather()` the data to create a new column indicating permutation number and another column indicating the cluster number.

Listing 18.8 Gathering the data, ready for plotting

```
swissClustersGathered <- gather(swissClusters,
                                key = "Permutation", value = "Cluster",
                                -Length, -Left, -Right,
                                -Bottom, -Top, -Diagonal)
```

```
swissClustersGathered

# A tibble: 16,200 x 8
   Length  Left Right Bottom   Top Diagonal Permutation Cluster
    <dbl> <dbl> <dbl>  <dbl> <dbl>    <dbl> <chr>         <int>
 1   215.  131   131.    9     9.7     141  V1                1
 2   215.  130.  130.    8.1   9.5     142. V1                2
 3   215.  130.  130.    8.7   9.6     142. V1                2
 4   215.  130.  130.    7.5  10.4     142  V1                2
 5   215   130.  130.   10.4   7.7     142. V1                3
 6   216.  131.  130.    9    10.1     141. V1                4
 7   216.  130.  130.    7.9   9.6     142. V1                5
 8   214.  130.  129.    7.2  10.7     142. V1                2
 9   215.  129.  130.    8.2  11       142. V1                2
10   215.  130.  130.    9.2  10       141. V1                6
# ... with 16,190 more rows
```

Great—now our tibble is in a format ready for plotting. Looking back at figure 18.8, we can see that the variables that most obviously separate clusters in the data are `Right` and `Diagonal`. As such, we'll plot these variables against each other by mapping them to the x and y aesthetics, respectively. We map the `Cluster` variable to the color aesthetic (wrapping it inside `as.factor()` so the colors aren't drawn as a single gradient). We then facet by `Permutation`, add a `geom_point()` layer, and add a theme. Because some of the cluster models have a large number of clusters, we suppress the drawing of what would be a very large legend, by adding the line `theme(legend.position = "none")`.

Listing 18.9 Plotting cluster memberships of permutations

```
ggplot(swissClustersGathered, aes(Right, Diagonal,
                                  col = as.factor(Cluster))) +
  facet_wrap(~ Permutation) +
  geom_point() +
  theme_bw() +
  theme(legend.position = "none")
```

> **TIP** The `theme()` function allows you to control the appearance of your plots (such as changing background colors, gridlines, font sizes, and so on). To find out more, call `?theme`.

The resulting plot is shown in figure 18.10. We can see that different combinations of *epsilon* and *minPts* have resulted in substantially different clustering models. Many of these models capture the two obvious clusters in the dataset, but most do not.

Exercise 2

Let's also visualize the number and size of the clusters returned by each permutation. Pass our `swissClustersGathered` object to `ggplot()` with the following aesthetic mappings:

- `x = reorder(Permutation, Cluster)`
- `y = fill = as.factor(Cluster)`

> ***(continued)***
>
> Also add a `geom_bar()` layer. Now draw the same plot again, but this time add a `coord_polar()` layer. Change the x aesthetic mapping to just `Permutation`. Can you see what the `reorder()` function was doing?

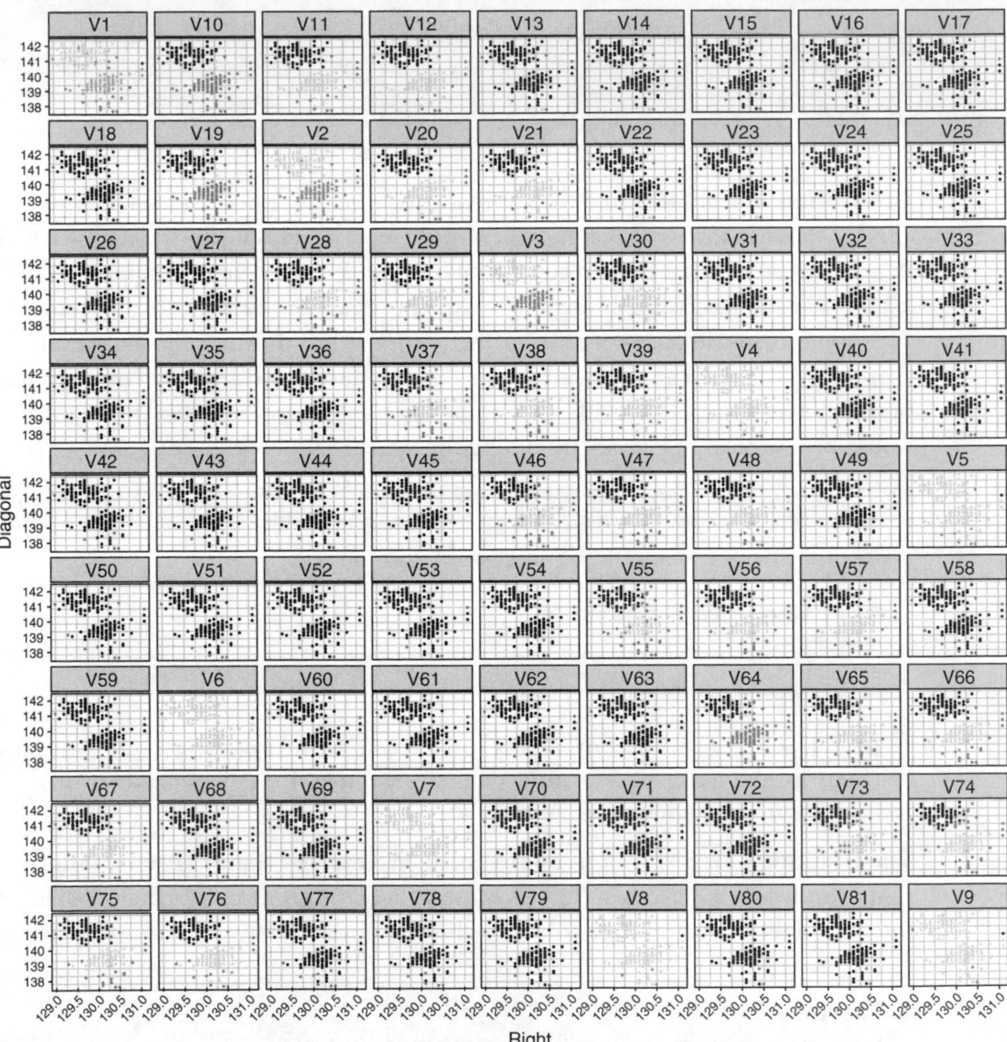

Figure 18.10 Visualizing the result of our tuning experiment. Each subplot shows the `Right` and `Diagonal` variables plotted against each other for a different permutation of *epsilon* and *minPts*. Cases are shaded by their cluster membership.

How are we going to choose the best-performing combination of *epsilon* and *minPts*? Well, as we saw in chapter 17, visually checking to make sure the clusters are sensible is important, but we can also calculate internal cluster metrics to help guide our choice.

In chapter 17, we defined our own function that would take the data and the cluster membership from a clustering model and calculate the Davies-Bouldin and Dunn indices and the pseudo F statistic. Let's redefine this function to refresh your memory.

Listing 18.10 Defining the `cluster_metrics()` function

```
cluster_metrics <- function(data, clusters, dist_matrix) {
  list(db   = clusterSim::index.DB(data, clusters)$DB,
       G1   = clusterSim::index.G1(data, clusters),
       dunn = clValid::dunn(dist_matrix, clusters),
       clusters = length(unique(clusters))
  )
}
```

To help us select which of our clustering models best captures the structure in the data, we're going to take bootstrap samples from our dataset and run DBSCAN using all 81 combinations of *epsilon* and *minPts* on each bootstrap sample. We can then calculate the mean of each of our performance metrics and see how stable they are.

> **NOTE** Recall from chapter 17 that a bootstrap sample is created by sampling cases from the original data, with replacement, to create a new sample that's the same size as the original.

Let's start by generating 10 bootstrap samples from our `swissScaled` dataset. We do this just as we did in chapter 17, using the `sample_n()` function and setting the `replace` argument equal to `TRUE`.

Listing 18.11 Creating bootstrap samples

```
swissBoot <- map(1:10, ~ {
  swissScaled %>%
    as_tibble() %>%
    sample_n(size = nrow(.), replace = TRUE)
})
```

Before we run our tuning experiment, DBSCAN presents a potential problem when calculating internal cluster metrics. As we saw from the discussion about them in chapter 16, these metrics work by comparing the separation between clusters and the spread within clusters (however they define these concepts). Think for a second about the noise cluster, and how it will impact these metrics. Because the noise cluster isn't a distinct cluster occupying one region of the feature space but is typically spread out across it, its impact on internal cluster metrics can make the metrics uninterpretable and difficult to compare. As such, once we have our clustering results, we're going to remove the noise cluster so we can calculate our internal cluster metrics using only non-noise clusters.

NOTE This doesn't mean it's not important to consider the noise cluster when evaluating the performance of a DBSCAN model. Two cluster models could theoretically give equally good cluster metrics, but one model may place cases in the noise cluster that you consider to be important. You should therefore always visually evaluate your cluster result (including noise cases), especially when you have domain knowledge of your task.

In the following listing, we run the tuning experiment on our bootstrap samples. The code is quite long, so we'll walk through it step by step.

Listing 18.12 Performing the tuning experiment

```
metricsTib <- map_df(swissBoot, function(boot) {
  clusterResult <- pmap(dbsParamSpace, dbscan, x = boot)

  map_df(clusterResult, function(permutation) {
    clust <- as_tibble(permutation$cluster)
    filteredData <- bind_cols(boot, clust) %>%
      filter(value != 0)

    d <- dist(select(filteredData, -value))

    cluster_metrics(select(filteredData, -value),
                    clusters = filteredData$value,
                    dist_matrix = d)
  })
})
```

First, we use the `map_df()` function, because we want to apply an anonymous function to each bootstrap sample and row-bind the results into a tibble. We run the DBSCAN algorithm using every combination of *epsilon* and *minPts* in our `dbsParamSpace` using `pmap()`, just as we did in listing 18.5.

Now that the cluster results have been generated, the next part of the code applies our `cluster_metric()` function to each permutation of *epsilon* and *minPts*. Again, we want this to be returned as a tibble, so we use `map_df()` to iterate an anonymous function over each element in `clusterResult`.

We start by extracting the cluster membership from each permutation, converting it into a tibble (of a single column), and using the `bind_cols()` function to stick this column of cluster membership onto the bootstrap sample. We then pipe this into the `filter()` function to remove cases that belong to the noise cluster (cluster 0). Because the Dunn index requires a distance matrix, we next define the distance matrix, `d`, using the filtered data.

At this point, for a particular permutation of *epsilon* and *minPts* for a particular bootstrap sample, we have a tibble containing the scaled variables and a column of cluster membership for cases not in the noise clusters. This tibble is then passed to our very own `cluster_metrics()` function (removing the `value` variable for the first argument and extracting it for the second argument). We pass the distance matrix as the `dist_matrix` argument.

Phew! That took quite a bit of concentration. I strongly suggest that you read back through the code and make sure each line makes sense to you. Print the `metricsTib` tibble. We end up with a tibble of four columns: one for each of our three internal cluster metrics, and one containing the number of clusters. Each row contains the result of a single DBSCAN model, 810 total (81 permutations of *epsilon* and *minPts* and 10 bootstrap samples for each).

Now that we've performed our tuning experiment, the easiest way to evaluate the results is to plot them.

Listing 18.13 Preparing the tuning result for plotting

```
metricsTibSummary <- metricsTib %>%
  mutate(bootstrap = factor(rep(1:10, each = 81)),
         eps = factor(rep(dbsParamSpace$eps, times = 10)),
         minPts = factor(rep(dbsParamSpace$minPts, times = 10))) %>%

  gather(key = "metric", value = "value",
         -bootstrap, -eps, -minPts) %>%

  mutate_if(is.numeric, ~ na_if(., Inf)) %>%
  drop_na() %>%

  group_by(metric, eps, minPts) %>%
  summarize(meanValue = mean(value),
            num = n()) %>%
  group_by(metric) %>%
  mutate(meanValue = scale(meanValue)) %>%
  ungroup()
```

We first need to `mutate()` columns indicating which bootstrap a particular case used, which *epsilon* value it used, and which *minPts* value it used. Read as far as the first line break in listing 18.13 to see this.

Next, we need to gather the data such that we have a column indicating which of our four metrics the row is indicating, so that we can facet by each metric. We do this using the `gather()` function before the second line break in listing 18.13.

At this point, we have a problem. Some of the cluster models contain only a single cluster. To return a sensible value, each of our three internal cluster metrics requires a minimum of two clusters. When we apply our `cluster_metrics()` function to the clustering models, the function will return `NA` for the Davies-Bouldin index and pseudo F statistic and `INF` for the Dunn index, for any model containing only a single cluster.

> **TIP** Run `map_int(metricsTib, ~sum(is.na(.)))` and `map_int(metricsTib, ~sum(is.infinite(.)))` to confirm this for yourself.

So let's remove `INF` and `NA` values from our tibble. We do this by first turning `INF` values into `NA`. We use the `mutate_if()` function to consider only the numeric variable (we could also have used `mutate_at(.vars = "value", …))`, and we use the `na_if()`

function to convert values to NA if they are currently INF. We then pipe this into drop_na() to remove all the NA values at once.

Finally, to generate mean values for each metric, for each combination of *epsilon* and *minPts*, we first group_by()metric, eps, and minPts, and summarize() both the mean and number of the value variable. Because the metrics are on different scales, we then group_by()metric, scale() the meanValue variable, and then ungroup().

That was some serious dplyring! Again, don't just gloss over this code. Start again from the top and read all of listing 18.13 to be sure you understand it. Also be comforted that I didn't just write this all out the first time; I knew what I wanted to achieve, and I worked through the problem line by line. At each step, I looked at the output to make sure what I had done was correct and to work out what I needed to do next. Print out the metricsTibSummary so you understand what we end up with.

Fantastic. Now that our tuning data is in the correct format, let's plot it. We're going to create a heatmap where *epsilon* and *minPts* are mapped to the x and y aesthetics, and the value of the metric is mapped to the fill of each tile in the heatmap. There will be a separate subplot for each metric. Also, because we removed rows containing NA and INF values, some combinations of *epsilon* and *minPts* have fewer than 10 bootstrap samples. To help guide our choice of hyperparameters, we're going to map the number of samples for each combination to the alpha aesthetic (transparency), because we may have less confidence in a combination of hyperparameters that has fewer bootstrap samples. We do this all in the following listing.

Listing 18.14 Plotting the results of the tuning experiment

```
ggplot(metricsTibSummary, aes(eps, minPts,
                              fill = meanValue, alpha = num)) +
  facet_wrap(~ metric) +
  geom_tile(col = "black") +
  theme_bw() +
  theme(panel.grid.major = element_blank())
```

Aside from mapping the num variable to the alpha aesthetic, the only new thing here is geom_tile(), which will create rectangular tiles for each combination of the x and y variables. Setting col = "black" simply draws a black border around each individual tile. To prevent major gridlines being drawn, we add the layer theme(panel.grid.major = element_blank()).

The resulting plot is shown in figure 18.11. We have four subplots: one for each of our three internal cluster metrics, and one for the number of clusters. A hole at the top right in each internal metric's subplot shows where this area of the hyperparameter tuning space resulted in only a single cluster (and we removed these values). Surrounding the hole are tiles that are semitransparent, because some of the bootstrap samples for these combinations of *epsilon* and *minPts* resulted in only a single cluster and so were removed.

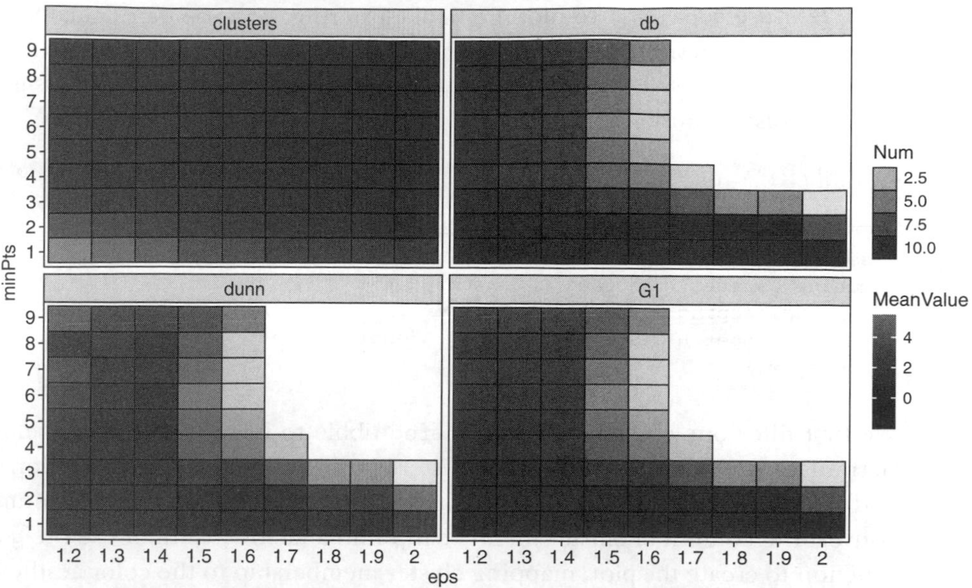

Figure 18.11 Visualizing the cluster performance experiment. Each subplot shows a heatmap for the number of clusters, Davies-Bouldin index (`db`), Dunn index (`dunn`), and pseudo F statistic (`G1`) returned by the cluster models. Each tile represents the combination of *epsilon* and *minPts*, and the depth of shading of the tile indicates its value for each metric. The blank region at the top right in the metric plots indicates a region with no data, and semitransparent tiles indicate fewer than 10 samples.

NOTE Your plot looking a little different than mine? This is because of the random sampling we used to create the bootstrap samples. A similar pattern should be present, however.

Let's use this plot to guide our final choice of *epsilon* and *minPts*. It isn't necessarily straightforward, because there is no single, obvious combination that all three internal metrics agree on. First, let's avoid combinations in or around the hole in the plot—I think that's a pretty clear starting point. Next, let's remind ourselves that, in theory, the best clustering model will be the one with the lowest Davies-Bouldin index and the largest Dunn index and pseudo F statistic. So we're looking for a combination that best satisfies those criteria. With this in mind, before reading on, look at the plots and try to decide which combination you would choose.

I think I would choose an *epsilon* of 1.2 and a *minPts* of 9. Can you see that with this combination of values (the top left in each subplot), the Dunn and pseudo F statistic are near their highest, and the Davies-Bouldin index is at its lowest? Let's find out which row of our `dbsParamSpace` tibble corresponds to this combination of values:

```
which(dbsParamSpace$eps == 1.2 & dbsParamSpace$minPts == 9)

[1] 73
```

Next, let's use ggpairs() to plot the final clustering. Because we calculated the internal cluster metrics, not considering the noise cluster, we'll plot the result with and without noise cases. This will allow us to visually confirm whether the assignment of cases as noise is sensible.

Listing 18.15 Plotting the final clustering with outliers

```
filter(swissClustersGathered, Permutation == "V73") %>%
  select(-Permutation) %>%
  mutate(Cluster = as.factor(Cluster)) %>%
  ggpairs(mapping = aes(col = Cluster),
          upper = list(continuous = "density")) +
  theme_bw()
```

We first filter our swissClustersGathered tibble to include only rows belonging to permutation 73 (these are the cases clustered using our chosen combination of *epsilon* and *minPts*). Next, we remove the column indicating the permutation number and convert the column of cluster membership into a factor. We then use the ggpairs() function to create the plot, mapping cluster membership to the color aesthetic.

The resulting plot is shown in figure 18.12. The model appears to have done a pretty good job of capturing the two obvious clusters in the dataset. Quite a lot of cases have been classified as noise. Whether this is reasonable will depend on your

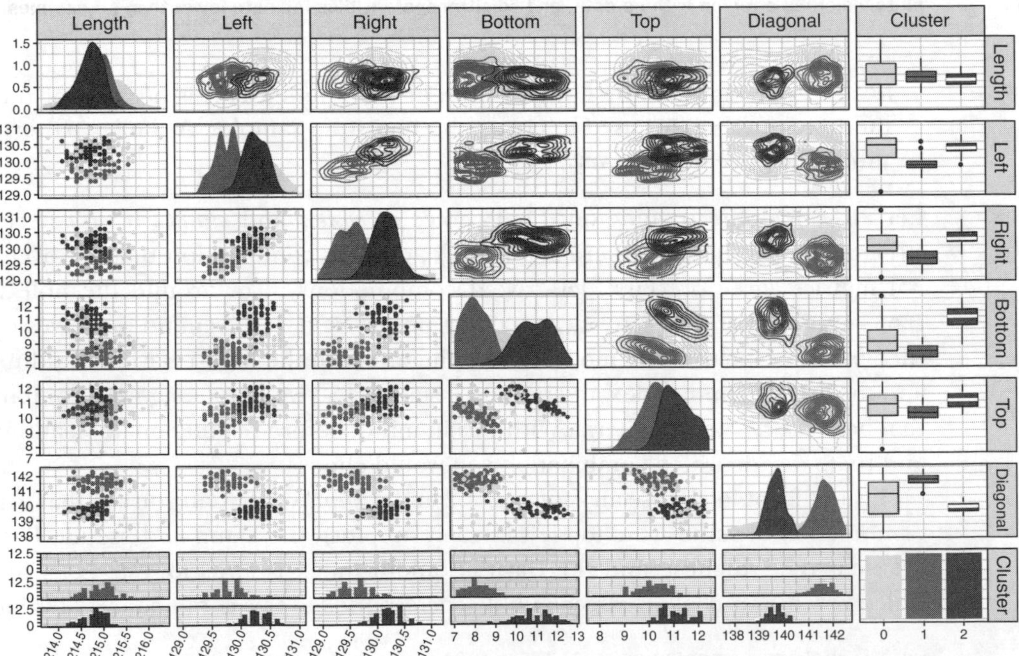

Figure 18.12 Plotting our final DBSCAN cluster model with ggpairs(). This plot includes the noise cluster.

goal and how stringent you want to be. If it's important to you that fewer cases are placed in the noise cluster, you may want to choose a different combination of *epsilon* and *minPts*. This is why relying on metrics alone isn't good enough: expert/domain knowledge should always be considered where it is available.

Now let's do the same thing, but without plotting outliers. All we change here is to add `Cluster != 0` in the `filter()` call.

Listing 18.16 Plotting the final clustering without outliers

```
filter(swissClustersGathered, Permutation == "V73", Cluster != 0) %>%
  select(-Permutation) %>%
  mutate(Cluster = as.factor(Cluster)) %>%
  ggpairs(mapping = aes(col = Cluster),
          upper = list(continuous = "density")) +
  theme_bw()
```

The resulting plot is shown in figure 18.13. Looking at this plot, we can see that the two clusters our DBSCAN model identified are quite neat and well separated.

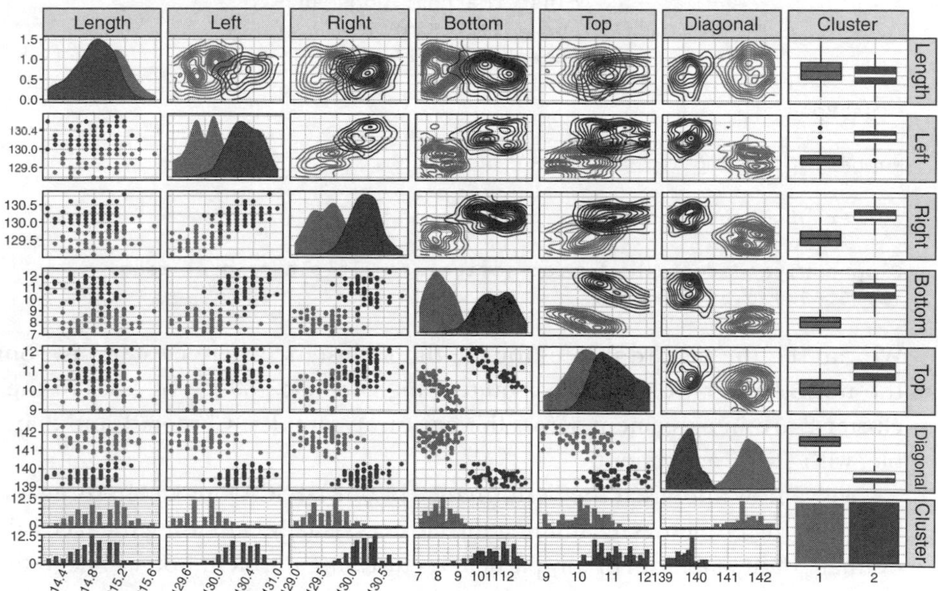

Figure 18.13 Plotting our final DBSCAN cluster model with `ggpairs()`. This plot excludes the noise cluster.

> **WARNING** Make sure you always look at your outliers. It's possible for DBSCAN to make clusters look more important than they are when outliers are removed.

Our clustering model seems pretty reasonable, but how stable is it? The final thing we're going to do to evaluate the performance of our DBSCAN model is calculate the

Jaccard index across multiple bootstrap samples. Recall from chapter 17 that the Jaccard index quantifies the agreement of cluster membership between clustering models trained on different bootstrap samples.

To do this, we first need to load the fpc package. Then we use the `clusterboot()` function the same way we did in chapter 17. The first argument is the data we're going to be clustering (our scaled tibble), `B` is the number of bootstraps (more is better, depending on your computational budget), and `clustermethod = dbscanCBI` tells the function to use the DBSCAN algorithm. We then set the desired values of *epsilon* and `MinPts` (careful: note the capital *M* this time), and set `showplots = FALSE` to avoid drawing 500 plots.

NOTE I've truncated the output to show the most important information.

Listing 18.17 Calculating the Jaccard index across bootstrap samples

```
library(fpc)

clustBoot <- clusterboot(swissScaled, B = 500,
                         clustermethod = dbscanCBI,
                         eps = 1.2, MinPts = 9,
                         showplots = FALSE)

clustBoot

Number of resampling runs:  500

Number of clusters found in data:  3

Clusterwise Jaccard bootstrap (omitting multiple points) mean:
[1] 0.6893 0.8074 0.6804
```

We can see the Jaccard indices for the three clusters (where cluster 3 is, confusingly, the noise cluster). Cluster 2 has quite a high stability: 80.7% of cases in the original cluster 2 are in agreement across the bootstrap samples. Clusters 1 and 3 are less stable, with ~68% agreement.

We've now appraised the performance of our DBSCAN model in three ways: using internal cluster metrics, examining the clusters visually, and using the Jaccard index to evaluate their stability. For any particular clustering problem, you will need to evaluate all this evidence together to make a decision as to whether your cluster model is appropriate for the task at hand.

Exercise 3

Use `dbscan()` to cluster our `swissScaled` dataset, keeping *epsilon* as 1.2 but setting *minPts* to 1. How many cases are in the noise cluster? Why? The `fpc` package also has a `dbscan()` function, so use `dbscan::dbscan()` to use the function from the dbscan package.

18.3 Building your first OPTICS model

In this section, I'm going to show you how we can use the OPTICS algorithm to create an ordering of cases in a dataset and how we can extract clusters from this ordering. We will directly compare the results we get using OPTICS to those we generated using DBSCAN.

To do this, we're going to use the `optics()` function from the dbscan package. The first argument is the dataset; just like DBSCAN, OPTICS is sensitive to the variable scale, so we're using our scaled tibble.

Listing 18.18 Ordering cases with OPTICS and extracting clusters

```
swissOptics <- optics(swissScaled, minPts = 9)

plot(swissOptics)
```

Just like the `dbscan()` function, `optics()` has the `eps` and *minPts* arguments. Because *epsilon* is an optional argument for the OPTICS algorithm and only serves to speed up computation, we'll leave it as the default of `NULL`, which means there is no maximum *epsilon*. We set *minPts* equal to 9 to match what we used in our final DBSCAN model.

Once we've created our ordering, we can inspect the reachability plot by simply calling `plot()` on the output from the `optics()` function; see figure 18.14. Notice that we have two obvious troughs separated by high peaks. Remember that this indicates regions of high density separated by regions of low density in the feature space.

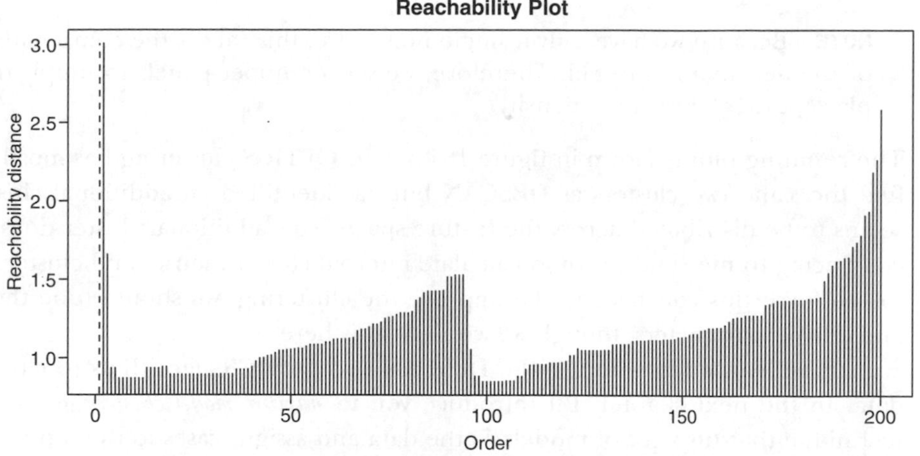

Figure 18.14 The reachability plot generated from applying the OPTICS algorithm to our data. The x-axis shows the processing order of the cases, and the y-axis shows the reachability distance for each case. We can see two main troughs in the plot, bordered by peaks of higher reachability distance.

Now let's extract clusters from this ordering using the steepness method. To do so, we use the `extractXi()` function, passing the output from the `optics()` function as the first argument, and specifying the argument *xi*:

```
swissOpticsXi <- extractXi(swissOptics, xi = 0.05)
```

Recall that *xi* (ξ) is a hyperparameter that determines the minimum steepness (1 – ξ) needed to start and end clusters in the reachability plot. How do we choose the value of ξ? Well, in this example, I've simply chosen a value of ξ that gives a reasonable clustering result (as you'll see in a moment). As we know, this isn't a very scientific or objective approach; for your own work, you should tune ξ as a hyperparameter, just as we did for *epsilon* and *minPts* for DBSCAN.

> **NOTE** The ξ hyperparameter is bounded between 0 and 1, so this gives you a fixed space to search within.

Let's plot the clustering result so we can compare it with our DBSCAN model. We mutate a new column in our dataset, containing the clusters we extracted using the steepness method. We then pipe this data into the `ggpairs()` function.

Listing 18.19 Plotting the OPTICS clusters

```
swissTib %>%
  mutate(cluster = factor(swissOpticsXi$cluster)) %>%
  ggpairs(mapping = aes(col = cluster),
          upper = list(continuous = "points")) +
  theme_bw()
```

> **NOTE** Because we have only a single noise case, this causes the computation of the density plots to fail. Therefore, we set the upper panels to simply display `"points"` instead of density.

The resulting plot is shown in figure 18.15. Our OPTICS clustering has mostly identified the same two clusters as DBSCAN but has identified an additional cluster that seems to be distributed across the feature space. This additional cluster doesn't look convincing to me (but we could calculate internal cluster metrics and cluster stability to reinforce this conclusion). To improve the clustering, we should tune the *minPts* and ξ hyperparameters, though we won't do this here.

You've learned how to use the DBSCAN and OPTICS algorithms to cluster your data. In the next chapter, I'll introduce you to *mixture model clustering*, a clustering technique that fits a set of models to the data and assigns cases to the most probable model. I suggest that you save your .R file, because we're going to continue using the same dataset in the next chapter. This is so we can compare the performance of our DBSCAN and OPTICS models to the output of our mixture model.

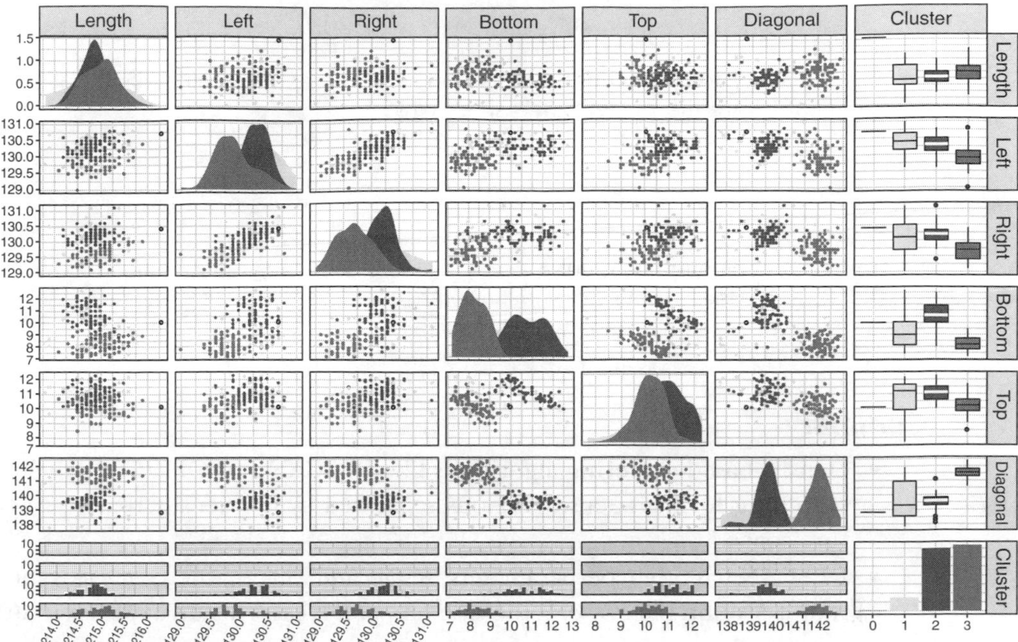

Figure 18.15 Plotting our final OPTICS cluster model with `ggpairs()`

18.4 Strengths and weaknesses of density-based clustering

While it often isn't easy to tell which algorithms will perform well for a given task, here are some strengths and weaknesses that will help you decide whether density-based clustering will perform well for you.

The strengths of density-based clustering are as follows:

- It can identify non-spherical clusters of different diameters.
- It is able to natively identify outlying cases.
- It can identify clusters of complex, non-spherical shapes.
- OPTICS is able to learn a hierarchical clustering structure and doesn't require the tuning of *epsilon*.
- OPTICS is able to find clusters of differing density.
- OPTICS can be sped up by setting a sensible *epsilon* value.

The weaknesses of density-based clustering are these:

- It cannot natively handle categorical variables.
- The algorithms cannot select the optimal number of clusters automatically.
- It is sensitive to data on different scales.
- DBSCAN is biased toward finding clusters of equal density.

Exercise 4

Use `dbscan()` to cluster our unscaled `swissTib` dataset, keeping *epsilon* at 1.2 and *minPts* at 9. Are the clusters the same? Why?

Exercise 5

Train extract clusters from our `swissOptics` object, using the *xi* values 0.035, 0.05, and 0.065. Use `plot()` to see how these different values change the clusters extracted from the reachability plot.

Summary

- Density-based clustering algorithms like DBSCAN and OPTICS find clusters by searching for high-density regions separated by low-density regions of the feature space.
- DBSCAN has two hyperparameters, *epsilon* and *minPts*, where *epsilon* is the search radius around each case. If the case has *minPts* cases inside its *epsilon*, that case is a core point.
- DBSCAN recursively scans *epsilon* of all cases density-connected to the starting case in any cluster, categorizing cases as either core points or border points.
- DBSCAN and OPTICS create a noise cluster for cases that lie too far away from high-density regions.
- OPTICS creates an ordering of the cases from which clusters can be extracted. This ordering can be visualized as a reachability plot where troughs separated by peaks indicate clusters.

Solutions to exercises

1 Print the result of using `expand.grid()`, and inspect the result to understand what the function does:

```
dbsParamSpace

# The function creates a data frame whose rows make up
# every combination of the input vectors.
```

2 Plot the tuning experiment to visualize the number and size of the clusters from each permutation:

```
ggplot(swissClustersGathered, aes(reorder(Permutation, Cluster),
                                  fill = as.factor(Cluster))) +
  geom_bar(position = "fill", col = "black") +
  theme_bw() +
  theme(legend.position = "none")
```

```
ggplot(swissClustersGathered, aes(reorder(Permutation, Cluster),
                                  fill = as.factor(Cluster))) +
  geom_bar(position = "fill", col = "black") +
  coord_polar() +
  theme_bw() +
  theme(legend.position = "none")

ggplot(swissClustersGathered, aes(Permutation,
                                  fill = as.factor(Cluster))) +
  geom_bar(position = "fill", col = "black") +
  coord_polar() +
  theme_bw() +
  theme(legend.position = "none")

# The reorder function orders the levels of the first argument
# according to the values of the second argument.
```

3 Use `dbscan()` with an *epsilon* of 1.2 and a *minPts* of 1:

```
swissDbsNoOutlier <- dbscan::dbscan(swissScaled, eps = 1.2, minPts = 1)

swissDbsNoOutlier

# There are no cases in the noise cluster because the minimum cluster
# size is now 1, meaning all cases are core points.
```

4 Use `dbscan()` to cluster our unscaled data:

```
swissDbsUnscaled <- dbscan::dbscan(swissTib, eps = 1.2, minPts = 9)

swissDbsUnscaled

# The clusters are not the same as those learned for the scaled data.
# This is because DBSCAN and OPTICS are sensitive to scale differences.
```

5 Extract different clusters from `swissOptics` using different values of *xi*:

```
swissOpticsXi035 <- extractXi(swissOptics, xi = 0.035)
plot(swissOpticsXi035)

swissOpticsXi05 <- extractXi(swissOptics, xi = 0.05)
plot(swissOpticsXi05)

swissOpticsXi065 <- extractXi(swissOptics, xi = 0.065)
plot(swissOpticsXi065)
```

19 Clustering based on distributions with mixture modeling

This chapter covers

- Understanding mixture model clustering
- Understanding the difference between hard and soft clustering

Our final stop in unsupervised learning techniques brings us to an additional approach to finding clusters in data: *mixture model clustering*. Just like the other clustering algorithms we've covered, mixture model clustering aims to partition a dataset into a finite set of clusters.

In chapter 18, I showed you the DBSCAN and OPTICS algorithms, and how they find clusters by learning regions of high and low density in the feature space. Mixture model clustering takes yet another approach to identify clusters. A *mixture model* is any model that describes a dataset by combining a mix of two or more probability distributions. In the context of clustering, mixture models help us to identify clusters by fitting a finite number of probability distributions to the data and iteratively modifying the parameters of those distributions until they best fit the underlying data. Cases are then assigned to the cluster of the distribution under which they are most likely. The most common form of mixture modeling is *Gaussian mixture modeling*, which fits Gaussian (or normal) distributions to the data.

By the end of this chapter, I hope you'll have a firm understanding of how mixture model clustering works and its differences and similarities when compared to some of the algorithms we've already covered. We'll apply this method to our Swiss banknote data from chapter 18 to help you understand how mixture model clustering differs from density-based clustering. If you no longer have the `swissTib` object defined in your global environment, just rerun listing 18.1.

19.1 What is mixture model clustering?

In this section, I'm going to show you what mixture model clustering is and how it uses an algorithm called *expectation-maximization* to iteratively improve the fit of the clustering model. The clustering algorithms we've met so far are all considered *hard* clustering methods, because each case is assigned wholly to one cluster and not to another. One of the strengths of mixture model clustering is that it is a *soft* clustering method: it fits a set of probabilistic models to the data and assigns each case a probability of belonging to each model. This allows us to quantify the probability of each case belonging to each cluster. Thus we can say, "This case has a 90% probability of belonging to cluster A, a 9% probability of belonging to cluster B, and a 1% probability of belonging to cluster C." This is useful because it gives us the information we need to make better decisions. Say, for example, a case has a 51% probability of belonging to one cluster and 49% probability of belonging to the other, how happy are we to include this case in its most probable cluster? Perhaps we're not confident enough to include such cases in our final clustering model.

> **NOTE** Mixture model clustering doesn't, in and of itself, identify outlying cases like DBSCAN and OPTICS do, but we can manually set a cut-off of probability if we like. For example, we could say that any case with less than a 60% probability of belonging to its most probable cluster should be considered an outlier.

So mixture model clustering fits a set of probabilistic models to the data. These models can be a variety of probability distributions but are most commonly Gaussian distributions. This clustering approach is called mixture modeling because we fit multiple (a mixture of) probability distributions to the data. Therefore, a Gaussian mixture model is simply a model that fits multiple Gaussian distributions to a set of data.

Each Gaussian in the mixture represents a potential cluster. Once our mixture of Gaussians fits the data as well as possible, we can calculate the probability of each case belonging to each cluster and assign cases to the most probable cluster. But how do we find a mixture of Gaussians that fits the underlying data well? We can use an algorithm called expectation-maximization (EM).

19.1.1 Calculating probabilities with the EM algorithm

In this section, I'll take you through some prerequisite knowledge you'll need to know in order to understand the EM algorithm. This focuses on how the algorithm calculates the probability that each case comes from each Gaussian.

Imagine that we have a one-dimensional dataset: a number line with cases distributed across it (see the top panel of figure 19.1). First, we must predefine the number of clusters to look for in the data; this sets the number of Gaussians we will be fitting. In this example, let's say we believe two clusters exist in the dataset.

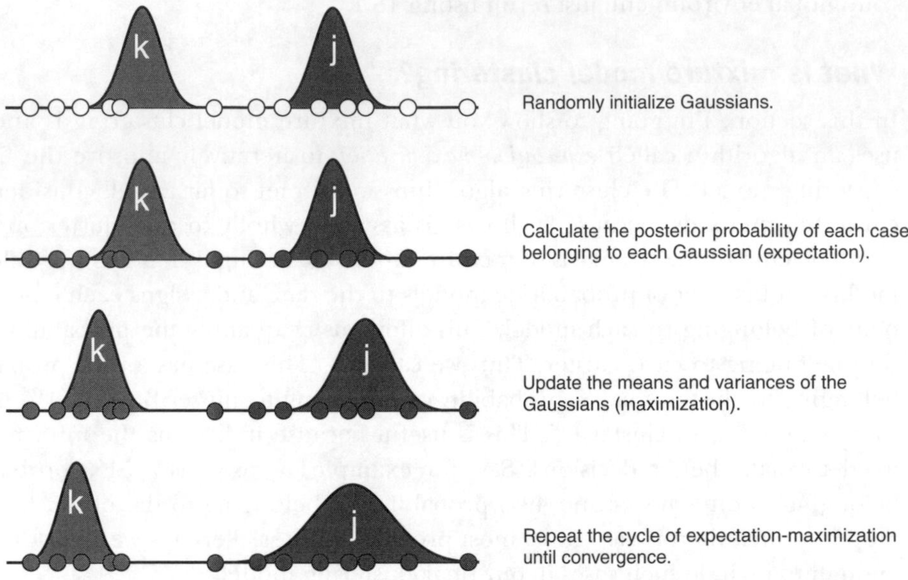

Figure 19.1 The expectation-maximization algorithm for two, one-dimensional Gaussians. Dots represent cases along a number line. Two Gaussians are randomly initialized along the line. In the expectation step, the posterior probability of each case for each Gaussian is calculated (indicated by shading). In the maximization step, the means, variances, and priors for each Gaussian are updated based on the calculated posteriors. The process continues until the likelihood converges.

> **NOTE** This is one of the ways in which mixture model clustering is similar to k-means. I'll show you the other way in which they are similar later in the chapter.

A one-dimensional Gaussian distribution needs two parameters to define it: the mean and the variance. So we randomly initialize two Gaussians along the number line by selecting random values for their means and variances. Let's call these Gaussians *j* and *k*. Then, given these two Gaussians, we calculate the probability that each case belongs to one cluster versus the other. To do this, we can use our good friend, Bayes' rule.

Recall from chapter 6 that we can use Bayes' rule to calculate the posterior probability of an event ($p(k|x)$) given the likelihood ($p(x|k)$), prior ($p(k)$), and evidence ($p(x)$).

$$p(k|x) = \frac{p(x|k) \times p(k)}{p(x)} \qquad \textbf{Equation 19.1}$$

In this case, $p(k|x)$ is the probability of case x belonging to Gaussian k; $p(x|k)$ is the probability of observing case x if you were to sample from Gaussian k; $p(k)$ is the probability of a randomly selected case belonging to Gaussian k; and $p(x)$ is the probability of drawing case x if you were to sample from the entire mixture model as a whole. The evidence, $p(x)$, is therefore the probability of drawing case x from either Gaussian.

When computing the probability of one event or the other occurring, we simply add together the probabilities of each event occurring independently. Therefore, the probability of drawing case x from Gaussian j or k is the probability of drawing it from Gaussian j plus the probability of drawing it from Gaussian k. The probability of drawing case x from one of the Gaussians is the likelihood multiplied by the prior for that Gaussian. With this in mind, we can write our Bayes' rule more fully, as shown in equation 19.2.

$$p(k|x_i) = \frac{p(x_i|k) \times p(k)}{p(x_i|k)p(k) + p(x_i|j)p(j)}$$ **Equation 19.2**

Notice that the evidence has been expanded to more concretely show how the probability of drawing case x_i from either Gaussian is the sum of the probabilities of drawing it from either independently. Equation 19.2 allows us to calculate the posterior probability of case x_i belonging to Gaussian k. Equation 19.3 shows the same calculation, but for the posterior probability of case x_i belonging to Gaussian j.

$$p(j|x_i) = \frac{p(x_i|j) \times p(j)}{p(x_i|k)p(k) + p(x_i|j)p(j)}$$ **Equation 19.3**

So far, so good. But how do we calculate the likelihood and the priors? The likelihood is the probability density function of the Gaussian distribution, which tells us the relative probability of drawing a case with a particular value from a Gaussian distribution with a particular combination of mean and variance. The probability density function for Gaussian distribution k is shown in equation 19.4, but it isn't necessary for you to memorize it:

$$p(x_i|k) = \frac{1}{\sqrt{2\pi\sigma_k^2}} e^{-\frac{(x_i - \mu_k)^2}{2\sigma_k^2}}$$ **Equation 19.4**

where μ_k and σ_k^2 are the mean and variance, respectively, for Gaussian k.

At the start of the algorithm, the prior probabilities are generated randomly, just like the means and variances of the Gaussians. These priors get updated at each iteration to be the sum of the posterior probabilities for each Gaussian, divided by the number of cases. You can think of this as the mean posterior probability for a particular Gaussian across all cases.

19.1.2 EM algorithm expectation and maximization steps

Now that you have the necessary knowledge to understand how the posterior probabilities are calculated, let's see how the EM algorithm iteratively fits the mixture model. The EM algorithm (as its name suggests) has two steps: expectation and maximization. The expectation step is where the posterior probabilities are calculated for each case, for each Gaussian. This is shown in the second panel from the top in figure 19.1.

At this stage, the algorithm uses Bayes' rule as we set out earlier, to calculate the posterior probabilities. The cases along the number line in figure 19.1 are shaded to indicate their posterior probabilities.

Next comes the maximization step. The job of the maximization step is to update the parameters of the mixture model, to maximize the likelihood of the underlying data. This means updating the means, variances, and priors of the Gaussians.

Updating the mean of a particular Gaussian involves adding up the values of each case, weighted by their posterior probability for that Gaussian, and dividing by the sum of all the posterior probabilities. This is shown in equation 19.5.

$$\mu_k = \frac{\sum_{i=1}^{n} p(k|x_i)x_i}{\sum_{i=1}^{n} p(k|x_i)}$$

Equation 19.5

Think about this for a second. Cases that are close to the mean of the distribution will have a high posterior probability for that distribution and so will contribute more to the updated mean. Cases far away from the distribution will have a small posterior probability and will contribute less to the updated mean. The result is that the Gaussian will move toward the mean of the cases that are most probable under this Gaussian. You can see this illustrated in the third panel of figure 19.1.

The variance of each Gaussian is updated in a similar way. We sum the squared difference between each case and the Gaussian's mean, multiplied by the case's posterior, and then divide by the sum of posteriors. This is shown in equation 19.6. The result is that the Gaussian will get wider or narrower, based on the spread of the cases that are most probable under this Gaussian. You can also see this illustrated in the third panel of figure 19.1.

$$\sigma_k^2 = \frac{\sum_{i=1}^{n} p(k|x_i)(x_i - \mu_k)^2}{\sum_{i=1}^{n} p(k|x_i)}$$

Equation 19.6

The last thing to be updated are the prior probabilities for each Gaussian. As mentioned already, the new priors are calculated by dividing the sum of the posterior probabilities for a particular Gaussian, and dividing by the number of cases, as shown in equation 19.7. This means that a Gaussian for which many cases have a large posterior probability will have a large prior probability.

Conversely, a Gaussian for which few cases have a large posterior probability will have a small prior probability. You can think of this as a soft or probabilistic equivalent to setting the prior equal to the proportion of cases belonging to each Gaussian.

$$p_k = \frac{\sum_{i=1}^{n} p(k|x_i)}{n}$$ **Equation 19.7**

Once the maximization step is complete, we perform another iteration of the expectation step, this time computing the posterior probabilities for each case under the new Gaussians. Once this is done, we then rerun the maximization step, again updating the means, variances, and priors for each Gaussian based on the posteriors. This cycle of expectation-maximization continues iteratively until either a specified number of iterations is reached or the overall likelihood of the data under the model changes by less than a specified amount (called *convergence*).

19.1.3 What if we have more than one variable?

In this section, we'll extend what you learned about how the EM algorithm works in one dimension, to clustering over multiple dimensions. It is rare to come across a univariate (one-dimensional) clustering problem. Usually, our datasets contain multiple variables that we wish to use to identify clusters. I limited my explanation of the EM algorithm for Gaussian mixture models in the previous section, because a univariate Gaussian has only two parameters: its mean and variance. When we have a Gaussian distribution in more than one dimension (a multivariate Gaussian), we need to describe it using its centroid and its *covariance matrix*.

We've come across centroids in previous chapters: a centroid is simply a vector of means, one for each dimension/variable in the dataset. A covariance matrix is a square matrix whose elements are the *covariance* between variables. For example, the value in the second row, third column of a covariance matrix indicates the covariance between variables 2 and 3 in the data. Covariance is an unstandardized measure of how much two variables change together. A positive covariance means that as one variable increases, so does the other. A negative covariance means that as one variable increases, the other decreases. A covariance of zero usually indicates no relationship between the variables. We can calculate the covariance between two variables using equation 19.8.

$$Cov(x,y) = \frac{\sum_{i=1}^{n} (x_i - \bar{x})(y_i - \bar{y})}{n-1}$$ **Equation 19.8**

NOTE While covariance is an unstandardized measure of the relationship between two variables, correlation is a standardized measure of the relationship between two variables. We can convert covariance into correlation by dividing it by the product of the variables' standard deviations.

The covariance between one variable and itself is simply that variable's variance. Therefore, the diagonal elements of a covariance matrix are the variances of each of the variables.

TIP Covariance matrices are often called *variance-covariance* matrices for this reason.

If the EM algorithm only estimated a variance for each Gaussian in each dimension, the Gaussians would be perpendicular to the axes of the feature space. Put another way, it would force the model to assume there were no relationships between the variables in the data. It's usually more sensible to assume there will be some degree of relationship between the variables, and estimating the covariance matrix allows the Gaussians to lie diagonally across the feature space.

NOTE Because we estimate the covariance matrix, Gaussian mixture model clustering is insensitive to variables on different scales. Therefore, we *don't* need to scale our variables before training the model.

When we're clustering over more than one dimension, the EM algorithm randomly initializes the centroid, covariance matrix, and prior for each Gaussian. It then calculates the posterior probability for each case, for each Gaussian in the expectation step. In the maximization step, the centroid, covariance matrix, and prior probability are updated for each Gaussian. The EM algorithm continues to iterate until either the maximum number of iterations is reached or the algorithm reaches convergence. The EM algorithm for a bivariate case is illustrated in figure 19.2.

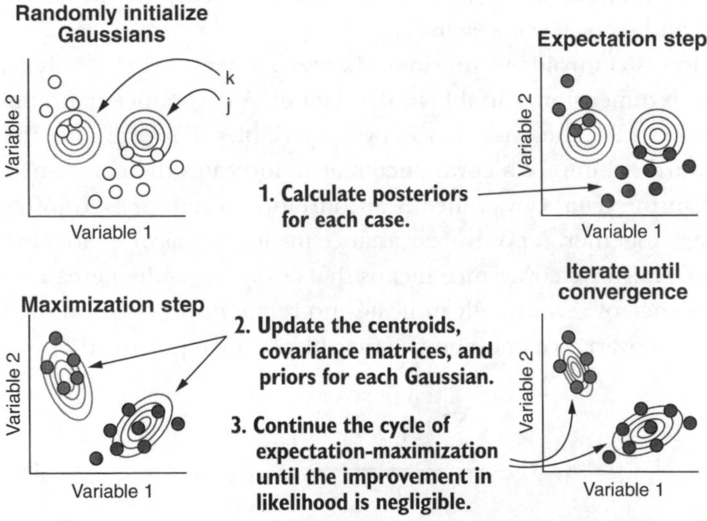

Figure 19.2 The expectation-maximization algorithm for two, two-dimensional Gaussians. Two Gaussians are randomly initialized in the feature space. In the expectation step, the posterior probabilities for each case are calculated for each Gaussian. In the maximization step, the centroids, covariance matrices, and priors are updated for each Gaussian, based on the posteriors. The process continues until the likelihood converges.

The mathematics for the multivariate case

The equations for updating the means and (co)variances are a little more complicated than those we encountered in the univariate case. If you're interested, here they are.

The mean of Gaussian *k* for variable *a* is

$$\mu_{k,a} = \sum_{i=1}^{n} \left(\frac{p(k|x_i)}{n \times p(k)} \right) x_{i,a}$$

The centroid of the Gaussian is therefore just a vector where each element is the mean of a different variable.

The covariance between variables *a* and *b* for Gaussian *k* is

$$(\sigma_k)_{a,b} = \sum_{i=1}^{n} \left(\frac{p(k|x_i)}{n \times p(k)} \right) (x_{i,a} - \mu_{k,a})(x_{i,b} - \mu_{k,b})$$

where σ_k is the covariance matrix for Gaussian *k*.

Finally, in the multivariate case, the likelihood ($p(x_i|k)$) now needs to take into account the covariance, and so it now becomes

$$p(x_i | k) = \frac{1}{\sqrt{2\pi|\Sigma_k|}} e^{-0.5(\vec{x}_i - \vec{\mu}_k)^T \Sigma_k^{-1} (\vec{x}_i - \vec{\mu}_k)}$$

Does this process seem familiar to you—iteratively updating the position of the clusters based on how far cases in the data are from them? We saw a similar procedure for the k-means algorithms in chapter 16. Gaussian mixture model clustering therefore extends k-means clustering to allow non-spherical clusters or different diameters (due to the covariance matrix) and soft clustering. In fact, if you were to constrain a Gaussian mixture model such that all clusters had the same variance, no covariance, and equal priors, you would get a result very similar to that provided by Lloyd's algorithm!

19.2 Building your first Gaussian mixture model for clustering

In this section, I'll show you how to build a Gaussian mixture model for clustering. We'll continue using the Swiss banknote dataset so we can compare the results to the DBSCAN and OPTICS clustering results. An immediate advantage of mixture model clustering over DBSCAN and OPTICS is that it is invariant to variables on different scales, so there's no need to scale our data first.

NOTE For correctness, I should say that there's no need to scale our data as long as we make no prior specification of the covariances of the model components. It's possible to specify our prior beliefs of the means and covariances of the components, though we won't do that here. If we were to do this, it would be important for the covariances to consider the scale of the data.

The mlr package doesn't have an implementation of the mixture modeling algorithm we're going to use, so instead we'll use functions from the mclust package. Let's start by loading the package:

```
library(mclust)
```

There are a few things I particularly like about using the mclust package for clustering. The first is that it's the only R package I know of that prints a cool logo to the console when you load it. The second is that it displays a progress bar to indicate how much longer your clustering will take (very important for judging whether there's time for a cup of tea). And third, its function for fitting the model will automatically try a range of cluster numbers and try to select the best-fitting number. We can also manually specify the number of clusters if we think we know better.

Let's use the `Mclust()` function to perform the clustering and then call `plot()` on the results.

Listing 19.1 Performing and plotting mixture model clustering

```
swissMclust <- Mclust(swissTib)

plot(swissMclust)
```

Plotting the `Mclust()` output does something a little odd (and irritating, as far as I'm concerned). It prompts us to enter a number from 1 to 4, corresponding to one of the following options:

1. BIC
2. Classification
3. Uncertainty
4. Density

Entering the number will draw the corresponding plot containing useful information. Let's look at each of these plots in turn.

The first plot available to us shows the *Bayesian information criterion* (BIC) for the range of cluster numbers and model types the `Mclust()` function tried. This plot is shown in figure 19.3. The BIC is a metric for comparing the fit of different models, and it penalizes us for having too many parameters in the model. The BIC is usually defined as in equation 19.9.

$$BIC = \ln(n)p - 2\ln(L) \quad \textbf{Equation 19.9}$$

where n is the number of cases, p is the number of parameters in the model, and L is the overall likelihood of the model.

Therefore, for a fixed likelihood, as the number of parameters increases, the BIC increases. Conversely, for a fixed number of parameters, as the model likelihood

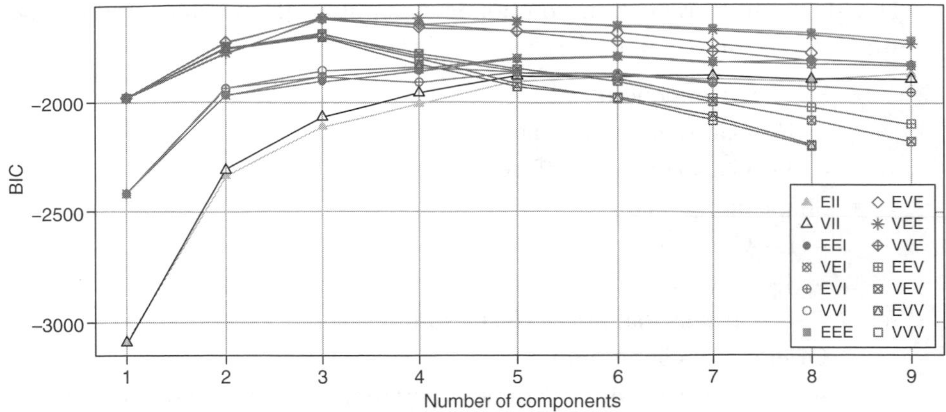

Figure 19.3 The BIC plot from our mclust model. The x-axis shows the number of clusters, the y-axis shows the Bayesian information criterion (BIC), and each line shows a different model, with the three-letter code indicating which constraints are put on the covariance matrix. In this arrangement of the BIC, higher values indicate better-fitting and/or more parsimonious models.

increases, the BIC decreases. Therefore, the smaller the BIC, the better and/or more parsimonious our model is. Imagine that we had two models, each of which fit the dataset equally well, but one had 3 parameters and the other had 10. The model with 3 parameters would have the lower BIC.

The form of BIC shown in the plot is actually sort of the other way around and takes the form shown in equation 19.10. After being rearranged this way, better fitting and/or more parsimonious models will actually have a higher BIC value.

$$BIC = L - 0.5 \times p \times \ln(n)$$ **Equation 19.10**

Now we know what the BIC is and how to interpret it, but what are all the lines in figure 19.3? Well, the `Mclust()` function tries a range of cluster numbers for us, for a range of different model types. For each combination of model type and cluster number, the function evaluates the BIC. This information is conveyed in our BIC plot. But what do I mean by *model types*? I didn't mention anything about this when I showed you how Gaussian mixture models work. When we train a mixture model, it's possible to put constraints on the covariance matrix to reduce the number of parameters needed to describe the model. This can help to prevent overfitting the data.

Each of the model types is represented by a different line in figure 19.3, and each has a strange three-letter code identifying it. The first letter of each code refers to the *volume* of each Gaussian, the second letter refers to the *shape*, and the third letter refers to the *orientation*. Each of these components can take one of the following:

- *E* for *equal*
- *V* for *variable*

The shape and orientation components can also take a value of *I* for *identity*. The effects of the values on models are as follows:

- Volume component:
  - *E*—Gaussians with equal volume
  - *V*—Gaussians with different volumes
- Shape component:
  - *E*—Gaussians with equal aspect ratios
  - *V*—Gaussians with different aspect ratios
  - *I*—Clusters that are perfectly spherical
- Orientation component:
  - *E*—Gaussians with the same orientation through the feature space
  - *V*—Gaussians with different orientations
  - *I*—Clusters that are orthogonal to the axes of the feature space

So really, the `Mclust()` function is performing a tuning experiment for us and will automatically select the model with the highest BIC value. In this case, the best model is the one that uses the VVE covariance matrix with three Gaussians (use `swissMclust$modelName` and `swissMclust$G` to extract this information).

That's the first plot, which is certainly useful. Perhaps the most useful plot, however, is the one obtained from option 2. It shows us our final clustering result from the selected model; see figure 19.4. The ellipses indicate the covariances of each cluster,

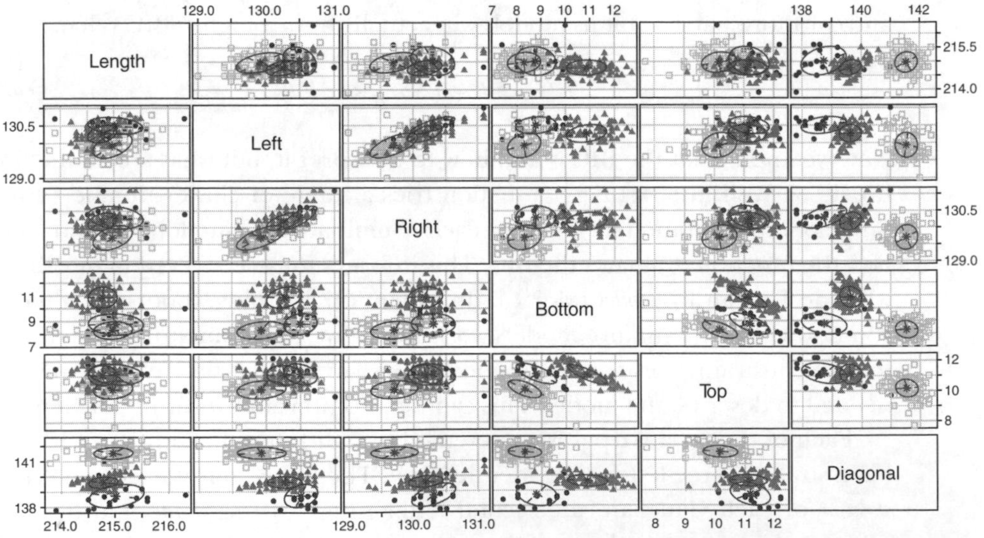

Figure 19.4 The classification plot from our mclust model. All variables in the original data are plotted against each other in a scatterplot matrix, with cases shaded and shaped according to their cluster. Ellipses indicate the covariances of each Gaussian, and stars indicate their centroids.

and the star at the center of each indicates its centroid. The model appears to fit the data well and seems to have identified three reasonably convincing clusters compared to the two identified by our DBSCAN model (though we should use internal cluster metrics and Jaccard indices to more objectively compare the models).

The third plot is similar to the second, but it sets the size of each case based on its uncertainty (see figure 19.5). A case whose posterior probabilities aren't dominated by a single Gaussian will have a high uncertainty, and this plot helps us identify cases that could be considered outliers.

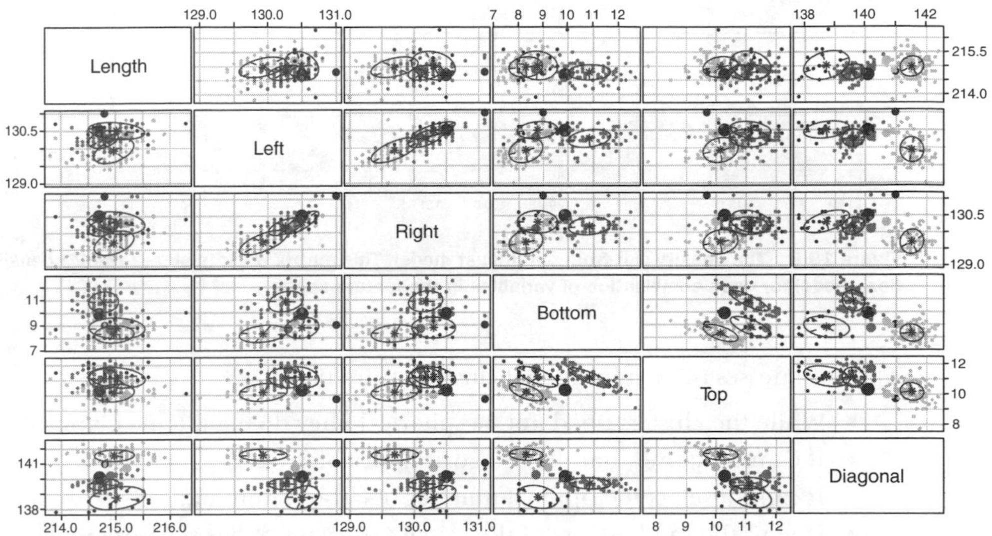

Figure 19.5 The uncertainty plot from our mclust model. This plot is similar to the classification plot, except that the size of each case corresponds to its uncertainty under the final model.

The fourth and final plot shows the density of the final mixture model (see figure 19.6). I find this plot less useful, but it looks quite cool. To exit `Mclust()`'s `plot()` method, you need to enter `0` (which is why I find this irritating).

19.3 Strengths and weaknesses of mixture model clustering

While it often isn't easy to tell which algorithms will perform well for a given task, here are some strengths and weaknesses that will help you decide whether mixture model clustering will perform well for you.

The strengths of mixture model clustering are as follows:

- It can identify non-spherical clusters of different diameters.
- It estimates the probability that a case belongs to each cluster.
- It is insensitive to variables on different scales.

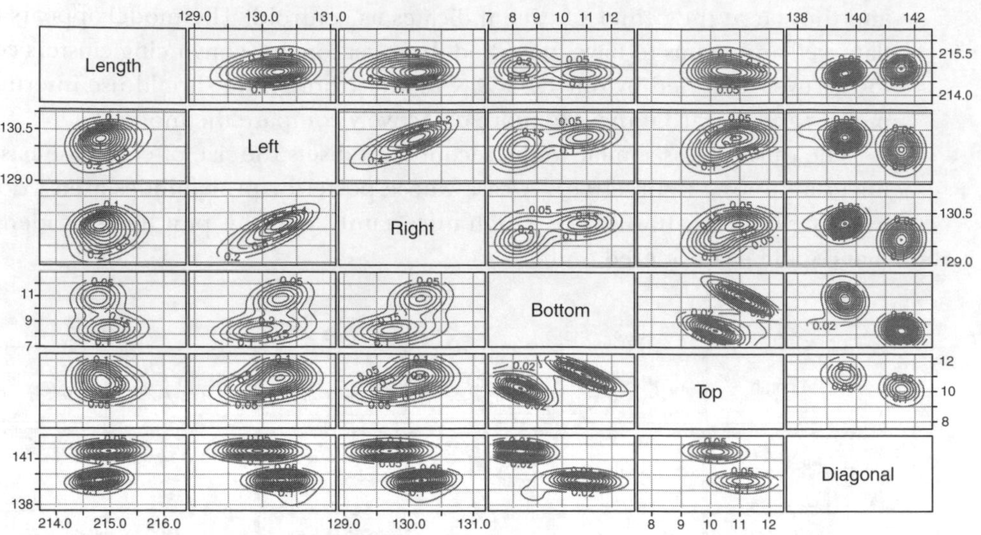

Figure 19.6 The density plot from our mclust model. This matrix of plots shows the 2D density of the final model for each combination of variables in the feature space.

The weaknesses of mixture model clustering are these:

- While the clusters need not be spherical, they do need to be elliptical.
- It cannot natively handle categorical variables.
- It cannot select the optimal number of clusters automatically.
- Due to the randomness of the initial Gaussians, it has the potential to converge to a locally optimal model.
- It is sensitive to outliers.
- If the clusters cannot be approximated by a multivariate Gaussian, it's unlikely the final model will fit well.

Exercise 1

Use the `Mclust()` function to train a model, setting the `G` argument to `2` and the `modelNames` argument to `"VVE"` to force a VVE model with two clusters. Plot the results, and examine the clusters.

Exercise 2

Using the `clusterboot()` function, calculate the stability of the clusters generated from a two-cluster and a three-cluster VVE model. Hint: Use `noisemclustCBI` as the `clustermethod` argument to use mixture modeling. Is it easy to compare the Jaccard indices of models with different numbers of clusters?

Summary

- Gaussian mixture model clustering fits a set of Gaussian distributions to the data and estimates the probability of the data coming from each Gaussian.
- The expectation-maximization (EM) algorithm is used to iteratively update the model until the likelihood of the data converges.
- Gaussian mixture modeling is a soft-clustering method that gives us a probability of each case belonging to each cluster.
- In one dimension, the EM algorithm only needs to update the mean, variance, and prior probability of each Gaussian.
- In more than one dimension, the EM algorithm needs to update the centroid, covariance matrix, and prior probability of each Gaussian.
- Constraints can be placed on the covariance matrix to control the volume, shape, and orientation of the Gaussians.

Solutions to exercises

1. Train a VVE mixture model with two clusters:

```
swissMclust2 <- Mclust(swissTib, G = 2, modelNames = "VVE")

plot(swissMclust2)
```

2. Compare the cluster stability of a two- and three-cluster mixture model:

```
library(fpc)

mclustBoot2 <- clusterboot(swissTib, B = 10,
                           clustermethod = noisemclustCBI,
                           G = 2, modelNames = "VVE",
                           showplots = FALSE)

mclustBoot3 <- clusterboot(swissTib, B = 10,
                           clustermethod = noisemclustCBI,
                           G = 3, modelNames = "VVE",
                           showplots = FALSE)


mclustBoot2

mclustBoot3

# It can be challenging to compare the Jaccard indices between models with
# different numbers of clusters. The model with three clusters may better
# represent nature, but as one of the clusters is small, the membership is
# more variable between bootstrap samples.
```

20 Final notes and further reading

This chapter covers

- A brief summary of what we've covered
- A roadmap to further your knowledge

Take a moment to look back at all the topics we've covered throughout this book. We've covered a huge amount of information, and now that we're near the end of the book, I'd like to put it all together to give you the bigger picture. At university, I used to get frustrated with lecturers who would assume that because they had taught something to us, we would simply remember it. I know this isn't how most people learn, and you may well have forgotten many of the details I tried to teach throughout the book. That's okay—I hope you feel that you can pick up this book as a reference for future machine learning projects you might be working on. And in this chapter, I summarize many of the broad, important concepts we touched on throughout the book.

After completing this book, you have a formidable number of machine learning algorithms in your toolbox—enough to tackle a huge range of problems. I also hope that you now know a general approach to machine learning and, importantly, how to objectively evaluate the performance of your model-building processes. While I've provided you with both "bread and butter" algorithms as well as modern ones, machine learning research is fast moving. There are many more algorithms I didn't cover, such as those used in deep learning, reinforcement learning, and anomaly detection. Therefore, in this chapter, I also provide you with several potential avenues for future learning. When learning something new, I get frustrated when I reach the end of the textbook and then have no idea where to go next; so, I'll recommend additional books and resources to further your learning.

20.1 A brief recap of machine learning concepts

In this section, I'll summarize the general machine learning concepts we covered throughout the book, referencing the relevant sections of the book as we go. These concepts include the following:

- Types of machine learning algorithms
- The bias-variance trade-off
- Model validation
- Hyperparameter tuning
- Missing value imputation
- Feature engineering and feature selection
- Ensemble techniques
- Regularization

My hope is that now that you've completed the book, these concepts will fit more concretely into your bigger picture of machine learning.

20.1.1 Supervised, unsupervised, and semi-supervised learning

Machine learning tasks can be divided into supervised and unsupervised tasks, based on whether the algorithm has access to labeled data: whether we have access to the ground truth when training the model. Algorithms that learn patterns in the data that can be used to predict the ground truth are said to be *supervised*. Supervised machine learning algorithms can be further distinguished, based on the kind of output variable they predict. Supervised learning algorithms that predict categorical variables (or classes) are said to be *classification algorithms*, while those that predict continuous variables are said to be *regression algorithms*.

NOTE Some algorithms—like k-nearest neighbors, random forest, and XGBoost—can be used for both classification *and* regression.

Unsupervised algorithms learn patterns in the data without any form of ground truth. We can differentiate these algorithms based on what their purpose is. Unsupervised learning algorithms that can compress the information in a high-dimensional dataset into a lower-dimensional representation are called *dimension-reduction algorithms*. Unsupervised learning algorithms that find groups of cases that are more similar to each other than cases in other groups are called *clustering algorithms*.

You first encountered these definitions in section 1.2, all the way back in chapter 1. I've reproduced figure 1.5 in figure 20.1: it summarizes the differences between supervised and unsupervised learning.

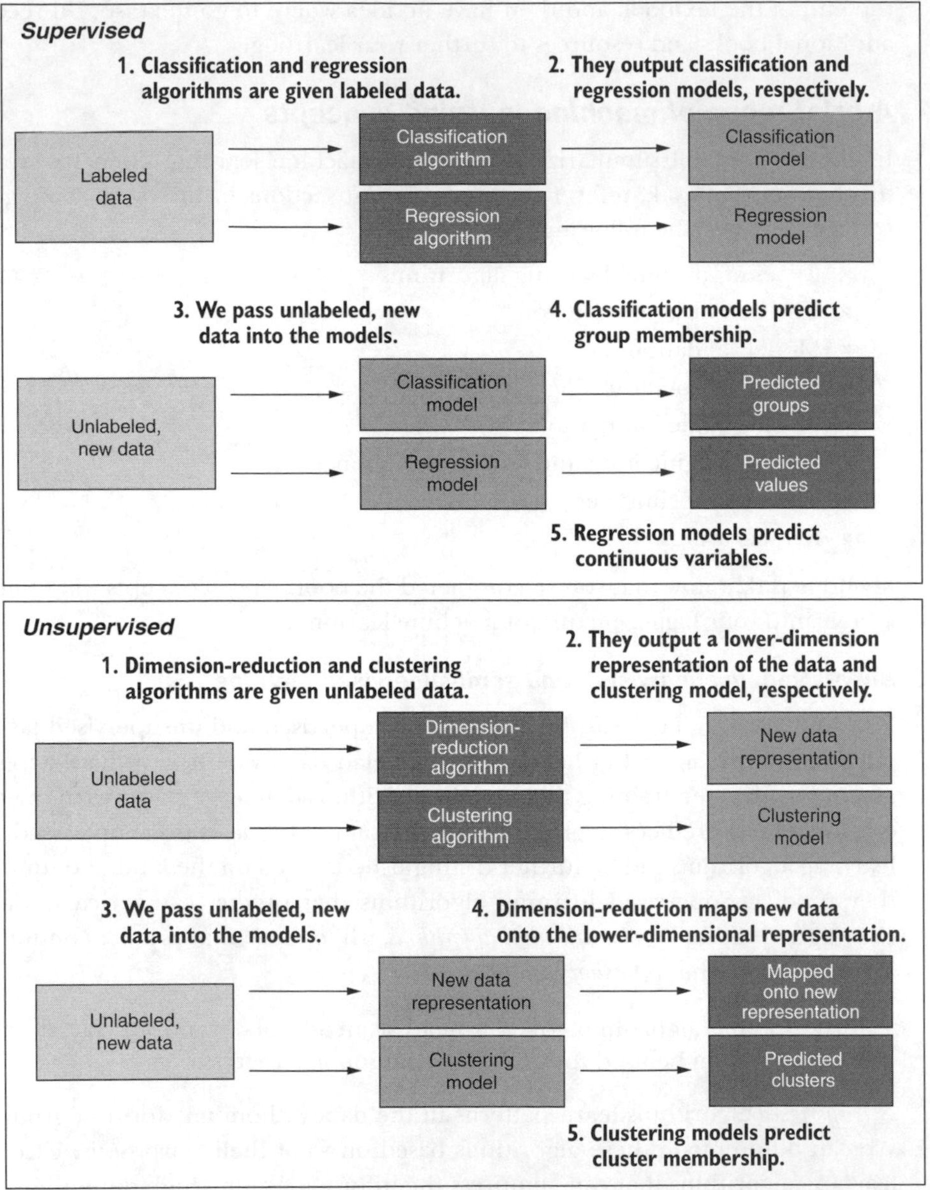

Figure 20.1 Supervised vs. unsupervised machine learning. Supervised algorithms take data already labeled with a ground truth and build a model that can predict the labels of new, unlabeled data. Unsupervised algorithms take unlabeled data and learn patterns within it, such that new data can be mapped onto these patterns.

NOTE Although I didn't mention this in chapter 1, not all unsupervised algorithms can make predictions on new data. For example, hierarchical clustering and t-SNE models are unable to make predictions on new data.

There is an approach partway between supervised and unsupervised machine learning called *semi-supervised learning*. Semi-supervised learning is an approach, rather than a type of algorithm, and is useful when we have access to partially labeled data. If we expertly label as many of the cases in a dataset as is feasibly possible, then we can build a supervised model using only these labeled data. We use this model to predict the labels of the rest of the dataset. Now we combine the data with the manual labels and pseudo-labels, and use this to train a new model.

Figure 20.2 shows all the machine learning algorithms we used throughout this book, partitioning them into supervised and unsupervised, and also classification, regression, dimension reduction, and clustering. My hope is that you can refer to this figure when deciding which algorithms are most suitable for the task at hand, and that you will add to the algorithms listed here as your knowledge grows.

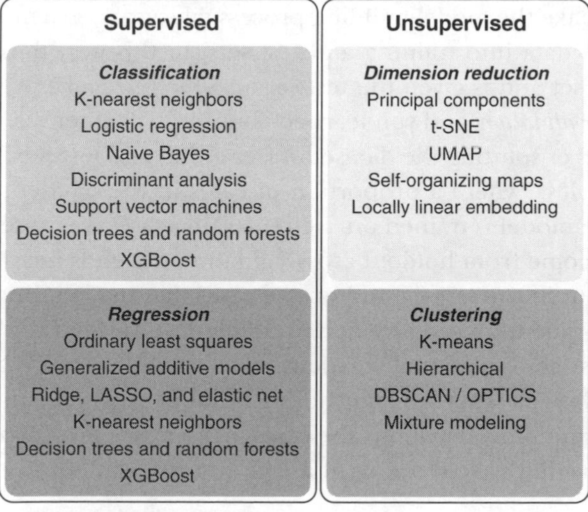

Figure 20.2 Summary of the algorithms we cover in the book, whether they are supervised or unsupervised learners, and whether they can be used for classification, regression, dimension reduction, or clustering

20.1.2 Balancing the bias-variance trade-off for model performance

When training a predictive model, it's important to evaluate how it will perform in the real world. When evaluating the performance of our models, we should *never* evaluate them using the data we used to train them. This is because models will almost always perform better when making predictions on the data used to train them than when making predictions on unseen data.

In chapter 3, you learned that an important concept to understand when evaluating model performance is the bias-variance trade-off. As the complexity of a model increases, and the more closely it fits the training set, the more variable its predictions will be on unseen data. Models that are too simple and don't capture the relationships in the data well are biased toward making consistently poor predictions. As we increase the complexity of our model, its variance will increase, and its bias will decrease; the inverse is also true.

The bias-variance trade-off therefore describes the balance between overfitting (training a model that fits the noise of the training set) and underfitting (training a model that poorly fits the training set). Somewhere between a model that overfits and a model that underfits is an optimally fitting model whose predictions generalize well to unseen data. The way to tell if we are underfitting or overfitting is to use cross-validation. However, even just passing the training set back through the model will tell you if you're underfitting, because the model will perform poorly.

20.1.3 Using model validation to identify over-/underfitting

To evaluate how well a model will make predictions on new data, we need to pass new, unseen data through the model and see how closely its predictions match the ground truth. One way of doing this would be to train the model on the data at hand and then, as new data is generated, pass that data through the model to evaluate its predictions. This process could make the model-building process take years, so a more realistic approach is to split the data into training and test sets. In this way, the model is trained using the training set and is given the test set on which to make predictions. This process is called *cross-validation*, and you learned about it in chapter 3.

There are multiple ways of splitting the dataset into training and test sets. Holdout cross-validation is the simplest, where a proportion of cases in the dataset are "held out" as the test set, and the model is trained on the remaining cases. Because the split is usually random, the outcome from holdout cross-validation depends heavily on the proportion of cases held out in the test set and on the cases that made it into the test set. As such, holdout cross-validation can give quite variable results when run multiple times, though it is the least computationally expensive method. I've reproduced figure 3.12 in figure 20.3: it shows a schematic illustrating holdout cross-validation.

K-fold cross-validation randomly partitions the cases into *k* near-equally sized folds. For each fold, the cases inside the fold are used as the test set, while the remaining

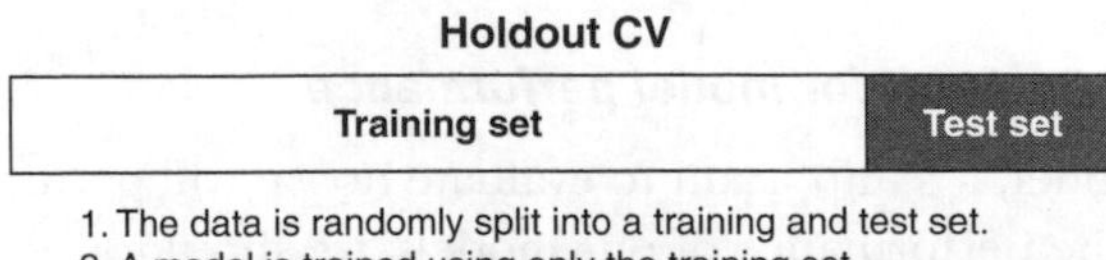

Holdout CV
Training set
Test set
1. The data is randomly split into a training and test set.
2. A model is trained using only the training set.
3. Predictions are made on the test set.
4. The predictions are compared to the true values.

Figure 20.3 Holdout cross-validation. The data is randomly split into a training set and a test set. The training set is used to train the model, which is then used to make predictions on the test set. The similarity of the predictions to the true values of the test set is used to evaluate model performance.

data is used as the training set. The mean performance metric of all the folds is then returned. The advantage of k-fold over holdout cross-validation is that because each case is used in the test set once, the results are less variable, although the results will be sensitive to our choice of the number of folds. To make the result even more stable, we can use repeated k-fold cross-validation, where the whole k-fold process is repeated multiple times, randomly shuffling the cases for each repetition. I've reproduced figure 3.13 in figure 20.4: it illustrates k-fold cross-validation.

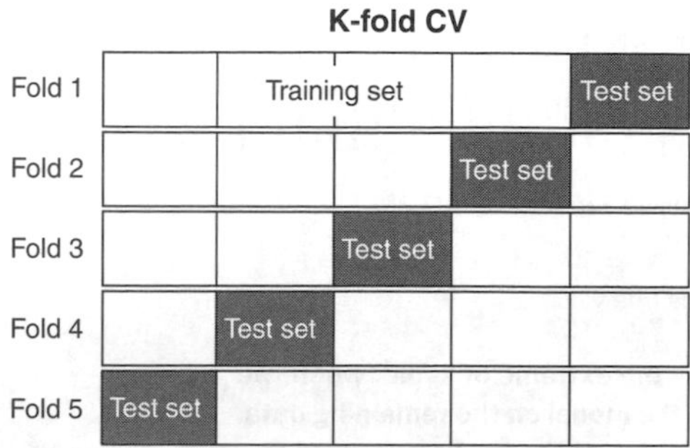
K-fold CV
Fold 1
Training set
Test set
Fold 2
Test set
Fold 3
Test set
Fold 4
Test set
Fold 5
Test set
1. The data is randomly split into K equal-sized folds.
2. Each fold is used as the test set once, where the rest of the data makes the training set.
3. For each fold, predictions are made on the test set.
4. The predictions are compared to the true values.

Figure 20.4 K-fold cross-validation. The data is randomly split into near equally sized folds. Each fold is used as the test set once, and the rest of the data is used as the training set. The similarity of the predictions to the true values of the test set is used to evaluate model performance.

Leave-one-out cross-validation is the extreme of k-fold cross-validation, where the number of folds is equal to the number of cases in the dataset. In this way, every case in the dataset is used as the test set once, with the model being trained using all of the other cases. Leave-one-out cross-validation tends to give more variable performance estimates than k-fold, except where the dataset is small, in which circumstance k-fold may give more variable estimates due to the small training set. I've reproduced figure 3.14 in figure 20.5; it illustrates leave-one-out cross-validation.

One of the most common mistakes many people make when training machine learning models is not including their data-dependent preprocessing steps in their cross-validation procedure. If this preprocessing includes the tuning of any hyperparameters, it's important to use nested cross-validation. Doing so ensures that the data we use for the final evaluation of the model hasn't been seen by the model at all.

Nested cross-validation starts by splitting the data into training and test sets (this can be done using the holdout, k-fold, or leave-one-out methods). This division is called the *outer loop*. The training set is used to cross-validate each value of our hyperparameter search space. This is called the *inner loop*. The hyperparameter that gives the best cross-validated performance from each inner loop is passed to the outer loop. A model is trained on each training set of the outer loop, using the best hyperparameter from its inner loop, and these models are used to make predictions on their test sets. The average performance metrics of these models across the outer loop are then

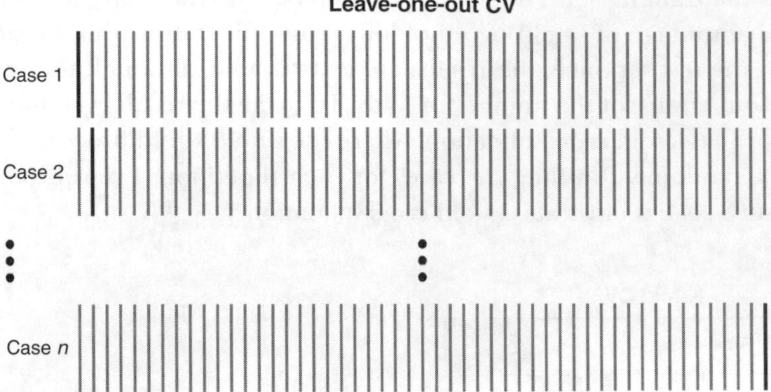

Figure 20.5 Leave-one-out cross-validation is the extreme of k-fold, where we reserve a single case as the test set and train the model on the remaining data. The similarity of the predictions to the true values of the test set is used to evaluate model performance.

reported as an estimate of how the model will perform on unseen data. I've reproduced figure 3.16 in figure 20.6; it illustrates nested cross-validation. In this example, we are using 3-fold cross-validation for the outer loop, and 4-fold for the inner loop.

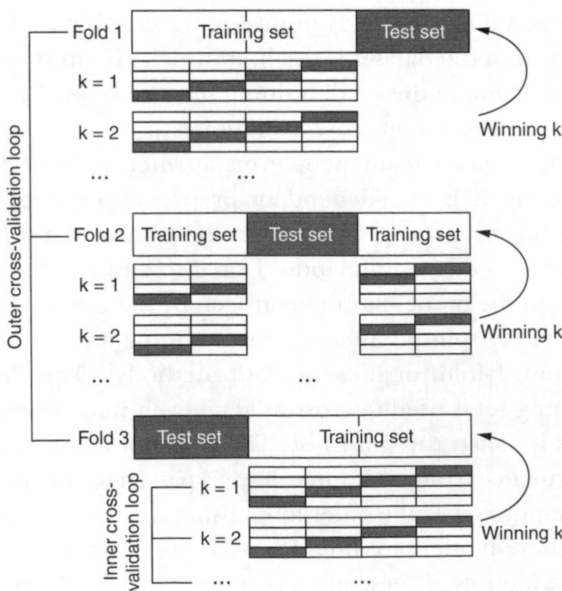

Figure 20.6 Nested cross-validation. The dataset is split into folds. For each fold, the training set is used to create sets of inner k-fold cross-validation. Each of these inner sets cross-validates a single hyperparameter value by splitting the data into training and test sets. For each fold in these inner sets, a model is trained using the training set and evaluated on the test set, using that set's hyperparameter value. The hyperparameter from each inner cross-validation loop that gives the best-performing model is used to train the models on the outer loop.

Training set, test set, and ... validation set?

You may see other people refer to splitting their data into a training set, a test set, and a *validation set*. I want to show you how this is just a special case of nested cross-validation. When using this approach, people train the model using the training set with a range of hyperparameter values and use the test set to evaluate the performance of these hyperparameter values. The model with the best-performing hyperparameter values is then given the validation set to make predictions on. The performance of the model on the validation set is used as the final indicator of the model-building process's performance. The importance of this is that the validation set isn't seen by the model during training, including during hyperparameter tuning, so there is no information leak for the model to learn patterns present in the validation set.

Now look again at the schematic in figure 20.6. Can you see that splitting the data into training, test, and validation sets is just nested cross-validation using holdout cross-validation for both the inner and outer loop? I explained this using the "nested" nomenclature because it gives us a much more flexible toolset for evaluating model performance than simply splitting the data into training, test, and validation sets. For example, it allows us to use more complex cross-validation strategies for our inner and outer loops, and even mix different strategies between them.

20.1.4 Maximizing model performance with hyperparameter tuning

Many machine learning algorithms have hyperparameters that control how they learn. A *hyperparameter* is a variable, setting, or option that cannot be estimated directly from the data itself. The best way to select the optimal combination of hyperparameters for any given algorithm and dataset is to use hyperparameter tuning.

Hyperparameter *tuning* is the process of iteratively trying models with different combinations of hyperparameters, and selecting the combination that gives the best-performing model. The tuning process should accompany cross-validation, where, for each combination of hyperparameters, a model is trained on the training set and evaluated on the test set.

If the range of hyperparameter values we need to search over is small, then it is often beneficial to employ a grid search method. In grid search, we simply try every combination of hyperparameter values that we define in our search space. Grid search is the only search method that is guaranteed to select the best-performing combination of hyperparameters in our search space.

But when dealing with multiple hyperparameters, or when the search space becomes very large, grid search can become prohibitively slow. In such situations, we can employ random search instead. Random search randomly samples combinations of hyperparameters from the search space, for as many iterations as we can afford. Random search is not guaranteed to find the best-performing combination of hyperparameters, but it can usually find a close approximation in a fraction of the time required by grid search.

Whichever search method we use, as a data-dependent preprocessing step, it is vital to include hyperparameter tuning in our cross-validation strategy, in the form of nested cross-validation.

20.1.5 Using missing value imputation to deal with missing data

Missing value imputation is the practice of using sensible values to fill in missing data in a dataset, such that we can still train a model using the full dataset. The alternative would be to discard cases with any missing data.

A naive way to impute missing values is to simply replace missing values with the mean or median for a continuous variable (as we did in chapter 4) or the mode for a categorical variable. The problem is that this approach adds bias to any models you train and throws away information about relationships in the data that may in fact have predictive value. A better approach, therefore, is to use another machine learning algorithm to estimate sensible values for the missing data, based on the values of the other variables for that case (as we did in chapters 9 and 10). For example, we could use the k-nearest neighbors algorithm to find what the cases most similar to the one in question have as their value for the missing value. As a data-dependent preprocessing step, missing value imputation should be included in the cross-validation process.

20.1.6 Feature engineering and feature selection

Feature engineering is the practice of extracting useful/predictive information from existing variables when the data is currently in a less useful format. For example, this could involve extracting gender from transcribed medical notes, or combining various financial metrics to create an index of market stability. Feature engineering usually requires some domain knowledge and some thought about what features are likely to impact the outcome variable. We first covered feature engineering in chapter 4, and we used it again in chapter 10.

Feature selection, on the other hand, is concerned with removing variables that contribute no or little predictive information to the model. In doing so, we can protect ourselves from both overfitting and the curse of dimensionality. You learned in chapter 9 that feature selection can be done in two different ways: filter methods and wrapper methods.

Filter methods are computationally less expensive but are less likely to result in an optimal selection of features. They rely on calculating some metric of the relationship between each feature and the outcome variable. This metric could simply be the correlation between each feature and the outcome, for example. We can then skim off a specific number or proportion of features that have a weaker relationship with the outcome.

Wrapper methods are more computationally expensive but are more likely to result in a better-fitting model. They consist of iteratively fitting and evaluating models with different permutations of the predictor variables. The combination of variables that gives the best-performing model is chosen.

Feature engineering and selection are extremely important—arguably more important than our choice of algorithm. We can use the most cutting-edge, high-performing algorithm ever developed, but if our features are not making the most of the predictive information they contain, or there are many irrelevant variables in the data, our model won't perform as well as it should. If our feature engineering/selection processes are data dependent, it's important to include them in cross-validation.

20.1.7 Improving model performance with ensemble techniques

The performance of most supervised machine learning algorithms can be improved by combining them with an ensemble technique. *Ensembling* is where, instead of training a single model, we train multiple models that help us reduce overfitting and improve the accuracy of predictions. There are three types of ensemble techniques:

- Bagging
- Boosting
- Stacking

You learned about ensemble techniques for classification and regression in chapters 8 and 12, respectively.

Bagging (also called *bootstrap aggregating*) consists of creating multiple bootstrap samples from the original dataset and training a model on each sample in parallel. New data is then passed to each individual model, and the modal or mean prediction is returned (for classification and regression problems, respectively). Bagging helps us to avoid overfitting and so can reduce the variance of our models. Bagging can be used for virtually any supervised learning algorithm (and some clustering algorithms), but its most famous implementation is in the random forest algorithm, which uses classification/regression trees.

While bagging trains models in parallel, *boosting* trains models sequentially, where each subsequent model seeks to improve on the mistakes of the existing chain of models. In adaptive boosting, cases that are incorrectly classified by the existing ensemble of models are weighted more heavily, such that they are more likely to be sampled in the next iteration. AdaBoost is the only well-known implementation of adaptive boosting. In gradient boosting, the residual error of the existing ensemble is minimized by each additional model. XGBoost is a famous implementation of gradient boosting that uses classification/regression trees; but just like bagging, boosting can be used with any supervised learning algorithm.

In *stacking*, we create base models that are good at learning different patterns in the feature space. One model may then be good at predicting in one area of the feature space, but make mistakes in another area. One of the other models may do a good job of predicting values in an area of the feature space where the others do poorly. Predictions made by the base models are used as predictor variables (along with all the original predictors) by a final stacked model. This stacked model is then able to learn from the predictions made by the base models to make more accurate predictions of its own.

20.1.8 Preventing overfitting with regularization

Regularization describes a set of techniques for limiting the magnitude of model parameters to prevent overfitting. Regularization is particularly important for guarding against overfitting due to the inclusion of predictors with little or no predictive value. You learned in chapter 11 that the two most common forms are L2 and L1 regularization.

In L2 regularization, the loss function of the model has a penalty added to it, which is the L2 norm of the model parameters weighted by a tunable hyperparameter, *lambda.* The L2 norm of the model parameters is the sum of squared parameter values. The effect of L2 regularization is that model parameters can be shrunk toward zero (but never to zero, unless the ordinary least squares [OLS] estimate is zero), with weaker predictors being penalized more greatly. Ridge regression is an example of L2 regularization being used to prevent overfitting in linear regression.

In L1 regularization, we add the L1 norm to the loss function, weighted by *lambda.* The L1 norm is the sum of the absolute parameter values. The effect of L1 regularization is that model parameters can be shrunk to zero, effectively removing them from the model. L1 regularization is therefore a form of automatic feature selection. LASSO is an example of L1 regularization being used to prevent overfitting in linear regression.

20.2 Where can you go from here?

You might be wondering what your next steps are in your machine learning education. That really is up to you and what you want to achieve, but in this section I'll point you in the direction of some excellent resources you can use to further develop your knowledge and skills. I'm a firm believer, though, that the best way to solidify new knowledge is to use it—so use the techniques and algorithms you learned throughout this book in your work, and teach them to your colleagues!

20.2.1 Deep learning

As I mentioned near the start of the book, I omitted deep learning (machine learning using artificial neural networks) because I felt it deserves a book of its own. But no machine learning education could be considered comprehensive without learning about this extraordinary field. Neural networks are powerful tools for any machine learning task, but if your work will revolve around computer vision, the classification of images/video, or building models on other complex data such as audio files, deep learning is a vital avenue for you to explore. For R, I cannot recommend more highly *Deep Learning with R* by Francois Chollet and Joseph J. Allaire (Manning, 2018, www.manning.com/books/deep-learning-with-r). This book is easily digestible by nonspecialists and will reinforce some of the basic machine learning concepts we have covered here.

20.2.2 Reinforcement learning

Reinforcement learning is a cutting-edge area of machine learning research and application, where algorithms learn from experience by being rewarded when they make a good decision. Often considered alongside supervised and unsupervised algorithms to be the third class of machine learning algorithms, it has been used to create chess bots that can outwit world champion chess players. If you're interested in reinforcement learning, I highly recommend *Deep Learning and the Game of Go* by Max Pumperla and Kevin Ferguson (Manning, 2019, www.manning.com/books/deep-learning-and-the-game-of-go).

20.2.3 General R data science and the tidyverse

If you want to improve your R data science skills in general, as well as become more proficient with tools from the tidyverse (including some we didn't use), I recommend *R for Data Science* by Garrett Grolemund and Hadley Wickham (O'Reilly Media, 2016).

If you want to become a ggplot2 master, then pick up a copy of *ggplot2* by Hadley Wickham (Springer International Publishing, 2016).

If your R skills are pretty good and you want to learn more about how the language works and how to do more advanced programming (such as object-oriented programming), you'll enjoy *Advanced R* by Hadley Wickham (CRC Press, 2019). You may notice that this guy Hadley keeps popping up; if you want to keep up to date with the R community and developments to the tidyverse, you can do worse than to follow him.

20.2.4 mlr tutorial and creating new learners/metrics

A few times in the book, I mentioned that a particular algorithm hadn't yet been implemented in mlr. The mlr package is meant to make your machine learning experience more streamlined, not less flexible; so if you wish to implement an algorithm in another package (or your own) or a new performance metric, it really isn't that hard to do so yourself. You can find a tutorial on how to do this (as well as other useful information and resources) on the mlr website: http://mng.bz/5APD.

20.2.5 Generalized additive models

If your work will involve modeling nonlinear relationships for regression tasks, I suggest you delve deeper into the inner workings of generalized additive models (GAMs). For R, a great place to do this is *Generalized Additive Models: An Introduction with R* by Simon Wood (Chapman and Hall/CRC, 2017).

20.2.6 Ensemble methods

Ensemble methods got you excited? We only touched the surface in this book, using ensembles for tree-based models. If you are convinced that ensembling can almost always make models better, I suggest you dip into *Ensemble Methods: Foundations and Algorithms* by Zhi-Hua Zhou (Chapman and Hall/CRC, 2012).

20.2.7 Support vector machines

Excited about how support vector machines (SVMs) can contort the feature space to create linear boundaries? SVMs are very popular, and their theory is quite complex. To learn more about how you can harness their predictive power, I recommend *Support Vector Machines* by Andreas Christmann and Ingo Steinwart (Springer, 2008).

20.2.8 Anomaly detection

Sometimes you're not interested in the common patterns in your data. Sometimes it's the unusual, outlying cases that you're really interested in. For example, you may be trying to identify fraudulent activity on a credit card, or trying to identify rare bursts of radiation from stars. Identifying such rare events in a dataset can be challenging, but an area of machine learning called *anomaly detection* is dedicated to solving these problems. Some of the algorithms you met in this book can be repurposed for anomaly detection, such as the SVM algorithm. If you have a penchant for the rare and unusual, take a look at *Anomaly Detection Principles and Algorithms* by Kishan G. Mehrotra, Chilukuri K. Mohan, and HuaMing Huang (Springer, 2017).

20.2.9 Time series

Something I didn't touch on in this book is time series forecasting. This is the area of machine learning and statistics concerned with predicting the future state of a variable, based on its previous states. Common applications of time series forecasting are predicting fluctuations in stock market variables and forecasting weather patterns. If you want to get rich or stay dry, I would start with *Introductory Time Series with R* by Paul Cowpertwait and Andrew Metcalfe (Springer, 2009).

20.2.10 Clustering

We've covered pretty good ground when it comes to clustering, but there is much more for you to get your teeth into. To learn more, I recommend *Data Clustering: Algorithms and Applications* by Charu Aggarwal (Chapman & Hall/CRC, 2013).

20.2.11 Generalized linear models

Impressed at how the general linear model can be extended to predict classes as we did in logistic regression? We can use the same principal to predict count data (as in Poisson regression) or percentages (as in beta regression). The extended form of the general linear model to handle situations where our outcome is not a normally distributed continuous variable is called the generalized linear model. It gives us extraordinary flexibility when building predictive models, while still allowing complete interpretability of the model parameters. To learn more, I recommend *Generalized Linear Models With Examples in R* by Peter K. Dunn and Gordon K. Smyth (Springer, 2018), though you may find it a tough read if you don't already have a good mathematical grounding in linear modeling.

20.2.12 Semi-supervised learning

If you have the common problem of data that is time-consuming and/or costly to label manually, you can probably benefit from the application of semi-supervised learning. To learn more, I recommend *Semi-Supervised Learning* by Olivier Chapelle, Bernhard Scholkopf, and Alexander Zien (MIT Press, 2006).

20.2.13 Modeling spectral data

If you're going to be working with spectral data, or data that can be represented by smooth functions, you'll want a good grounding in functional data analysis (briefly mentioned in chapter 10). Functional data analysis is where we use functions as variables in our models, rather than individual values. To learn more, I recommend *Functional Data Analysis* by James Ramsay (Springer, 2005).

20.3 The last word

I really hope that the skills you've acquired through reading this book will help you gain insight into a part of nature you're studying, help you streamline and improve your business practices, or just help you get more from your hobby data science projects. I also hope that the tidyverse skills we used throughout the book will help you to write easier, more readable code, and that your new mlr skills will continue to make your machine learning projects simpler.

Thank you for reading!

appendix Refresher on statistical concepts

If you don't come from a statistical background, or perhaps just want to refresh your memory about some statistical concepts, this appendix aims to get you up to speed with the basic knowledge you'll need to get the most out of this book. If you're unsure whether you need to use this refresher, flick through the section headings and make sure there's nothing you don't feel confident with. You won't need to memorize any of this material, only be aware of the important concepts. Also feel free to reference any of the definitions here as you progress through the book.

A.1 Data vocabulary

Let's start with some basic vocabulary we'll be using to describe data. There are some variations in the way data scientists and statisticians use the terminology, so I'll try to make it clear which terms are equivalent and which I opt to use throughout the book. In this section, we'll discuss

- The difference between a sample and a population
- What we mean by rows, columns, cases, and variables
- What the different types of variables are and how they differ

A.1.1 Sample vs. population

In data science and statistics, we're usually trying to learn something about, or predict something in, the real world. Let's say we're interested in the tusk length of hippos. It would be impossible to measure the tusk length of every hippo in the world—there are simply too many, and they aren't keen on us putting a ruler inside their mouth. So instead, we measure as many hippos' tusks as is feasible, both in terms of finance and hours of work. This smaller, more manageable number of hippos is called our *sample*. We hope that the tusk lengths in our sample do a good job of representing the tusk lengths of all the hippos in the world, which is the *population* to which we are trying to generalize our findings. This distinction between the sample and the population is illustrated in figure A.1.

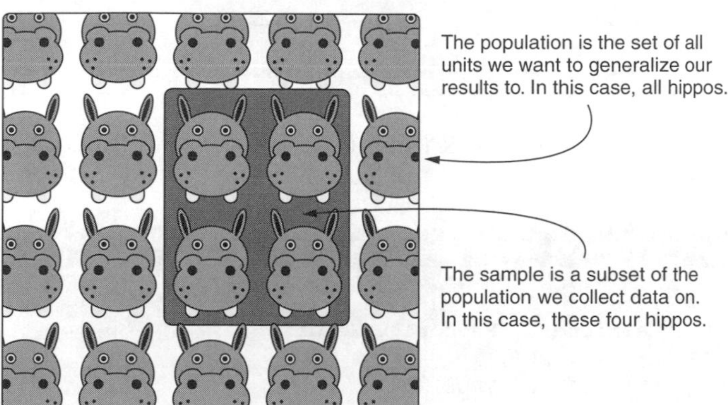

The population is the set of all units we want to generalize our results to. In this case, all hippos.
The sample is a subset of the population we collect data on. In this case, these four hippos.

Figure A.1 The difference between the population and the sample. The population is the set of all units we would like to generalize our results to. The population is often considered nearly infinite in size. The sample is a more manageable subset we measure, which we hope will represent the population.

A difference between the sample and the population is referred to as *sampling error* and arises because the sample is almost never a perfect representation of the population. We hope to make sampling error as small as possible by using a sample that is as large as possible and by not introducing bias when creating our sample (for example, not selecting smaller hippos because they are less scary). If sampling error is too large, we won't be able to generalize our findings to the wider population.

A.1.2 Rows and columns

Once we've collected our data, most of the time we can structure it into a tabular format with rows and columns. A common way of representing data of this type in R is by using a data frame.

As explained in chapter 2, we often need to rearrange how tabular data is structured, depending on our goal. But most of the time, it's desirable to format data such that each row represents a single unit of our sample, and each column represents a different *variable*. For our hippo example, each hippo would be a single unit in our dataset, so each row would correspond to measurements made on a single hippo, as shown in table A.1.

Table A.1 An example of data arranged in tabular format, where each row corresponds to a single hippo and each column corresponds to a different variable. Note that, culturally, hippos give their children names beginning with *H*.

Name	TuskLength	Female
Harry	32	FALSE
Hermione	15	TRUE
Hector	45	FALSE
Heidi	20	TRUE

We can create a data frame like this in R using the `data.frame()` function, as shown in the following listing.

Listing A.1 Creating our hippo data frame

```
hippos <- data.frame(
  Name = c("Harry", "Hermione", "Hector", "Heidi"),
  TuskLength = c(32, 15, 45, 20),
  Female = c(FALSE, TRUE, FALSE, TRUE)
  )
```

In statistics, when the data is formatted like this, each row is said to correspond to one *subject* in the data, with a subject here being a single hippo. In data science and machine learning, it's more common to see the term *case* to describe a single unit in the data, so this is the term I use throughout the book.

Columns that contain measurements made on each case are referred to as *variables.* When we're trying to predict the value of one variable based on its relationships with the others, we use terms to distinguish between the variable we want to predict and the ones we are using to make the predictions. Statisticians call the variable we're trying to predict the *dependent variable,* while the variables we used to make these predictions are called the *independent variables.* In data science, you might be more likely to hear the term *outcome* or *response* variable for the dependent variable and *predictor variables* or *features* for the independent variables. I use the data science terminology throughout the book.

A.1.3 Variable types

Different variables might be measured using different types of scales, meaning we need to handle them differently. Throughout the book, I mention continuous variables, categorical variables, and sometimes logical variables.

Continuous variables represent some measurement on a numeric continuum. For example, the length of a hippo's tusk would be represented as a continuous variable. We can apply mathematical transformations to continuous variables. In R, continuous variables are most commonly represented as *integers* or as *doubles.* An integer variable can only have whole numbers, whereas a double can also include non-zero digits after a decimal point. In the data shown in table A.1, the `TuskLength` variable is numeric.

Categorical variables have *levels*, each of which represents a different group or category of objects. For example, let's say we were comparing tusk length between common hippos and pygmy hippos. Our data would contain a categorical variable indicating which species of hippo each case in the data belonged to. In R, it's common to represent categorical variables as *factors*, where the possible levels of the factor are predefined. In the data shown in table A.1, the `Name` variable is categorical.

Logical variables can take a value of `TRUE` or `FALSE` to indicate a binary outcome. For example, we could include a logical variable to indicate whether the hippo tried to bite us. Logical variables are most useful as arguments to functions, to control the way they behave, or to select cases that are most interesting to us. In the data shown in table A.1, the `Female` variable is logical.

The next listing shows how we can use the `class()` function to determine what kind of variable we're working with.

Listing A.2 Using `class()` to determine variables types

```
class(hippos$Name)
[1] "factor"

class(hippos$TuskLength)
[1] "numeric"

class(hippos$Female)
[1] "logical"
```

A.2 Vectors

A *vector* is a set of numbers that encodes both magnitude and direction. Imagine a coordinate system with an x-axis and a y-axis, as shown in figure A.2. If we pick a point on the coordinate system, that point will have a value for each axis: let's say x = 3 and y = 5. We can represent this point as the vector (3,5). The vector encodes magnitude, because we can calculate the distance between the point defined by this vector and the origin of the coordinate system (0,0). The vector also encodes direction, because if we draw a line connecting the origin (0,0) to this point (3,5), we can calculate the angle

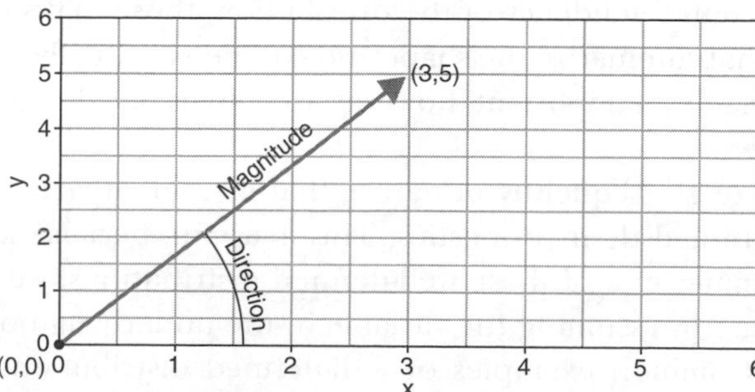

Figure A.2 An example of a two-dimensional vector at point x = 3, y = 5. The arrow shows how vectors encode magnitude, which we can represent as their distance from the origin (or another vector). The curved line representing the angle between the x-axis and the arrow indicates how vectors encode direction.

between this line and the axes of the coordinate space. Figure A.2 is an example of a two-dimensional vector, but vectors can have as many dimensions as we like.

We can perform operations with vectors, such as addition, subtraction, and multiplication, to create new vectors. We don't do any complex mathematics using vectors throughout the book, but I sometimes refer to vectors when we're dealing with concepts in more than two dimensions. For example, in some parts of the book I refer to a vector of means, where each element in the vector is the mean of a different variable.

Confusingly, R has a data structure called an *atomic vector* that may or may not represent a mathematical vector. An atomic vector in R contains a set of values that must all be the same type (this is where the word *atomic* comes from in the name). If the atomic vector's elements are numeric, then it will also be a vector in the mathematical sense, because the values encode magnitude and direction. But if we have atomic vectors with character or logical elements, neither of these can encode magnitude and direction; so while we refer to them as vectors within R, they are not vectors in the mathematical sense. Here is how we can create numeric, character, and logical atomic vectors using the `c()` function.

Listing A.3 Creating atomic vectors in R

```
numericVector <- c(1, 31, 10)

characterVector <- c("common hippo", "pygmy hippo")

logicalVector <- c(TRUE, TRUE, FALSE)
```

A.3 Distributions

When we measure a variable, it's often desirable to examine the range of values taken on by the variable. We can do this, for example, using a histogram, where we plot the possible values of our variable against the frequency with which we observed each of them. The shape we get from plotting such a histogram represents the *distribution* of our variable and tells us information such as where our variable is centered, how dispersed it is, whether its values are symmetrically distributed around its center, and how many peaks it has.

We can summarize distributions of variables using a variety of statistics, such as those that summarize the central tendency of the distribution, those that summarize the dispersion, and those that summarize the shape and symmetry. Visually inspecting the distributions of our variables is important, however, to help us decide the best way to handle different variables.

Some distributions occur so frequently in nature that mathematicians have formally defined them and studied their properties. This is useful, because if we find that our variable approximates one of these well-defined distributions, we can simplify our statistical modeling by assuming the variable in the underlying population follows this distribution. Common examples of well-defined distributions are the

Gaussian (also called the normal) distribution, which is one of many bell-shaped distributions, and the Poisson distribution, which variables representing discrete counts often follow.

If we measured 1,000 hippo tusks and plotted a histogram of their lengths, we might get something like the distribution shown in figure A.3. The bars of the histogram represent the frequency with which a particular tusk length occurs in the dataset. I've overlaid a theoretical normal distribution (the smooth line) over the histogram, whose mean and standard deviation correspond to those of the data.

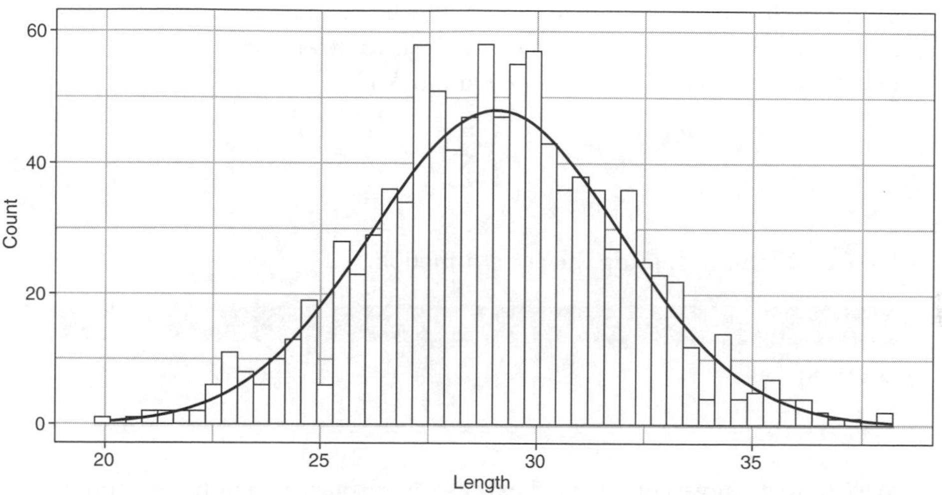

Figure A.3 A histogram showing the distribution of an imaginary sample of hippo tusk lengths. The distribution approximates a Gaussian distribution. The curved line represents the probability density function of a Gaussian distribution with the same mean and standard deviation as the sample.

Distributions that are mathematically defined are often called *probability distributions*, and they have a defined *probability density function*. The probability density function for a particular distribution is an equation that we can use to calculate the probability that a particular value came from that distribution. For example, let's say we measured a hippo tusk as being 32 cm long. If we know the distribution that best represents the lengths of all hippo tusks, we can use the probability density function to estimate the probability of finding a hippo with a 32-cm tusk. You don't need to know or memorize any probability density functions before reading the book, but I refer to them on occasion, so it's useful for you to know what they are. Look back at figure A.2: the smooth line I overlaid onto the histogram is the probability density function for the Gaussian distribution with the same mean and standard deviation as the data.

A.4 Sigma notation

Mathematical notation can look intimidating to those not formally trained in its use. But mathematical notation is really there to make our lives easier. While there are some equations in this book, not one of them uses anything more complicated than addition, subtraction, multiplication, and division. I do, however, use one symbol that makes my life a lot easier; and once you get the hang of it, it will make your life easier too (and make lots of equations seem less impenetrable). That symbol is the capital Greek letter *sigma*, which looks like a strange "E" (Σ).

In equations, capital sigma simply means to sum whatever is on the right-hand side of it. You'll usually see indices above and below the sigma that tell us where to start and stop summing from. For example, instead of writing 1 + 2 + 3 + 4 + 5 = 15, we can use the sigma notation shown in equation A.1.

$$\sum_{i=1}^{5} i = 15$$

Equation A.1

We can do this in R using the `sum()` function.

Listing A.4 Using the `sum()` function in R

```
sum(1:5)

[1] 15
```

We can write more complicated expressions using sigma notation, and the indices give us control over the range of values we want to sum over. Take a look at equation A.2 and try to work out what the value of x is.

$$\sum_{i=3}^{6} 2^i - i = x$$

Equation A.2

If the answer isn't clear to you, perhaps thinking like a programmer will help. You can think of sigma notation as a `for` loop for addition. If I was going to read equation A.2 aloud as a `for` loop, I would say, "For all values of *i* between 3 and 6, take the *i*th power of 2 and subtract *i*, and then add up all these values." This then becomes

- $2^3 - 3 = 5$
- $2^4 - 4 = 12$
- $2^5 - 5 = 27$
- $2^6 - 6 = 58$

and 5 + 12 + 27 + 58 = 102.

We can do this in R by creating a function that calculates the value on the right-hand side of the sigma sign, and passing it to the `sum()` function.

Listing A.5 Using `sum()` for more complex functions

```
fun <- function(i) (2^i) - i

sum(fun(3:6))

[1] 102
```

Using sigma notation means that when we are summing dozens, hundreds, or even thousands of numbers, we don't have to write them all. So I hope you can see how sigma notation makes out lives easier! I'm introducing it to you here because I'm going to use it in the next section to remind you how to calculate the arithmetic mean.

A.5 Central tendency

When working with variables, it's often important to get a sense of the center of their distributions. There are multiple statistics we can use to summarize the center of a distribution; they give different information and are appropriate in different situations. Statistics that provide such information are referred to as measures of *central tendency*, and the three most common are the *arithmetic mean*, the *median*, and the *mode*.

A.5.1 Arithmetic mean

Much to the surprise of spreadsheet users, there is no formal mathematical concept of an "average." But when people colloquially speak of an "average," what they usually mean (pun intended) is the arithmetic mean. The *arithmetic mean* (or just the *mean*) is simply the sum of all the values in a vector, divided by the number of elements. For example, if I measure the tusk lengths of 5 hippos as being 32, 15, 45, 20, and 54, then the mean is (32 + 15 + 45 + 20 + 54) / 5 = 33.2.

Writing that out for just five hippo tusks is cumbersome enough, but imagine if I had to write this for dozens of tusks! Instead, we can use our new friend, sigma notation. The arithmetic mean in sigma notation is shown in equation A.3.

$$\text{mean} = \frac{\sum_{i=1}^{n} x_i}{n}$$

Equation A.3

For our hippo example, x represents our vector of tusk lengths, i is an index telling us which element of that vector to consider, and n is the total number of elements in the vector. Then we can read equation A.3 aloud as "For each element of x between the first and the last element, add the values of x. Then divide this value by the number of elements in x." We can do this in R using the `mean()` function.

Listing A.6 Using the `mean()` function in R

```
mean(c(32, 15, 45, 20, 54))

[1] 33.2
```

NOTE Wonder why I'm bothering to specify that this is the *arithmetic* mean? That's because there are two other types of mean, appropriate in other situations, called the *geometric* mean and the *harmonic* mean. I don't mention them in the book, so I won't elaborate on them, but I suggest you find out more about their uses.

The arithmetic mean is useful for summarizing the center of symmetrical distributions with a single peak, such as the Gaussian distribution. For distributions that are asymmetric, have multiple peaks, or have outliers, however, the mean may not be a good representative of the distribution's central tendency.

NOTE The term *outlier* is used to describe a case that is considerably different from the majority of the cases. It is a case that has an unusually high or low value for one or more variables. There are many methods for identifying whether a case is an outlier, but it really depends on the task at hand.

A.5.2 Median

The median is a *robust* measure of central tendency, meaning it is not severely influenced by asymmetry or outlying cases in a distribution like the mean is. The median also has a very simple interpretation: it is the value for which 50% of the cases are larger and 50% of the cases are smaller. To calculate the median, we simply arrange the elements of a vector in order of their size and pick the middle value.

Let's look back at the tusk lengths from earlier: 32, 15, 45, 20, and 54. Rearranging the tusks in order of size gives us 15, 20, 32, 45, and 54, so the median is 32 because it's the middle value. If the vector has an even number of elements, the median is the value that is midway between them. So if we measure another hippo tusk to be only 5, arranging the elements in order now gives 5, 15, 20, 32, 45, and 54. This means the median is midway between 20 and 32, which is 26. We can calculate the median in R using the `median()` function.

Listing A.7 Using the `median()` function in R

```
median(c(32, 15, 45, 20, 54))

[1] 32

median(c(32, 15, 45, 20, 54, 5))

[1] 26
```

A.5.3 Mode

The mode is generally used in slightly different situations than the mean and median. Whereas the mean and median summarize the center of the distribution, the mode tells us which individual value is most commonly observed across the distribution.

NOTE There is no function for calculating the mode in base R, but you can write one yourself if you need to.

A.6 Measures of dispersion

In addition to summarizing the center of a distribution, it's often important to also summarize how dispersed or spread out the values of the distribution are. There are many different measures of dispersion that tell us slightly different information and are appropriate in different situations, but they all give us an indication as to how skinny or wide our distribution of values is. I'm going to remind you of four of these: *mean absolute deviation*, *standard deviation*, *variance*, and the *interquartile range*.

A.6.1 Mean absolute deviation

Let's start by talking about what I mean by the word *deviation* (this isn't the same meaning as your grandparents might use when chastising immoral behavior). The deviation of an element in a distribution is how far that element's value is from the mean of the distribution. So if the mean length of our hippo tusks is 33.2 cm, the deviation of a 16.1-cm tusk is –17.1 cm. Notice that this deviation is signed: it's negative if the element is smaller than the mean, and it's positive if the element is larger than the mean.

NOTE The deviation between a value and an estimated value is called a *residual*, and I elaborate more on this in the body of the book.

To get an idea of the average (there's that nondescript word again) difference between all the elements and the mean of the distribution, we could take the mean of all the deviations. The problem with this is that in an approximately symmetrical distribution, the positive and negative deviations will cancel each other out, and we'll get a mean deviation close to zero.

Instead, we can take the *absolute* deviations by changing the sign of the negative deviations to positive, and take the mean of these. This gives us the mean absolute deviation, which will be larger when the data is spread out and smaller when the data is concentrated around the center of the distribution. The equation for the mean absolute deviation is shown in equation A.4, where the vertical lines indicate the absolute value of the expression between them, and $\bar{x}$ indicates the mean.

$$\text{MAD} = \frac{\sum_{i=1}^{n} \left| x_i - \bar{x} \right|}{n}$$ **Equation A.4**

We can calculate the mean absolute deviation in R using the `mad()` function. By default, this function calculates the *median absolute deviation*, which is also commonly used, so we use the `center` argument to specify that we want the mean.

Listing A.8 Using the `mad()` function in R

```
tusks <- c(32, 15, 45, 20, 54)

mad(tusks, center = mean(tusks))

[1]
```

A.6.2 Standard deviation

While the mean absolute deviation is a very intuitive and sensible measure of dispersion, you won't see it reported very often. That's because people more commonly use and report the standard deviation. The standard deviation is similar to the mean absolute deviation, except for a few differences. First, instead of summing the absolute deviations from the mean, we sum the squared deviations. We then divide this sum by $n-1$ (one fewer than the number of elements in the vector) and take the square root. You can see this shown in equation A.5, where S is the standard deviation.

$$S = \sqrt{\frac{\sum_{i=1}^{n}(x_i - \bar{x})^2}{n-1}}$$

Equation A.5

We can calculate this in R using the `sd()` function.

Listing A.9 Using the `sd()` function in R

```
sd(c(32, 15, 45, 20, 54))

[1] 16.42
```

Why use the standard deviation when the mean absolute deviation is much more intuitive? Because the standard deviation has some nice mathematical properties that make it more convenient to work with. One important consequence of using the standard deviation rather than the mean absolute deviation is that because the differences are squared, it is more greatly influenced by cases that are far from the mean. Another convenience of the standard deviation is that if the data follows a Gaussian (normal) distribution, then known proportions of the data will fall within certain standard deviations away from the mean. This is elaborated on in figure A.4, which shows that for a perfect Gaussian distribution, 68%, 95%, and 99.7% of the cases fall within one, two, and three standard deviations of the mean, respectively.

A.6.3 Variance

The variance is very easy to calculate: it is simply the square of the standard deviation. Its formula is the same as for the standard deviation, except of course that we drop the square root symbol. This is shown in equation A.6, where S^2 is the variance.

$$S^2 = \frac{\sum_{i=1}^{n}(x_i - \bar{x})^2}{n-1}$$

Equation A.6

If the variance and standard deviation are transformations of each other, why do we need both? We don't, really; but while the variance makes some statistical computations slightly simpler, the standard deviation has the advantage of having the same units as the variable for which it's calculated.

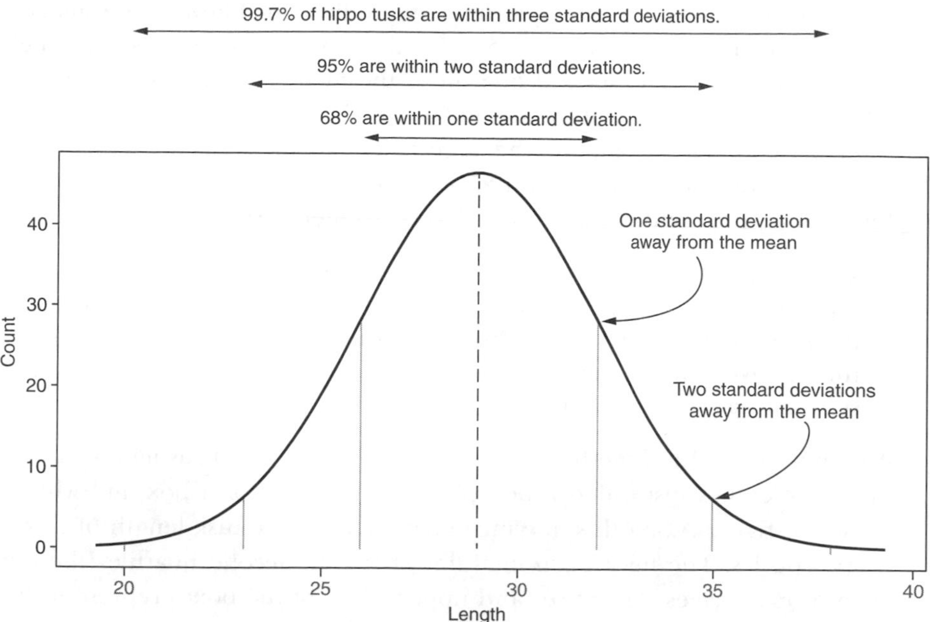

Figure A.4 For a perfect, Gaussian-distributed variable, 68% of the cases lie within one standard deviation's distance of the mean. 95% and 99.7% of cases lie within two and three standard deviations, respectively.

We can calculate the variance in R using the `var()` function or by taking the square of the standard deviation.

Listing A.10 Using the `var()` function in R

```
var(c(32, 15, 45, 20, 54))

[1] 269.7

sd(c(32, 15, 45, 20, 54))^2

[1] 269.7
```

A.6.4 Interquartile range

While the standard deviation and variance, in particular, are well suited for summarizing the dispersion of symmetrical distributions with no outliers, we need ways to summarize the dispersion of distributions that don't play by these rules. The interquartile range (IQR) is a good choice in such situations, because it is a robust statistic that isn't heavily influenced by outliers and asymmetry. Simply put, the IQR is the difference between the first quartile and the third quartile.

If we arrange the elements of a vector in order of their values, the *quartiles* of the vector are the elements for which 25%, 50%, 75%, and 100% of the other elements have smaller values. The first quartile is a middle value between the smallest element and the median: it splits the vector such that 25% of the elements are below it and 75% are above it. The second quartile is the median, splitting the vector such that 50% of the elements are above it and 50% are below it. The third quartile is a middle value between the median and the largest element and splits the vector such that 75% of the elements are below it and 25% of the elements are above it. The zeroth and fourth quartiles are the smallest and largest elements, respectively.

> **NOTE** I've left the definition of the first and third quartiles relatively ambiguous, because there are no less than nine different methods of calculating their exact values! These methods don't always agree with each other, but they always divide the elements of the vector into 25% and 75%, so we won't split hairs about them here.

A common graphical method of displaying the quartiles is using a box and whiskers plot (sometimes just called a box plot). An example of a box and whiskers plot is shown in figure A.5, with some imaginary data for the tusk length of three different hippo species. The thick horizontal line shows the second quartile (the median) for each hippo species. The lower and upper edges of the boxes represent the first and third quartiles, respectively. The whiskers (the vertical lines extending out of the boxes) connect the lowest and highest value for each species and therefore represent the full range of the data.

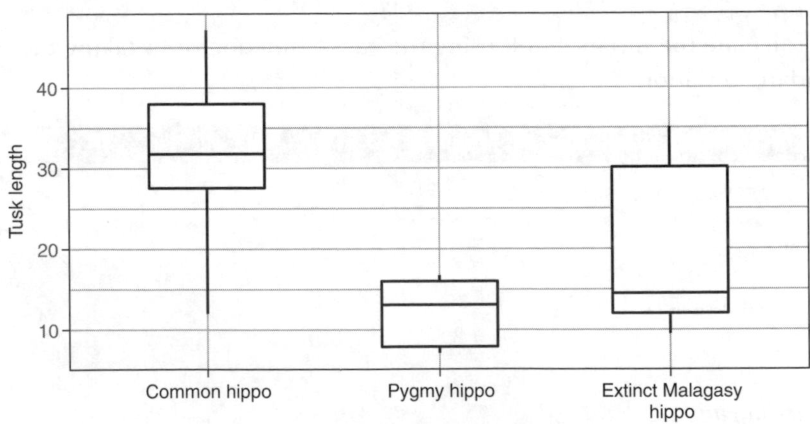

Figure A.5 Box and whiskers plots for imaginary hippo tusk data. The thick horizontal lines are the medians, the edges of the boxes represent the first and third quartiles, and the vertical whiskers represent the full range.

> **NOTE** Sometimes the whiskers *don't* represent the full range. Often they indicate the *Tukey range*, which is 1.5 times the IQR below and above the first and third quartiles, respectively. Any cases outside this range are drawn as a dot to highlight them as potential outliers.

The IQR is the difference between the first and third quartiles of the vector and thus tells us the range of the middle 50% of the elements in the vector. It is useful in situations where we have outlying cases and/or non-Gaussian-distributed data.

We can calculate the IQR in R using the `IQR()` function (which is unusual in that the function name is capitalized).

Listing A.11 Using the `IQR()` function in R

```
IQR(c(32, 15, 45, 20, 54))

[1] 25
```

A.7 Measures of the relationships between variables

It's very common to find that there are relationships between pairs of variables we are working with. Even if two variables have no causal relationship, it's not uncommon that they will have a relationship. This could be a positive relationship, such that when one variable increases in value, so does the other; or a negative relationship, where, as one variable increases, the other decreases.

It's important to be able to summarize relationships between pairs of variables in terms of both their direction (positive, negative, or no relationship) and magnitude (no relationship to perfect relationship). The two most common statistics used to summarize the direction and magnitude of the relationship between two variables are the *covariance* and the *Pearson correlation coefficient*.

A.7.1 Covariance

The covariance between two variables tells us how they covary. If the pair of variables increase and decrease together, the covariance is positive; and if one variable increases as the other decreases, the covariance is negative. If there is no relationship between the pair of variables, the covariance is zero (but this practically never happens in the real world).

It's possible for two variables to have a covariance of zero (or near zero) but actually have a nonlinear relationship. Run the following code and see for yourself (note how small the covariance value is):

```
x <- seq(-1, 1, length = 1e6)

y <- x^4

plot(x, y, type = "l")

cov(x, y)
```

To calculate the covariance, we consider a single case and find its deviation from the mean of the first variable and then also from the second variable. We then find the product of these deviations. This is done for all of the cases in the dataset, and these products of deviations are added up and divided by $n - 1$ (one fewer than the number of elements in the vector). This process is illustrated in equation A.7.

$$Cov(x,y) = \frac{\sum_{i=1}^{n} (x_i - \bar{x})(y_i - \bar{y})}{n-1} \quad \text{Equation A.7}$$

We can calculate the covariance between two vectors in R using the `cov()` function.

Listing A.12 Using the `cov()` function in R

```
tusks <- c(32, 15, 45, 20, 54)

weight <- c(18, 11, 19, 15, 18)

cov(tusks, weight)

[1] 44.7
```

The covariance is very useful mathematically, but as its units are the product of the values of both variables, its magnitude can be difficult to interpret. Covariance is therefore said to be an *unstandardized* measure of the relationship between variables, which means we cannot compare covariances between pairs of variables measured on different scales. A standardized version of covariance is correlation—or, more formally, the Pearson correlation coefficient.

A.7.2 Pearson correlation coefficient

The Pearson correlation coefficient (or just the correlation coefficient) is a standardized version of the covariance that is unitless and is bounded between –1 and +1. A correlation of –1 indicates a perfect negative relationship between the pair of variables, a correlation of +1 indicates a perfect positive relationship, and a correlation of zero indicates no relationship at all. These three extremes rarely occur in the real world (if you get +1, check that you haven't calculated the correlation between a variable and itself), and a value somewhere between them is much more likely.

> **NOTE** I've made it a point to call this the Pearson correlation coefficient (after the statistician Karl Pearson) to distinguish it from other, perhaps less commonly used, types: Kendall rank, Spearman, and point-biserial correlation. These other types are useful in situations when the variables are not both continuous and follow a Gaussian distribution, as is assumed by the Pearson correlation coefficient, but we don't consider them in this book.

Calculating the Pearson correlation coefficient is simple if we know how to calculate the covariance; we simply divide the covariance by the product of the standard deviations of the variables. This is shown in equation A.8.

$$r_{xy} = \frac{Cov(x, y)}{S_x S_y} \quad \text{Equation A.8}$$

Because the correlation coefficient (often represented by *r*) is standardized and unitless, we can compare its value between pairs of variables on different scales. We can calculate the Pearson correlation coefficient between two vectors in R using the `cor()` function.

Listing A.13 Using the `cov()` function in R

```
tusks <- c(32, 15, 45, 20, 54)

weight <- c(18, 11, 19, 15, 18)

cor(tusks, weight)

[1] 0.8321
```

A.8 Logarithms

Logarithms, or logs, are mathematical functions that are the opposite of exponentiation. For example, if $2^5 = 32$, then $\log_2(32) = 5$. In this example, the *base* of the logarithm is 2. In other words, the result of $\log_2(32)$ is the exponent to which 2 must be raised to get 32. Logarithms can have any base we like, depending on our reasons for wanting to use a logarithmic function. The three most common choices are logs with bases 2, 10, and Euler's number (*e*), which is an important constant with a value of approximately 2.718. The base of a logarithm is usually denoted as a subscript after the log symbol (for example, $\log_2$ or $\log_{10}$); but when the base is *e*, the log is called the *natural logarithm* and is usually denoted as *ln*.

NOTE You may see something like $\log(x)$ with no subscript. Depending on the intended audience, this may be interpreted as $\log_{10}(x)$ or $\log_e(x)$. It's much better to be explicit about which one you mean.

Logarithms have many useful properties in mathematics and statistics. One is that they can be used to compress extremely large values on a scale together with much smaller values. For example, the $\log_{10}$ of the vector 1, 10, 100, 1,000, 10,000, 100,000 is 0, 1, 2, 3, 4, 5. So if we have a variable containing both very small and very large numbers, this variable can be made easier to work with if we $\log_{10}$-transform it.

Another useful property of logs, particularly the natural logarithm, is that if there is an exponential relationship between two variables (say, time and bacterial growth), taking the log of one of the variables can linearize the relationship. Working with a linear relationship between variables is often mathematically simpler.

Take a look at the example in figure A.6. The left-hand plot shows a *y* variable with both very small and very large values, where the relationship between the *x* and *y* variables is exponentially increasing. The right-hand plot shows the same data, but after $\log_{10}$-transforming the *y* variable. You can see that, after the transformation, the *y* variable can now be more easily visualized on a plot, and the relationship between the *x* and *y* variables has been linearized.

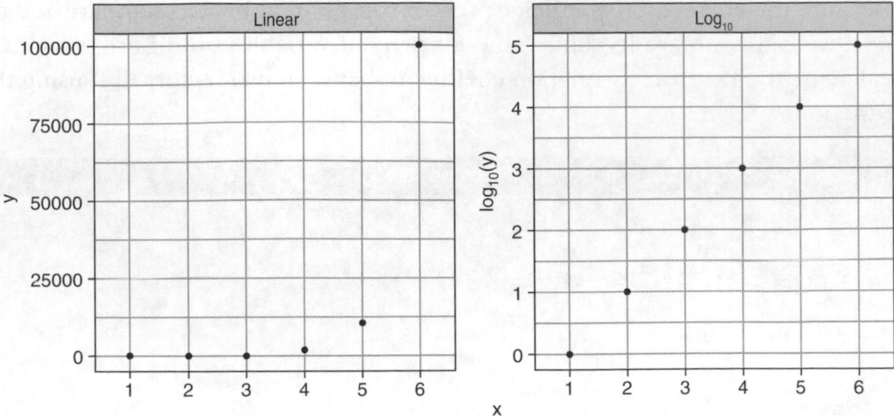

Figure A.6 The impact of $\log_{10}$ transformation on variables. The left-side plot shows a *y* variable with both very small and very large values. In the right-side plot, the *y* variable has been $\log_{10}$-transformed.

index

Symbols

A

B

D

M

N

U

V

W

RELATED MANNING TITLES

Deep Learning with R
by François Chollet, with J. J. Allaire

ISBN 9781617295546
360 pages, $49.99
January 2018

Practical Data Science with R, Second Edition
by Nina Zumel and John Mount

ISBN 9781617295874
568 pages, $49.99
November 2019

Beyond Spreadsheets with R
by Dr. Jonathan Carroll

ISBN 9781617294594
352 pages, $49.99
December 2018

R in Action, Third Edition
by Robert I. Kabacoff

ISBN 9781617296055
625 pages, $59.99
Summer 2020

For ordering information go to www.manning.com